S0-AGH-487

The Humanities

VOLUME I

Mary Ann Frese Witt

North Carolina State University at Raleigh

Charlotte Vestal Brown

Duke University

Roberta Ann Dunbar

University of North Carolina at Chapel Hill

Frank Tirro

Yale University

Ronald G. Witt

Duke University

With the collaboration of

Ernest D. Mason

North Carolina Central University

The

HUMANITIES

CULTURAL ROOTS AND CONTINUITIES

Volume I—Three Cultural Roots

D. C. HEATH AND COMPANY   Lexington, Massachusetts   •   Toronto

COVER ILLUSTRATION: *The Ambassadors*, by Hans Holbein.
Reproduced by courtesy of the Trustees, The National Gallery, London.

Drawings by Eugene Brown.

Copyright © 1980 by D. C. Heath and Company.

All rights reserved. No part of this publication may be reproduced or transmitted in any form or by any means, electronic or mechanical, including photocopy, recording, or any information storage or retrieval system, without permission in writing from the publisher.

Published simultaneously in Canada.

Printed in the United States of America.

International Standard Book Number: 0-669-01450-8

Library of Congress Catalog Card Number: 78-78360

CREDITS

African Arts Efe ceremony excerpts are reprinted by permission from "Efe: Voiced Power and Pageantry" by Henry John Drewal in *African Arts*, Volume III, No. 2 (Winter, 1974).

American Folklore Society Yoruba riddles reproduced by permission of the American Folklore Society from the *Journal of American Folklore*, Vol. 62, No. 243, 1949.

Bantam Books, Inc. *The Aeneid of Virgil*, A verse translation by Allen Mandelbaum. Copyright © 1971 by Allen Mandelbaum. By permission of Bantam Books, Inc. All rights reserved.

Ulli Beier "Oriki Obatala," "Oriki Eshu," "Oriki Ogun," "Adiye," "Etu-Duiker," "New Yam," "Children," Yoruba funeral poems, Yoruba proverbs, and six Yoruba riddles reprinted by permission of Ulli Beier. Translated by Bakare Gbadamosi and Ulli Beier.

Black Orpheus Two Yoruba Myths of Creation from *Black Orpheus*, VIII (June 1960), reprinted by permission of *Black Orpheus*.

Frank Cass & Co., Ltd. "The Kano Man" from *Hausa Tales and Traditions*, an English translation of Tatsuniyoyi na Hausa originally compiled by Frank Edgar. Reprinted by permission of Frank Cass & Co., Ltd.

Crown Publishers, Inc. "Forefathers," by Birago Diop, is taken from *An African Treasury* by Langston Hughes. Copyright © 1960 by Langston Hughes. Used by permission of Crown Publishers, Inc.

Doubleday & Company, Inc. "Generation Gap" from *Christmas in Biafra and Other Poems* by Chinua Achebe. Reprinted by permission of Doubleday & Company, Inc. and Harold Ober Associates Incorporated. Copyright © 1973 by Chinua Achebe.

Hakluyt Society "The Discovery of the Kingdom of Benin" from *Europeans in West Africa, 1450–1560*, Vol. I, J. W. Blake, translator and editor; "Esmeraldo de situ Orbis" by Duarte Pacheco Hereira, George T. Kimble, translator, reprinted by permission of the Hakluyt Society.

Harcourt Brace Jovanovich, Inc. *Oedipus Rex of Sophocles: An English Version* by Dudley Fitts and Robert Fitzgerald, copyright, 1949, by Harcourt Brace Jovanovich, Inc.; renewed, 1977, by Cornelia Fitts and Robert Fitzgerald. Reprinted by permission of the publisher.
CAUTION: All rights, including professional, amateur, motion picture, recitation, lecturing, performance, public reading, radio broadcasting, and television are strictly reserved. Inquiries on all rights should be addressed to Harcourt Brace Jovanovich, Inc., 757 Third Avenue, New York, N.Y. 10017.

Aristophanes' *Lysistrata: An English Version* by Dudley Fitts, copyright, 1954, by Harcourt Brace Jovanovich, Inc.; © 1962 by Dudley Fitts. Reprinted by permission of the publisher.
CAUTION: All rights, including professional, amateur, motion picture, recitation, lecturing, performance, public reading, radio broadcasting, and television are strictly reserved. Inquiries on all rights should be addressed to Harcourt Brace Jovanovich, Inc., 757 Third Avenue, New York, N.Y. 10017.

The Johns Hopkins University Press Music for "Quant'e bella giovinezza" transcribed and edited by Walter H. Rubsamen in "The Music for 'Quant'e bella giovinezza' and Other Carnival Songs by Lorenzo de' Medici" from *Art, Science and History in the Renaissance* edited by Charles S. Singleton. Copyright © 1967 by The Johns Hopkins University Press. Reprinted by permission of the publisher.

Ibadan University Press Excerpts from Benin oral traditions reprinted from *A Short History of Benin* by J. V. Egharevba. By permission of Ibadan University Press, Ibadan, Nigeria.

Longman Group Ltd. This condensed version of *Sundiata: An Epic of Old Mali* is reproduced by permission of Longman Group Ltd., (1965) and the original editor, Présence Africaine, Paris (1960). All rights reserved. Also by permission of Humanities Press, Inc., New Jersey.

The New American Library, Inc. From *The Paradiso* by Dante Alighieri as translated by John Ciardi. Copyright 1961, 1965, 1967, 1970 by John Ciardi. Reprinted by arrangement with The New American Library, Inc., New York, N.Y.

Nigeria Magazine "The Oba of Benin" reprinted by permission of *Nigeria Magazine*.

Northern Nigerian Publishing Company, Ltd. "Squirrel and Hedgehog," "The Blind Man with the Lamp," "Life Is Better than Wealth," "Hasara and Riba," and "The Rivals" from *Ka K'ara Karatu* (anonymous) translated by Roberta Ann Dunbar. Reprinted by permission of Northern Nigerian Publishing Company, Ltd., publishers of the Hausa version.

W. W. Norton & Company, Inc. Music and English version of "Be m'an perdut" are reprinted from *A Treasury of Early Music*, Compiled and Edited by Carl Parrish, with the permission of W. W. Norton & Company, Inc. Copyright © 1958 by W. W. Norton & Company, Inc. The selection on the destruction of the church at Chartres is reprinted from *Chartres Cathedral*, Edited by Robert Branner, with the permission of W. W. Norton & Company, Inc. Copyright © 1969 by Robert Branner.

Oxford University Press "The Introduction of Brass-Casting from Ife" from *Nigerian Perspectives* by Thomas Hodgkin. Copyright © 1960 Oxford University Press. Reprinted by permission of the Oxford University Press.

Présence Africaine "The Beloved" by Amadou Hampaté Ba from *African Poetry*, Ulli Beier, ed. Reprinted by permission of *Présence Africaine*, Paris.

Routledge & Kegan Paul Ltd. Music for "The Willow Song" reprinted from *Music in Shakespearean Tragedy* by F. W. Sternfeld (1963). Reprinted by permission of Routledge & Kegan Paul Ltd., London.

Schocken Books Inc.   Selections by Sappho are reprinted by permission of Schocken Books Inc. from *Greek Lyric Poetry* edited by Willis Barnstone. Copyright © 1962, 1967 by Willis Barnstone.

UCLA Art Council   Condensed version of Robert Farris Thompson material is adapted from "African Art in Motion" by Robert Farris Thompson. Reprinted by permission of UCLA Art Council, University of California, Los Angeles.

The University of Chicago Press   "The Town Mouse and the Country Mouse" and "My Slave Is Free to Speak Up for Himself" from *The Satires and Epistles of Horace* translated by Smith Palmer Bovie. Copyright © 1959 by The University of Chicago. Reprinted by permission of The University of Chicago Press and Smith Palmer Bovie.

The University of Wisconsin Press   Ballade "For His Mother to Our Lady" by François Villon from *French Lyrics in English Verse* translated by William Frederic Giese. Reprinted by permission of The University of Wisconsin Press. "The Origin of All Kings" from *Hausa Readings* by Neil Skinner, The University of Wisconsin Press, 1968. Reprinted by permission of The University of Wisconsin Press. This translation by Roberta Ann Dunbar.

Wole Soyinka   "Death in the Dawn" reprinted by permission of the author from *Modern Poetry from Africa*, Second Edition, Gerald Moore and Ulli Beier, editors.

CONTENTS

COLOR ILLUSTRATIONS

MAPS

PREFACE

This book is designed to introduce students to the humanities in an interdisciplinary context. We feel that in an introductory humanities course the student's personal growth should take place on three levels: 1) historical, 2) aesthetic, and 3) philosophical. The overall purpose of the two volumes can best be described by breaking it down into these three categories.

The Historical Level

We stress the concept of "cultural roots" because one cannot understand the culture in which one lives without some notion of what went into its making. Therefore, we have made every effort here to link the "roots" discussed to aspects of the contemporary American cultural environment. This can be a knotty problem because such links can sometimes be too facile, and we would also like students to discover that cultures remote in time or space can be worth studying simply for themselves. This, too, is part of a growth process in historical depth. Volume I treats three cultural roots: Greco-Roman, Judeo-Christian, and West African. This choice needs some justification, since many Americans have other cultural roots as well: oriental, Middle Eastern, north European, Latin American, American Indian, to name a few. Still, the Greco-Roman and the

Judeo-Christian traditions undoubtedly constitute the bases of the Western humanities. African culture, a long neglected field of study, has contributed significantly to modern Afro-American art and thought and in many ways to Western culture in general. In addition, African culture offers the opportunity to study some fundamental aspects of the humanities in a truly interdisciplinary context.

In the discussion of each of these "roots," we adopted the policy of focusing on one period and/or place. The focus for the Greco-Roman root is on fifth-century B.C. Athens, that for the Judeo-Christian on medieval Europe, that for Africa on the Yoruba people. This means, for example, that some significant monuments of classical Greek drama, sculpture, and architecture can be examined rather extensively, while early Greece and Rome receive a briefer treatment. In our discussion of the Renaissance and Reformation periods we emphasize the fusion of the Greco-Roman and Judeo-Christian roots and focus on the development of humanism in fifteenth-century Italy and its diffusion in the north.

If we pursued the same metaphor, Volume II might be called "stems, leaves, and flowers." Here, too, an attempt is made to focus and spread out, more than to survey and to spread thin. The court of Louis XIV in the seventeenth century, the Enlightenment in France and America, the romantic movement, the Industrial Revolution, the modernist movement and Black culture in the United States all provide centers around which interrelated humanities can be discussed.

The Aesthetic Level

On the whole, we follow the same "focal" principle in the aesthetic domain. In presenting music, we operate on the assumption that a student will retain more from listening to and analyzing an entire work than from reading music history and theory and hearing snippets. In dealing with art and literature, it is sometimes possible to make an important point with a photograph and a caption or with a close analysis of a brief literary passage. Nevertheless, in the presentation of major works in the focal periods, we assume that it is more useful for a student to look at the whole of Chartres cathedral than to skim the history of medie-

val art, and to read all of *Oedipus Rex* rather than bits and summaries from several Greek tragedies. With lengthy works such as epics and novels this is, of course, not possible. The analyses of extremely short passages such as those from the *Iliad* and the *Aeneid* are intended to serve as introductions to the works. A teacher may well wish to assign one or more epics or novels as supplementary reading.

Dance, an often neglected art form, is given more extensive treatment here than in other humanities texts. Entire dance compositions can, of course, be appreciated only in live performance or film, and we will list resources for the latter in the Instructor's Guide. Also in the guide will be some suggestions for "sensitivity exercises" designed to involve students actively in the aesthetic process and in interrelating the arts. These may be used as warm-ups during the first few days of class or introduced at any point. It has been our experience that a long introductory chapter on how to look, listen, and read is largely wasted; therefore, we treat such matters in the introductions to individual works. Questions on the nature of genre are treated in the cultural context in which they originate, notably in ancient Greece. We place much importance on study questions that require the student to read, look, and listen carefully.

While we try to avoid jargon, we feel that some knowledge of the technical vocabulary of criticism in the arts is essential for literate discussion. Difficult or unfamiliar terms appear in italics the first time they are used in any given chapter, indicating that they are defined in the Glossary.

The Philosophical Level

It may well be objected that we compromise the focal method in our presentation of philosophy since no entire philosophical works appear in the book. This is largely due to considerations of space; but it is also true that, when dealing with a work in terms of certain fundamental ideas rather than in terms of aesthetic wholeness, the "snippet" method is not so objectionable. Beginning humanities students are probably not ready to read Aristotle's *Ethics* in its entirety, yet they should be able to see how Aristotle's ideas are essential to the cultural roots of the modern world.

The student's personal growth in the philosophical area means, however, something much broader than his or her contact with formal philosophy. The (ideal) student whose historical awareness is increased by an understanding of cultural roots and whose aesthetic sensitivity is heightened by personal confrontation with a variety of works of art should also be able to expand his or her mind through contact with diverse ideas. A humanities course should enable students to refine their thinking on the basic questions that affect all mankind, to formulate more clearly their personal values, and to discuss these with intellectual rigor rather than in vaporous bull sessions. Teachers should welcome debates that might arise from a comparison between Genesis and African mythology, the "woman" question in *Lysistrata* and in John Stuart Mill, and the relative merits of realistic and abstract art or tonal and atonal music. We offer some topics for controversial discussion in the guide, but teachers and students will find many more.

Individual teachers will decide which aspects of the humanities and which cultural roots they wish to emphasize. We hope that this book will offer enough flexibility to be useful for a variety of approaches.

MARY ANN FRESE WITT
CHARLOTTE VESTAL BROWN
ROBERTA ANN DUNBAR
FRANK TIRRO
RONALD G. WITT

ACKNOWLEDGMENTS

Many people have contributed time, work, ideas, and encouragement to the creation of this book. Gratitude is due first of all to those who provided their own research and writing: Professor Edmund Reiss of Duke University wrote the section on courtly love in Volume I, translated *Equitan* and *The Miller's Tale*, and provided introductions to those selections, as well as to the two anonymous medieval English poems; Professor Alan Gonzalez of North Carolina State University wrote the sections on literature and social commitment and on writers and the Spanish Civil War in Volume II and translated *El Cojo*; Professor Ernest Mason of North Carolina Central University wrote the introduction to Freud as well as the unit on Afro-American culture in Volume II; D. D. Williams of Raleigh, North Carolina wrote the film section in Volume II.

The plan for this textbook grew out of the four years I spent initiating and directing an interdisciplinary humanities program at North Carolina Central University in Durham. It would not have been possible without the stimulation and aid of my students and colleagues there. Professor Charles Ray and Dean Cecil Patterson, who provided me with the time, encouragement, and wherewithal to create the program, deserve a special word of thanks. The professors who worked closely with me, Elizabeth Lee, Phyllis Lotchin, Ernest Mason, Norman Pendergraft, Earl Sanders, Winifred Stoelting, and Randolph Umberger, have all left their mark on this book. The generous support of the Kenan Foundation, which provided the humanities program with a four-year grant, enabled me to research and compile much of the material here. The Kenan Foundation also provided me with the opportunity to attend numerous conferences on the humanities. The stimulating workshops given at North Carolina Central University by Clifford Johnson, of the Institute for Services to Education, also provided inspiration for this book.

The preparation of the manuscript, often a difficult and time-consuming task, has also been the work of several people. I would especially like to thank Jane Birken, Deborah Crowder, Anita Hix, Lorraine Hollis, Jan Krob, and Dorothy Sapp.

Others helped to improve the quality of the manuscript by their reading and suggestions. Professor Christina Sorum of North Carolina State University gave a critical reading of the Greek and Roman material; Professor Peter Wood of Duke University was of great assistance in the material dealing with American history and culture; Paul Clifford of the Duke Art Museum offered many valuable suggestions for the African art section. The analysis and suggestions of Professor J. Lee Greene of the University of North Carolina at Chapel Hill informed the discussion of Afro-American literature in the section on African continuities. Professors Brian Lindsay, University of South Carolina at Spartanburg; Walter Klarner, Johnson County Community College; Aurelia N. Young, Jackson State University; Michael Geis, Western Michigan University; Dorothy J. Corsberg, Northeastern Junior College; Judith Krabbe, Jackson State University; and Brother Paul French, Lewis University, read versions of the manuscript and made many helpful comments.

I have been fortunate to work with co-authors who combine intelligence and sensitivity with a spirit of co-operation. We have all been most fortunate to have been guided by the interest and the diligence of assistant editor Jessie Solodar and the tact, patience, enthusiasm and sound judgments of editor Holt Johnson, both of D. C. Heath and Company.

MARY ANN FRESE WITT

Chronicle of Events

Chronicle of Events

Date	AFRICA	MESOPOTAMIA-SYRIA-PALESTINE	GREECE
3000 B.C.	Lower and Upper Egypt unite First to Second Dynasty (3110–2615)	Sumerian city-states Successive waves of Semites occupy Palestine	
2900			
2800			
2700	Age of Pyramids (c. 2650–2150)		
2600			
2500			
2400			
2300			
2200			
2100			Minoan palace construction begins on island of Crete
2000		Phoenician (Canaanite) city culture	
1900			
1800		Babylonian Dynasty established	
1700	Hyksos invasions (1678–1570)		
1600			High point of Minoan civilization (1600–1400)
1500	Eighteenth Dynasty and Imperial Age (1525–1075)		
1400		Phoenicians develop alphabet	
1300	Akhenaten introduces monotheism (1370–1353)		Destruction of Minoan palace Mycenaean expansion
1200		Hebrews enter Palestine Phoenicians flourish (1200–900)	Traditional date for sack of Troy (c. 1184)

Date	AFRICA	MESOPOTAMIA-SYRIA-PALESTINE	ROME	GREEK POLITICAL EVENTS	GREEK CULTURAL EVENTS
1100					
		Early Assyrian Empire Early Biblical books written Saul made King of Hebrews (c. 1025)			Greek cities on Aegean coast and Greek colonies in Asia Minor established
1000 B.C.		David King of Hebrews (1000–961)			
		Solomon (961–922)			
		Hebrew kingdom divides into Israel and Judah (922)			
900		Assyria conquers Phoenicians and Israel (876–605)			
800	Phoenicians found Carthage (814)		Traditional date for founding of Rome (753)	Beginning of polis	Homer?
700					
600	Iron age begins at Meroe	Nineveh falls (612) Neo-Babylonian Empire of Nebuchadrezzar			Sappho (c. 600)
		Jews taken captive to Babylon (586)			Beginning of Drama and Panathenian Festivals
		Persians take Babylon (539)			
	Persia conquers Egypt (525)	Jews return home (538) Darius of Persia (521–486)	Kings expelled and Republic created (509)		Aeschylus (525–456)
500				Persian Wars (499–479) Pericles (498–427)	Euripides (480–406) Thucydides (470–400) Socrates (470–399) Building of Parthenon (447–432)
				Peloponnesian War (431–404)	Plato (427–347) Aristophanes' *Lysistrata* (411) Sophocles' *Oedipus* (406)
400				Philip of Macedon (382–336)	Aristotle (384–322)

Archaic Age (750–480)

Classical Age (480–350)

Timeline (400 B.C. – A.D. 200)

Time	AFRICA	MESOPOTAMIA-SYRIA-PALESTINE	ROME	GREEK POLITICAL EVENTS	GREEK CULTURAL EVENTS
400 B.C.	Alexander conquers Egypt (332); Greek dynasty rules (331–304)		Vigorous program of Roman conquest of Italy begins (343)	Alexander of Macedon (the Great) (356–323)	Epicurus (342–270); Zeno (336–264) and founding of Stoic school
300			I Punic War (264–241); Sardinia and Corsica annexed (238)		*Hellenistic Age (350–150)*
200	Nok civilization at its height (200 B.C.–200 A.D.)		II Punic War (218–201); Terence (195–159)	Rome begins conquest of Greece	
	Carthage sacked (146); Rome conquers North Africa		III Punic War (149–146); Cicero (106–43); Caesar (100–44); Lucretius (99–55)		
100		Occupation of Israel by Romans (63); Reign of Herod the Great in Palestine (37 B.C.–4 A.D.)	Horace's *Satires* (35–29); Virgil's *Aeneid* (29–19); Augustus begins reign (27)		

Time	AFRICA	ROME AND EUROPE	PAGAN AND CHRISTIAN CULTURE
A.D.		Death of Augustus (14); Conquest of Britain (43–51); Sack of Jerusalem (70)	Birth of Jesus Christ; Persecution of Christians by Nero (64)
100			Juvenal's *Satires* (c. 100); Roman Pantheon built (118–125)
200		Period of disorder (235–284)	Plotinus (205–270) and Neo-Platonism

Timeline (c. 300–975)

- Reforms of Diocletian (285–305)
- Edict of Toleration by Constantine (313)
- Building of Old St. Peter's (330–340)
- Alaric sacks Rome (410)
- Vandals sack Rome (455)
- Traditional date for end of Western Roman Empire (476)
- Justinian (483–565) extends Roman Empire in East and temporarily conquers parts of Italy, Africa, and Spain—Codifies Roman Law
- Moslem conquest of Africa
- Empire of Ghana (700–1230)
- Moslem conquest of Spain (711)
- Defeat of Moslems at Poitiers (732)
- Charlemagne (768–814)
- Second period of invasions (c. 800–950): Northmen, Hungarians, and Saracens
- Northmen establish Normandy (911)
- Otto I founds German Empire (962)
- Hugh Capet King of France (987)
- First systematic teaching of Aristotle's Logic (975)
- Beginnings of Benin

	300	400	500	600	700	800	900

Timeline (1000–1200)

EUROPEAN CULTURE	EUROPE	AFRICA
Building of St. Sernin—Romanesque (11th and 12th centuries)		
Romanesque Style (11th and 12th centuries)		
	Norman invasion of England (1066)	
St. Bernard (1090–1153)	First Crusade (1095)	
Play of Daniel (12th century)		
Rebuilding of St. Denis on new lines—early Gothic		
Bernart de Ventadorn (late 12th century)		
Marie de France (late 12th century)		
Chartres Cathedral begun (1194)	Mongol invasion of Russia	Revolt of Mande peoples against Ghana (c. 1200) and rise of Mali Empire
Aquinas (1225–1274)	European embassy sent to China	

Dates: 1000, 1050, 1100, 1150, 1200

EUROPEAN CULTURE

- Giotto (1276–1337)
- Dante's *Divine Comedy* (1300–1321)
- Petrarch (1304–1374)
- Boccaccio (1310–1375)

Gothic Style (12th–15th centuries)

- Bruni (1370–1444)
- Brunelleschi (1377–1446)
- Chaucer's *Canterbury Tales* (1390–1400)
- Masaccio (1401–1428)
- Henry the Navigator founds navigation school at Sagres (1419)
- Piero della Francesca (1420–1492)
- Medici dominate Florence (1434)
- Alberti's *On Painting* (1435)
- Leonardo da Vinci (1442–1519)
- Botticelli (1444–1510)
- Lorenzo il Magnifico (1449–1492)
- Pico della Mirandola (1463–1494)
- Isaac's *On the Death of Lorenzo*

Renaissance Style (15th and 16th centuries) ←

EUROPE

- St. Louis (1214–1270)
- Hundred Years War begins (1337)
- First appearance of Black Death (1348–1350)
- Jeanne d'Arc burned (1431)
- Spanish Inquisition established (1478)
- Columbus discovers America (1492)
- DaGama sails for India (1497)

AFRICA

- Mansa Musa pilgrimage to Mecca (1324)
- Exploration of Canaries (1330's and 1340's)
- John Affonso d'Aveiro visits Benin (1485–1486)

Years: 1250, 1300, 1350, 1400, 1450

NEW WORLD

- First black slaves in New World (1505)
- Magellan circumnavigates the globe (1519)
- Cortez in Mexico (1519–1521)
- Verrazano establishes French claims in North America (1524)

EUROPEAN CULTURE

- Michelangelo's *David* (1504)
- Raphael's *School of Athens* (1510–1511)
- Machiavelli's *Prince* (1513)
- First edition of Erasmus' *Colloquies* (1516)
- Luther publishes German *New Testament* (1521)

Renaissance Style (15th and 16th centuries)

- First edition of Calvin's *Institutes* (1536)
- Copernicus' *Revolution of Heavenly Bodies* (1543)
- Titian (1477–1576)
- Bruegel (1520–1569)

EUROPE

- Peasants' Revolt in Germany (1525)
- Henry VIII declares himself head of Church of England (1534)
- Jesuit Order founded (1540)
- Council of Trent (1545–1563)
- Peace of Augsburg legalizes Lutheranism in Germany (1555)

AFRICA

- Duarte Pacheco Pereira's *Esmeraldo de situ orbis* (1507)
- Benin at the height of its power (16th and 17th centuries)

Years: 1500, 1525, 1550

Timeline

Dates: 1575 — 1600 — 1625 — 1650 — 1700

Exploration and the Americas

- Building of St. Augustine in Florida (1565)
- Settlement at Jamestown (1607)
- Founding of Quebec (1608)
- First slaves in Virginia (1619)
- Plymouth colony established (1620)
- New York City taken by English from Dutch (1664)
- Salem Witch Trials (1692)

Arts and Sciences

- First edition of Montaigne's *Essays* (1580–1588)
- Shakespeare (1564–1616)
- Kepler (1571–1630)
- Caravaggio's *Calling of St. Matthew* (1599–1600)
- Rubens' *Raising of the Cross* (1609–1610)
- Giambattista Marino (1569–1625)
- John Donne (1572–1631)
- Descartes (1596–1650)
- Corneille (1606–1684)
- Harvey demonstrates circulation of blood (1628)
- French Academy founded (1635)
- Galileo's *Discourse on Two New Sciences* (1638)
- Richard Crashaw (1612–1649)
- Rome's Cornaro Chapel (1645–1652)
- Rembrandt (1606–1669)
- Milton (1609–1674)
- Lully (1632–1687)
- Royal Society of London created (1662)
- Construction of Versailles begins (1669)
- Molière's *Le Bourgeois Gentilhomme* (1670)
- Robert Boyle (1627–1691)
- Newton publishes *Mathematical Principles* (1687)
- Locke's *An Essay Concerning Human Understanding* (1690)
- Darby cokes coal (1709)
- Johann Sebastian Bach (1685–1750)

Political Events

- Reign of Queen Elizabeth I of England (1558–1603)
- Wars of Religion begin in France (1561)
- Massacre of French Protestants (1572)
- Defeat of Spanish Armada (1588)
- Edict of Nantes (1598)
- Thirty Years War begins (1618)
- Civil War in England begins (1643)
- Peace of Westphalia in Germany (1648)
- Restoration of English Monarchy (1660)
- Louis XIV (1638–1715)
- Louis revokes Edict of Nantes (1685)
- Union of Scotland and England (1707)
- War of Spanish Succession (1701–1713)
- Hanover (Windsor) dynasty begins in England (1714)
- Foundation of Ashanti Confederacy (1701)

Year	AFRICA	EUROPE	EUROPEAN CULTURE	NEW WORLD
1725			Building of Hotel Soubise (1732) Kay's Flying Shuttle (1733) English repeal laws against witchcraft (1736) Voltaire's *Micromegas* (1739) Handel's *Messiah* (1742) Montesquieu's *Spirit of the Laws* (1748)	Georgia, last of original thirteen colonies, founded (1733)
		War of Austrian Succession (1740–1748)		
1750		Death of George II (1760)	Volume I of the *Encyclopédie* (1751) Mozart (1756–1791) Rousseau's *On the Origins of Inequality* (1755) First blast furnace (1761) Rousseau's *Social Contract* (1762) Watt patents steam engine (1769) Schiller (1759–1805)	French and Indian War (1754–1763) English take Quebec (1759) English acquire Canada by Treaty of Paris (1763) Boston Massacre (1770) Revolutionary War begins (1775)
1775		Accession of Louis XVI (1774) Meeting of Estates General (May, 1789) Taking of Bastille (July, 1789) Fall of Robespierre (1794) Napoleon's coup d'état (1799)	Goethe's *Werther* (1787) Wollstonecraft's *Vindication of Rights of Women* (1792)	Treaty of Paris ends war (1783) Constitution goes into effect (1789) Washington dies (1799)

Year	AFRICA	EUROPE	EUROPEAN CULTURE	AMERICA
1800	Rise of Fulani Empire (19th century)	Napoleon Consul for life (1802) Napoleon crowned Emperor (1804)	David (1748–1825) Madame de Staël (1766–1817) Wordsworth (1770–1850) Constable (1776–1837)	Jefferson elected President (1801)
1810	Britain abolishes slave trade (1807)	End of Holy Roman Empire (1806)	Stephenson's locomotive (1814) Byron (1788–1824) Goya *Executions of the 3rd of May* (1814) Blake (1757–1827)	War of 1812 (1812–1814) Founding of North American Review (1815)
1820	France abolishes slave trade (1815)	Defeat of Napoleon and Congress of Vienna (1815) Industrialization of England (1815–1850)		
	Liberia established (1822)	Greek War of Independence (1821–1829)	Beethoven's Ninth Symphony (1824)	
1830	France annexes Algeria (1830)	Revolutions in France, Germany, Italy, Belgium, and Poland (1830) Industrialization of France and Belgium (1830–1860) Industrialization of Germany (1840–1870)	Heine (1797–1856)	Emerson (1803–1882) Poe (1809–1849)
1840		Revolutions in France, Italy, Germany, and Austria (1848)	Delacroix (1799–1863) Dickens' *Old Curiosity Shop* (1840) *Giselle* (1841) Chopin (1810–1849) Turner's *Rain, Steam, and Speed* (1845) *Communist Manifesto* (1848)	Mexican War (1846–1848) Gold discovered in California (1848)

	AFRICA	INTERNATIONAL POLITICS	EUROPEAN CULTURE	AMERICAN CULTURE
1850	Livingstone at Victoria Falls (1853–1856)	Second Empire founded in France (1852) Crimean War (1855)	Crystal Palace (1851) Millet (1814–1875) Courbet's Manifesto (1855) Baudelaire (1821–1867) Darwin's Origin of Species (1859)	Walt Whitman (1819–1892)
1860		Foundation of Kingdom of Italy (1860) Emancipation of serfs in Russia (1861)	Mill's On Subjection of Women (1861) Ford Maddox Brown's Work (1862–1863) van Gogh (1853–1890)	Civil War (1861–1865) Emily Dickinson (1830–1886) Period of Reconstruction (1867–1877)
1870	Opening of Suez Canal (1869) Brazza explores Lower Congo (1875)	Creation of Dual Monarchy Austria-Hungary (1867) Franco-Prussian War (1870–1871) German Empire and Third French Republic created (1871)	Nietzsche (1844–1900) Monet's Impressions: Sunrise (1873) Gauguin (1848–1903)	Stephen Crane (1871–1900)
1880	France occupies Tunisia (1881) Britain occupies Egypt (1882) Germans in Togo and Cameroon (1886) Gold found in South Africa (1886) Rhodes establishes Rhodesia (1889–1891)	Dual Alliance: Germany and Austria-Hungary (1879) Triple Alliance: Germany, Austria-Hungary, and Italy (1882) German-Russian Reinsurance Treaty (1887)	Dostoevsky's Brothers Karamazov (1880) Mallarmé (1842–1898) Verlaine (1844–1896) Rimbaud (1854–1891)	William Dean Howells (1837–1920) Henry James (1843–1916)

	AFRICA	INTERNATIONAL POLITICS	EUROPEAN CULTURE	AMERICAN CULTURE
1890	French annex Guinea and Ivory Coast (1893)	Industrialization of Russia (1890–1914) Franco-Russian Alliance (1894)	Cézanne (1839–1906)	Reliance Building (1891) Spanish-American War (1898) Chesnutt's The Conjure Woman (1899)
1900	British conquest of N. Nigeria (1900–1903) Senghor born (1903)	Entente Cordiale: France and Great Britain (1902) First Russian Revolution (1905)	Matisse (1869–1954) Apollinaire (1880–1918) Picasso's Les demoiselles d'Avignon (1907)	Louis H. Sullivan (1856–1924)
1910	Morocco becomes French protectorate (1912) Conquest of German colonies (1914–1915)	Balkan Wars (1912–1913) First World War (1914–1918) Russian Revolution (1917) Treaty of Versailles (1919) German Weimar Republic created (1919)	Duchamp's Nude Descending a Staircase (1912) Mondrian (1872–1944) Kandinsky's On the Spiritual in Art (1912) Rite of Spring (1913) Kirchner's Street (1914) Bauhaus founded (1919)	U.S. declares war on Germany and Austria-Hungary (1917) Harlem Renaissance (1919–1932)
1920		Irish Free State (1922) Mussolini establishes Fascism in Italy (1922) Great Depression begins (1929)	Kafka (1883–1924) Nijinsky (1890–1950) Lipchitz' Figure (1926–1928) Brancusi's Bird in Space (1928)	W.E.B. Dubois (1868–1963) Davis' Egg Beater No. 1 (1927) Stock Market Crash (1929)

	AMERICAN CULTURE	EUROPEAN CULTURE	INTERNATIONAL POLITICS	AFRICA
1930	Shahn's *Passion of Sacco and Vanzetti* (1930) New Deal begins (1933) Louis Armstrong (1900–1971)	Freud's *Civilization and Its Discontents* (1930) Le Corbusier's *Villa Savoye* (1929–1930) James Joyce (1882–1941) Picasso's *Guernica* (1937)	Hitler rises to power (1933) Official rearmament of Germany (1935) Spanish Civil War (1936–1939) Second World War begins (1939)	Nigerian youth movement begins (early 1930's) Italy conquers Ethiopia (1936)
1940	T. S. Eliot (1888–1965) Jackson Pollock (1912–1956) Japanese attack Pearl Harbor (1941) Richard Wright (1908–1960) E. E. Cummings (1894–1962)	Einstein (1879–1955) Sartre (1905–)	Formation of United Nations (1945) Fourth French Republic established (1945) Communist takeover in E. Europe (1946–1948) China becomes communist (1949) Korean War (1950–1953)	Ethiopia liberated (1941)
1950	Langston Hughes (1902–1967) Ezra Pound (1885–1972) Duke Ellington (1899–1974) Martha Graham (1895–)	Camus (1913–1960) Charlie Chaplin (1889–1977) Arrabal's *Picnic on the Battlefield* (1952) Beckett's *Endgame* (1957)	Russian Sputnik (1957) Common Market (1957) de Gaulle's Fifth Republic (1958)	Algerian War begins (1954) Morocco and Tunisia freed (1955) Ghana first colony to gain independence (1957) Guinea independent (1958)
1960	Ralph Ellison (1914–) Katherine Dunham (1919–) Kurt Vonnegut, Jr. (1922–) James Baldwin (1924–) Miles Davis (1926–)		Berlin Wall (1961) Beginning of Russia-China split (1962) Great Cultural Revolution in China (1966)	Nigeria and most French colonies independent (1960) Algeria and Tanganyika freed (1962)
1970	Adrienne Rich (1929–) Alvin Ailey (1931–) LeRoi Jones (1938–) Nikki Giovanni (1943–)		Withdrawal of U.S. from Vietnam (1972)	Amin gains power in Uganda (1971) Breakdown of Portuguese African Empire (1974)
1980				

APPROACHING
THE HUMANITIES

What Are the Humanities?

About fifty years ago almost any educated person would have felt able to give a confident and straightforward answer to the above question. Now, however, people involved with the humanities tend to discuss such topics as "the humanities in crisis," "the humanities in revolution," or "the changing role of the humanities." They also have a variety of ideas on what the humanities include and what they are about. One thing they agree upon: the humanities are in some way vital to the education of human beings. Those who formulate educational policy seem, at least on the surface, to agree—the category "humanities" includes a wide variety of courses offered or even required at colleges and high schools—and a typical college catalog gives the impression that all knowledge is divided into three parts: sciences, social sciences, and humanities.

There is certainly no one pat, inclusive definition of the humanities.

Even if one approaches such a definition from the most simplified point of view—we might call it the "college catalog approach"—it is difficult for everyone to agree on a list of disciplines that should be included under "humanities." Classical and modern languages and literature, English literature and philosophy, art history, music history, and even dance history usually pose no problem; but what about drama, studio art and music, dance, film, media studies, religion? While it is traditionally assumed that artists perform or practice the arts while humanists analyze and study them, rigidly exclusive categories benefit neither group. No one denies that social sciences such as history and anthropology and natural sciences such as biology have "humanistic" aspects, but what are they?

It may be helpful to attempt a basic distinction between the sciences and the humanities. Scientists, on the whole, claim to be objective: they collect data, conduct experiments, formulate laws or theories, and remain essentially detached from the process. Humanists, on the other hand, are vitally concerned with the expression of human values, beliefs, and emotions; thus their involvement with their material is necessarily a less detached, more subjective one. Consider a topic that you might study in the sciences, the social sciences, and the humanities. Let us take as an example a human emotion—fear. In a course in biology or physiology you might analyze the secretions produced when an animal or a human being experiences fear; in a psychology or sociology course you might be asked to define causes of situations that produce fear; and in an art or English course you might study the expression of fear in a painting or a poem. If you respond fully to the painting or the poem, it is probable that your own feelings about fear will become more fully involved in the third type of study than in the first two. Through your emotional involvement, you might then begin to develop new values and beliefs on the subject of fear. But are the lines that we have drawn here really hard and fast ones? Doesn't a doctor or a psychologist who attempts to help a patient overcome his fears necessarily hold some values and beliefs on the subject? On the other hand, can a student of the humanities respond fully to a painting or a poem merely through emotional involvement without detached observation and objec-

tive analysis? The question is not one of absolute definition but one of emphasis.

Another way to approach the concept "humanities" is to look at the word itself. Obviously, its root is "human." We have already implied that humanists, or people concerned with the humanities, are primarily interested in human values, beliefs, and emotions—one might say simply with total human beings. The first people to call themselves humanists believed that man was the very highest point of creation and that everything else should be measured by human standards. We are perhaps not quite so confident today, but in the humanities we still begin our inquiries about the world from a *human* point of view.

Historical Development of the Humanities

This leads us to another approach to the concept "humanities": the historical one. The establishment of humanities as a body of knowledge is the result of something that a few people thought was important some five hundred years ago. The Renaissance humanists, reacting against a curriculum dominated by theology in the Middle Ages, passionately edited and commented on ancient Greek and Latin texts because they believed that human-centered inquiry should be revived. The studies that they called the humanities—in Latin, *studia humanitatis*—centered around the literature of antiquity. The humanists did not study the rediscovered works of Greek and Latin literature merely out of historical curiosity: they did so because they believed that this type of mental exercise would have a vital and profound impact on the present. By studying the grammar and the rhetoric of the ancients, they would learn how to express themselves more effectively in speaking and writing. By reading what they called the moral philosophy of Greek and Latin writers, they could understand what some of the great minds of the past had to say on complex moral issues. Thus the study of what we call form and content in literature was to lead not to slavish imitation of rules of grammar or traditional morality but to the refinement and development of the human mind. From the study of classical literature came the belief we most often associate with the Renaissance humanists, the belief in the dignity of man. A respect for the humanity of all persons and an admiration for the freedom and creativity of the human mind are humanist ideals that subsequent generations have interpreted in their own ways.

In spite of their affirmation of the basic dignity of all human beings, the Renaissance humanists definitely believed that some were more "human" than others. People who studied the humanities, according to them, actually acquired more humanity not only because they were able to think for themselves more creatively and to express themselves more subtly but also because they acquired a deeper understanding of human beings. Ideally, this kind of humanistic growth should be available to all. In practice, however, it was available only to those with enough wealth, family support, or adequate patronage to have a certain amount of leisure. As an influence of Renaissance humanism, the study of Greek and Latin became the mark of a "cultured" man or woman. As a distortion of humanist ideals, "culture" became associated with class privilege and snobbery. The association between culture and class survived the revolutions of the eighteenth century and transferred itself from the aristocracy to the middle classes. At their worst, professors and students of the humanities became caricatures of humanism. At certain times and places, both in Europe and the United States, you were "in" if you could drop the right Greek and Latin quotations at the right point, along with some memorized clichés about the beauty of certain accepted works. You were said to be "cultured" or "cultivated" if you said the right things about the right works of literature, art, and music, and showed exquisite table manners as well. In recent years, as we came to see the importance of the humanities in all human cultures and for all human minds, this kind of snobbishness has come in for a good deal of ridicule.

This should not be understood to imply that the humanities simply fell into decadence after the Renaissance. What happened, in fact, is that they branched out and went in all sorts of different directions. Cultural snobbery and blind worship of tradition and class privilege were the banners of a very narrow faction. Creative men and women have always carried the spirit of the humanities into the present and the future, stimulated by, but not bound by the past. Seven-teenth-century humanists in Europe allied themselves with scientists to fight for the liberty of the questioning human mind against the dictates of established authority. Eighteenth-century humanists speaking out for religious tolerance, for liberty, equality, and fraternity, helped to create revolutions. Nineteenth-century humanists struggled to save the human spirit from a threatening emphasis on industrial growth and technical progress. They also broadened considerably the areas encompassed by humanistic study through the creation of new fields such as folklore, comparative religions, art history, and music history. Pioneers in oriental and African studies began to help Western humanists to emerge from their cultural prison.

The Humanities Today

In our own century, fields allied with the humanities, including the interdisciplinary approaches to them with which we are concerned here, have proliferated. Some (though not all) students of the humanities have branched out to fields like film, TV, dance, and crafts. The scope of the humanities has also broadened considerably. We in the West are beginning to see more clearly that there are other humanistic traditions besides our own, not only in the great past civilizations of India, China, Africa, and the Arab world, but also in the cultures of the American Indians or the Polynesians. We have come a long way from a study confined to Greek and Roman literature, but these are still relevant to our present concerns. A line from the Roman poet Terence, a slave of African origins, might in fact best define the ideal modern humanist.

Homo sum; humani nihil a me alienum puto.
(I am a man; I hold nothing human foreign to me.)

If the humanities have developed and flourished in certain respects, they have, especially in our own time, undergone numerous crises. Certainly there are modern humanists of various political persuasions and cultural attachments who continue to fight the battle for the freedom and creativity of the human spirit against those they perceive to be its enemies. The teaching of the humanities was greatly enriched in the United States and Canada during the 1930s and 1940s because many humanists fled to North America from Germany in protest against one of the most massive repressions of the human spirit in our history. On the other hand, survivors of Hitler's concentration camps found that they had lost, or had to revise drastically, their traditional concepts of "the dignity of man." More recently, leaders of the New Left movement in the 1960s and early 1970s declared the teaching of traditional humanities in colleges to be an instrument of ruling class oppression, while others found their quest for liberation furthered by their reading of writers like Dostoevsky or Hesse. Each generation must redefine the spirit and the content of the humanities for itself.

The humanities must, of course, change and grow if they are not to stagnate. Yet humanists, perhaps more than others, remain aware of the value of tradition. Change in the humanities comes about primarily through the reinterpretation and reevaluation of tradition. Throughout the development of the humanities, certain humanist values have emerged as constants. Among them are a commitment to full, individual development of the whole human being, a belief in the freedom of intellectual inquiry and artistic expression, an opposition to oppression, intolerance, fanaticism. The ways in which these values are embodied vary widely, but the humanist is often apt to run afoul of various establishments.

Are traditional humanistic values adequate in a world that has seen Auschwitz and Hiroshima, My Lai and Kent State, the dangers of pollution, radiation, and energy shortages? Technological and economic events seem to shape the world in a way remote from individual minds. Some contemporary writers speak of the necessary formation of a posthumanism. Today's students of the humanities will be charged with carrying on a tradition and radically restructuring its values.

What, it may well be asked, can the study of the humanities do for a student in the last decades of the twentieth century? We have seen that traditionally humanists believed that the study of the humanities would increase one's moral capabilities, make one a better person. It is clear that we are no longer confident of this. What most humanists do still believe, however, is that the study of the humanities can and should have an impact on the personal growth and develop-

ment of every human being. True involvement with the humanities means involvement with one's self. It means stretching and expanding one's capacity for thought, sensitivity, and creativity; it means asking some basic questions. Who am I? What are my goals in life? What religious or moral beliefs do I really hold? Are human beings basically good or evil? Is equality possible? What is beauty? What is love? What are the roles of men and women? These are only a few examples.

The humanities, as this brief introduction shows, undoubtedly raise more questions than they answer. This is perhaps their most important function: to lead human beings to ask questions and to provide them with means for developing individual responses. It is vital for the humanities to maintain an interaction with developing, creative human life.

Interrelating the Arts within the Humanities

What justifies studying a poem or story, a building, a statue, a dance, a musical composition, and a work of philosophy together? One reason often given is enriched understanding of a particular human culture: the study of the masks, dances, poetry, music, and religion of the Yoruba people will give more insight into their culture than will the study of their poetry alone. Another reason lies in the fact that the comparative method enables one art form to shed light on another. A third, more general, reason is that all of these enable us to understand more about the human spirit and its creative capacity.

We have seen that the humanities are primarily concerned with human values, beliefs, and emotions and with the way in which these are expressed through human creations. Philosophy and religion embody more or less systematically organized values and beliefs, while works of art (in literature, painting, music, or other) embody the creative expression of these values and beliefs. But these distinctions are not hard and fast. A philosophical tract may also be artistic, and a play or a statue may open up new dimensions in philosophy. The study of cultural history—of values and beliefs prevalent at certain times and places—helps to bind the humanities together, though sometimes a work of genius may go *against* prevailing values and systems.

If we limit ourselves to the study of the arts for the moment, some essential common elements in the humanities will perhaps become clearer. Let us hypothesize that for the creation of a work of art basically two things are needed: some kind of raw material and a creative mind. Some examples come to mind: Michelangelo and a block of marble, Shakespeare and the English language, Beethoven and the notes in the Western scale. The creative mind (as well as the muscles, you might argue in the first case) of the artist works on the raw material, giving it shape or form. It then bears the imprint of his individual genius, but it also shows the influence of the cultural tradition and the era from which it comes. The combination of these will constitute its style. It will also have certain subject matters, structures, and themes that will be composed of the "fundamentals" of the art form used. All of these can be analyzed, in various ways, step by step. A technical analysis of a work of art, while a necessary and useful step in the process of understanding, is still only a means to an end. The end can be called "aesthetic awareness"—the expansion of one's capacity to perceive meaning and to react to it.

The artist gives shape, power, and expression to stone, words, or notes; and you, the humanities student, through some technical and historical knowledge and a willingness to expand your creative awareness, prepare yourself to receive a personal impact from the work of art. Of course, you can choose not to expand but instead to judge through the limits and prejudices of your present experience, deciding immediately that you simply "like" or "dislike" or "agree with" or "don't agree with" certain works or ideas. In that case, you will not be receiving an education in the humanities. You are not expected to venerate and worship any prescribed set of masterpieces, but you are invited to open your mind and senses and grapple with the unexpected.

Culture, Cultural Roots, and the Humanities

"Culture," a word that has acquired many meanings in recent years, is in need of some definition. We all feel that we belong to a group culture, whose values we may either defend or reject; and in the educational process (broadly speaking, *not* limited to schooling) we also acquire an individual culture. This latter may sometimes take on the connotation of "overrefined."

It may be useful to look at the root meaning of the word. In Latin, the verb *colere* means "to cultivate or till," and the noun *cultura*, "soil cultivation." Our word *agriculture* comes from this root and from the Latin word for *field*. Language often grows by metaphors, and here the word culture, applied to human beings, suggests that the human mind, especially the mind of a child, is like a field that must be tilled, fertilized, planted, and *cultivated* by parents, teachers, and other influential members of the society in which the child lives. Applied to an adult, it implies the acquisition of learning and knowledge not merely for their practical value but also for the growth of the mind in its intellectual, moral, and aesthetic capacities. It is in this sense that the black American poet Dudley Randall, describing the beliefs of the humanist W.E.B. DuBois, speaks of "the right to cultivate the brain." [1] We are, of course, vitally concerned with culture in this sense of individual development in the humanities. The Renaissance humanists, initiators of the tradition in which DuBois was educated, believed, as we have seen, that this sort of culture was best acquired through the study of Greek and Latin literature. Today we see all of the humanities as a means necessary for the acquisition of culture.

If the humanities are concerned with culture in an individual sense, they are also concerned with it in a social or sociological sense. Let us return for a moment to the comparison between the child's mind and the farmer's field. As it is cultivated, that mind not only develops as an individual, but it also acquires certain habits, values, beliefs, ways of thinking, seeing, feeling, and expressing that attach the child to a certain culture. When we use the word in this sense, it might help to think of its meaning in the biological sciences. Certain types of bacteria growing in certain types of environments are called "cultures." When we extend this

---

[1] In "Booker T. and W.E.B." The relevant lines are: "Some men rejoice in skill of hand, /And some in cultivating land, /But there are others who maintain /The right to cultivate the brain."

notion to human beings, we are aware of what it means to speak of a Western culture, an Oriental culture, an African culture. More specifically, we may speak of Slavic or Germanic or Latin culture, of Ibo or Bantu culture, of Japanese culture. We may speak of American culture, or we may break it down into Black culture, Italo-American culture, Midwestern culture, urban culture, rural culture, and so on. We may make other sorts of categories such as youth culture, female culture, male culture, and Baptist culture. There are, in other words, a variety of ways to slice the cultural pie.

Anthropologists looking at a culture are interested in its language, religion, social customs, food, and clothing; its moral and philosophical beliefs; its political, economic, and familial systems; and its plastic arts, poetry, tales, music, and dance. Humanists are interested in all of these things too, but especially in a given culture's intellectual and artistic achievements. Ideally, in the study of the humanities, we should combine the two meanings of the word *culture* discussed here: we should both acquire individual culture and learn about a social culture. As you read a Greek tragedy or examine a piece of African sculpture, you learn something about the values, beliefs, and aesthetics of a particular people; but you also cultivate your own brain through new ideas and expanded senses. Human beings differ from bacteria in that they can flourish and develop through exposure to cultures different from their own.

The success of Alex Haley's book *Roots* and the film made of it shows how deeply interested people are in the idea of "roots." For black Americans, tracing family origins is perhaps doubly interesting because doubly difficult. Tracing one's *cultural* roots, however, can be even more complex a matter. On the American continent, particularly, where so many of us have so many different origins, we have all been influenced by a number of cultures. Thus an Afro-American may discover that he has some Irish cultural roots; an Anglo-American may find that certain aspects of his culture are native American (Indian) or African. As we learn more about a world with ever faster communications, we also become more acquainted with totally foreign cultures, which in turn become a part of our personal, individual culture. We begin to discover unexpected cultural roots when we ask questions like "what lies at

the root of the ways in which I think, perceive, and express myself?" or "what are the origins of the books, films, TV programs, buildings, music, and visual stimuli of my culture?"

This book focuses on three basic cultural roots: Greco-Roman, Judeo-Christian, and West African. Though many others—such as American Indian, Egyptian, and Chinese—could have been included, they were not, primarily because of limits of space and the scope of a single course. Perhaps we should explain why we have chosen to concentrate on the three cultural roots listed above and what we mean by them.

The art, thought, languages, political institutions, and religious systems of North America and Europe have developed primarily from what we can loosely call Western or Occidental culture. (Naturally many non-Western elements, especially the native American cultures, remain.) Thus if we are to understand an overwhelming influence in our lives, we must come to terms with some of the most outstanding components of Western culture. Intellectually and artistically, as well as in more practical ways, the mainstreams composing this culture are generally thought to be two: one from the civilizations of ancient Greece and Rome; the other from the Bible, which originated in the culture of the ancient Hebrews. The religion of the latter, Judaism, gave rise to two world religions, Islam and Christianity, and continues as an important cultural force itself. The beliefs and institutions of Christianity as they developed from Judaism (and were influenced by Greco-Roman culture) have been major forces in the formation of Western culture. The Renaissance gave rise to the study of the humanities with literary, philosophical, and political ideas from the Greco-Roman tradition and a mentality formed by the Judeo-Christian one. These two roots, fused in various ways and influenced by a variety of other cultures, have continued to exert their influence on the art, thought, and institutions of the West.

The study of African culture should provide some needed balance and some interesting comparisons with the Western humanistic tradition. Knowledge of Africa is becoming important not only because Black Americans are more and more concerned with understanding African origins of their culture, but also because all of us are becoming more aware that African culture has influenced the West more generally. Since our interest in the first volume of this book is in "roots" and thus in ancient cultures, we will focus here on some ancient West African empires that flourished around the time of the Middle Ages and Renaissance in Europe. We will, however, also look at some West African art forms that may have been produced or recorded in recent years but that express the continuity of traditional African values. The sense of chronological time, so natural to us in the West, is perceived quite differently in Africa.

We stressed in the preface that our treatment of cultural roots will be in the form of concentration on a few periods and works rather than in the form of an ex-haustive survey. As we begin our study of modern culture—from the seventeenth century to the present—we will observe the continuities from the three original cultural roots and pick up some new roots along the way. There, too, we will be looking at a few works, places, and periods of particular significance to the formation of contemporary culture.

You may consider the works you encounter here to be roots of your culture, or you may consider them totally foreign; you may even go through a shift in your attitude. What counts in the end is your humanistic involvement with them. If you experience them openly and creatively, they will in any case become a vital part of your personal culture.

PART ONE
THE GRECO-ROMAN ROOT

1

EARLY GREECE

The civilization of ancient Greece, which we can date roughly from about the eighth century to the first century B.C., and the civilization of ancient Rome, lasting from about the first century B.C. to the fifth century A.D., are often referred to collectively as *Greco-Roman* or as *classical.* This should not be interpreted to mean that their cultures were identical. There are many points of contrast, and, although the Romans assimilated a good deal of Greek culture, they added many unique features of their own. Still, they do share a common cluster of ways of thinking and creating that differ from those of other ancient cultures and that have clearly influenced the development of the Western humanistic tradition. Both Greeks and Romans gave human reason, in forms like rule by law and discussion through philosophy, more importance than mystical experience or reliance on tradition. In literature, art, and architecture, both cultures stressed balance, proportion, simplicity, and nobility as their criteria for beauty. Yet their view of human beings was not cold or merely rationalistic. The whole man was very much in view; and, if reason was to dominate the passions, the emotional, ecstatic side of human nature was also recognized as essential.

It is quite possible to argue that Western culture, particularly North American culture, has been more influenced by the Romans than by the Greeks. Yet we have chosen to focus attention here on Greek culture for three reasons: 1) the Greeks obviously came first and laid the basis for the later culture; 2) Greek culture was more concentrated and it is somewhat easier to get a coherent view of its lifestyle, art, and thought; and 3) in many instances the Greek cultural monuments, especially the tragedies, are more alive and significant for us today than are their Roman counterparts. We will devote most attention to the "classical" phase of Greek culture; but, to avoid confusion, it is necessary to remember that *all* of Greco-Roman culture is sometimes called classical, as when we speak of classical languages (Greek and Latin) or classical literature. The word was first adopted by Renaissance scholars, who used it in the sense of "first class" or "best" because they considered the artistic and literary style of the ancient Greeks and Romans as the model for all good art. That ideal model was generally accepted until the nineteenth century in the West. Now we also use the term *classical* to refer to the particular phase of Greek art and literature that, according to most historians of Greek culture, most perfectly expresses the ideals of the Greek aesthetic and the Greek view of life—Athens in the fifth century B.C., specifically 480–404. We will define the classical canons more specifically when examining the creations from this phase. First, however, it will be necessary to examine briefly the rise of Greek civilization and some important prior cultural developments.

Hellenism—The Rise of Greek Culture

What was so important about a small Mediterranean civilization that flourished over two thousand years ago in a country we now call Greece? History books and anthologies of literature often begin with the Greeks as if culture itself had begun there, but we know that is false. If we look at Greek civilization in the context of world history, we can see that it is a relative latecomer. The first human cultures arose in Africa; the first large-scale civilization was in the Middle East, in Mesopotamia. Great civilizations in Asia and Africa—notably those in the Indus valley in India, in China, and in Egypt—were highly developed while savage tribes still roamed in Greece. In fact, all of Western civilization can be seen as the child of Eastern civilization. The Greeks were not the first to create a written literature, painting, sculpture, music, or science. In many of these fields they borrowed heavily from Egypt. Yet the ways in which they developed the humanities and sciences were unique. Those developments are significant for our search for cultural roots because the Greeks were the first to express themselves in ways that can be designated as characteristically Western.

There is a more specific reason why the culture of the ancient Greeks is especially important to the study of the humanities. Theirs was the first culture that we can truly call humanistic. The Greeks were the first to be interested in, and indeed to glorify, human beings simply as human beings—for themselves and their own unique qualities rather than because of their place in a religious, familial, or social order. This stress on the value of the individual made Greek culture less conservative than its predecessors. In contrast to the stable, slowly changing, and long-lasting Egyptian culture, Greek culture was dynamic, rapidly changing, and short-lived.

Unfortunately, it used to be fairly commonplace for Western historians to assume that because the Greeks were different they were better, or because their culture changed more rapidly they contributed more to the development of the human spirit. We are now perhaps better able to see that the restless, dynamic character of Western culture has created its own problems, and also that we have much to learn from the older cultures of the rest of the world. At the risk of making too great a generalization, we might say that a religious sense of life, or the sense of being in touch with a supernatural, spiritual world, and the use of symbolism or suggestion to convey this in art, have characterized the African and Asiatic contributions to world culture. Philosophy, or the rational analysis of problems from a human point of view and a corresponding naturalism in art have been the legacies of the Greeks and their successors, the Romans.

Hellenism and Hebraism The Greek view of life can also be effectively contrasted with that of the ancient Hebrews, whose culture gave rise to the other main root of Western culture. The adjective *Hellenic* and the noun *Hellenism* have come to stand for certain ways of thinking and feeling that can be traced back to the ancient Greeks. They derive from the Greek word for Greece, Ελλας, *Hellas* in the Roman alphabet. In an influential essay, "Culture and Anarchy," written about a hundred years ago, the English poet and critic Matthew Arnold set down what he perceived to be the important contrasts between the two main sources of Western culture: Hellenism and Hebraism. The aim of Hellenism, in his opinion, is "to see things as they really are," while the aim of Hebraism is "conduct and obedience." The one stresses "right thinking," or reasoning for oneself; the other stresses "right acting," or obeying God's commandments. While scholars and thinkers have since attacked Arnold's oversimplified view, pointing out in particular that Greek culture was not all "sweetness and light" (as he put it), his basic categories still make sense.

"Man is the measure of all things," a statement by the Greek philosopher Protagoras, would have been inconceivable in an African or Far Eastern culture or in a Near Eastern one such as that of the ancient Hebrews. Contrast this with a question from the Bible, in Psalm 8, "What is man that Thou art mindful of him?" Although Greek thinkers were aware of the frailty of man, this question would not have occurred to them. Greek culture assumed that human beings were the primary interest of the gods, just as the gods themselves were glorified human beings. It was natural for men to be curious about, and attempt to interpret, the world around them.

Crete How did the Hellenes (the Greeks) develop their particular form of culture? The first civilization to exist in the country now called Greece developed on the island of Crete in the Mediterranean Sea (see map) around 2000 B.C. The island's location between Egypt and mainland Greece is symbolic of its role in helping to transmit one culture to the other. The Minoans, as they were called after their legendary king, Minos, seem to have developed trade with Egypt (whose civilization had already been in existence for a thousand years) and to have led peaceful and creative lives. The form of government in Crete was apparently matriarchal; that is, it was ruled by a queen whose husband, the king, was ritually sacrificed each year. A mother-earth goddess was the principal deity in Minoan religion. A modern African scholar has interpreted the importance given to the female principle in Crete as evidence that Minoan civilization is basically African in its origins. Whether or not this theory is true, the matriarchal emphasis in Minoan culture certainly contrasts with the male-dominated later Greek culture.

Minoan artists used natural forms—plants, animals, fish, and fowl—to decorate walls, pottery, and gems. Their loosely structured, vividly colorful designs suggest a deep love for, and profound observation of, nature. The unfortified, elaborate, and labyrinthine palaces at Knossos (Fig. 1-1), Phaistos, and Mallia contrast sharply with the hierarchical, ceremonial, ritualistic tomb and temple complexes of Egypt. Built of wood, mudbrick, and stone, the multileveled palaces had light wells, folding doors, and winding stairs that connected apartments, ceremonial rooms, workshops, and storage areas. The beautiful *frescoes*, seal stones, jewelry, and other artifacts suggest a lifestyle in which satisfaction and pleasure were more important than ceremonial or military discipline.

1–1 Knossos, Crete: Palace, East Wing. (Eugene Brown)

CLASSICAL GREECE

In 1400 B.C. Crete was conquered by a more warlike people, the first we can truly call Greek. Wandering tribes from Europe, settling in mainland Greece, eventually developed a rich civilization centered in the city of Mycenae, which flourished between 1600 and 1200 B.C. This civilization is referred to either as Achaean, from the name of its principal tribe, or Mycenaean, from the name of the city. Within it a number of kings ruled over small, independent states. The most famous of these kings were Agamemnon, who ruled in My-

cenae with Queen Clytemnestra, and his brother Menelaus, who ruled in Sparta with Helen. Their names have become familiar to us because of the legend of the Trojan War. According to this legend Helen, the most beautiful woman in the world, ran away from her husband with Paris, the son of Priam, king of Troy. Troy was located in Asia Minor, and its ruins have been excavated in what is now Turkey. Determined to recapture Helen, the kings of Greece raised a huge fleet of ships commanded by Agamemnon. They sailed for

Troy and remained there for nine years, fighting and plundering but unable to take the city. In the tenth year Agamemnon quarreled with his most powerful fighter, Achilles. As Achilles and his followers withdrew from the fighting, the brother of Paris, Hektor, began to lead the Trojans toward victory. Achilles then returned to battle, succeeding in entering Troy; he killed Hektor but was soon killed himself. Although the Greeks were aided by powerful new allies such as Memnon, the black prince from Ethiopia, and Penthisilea, queen of the Amazons, with her female warriors, Troy still continued to hold out. It was finally overcome by a ruse devised by the "wily" Greek, Odysseus. The Greeks, pretending to acknowledge defeat, actually boarded their ships to prepare for departure, leaving behind them a huge wooden horse as an offering to the gods. The horse was, in fact, full of armed Greek soldiers. When the Trojans, overcome with curiosity, took it into their city, the Greeks came out and set fire to Troy. Thus the will of the gods was accomplished: Troy was subdued by the Achaeans, and Helen returned to Menelaus. Historians today believe that the Trojan war (ca. 1200 B.C.) was actually fought, but probably for economic reasons. More important for our cultural roots is the legendary material that has spawned a wealth of Western literature, beginning with the *Iliad* and the *Odyssey*.

Mycenae   The Mycenaean age of Greek culture, about which we have little factual information, is often called the heroic age because most of the heroic deeds such as the Trojan War that were later written and sung about took place then. In contrast to matriarchal Crete, it was a masculine-oriented and male-ruled society. The painting, sculpture, and architecture of Mycenae affirm this orientation. The citadel (Fig. 1-2) at Mycenae, overlooking the plain and visible from the sea, was heavily fortified. One entered it through the Lion Gate, so called for its monumental *relief sculpture* of two lions. The king's palace dominated the entire complex. A rectangular building with a deep porch on its narrow end, it contained a main room where the king received dignitaries, held court, and entertained. Frescoes of shields and warriors decorated the walls. The heraldic lions at the gate and the massive scale of the masonry create an image of power controlled by will, solemnity, and ritual.

Mycenae "rich in gold" was eventually destroyed by uncivilized invaders from the north, the Dorians. The next four hundred years are often called the "dark ages" of Greece. We know little about this period except that what would later become the classical city-states—Athens, Corinth, Argos, and finally Sparta—were beginning to emerge as centers of power.

Archaic Period   The next epoch of Greek culture is sometimes referred to as the Archaic period. *Archaic* refers to something in its initial stages. This period, which we can date from approximately 700–480 B.C., indeed saw the beginnings of several forms of Greek culture. In politics the unit of the city-state, or *polis*, was formed; and the form of government known as "democracy," which means in Greek "rule by the people," evolved. In architecture the Doric temple was created, and in sculpture the first free-standing human figures appeared. Greek vase painting was also developed during this time, and the first people who can properly be called philosophers began to speculate and

1–2   Mycenae, Lion Gate, c. 1250 B.C. (Eugene Brown)

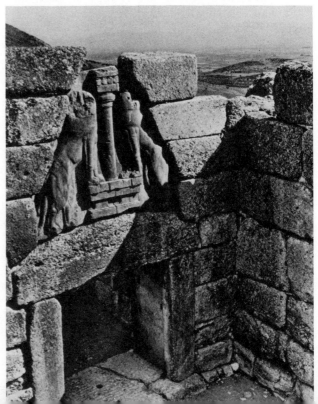

reason about the nature of the universe. Early forms of drama evolved throughout this period; and Thespis, the founder of Greek drama as we know it, won the first dramatic contest in Athens in the sixth century B.C. We will discuss all of these forms in connection with their classical stages in the next chapter. Here we look at two elements of Greek culture that reached a kind of culmination in the Archaic period: religion and poetry—specifically the forms of the *epic* and the *lyric*.

Greek Religion and Mythology

The Greeks, in contrast to the ancient peoples of India and the Middle East, did not have what we might call a religious genius. They seem to have been too much oriented toward this world to have devised either a great theology or a literature of mystical experience. Unlike the early Hindu scriptures or the laws of the God of the Hebrews, the stories of the gods on Mount Olympus have given rise to no enduring religion. Why, then, have these stories been so appealing to people for so many generations, and why are names of gods and goddesses like Zeus, Apollo, and Aphrodite still familiar to us? Unlike the Hebrew and Christian God, who belongs to a realm inaccessible to humans except through faith, the Greek gods are comprehensible to human beings. They may be seen as a kind of wish fulfillment—they are like us but powerful, beautiful, and immortal; they live "at ease." Created through prescientific attempts to explain the universe, they embody deep, intuitive understandings of human psychology.

The terms *myth* and *mythology*, used in a variety of ways, need some clarification. In popular usage, a myth designates something that the person using the word believes to be untrue even though many people may accept it as true. Thus we speak of myths created by advertising or the myth of pure and honest government. Used by psychologists, anthropologists, or literary critics, however, the word has a much broader meaning, one that is nearly the opposite of its popular one. It comes from the Greek μυθος (mythos), which can mean "a word" or "a story." Every culture in the world has, or has had a set of stories passed down orally from one generation to the next that are called its myths; the body of a culture's myths is its mythology. Myths differ

from legends (such as that of the Trojan War) in that they are not usually based on a historical event, situated in time. Myths take place outside of historical time, in what students of mythology call "sacred time" and the Australian aborigines call "dream time." They often attempt to explain the origins of some phenomenon of nature such as the creation of man or why the sun rises and sets. Their characters are gods, sacred beings, or semidivine heroes and heroines. Studies in comparative mythology show that many figures such as the sky god, the earth goddess, the vegetation god, the divine child, and the virgin mother are, with different names and in various forms, found in widely divergent cultures that apparently had no influence on each other. Calling such figures *archetypes*, the psychologist Carl Gustav Jung postulated a "collective unconscious" from which human beings drew their vital myths.

Far from being a pack of lies, as popular usage would have it, the myths of a particular culture represent for that culture the deepest form of truth—a reality which is lived and practiced through ritual. For those outside of the culture they may also portray profound human truths, whether in a psychological, sociological, or spiritual sense. Thus we may distinguish between mythological truth and factual truth. Because of the insights it offers on the human mind and emotions, Greek mythology has continuously inspired Western art, literature, and even science.

The notion of "mythological truth" also informs the way in which Western culture views its own religions. After the work of Charles Darwin and of Biblical criticism in the nineteenth century, many believing Jews and Christians found that they could no longer accept the account of the origin of the world and of man given in Genesis to be true in a literal sense; and yet most believers today accept it as true in a symbolical, religious, or mythological sense. Religion, of course, is much more than a particular set of myths, although these are part of it. The word means a "binding together" and implies a system of beliefs, rituals, and standards of conduct. Great world religions such as Judaism, Christianity, Islam, Hinduism, and Buddhism have given human beings a core of meaning to their lives outlasting political change, scientific discoveries, and other cultural developments. The religion of the ancient Greeks, despite the beauty of its mythology, was not one of these.

Gods and Goddesses It is not possible to mention all the Greek gods and goddesses and religious doctrines here, but we will look briefly at the Greek account of the origin of the world and at some of the major figures.

The Greeks believed that the creation of the universe came from Chaos, a great mass in which everything now existing was jumbled. The first beings to spring forth were a female divinity, earth (Gaea), and a male divinity, heaven (Uranus). It is worth noting here that nearly all myths of creation and religious systems except Judaism and Christianity have seen the need for a divine female role in creation. The children of Gaea and Uranus were the Titans, the first gods, whose leader was Cronos (Saturn, in Latin). (The Romans largely assimilated Greek religion, and all of the Greek gods and goddesses are probably more familiar under their Latin names, which will appear here in parentheses.) Cronos was deposed by his son Zeus (Jupiter). Zeus became lord of the heavens, his brother Poseidon (Neptune) lord of the sea, and their brother Dis (Pluto) lord of the underworld, or the realm of the dead. Hera (Juno), the wife of Zeus, was goddess of childbirth and protector of married women. Because the family of Zeus was said to live on Mount Olympus, its members were called the Olympian gods and goddesses. Some of the others are these:

Athena (Minerva), patron of the city of Athens and goddess of wisdom. She sprang full-grown from the head of Zeus.

Phoebus Apollo, god of the sun, reason, music, and medicine. He established the oracle at Delphi where the Greeks went to receive enigmatic prophecies about their future. He is associated with two Greek sayings: "Know thyself" and "Nothing in excess."

Dionysus (Bacchus), god of wine, ecstasy, fertility, and the theater.

Aphrodite (Venus), goddess of love and beauty. She caused amorous complications among gods and mortals as well as great happiness. Her son Eros (Cupid) was well known for shooting his arrows in the wrong place at the wrong time.

There were, of course, other gods and goddesses in the Olympian pantheon as well as demigods and semidivine heroes, but none of them, not even Zeus, was all-powerful in the way of the Jewish and Christian God. Above the gods was a concept of fate, or destiny. It was believed that every individual on earth had a *moira*, or pattern of life, to fulfill. Though the gods could predict what it would be, they did not directly intervene. Just how it would be fulfilled depended on the individual's character and the choices that he made in his life. We will see how this problem of the relations between man, gods, and fate is examined in the tragedy *Oedipus Rex*.

Greek religion was practiced throughout the "heroic" or Mycenaean age but was not systematically written down and explained until the Archaic period. Religious practices consisted of the sacrifice of animals and the pouring of libations (usually wine or oil) to the gods. Each god or goddess had a temple where his or her sacred image was kept and the gifts of the worshipers were stored. The rites usually took place before, not within, the temple. Thus the building and the area around it became a sanctuary. Here statues and *stele* (standing slabs of stone, painted or carved) were placed as offerings and commemoratives of events such as victories. Some of the important sanctuaries, like Delphi, belonged to all Greeks and had statues, stele, and small treasuries to hold offerings from each of the great city-states. Others, like the Athenian Acropolis, were the manifestation of the power and glory of a particular city.

The gods, for the Greeks, could take part in human affairs. This divine intervention is also reflected in the close association of a particular divinity with a city. Athens and Athena is the most famous example: Athena was said to be directly involved with the evolution of Athenian law and justice. Thus, religious observances became intermingled with political life in a complex way that enhanced the city's vitality and cohesiveness.

Long before Athens became the principal Greek city, the epic poems of Homer show to what extent the Greek gods were seen as involved with human activities.

Homer and the Epic

The poet Homer, who probably lived around 800 B.C., has been traditionally revered as the first writer of Western literature. Yet he was not a writer at all in the sense that we use the word today, and it is possible that he did not even know how to read and write. Homer belonged to an oral tradition, the nature of which we will study more fully in the chapter on African literature, and he was "a singer of tales." He composed, rather than wrote, his poems, probably basing them on a long tradition of singers who recited stories about the Trojan War, accompanied by the music of a stringed instrument, the lyre. The original purpose of this *epic* poetry was to "sing the famous deeds of men": to teach people in a pleasurable way about the great heroes of their culture. It should be stressed that Homer's poetry is not folk poetry—it is highly polished poetry, composed according to strict rules, but it was composed orally. Other cultures—African, Babylonian, Assyrian, Indian—have also produced great oral epics; and oral epics are still being created in the Balkan countries of Europe and other places (including Africa) that have retained an oral tradition. When we read Homer, we are reading an English text translated from an ancient Greek text that is a written version of the chanted oral epic. We do not know who decided to write down the Homeric poems or why and when this was done, but that act was in itself a momentous event for our cultural history. Homer's two great epics, the *Iliad* and the *Odyssey*, have been translated by generations of poets and scholars and are still widely read. They have also been instrumental in the creation of a long tradition of written epics.

The epic as a literary type was first defined by the first critic of Western literature, Aristotle (384–322 B.C.). Using Aristotle's definition, Thrall, Hibbard, and Holman in their *Handbook to Literature* define the epic for the modern reader thus: "A long narrative poem in elevated style presenting characters of high position in a series of adventures which form an organic whole through their relation to a central figure of heroic proportions and through their development of episodes important to the history of a nation or race."[1] There are four important elements to retain from this definition: style, hero, action, and culture. In spite of its folk origins, the epic uses a noble rhythmic pattern or *meter* (in Greek the six-foot line, dactylic hex-

ameter) and intricate figures of speech. The epic hero, though he may have human faults, must be almost superhuman in courage, strength, and greatness of character. Epic actions often include great wars and range over an entire country or continent. Supernatural beings, in Homer's case the gods, are usually involved in these actions. The actions must be important ones in the history of a nation or race and the hero in some sense a savior of that nation or race. Thus the hero is not only a great individual but also a culture-hero. Achilles, the hero of the *Iliad*, exemplifies what Homer perceived to be the greatness of the Greeks, and he is instrumental in an event highly significant for their culture: the downfall of Troy.

The Homeric poems were written down and read years after they were composed. The epic became a written form in Western literature with the Latin poet Virgil's *Aeneid*. Important examples of the epic in English literature are *Beowulf* and Milton's *Paradise Lost*. The epic as a literary form began to die out in the nineteenth century when it was replaced by the novel. In American culture the film industry attempted to take over the form—think how many movies have been advertised as "epic." Even this form seems to be on its way out in the contemporary world. It could be argued that our culture no longer produces events and heroes of "epic" proportions.

Both of Homer's epics are concerned with the Trojan War. The *Iliad* (Greek for "Song of Troy") depicts the war itself, while the *Odyssey* depicts the long and adventurous return home of the hero of the Trojan horse episode, Odysseus. The *Iliad* has thus been called the epic of war and the *Odyssey* the epic of peace; yet both investigate the nature of these two fundamental states of human society. The *Iliad* presents war both in its terror and its glory. Through our own experience of these matters we can, as modern readers, relate to Homer's vivid portrayal of the human urge for violence and the human yearning for peace.

The ILIAD   Neither of these epics can really be studied in brief snippets, so the reader is encouraged to read one or both in its entirety. Still, by way of introduction, we may look briefly here at the story of the first epic, the *Iliad*, and at the way that Homer treats his material. The opening lines of the epic tell the reader (or lis-

---

[1] William Flint Thrall, Addison Hibbard, and C. Hugh Holman, *A Handbook to Literature* (New York: The Odyssey Press, 1960), pp. 174–75.

tener) exactly what the poet intends to do, and set the tone for the rest.

> Sing, goddess, the anger of Peleus' son Achilleus
> and its devastation, which put pains thousandfold
>   upon the Achaians,
> hurled in their multitudes to the house of Hades
>   strong souls
> of heroes, but gave their bodies to be the delicate feasting
> of dogs, of all birds, and the will of Zeus was accomplished
> since that time when first there stood in division
>   of conflict
> Atreus' son the lord of men and brilliant Achilleus.

The translator of this passage, Richard Lattimore, has attempted to render in English the stately rhythm of the Greek hexameter. You should be able to count six beats in each line. Even this short passage reveals Homer's attention to realistic detail—the line about the dead bodies—and his use of *epithets* or repeated modifiers that succinctly characterize a person or thing, such as "lord of men" for Atreus' son Agamemnon and "brilliant" for Achilles (Achilleus). One of the most famous of these (not in this passage) is "the rosy-fingered dawn."

The goddess invoked by Homer is the muse, who was supposed to inspire the poet to sing. The poem's subject as stated is not the general one of the war but the immediate one of the anger of Achilles. Yet the poet branches out from this internal theme of the individual character of his hero to the external one of the war and its destruction. He then extends his point of view to an even more universal one—this war and its outcome were the will of the supreme god Zeus. The introduction is rounded out by a return to the original subject. We now learn that Achilles was "angry" because of a conflict with Atreus' son (Agamemnon), and the poet is ready to begin his tale.

These three levels—which we might call the internal, the external, and the universal—remain in interplay throughout the *Iliad*. The story begins with an explanation of how Achilles came to be angry with Agamemnon. Briefly, Achilles feels that he has been dishonored because Agamemnon took from him his war prize and concubine, a girl named Briseis. We are in the tenth year of the Trojan War, and Achilles withdraws himself from the fighting to prove to the Greeks how necessary he is to them. The gods become in-

volved in this personal quarrel when Achilles prays to his mother Thetis, a sea divinity, to let the Greeks be defeated in his absence; she carries his prayer to Zeus. This is the situation at the end of the first book of the *Iliad*. Books 2–7 describe the fighting between the Greeks and Trojans and develop individual characters, human and divine. By the end of Book 8 the Greek leaders are discouraged, and Agamemnon offers to give Briseis back to Achilles, along with many other gifts, if he will rejoin the fighting. Achilles is too angry to accept. It is only when his best friend, Patroklos, has been killed by Hektor, son of King Priam of Troy, that he is moved to return to battle. He succeeds in driving the Trojans back, slays Hektor, and drags his body behind his chariot. The Greeks hold an elaborate funeral for Patroklos. The body of Hektor remains unburied, a sign of dishonor; but, when King Priam comes to Achilles to ask for his son's body, Achilles takes pity on the old man and the *Iliad* ends with the Trojans' funeral for Hektor.

This brief outline cannot give any sense of the power of the *Iliad*, but it may serve as a guideline to the nature of the Homeric epic. The *Iliad* is not the story of the Trojan War; it is the story of an event in the life of Achilles. And yet the destiny of the hero is intertwined with the destiny of his people, and that in turn with the designs of the gods. An individual personality is at its core, but the great world of war and peace is the domain of this epic.

Sappho and the Lyric

Some two centuries after Homer, another Greek poet perfected a very different poetic form that was to influence, and is still influencing, the course of Western literature. The poet was a woman named Sappho who lived on the island of Lesbos in the Aegean Sea, and the form she used was the *lyric*. Sappho was something like the headmistress of a school of girls who were devoted to poetry and to the service of the goddess of love and beauty, Aphrodite. The term "Lesbian" comes from this island and its customs, and it is true that Sappho formed passionate attachments to her pupils. It is perhaps difficult for us to understand that these relationships and Sappho's love poems about them were also religious in nature. Aphrodite was, after all, a real goddess for the Greeks, and the cultivation and admiration of the beauty of young girls was a form of worship. A wife and mother, Sappho also wrote poems about love between men and women. The primary subject of all her lyrics, whose freshness and beauty are still moving even in translation, is the power of love and its effects on the entire human personality. In contrast to the epic, the lyric is entirely concentrated on personal, individual emotions, and it is a great deal shorter. Before reading some of Sappho's poems (most of which have come down to us only in fragments), let us examine briefly the nature and development of the lyric form.

The Greeks were not the first to write intimate love poetry—there are some beautiful Egyptian examples, and India and China have their own traditions in this form. The Western world's lyric, however, and indeed the word itself, derives from its practice on the Aegean islands. We use the word *lyric* today for words set to music (song lyrics) or to describe a particular kind of poetry characterized by a subjective presentation of an intense emotion, often but not necessarily love. Even if not set to music, the lyric poem usually has a musical effect on the reader or listener. The lyric in Greece was inseparable from music; melody and rhythm were tied intimately to the words of the poem. *Lyric* comes from the name of a stringed musical instrument, the lyre (Fig. 1-3), the characteristic instrument of the cult of Apollo. The lyre was played as an independent solo instrument, and we assume that it was also used as a kind of background accompaniment to the chanted or recited epic. Probably there was a great deal of improvisational folk poetry and song in early Greek times, but the development of a complex system of music theory and of expressive musical scales, called *modes*, opened up new possibilities for formal composition. A musician from Lesbos, Terpander, who played a large lyre called a cithara, is regarded as the founder of Greek classical music.

The earliest lyric poets were primarily musicians who simultaneously composed both words and music. Their musical pieces (all of which have been lost) were probably simple tunes—at least they lacked any harmony in the modern sense. Lyric poetry, which meant poetry to be sung to the music of a lyre, developed along two lines: choral and monodic (solos). The

1–3   Lyre Player from Keros, c. 2000 B.C. (National Archaeological Museum, Athens)

choral songs, sung by groups and usually performed at religious or festive occasions, were accompanied not only by the lyre but also by dancing. The combined arts of the choral spoken word, music, and dance passed into the choruses of the classical Greek dramas.

The other type of lyric poetry was sung by one person rather than by a group. It was more personal, used more colloquial language, and was sung on less formal occasions. Many solo poems are wedding songs. These poems are the first in Western literature that speak about the poet's personal feelings or that describe scenes from everyday life. Many of these lyrics, although often in fragments, have come down to us. Sappho was not the only lyric poet who wrote for solo performance, but she was acknowledged by later Greeks as the greatest. She wrote without reservation about her personal world of emotions. Her poetry seems straightforward, spontaneous, even simple; yet she wrote in a subtle, fixed *meter* (the "sapphic"), and her apparently plain images have great evocative power. Perhaps most important for us is that in a world which was, on the whole, dominated by men, she was an independent woman and sang proudly about the woman's sphere in which she lived. A modern feminist might not agree with her lack of interest in entering the world of men, but she seems to have believed that her world of intimate, personal emotions and friendships and her cult of the goddess Aphrodite were in fact superior to politics or warfare. The contrast between her view of the Trojan War in the first poem printed here and that of Homer in the *Iliad* makes this clear. It also makes clear a fundamental difference between the epic and the lyric.

The poems read on the printed page are at some remove from their original state. They are without music, many of them are fragments, and they are translations. The translations printed here are by a contemporary American poet and scholar, Willis Barnstone.

SAPPHO

Lyrics

TO ANAKTORIA, NOW A SOLDIER'S WIFE IN LYDIA

Some say cavalry and some would claim
infantry or a fleet of long oars
is the supreme sight on the black earth.
   I say it is

the girl you love. And easily proved.
Did not Helen, who was queen of mortal
beauty, choose as first among mankind
   the very scourge

of Trojan honor? Haunted by Love
she forgot kinsmen, her own dear child,
and wandered off to a remote country.
   O weak and fitful

Woman bending before any man:
So Anaktoria, although you are
Far, do not forget your loving friends.
   And I for one

Would rather listen to your soft step
and see your radiant face—than watch
all the dazzling horsemen and armored
   Hoplites of Lydia.

PARALYSIS

Mother darling, I cannot work the loom
for the Cyprian[1] has almost crushed me,
broken me with love for a slender boy.

TO EROS

From all the offspring
of the earth and heaven
Love is the most precious.

HOMAGE

Our slender Adonis is dying, Kytherea,
   tell us what to do.
Tear open your dresses, virgins, and
   batter your breasts!

TO THE QUEEN OF LOVE

   Cyprian, come
and gently pour nectar in our
golden cups, and pour joy too
in all our hearts.

THE LYRIC POEM

Come, holy tortoise shell,
my lyre, and become a poem.

LIGHT VANISHING

The moon has gone down,
the Pleiades have set.
Night is half gone,
and life speeds by.
I lie in bed, alone.

THE BLAST OF LOVE

Like a windstorm
punishing the oak trees,
love shakes my heart.

---

[1] Aphrodite, who was born on the island of Cypros.

SEIZURE

To me that man equals a god
as he sits before you and listens
closely to your sweet voice

and lovely laughter—which troubles
the heart in my ribs. For Brocheo,
when I look at you my voice fails,

my tongue is broken and thin fire
runs like a thief through my body.
My eyes are dead to light, my ears

pound, and sweat pours down over me.
I shudder, I am paler than grass,
and am intimate with dying—but

I must suffer everything, being poor.

WORLD

I could not hope
to touch the sky
with my two arms.

BEACH COLOR

The furzy flower of the golden broom
grew along the shore.

FULL MOON

The glow and beauty of the stars
are nothing near the splendid moon
when in her roundness she burns silver
about the world.

THEN

In gold sandals
dawn like a thief
fell upon me.

SHRILL SONG

When sun sprays the earth
with straight-falling flames,
a cricket rubs his wings,
scraping up thin sweet song.

THE HERALD

Nightingale, with your
lovely voice, you are
the herald of spring.

CONFESSION

But I love refinement, and the bright
and beautiful are for me the same
as desire for sunlight.

EVENING STAR

Hesperos, of all stars,
is the most beautiful.

TO APHRODITE OF THE FLOWERS, AT KNOSSOS

Come to the holy temple of the virgins
where the pleasant grove of apple trees
circles an altar smoking with frankincense.

The roses leave shadow on the ground
and cool springs murmur through apple
branches
where shuddering leaves pour down profound sleep.

In that meadow where horses have grown
glossy, and all spring flowers grow wild,
the anise shoots fill the air with a-
roma.

And there our queen Aphrodite pours
celestial nectar in the gold cups,
which she fills gracefully with sudden joy.

A LETTER TO ATTHIS   I

My Atthis, although our dear Anaktoria
lives in distant Sardis,
she thinks of us constantly, and

of the life we shared in days when for her
you were a splendid goddess,
and your singing gave her deep joy.

Now she shines among Lydian women as
when the red-fingered moon
rises after sunset, erasing

stars around her, and pouring light equally
across the salt sea
and over densely flowered fields;

and lucent dew spreads on the earth to
    quicken
roses and fragile thyme
and the sweet-blooming honey-lotus.

Now while our darling wanders she remem-
    bers lovely Atthis' love,
and longing sinks deep in her breast.

She cries loudly for us to come! We hear,
for the night's many tongues
carry her cry across the sea.

QUESTIONS

1. How would you describe Sappho's lyric quality? Is her poetic talent apparent even in fragments and translation?
2. What types of *images* does Sappho use? What effects do they have?
3. What concept of love emerges from your reading of these poems?

2

CLASSICAL GREECE: LIFE AND ART

The time between the world of Homer and Sappho and the world of "classical" Athens saw a growth in the population of Greece, greater material prosperity, and shifts in political power. The city-states in Mycenaean times had been governed by kings, but control had then passed to the nobles; now, in the seventh century B.C., a rising merchant class began to make its power felt. Through revolutions against the nobles, this class assumed control in several of the city-states through a strong man or *tyrant*. This word originally had no bad connotations; but, as these men began to depend more and more on force to impose their wills, the word took on its modern significance. Other governments soon replaced the tyrannies. The form of government that arose in the city-state of Athens was called *democracy*, which means in Greek "rule by the people." Athens' rival city-state, Sparta, did not go through the tyrant stage but retained an aristocratic government or *oligarchy*, which means in Greek "rule by the few." The relative advantages and disadvantages of these two opposing forms of government became an important theme in Greek thought during the period with which we are concerned here.

Athens and Sparta began as allies in a series of wars that were decisive for the political, economic, and cultural importance that Greece was to assume. Persia, the last great power of the Middle East, controlled an empire stretching from India and the Asiatic steppes to the Aegean and the Nile. Naturally, the Persians attempted to annex the tiny land of Greece to their empire. The surprise on all sides was great when the Greek allies, led by the Athenians, defeated the mighty Persian army, led by King Xerxes, at the naval battle of Salamis in 480 B.C. Prior to the battle, however, the Athenians themselves had had to evacuate their city before the advancing Persians. Xerxes took the city and burned the Acropolis but, defeated at Salamis, was forced to abandon Athens and return to Persia.

The Greeks saw this battle not only as a great military victory but, perhaps more importantly, as a cultural one. Persia represented to the Athenians in particular all the values that were anti-Greek. The Persian empire, with its political hierarchy and remote, powerful king at the top, was a far cry from the small state with its "rule by the people." Another negative value that the Persians represented is summed up by the Greek word *hubris*. This is best translated as arrogance, unbridled ambition, or stepping out of the boundaries that the gods have set for men. Xerxes' ambition to conquer the world and his manner of acting and treating himself more like a god than a man were seen to be examples of hubris. In the example of Xerxes' defeat, the Greeks could see a rhythm of tragedy: hubris leads man into folly, or actions which are contrary to reason; such acts bring on *nemesis*. Nemesis was the name of a Greek goddess, but the word is translated as retribution, punishment, or disaster. A tragedy written by Aeschylus in 472 B.C. entitled *The Persians* showed just this cycle. In opposition, the Greeks upheld an ideal they called *sophrosyne*, which means wisdom and moderation. It is perhaps best expressed by the famous motto of the oracle at Delphi: "Nothing in excess." We will see the importance of this concept to the art and thought that we call classical.

Politics and Life in Ancient Athens

Greek culture was concentrated in the *polis* (from which comes the word politics), a city-state. Territorially the polis included the city and the surrounding countryside; but, as it was customarily observed, no citizen should live more than a day's walk from the center. The contrast between the care lavished on public buildings and the humble construction of private houses demonstrates the important role of the polis in the lives of its citizens. The market, the courts, the temples were the focuses of activity, not private gardens and domiciles. It was generally believed that man could realize his humanity only through participation in its political processes. The polis provided the religious forms and the moral and cultural values that gave meaning and fullness to a citizen's existence. Citizenship was a privilege acquired by males through birth; normally both one's father and mother had to be natives of the state. Citizenship guaranteed membership in a political community and at least some share in the government of the polis. While in more aristocratic city-states participation was often limited to membership in an assembly with minimal powers, in fifth-century Athens every citizen over twenty-five was eligible for the whole range of state offices, which were filled for short terms either by election or by drawing lots.

All policy decisions and laws were made by the Assembly of the People, composed of the whole body of male citizens. Day-to-day matters and the responsibility of preparing an agenda for the frequent meetings of the Assembly were in the hands of a Council of Five Hundred. Elected annually, this council functioned by means of a rotating committee meeting daily. A variety of magistrates performed specialized tasks relating to finance and military matters, but the closely defined powers delegated them allowed almost no room for personal initiative. Ultimately all public officials were responsible to the Assembly, and anyone wishing to exert political authority in the state had to do so through his leadership within that body.

Despite its democratic constitution, Athens, like all Greek city-states, was a slaveholding society. Slaves numbered about 125,000, while citizens and their families made up about 100,000. A majority of the slaves were employed in domestic service, but about fifty thousand worked in industry and another ten thousand (surely the most unfortunate) toiled in the silver mines of Laurion. Apart from the mines, Athenian slavery was not oppressive. Citizens worked alongside slaves in industrial production, and it was usually difficult to distinguish slaves from free men by their dress. In a society where the productive capacity was low and consumption needs relatively simple, the use of slaves was not motivated by a desire for the luxurious life but rather for the creation of an amount of leisure so that citizens could carry out their duties as members of the polis.

The status of women in this society is a matter of debate. They were not citizens nor did they have rights in law. Marriage seems to have meant the passing from the protection of the father to that of the husband. Wives were expected to remain at home to supervise their household and the children. The women free to attend gatherings of men outside the home were either prostitutes or high-class courtesans—foreign women called *hetaerae*. On the other hand, tender scenes between husband and wife depicted on funeral vases suggest the existence of deep ties of affection between some married couples. Representations of strong, intelligent women in Greek tragedy and comedy indicate that such women, at least in the upper class, did exist; but, on the whole, we must think of Greek women as excluded from active roles in the community.

The great age of Athens fell between the end of the Persian Wars in 480 B.C. and the end of the Peloponnesian Wars in 404 B.C., when Athens was defeated by Sparta. The Peloponnesian Wars are so called because Sparta is located in that section of Greece called the Peloponnesus (see map). As rivals for commercial power and representatives of conflicting political ideologies, the two cites of Athens and Sparta came to an inevitable clash. The Athenian Thucydides, one of the first historians of Western culture, has given us both a chronicle of the war between the two city-states and a vision of the workings of history in his *History of the Peloponnesian War*, probably completed about 400 B.C. His history is conceived in terms related to classical tragedy. In particular, he sees the reckless Athenian attack on the city of Syracuse in Sicily as a manifestation of hubris, which led to the downfall of the Athenians. The most famous passage of this history, reprinted here, is a funeral oration for some young Athenian soldiers by the Athenian statesman Pericles. Pericles, who headed the Athenian democracy during its greatest (classical) period, speaks for the young men who died. He does so by praising the way of life for which they gave their own lives. The translation is by Benjamin Jowett.

THUCYDIDES

Pericles' Funeral Oration

I will speak first of our ancestors, for it is right and becoming that now, when we are lamenting the dead, a tribute should be paid to their memory. There has never been a time when they did not inhabit this land, which by their valor they have handed down from generation to generation, and we have received from them a free state. But if they were worthy of praise, still more were our fathers, who added to their inheritance, and after many a struggle transmitted to us their sons this great empire. And we ourselves assembled here to-day, who are still most of us in the vigor of life, have chiefly done the work of improvement, and have richly endowed our city with all things, so that she is sufficient for herself both in peace and war. Of the military exploits by which our various possessions were acquired, or of the energy with which we or our fathers drove back the tide of war, Hellenic or Barbarian, I will not speak; for the tale would be long and is familiar to you. But before I praise the dead, I should like to point out by what principles of action we rose to power, and under what institutions and through what manner of life our empire became great. For I conceive that such thoughts are not unsuited to the occasion, and that this numerous assembly of citizens and strangers may profitably listen to them.

Our form of government does not enter into rivalry with the institutions of others. We do not copy our neighbors, but are an example to them. It is true that we are called a democracy, for the administration is in the hands of the many and not of the few. But while the law secures equal justice to all alike in their private disputes, the claim of excellence is also recognized; and when a citizen is in any way distinguished, he is preferred to the public service, not as a matter of privilege, but as the reward of merit. Neither is poverty a bar, but a man may benefit his country whatever be the obscurity of his condition. There is no exclusiveness in our public life, and in our private intercourse we are not suspicious of one another, nor angry with our neighbor if he does what he likes; we do not put on sour looks at him which, though harmless, are not pleasant. While we are thus unconstrained in our private intercourse, a spirit of reverence pervades our public acts; we are prevented from doing wrong by respect for authority and for the laws, having an especial regard to those which are ordained for the protection of the injured as well as to those unwritten laws which bring upon the transgressor of them the reprobation of the general sentiment.

And we have not forgotten to provide for our weary spirits many relaxations from toil; we have regular games and sacrifices throughout the year; at home the style of our life is refined; and the delight which we daily feel in all these things helps to banish melancholy. Because of the greatness of our city the fruits of the whole earth flow in upon us; so that we enjoy the goods of other countries as freely as of our own.

Then, again, our military training is in many respects superior to that of our adversaries. Our city is thrown open to the world, and we never expel a foreigner or prevent him from seeing or learning anything of which the secret if revealed to an enemy might profit him. We rely not upon management or trickery, but upon our own hearts and hands. And in the matter of education, whereas they from early youth are always undergoing laborious exercises which are to make them brave, we live at ease, and yet are equally ready to face the perils which they face. And here is the proof. The Lacedaemonians come into Attica not by themselves, but with their whole confederacy following; we go alone into a neighbor's country; and although our opponents are fighting for their homes and we on a foreign soil, we have seldom any difficulty in overcoming them. Our enemies have never yet felt our united strength; the care of a navy divides our attention, and on land we are obliged to send our own citizens everywhere. But they, if they meet and defeat a part of our army, are as proud as if they had routed us all, and when defeated they pretend to have been vanquished by us all.

If then we prefer to meet danger with a light heart but without laborious training, and with a courage which is gained by habit and not enforced by law, are we not greatly the gainers? Since we do not anticipate the pain, although, when the hour comes, we can be as brave as those who never allow themselves to rest; and thus too our city is equally admirable in peace and in war. For we are lovers of the beautiful, yet simple in our tastes, and we cultivate the mind without loss of manliness. Wealth we employ, not for talk and ostentation, but when there is a real use for it. To avow poverty with us is no disgrace: the true disgrace is in doing nothing to avoid it. An Athenian citizen does not neglect the state because he takes care of his own household; and even those of us who are engaged in business have a very fair idea of politics. We alone regard a man who takes no interest in public affairs, not as a harmless, but as a useless character; and if few of us are originators, we are all sound judges of a policy. The great impediment to action is, in our opinion, not discussion, but the want of that knowledge which is gained by discussion preparatory to action. For we have a peculiar power of thinking before we act and of acting too, whereas other men are courageous from ignorance but hesitate upon reflection. And they are surely to be esteemed the bravest spirits who, having the clearest sense both of the pains and pleasures of life, do not on that account shrink from danger. In doing good, again, we are unlike others; we make our friends by conferring, not by receiving favors. Now he who confers a favor is the firmer friend, because he would fain by kindness keep alive the memory of an obligation; but the recipient is colder in his feelings, because he knows that in requiting another's generosity he will not be winning gratitude, but only paying a debt. We alone do good to our neighbors not upon a calculation of interest, but in the confidence of freedom and in a frank and fearless spirit. To sum up: I say that Athens is the school of Hellas, and that the individual Athenian in his own person seems to have the power of adapting himself to the most varied forms of action with the utmost versatility and grace. This is no passing and idle word, but truth and fact; and the assertion is verified by the position to which these qualities have raised the state. For in the hour of trial Athens alone among her contemporaries is superior to the report of her. No enemy who comes against her is indignant at the reverses which he sustains at the hands of such a city; no subject complains that his masters are unworthy of him. And we shall assuredly not be without witnesses; there are mighty monuments of our power which will make us the wonder of this and of succeeding ages; we shall not need the praises of Homer or of any other panegyrist whose poetry may please for the moment, although his representation of the facts will not bear the light of day. For we have compelled every land and every sea to open a path for our valor, and have everywhere planted eternal memorials of our friendship and of our enmity. Such is the city for whose sake these men nobly fought and died; they could not bear the thought that she might be taken from them; and every one of us who survive should gladly toil on her behalf.

COMMENTS AND QUESTIONS

1. Thucydides, through his spokesman Pericles, is defining a balanced system of government in a style that is also balanced. Define and point out the balances in style and content.
2. Where does Pericles describe the Athenian taste in art, and what is it?
3. What are the potential disadvantages of a democracy, and how does Athenian democracy avoid these disadvantages, according to Pericles?
4. How does Athenian democracy compare with modern democracies?

Classical Greek Architecture and Sculpture

When the Athenians returned to Athens after their triumph over Xerxes at Salamis, they found a ravaged city. On the Acropolis, temples had been burned, statues toppled, and inscriptions destroyed or defaced. After the city rebuilt its fortifications, its leaders began the great rebuilding project on the Acropolis. This activity not only built morale, as Pericles said, but also provided jobs. The majestic buildings on the Acropolis, now ruined by time and subsequent wars, are the results of Pericles' building program. They and the sculpture adorning them constitute the best models for the ideals of the classical style (Fig. 2-1).

Like all cultural monuments, the buildings on the Acropolis have a history. To understand the accomplishments of the master builders and artisans who created the buildings, it is necessary to know something of the origins of architecture.

The Beginnings of Architecture Architecture surely began with the need for shelter, but people quickly sensed its potential for physical, visual representation of ideas like power, permanence, magic, and the sacred. People attended to houses and fortifications, but the greatest care was lavished on those buildings that served the king or god. The first sacred buildings may have been built of nothing more than walls of mud, mudbrick, or stones enclosing a small, irregular space without windows. The walls were probably

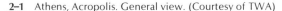

2–1 Athens, Acropolis. General view. (Courtesy of TWA)

thicker at the bottom and sloped inward toward the top. The first temples built by the Greeks were simple rectangular boxes, sometimes curved at one end. The *groundplan*—the term we use to designate a drawing of any building that shows in outline the walls, openings and supports—includes one room whose walls extend to flank the doorway. This room, called a *naos,* was for the cult statue, while the extended walls made an entrance porch, the *pronaos;* together they form the *cella.* Beams for the roof rested on the top edge of the cella walls and, when crossed to form a triangular shape, could carry a wooden *gable* or ridge pole that followed the long axis of the cella, leaving an open triangular space at each end called the *pediment.* The roof would slope down from the center to the sides, creating a deep overhang. Any opening or door in the wall weakened the wall structure, necessitating on either side of the opening a reinforcement in the form of wooden posts that supported a horizontal wooden beam, the *lintel,* spanning the posts. The combination of posts and lintels could carry the weight of the roof (Fig. 2-2).

Combining walls with posts and lintels made possible a variety of spatial arrangements of rooms, doors, and windows. A comparison of Greek, Egyptian, Minoan, and Mycenaean architecture shows different uses of these simple elements. The Greeks, enclosing the cult statue in the cella, soon surrounded it with rows of columns or posts on all four sides to create a *colonnade.* Ceremonies took place outside at an altar placed on the long axis of the building that faced east.

RIDGE BEAM

PRINCIPAL RAFTER

TIE BEAM

KINGPOST

WALLPLATE

LINTEL

POST

2-2 Basic post-and-lintel construction.

Our description of these simple forms of architecture may enable us to define architecture. We use the word to describe the total process that begins with an idea or need, employs building systems (like post and lintel), applies local technology, and produces a structure. Architecture grows and changes with tradition and in response to need.

The creation of a building involves one set of events and actions. Our experience of the building becomes another series of events depending on a number of factors. One is our knowledge of what a building stands for—what it means to those who built it. Another is our knowledge of what a building is used for—its function. Yet another is our perception of how it stands up. Our bodies respond to the way in which weight and lift, support and balance occur in the built form. The Greeks used the smooth mass of the wall and the great downward pressing weight of the roof with its overhang to contrast with the dynamic power of the upward thrusting post or column. Similarly, the *rhythm* of light and dark created by the columns against the smooth cella wall also play a part in our perception of the temple.

The Greek Temple The architectural factor that became the most significant formal element of the Greek temple was the shape and scale of the column and its combination with other specific features—its capital (the cushion and flat block under the lintel) and the lintel, or *entablature,* above. The two most important combinations of *orders* are the *Doric* and the *Ionic.* Documents tell us that the Doric order evolved in the Dorian Peloponnesus. The Ionic order was first found in Asia Minor. Both were used by the Greeks of the fifth century (Fig. 2-3).

Observing the orders side by side, you can see that there is a difference in the height and thickness of the column, the presence or absence of a base for the column, the forms of the capital, and the lintel and *frieze* above the column. Vitruvius, a first-century B.C. Roman who wrote a treatise on architecture, tells us that the Doric was the most ancient order and was serious, grave, dignified, and masculine. The slender, lighter, more elegant Ionic was considered feminine. Femininity, in this case, was not associated with the gender of the gods but with the universal aspects of the female principle.

2–3 Classical Greek orders.

DORIC ORDER

ENTABLATURE
- PEDIMENT
- RAKING CORNICE
- CORNICE
- FRIEZE
- METOPE
- TRIGLYPH
- ARCHITRAVE

COLUMN
- CAPITAL
  - ABACUS
  - ECHINUS
- SHAFT

STYLOBATE
STEREOBATE

IONIC ORDER
- FRIEZE
- ARCHITRAVE
- FACIAE
- CAPITAL
- VOLUTE
- BASE

CORINTHIAN ORDER
- FRIEZE
- ARCHITRAVE
- CAPITAL

The Parthenon The temple form, a cella with a colonnade on all four sides, became the rule for major temples; but its builders enriched and elaborated it, as we will see in the Parthenon. The Parthenon, built between 477 and 438 B.C., was designed and executed under the direction of Ictinus and Kallicrates, master builders (Figs. 2-4, 2-5). The sculptural program was directed by the sculptor, Phideas, who did some images himself and was solely responsible for the cult statue of Athena, placed in the cella. Tradition dictated that the temple be Doric; this one has six columns on its ends and seventeen down each flank. Located on the highest point of the Acropolis, the third temple to Athena Parthenos on that site, it was the crown of the complex. Forms originally built in mudbrick and wood, then in local stone, were now interpreted in gleaming white marble. The *pediment* on the west end, facing the sea, had its triangular space filled with sculptures depicting

2–4 Athens, Parthenon. (Greek National Tourist Organization)

A **Propylaea**
B **Statue of Athena**
C **Parthenon**
D **Erectheum**
E **Site of Older Parthenon**
F **Temple of Athena Nike**

2–5 Athens, Acropolis. Groundplan.

the story of Athena's rivalry with Poseidon for the homage of the city. The sculpture of the east pediment showed Athena's birth. The *metopes*, the spaces between the ends of the lateral beams of the roof, above the lintel, were sculpted in *low relief* with scenes from the Trojan War, the Battle of Gods and Giants, Lapiths and Centaurs, Greeks and Amazons, all historical allusions to the Greeks' struggle with the Persians—allegories for the struggle between light and darkness, civilization and barbarism. At the top of the cella walls was a sculpted frieze, showing the procession of the Panathenaea, the festival held every four years to honor Athena. Finally, the whole building was painted and polished. Capitals and moldings received color: blue, red, and gilding. Sculpture was given natural coloring;

weapons, horse tack, shields, and other objects were bronze, brass, or gold. Within the cella, the gold and ivory cult statue was placed, at the far end from the door.

Surrounded by terraces, trees, statues, and stele, as well as the other buildings that soon rose around it, the Parthenon dominated the Acropolis. The entire complex was so moving that even the embittered Spartans did not destroy it when they finally defeated the Athenians in 404 B.C. Time and wars following the fall of the Roman empire ravaged the site, the worst destruction being the Venetian bombardment of 1678.

Even in the ruined state in which the Parthenon stands today, one senses an order of intractable stone formed into an ideal relationship between weight and support, repose and response, symmetry and rhythm. These characteristics recall the system of balances in Pericles' *Funeral Oration* or the search for a mean between passion and will, intuition and reason that we will observe in Greek philosophy. Perhaps we can better understand the Parthenon by looking now at Greek sculpture, whose origins lie in the same past and whose possibilities, like the temple form, seem completely realized by the late fifth century.

Greek Sculpture   Greek sculpture seems born of two almost contradictory desires: the desire to attain complete naturalism and the desire to make the figures ideal types. The gods and goddesses, votive figures, and even the more personalized portraits seem both human and divine.

Archaic Sculpture   The *Kouros* of Sounion (*Kouros* is Greek for youth, a standing male nude) was made in the *Archaic* period about 600 B.C. (Fig. 2-6). Over life size (ten feet) this free-standing male nude is characteristic of many such figures that exhibit some attempt to appear natural but are still confined to the stone block from which they were carved. One foot steps forward, but the body weight does not shift. The body itself is really perceived as a columnar shape in which anatomical details are arranged in a symmetrical, stylized way.

Beginning with the head, the face, jawline, ears, and back of the head are seen as almost separate flat sections. The forehead, eyebrow ridge, and nose form one smooth plane, and the eyes are simplified into a wide open stare, the eyelids marked only by a groove. Similarly, the shoulders and chest flow into another smooth plane, where slight ridges, grooves, and swellings incorrectly delineate the body but are formally pleasing and symmetrical. The hip joint and the hips are reduced to one generalized swell into the thighs. Kneecaps are rigid designs, and the calves have some incised ridges for musculature. The spinal column is almost perfectly straight, and shoulder blades are incised grooves. The arms mask the sides of the body, and the clenched fists make the arms seem to press in toward the body.

The total impression is one of a compact, sculptural solid. It is a memorable and commanding form that deserves our attention because it is a familiar form—a human body—transformed into something timeless. The *Kouros* can be walked around and studied; touched and compared mentally with our own body's surface, texture, articulation, and movement. When we compare our flexible elbow, the soft flesh behind the knee, the loose, floating oval kneecap, and the soft ridges behind the neck and ears with those of this figure, we begin to realize that while the statue is *not* lifelike, its own symmetry, the incised ridges, and the contrast between the way it is and what it seems to be—a human body—create a pleasing and enlightening experience. The *Kouros*, made to commemorate an event, inhabits a space different from our own, and we, like it, are confined to a different place and space. The columnar

2-6   Kouros of Sounion, c. 600 B.C. (National Archaeological Museum, Athens)

2–7   Kore from Auxerre. Louvre, Paris. (© Arch. Phot. Paris/S.P.A.D.E.M., 1980)

2–8   Kritios Boy, c. 480 B.C. (Acropolis Museum, Athens)

Kore, a female, is equally rigid and posed, yet the symmetry, balance, and harmony of the drapery of the figure, the hair, and the very stylized face are pleasing (Fig. 2-7).

Early Classical Sculpture   The *Kritios Boy* found on the Acropolis was made about 480 B.C. (Fig. 2-8). How different he seems from the previous figures! The body now moves and turns—weight flows into one leg as the figure poses and balances. The body has become a flexible, smooth-muscled, and tactile form. One

feels that a touch would reveal a yielding surface of skin and flesh. The body is perceived in the round; it reaches outside the imaginary lines of the block from which it was carved. Yet, because of its perfection, the sculpture remains separate from us. Not a blemish or scar, an undeveloped muscle, or unhappy emotion breaks the graceful forms of the body and face. Our own form would rarely compare favorably with this athletic perfection that seems to speak of self-restraint and control; perpetual youth and self-awareness. This is humanity idealized into what one *might* become.

Classical Sculpture The development of free-standing figures toward this expressive perfection is paralleled in other kinds of sculpture. The frieze of the Panathenaic procession gives us more insight into the qualities of the ideal and the real that combine to make the expressive and dramatic scenes of classical art. The frieze has a rhythm that grows like that of an anthem.

On the southeast side, where the procession begins, figures stand or begin to walk slowly. Riders hold their horses, and the sacrificial beasts are readied. As the procession moves along the south flank and turns the western corner, the participants move more rapidly, clustering together. In the section illustrated here (Fig. 2-9), horses and riders, bodies mingling in the low sculpted relief, seem to push eagerly forward. Cloaks blow in the wind; manes and hair are breeze-tossed. As the procession reaches the east end, movement becomes quiet and figures halt in the presence of the gods and goddesses on Mount Olympus. The participants are almost anonymous, the ideally beautiful youths and maids of a procession still going on. The older priest-celebrants will always remain so, as will for all time the gods watching the ceremony.

In the blasted, broken fragments that remain from the Parthenon's pedimental sculptures, scholars and students of Greek sculpture see some of the most beautiful forms of the fifth century. Yet it is difficult for us, as novices, to penetrate the veil of destruction and time that lies over these forms. Only in the *Dionysus* (Fig. 2-10) or the now headless figures of the goddesses from the pediment can we begin to perceive the magnificent beauty of the body, perfectly harmonized with an ex-pressive ideal (Fig. 2-11). The three ladies sit, lean, and recline to fit the space of the triangular pediment. Their bodies are substantial, weighty volumes. Their clothes do not conceal, but cling, turn, reveal, and emphasize the physical presence of these figures.

Let us now concentrate on a single classical sculpture, *The Spearbearer* by Polykleitos (Fig. 2-12). This figure is a bronze sculpture (the Greeks worked in bronze as much as stone), but the medium does not deny a comparison with the *Kritios Boy*. Of the two figures, which seems more confined in an imaginary blocklike space? How is movement suggested? Of the two bodies, which is more convincingly lifelike, which is more nearly perfect? Compare both works with a present-day athlete of the same general build. What does this tell you about the classical ideal? What is the mental or emotional state of each figure? Is it appealing? Does it enhance or contrast with the forms of the figures? What devices, like the material itself, help maintain the figures' physical and psychological distance?

Classical Architecture and Sculpture Compared Just as *The Spearbearer* harmonizes nature—the real with the ideal, of what one might be—the Parthenon harmonizes the forces of gravity and weight and the characteristics of the building system itself into a perfect balance of vertical and horizontal, compression and support (Fig. 2-4). The Parthenon's colonnade is not too tall or it would seem spindly; the columns are not too thick or they would be stumpy; the spaces between the columns are not too great or the rhythm they create would be broken; the lintels are

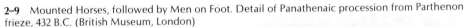

2–9   Mounted Horses, followed by Men on Foot. Detail of Panathenaic procession from Parthenon frieze, 432 B.C. (British Museum, London)

2–10 Dionysus from east pediment of the Parthenon, c. 438–432 B.C. (Reproduced by Courtesy of the Trustees of the British Museum)

2–11 Three Goddesses from east pediment of the Parthenon, c. 438–432 B.C. (Reproduced by Courtesy of the Trustees of the British Museum)

2–12 Polykleitos, Spearbearer, bronze. (Staatliche Antikensammlungen und Glyptothek, München)

not too long; neither are the capitals too large or small. The floor rises slightly to the center on both the long and short axis; the columns lean inward ever so slightly to counter visually the outward, downward pressure of the roof. The columns at the corner are slightly larger since they, as Vitruvius says, would seem too slender because they must be seen against light from both sides. The columns themselves swell slightly as though in vigorous, elastic response to the downward pressure of the roof. Greek architects grasped these fine points in the way that sculptors came to know the body. As head, neck, and chest become understood, as surface dissolves so that muscles swell and move rather than appear as ridges and grooves, as the body turns in space and becomes free of the solid compact mass of stone, so the Parthenon is lifted from the intractable marble to sit lightly in its landscape, its mass balanced between the reality of gravity and a thrust into bright light. To be seen from all sides, experienced during ceremonies, the building is like an ideal body, completely harmonious, self-aware and whole, mysterious and moving.

Other Classical Greek Buildings The temple form is a complete entity with its traditional, ritual, and formal demands; nevertheless, we should remember that it was not the only type of Greek building. There were theaters, meeting houses, and the colonnaded porticos of the market place. Moreover, the basic temple form itself was capable of elaborate variation,

and it is in this context that we should see the Parthenon. Two buildings on the Acropolis help us to do so.

Built after the Parthenon, the Propylaea is a monumental gateway providing a secondary focus for processions, bridging the physical changes in the levels of entry and creating a place of passage from which one can focus on the sanctuary (Fig. 2-13). The master builders employed the Doric and Ionic orders; on the porticoes and exterior passages the Doric order gives substance to the idea of gateway and entrance. As the levels change, the interior Ionic columns stretch upward easily to carry the roof and visually lighten its weight. The complete gateway once acted also as entrance to the two wings, which were picture galleries containing scenes of Athenian victories.

The Erechtheum, on the north side of the Parthenon, is a very irregular but equally harmonious adjustment of building to the land and to the variety of functions it had to serve (Fig. 2-14). A number of shrines and ancient artifacts of the city had to be accommodated. To the east was a shallow Ionic portico; on the north side was a deeper, richer Ionic porch for entry to the rooms that contained ancient relics; on the south side was the Porch of the Maidens, its flat roof supported by columns transformed into maidens, the *caryatid* order. Instead of a uniform building with a single *gable*, there are intersecting gables and two stories united with one. The Ionic order not only stretches but, along the west side, is also flattened into half-columns that unite the north and south porches,

2-13 Acropolis, Propylaea from the west. (Alinari/Editorial Photocolor Archives)

2-14 Acropolis, Erechtheum from the west side with porch of the Maidens. (Greek National Tourist Office)

2-15 Praxiteles, Aphrodite of Cnidos, c. 350 B.C. (Vatican Museums, Rome—Alinari/Editorial Photocolor Archives)

2-16 Altar of Zeus, from Pergamon, c. 181–159 B.C. (Staatliche Museen zu Berlin, Antiken-Sammlung/Photographische Abteilung)

minimizing the change in location and in scale. Each porch has its own symmetry; but, in the balance of each against each, harmony is attained by the contrast of height and weight, openness and enclosure, shallowness and depth.

Greek architecture and sculpture were accompanied and enhanced by all the other arts: painting, music, dance, and drama. We know about painting only through written accounts, surviving vase painting, and later Roman copies of Greek work. But we do know that other arts shared in the conquest of space and movement and that, after the Parthenon, the builders' art continued to grow, flourish, and change. New needs inspired new ideas that provided a growing and changing art. After the Peloponnesian Wars new states acquired power and wealth; their ideals and beliefs were manifested in sculpture, painting, and building.

From Classical to Hellenistic Sculpture   The Cnidian *Aphrodite*, made in the fourth century, is among the first female nudes, her form suggesting that of the Parthenon goddesses, who were still clothed (Fig. 2-15). The island of Cnidos had become an important shrine, and portraying the goddess nude had become an acceptable practice. Compare this statue with *The Spearbearer*. Does the Greek ideal extend to women? Is there any change from the previous century?

Another example of later Greek art is the great Altar of Zeus at Pergamon (Fig. 2-16). It is a radically different complex from that of the Athenian Acropolis, and the sculpture of the frieze is much more dramatic and graphically expressive. Compare these figures with those of the horsemen in the Panathenaea. Consider the striking differences of scale, depth of relief, movement of figures, and quality of emotional expression on their faces and in the bodies of the Pergamon figures.

For centuries it was held that the diffusion of artists and builders, along the evolution of new and more complex forms, represented a decline in the power and quality of Greek art and architecture, which reached its highest state in the classical period. Although modern taste questions this judgment against Hellenistic art (the term used to refer to the art of the third and second centuries B.C.), it is in any case a tribute to the classical period that its goals and forms could provide sources and ideas for two millennia.

3

CLASSICAL GREECE: DRAMA

Along with its creativity in the visual arts, the age of Pericles saw a flourishing of drama. Drama, as we know it in the West, is in fact a creation of the Greeks. Theatergoing was more than a festive activity for Athenians; it was regarded as an important part of a citizen's education and was supported by the state. *Tragedies* and *comedies*, as well as other theatrical events, were performed annually at the festival of Dionysus, the god of wine, fertility, and ecstasy. The Athenian theatergoer, rather than going out for an evening's entertainment as we do, would devote a whole day to this activity. During the festival of Dionysus, which lasted for several days, business activities would cease, prisoners would be released from jail, and everyone—young, old, rich, poor, male, female, free, slave—would congregate at daybreak in a type of outdoor auditorium from which our football stadiums have been developed. There they would sit on stone benches, often to watch three tragedies, a *satyr play* (a grotesque skit in which the actors wore horses' tails and ears), and a comedy. The ruins of the theater of Dionysus on the Acropolis and the better-preserved theater at Epidaurus (Fig. 3-1) give us a clear idea of the circular orchestra, where the chorus sang and danced, and the *theatron*, the horseshoe-shaped area for the audience. A *skene*, or backdrop against which the actors performed, would have been set up in the back of the orchestra, facing the audience. Acoustics in this theater are still remarkable. A clear voice from the orchestra is deflected by the stone sides and can be heard without any form of artificial amplification.

Even though the Athenian theatergoer's experience was different from ours, it is recognizable to us because it is at the base of our own experience with the theater. We are all familiar with actors who act out a story and come into conflict with each other, but fifth-century B.C. Athens was, as far as we know, the first place in the world where this type of performance had been or was being staged. How did it come to be? Was the drama someone's invention or a long-standing development? It should be stated immediately that no one knows the definitive answer to this question. We can best examine it in relation to the two principal forms themselves, tragedy and comedy.

The Development of Tragedy

Tragedy developed into a full-fledged dramatic form sometime before the classical age and earlier than comedy. Τραγωιδια *(tragoidia)* in Greek comes from words meaning "goat" and "song." For this reason it has been assumed that tragedy developed from "goat songs" or choric performances similar to, or identical with, the grotesque satyr plays mentioned earlier. According to this theory, the serious play that we now know as tragedy would have begun as a kind of ecstatic comedy, perhaps far from Athens, in the Peloponnesus. Since tragedy was performed at the festival of Dionysus, many have also assumed that it grew out of some sort of religious ritual. According to one of these theories,

3-1   Epidaurus, theater from above. Polykleitos the Younger, c. 350 B.C. (Eugene Brown)

the chants of the priest and the response of the worshipers gave rise to the actors and chorus respectively. A recent theory holds that Greek tragedy had nothing to do with religious rituals but was essentially the creation of the first man of the theater, Thespis, who created drama out of poetic recitations of stories from Homer.

The tragedies written by Thespis probably had only one actor, along with a chorus. The actor, who probably represented an epic hero from Homer, would have to present his own story, which would be concentrated on his *pathos*, or suffering. The chorus would begin the play with a hymn. to the gods and end with a lamentation over the hero. The *aulos*, a type of oboe and the characteristic instrument of the Dionysian cult, was employed in the performance of elegies, or songs of mourning; and it is likely that it was also used for instrumental preludes and interludes in the drama. In between the short scenes or *episodes* during which the hero spoke, the chorus would sing lyrics as a comment on his sufferings.

The Role of Music and Dance in Tragedy

From the beginning, tragedy was intimately associated with the arts of music and dance. The Greek word for *chorus*, which comes from the verb "to dance," indicates that the choruses were originally groups of dancers as well as singers (all men, as were the actors). It is probable that individual actors danced, too. Although there is little evidence on what the dances were like, we do know that they were mimetic; that is, they mimed or imitated the action of the play. The use of the hands was very important in expressing emotion, just as it is in oriental dancing today.

Music, instrumental as well as choral, also played an important role in creating emotional effects in tragedy. Just as the lyre was the instrument of lyric poetry, the aulos, a double-reeded wind instrument, was seen as most appropriate for tragedy. It had a shrill, piercing tone, perhaps associated with the ecstatic worship of Dionysus. The Greeks composed music in several *modes*, scales whose organization of notes differs from our modern major and minor system. Each mode was said to produce a special kind of feeling. In modern music, we distinguish between the forceful major mode and the wistful or melancholy minor mode. The Greek theory of modes was more complicated. The Dorian mode was considered manly and strong, appropriate for the training of young men, whereas the emotional Mixolydian mode was considered piercing and suitable for lamentations. Both, however, were appropriate for tragedy. The Greeks, as we will see in the section on philosophy, had great faith in the ability of music to influence and mold the characters of human beings. Unfortunately, very little Greek music remains—none from the classical period—so we can only conjecture what the total spectacle of an Athenian drama would have been like.

The Principal Greek Tragedians

Aeschylus   The first tragedian whose plays are known to us is Aeschylus, who lived from 525 to 456 B.C. and thus participated in the growth and the glory of Athens. He was proud of having fought at the battle of Marathon. Aeschylus had the genius to add a second actor to the tragic form; thus, in his plays two actors appear at once on the stage. There is still a principal hero, whose sufferings are the main subject of the tragedy, but now he can be seen interacting with other human beings. The chorus, though, is still of major importance in the dramas of Aeschylus, who was himself a musician and was said to have been most attentive in fitting his choral songs to music. Aeschylus' most famous work is the trilogy, or series of three plays, entitled the *Oresteia* (Orestes plays). The first play in the trilogy is *Agamemnon*, the name of the king of Mycenae and leader of the Greeks in the Trojan War. In the play Agamemnon returns from the war, a glorious hero, only to be murdered by his wife Clytemnestra. In the second play, *The Libation Bearers*, Agamemnon's son Orestes avenges his father's death by killing his mother and her lover. In the final part of the trilogy Orestes is pursued by the Eumenides, horrible furies who torment him because of the slaying of his mother; but he is finally put on trial, judged, and acquitted by Athena, the patron goddess of Athens. The outcome of the trilogy shows the belief in law and the new system of justice developing in Athens.

Aeschylus wrote about ninety tragedies altogether. Besides the *Oresteia* those that survive are *The Persians*, *The Seven Against Thebes*, *Prometheus Bound*, and *The Suppliants*. The plots of all of Aeschylus' tragedies are extremely simple, and the characters are not what we would call "well rounded," but rather embodiments of a single passion. Everything is concentrated on the tragic event and the emotional and spiritual meaning of that event. This simplicity and concentration is, as we have seen in other art forms, part of what we mean by classical. Aeschylus' plays, in their spareness and grandeur, have been compared to early classical sculpture such as the *Kritios Boy*.

Sophocles   Sophocles (496–406 B.C.), a younger contemporary of Aeschylus, further developed the tragic form by adding a third actor. During his long life he wrote about 125 plays, of which only eight have come down to us. Of these, the best known are the plays of the Oedipus cycle: *Antigone*, *Oedipus Rex*, and *Oedipus at Colonnus*. Unlike the *Oresteia*, these plays were not written as a trilogy but at different points of Sophocles' career. They are thus meant to be performed as individual plays. It is *Oedipus Rex*, the most renowned of all Greek tragedies, that we will study in detail here. Sophocles' characters, while maintaining a sense of classical balance and restraint, seem more human and alive than those of Aeschylus. They may be compared, as we shall see later, to "high" classical sculpture. The chorus has less importance relative to the actors than in Aeschylus' drama, but we should bear in mind that music and dance still played a vital role. Sophocles was himself a dancer.

Euripides   The next great tragedian, Euripides (480–406 B.C.), began to break out of the limits of classicism by creating more realistic characters and more complex plots. The traditional critical judgment on Euripides and his older contemporary holds that "Sophocles shows man as he ought to be and Euripides shows man as he is." Euripides' interest in individual psychology and in extreme real-life situations makes him in many ways closer to modern sensibilities. Although, like all ancient Greek playwrights, he uses old myths as the basis for his plots, Euripides appears to many readers as a religious skeptic or even an atheist. Euripides also wrote an *Orestes*, which differs considerably from the trilogy by Aeschylus. Like all great psychological writers, he had a considerable interest in women, as shown in plays such as *Hippolytus*, which treats the myth of Phaedra driven mad by love, *The Trojan Women*, and *Medea*. The realism, emotionalism, and individuality of Euripides' characters make them comparable to postclassical or Hellenistic sculptures.

Oedipus Rex

The tragedy we will study here, Sophocles' *Oedipus Rex*, written about 430 B.C., has traditionally, since the philosopher-critic Aristotle first wrote about it, been taken as *the* best example of tragedy in world literature. If we want to understand the meaning of "tragedy" and "tragic," the best place to start is still with Oedipus.

One important notion to bear in mind while reading a Greek tragedy is that, unlike modern audiences, the Greeks who attended the festival of Dionysus did not attend a play for its plot suspense or to find out "what happens next." Today, when recommending a movie to a friend, we do not tell the plot for fear of spoiling it for him. Greek tragedies were all based on myths or legends that the theatergoers already knew. Thus, when they went to see *Oedipus*, they did not wonder what the play would be about, but rather what Sophocles had done with an old, familiar story. Since the tragedies at the festival of Dionysus were presented as a contest, the judges would also choose the best three tragedies on the basis of how well the already given material had been worked into dramatic form. It will therefore be useful to know something about the myth of Oedipus before approaching the tragedy.

The story takes place in an early, legendary period of Greek history when the city-states were ruled by kings. The city of Thebes, it was told, was ruled by King Laius (Laïos) and his queen, Jocasta (Iokastê). Thebes was founded by Laius' ancestor Cadmus, who was cursed by the gods and told that all of his descendants would receive some form of this curse. Thus Laius was told by a prophet of the god Apollo that he and Jocasta would bear a son who would kill his father and marry his mother. Hoping to avert this fate, the king and queen asked one of their shepherds to take their first-born son to Mount Cithaeron (Kithairon) near Thebes, to leave the baby to be exposed to die. The shepherd, out of pity for the child, gave him to a slave from the Greek city of Corinth, on the other side of the mountain, hoping that he would remain in that city and thus have no chance to fulfill the dreadful prophecy. The child is, of course, Oedipus, whose name means "swollen foot," a deformity he acquired from the pins put in his feet when he was left to die. He grows up believing that he is the natural son of King Polybus (Polybos) and Queen Meropê of Corinth, but one day he, too, receives a prophecy declaring that he will kill his father and marry his mother. He then flees Corinth and vows never to see his parents again.

During his travels Oedipus arrives at the outskirts of Thebes. There he gets into a quarrel with an old man whom he kills in a fit of anger—the man is Laius. He then finds that Thebes is under the control of a monster called the Sphinx, who has stationed herself outside the city and demands a yearly tribute from its citizens. Her power over Thebes can only be overcome if someone answers her riddle: "What walks on four legs in the morning, on two in the afternoon, and on three in the evening and is strongest when it uses the fewest number of legs?" Oedipus solves the riddle: the answer is *man*, who crawls on all fours as a baby, walks on two legs as an adult, and with a stick as an old man. Oedipus is hailed in Thebes as the savior of the city and given the hand of Laius' widow, Queen Jocasta, in marriage. Sophocles' play opens several years after this event, at a time when the city is again in peril and the people again look to Oedipus to help them. This time the trouble is a plague, a disease that is spreading among the people of Thebes, killing many of them. The people of Athens, by the way, would have recognized their own plight in the performance since they had just undergone a terrible plague at the time that *Oedipus* was written.

This story, then, is the material with which Sophocles worked. Notice that it resembles familiar fairy tales or folk tales—the curse, the prophecies, the riddle, and the hero-savior are all elements found in popular tales. Imagine possible ways of treating this story or parts of it. Could it be made into a poem or a tale for children, a lyric, an epic, a domestic drama, a comedy? Now let us see what Sophocles has done.

First of all, Sophocles does not begin his tragedy at the beginning. Since the Greeks, it has been the rule in Western drama and fiction to begin "in the middle of things" rather than, as in the oral folk tale, "once upon a time." *Oedipus* begins in the midst of a tense situation that demands a solution: a plague is raging; what will the king do? In fact, Sophocles begins his story after the important events have already occurred. The action of the play takes place in less than a day; yet the entire life of Oedipus, from his birth to his preparation for death, is brought into the development. Also, although we hear about Corinth and other parts of Thebes, the stage setting is in only one place—just outside the palace of the king and queen. There is only one plot or action in the play—no subplots or other distractions. There is certainly no comic relief, as found in Shakespeare. This simplicity of structure and unity of tone contribute to the play's classical quality. Just as in the Parthenon or the statue of *The Spearbearer*, everything nonessential is stripped away. What is left is a clear and balanced presentation of the essence of an aspect of life, rather than a realistic "slice of life." Part of the force and the impact of Greek tragedy lies in this classical simplicity.

If most of the story of Oedipus has taken place before the play begins, what *is* the plot or action of this tragedy? Most of it lies in the discovery of previous events. In this sense it resembles a detective story that opens after the crime has been committed. Oedipus begins by trying to find the answer to the question, "Who killed King Laius?" He ends by asking, and then answering, a much more profound question, "Who am I?" His tragedy, or his downfall, occurs when he finds the answer to his questions. As you read the play, notice how Sophocles builds up to the climactic point step by step. Try to determine, too, what emotional effect the tragic discovery of Oedipus has on you, the reader or spectator, and whether or not this changes by the end of the play. Notice how Sophocles has interpreted and portrayed the character of Oedipus. Finally, try to define for yourself what constitutes the personal tragedy of Oedipus and what makes the play a tragedy. This translation is by Dudley Fitts and Robert Fitzgerald.

SOPHOCLES

Oedipus Rex

CHARACTERS

OEDIPUS, *King of Thebes, supposed son of Polybos and Meropê, King and Queen of Corinth*
IOKASTÊ, *wife of Oedipus and widow of the late King Laïos*
KREON, *brother of Iokastê, a prince of Thebes*
TEIRESIAS, *a blind seer who serves Apollo*
PRIEST
MESSENGER, *from Corinth*
SHEPHERD, *former servant of Laïos*
SECOND MESSENGER, *from the palace*
CHORUS OF THEBAN ELDERS
CHORAGOS, *leader of the Chorus*
ANTIGONE *and* ISMENE, *young daughters of Oedipus and Iokastê. They appear in the Éxodos but do not speak.*
SUPPLIANTS, GUARDS, SERVANTS

THE SCENE.   *Before the palace of* OEDIPUS, *King of Thebes. A central door and two lateral doors open onto a platform which runs the length of the façade. On the platform, right and left, are altars; and three steps lead down into the orchêstra or chorus-ground. At the beginning of the action these steps are crowded by suppliants who have brought branches and chaplets of olive leaves and who sit in various attitudes of despair.* OEDIPUS *enters.*

PROLOGUE

OEDIPUS   My children, generations of the living
In the line of Kadmos,[1] nursed at his ancient hearth:
Why have you strewn yourselves before these altars
In supplication, with your boughs and garlands?
The breath of incense rises from the city
With a sound of prayer and lamentation.
                                    Children,
I would not have you speak through messengers,
And therefore I have come myself to hear you—
I, Oedipus, who bear the famous name.
(*To a* PRIEST) You, there, since you are eldest in the
   company,
Speak for them all, tell me what preys upon you,
Whether you come in dread, or crave some blessing:
Tell me, and never doubt that I will help you
In every way I can; I should be heartless
Were I not moved to find you suppliant here.

---
[1] Founder of Thebes.

PRIEST   Great Oedipus, O powerful king of Thebes!
You see how all the ages of our people
Cling to your altar steps: here are boys
Who can barely stand alone, and here are priests
By weight of age, as I am a priest of God,
And young men chosen from those yet unmarried;
As for the others, all that multitude,
They wait with olive chaplets in the squares,
At the two shrines of Pallas, and where Apollo
Speaks in the glowing embers.
                              Your own eyes
Must tell you: Thebes is tossed on a murdering sea
And can not lift her head from the death surge.
A rust consumes the buds and fruits of the earth;
The herds are sick; children die unborn,
And labor is vain. The god of plague and pyre
Raids like detestable lightning through the city,
And all the house of Kadmos is laid waste,
All emptied, and all darkened: Death alone
Battens upon the misery of Thebes.

You are not one of the immortal gods, we know;
Yet we have come to you to make our prayer
As to the man surest in mortal ways
And wisest in the ways of God. You saved us
From the Sphinx, that flinty singer, and the tribute
We paid to her so long; yet you were never
Better informed than we, nor could we teach you:
A god's touch, it seems, enabled you to help us.

Therefore, O mighty power, we turn to you:
Find us our safety, find us a remedy,
Whether by counsel of the gods or of men.
A king of wisdom tested in the past
Can act in a time of troubles, and act well.
Noblest of men, restore
Life to your city! Think how all men call you
Liberator for your boldness long ago;
Ah, when your years of kingship are remembered,
Let them not say *We rose, but later fell*—
Keep the State from going down in the storm!
Once, years ago, with happy augury,
You brought us fortune; be the same again!
No man questions your power to rule the land:
But rule over men, not over a dead city!
Ships are only hulls, high walls are nothing,
When no life moves in the empty passageways.

OEDIPUS   Poor children! You may be sure I know
  All that you longed for in your coming here.
  I know that you are deathly sick; and yet,
  Sick as you are, not one is as sick as I.
  Each of you suffers in himself alone
  His anguish, not another's; but my spirit
  Groans for the city, for myself, for you.

  I was not sleeping, you are not waking me.
  No, I have been in tears for a long while
  And in my restless thought walked many ways.
  In all my search I found one remedy,
  And I have adopted it: I have sent Kreon,
  Son of Menoikeus, brother of the queen,
  To Delphi, Apollo's place of revelation,
  To learn there, if he can,
  What act or pledge of mine may save the city.
  I have counted the days, and now, this very day,
  I am troubled, for he has overstayed his time.
  What is he doing? He has been gone too long.
  Yet whenever he comes back, I should do ill
  Not to take any action the god orders.
PRIEST   It is a timely promise. At this instant
  They tell me Kreon is here.
OEDIPUS   O Lord Apollo!
  May his news be fair as his face is radiant!
PRIEST   Good news, I gather! he is crowned with bay,
  The chaplet is thick with berries.
OEDIPUS   We shall soon know;
  He is near enough to hear us now.

  (*Enter* KREON)

                    O prince:
  Brother: son of Menoikeus:
  What answer do you bring us from the god?
KREON   A strong one. I can tell you, great afflictions
  Will turn out well, if they are taken well.
OEDIPUS   What was the oracle? These vague words
  Leave me still hanging between hope and fear.
KREON   Is it your pleasure to hear me with all these
  Gathered around us? I am prepared to speak,
  But should we not go in?
OEDIPUS   Speak to them all,
  It is for them I suffer, more than for myself.
KREON   Then I will tell you what I heard at Delphi.
  In plain words

The god commands us to expel from the land of
    Thebes
  An old defilement we are sheltering.
  It is a deathly thing, beyond cure;
  We must not let it feed upon us longer.
OEDIPUS   What defilement? How shall we rid ourselves
  of it?
KREON   By exile or death, blood for blood. It was
  Murder that brought the plague-wind on the city.
OEDIPUS   Murder of whom? Surely the god has named
  him?
KREON   My lord: Laïos once ruled this land,
  Before you came to govern us.
OEDIPUS   I know;
  I learned of him from others; I never saw him.
KREON   He was murdered; and Apollo commands us
  now
  To take revenge upon whoever killed him.
OEDIPUS   Upon whom? Where are they? Where shall
  we find a clue
  To solve that crime, after so many years?
KREON   Here in this land, he said. Search reveals
  Things that escape an inattentive man.
OEDIPUS   Tell me: Was Laïos murdered in his house,
  Or in the fields, or in some foreign country?
KREON   He said he planned to make a pilgrimage.
  He did not come home again.
OEDIPUS   And was there no one,
  No witness, no companion, to tell what happened?
KREON   They were all killed but one, and he got away
  So frightened that he could remember one thing
  only.
OEDIPUS   What was the one thing? One may be the
  key
  To everything, if we resolve to use it.
KREON   He said that a band of highwaymen attacked
  them,
  Outnumbered them, and overwhelmed the king.
OEDIPUS   Strange, that a highwayman should be so
  daring—
  Unless some faction here bribed him to do it.
KREON   We thought of that. But after Laïos' death
  New troubles arose and we had no avenger.
OEDIPUS   What troubles could prevent your hunting
  down the killers?
KREON   The riddling Sphinx's song

Made us deaf to all mysteries but her own.

OEDIPUS   Then once more I must bring what is dark to
    light.
It is most fitting that Apollo shows,
As you do, this compunction for the dead.
You shall see how I stand by you, as I should,
Avenging this country and the god as well,
And not as though it were for some distant friend,
But for my own sake, to be rid of evil.
Whoever killed King Laïos might—who knows?—
Lay violent hands even on me—and soon.
I act for the murdered king in my own interest.

Come, then, my children: leave the altar steps,
Lift up your olive boughs!
                           One of you go
And summon the people of Kadmos to gather here.
I will do all that I can; you may tell them that.

(*Exit a* PAGE)

So, with the help of God,
We shall be saved—or else indeed we are lost.

PRIEST   Let us rise, children. It was for this we came,
And now the king has promised it.
Phoibos[2] has sent us an oracle; may he descend
Himself to save us and drive out the plague.

(*Exeunt* OEDIPUS *and* KREON *into the palace by the central door. The* PRIEST *and the* SUPPLIANTS *disperse R and L. After a short pause the* CHORUS *enters the* orchêstra)

PARODOS [3]

Strophe 1

CHORUS   What is God singing in his profound
    Delphi of gold and shadow?

---

[2] Apollo.

[3] *Parodos* is the song or ode chanted by the chorus on their entry. It is accompanied by dancing and music played on an oboe. The chorus, in this play, represents elders of the city of Thebes. They remain on stage (on a level lower than the principal actors) for the remainder of the play. The choral odes and dances serve to separate one scene from another (there was no curtain in Greek theater) as well as to comment on the action, reinforce the emotion, and interpret the situation. The chorus also performs dance movements during certain portions of the scenes themselves. *Strophe* and *antistrophe* are terms denoting the movement and countermovement of the chorus from one side of their playing area to the other. When the chorus participates in dialogue with the other characters, their lines are spoken by the Choragos, their leader.

What oracle for Thebes, the sunwhipped city?
Fear unjoints me, the roots of my heart tremble.
Now I remember, O Healer, your power, and
    wonder:
Will you send doom like a sudden cloud, or weave it
Like nightfall of the past?
Speak to me, tell me, O
Child of golden Hope, immortal Voice.

Antistrophe 1

Let me pray to Athenê, the immortal daughter of
    Zeus,
And to Artemis her sister
Who keeps her famous throne in the market ring,
And to Apollo, archer from distant heaven—
O gods, descend! Like three streams leap against
The fires of our grief, the fires of darkness;
Be swift to bring us rest!
As in the old time from the brilliant house
Of air you stepped to save us, come again!

Strophe 2

Now our afflictions have no end,
Now all our stricken host lies down
And no man fights off death with his mind;
The noble plowland bears no grain,
And groaning mothers can not bear—
See, how our lives like birds take wing,
Like sparks that fly when a fire soars,
To the shore of the god of evening.

Antistrophe 2

The plague burns on, it is pitiless,
Though pallid children laden with death
Lie unwept in the stony ways,
And old gray women by every path
Flock to the strand about the altars
There to strike their breasts and cry
Worship of Phoibos in wailing prayers:
Be kind, God's golden child!

Strophe 3

There are no swords in this attack by fire,
No shields, but we are ringed with cries.
Send the besieger plunging from our homes
Into the vast sea-room of the Atlantic
Or into the waves that foam eastward of Thrace—
For the day ravages what the night spares—

Destroy our enemy, lord of the thunder!
Let him be riven by lightning from heaven!

Antistrophe 3

Phoibos Apollo, stretch the sun's bowstring,
That golden cord, until it sing for us,
Flashing arrows in heaven!
                              Artemis, Huntress,
Race with flaring lights upon our mountains!
O scarlet god, O golden-banded brow,
O Theban Bacchos in a storm of Maenads,

(Enter OEDIPUS, *C)*

Whirl upon Death, that all the Undying hate!
Come with blinding torches, come in joy!

SCENE I

OEDIPUS   Is this your prayer? It may be answered.
    Come,
    Listen to me, act as the crisis demands,
    And you shall have relief from all these evils.

    Until now I was a stranger to this tale,
    As I had been a stranger to the crime.
    Could I track down the murderer without a clue?
    But now, friends,
    As one who became a citizen after the murder,
    I make this proclamation to all Thebans:
    If any man knows by whose hand Laïos, son of
        Labdakos,
    Met his death, I direct that man to tell me
        everything,
    No matter what he fears for having so long withheld
        it.
    Let it stand as promised that no further trouble
    Will come to him, but he may leave the land in
        safety.

    Moreover: If anyone knows the murderer to be
        foreign,
    Let him not keep silent: he shall have his reward
        from me.
    However, if he does conceal it; if any man
    Fearing for his friend or for himself disobeys this
        edict,
    Hear what I propose to do:

    I solemnly forbid the people of this country,

Where power and throne are mine, ever to receive
    that man
Or speak to him, no matter who he is, or let him
Join in sacrifice, lustration, or in prayer.
I decree that he be driven from every house,
Being, as he is, corruption itself to us: the Delphic
Voice of Apollo has pronounced this revelation.
Thus I associate myself with the oracle
And take the side of the murdered king.

As for the criminal, I pray to God—
Whether it be a lurking thief, or one of a number—
I pray that that man's life be consumed in evil and
    wretchedness.
And as for me, this curse applies no less
If it should turn out that the culprit is my guest here,
Sharing my hearth.
                        You have heard the penalty.
I lay it on you now to attend to this
For my sake, for Apollo's, for the sick
Sterile city that heaven has abandoned.
Suppose the oracle had given you no command:
Should this defilement go uncleansed for ever?
You should have found the murderer: your king,
A noble king, had been destroyed!
                                Now I,
Having the power that he held before me,
Having his bed, begetting children there
Upon his wife, as he would have, had he lived—
Their son would have been my children's brother,
If Laïos had had luck in fatherhood!
(And now his bad fortune has struck him down)—
I say I take the son's part, just as though
I were his son, to press the fight for him
And see it won! I'll find the hand that brought
Death to Labdakos' and Polydoros' child,
Heir of Kadmos' and Agenor's line.[4]
And as for those who fail me,
May the gods deny them the fruit of the earth,
Fruit of the womb, and may they rot utterly!
Let them be wretched as we are wretched, and worse!

For you, for loyal Thebans, and for all
Who find my actions right, I pray the favor
Of justice, and of all the immortal gods.

---

[4] Father, grandfather, great-grandfather, and great-great-grandfather
of Laïos.

CHORAGOS   Since I am under oath, my lord, I swear
  I did not do the murder, I can not name
  The murderer. Phoibos ordained the search;
  Why did he not say who the culprit was?
OEDIPUS   An honest question. But no man in the
    world
  Can make the gods do more than the gods will.
CHORAGOS   There is an alternative, I think—
OEDIPUS   Tell me.
  Any or all, you must not fail to tell me.
CHORAGOS   A lord clairvoyant to the lord Apollo,
  As we all know, is the skilled Teiresias.
  One might learn much about this from him,
    Oedipus.
OEDIPUS   I am not wasting time:
  Kreon spoke of this, and I have sent for him—
  Twice, in fact; it is strange that he is not here.
CHORAGOS   The other matter—that old report—seems
    useless.
OEDIPUS   What was that? I am interested in all reports.
CHORAGOS   The king was said to have been killed by
    highwaymen.
OEDIPUS   I know. But we have no witnesses to that.
CHORAGOS   If the killer can feel a particle of dread,
  Your curse will bring him out of hiding!
OEDIPUS   No.
  The man who dared that act will fear no curse.

(*Enter the blind seer* TEIRESIAS, *led by a* PAGE)

CHORAGOS   But there is one man who may detect the
    criminal.
  This is Teiresias, this is the holy prophet
  In whom, alone of all men, truth was born.
OEDIPUS   Teiresias: seer: student of mysteries,
  Of all that's taught and all that no man tells,
  Secrets of Heaven and secrets of the earth:
  Blind though you are, you know the city lies
  Sick with plague; and from this plague, my lord,
  We find that you alone can guard or save us.

  Possibly you did not hear the messengers?
  Apollo, when we sent to him,
  Sent us back word that this great pestilence
  Would lift, but only if we established clearly
  The identity of those who murdered Laïos.
  They must be killed or exiled.

                              Can you use
  Birdflight[5] or any art of divination
  To purify yourself, and Thebes, and me
  From this contagion? We are in your hands.
  There is no fairer duty
  Than that of helping others in distress.
TEIRESIAS   How dreadful knowledge of the truth
    can be
  When there's no help in truth! I knew this well,
  But did not act on it: else I should not have come.
OEDIPUS   What is troubling you? Why are your eyes so
    cold?
TEIRESIAS   Let me go home. Bear your own fate, and
    I'll
  Bear mine. It is better so: trust what I say.
OEDIPUS   What you say is ungracious and unhelpful
  To your native country. Do not refuse to speak.
TEIRESIAS   When it comes to speech, your own is
    neither temperate
  Nor opportune. I wish to be more prudent.
OEDIPUS   In God's name, we all beg you—
TEIRESIAS   You are all ignorant.
  No; I will never tell you what I know.
  Now it is my misery; then, it would be yours.
OEDIPUS   What! You do know something, and will not
    tell us?
  You would betray us all and wreck the State?
TEIRESIAS   I do not intend to torture myself, or you.
  Why persist in asking? You will not persuade me.
OEDIPUS   What a wicked old man you are! You'd try a
    stone's
  Patience! Out with it! Have you no feeling at all?
TEIRESIAS   You call me unfeeling. If you could only
    see
  The nature of your own feelings . . .
OEDIPUS   Why,
  Who would not feel as I do? Who could endure
  Your arrogance toward the city?
TEIRESIAS   What does it matter?
  Whether I speak or not, it is bound to come.
OEDIPUS   Then, if "it" is bound to come, you are
    bound to tell me.
TEIRESIAS   No, I will not go on. Rage as you please.

―――――
5 Prophets predicted the future or divined the unknown by observing
  the flight of birds.

OEDIPUS   Rage? Why not!
                                    And I'll tell you what I think:
You planned it, you had it done, you all but
Killed him with your own hands: if you had eyes,
I'd say the crime was yours, and yours alone.

TEIRESIAS   So? I charge you, then,
Abide by the proclamation you have made:
From this day forth
Never speak again to these men or to me;
You yourself are the pollution of this country.

OEDIPUS   You dare say that! Can you possibly think you have
Some way of going free, after such insolence?

TEIRESIAS   I have gone free. It is the truth sustains me.

OEDIPUS   Who taught you shamelessness? It was not your craft.

TEIRESIAS   You did. You made me speak. I did not want to.

OEDIPUS   Speak what? Let me hear it again more clearly.

TEIRESIAS   Was it not clear before? Are you tempting me?

OEDIPUS   I did not understand it. Say it again.

TEIRESIAS   I say that you are the murderer whom you seek.

OEDIPUS   Now twice you have spat out infamy. You'll pay for it!

TEIRESIAS   Would you care for more? Do you wish to be really angry?

OEDIPUS   Say what you will. Whatever you say is worthless.

TEIRESIAS   I say you live in hideous shame with those
Most dear to you. You can not see the evil.

OEDIPUS   Can you go on babbling like this for ever?

TEIRESIAS   I can, if there is power in truth.

OEDIPUS   There is:
But not for you, not for you,
You sightless, witless, senseless, mad old man!

TEIRESIAS   You are the madman. There is no one here
Who will not curse you soon, as you curse me.

OEDIPUS   You child of total night! I would not touch you;
Neither would any man who sees the sun.

TEIRESIAS   True: it is not from you my fate will come.
That lies within Apollo's competence,
As it is his concern.

OEDIPUS   Tell me, who made
These fine discoveries? Kreon? or someone else?

TEIRESIAS   Kreon is no threat. You weave your own doom.

OEDIPUS   Wealth, power, craft of statesmanship!
Kingly position, everywhere admired!
What savage envy is stored up against these,
If Kreon, whom I trusted, Kreon my friend,
For this great office which the city once
Put in my hands unsought—if for this power
Kreon desires in secret to destroy me!

He has bought this decrepit fortune-teller, this
Collector of dirty pennies, this prophet fraud—
Why, he is no more clairvoyant than I am!
                                    Tell us:
Has your mystic mummery ever approached the truth?
When that hellcat the Sphinx was performing here,
What help were you to these people?
Her magic was not for the first man who came along:
It demanded a real exorcist. Your birds—
What good were they? or the gods, for the matter of that?
But I came by,
Oedipus, the simple man, who knows nothing—
I thought it out for myself, no birds helped me!
And this is the man you think you can destroy,
That you may be close to Kreon when he's king!
Well, you and your friend Kreon, it seems to me,
Will suffer most. If you were not an old man,
You would have paid already for your plot.

CHORAGOS   We can not see that his words or yours
Have been spoken except in anger, Oedipus,
And of anger we have no need. How to accomplish
The god's will best: that is what most concerns us.

TEIRESIAS   You are a king. But where argument's concerned
I am your man, as much a king as you.
I am not your servant, but Apollo's.
I have no need of Kreon or Kreon's name.

Listen to me. You mock my blindness, do you?
But I say that you, with both your eyes, are blind:
You can not see the wretchedness of your life,
Nor in whose house you live, no, nor with whom.
Who are your father and mother? Can you tell me?

You do not even know the blind wrongs
That you have done them, on earth and in the world
  below.
But the double lash of your parents' curse will whip
  you
Out of this land some day, with only night
Upon your precious eyes.
Your cries then—where will they not be heard?
What fastness of Kithairon[6] will not echo them?
And that bridal-descant of yours—you'll know it
  then,
The song they sang when you came here to Thebes
And found your misguided berthing.
All this, and more, that you can not guess at now,
Will bring you to yourself among your children.

Be angry, then. Curse Kreon. Curse my words.
I tell you, no man that walks upon the earth
Shall be rooted out more horribly than you.
OEDIPUS   Am I to bear this from him?—Damnation
  Take you! Out of this place! Out of my sight!
TEIRESIAS   I would not have come at all if you had not
  asked me.
OEDIPUS   Could I have told that you'd talk nonsense,
  that
  You'd come here to make a fool of yourself, and of
  me?
TEIRESIAS   A fool? Your parents thought me sane
  enough.
OEDIPUS   My parents again!—Wait: who were my
  parents?
TEIRESIAS   This day will give you a father, and break
  your heart.
OEDIPUS   Your infantile riddles! Your damned
  abracadabra!
TEIRESIAS   You were a great man once at solving
  riddles.
OEDIPUS   Mock me with that if you like; you will find
  it true.
TEIRESIAS   It was true enough. It brought about your
  ruin.
OEDIPUS   But if it saved this town?
TEIRESIAS   (to the PAGE)   Boy, give me your hand.
OEDIPUS   Yes, boy; lead him away.

_____
[6] The mountain where Oedipus was taken to be exposed as an infant.

                              —While you are here
We can do nothing. Go; leave us in peace.
TEIRESIAS   I will go when I have said what I have to
  say.
  How can you hurt me? And I tell you again:
  The man you have been looking for all this time,
  The damned man, the murderer of Laïos,
  That man is in Thebes. To your mind he is foreign-
  born,
  But it will soon be shown that he is a Theban,
  A revelation that will fail to please.
                              A blind man,
  Who has his eyes now; a penniless man, who is rich
  now;
  And he will go tapping the strange earth with his
  staff.
  To the children with whom he lives now he will be
  Brother and father—the very same; to her
  Who bore him, son and husband—the very same
  Who came to his father's bed, wet with his father's
  blood.

  Enough. Go think that over.
  If later you find error in what I have said,
  You may say that I have no skill in prophecy.

(Exit TEIRESIAS, led by his PAGE. OEDIPUS goes into the
palace)

ODE I

Strophe 1

CHORUS   The Delphic stone of prophecies
  Remembers ancient regicide
  And a still bloody hand.
  That killer's hour of flight has come.
  He must be stronger than riderless
  Coursers of untiring wind,
  For the son[7] of Zeus armed with his father's thunder
  Leaps in lightning after him;
  And the Furies hold his track, the sad Furies.

Antistrophe 1

Holy Parnassos'[8] peak of snow
Flashes and blinds that secret man,

_____
[7] Apollo.
[8] Mountain sacred to Apollo.

That all shall hunt him down:
Though he may roam the forest shade
Like a bull gone wild from pasture
To rage through glooms of stone.
Doom comes down on him; flight will not avail him;
For the world's heart calls him desolate,
And the immortal voices follow, for ever follow.

Strophe 2

But now a wilder thing is heard
From the old man skilled at hearing Fate in the wing-
   beat of a bird.
Bewildered as a blown bird, my soul hovers and can
   not find
Foothold in this debate, or any reason or rest of
   mind.
But no man ever brought—none can bring
Proof of strife between Thebes' royal house,
Labdakos' line, and the son of Polybos;
And never until now has any man brought word
Of Laïos' dark death staining Oedipus the King.

Antistrophe 2

Divine Zeus and Apollo hold
Perfect intelligence alone of all tales ever told;
And well though this diviner works, he works in his
   own night;
No man can judge that rough unknown or trust in
   second sight,
For wisdom changes hands among the wise.
Shall I believe my great lord criminal
At a raging word that a blind old man let fall?
I saw him, when the carrion woman[9] faced him of
   old,
Prove his heroic mind. These evil words are lies.

SCENE II

KREON   Men of Thebes:
   I am told that heavy accusations
   Have been brought against me by King Oedipus.

   I am not the kind of man to bear this tamely.

   If in these present difficulties
   He holds me accountable for any harm to him

---

[9] The Sphinx.

Through anything I have said or done—why, then,
I do not value life in this dishonor.
It is not as though this rumor touched upon
Some private indiscretion. The matter is grave.
The fact is that I am being called disloyal
To the State, to my fellow citizens, to my friends.
CHORAGOS   He may have spoken in anger, not from
   his mind.
KREON   But did you not hear him say I was the one
   Who seduced the old prophet into lying?
CHORAGOS   The thing was said: I do not know how
   seriously.
KREON   But you were watching him! Were his eyes
   steady?
   Did he look like a man in his right mind?
CHORAGOS   I do not know.
   I can not judge the behavior of great men.
   But here is the king himself.

(*Enter* OEDIPUS)

OEDIPUS   So you dared come back.
   Why? How brazen of you to come to my house,
   You murderer!
                     Do you think I do not know
   That you plotted to kill me, plotted to steal my
      throne?
   Tell me, in God's name: am I coward, a fool,
   That you should dream you could accomplish this?
   A fool who could not see your slippery game?
   A coward, not to fight back when I saw it?
   You are the fool, Kreon, are you not? hoping
   Without support or friends to get a throne?
   Thrones may be won or bought: you could do
      neither.
KREON   Now listen to me. You have talked; let me
   talk, too.
   You can not judge unless you know the facts.
OEDIPUS   You speak well: there is one fact; but I find
   it hard
   To learn from the deadliest enemy I have.
KREON   That above all I must dispute with you.
OEDIPUS   That above all I will not hear you deny.
KREON   If you think there is anything good in being
   stubborn
   Against all reason, then I say you are wrong.

OEDIPUS   If you think a man can sin against his own kind
And not be punished for it, I say you are mad.

KREON   I agree. But tell me: What have I done to you?

OEDIPUS   You advised me to send for that wizard, did you not?

KREON   I did. I should do it again.

OEDIPUS   Very well. Now tell me:
How long has it been since Laïos—

KREON   What of Laïos?

OEDIPUS   Since he vanished in that onset by the road?

KREON   It was long ago, a long time.

OEDIPUS   And this prophet,
Was he practicing here then?

KREON   He was; and with honor, as now.

OEDIPUS   Did he speak of me at that time?

KREON   He never did,
At least, not when I was present.

OEDIPUS   But . . . the enquiry?
I suppose you held one?

KREON   We did, but we learned nothing.

OEDIPUS   Why did the prophet not speak against me then?

KREON   I do not know; and I am the kind of man
Who holds his tongue when he has no facts to go on.

OEDIPUS   There's one fact that you know, and you could tell it.

KREON   What fact is that? If I know it, you shall have it.

OEDIPUS   If he were not involved with you, he could not say
That it was I who murdered Laïos.

KREON   If he says that, you are the one that knows it!—
But now it is my turn to question you.

OEDIPUS   Put your questions. I am no murderer.

KREON   First, then: You married my sister?

OEDIPUS   I married your sister.

KREON   And you rule the kingdom equally with her?

OEDIPUS   Everything that she wants she has from me.

KREON   And I am the third, equal to both of you?

OEDIPUS   That is why I call you a bad friend.

KREON   No. Reason it out, as I have done.
Think of this first: Would any sane man prefer
Power, with all a king's anxieties,
To that same power and the grace of sleep?

Certainly not I.
I have never longed for the king's power—only his rights.
Would any wise man differ from me in this?
As matters stand, I have my way in everything
With your consent, and no responsibilities.
If I were king, I should be a slave to policy.

How could I desire a scepter more
Than what is now mine—untroubled influence?
No, I have not gone mad; I need no honors,
Except those with the perquisites I have now.
I am welcome everywhere; every man salutes me,
And those who want your favor seek my ear,
Since I know how to manage what they ask.
Should I exchange this ease for that anxiety?
Besides, no sober mind is treasonable.
I hate anarchy
And never would deal with any man who likes it.
Test what I have said. Go to the priestess
At Delphi, ask if I quoted her correctly.
And as for this other thing: if I am found
Guilty of treason with Teiresias,
Then sentence me to death. You have my word
It is a sentence I should cast my vote for—
But not without evidence!
                              You do wrong
When you take good men for bad, bad men for good.
A true friend thrown aside—why, life itself
Is not more precious!
                              In time you will know this well:
For time, and time alone, will show the just man,
Though scoundrels are discovered in a day.

CHORAGOS   This is well said, and a prudent man would ponder it.
Judgments too quickly formed are dangerous.

OEDIPUS   But is he not quick in his duplicity?
And shall I not be quick to parry him?
Would you have me stand still, hold my peace, and let
This man win everything, through my inaction?

KREON   And you want—what is it, then? To banish me?

OEDIPUS   No, not exile. It is your death I want,
So that all the world may see what treason means.

KREON   You will persist, then? You will not believe
    me?
OEDIPUS   How can I believe you?
KREON   Then you are a fool.
OEDIPUS   To save myself?
KREON   In justice, think of me.
OEDIPUS   You are evil incarnate.
KREON   But suppose that you are wrong?
OEDIPUS   Still I must rule.
KREON   But not if you rule badly.
OEDIPUS   O city, city!
KREON   It is my city, too!
CHORAGOS   Now, my lords, be still. I see the queen,
    Iokastê, coming from her palace chambers;
    And it is time she came, for the sake of you both.
    This dreadful quarrel can be resolved through her.

(*Enter* IOKASTÊ)

IOKASTÊ   Poor foolish men, what wicked din is this?
    With Thebes sick to death, is it not shameful
    That you should rake some private quarrel up?
    (*To* OEDIPUS) Come into the house.
                 —And you, Kreon, go now:
    Let us have no more of this tumult over nothing.
KREON   Nothing? No, sister: what your husband plans
    for me
    Is one of two great evils: exile or death.
OEDIPUS   He is right.
            Why, woman I have caught him squarely
    Plotting against my life.
KREON   No! Let me die
    Accurst if ever I have wished you harm!
IOKASTÊ   Ah, believe it, Oedipus!
    In the name of the gods, respect this oath of his
    For my sake, for the sake of these people here!

Strophe 1

CHORAGOS   Open your mind to her, my lord. Be ruled
    by her, I beg you!
OEDIPUS   What would you have me do?
CHORAGOS   Respect Kreon's word. He has never
    spoken like a fool,
    And now he has sworn an oath.
OEDIPUS   You know what you ask?
CHORAGOS   I do.
OEDIPUS   Speak on, then.

CHORAGOS   A friend so sworn should not be baited so,
    In blind malice, and without final proof.
OEDIPUS   You are aware, I hope, that what you say
    Means death for me, or exile at the least.

Strophe 2

CHORAGOS   No, I swear by Helios, first in Heaven!
    May I die friendless and accurst,
    The worst of deaths, if ever I meant that!
        It is the withering fields
            That hurt my sick heart:
        Must we bear all these ills,
            And now your bad blood as well?
OEDIPUS   Then let him go. And let me die, if I must,
    Or be driven by him in shame from the land of
        Thebes.
    It is your unhappiness, and not his talk,
    That touches me.
                As for him—
    Wherever he goes, hatred will follow him.
KREON   Ugly in yielding, as you were ugly in rage!
    Natures like yours chiefly torment themselves.
OEDIPUS   Can you not go? Can you not leave me?
KREON   I can.
    You do not know me; but the city knows me,
    And in its eyes I am just, if not in yours.

(*Exit* KREON)

Antistrophe 1

CHORAGOS   Lady Iokastê, did you not ask the King to
    go to his chambers?
IOKASTÊ   First tell me what has happened.
CHORAGOS   There was suspicion without evidence;
    yet it rankled
    As even false charges will.
IOKASTÊ   On both sides?
CHORAGOS   On both.
IOKASTÊ   But what was said?
CHORAGOS   Oh let it rest, let it be done with!
    Have we not suffered enough?
OEDIPUS   You see to what your decency has brought
    you:
    You have made difficulties where my heart saw
    none.

Antistrophe 2

CHORAGOS   Oedipus, it is not once only I have told
   you—
   You must know I should count myself unwise
   To the point of madness, should I now forsake you—
        You, under whose hand,
            In the storm of another time,
        Our dear land sailed out free.
            But now stand fast at the helm!

IOKASTÊ   In God's name, Oedipus, inform your wife
   as well:
   Why are you so set in this hard anger?

OEDIPUS   I will tell you, for none of these men
   deserves
   My confidence as you do. It is Kreon's work,
   His treachery, his plotting against me.

IOKASTÊ   Go on, if you can make this clear to me.

OEDIPUS   He charges me with the murder of Laïos.

IOKASTÊ   Has he some knowledge? Or does he speak
   from hearsay?

OEDIPUS   He would not commit himself to such a
   charge,
   But he has brought in that damnable soothsayer
   To tell his story.

IOKASTÊ   Set your mind at rest.
   If it is a question of soothsayers, I tell you
   That you will find no man whose craft gives
      knowledge
   Of the unknowable.
                  Here is my proof:
   An oracle was reported to Laïos once
   (I will not say from Phoibos himself, but from
   His appointed ministers, at any rate)
   That his doom would be death at the hands of his
      own son—
   His son, born of his flesh and of mine!

   Now, you remember the story: Laïos was killed
   By marauding strangers where three highways meet;
   But his child had not been three days in this world
   Before the king had pierced the baby's ankles
   And left him to die on a lonely mountainside.

   Thus, Apollo never caused that child
   To kill his father, and it was not Laïos' fate
   To die at the hands of his son, as he had feared.
   This is what prophets and prophecies are worth!

Have no dread of them.
                  It is God himself
   Who can show us what he wills, in his own way.

OEDIPUS   How strange a shadowy memory crossed my
   mind,
   Just now while you were speaking; it chilled my
   heart.

IOKASTÊ   What do you mean? What memory do you
   speak of?

OEDIPUS   If I understand you, Laïos was killed
   At a place where three roads meet.

IOKASTÊ   So it was said;
   We have no later story.

OEDIPUS   Where did it happen?

IOKASTÊ   Phokis, it is called: at a place where the
      Theban Way
   Divides into the roads toward Delphi and Daulia.

OEDIPUS   When?

IOKASTÊ   We had the news not long before you came
   And proved the right to your succession here.

OEDIPUS   Ah, what net has God been weaving for me?

IOKASTÊ   Oedipus! Why does this trouble you?

OEDIPUS   Do not ask me yet.
   First, tell me how Laïos looked, and tell me
   How old he was.

IOKASTÊ   He was tall, his hair just touched
   With white; his form was not unlike your own.

OEDIPUS   I think that I myself may be accurst
   By my own ignorant edict.

IOKASTÊ   You speak strangely.
   It makes me tremble to look at you, my king.

OEDIPUS   I am not sure that the blind man can not see.
   But I should know better if you were to tell me—

IOKASTÊ   Anything—though I dread to hear you ask
   it.

OEDIPUS   Was the king lightly escorted, or did he ride
   With a large company, as a ruler should?

IOKASTÊ   There were five men with him in all: one
      was a herald.
   And a single chariot, which he was driving.

OEDIPUS   Alas, that makes it plain enough!
                            But who—
   Who told you how it happened?

IOKASTÊ   A household servant,
   The only one to escape.

OEDIPUS   And is he still

A servant of ours?

IOKASTÊ   No; for when he came back at last
And found you enthroned in the place of the dead
    king,
He came to me, touched my hand with his, and
    begged
That I would send him away to the frontier district
Where only the shepherds go—
As far away from the city as I could send him.
I granted his prayer; for although the man was a
    slave,
He had earned more than this favor at my hands.

OEDIPUS   Can he be called back quickly?

IOKASTÊ   Easily.
But why?

OEDIPUS   I have taken too much upon myself
Without enquiry; therefore I wish to consult him.

IOKASTÊ   Then he shall come.
                                      But am I not one also
To whom you might confide these fears of yours?

OEDIPUS   That is your right; it will not be denied you,
Now least of all; for I have reached a pitch
Of wild foreboding. Is there anyone
To whom I should sooner speak?

Polybos of Corinth is my father.
My mother is a Dorian: Meropê.
I grew up chief among the men of Corinth
Until a strange thing happened—
Not worth my passion, it may be, but strange.
At a feast, a drunken man maundering in his cups
Cries out that I am not my father's son! [10]

I contained myself that night, though I felt anger
And a sinking heart. The next day I visited
My father and mother, and questioned them. They
    stormed,
Calling it all the slanderous rant of a fool;
And this relieved me. Yet the suspicion
Remained always aching in my mind;
I knew there was talk; I could not rest;
And finally, saying nothing to my parents,
I went to the shrine at Delphi.

---

[10] Oedipus perhaps interprets this as an allegation that he is a bastard,
the son of Meropê but not of Polybos. The implication, at any rate,
is that he is not of royal birth, not the legitimate heir to the throne
of Corinth.

The god dismissed my question without reply;
He spoke of other things.
                                      Some were clear,
Full of wretchedness, dreadful, unbearable:
As, that I should lie with my own mother, breed
Children from whom all men would turn their eyes;
And that I should be my father's murderer.

I heard all this, and fled. And from that day
Corinth to me was only in the stars
Descending in that quarter of the sky,
As I wandered farther and farther on my way
To a land where I should never see the evil
Sung by the oracle. And I came to this country
Where, so you say, King Laïos was killed.

I will tell you all that happened there, my lady.

There were three highways
Coming together at a place I passed;
And there a herald came towards me, and a chariot
Drawn by horses, with a man such as you describe
Seated in it. The groom leading the horses
Forced me off the road at his lord's command;
But as this charioteer lurched over towards me
I struck him in my rage. The old man saw me
And brought his double goad down upon my head
As I came abreast.
                                      He was paid back, and more!
Swinging my club in this right hand I knocked him
Out of his car, and he rolled on the ground.
                                                      I killed him.

I killed them all.
Now if that stranger and Laïos were—kin,
Where is a man more miserable than I?
More hated by the gods? Citizen and alien alike
Must never shelter me or speak to me—
I must be shunned by all.
                                      And I myself
Pronounced this malediction upon myself!

Think of it: I have touched you with these hands,
These hands that killed your husband. What
    defilement!

Am I all evil, then? It must be so,
Since I must flee from Thebes, yet never again
See my own countrymen, my own country,

For fear of joining my mother in marriage
And killing Polybos, my father.
                              Ah,
If I was created so, born to this fate,
Who could deny the savagery of God?

O holy majesty of heavenly powers!
May I never see that day! Never!
Rather let me vanish from the race of men
Than know the abomination destined me!

CHORAGOS   We too, my lord, have felt dismay at this.
  But there is hope: you have yet to hear the shepherd.

OEDIPUS   Indeed, I fear no other hope is left me.

IOKASTÊ   What do you hope from him when he
      comes?

OEDIPUS   This much:
  If his account of the murder tallies with yours,
  Then I am cleared.

IOKASTÊ   What was it that I said
  Of such importance?

OEDIPUS   Why, "marauders," you said,
  Killed the king, according to this man's story.
  If he maintains that still, if there were several,
  Clearly the guilt is not mine: I was alone.
  But if he says one man, singlehanded, did it,
  Then the evidence all points to me.

IOKASTÊ   You may be sure that he said there were
      several;
  And can he call back that story now? He can not.
  The whole city heard it as plainly as I.
  But suppose he alters some detail of it:
  He can not ever show that Laïos' death
  Fulfilled the oracle: for Apollo said
  My child was doomed to kill him; and my child—
  Poor baby!—it was my child that died first.
  No. From now on, where oracles are concerned,
  I would not waste a second thought on any.

OEDIPUS   You may be right.
                          But come: let someone go
  For the shepherd at once. This matter must be
      settled.

IOKASTÊ   I will send for him.
  I would not wish to cross you in anything,
  And surely not in this.—Let us go in.

(Exeunt into the palace)

ODE II

Strophe 1

CHORUS   Let me be reverent in the ways of right,
  Lowly the paths I journey on;
  Let all my words and actions keep
  The laws of the pure universe
  From highest Heaven handed down.
  For Heaven is their bright nurse,
  Those generations of the realms of light;
  Ah, never of mortal kind were they begot,
  Nor are they slaves of memory, lost in sleep:
  Their Father is greater than Time, and ages not.

Antistrophe 1

The tyrant is a child of Pride
Who drinks from his great sickening cup
Recklessness and vanity,
Until from his high crest headlong
He plummets to the dust of hope.
That strong man is not strong.
But let no fair ambition be denied;
May God protect the wrestler for the State
In government, in comely policy,
Who will fear God, and on His ordinance wait.

Strophe 2

Haughtiness and the high hand of disdain
Tempt and outrage God's holy law;
And any mortal who dares hold
No immortal Power in awe
Will be caught up in a net of pain:
The price for which his levity is sold.
Let each man take due earnings, then,
And keep his hands from holy things,
And from blasphemy stand apart—
Else the crackling blast of heaven
Blows on his head, and on his desperate heart.
Though fools will honor impious men,
In their cities no tragic poet sings.

Antistrophe 2

Shall we lose faith in Delphi's obscurities,
We who have heard the world's core
Discredited, and the sacred wood
Of Zeus at Elis praised no more?
The deeds and the strange prophecies
Must make a pattern yet to be understood.

Zeus, if indeed you are lord of all,
Throned in light over night and day,
Mirror this in your endless mind:
Our masters call the oracle
Words on the wind, and the Delphic vision blind!
Their hearts no longer know Apollo,
And reverence for the gods has died away.

SCENE III

(*Enter* IOKASTÊ)

IOKASTÊ   Princes of Thebes, it has occurred to me
To visit the altars of the gods, bearing
These branches as a suppliant, and this incense.
Our king is not himself: his noble soul
Is overwrought with fantasies of dread,
Else he would consider
The new prophecies in the light of the old.
He will listen to any voice that speaks disaster,
And my advice goes for nothing.

(*She approaches the altar, R*)

                                     To you, then, Apollo,
Lycéan lord, since you are nearest, I turn in prayer.
Receive these offerings, and grant us deliverance
From defilement. Our hearts are heavy with fear
When we see our leader distracted, as helpless sailors
Are terrified by the confusion of their helmsman.

(*Enter* MESSENGER)

MESSENGER   Friends, no doubt you can direct me:
Where shall I find the house of Oedipus,
Or, better still, where is the king himself?
CHORAGOS   It is this very place, stranger; he is inside.
This is his wife and mother of his children.
MESSENGER   I wish her happiness in a happy house,
Blest in all the fulfillment of her marriage.
IOKASTÊ   I wish as much for you: your courtesy
Deserves a like good fortune. But now, tell me:
Why have you come? What have you to say to us?
MESSENGER   Good news, my lady, for your house and
    your husband.
IOKASTÊ   What news? Who sent you here?
MESSENGER   I am from Corinth.
The news I bring ought to mean joy for you,
Though it may be you will find some grief in it.

IOKASTÊ   What is it? How can it touch us in both
    ways?
MESSENGER   The word is that the people of the
    Isthmus
Intend to call Oedipus to be their king.
IOKASTÊ   But old King Polybos—is he not reigning
    still?
MESSENGER   No. Death holds him in his sepulchre.
IOKASTÊ   What are you saying? Polybos is dead?
MESSENGER   If I am not telling the truth, may I die
    myself.
IOKASTÊ   (*to a* MAIDSERVANT)   Go in, go quickly;
    tell this to your master.

O riddlers of God's will, where are you now!
This was the man whom Oedipus, long ago,
Feared so, fled so, in dread of destroying him—
But it was another fate by which he died.

(*Enter* OEDIPUS, *C*)

OEDIPUS   Dearest Iokastê, why have you sent for me?
IOKASTÊ   Listen to what this man says, and then tell
    me
What has become of the solemn prophecies.
OEDIPUS   Who is this man? What is his news for me?
IOKASTÊ   He has come from Corinth to announce
    your father's death!
OEDIPUS   Is it true, stranger? Tell me in your own
    words.
MESSENGER   I can not say it more clearly: the king is
    dead.
OEDIPUS   Was it by treason? Or by an attack of illness?
MESSENGER   A little thing brings old men to their rest.
OEDIPUS   It was sickness, then?
MESSENGER   Yes, and his many years.
OEDIPUS   Ah!
Why should a man respect the Pythian hearth,[11] or
Give heed to the birds that jangle above his head?
They prophesied that I should kill Polybos,
Kill my own father; but he is dead and buried,
And I am here—I never touched him, never,
Unless he died of grief for my departure,
And thus, in a sense, through me. No. Polybos
Has packed the oracles off with him underground.

----

[11] Delphi.

They are empty words.

IOKASTÊ   Had I not told you so?

OEDIPUS   You had; it was my faint heart that betrayed me.

IOKASTÊ   From now on never think of those things again.

OEDIPUS   And yet—must I not fear my mother's bed?

IOKASTÊ   Why should anyone in this world be afraid,
Since Fate rules us and nothing can be foreseen?
A man should live only for the present day.

Have no more fear of sleeping with your mother:
How many men, in dreams, have lain with their mothers!
No reasonable man is troubled by such things.

OEDIPUS   That is true; only—
If only my mother were not still alive!
But she is alive. I can not help my dread.

IOKASTÊ   Yet this news of your father's death is wonderful.

OEDIPUS   Wonderful. But I fear the living woman.

MESSENGER   Tell me, who is this woman that you fear?

OEDIPUS   It is Meropê, man; the wife of King Polybos.

MESSENGER   Meropê? Why should you be afraid of her?

OEDIPUS   An oracle of the gods, a dreadful saying.

MESSENGER   Can you tell me about it or are you sworn to silence?

OEDIPUS   I can tell you, and I will.
Apollo said through his prophet that I was the man
Who should marry his own mother, shed his father's blood
With his own hands. And so, for all these years
I have kept clear of Corinth, and no harm has come—
Though it would have been sweet to see my parents again.

MESSENGER   And is this the fear that drove you out of Corinth?

OEDIPUS   Would you have me kill my father?

MESSENGER   As for that
You must be reassured by the news I gave you.

OEDIPUS   If you could reassure me, I would reward you.

MESSENGER   I had that in mind, I will confess: I thought
I could count on you when you returned to Corinth.

OEDIPUS   No: I will never go near my parents again.

MESSENGER   Ah, son, you still do not know what you are doing—

OEDIPUS   What do you mean? In the name of God tell me!

MESSENGER   —if these are your reasons for not going home.

OEDIPUS   I tell you, I fear the oracle may come true.

MESSENGER   And guilt may come upon you through your parents?

OEDIPUS   That is the dread that is always in my heart.

MESSENGER   Can you not see that all your fears are groundless?

OEDIPUS   Groundless? Am I not my parents' son?

MESSENGER   Polybos was not your father.

OEDIPUS   Not my father?

MESSENGER   No more your father than the man speaking to you.

OEDIPUS   But you are nothing to me!

MESSENGER   Neither was he.

OEDIPUS   Then why did he call me son?

MESSENGER   I will tell you:
Long ago he had you from my hands, as a gift.

OEDIPUS   Then how could he love me so, if I was not his?

MESSENGER   He had no children, and his heart turned to you.

OEDIPUS   What of you? Did you buy me? Did you find me by chance?

MESSENGER   I came upon you in the woody vales of Kithairon.

OEDIPUS   And what were you doing there?

MESSENGER   Tending my flocks.

OEDIPUS   A wandering shepherd?

MESSENGER   But your savior, son, that day.

OEDIPUS   From what did you save me?

MESSENGER   Your ankles should tell you that.

OEDIPUS   Ah, stranger, why do you speak of that childhood pain?

MESSENGER   I pulled the skewer that pinned your feet together.

OEDIPUS   I have had the mark as long as I can remember.

MESSENGER   That was why you were given the name you bear.

OEDIPUS   God! Was it my father or my mother who did it?
Tell me!

MESSENGER   I do not know. The man who gave you to
me
Can tell you better than I.

OEDIPUS   It was not you that found me, but another?

MESSENGER   It was another shepherd gave you to me.

OEDIPUS   Who was he? Can you tell me who he was?

MESSENGER   I think he was said to be one of Laïos'
people.

OEDIPUS   You mean the Laïos who was king here years
ago?

MESSENGER   Yes; King Laïos; and the man was one of
his herdsmen.

OEDIPUS   Is he still alive? Can I see him?

MESSENGER   These men here
Know best about such things.

OEDIPUS   Does anyone here
Know this shepherd that he is talking about?
Have you seen him in the fields, or in the town?
If you have, tell me. It is time things were made
plain.

CHORAGOS   I think the man he means is that same
shepherd
You have already asked to see. Iokastê perhaps
Could tell you something.

OEDIPUS   Do you know anything
About him, Lady? Is he the man we have summoned?
Is that the man this shepherd means?

IOKASTÊ   Why think of him?
Forget this herdsman. Forget it all.
This talk is a waste of time.

OEDIPUS   How can you say that,
When the clues to my true birth are in my hands?

IOKASTÊ   For God's love, let us have no more
questioning!
Is your life nothing to you?
My own is pain enough for me to bear.

OEDIPUS   You need not worry. Suppose my mother a
slave,
And born of slaves: no baseness can touch you.

IOKASTÊ   Listen to me, I beg you: do not do this thing!

OEDIPUS   I will not listen; the truth must be made
known.

IOKASTÊ   Everything that I say is for your own good!

OEDIPUS   My own good
Snaps my patience, then! I want none of it.

IOKASTÊ   You are fatally wrong! May you never learn
who you are!

OEDIPUS   Go, one of you, and bring the shepherd here.
Let us leave this woman to brag of her royal name.

IOKASTÊ   Ah, miserable!
That is the only word I have for you now.
That is the only word I can ever have.

(Exit into the palace)

CHORAGOS   Why has she left us, Oedipus? Why has
she gone
In such a passion of sorrow? I fear this silence:
Something dreadful may come of it.

OEDIPUS   Let it come!
However base my birth, I must know about it.
The Queen, like a woman, is perhaps ashamed
To think of my low origin. But I
Am a child of Luck; I can not be dishonored.
Luck is my mother; the passing months, my
brothers,
Have seen me rich and poor.
                              If this is so,
How could I wish that I were someone else?
How could I not be glad to know my birth?

ODE III

Strophe

CHORUS   If ever the coming time were known
To my heart's pondering,
Kithairon, now by Heaven I see the torches
At the festival of the next full moon,
And see the dance, and hear the choir sing
A grace to your gentle shade:
Mountain where Oedipus was found,
O mountain guard of a noble race!
May the god [12] who heals us lend his aid,
And let that glory come to pass
For our king's cradling-ground.

Antistrophe

Of the nymphs that flower beyond the years,
Who bore you,[13] royal child,
To Pan of the hills or the timberline Apollo,
Cold in delight where the upland clears,
Or Hermês for whom Kyllenê's heights are piled?

---

[12] Apollo.

[13] The chorus is suggesting that perhaps Oedipus is the son of one of
the immortal nymphs and of a god—Pan, Apollo, Hermes, or Dionysus. The "sweet god-ravisher" (below) is the presumed mother.

Or flushed as evening cloud,
Great Dionysos, roamer of mountains,
He—was it he who found you there,
And caught you up in his own proud
Arms from the sweet god-ravisher
Who laughed by the Muses' fountains?

SCENE IV

OEDIPUS   Sirs: though I do not know the man,
I think I see him coming, this shepherd we want:
He is old, like our friend here, and the men
Bringing him seem to be servants of my house.
But you can tell, if you have ever seen him.

(*Enter* SHEPHERD *escorted by* SERVANTS)

CHORAGOS   I know him, he was Laïos' man. You can
trust him.
OEDIPUS   Tell me first, you from Corinth: is this the
shepherd
We were discussing?
MESSENGER   This is the very man.
OEDIPUS   (*to* SHEPHERD)   Come here. No, look at me.
You must answer
Everything I ask.—You belonged to Laïos?
SHEPHERD   Yes: born his slave, brought up in his
house.
OEDIPUS   Tell me: what kind of work did you do for
him?
SHEPHERD   I was a shepherd of his, most of my life.
OEDIPUS   Where mainly did you go for pasturage?
SHEPHERD   Sometimes Kithairon, sometimes the hills
near-by.
OEDIPUS   Do you remember ever seeing this man out
there?
SHEPHERD   What would he be doing there? This man?
OEDIPUS   This man standing here. Have you ever seen
him before?
SHEPHERD   No. At least, not to my recollection.
MESSENGER   And that is not strange, my lord. But I'll
refresh
His memory: he must remember when we two
Spent three whole seasons together, March to
September,
On Kithairon or thereabouts. He had two flocks;
I had one. Each autumn I'd drive mine home
And he would go back with his to Laïos' sheepfold.—

Is this not true, just as I have described it?
SHEPHERD   True, yes; but it was all so long ago.
MESSENGER   Well, then: do you remember, back in
those days,
That you gave me a baby boy to bring up as my own?
SHEPHERD   What if I did? What are you trying to say?
MESSENGER   King Oedipus was once that little child.
SHEPHERD   Damn you, hold your tongue!
OEDIPUS   No more of that!
It is your tongue needs watching, not this man's.
SHEPHERD   My king, my master, what is it I have done
wrong?
OEDIPUS   You have not answered his question about
the boy.
SHEPHERD   He does not know . . . He is only making
trouble . . .
OEDIPUS   Come, speak plainly, or it will go hard with
you.
SHEPHERD   In God's name, do not torture an old man!
OEDIPUS   Come here, one of you; bind his arms
behind him.
SHEPHERD   Unhappy king! What more do you wish to
learn?
OEDIPUS   Did you give this man the child he speaks
of?
SHEPHERD   I did.
And I would to God I had died that very day.
OEDIPUS   You will die now unless you speak the truth.
SHEPHERD   Yet if I speak the truth, I am worse than
dead.
OEDIPUS   (*to* ATTENDANT)   He intends to draw it
out, apparently—
SHEPHERD   No! I have told you already that I gave him
the boy.
OEDIPUS   Where did you get him? From your house?
From somewhere else?
SHEPHERD   Not from mine, no. A man gave him to
me.
OEDIPUS   Is that man here? Whose house did he
belong to?
SHEPHERD   For God's love, my king, do not ask me any
more!
OEDIPUS   You are a dead man if I have to ask you
again.
SHEPHERD   Then . . . Then the child was from the
palace of Laïos.

OEDIPUS   A slave child? or a child of his own line?

SHEPHERD   Ah, I am on the brink of dreadful speech!

OEDIPUS   And I of dreadful hearing. Yet I must hear.

SHEPHERD   If you must be told, then . . .

They said it was Laïos' child;

But it is your wife who can tell you about that.

OEDIPUS   My wife!—Did she give it to you?

SHEPHERD   My lord, she did.

OEDIPUS   Do you know why?

SHEPHERD   I was told to get rid of it.

OEDIPUS   Oh heartless mother!

SHEPHERD   But in dread of prophecies . . .

OEDIPUS   Tell me.

SHEPHERD   It was said that the boy would kill
his own father.

OEDIPUS   Then why did you give him over to this old
man?

SHEPHERD   I pitied the baby, my king,

And I thought that this man would take him far
away

To his own country.

He saved him—but for what a fate!

For if you are what this man says you are,

No man living is more wretched than Oedipus.

OEDIPUS   Ah God!

It was true!

All the prophecies!

—Now,

O Light, may I look on you for the last time!

I, Oedipus,

Oedipus, damned in his birth, in his marriage
damned,

Damned in the blood he shed with his own hand!

(He rushes into the palace)

ODE IV

Strophe 1

CHORUS   Alas for the seed of men.

What measure shall I give these generations

That breathe on the void and are void

And exist and do not exist?

Who bears more weight of joy

Than mass of sunlight shifting in images,

Or who shall make his thought stay on

That down time drifts away?

Your splendor is all fallen.

O naked brow of wrath and tears,

O change of Oedipus!

I who saw your days call no man blest—

Your great days like ghosts gone.

Antistrophe 1

That mind was a strong bow.

Deep, how deep you drew it then, hard archer,

At a dim fearful range,

And brought dear glory down!

You overcame the stranger[14]—

The virgin with her hooking lion claws—

And though death sang, stood like a tower

To make pale Thebes take heart.

Fortress against our sorrow!

True king, giver of laws,

Majestic Oedipus!

No prince in Thebes had ever such renown,

No prince won such grace of power.

Strophe 2

And now of all men ever known

Most pitiful is this man's story:

His fortunes are most changed, his state

Fallen to a low slave's

Ground under bitter fate.

O Oedipus, most royal one!

The great door[15] that expelled you to the light

Gave at night—ah, gave night to your glory:

As to the father, to the fathering son.

All understood too late.

How could that queen whom Laïos won,

The garden that he harrowed at his height,

Be silent when that act was done?

Antistrophe 2

But all eyes fail before time's eye,

All actions come to justice there.

Though never willed, though far down the deep past,

Your bed, your dread sirings,

Are brought to book at last.

Child by Laïos doomed to die,

Then doomed to lose that fortunate little death,

---

14 The Sphinx.

15 Iokastê's womb.

Would God you never took breath in this air
That with my wailing lips I take to cry:
For I weep the world's outcast.
I was blind, and now I can tell why:
Asleep, for you had given ease of breath
To Thebes, while the false years went by.

EXODOS [16]

(Enter, from the palace, SECOND MESSENGER)

SECOND MESSENGER   Elders of Thebes, most honored
    in this land,
What horrors are yours to see and hear, what weight
Of sorrow to be endured, if, true to your birth,
You venerate the line of Labdakos!
I think neither Istros nor Phasis, those great rivers,
Could purify this place of all the evil
It shelters now, or soon must bring to light—
Evil not done unconsciously, but willed.

The greatest griefs are those we cause ourselves.
CHORAGOS   Surely, friend, we have grief enough
    already;
    What new sorrow do you mean?
SECOND MESSENGER   The queen is dead.
CHORAGOS   O miserable queen! But at whose hand?
SECOND MESSENGER   Her own.
The full horror of what happened you can not know,
For you did not see it; but I, who did, will tell you
As clearly as I can how she met her death.

When she had left us,
In passionate silence, passing through the court,
She ran to her apartment in the house,
Her hair clutched by the fingers of both hands.
She closed the doors behind her; then, by that bed
Where long ago the fatal son was conceived—
That son who should bring about his father's
    death—
We heard her call upon Laïos, dead so many years,
And heard her wail for the double fruit of her
    marriage,
A husband by her husband, children by her child.

Exactly how she died I do not know:
For Oedipus burst in moaning and would not let us

Keep vigil to the end: it was by him
As he stormed about the room that our eyes were
    caught.
From one to another of us he went, begging a sword,
Hunting the wife who was not his wife, the mother
Whose womb had carried his own children and
    himself.
I do not know: it was none of us aided him,
But surely one of the gods was in control!
For with a dreadful cry
He hurled his weight, as though wrenched out of
    himself,
At the twin doors: the bolts gave, and he rushed in.
And there we saw her hanging, her body swaying
From the cruel cord she had noosed about her
    neck.
A great sob broke from him, heartbreaking to hear,
As he loosed the rope and lowered her to the ground.

I would blot out from my mind what happened next!
For the king ripped from her gown the golden
    brooches
That were her ornament, and raised them, and
    plunged them down
Straight into his own eyeballs, crying, "No more,
No more shall you look on the misery about me,
The horrors of my own doing! Too long you have
    known
The faces of those whom I should never have seen,
Too long been blind to those for whom I was
    searching!
From this hour, go in darkness!" And as he spoke,
He struck at his eyes—not once, but many times;
And the blood spattered his beard,
Bursting from his ruined sockets like red hail.

So from the unhappiness of two this evil has sprung,
A curse on the man and woman alike. The old
Happiness of the house of Labdakos
Was happiness enough: where is it today?
It is all wailing and ruin, disgrace, death—all
The misery of mankind that has a name—
And it is wholly and for ever theirs.
CHORAGOS   Is he in agony still? Is there no rest for
    him?
SECOND MESSENGER   He is calling for someone to open
    the doors wide

---

[16] Final scene.

So that all the children of Kadmos may look upon
His father's murderer, his mother's—no,
I can not say it!
                And then he will leave Thebes,
Self-exiled, in order that the curse
Which he himself pronounced may depart from the
    house.
He is weak, and there is none to lead him,
So terrible is his suffering.
                   But you will see:
Look, the doors are opening; in a moment
You will see a thing that would crush a heart of
    stone.

(The central door is opened; OEDIPUS, *blinded, is led in)*

CHORAGOS   Dreadful indeed for men to see.
  Never have my own eyes
  Looked on a sight so full of fear.

  Oedipus!
  What madness came upon you, what daemon
  Leaped on your life with heavier
  Punishment than a mortal man can bear?
  No: I can not even
  Look at you, poor ruined one.
  And I would speak, question, ponder,
  If I were able. No.
  You make me shudder.
OEDIPUS   God. God.
  Is there a sorrow greater?
  Where shall I find harbor in this world?
  My voice is hurled far on a dark wind.
  What has God done to me?
CHORAGOS   Too terrible to think of, or to see.

Strophe 1

OEDIPUS   O cloud of night,
  Never to be turned away: night coming on,
  I can not tell how: night like a shroud!
  My fair winds brought me here.
                  O God. Again
  The pain of the spikes where I had sight,
  The flooding pain
  Of memory, never to be gouged out.
CHORAGOS   This is not strange.
  You suffer it all twice over, remorse in pain,
  Pain in remorse.

Antistrophe 1

OEDIPUS   Ah dear friend
  Are you faithful even yet, you alone?
  Are you still standing near me, will you stay here,
  Patient, to care for the blind?
                  The blind man!
  Yet even blind I know who it is attends me,
  By the voice's tone—
  Though my new darkness hide the comforter.
CHORAGOS   Oh fearful act!
  What god was it drove you to rake black
  Night across your eyes?

Strophe 2

OEDIPUS   Apollo. Apollo. Dear
  Children, the god was Apollo.
  He brought my sick, sick fate upon me.
  But the blinding hand was my own!
  How could I bear to see
  When all my sight was horror everywhere?
CHORAGOS   Everywhere; that is true.
OEDIPUS   And now what is left?
  Images? Love? A greeting even,
  Sweet to the senses? Is there anything?
  Ah, no, friends: lead me away.
  Lead me away from Thebes.
                  Lead the great wreck
  And hell of Oedipus, whom the gods hate.
CHORAGOS   Your misery, you are not blind to that.
  Would God you had never found it out!

Antistrophe 2

OEDIPUS   Death take the man who unbound
  My feet on that hillside
  And delivered me from death to life! What life?
  If only I had died,
  This weight of monstrous doom
  Could not have dragged me and my darlings down.
CHORAGOS   I would have wished the same.
OEDIPUS   Oh never to have come here
  With my father's blood upon me! Never
  To have been the man they call his mother's
    husband!
  Oh accurst! Oh child of evil,
  To have entered that wretched bed—
                  the selfsame one!
  More primal than sin itself, this fell to me.

CHORAGOS   I do not know what words to offer you.
 You were better dead than alive and blind.

OEDIPUS   Do not counsel me any more. This
   punishment
 That I have laid upon myself is just.
 If I had eyes,
 I do not know how I could bear the sight
 Of my father, when I came to the house of Death,
 Or my mother: for I have sinned against them both
 So vilely that I could not make my peace
 By strangling my own life.
                    Or do you think my children,
 Born as they were born, would be sweet to my eyes?
 Ah never, never! Nor this town with its high walls,
 Nor the holy images of the gods.
                    For I,
 Thrice miserable!—Oedipus, noblest of all the line
 Of Kadmos, have condemned myself to enjoy
 These things no more, by my own malediction
 Expelling that man whom the gods declared
 To be a defilement in the house of Laïos.
 After exposing the rankness of my own guilt,
 How could I look men frankly in the eyes?
 No, I swear it,
 If I could have stifled my hearing at its source,
 I would have done it and made all this body
 A tight cell of misery, blank to light and sound:
 So I should have been safe in my dark mind
 Beyond external evil.
                    Ah Kithairon!
 Why did you shelter me? When I was cast upon you,
 Why did I not die? Then I should never
 Have shown the world my execrable birth.

 Ah Polybos! Corinth, city that I believed
 The ancient seat of my ancestors: how fair
 I seemed, your child! And all the while this evil
 Was cancerous within me!
                    For I am sick
 In my own being, sick in my origin.

 O three roads, dark ravine, woodland and way
 Where three roads met: you, drinking my father's
   blood,
 My own blood, spilled by my own hand: can you
   remember

The unspeakable things I did there, and the things
 I went on from there to do?
                    O marriage, marriage!
 That act that engendered me, and again the act
 Performed by the son in the same bed—
                    Ah, the net
 Of incest, mingling fathers, brothers, sons,
 With brides, wives, mothers: the last evil
 That can be known by men: no tongue can say
 How evil!
                    No. For the love of God, conceal me
 Somewhere far from Thebes; or kill me; or hurl me
 Into the sea, away from men's eyes for ever.

 Come, lead me. You need not fear to touch me.
 Of all men, I alone can bear this guilt.

(*Enter* KREON)

CHORAGOS   Kreon is here now. As to what you ask,
 He may decide the course to take. He only
 Is left to protect the city in your place.
OEDIPUS   Alas, how can I speak to him? What right
   have I
 To beg his courtesy whom I have deeply wronged?
KREON   I have not come to mock you, Oedipus,
 Or to reproach you, either. (*To* ATTENDANTS)
                    —You, standing there:
 If you have lost all respect for man's dignity,
 At least respect the flame of Lord Helios:
 Do not allow this pollution to show itself
 Openly here, an affront to the earth
 And Heaven's rain and the light of day. No, take him
 Into the house as quickly as you can.
 For it is proper
 That only the close kindred see his grief.
OEDIPUS   I pray you in God's name, since your
   courtesy
 Ignores my dark expectation, visiting
 With mercy this man of all men most execrable:
 Give me what I ask—for your good, not for mine.
KREON   And what is it that you turn to me begging
   for?
OEDIPUS   Drive me out of this country as quickly as
   may be
 To a place where no human voice can ever greet me.
KREON   I should have done that before now—only,

God's will had not been wholly revealed to me.
OEDIPUS   But his command is plain: the parricide
Must be destroyed. I am that evil man.
KREON   That is the sense of it, yes; but as things are,
We had best discover clearly what is to be done.
OEDIPUS   You would learn more about a man like me?
KREON   You are ready now to listen to the god.
OEDIPUS   I will listen. But it is to you
That I must turn for help. I beg you, hear me.

The woman in there—
Give her whatever funeral you think proper:
She is your sister.
                    —But let me go, Kreon!
Let me purge my father's Thebes of the pollution
Of my living here, and go out to the wild hills,
To Kithairon, that has won such fame with me,
The tomb my mother and father appointed for me,
And let me die there, as they willed I should.

And yet I know
Death will not ever come to me through sickness
Or in any natural way: I have been preserved
For some unthinkable fate. But let that be.

As for my sons, you need not care for them.
They are men, they will find some way to live.
But my poor daughters, who have shared my table,
Who never before have been parted from their
        father—
Take care of them, Kreon; do this for me.

And will you let me touch them with my hands
A last time, and let us weep together?
Be kind, my lord,
Great prince, be kind!
                    Could I but touch them,
They would be mine again, as when I had my eyes.

(Enter ANTIGONE and ISMENE, attended)

Ah, God!
Is it my dearest children I hear weeping?
Has Kreon pitied me and sent my daughters?
KREON   Yes, Oedipus: I knew that they were dear to
        you
In the old days, and know you must love them still.
OEDIPUS   May God bless you for this—and be a
        friendlier

Guardian to you than he has been to me!

Children, where are you?
Come quickly to my hands: they are your
        brother's—
Hands that have brought your father's once clear
        eyes
To this way of seeing—
                    Ah dearest ones,
I had neither sight nor knowledge then, your father
By the woman who was the source of his own life!
And I weep for you—having no strength to see you—,
I weep for you when I think of the bitterness
That men will visit upon you all your lives.
What homes, what festivals can you attend
Without being forced to depart again in tears?
And when you come to marriageable age,
Where is the man, my daughters, who would dare
Risk the bane that lies on all my children?
Is there any evil wanting? Your father killed
His father; sowed the womb of her who bore him;
Engendered you at the fount of his own existence!
That is what they will say of you.
                            Then, whom
Can you ever marry? There are no bridegrooms for
        you,
And your lives must wither away in sterile
        dreaming.

O Kreon, son of Menoikeus!
You are the only father my daughters have,
Since we, their parents, are both of us gone for ever.
They are your own blood: you will not let them
Fall into beggary and loneliness;
You will keep them from the miseries that are mine!
Take pity on them; see, they are only children,
Friendless except for you. Promise me this,
Great prince, and give me your hand in token of it.

(KREON clasps his right hand)

Children:
I could say much, if you could understand me,
But as it is, I have only this prayer for you:
Live where you can, be as happy as you can—
Happier, please God, than God has made your father.
KREON   Enough. You have wept enough. Now go
        within.

OEDIPUS   I must; but it is hard.

KREON   Time eases all things.

OEDIPUS   You know my mind, then?

KREON   Say what you desire.

OEDIPUS   Send me from Thebes!

KREON   God grant that I may!

OEDIPUS   But since God hates me . . .

KREON   No, he will grant your wish.

OEDIPUS   You promise?

KREON   I can not speak beyond my knowledge.

OEDIPUS   Then lead me in.

KREON   Come now, and leave your children.

OEDIPUS   No! Do not take them from me!

KREON   Think no longer
    That you are in command here, but rather think
    How, when you were, you served your own
        destruction.

(Exeunt into the house all but the CHORUS; *the*
CHORAGOS *chants directly to the audience)*

CHORAGOS   Men of Thebes: look upon Oedipus.

This is the king who solved the famous riddle
And towered up, most powerful of men.
No mortal eyes but looked on him with envy,
Yet in the end ruin swept over him.

Let every man in mankind's frailty
Consider his last day; and let none
Presume on his good fortune until he find
Life, at his death, a memory without pain.

COMMENTS AND QUESTIONS

1. Define the character of Oedipus. Is he heroic or superhuman or merely human? How well do we get to know him?
2. Is Oedipus a puppet of the gods or a free man? Give examples to support your opinion.
3. Trace the uses of images of blindness and insight in the play.
4. Define the character of Iokastê. How does she serve as a foil to Oedipus?
5. Sophocles delights in the use of tragic *irony*—having characters say something "all too true" of which they are unaware. Find examples of this in the play.
6. Aristotle, the Greek philosopher and literary critic,

maintained that a tragic hero is one who falls from a high position of power and success to a low one, not because he is morally weak and deserves his fate, but through a slight flaw in his otherwise noble character. A modern scholar holds rather that tragedy occurs from the clash of two strong forces: that of man and that of the gods. Which theory seems to you to best describe the tragedy of Oedipus?
7. What is Oedipus' attitude at the end of the play? What has he learned about himself and life? What is the difference between a tragic view of life and a merely pessimistic one?
8. Many people maintain that modern Westerners, particularly Americans, have lost a sense of tragedy. During the Vietnam War, one writer ascribed America's moral failure to terminate an obviously useless course to a lack of a sense of tragedy.[1] We were unable to say, "This is our fate, we were wrong, we have lost." We would make everything all right by throwing in just a few more bombs. What would a modern American Oedipus do about his situation? Do we have any tragic heroes?
9. *Oedipus* has been interpreted both as a glorification of man and as a defense of religion that points out the limitations of man. Which view seems close to the truth in your opinion?

Humanism and Tragedy

During the great classical age of Athens, intellectuals, intrigued with new developments in science and philosophy, began to challenge the old, accepted religious beliefs. In art, in politics, as in thought, man (rather than the gods) was becoming, as the philosopher Protagoras said, "the measure of all things." Man's confidence in his own abilities and powers has perhaps never been greater than at this time. We see this in *Oedipus* in the hero's self-confidence at the beginning of the play. The people of Thebes who look to him as their savior treat him almost like a god. We see an extreme confidence in man's reason and a denial of the power of the gods over man in Iokastê's scoffing at prophecies. But here, as in other aspects, Sophocles portrays a balance between extremes. The outcome of the

---

[1] Rollo May, "The Tragic Sense," The *New York Times,* January 7, 1973.

tragedy shows that the gods, or fate, have the last word, but it certainly does not show man to be a little puppet whose destiny is simply to obey the divine will. Oedipus is "blind" in that he does not recognize the limits set by divine power, but great in that he struggles to find the truth through his own individual human reason. Sophocles wanted to warn his fellow Athenians not to neglect religion but he also wanted to demonstrate to them the greatness of human character and intelligence. Sophocles' faith in man, or his "humanism," is perhaps best exemplified in the famous choral ode in another of his tragedies, *Antigone* (translated by Elizabeth Wyckoff):

Many the wonders but nothing walks stranger than man.
This thing crosses the sea in the winter's storm,
making his path through the roaring waves.
And she, the greatest of gods, the earth—
ageless she is, and unwearied—he wears her away
as the ploughs go up and down from year to year
and his mules turn up the soil.

Gay nations of birds he snares and leads,
wild beast tribes and the salty brood of the sea,
with the twisted mesh of his nets, this clever man.
He controls with craft the beasts of the open air,
walkers on hills. The horse with his shaggy mane
he holds and harnesses, yoked about the neck,
and the strong bull of the mountain.

Language, and thought like the wind
and the feelings that make the town;
he has taught himself, and shelter against the cold,
refuge from rain. He can always help himself.
He faces no future helpless. There's only death
that he cannot find an escape from. He has contrived
refuge from illnesses once beyond all cure.

Clever beyond all dreams
the inventive craft that he has
which may drive him one time or another to well or ill.

Classical tragedy shows that a belief in the dignity and greatness of human beings is not incompatible with a full awareness of their limitations.

Greek Comedy

Tragedy, according to the philosopher Aristotle, provided a release for the emotions of pity and terror. Spectators would pity the unfortunate protagonist and would fear that they themselves might undergo a disaster, thus purging themselves of those emotions. Whatever else went on at the festival of Dionysus, it must have offered an opportunity for the release of pent-up feelings. The people who attended it "let off steam" in all sorts of ways—first of all by feeling liberated from the everyday world of work and duty. There was drinking, feasting, carousing. At the plays themselves the idea was to participate emotionally as a spectator rather than merely to view passively. The Greeks, like most peoples of the world, recognized society's need for a true holiday, or festival—a time of collective celebration and liberation. The way that a culture celebrates, or organizes its festivals, says a great deal about its values. (Bear this in mind as we study festivals in medieval and Renaissance Europe and in Africa.) One might well ask if our contemporary society recognizes this need adequately. Do people who spend their days off at home watching television experience a release and liberation from the everyday world? Is there a basic difference between the theatrical and the media experience? Or do we provide other, communal ceremonies of celebration?

Comedy is one response to the human need to "let go" or to transcend the everyday world. Human beings, if they remain truly human, never lose the childlike need to play, and they certainly need to be able to laugh at their own and at others' shortcomings and to remember that life is not all earnestness and work. If we transcend the everyday world with tragedy through an almost religious sense of awe, we transcend it with comedy through our laughter. We laugh at a comic character either because he is quick, witty, and always able to outsmart the "bad guys" or, on the contrary, because he is always getting into trouble. Comedy is often worked out on the level of *action*, whereas tragedy is often worked out on the level of *thought*. While tragic writers tend to view man in the context of a universal human condition, comic writers often take a hard look at their immediate society, satirizing its customs and institutions. For this reason, it will be useful to look at the development of comedy in Greece and at the society in which Aristophanes was writing.

The word *comedy* comes from *komos*, which means a revel. It seems probable that fertility rituals and celebrations are at the origins of comedy. From the earliest days of Greece, groups of men, revelers, would go around from village to village, wearing huge artificial phalluses, telling jokes (often obscene ones), singing, and dancing. The community would participate in the revels. These were not only for fun but were also intended to increase fertility—in the land, in people, in animals. Worship of the phallus as a symbol of fertility is common among all "primitive" peoples, and Freud and Jung have shown that phallic symbols appear in the dreams of "civilized" people as well. Often, the *komos* would end with some sort of sexual union—a ritual orgy, a pairing off with mates, or a marriage. This was not meant to encourage free sex on all occasions but to ensure fertility.

We do not know exactly how comedy as an art form grew from these revels, but it was recognized as such at the festival of Dionysus in Athens around 486 B.C., thus later than tragedy. Aristophanes, the only Greek classical comic author whose works survive, composed "old comedies." In his comedies, many of the old ritual features of the *komos*—the big phalluses, padding, animal costumes, grotesque masks, colloquial speech, and obscene jokes—are retained. There are often two choruses in opposition to each other (in *Lysistrata*, the choruses of old men and old women). Certainly music and dance were of great importance. Of course, the purpose was no longer to promote fertility but to entertain people.

The situations in old comedy are often fantastic ones (in some, such as *The Birds* and *The Frogs*, the characters are dressed like animals), but the people or the institutions made fun of were real enough. About a hundred years after Aristophanes we find "new comedy," in the hands of its most famous practitioner, Menander, without phalluses, grotesque costumes, or indecent jokes. The new comedy was realistic rather than fantastic—it reflected everyday life and created stock, yet individualized characters. New comedy, such as that practiced by the Romans Plautus and Terence, is more similar to the comedies of manners with which we are familiar in modern theater, films, and television. The situations in new comedy often arise from misunderstandings, there is often a great deal of verbal play and wit, and the endings are happy. New comedy has lost touch with its origins in ritual fertility except that—even today—it often ends with a marriage or a happy love.

Lysistrata, first performed in 411 B.C., is essentially a comic fantasy about a real contemporary event. Athens and Sparta, as we saw in the section on politics, were the rival leaders in a series of battles, lasting from 431 to 404 B.C., called the Peloponnesian Wars. Aristophanes had long been a spokesman for peace—in one of his plays he even went so far as to suggest that in some instances the Athenians had treated the Spartans unfairly. Like many of his countrymen, he deplored the evolution of Athens from a democracy to a dictatorship, a seeming necessity in wartime. He was particularly opposed to the foolhardy naval expedition that the Athenians sent to Sicily in 415 B.C. This attack, which ended in defeat and brought the Athenians vast losses in ships and men, was really the turning point of the war. By the time of the writing of *Lysistrata*, it must have been apparent that the Spartans were winning the war and that a genuine negotiated peace treaty, which might have been possible earlier, was no longer possible. There are some sad underpinnings to this comedy: an idyllic dream of peace; a memory of the time when Athens and Sparta were allies and fought bravely together during the Persian Wars. Yet these serious concerns do not prevent *Lysistrata* from being a total comedy. Perhaps the human need to laugh at the world is even greater at times of disaster than in normal times. And perhaps Aristophanes is suggesting something that is of concern to us today: if men have been such failures at keeping peace in the world, might not women do better?

The play's title character (her name means "she who dissolves the armies") shows herself superior to the men in every way. She is the only one who keeps a cool head; she plans an effective strategy and negotiates the peace. Her plan for forcing peace negotiations—organizing the women of Athens and Sparta in a sex strike against their husbands—is highly comic but also effective. Because of its explicitness about sex, *Lysistrata* was forbidden reading in schools for a long time. Most modern readers, however, with less puritanical attitudes, find it extremely funny. Aristophanes' comedies, because of their use of Greek dialects and plays on words, are particularly difficult to translate. In this English version by Dudley Fitts, the woman from Sparta, Lampito, is given a Southern accent as the American equivalent of her Spartan dialect.

ARISTOPHANES

Lysistrata

CHARACTERS

LYSISTRATA ⎫
KALONIKE ⎬ *Athenian women*
MYRRHINE ⎭
LAMPITO, *a Spartan woman*
CHORUS
MAGISTRATE
KINESIAS, *husband of Myrrhine*
SPARTAN HERALD
SPARTAN AMBASSADOR
A SENTRY
ATHENIAN DRUNKARD

The supernumeraries include the BABY SON *of Kinesias;* STRATYLLIS, *a member of the hemichorus of Old Women; various individual speakers, both Spartan and Athenian.*
Until the exodos, *the* CHORUS *is divided into two hemichori: the first, of Old Men; the second, of Old Women. Each of these has its* CHORAGOS. *In the* exodos, *the hemichori return as Athenians and Spartans.*

THE SCENE.   *Athens. First, a public square; later, beneath the walls of the Acropolis; later, a courtyard within the Acropolis. Time: early in 411* B.C.

Athens; a public square; early morning; LYSISTRATA *sola.*

LYSISTRATA   If someone had invited them to a
    festival—
Bacchus's, say, or Pan's, or Aphrodite's, or
that Genetyllis business[1]—, you couldn't get through
    the streets,
what with the drums and the dancing. But now,
not a woman in sight!
                        Except—oh, yes!

(*Enter* KALONIKE)

Here's one, at last. Good
morning, Kalonike.
KALONIKE   Good morning, Lysistrata.
                                        Darling,
    don't frown so! You'll ruin your face!
LYSISTRATA   Never mind my face.
    Kalonike,

the way we women behave! Really, I don't blame the
    men
for what they say about us.
KALONIKE   No; I imagine they're right.
LYSISTRATA   For example: I call a meeting
    to think out a most important matter—and what
        happens?
The women all stay in bed!
KALONIKE   Oh, they'll be along.
    It's hard to get away, you know: a husband, a cook,
    a child . . . Home life can be *so* demanding!
LYSISTRATA   What I have in mind is even more
    demanding.
KALONIKE   Tell me: what is it?
LYSISTRATA   Something big.
KALONIKE   Goodness! *How* big?
LYSISTRATA   Big enough for all of us.
KALONIKE   But we're not all here!
LYSISTRATA   We would be, if *that's* what was up!
                        No, Kalonike,
    this is something I've been turning over for nights;
    and, I may say, sleepless nights.
KALONIKE   Can't be so hard, then,
    if you've spent so much time on it.
LYSISTRATA   Hard or not,
    it comes to this: Only we women can save Greece!
KALONIKE   Only we women? Poor Greece!
LYSISTRATA   Just the same,
    it's up to us. First, we must liquidate
    the Peloponnesians—
KALONIKE   Fun, fun!
LYSISTRATA   —and then the Boeotians.
KALONIKE   Oh! But not those heavenly eels![2]
LYSISTRATA   You needn't worry.
    Athens shall have her sea food.—But here's the
        point:
    If we can get the women from those places
    to join us women here, why, we can save
    all Greece!
KALONIKE   But dearest Lysistrata!
    How can women do a thing so austere, so
    political? We belong at home. Our only armor's
    our transparent saffron dresses and
    our pretty little shoes!

---

[1] References to cults of love and wine.

[2] Boeotia was famous for its sea food, especially its eels.

LYSISTRATA   That's it exactly.
Those transparent saffron dresses, those little shoes—
well, there we are!

KALONIKE   Oh?

LYSISTRATA   Not a single man would lift
his spear—

KALONIKE   I'll get my dress from the dyer's tomorrow!

LYSISTRATA   —or need a shield—

KALONIKE   The sweetest little negligée—

LYSISTRATA   —or bring out his sword.

KALONIKE   I know where I can buy
the dreamiest sandals!

LYSISTRATA   Well, so you see. Now, shouldn't
the women have come?

KALONIKE   Come? they should have *flown!*

LYSISTRATA   Athenians are always late.
                              But imagine!
There's no one here from the South Shore.

KALONIKE   They go to work early,
I can swear to that.

LYSISTRATA   And nobody from Acharnai.
They should have been here hours ago!

KALONIKE   Well, you'll get
that awful Theagenes woman: she's been having
her fortune told at Hecate's shrine.[3]
                            But look!
Someone at last! Can you see who they are?

(Enter MYRRHINE *and other women*)

LYSISTRATA   People from the suburbs.

KALONIKE   Yes! The entire
membership of the Suburban League!

MYRRHINE   Sorry to be late, Lysistrata.
                            Oh, come,
don't scowl so! Say something!

LYSISTRATA   My dear Myrrhine,
what is there to say? After all,
you've been pretty casual about the whole thing.

MYRRHINE   Couldn't find
my girdle in the dark, that's all.
                          But what *is*
"the whole thing"?

LYSISTRATA   Wait for the rest of them.

---

[3] Theagenes was notoriously superstitious; his practice of never leaving home without consulting Hecate is here transferred to his wife.

KALONIKE   I suppose so. But, look!
Here's Lampito!

(Enter LAMPITO *with women from Sparta*)

LYSISTRATA   Darling Lampito,
how pretty you are today! What a nice color!
Goodness, you look as though you could strangle a
   bull!

LAMPITO   Ah think Ah could! It's the work-out
in the gym every day; and, of co'se that dance of ahs
where y' kick yo' own tail.[4]

LYSISTRATA   What lovely breasts!

LAMPITO   Lawdy, when y' touch me lahk that,
Ah feel lahk a heifer at the altar!

LYSISTRATA   And this young lady?
Where is she from?

LAMPITO   Boeotia. Social-Register type.

LYSISTRATA   Good morning, Boeotian. You're as pretty
   as green grass.

KALONIKE   And if you look,
you'll find that the lawn has just been cut.

LYSISTRATA   And this lady?

LAMPITO   From Corinth. But a good woman.

LYSISTRATA   Well, in Corinth
anything's possible.

LAMPITO   But let's get to work. Which one of you
called this meeting, and why?

LYSISTRATA   I did.

LAMPITO   Well, then:
what's up?

MYRRHINE   Yes, what *is* "the whole thing," after all?

LYSISTRATA   I'll tell you.—But first, one question.

MYRRHINE   Ask away!

LYSISTRATA   It's your husbands. Fathers of your
   children. Doesn't it bother you
that they're always off with the Army? I'll stake my
   life,
not one of you has a man in the house this minute!

KALONIKE   Mine's been in Thrace the last five
   months, keeping an eye
on that General.[5]

---

[4] Among the physical exercises practiced by Greek girls was the strenuous *bibasis,* a dance in which the dancer kicked her buttocks with her heels.

[5] A certain Eukrates about whom nothing is known.

MYRRHINE   Mine's been in Pylos for seven.

LAMPITO   And mahn,
whenever he gets a *dis*charge, he goes raht back
with that li'l ole speah of his, and enlists again!

LYSISTRATA   And not the ghost of a lover to be found!
From the very day the war began—
                              those Milesians!
I could skin them alive!
                    —I've not seen so much, even,
as one of those devices they call Widow's Delight.
But there! What's important is: I've found a way
to end the war, are you with me?

MYRRHINE   I should *say* so!
Even if I have to pawn my best dress and
drink up the proceeds.[6]

KALONIKE   Me, too! Even if they split me
right up the middle, like a flounder.

LAMPITO   Ah'm shorely with you.
Ah'd crawl up Taygetos[7] on mah knees
if that'd bring peace.

LYSISTRATA   Then here it is.
Women! Sisters!
If we really want our men to make an armistice,
we must be ready to give up—

MYRRHINE   Give up what?
Quick, tell us!

LYSISTRATA   But *will* you?

MYRRHINE   We will, even if it kills us.

LYSISTRATA   Then we must give up sleeping with our
    men. *(Long silence)*
Oh? So now you're sorry? Won't look at me?
Doubtful? Pale? All teary-eyed?
                    But come: be frank with me,
as I've certainly been with you. Will you do it?

MYRRHINE   I couldn't. No.
Let the war go on.

KALONIKE   Nor I. Let the war go on.

LYSISTRATA   You, you little flounder,
ready to be split up the middle?

KALONIKE   Lysistrata, no!
I'd walk through fire for you—you *know* I would!—,
    but don't
ask us to give up *that!* Why, there's nothing like it!

LYSISTRATA   And you?

BOEOTIAN   No. I must say *I'd* rather walk through fire.

LYSISTRATA   You little salamanders!
No wonder poets write tragedies about women.
All we want's a quick tumble!
                              But you from Sparta:
if you stand by me, we may win yet! Will you?
It means so much!

LAMPITO   Ah sweah, it means *too* much!
By the Two Goddesses,[8] it does! Asking a girl
to sleep—Heaven knows how long!—in a great big
    bed
with nobody there but herself! But Ah'll stay with
    you!
Peace comes first!

LYSISTRATA   Spoken like a true Spartan!

KALONIKE   But, if—
            oh dear!
                    —if we give up what you tell us to,
will there *be* any peace?

LYSISTRATA   Why, mercy, of course there will!
We'll just sit snug in our very thinnest gowns,
perfumed and powdered from top to bottom, and
    those men
simply won't stand still! And when we say No,
they'll go out of their minds! And there's your peace.
You can take my word for it.

LAMPITO   Ah seem to remember
that Colonel Menelaus threw his sword away
when he saw Helen's breast all bare.

KALONIKE   But, goodness me!
What if they just get up and leave us?

LYSISTRATA   Well,
we'd have to fall back on ourselves, of course.
But they won't.

KALONIKE   What if they drag us into the bedroom?

LYSISTRATA   Hang on to the door.

KALONIKE   What if they slap us?

LYSISTRATA   If they do, you'd better give in.
But be sulky about it. Do I have to teach you how?
You know there's no fun for men when they have to
    force you.
There are millions of ways of getting them to see
    reason.

---

[6] Athenian women were frequently satirized for heavy drinking.
[7] A rugged mountain range in the Peloponnesus.

[8] Demeter and Persephone; a woman's oath.

Don't you worry: a man
doesn't like it unless the girl co-operates.

KALONIKE   I suppose so. Oh, all right! We'll go along!

LAMPITO   Ah imagine us Spahtans can arrange a
    peace. But you
Athenians! Why, you're just war-mongerers!

LYSISTRATA   Leave that to me.
I know how to make them listen.

LAMPITO   Ah don't see how.
After all, they've got their boats; and there's lots of
    money
piled up in the Acropolis.

LYSISTRATA   The Acropolis? Darling,
we're taking over the Acropolis today!
That's the older women's job. All the rest of us
are going to the Citadel to sacrifice—you understand
    me?
And once there, we're in for good!

LAMPITO   Whee! Up the rebels!
Ah can see you're a good strateegist.

LYSISTRATA   Well, then, Lampito,
let's take the oath.

LAMPITO   Say it. We'll sweah.

LYSISTRATA   This is it.
—But Lord! Where's our Inner Guard? Never mind.
                —You see this
shield? Put it down there. Now bring me the victim's
    entrails.

KALONIKE   But the oath?

LYSISTRATA   You remember how in Aeschylus' *Seven*[9]
they killed a sheep and swore on a shield? Well, then?

KALONIKE   But I don't see how you can swear for
    peace on a shield.

LYSISTRATA   What else do you suggest?

KALONIKE   Why not a white horse?
We could swear by that.

LYSISTRATA   And where will you get a white horse?

KALONIKE   I never thought of that. *What* can we do?

MYRRHINE   I have it!
Let's set this big black wine-bowl on the ground
and pour in a gallon or so of Thasian,[10] and swear
not to add one drop of water.

LAMPITO   Ah lahk *that* oath!

---

[9] *Seven Against Thebes.*
[10] A popular wine from Thasos.

LYSISTRATA   Bring the bowl and the wine-jug.

KALONIKE   Oh, what a simply *huge* one!

LYSISTRATA   Set it down; and, women, place your
    hands on the gift-offering.

O Goddess of Persuasion! And thou, O Loving-cup!
Look upon this our sacrifice, and
be gracious!

KALONIKE   It spills out like blood. How red and pretty
    it is!

LAMPITO   And Ah must say it smells good.

MYRRHINE   Let me swear first!

KALONIKE   No, by Aphrodite, let's toss for it!

LYSISTRATA   Lampito: all of you women: come, touch
    the bowl, and repeat after me:
I WILL HAVE NOTHING TO DO WITH MY
HUSBAND OR MY LOVER

KALONIKE   *I will have nothing to do with my
    husband or my lover*

LYSISTRATA   THOUGH HE COME TO ME IN
PITIABLE CONDITION

KALONIKE   *Though he come to me in pitiable
    condition*
(Oh, Lysistrata! This is killing me!)

LYSISTRATA   I WILL STAY IN MY HOUSE
UNTOUCHABLE

KALONIKE   *I will stay in my house untouchable*

LYSISTRATA   IN MY THINNEST SAFFRON SILK

KALONIKE   *In my thinnest saffron silk*

LYSISTRATA   AND MAKE HIM LONG FOR ME.

KALONIKE   *And make him long for me.*

LYSISTRATA   I WILL NOT GIVE MYSELF

KALONIKE   *I will not give myself*

LYSISTRATA   AND IF HE CONSTRAINS ME

KALONIKE   *And if he constrains me*

LYSISTRATA   I WILL BE AS COLD AS ICE AND
NEVER MOVE

KALONIKE   *I will be as cold as ice and never move*

LYSISTRATA   I WILL NOT LIFT MY SLIPPERS
TOWARD THE CEILING

KALONIKE   *I will not lift my slippers toward the
    ceiling*

LYSISTRATA   OR CROUCH ON ALL FOURS LIKE THE
LIONESS IN THE CARVING

KALONIKE   *Or crouch on all fours like the lioness in
    the carving*

LYSISTRATA   AND IF I KEEP THIS OATH LET ME
DRINK FROM THIS BOWL

KALONIKE   *And if I keep this oath let me drink from
this bowl*

LYSISTRATA   IF NOT, LET MY OWN BOWL BE
FILLED WITH WATER.

KALONIKE   *If not, let my own bowl be filled with
water.*

LYSISTRATA   You have all sworn?

MYRRHINE   We have.

LYSISTRATA   Then thus
I sacrifice the victim. *(Drinks largely)*

KALONIKE   Save some for us!
Here's to you, darling, and to you, and to you! It's all
for us women. *(Loud cries off-stage)*

LAMPITO   What's all *that* whoozy-goozy?

LYSISTRATA   Just what I told you.
The older women have taken the Acropolis. Now
you, Lampito,
rush back to Sparta. We'll take care of things here.
And
be sure you get organized!
                                    The rest of you girls,
up to the Citadel: and mind you push in the bolts.

KALONIKE   But the men? Won't they be after us?

LYSISTRATA   Just you leave
the men to me. There's not fire enough in the world
to make me open *my* door.

KALONIKE   I hope so, by Aphrodite!
At any rate,
let's remember the League's reputation for hanging
on!

(Exeunt)

The hillside just under the Acropolis.

(Enter CHORUS OF OLD MEN *with burning torches and
braziers; much puffing and coughing)*

MALE CHORAGOS   Easy, Drakes, old friend! Don't skin
your shoulders
with those damnable big olive-branches. What a job!

Strophe 1

OLD MEN   Forward, forward, comrades! Whew!
The things that old age does to you!
Neighbor Strymodoros, would you have thought it?

We've caught it—
                          And from women, too!
Women that used to board with us, bed with us—
Now, by the gods, they've got ahead of us,
Taken the Acropolis (Heaven knows why!),
Profaned the sacred statuar-y,
                          And barred the doors,
                              The aggravating whores!

MALE CHORAGOS   Come, Philourgos, quick, pile your
brushwood
next to the wall there.
                              These traitors to Athens and to us,
we'll fry each last one of them! And the very first
will be old Lykon's wife.[11]

Antistrophe 1

OLD MEN   By Demeter I swear it—(ouch!),
I'll not perform the Kleomenes-crouch!
How he looked—and a good soldier, too—
When out he flew,
                          That filthy pouch
Of a body of his all stinking and shaggy,
Bare as an eel, except for the bag he
Covered his rear with. Lord, what a mess!
Never a bath in six years, I'd guess!
                          Unhappy Sparta,
                              With such a martyr! [12]

MALE CHORAGOS   What a siege, friends! Seventeen
ranks strong
we stood at the Gate, and never a chance for a nap.
And all because of women, whom the gods hate
(and so does Euripides).
                              It's enough to make a veteran
turn in his medals from Marathon!

Strophe 2

OLD MEN   Forward, men! Just up the hillside,
And we're there!
Keep to the path! A yoke of oxen
Wouldn't care
            To haul this lumber. Mind the fire,
            Or it'll die before we're higher!
                  Puff! Puff!
                  This smoke will strangle me, sure enough!

---

[11] Rhodia, a famous belle of the day.

[12] Kleomenes, a king of Sparta, had captured the Acropolis but had
been forced to give it up.

Antistrophe 2

Holy Heracles, I'm blinded,
    Sure as fate!
  It's Lemnos-fire[13] we've been toting;
     And isn't it great
        To be singed by this infernal flame?
       (Laches, remember the Goddess: for shame!)
         Woof! Woof!
    A few steps more, and we're under the roof!
MALE CHORAGOS   It catches! It's blazing!
  Down with your loads!
  We'll sizzle 'em now,
  By all the gods!
  Vine-branches here, quick!
  Light 'em up,
  And in through the gate with 'em!
  If that doesn't stop
  Their nonsense—well,
  We'll smoke 'em to Hell.
  Ker*shoo*!
  (What we really need
  Is a grad-u-ate,
  Top of his class,
  From Samos Military State.[14]
  Achoo!)
  Come, do
  Your duty, you!
  Pour out your braziers,
  Embers ablaze!
  But first, Gentlemen, allow me to raise
  The paean:
        Lady
  Victory, now
  Assist thine adherents
  Here below!
  Down with women!
  Up with men!
  Io triumphe! [15]
OLD MEN   Amen!

(*Enter* CHORUS OF OLD WOMEN *on the walls of the Acropolis, carrying jars of water to extinguish the fire set by the* CHORUS OF OLD MEN)

FEMALE CHORAGOS   Fire, fire!
  Quickly, quickly, women, if we're to save ourselves!

Strophe

OLD WOMEN   Nikodike, run!
  Or Kalyke's done
  To a turn, and poor Kratylla's
  Smoked like a ham.
         Damn
  These men and their wars,
  Their hateful ways!
  I nearly died before I got to the place
  Where we fill our jars:
    Slaves pushing and jostling—
    Such a hustling
  I never saw in all my days!

Antistrophe

  But here's water at last.
  Sisters, make haste
  And slosh it down on them,
  The silly old wrecks!
         Sex
  Almighty! What they want's
  A hot bath? Send it down!
  And thou, Athena of Athens town,
  Assist us in drowning their wheezy taunts!
    O Trito-born! [16] Helmet of Gold!
    Help us to cripple their backs, the old
  Fools with their semi-incendiary brawn!

(*The* OLD MEN *capture a woman,* STRATYLLIS)

STRATYLLIS   Let me go! Let me go!
FEMALE CHORAGOS   You walking corpses,
  have you no shame?
MALE CHORAGOS   I wouldn't have believed it!
  An army of women in the Acropolis!
FEMALE CHORAGOS   So we scare you, do we? Grandpa,
  you've seen
  only our pickets yet!
MALE CHORAGOS   Hey, Phaidrias!
  Help me with the necks of these jabbering hens!

---

[13] Volcanic; Mount Moschylus on the island of Lemnos was the site of Vulcan's forge.

[14] At this time Samos was the headquarters of Athenian military activities.

[15] A ritual cry of triumph.

[16] Athena; according to some versions of her story, she was born at Lake Tritonis in Libya.

FEMALE CHORAGOS   Down with your pots, girls! We'll
    need both hands
  if these antiques attack us.
MALE CHORAGOS   Want your face kicked in?
FEMALE CHORAGOS   Want to try my teeth?
MALE CHORAGOS   Look out! I've got a stick!
FEMALE CHORAGOS   You lay a half-inch of your stick
    on Stratyllis,
  And you'll never stick again!
MALE CHORAGOS   Fall apart!
FEMALE CHORAGOS   I'll chew your guts!
MALE CHORAGOS   Euripides! Master!
  How well you knew women!
FEMALE CHORAGOS   Listen to him! Rhodippe,
  up with the pots!
MALE CHORAGOS   Demolition of God,
  what good are your pots?
FEMALE CHORAGOS   You refugee from the tomb,
  What good is your fire?
MALE CHORAGOS   Good enough to make a pyre
  to barbecue you!
FEMALE CHORAGOS   We'll squizzle your kindling!
MALE CHORAGOS   You think so?
FEMALE CHORAGOS   Yah! Just hang around a while!
MALE CHORAGOS   Want a touch of my torch?
FEMALE CHORAGOS   Your torch needs a bath.
MALE CHORAGOS   How about you?
FEMALE CHORAGOS   Soap for a senile bridegroom!
MALE CHORAGOS   Senile? Hold your trap!
FEMALE CHORAGOS   Just *you* try to hold it!
MALE CHORAGOS   The yammer of women!
FEMALE CHORAGOS   The yatter of men!
  But you'll never sit in the jury-box again.
MALE CHORAGOS   Gentlemen, I beg you, burn off that
    woman's hair!
FEMALE CHORAGOS   Let it come down! *(They empty*
  their pots on the men)
MALE CHORAGOS   What a way to drown!
FEMALE CHORAGOS   Hot, hey?
MALE CHORAGOS   Say,
    enough!
FEMALE CHORAGOS   Dandruff
    needs watering. I'll make you
    nice and fresh.
MALE CHORAGOS   For God's sake, you
  sluts, hold off!

(Enter a MAGISTRATE *accompanied by four constables)*

MAGISTRATE   These degenerate women! What a
    racket of little drums,
  what a yapping for Adonis on every house-top!
  It's like the time in the Assembly when I was
    listening
  to a speech—out of order, as usual—by that fool
  Demostratos,[17] all about troops for Sicily,
  that kind of nonsense—
                 and there was his wife
  trotting around in circles howling
  Alas for Adonis!—
              and Demostratos insisting
  we must draft every last Zakynthian that can walk—
  and his wife up there on the roof,
  drunk as an owl, yowling
  Oh weep for Adonis!—
            and that damned ox Demostratos
  mooing away through the rumpus. That's what we
    get
  for putting up with this wretched woman-business!
MALE CHORAGOS   Sir, you haven't heard the half of it.
    They laughed at us!
  Insulted us! They took pitchers of water
  and nearly drowned us! We're still wringing out our
    clothes,
  for all the world like unhousebroken brats.
MAGISTRATE   And a good thing, by Poseidon!
  Whose fault is it if these women-folk of ours
  get out of hand? We coddle them,
  we teach them to be wasteful and loose. You'll see a
    husband
  go into a jeweler's. "Look," he'll say,
  "jeweler," he'll say, "you remember that gold choker
  "you made for my wife? Well, she went to a dance
    last night
  "and broke the clasp. Now, I've got to go to Salamis,
  "and can't be bothered. Run over to my house
    tonight,
  "will you, and see if you can put it together for her."

---

[17] A well known demagogue; the speech alludes to the festival in
honor of Adonis which four years earlier had coincided with the
decision to undertake the disastrous Sicilian expedition. It was believed that the women's madness in lamenting Adonis had influenced the decision.

Or another one
goes to a cobbler—a good strong workman, too,
with an awl that was never meant for child's play.
    "Here,"
he'll tell him, "one of my wife's shoes is pinching
"her little toe. Could you come up about noon
"and stretch it out for her?"
                                    Well, what do you expect?
Look at me, for example. I'm a Public Officer,
and it's one of my duties to pay off the sailors.
And where's the money? Up there in the Acropolis!
And those blasted women slam the door in my face!
But what are we waiting for?
                        —Look here, constable,
stop sniffing around for a tavern, and get us
some crowbars. We'll force their gates! As a matter of
    fact,
I'll do a little forcing myself.

(*Enter* LYSISTRATA, *above, with* MYRRHINE, KALONIKE,
and the BOEOTIAN)

LYSISTRATA   No need of forcing.
Here I am, of my own accord. And all this talk
about locked doors—! We don't need locked doors,
but just the least bit of common sense.
MAGISTRATE   Is that so, ma'am!
                            —Where's my constable?
                                    —Constable,
arrest that woman, and tie her hands behind her.
LYSISTRATA   If he touches me, I swear by Artemis
    there'll be one scamp dropped from the public pay-
    roll tomorrow!
MAGISTRATE   Well, constable? You're not afraid, I
    suppose? Grab her,
two of you, around the middle!
KALONIKE   No, by Pandrosos! [18]
Lay a hand on her, and I'll jump on you so hard
your guts will come out the back door!
MAGISTRATE   That's what *you* think!
Where's the sergeant?—Here, you: tie up that trollop
    first,
the one with the pretty talk!
MYRRHINE   By the Moon-Goddess! [19]

Just you try it, and you'd better call a surgeon!
MAGISTRATE   Another one!
                    Officer, seize that woman!
                                        I swear
I'll put an end to this riot!
BOEOTIAN   By the Taurian,[20]
one inch closer and you won't have a hair on your
    head!
MAGISTRATE   Lord, what a mess! And my constables
    seem to have left me.
But—women get the best of us? By God, no!
                                —Scythians! [21]
Close ranks and forward march!
LYSISTRATA   "Forward," indeed!
By the Two Goddesses, what's the sense in *that*?
They're up against four companies of women
armed from top to bottom.
MAGISTRATE   Forward, my Scythians!
LYSISTRATA   Forward, yourselves, dear comrades!
You grainlettucebeanseedmarket girls!
You garlicandonionbreadbakery girls!
Give it to 'em! Knock 'em down! Scratch 'em!
Tell 'em what you think of 'em! (*General mêlée; the
    Scythians yield*)
                            —Ah, that's enough!
Sound a retreat; good soldiers don't rob the dead!
MAGISTRATE   A nice day *this* has been for the police!
LYSISTRATA   Well, there you are.—Did you really
    think we women
would be driven like slaves? Maybe now you'll admit
that a woman knows something about glory.
MAGISTRATE   Glory enough,
especially glory in bottles! Dear Lord Apollo!
MALE CHORAGOS   Your Honor, there's no use talking
    to them. Words
mean nothing whatever to wild animals like these.
Think of the sousing they gave us! and the water
was not, I believe, of the purest.
FEMALE CHORAGOS   You shouldn't have come after us.
    And if you try it again,
you'll be one eye short!—Although, as a matter of
    fact,
what I like best is just to stay at home and read,

---

[18] One of the daughters of the founder of Athens; a woman's oath.
[19] Artemis.

[20] Again Artemis, who was worshiped at Taurica Chersonesos.
[21] Athens' finest archers.

like a sweet little bride: never hurting a soul, no,
never going out. But if you *must* shake hornets'
    nests,
look out for the hornets!

Strophe

OLD MEN   Good God, what can we do?
        What are we coming to?
These women! Who could bear it? But, for that
    matter, who
            Will find
            What they had in mind
            When they seized Cranaos' city
            And held it (more's the pity!)
Against us men of Athens, and our police force, too?

MALE CHORAGOS   We might question them, I suppose.
    But I warn you, sir,
don't believe anything you hear! It would be un-
    Athenian
not to get to the bottom of this plot.
MAGISTRATE   Very well.
    My first question is this: Why, so help you God,
    did you bar the gates of the Acropolis?
LYSISTRATA   Why?
    To keep the money, of course. No money, no war.
MAGISTRATE   You think that money's the cause of
    war?
LYSISTRATA   I do.
    Money brought about the Peisandros business[22]
    and all the other attacks on the State. Well and good!
    They'll not get another cent here!
MAGISTRATE   And what will you do?
LYSISTRATA   What a question! From now on, we
    intend
    to control the Treasury.
MAGISTRATE   Control the Treasury!
LYSISTRATA   Why not? Does that seem strange? After
    all,
    we control our household budgets.
MAGISTRATE   But that's different!
LYSISTRATA   "Different"? What do you mean?
MAGISTRATE   I mean simply this:

---

it's the Treasury that pays for National Defense.
LYSISTRATA   Unnecessary. We propose to abolish war!
MAGISTRATE   Good God.—And National Security?
LYSISTRATA   Leave that to us.
MAGISTRATE   You?
LYSISTRATA   Us.
MAGISTRATE   We're done for, then!
LYSISTRATA   Never mind.
    We women will save you in spite of yourselves.
MAGISTRATE   What nonsense!
LYSISTRATA   If you like. But you must accept it, like it
    or not.
MAGISTRATE   Why, this is downright subversion!
LYSISTRATA   Maybe it is.
    But we're going to save you, Judge.
MAGISTRATE   I don't *want* to be saved!
LYSISTRATA   Tut. The death-wish. All the more
    reason.
MAGISTRATE   But the idea of women bothering
    themselves about peace and war!
LYSISTRATA   Will you listen to me?
MAGISTRATE   Yes. But be brief, or I'll—
LYSISTRATA   This is no time for stupid threats.
MAGISTRATE   By the gods,
    I'm losing my mind!
AN OLD WOMAN   That's nice. If you do, remember
    you've less to lose than *we* have.
MAGISTRATE   Quiet, you old buzzard!
    Now, Lysistrata: tell me what you're thinking.
LYSISTRATA   Glad to.
                    Ever since this war began
    we women have been watching you men, agreeing
        with you,
    keeping our thoughts to ourselves. That doesn't
        mean
    we were happy: we weren't, for we saw how things
        were going;
    but we'd listen to you at dinner
    arguing this way and that.
                    —Oh you, and your big
Top Secrets!—
                And then we'd grin like little patriots
    (though goodness knows we didn't feel like
        grinning) and ask you:
    "Dear, did the Armistice come up in Assembly
        today?"

---

[22] A politician who, even as Aristophanes was completing this play, was bringing about the revolution of the Four Hundred, which overthrew Athenian democracy.

And you'd say, "None of your business! Pipe
down!," you'd say.
And so we would.

AN OLD WOMAN   *I wouldn't have, by God!*

MAGISTRATE   You'd have taken a beating, then!
—Please go on.

LYSISTRATA   Well, we'd be quiet. But then, you know,
all at once
you men would think up something worse than ever.
Even *I* could see it was fatal. And, "Darling," I'd say,
"have you gone completely mad?" And my husband
would look at me
and say, "Wife, you've got your weaving to attend to.
"Mind your tongue, if you don't want a slap. 'War's
" 'a man's affair!' " [23]

MAGISTRATE   Good words, and well pronounced!

LYSISTRATA   You're a fool if you think so.
It was hard enough
to put up with all this banquet-hall strategy.
But then we'd hear you out in the public square:
"Nobody left for the draft-quota here in Athens?"
you'd say; and, "No," someone else would say, "not
a man!"
And so we women decided to rescue Greece.
You might as well listen to us now: you'll have to,
later.

MAGISTRATE   *You* rescue Greece? Absurd!

LYSISTRATA   You're the absurd one!

MAGISTRATE   You expect me to take orders from a
woman?

LYSISTRATA   Heavens, if that's what's bothering you,
take my veil,
here, and my girdle, and my market-basket. Go
home
to your weaving and your cooking! I tell you, "War's
a woman's affair!"

FEMALE CHORAGOS   Down with your pitchers,
comrades,
but keep them close at hand. It's time for a rally!

Antistrophe

OLD WOMEN   Dance, girls, dance for peace!
Who cares if our knees

Wobble and creak? Shall we not dance for such allies
as these?
Their wit! their grace! their beauty!
It's a municipal duty
To dance them luck and happiness who risk their all
for Greece!

FEMALE CHORAGOS   Women, remember your
grandmothers! Remember, you were born
among brambles and nettles! Dance for victory!

LYSISTRATA   O Eros, god of delight! O Aphrodite!
Cyprian!
Drench us now with the savor of love!
Let these men, getting wind of us, dream such joy
that they'll tail us through all the provinces of
Hellas!

MAGISTRATE   And if we do?

LYSISTRATA   Well, for one thing, we shan't have to
watch you
going to market, a spear in one hand, and heavens
knows
what in the other.

FEMALE CHORAGOS   Nicely said, by Aphrodite!

LYSISTRATA   As things stand now, you're neither men
nor women.
Armor clanking with kitchen pans and pots—
you sound like a pack of Corybantes! [24]

MAGISTRATE   A man must do what a man must do.

LYSISTRATA   So I'm told.
But to see a General, complete with Gorgon-shield,
jingling along the dock to buy a couple of herrings!

FEMALE CHORAGOS   *I* saw a Captain the other day—
lovely fellow he was,
nice curly hair—sitting on his horse; and—can you
believe it?—
he'd just bought some soup, and was pouring it into
his helmet!
And there was a soldier from Thrace
swishing his lance like something out of Euripides,
and the poor fruit-store woman got so scared
that she ran away and let him have his figs free!

MAGISTRATE   All this is beside the point.
Will you be so kind
as to tell me how you mean to save Greece?

---

[23] Quoted from Hektor's farewell to Andromache, *Iliad*, VI, 492.

[24] Wild and frenzied dancers; attendants of the goddess Cybele.

LYSISTRATA   Of course!
Nothing could be simpler.

MAGISTRATE   I assure you, I'm all ears.

LYSISTRATA   Do you know anything about weaving?
Say the yarn gets tangled: we thread it
this way and that through the skein, up and down,
until it's free. And it's like that with war.
We'll send our envoys
up and down, this way and that, all over Greece,
until it's finished.

MAGISTRATE   Yarn? Thread? Skein?
Are you out of your mind? I tell you,
war is a serious business.

LYSISTRATA   So serious
that I'd like to go on talking about weaving.

MAGISTRATE   All right. Go ahead.

LYSISTRATA   The first thing we have to do
is to wash our yarn, get the dirt out of it.
You see? Isn't there too much dirt here in Athens?
You must wash those men away.
                    Then our spoiled wool—
that's like your job-hunters, out for a life
of no work and big pay. Back to the basket,
citizens or not, allies or not,
or friendly immigrants!
                    And your colonies?
Hanks of wool lost in various places. Pull them
together, weave them into one great whole,
and our voters are clothed for ever.

MAGISTRATE   It would take a woman
to reduce state questions to a matter of carding and
    weaving!

LYSISTRATA   You fool! Who were the mothers whose
    sons sailed off
to fight for Athens in Sicily?

MAGISTRATE   Enough!
I beg you, do not call back those memories.

LYSISTRATA   And then,
instead of the love that every woman needs,
we have only our single beds, where we can dream
of our husbands off with the Army.
                        Bad enough for wives!
But what about our girls, getting older every day,
and older, and no kisses?

MAGISTRATE   Men get older, too.

LYSISTRATA   Not in the same sense.

                        A soldier's discharged,
and he may be bald and toothless, yet he'll find
a pretty young thing to go to bed with.
                        But a woman!
Her beauty is gone with the first grey hair.
She can spend her time
consulting the oracles and the fortune-tellers,
but they'll never send her a husband.

MAGISTRATE   Still, if a man can rise to the occasion—

LYSISTRATA (Furiously)   Rise? Rise, yourself!
Go invest in a coffin!
                You've money enough.
                        I'll bake you
a cake for the Underworld.[25]
                    And here's your funeral
wreath! (She pours water upon him)

MYRRHINE   And here's another! (More water)

KALONIKE   And here's
my contribution! (More water)

LYSISTRATA   What are you waiting for?
All aboard Styx Ferry![26]
                    Charon's calling for you!
It's sailing-time: don't disrupt the schedule!

MAGISTRATE   The insolence of women! And to me!
No, by God, I'll go back to court and show
the rest of the Bench the things that might happen to
    them!

(Exit MAGISTRATE)

LYSISTRATA   Really, I suppose we should have laid out
    his corpse
on the doorstep, in the usual way.
                        But never mind!
We'll give him the rites of the dead tomorrow
    morning!

(Exit LYSISTRATA with MYRRHINE and KALONIKE)

Strophe 1

OLD MEN   Sons of Liberty, strip off your clothes for
    action! Men arise!

---

[25] A honey cake was usually placed in the hand of the dead to be
given to Cerberus, the three-headed dog guarding the gates of
Hades.

[26] The Styx was the river over which Charon ferried the souls of the
dead.

Shall we stand here limp and useless while old
　　Cleisthenes'[27] allies
Prod a herd of furious grandmas to attempt to bring
　　to pass
A female restoration of the Reign of Hippias?[28]
　　　　Forbid it, gods misogynist!
　　　　Return our Treasury, at least!
We must clothe ourselves and feed ourselves to face
　　these civic rages,
And who can do a single thing if they cut off our
　　wages?

MALE CHORAGOS   Gentlemen, we are disgraced
　　forever if we allow
these madwomen to jabber about spears and shields
and make friends with the Spartans. What's a
　　Spartan? a wild
wolf's a safer companion any day! No; their plan's
to bring back Dictatorship; and we won't stand for
　　that!
From now on, let's go armed, each one of us
a new Aristogeiton!
　　　　　　　And to begin with,
I propose to poke a number of teeth
down the gullet of that harridan over there.

Antistrophe 1

OLD WOMEN   Hold your tongues, you senile bravoes,
　　or I swear, when you get home
Your own mothers wouldn't know you! Strip for
　　action, ladies, come!
I bore the holy vessels in my eighth year,[29] and at ten
I was pounding out the barley for Athena Goddess,[30]
　　then
　　　　　They elected me Little Bear
　　　　　For Artemis at Brauron Fair,[31]
I'd been made a Basket-Carrier[32] by the time I came
　　of age:

So trust me to advise you in this feminist rampage!

FEMALE CHORAGOS   As a woman, I pay my taxes to the
　　State,
though I pay them in baby boys. What do you
　　contribute,
you impotent horrors? Nothing but waste:
our treasury, the so-called Glory of the Persian Wars,
gone! rifled! parceled out for privilege! And you
have the insolence to control public policy,
leading us all to disaster!
　　　　　　　　　No, don't answer back
unless you want the heel of my slipper
slap against that ugly jaw of yours!

Strophe 2

OLD MEN   What impudence!
　　　　What malevolence!
　　　　Comrades, make haste,
All those of you who still are sensitive below the
　　waist!
　　　　Off with your clothes, men!
　　　　Nobody knows when
　　　　　We'll put them back on.
　　　　　Remember Leipsydrion![33]
　　　　We may be old,
　　　　But let's be bold!

MALE CHORAGOS   Give them an inch, and we're done
　　for! We'll have them
launching boats next and planning naval strategy.
Or perhaps they fancy themselves as cavalry!
That's fair enough: women know how to ride,
they're good in the saddle. Just think of Mikon's
　　paintings,[34]
all those Amazons wrestling with men! No, it's time
to bridle these wild mares!

Antistrophe 2

OLD WOMEN   Hold on, or
　　　　You *are* done for,
　　　　By the Two Goddesses above!
Strip, strip, my women: we've got the veterans on the
　　move!
　　　　Tangle with me, Gramps,

---

[27] An Athenian of notorious bisexual tendencies.

[28] Last of the Athenian tyrants. He had ruled with his brother Hipparchos until the latter's death at the hands of the patriots Aristogeiton and Harmonius: Hippias was killed later at Marathon.

[29] Four girls of high birth between the ages of seven and eleven were appointed to service in the Temple of Athena in the Acropolis.

[30] At ten a girl of aristocratic family was eligible to be Millmaid and to grind the sacred grain of Athena.

[31] Brauron was a town on the coast of Attica where a ceremony to Artemis was celebrated in which a little girl impersonated a bear.

[32] Girls carried baskets containing precious objects sacred to Athena.

---

[33] After the patriots had killed Hipparchos, they fled and fortified themselves in Leipsydrion; after a heroic defense they were forced to surrender.

[34] Mikon was one of the many painters who dealt with the invasion of Attica by the Amazons, a fabulous race of warrior-women.

And you'll have cramps
>For the rest of your days!
>>No more beans! No more cheese!
>My two legs
>Will scramble your eggs!

FEMALE CHORAGOS   If Lampito stands by me, and that elegant
Theban girl, Ismenia—what good are *you?*
>>>>>>>>Pass your laws!

Laws upon laws, you decrepit legislators!
At the worst you're just a nuisance, rationing Boeotian eels
on the Feast of Hecate, making our girls go without!
That was statesmanship! And we'll have to put up with it
until some patriot slits your silly old gizzards!

(Exeunt omnes)

The scene shifts to a court within the Acropolis.

(Re-enter LYSISTRATA)

FEMALE CHORAGOS   But Lysistrata! Leader! Why such a grim face?

LYSISTRATA   Oh the behavior of these idiotic women!
There's something about the female temperament that I can't bear!

FEMALE CHORAGOS   What in the world do you mean?

LYSISTRATA   Exactly what I say.

FEMALE CHORAGOS   What dreadful thing has happened?
Come, tell us: we're all your friends.

LYSISTRATA   It isn't easy
to say it; yet, God knows, we can't hush it up.

FEMALE CHORAGOS   Well, then? Out with it!

LYSISTRATA   To put it bluntly,
we're desperate for men.

FEMALE CHORAGOS   Almighty God!

LYSISTRATA   Why bring God into it?—No, it's just as I say.
I can't manage them any longer: they've gone man-crazy,
they're all trying to get out.
>>>>Why, look:
one of them was sneaking out the back door
over there by Pan's cave,[35] another
was sliding down the walls with rope and tackle;

another was climbing aboard a sparrow,[36] ready to take off
for the nearest brothel—I dragged *her* back by the hair!
They're all finding some reason to leave.
>>>>>>>>Look there!
There goes another one.
>>>>>>>—Just a minute, you!
Where are you off to so fast?

FIRST WOMAN   I've got to get home!
I've a lot of Milesian wool, and the worms are spoiling it.

LYSISTRATA   Oh bother you and your worms! Get back inside!

FIRST WOMAN   I'll be back right away, I swear I will!
I just want to get it stretched out on my bed.

LYSISTRATA   You'll do no such thing. You'll stay right here.

FIRST WOMAN   And my wool?
You want it ruined?

LYSISTRATA   Yes, for all I care.

SECOND WOMAN   Oh dear! My lovely new flax from Amorgos—[37]
I left it at home, all uncarded!

LYSISTRATA   Another one!
And all she wants is someone to card her flax.
Get back in there!

SECOND WOMAN   But I swear by the Moon-Goddess,
the minute I get it done, I'll be back!

LYSISTRATA   I say No!
If you, why not all the other women as well?

THIRD WOMAN   O Lady Eileithyia![38] Radiant goddess! Thou
intercessor for women in childbirth! Stay, I pray thee,
oh stay this parturition! Shall I pollute
a sacred spot?

LYSISTRATA   And what's the matter with *you?*

THIRD WOMAN   I'm having a baby—any minute now!

LYSISTRATA   But you weren't pregnant yesterday.

THIRD WOMAN   Well, I am today!

---

[35] A grotto on the north side of the Acropolis.

[36] A bird sacred to Aphrodite; it had been harnessed to the chariot of the goddess.

[37] An island in the Aegean famed for its flax.

[38] The goddess invoked by women at childbirth; it was unlawful to bear children on the Acropolis because it was holy ground.

Let me go home for a midwife, Lysistrata:
there's not much time.
LYSISTRATA   I never heard such nonsense.
What's that bulging under your cloak?
THIRD WOMAN   A little baby boy.
LYSISTRATA   It certainly isn't. But it's something
    hollow,
like a basin or— Why, it's the helmet of Athena!
And you said you were having a baby!
THIRD WOMAN   Well, I am! So there!
LYSISTRATA   Then why the helmet?
THIRD WOMAN   I was afraid that my pains
    might begin here in the Acropolis; and I wanted
    to drop my chick into it, just as the dear doves do.
LYSISTRATA   Lies! Evasions!—But at least one thing's
    clear:
you can't leave the place before your purification.
THIRD WOMAN   But I can't stay here in the Acropolis!
    Last night I dreamed
of a snake.[39]
FIRST WOMAN   And those horrible owls,[40] the noise
    they make!
I can't get a bit of sleep; I'm just about dead.
LYSISTRATA   You useless girls, that's enough: Let's
    have no more lying.
Of course you want your men. But don't you
    imagine
that they want you just as much? I'll give you my
    word,
their nights must be pretty hard.
                    Just stick it out!
A little patience, that's all, and our battle's won.
I have heard an Oracle. Should you like to hear it?
FIRST WOMAN   An Oracle? Yes, tell us!
LYSISTRATA   Quiet, then.—Here
is what it said:
IF EVER THE SWALLOWS, ESCHEWING HOOPOE-
    BIRDS,
SHALL CONSPIRE TOGETHER TO DENY THEM
    ALL ACCESS,
THEIR GRIEF IS FOREVER OVER.
                    These are the words

from the Shrine itself.
                    AYE, AND ZEUS WILL REDRES
THEIR WRONGS, AND SET THE LOWER ABOVE
THE HIGHER.
FIRST WOMAN   Does that mean we'll be on top?
LYSISTRATA   BUT IF THEY RETIRE,
    EACH SWALLOW HER OWN WAY, FROM THIS
        HOLY PLACE,
    LET THE WORLD PROCLAIM NO BIRD OF
        SORRIER GRACE
    THAN THE SWALLOW.
FIRST WOMAN   I swear, *that* Oracle makes sense!
LYSISTRATA   Now, then, by all the gods,
    let's show that we're bigger than these annoyances.
    Back to your places! Let's not disgrace the Oracle.

(*Exeunt* LYSISTRATA *and the dissident women; the*
CHORUSES *renew their conflict*)

Strophe

OLD MEN   I know a little story that I learned way back
    in school
Goes like this:
Once upon a time there was a young man—and no
    fool—
Named Melanion,[41] and his
One aversi-on was marriage. He loathed the very
    thought!
So he ran off to the hills, and in a special grot
Raised a dog, and spent his days
Hunting rabbits. And it says
That he never never never did come home.
It might be called a refuge *from* the womb.
All right,
            all right,
                    all right!
We're as pure as young Melanion, and we hate the
    very sight
Of you sluts!
A MAN   How about a kiss, old woman?
A WOMAN   Here's an onion in your eye!
A MAN   A kick in the guts, then?
A WOMAN   Try, old bristle-tail, just try!

---

[39] The sacred snake of the Acropolis; it was never seen but was believed to guard the holy ground.
[40] Birds sacred to Athena.

[41] The suitor of Atalanta, who hated men. The Chorus of Old Men
have made him a hater of women.

A MAN   Yet they say Myronides[42]
   On hands and knees
   Looked just as shaggy fore and aft as I!

Antistrophe

OLD WOMEN   Well, *I* know a little story, and it's just as
      good as yours.
   Goes like this:
   Once there was a man named Timon[43]—a rough
      diamond, of course,
   And that whiskery face of his
   Looked like murder in the shrubbery. By God, he
      was a son
   Of the Furies, let me tell you! And what did he do
      but run
   From the world and all its ways,
   Cursing mankind! And it says
   That his choicest execrations as of then
   Were leveled almost wholly at *old* men.
   All right,
         all right,
               all right!
   But there's one thing about Timon: he could always
      stand the sight
   Of us "sluts"!

A WOMAN   How about a crack in the jaw, Pop?
A MAN   I can take it, Ma—no fear!
A WOMAN   How about a kick in the face?
A MAN   You'd show your venerable rear.
A WOMAN   I may be old;
   But I've been told
   That I've nothing to worry about down there!

   (*Re-enter* LYSISTRATA)

LYSISTRATA   Oh, quick, girls, quick! Come here!
FEMALE CHORAGOS   What is it?
LYSISTRATA   A man!
   A man simply bulging with love!
                  O Cyprian Queen,
   O Paphian, O Cythereian! Hear us and aid us!
FEMALE CHORAGOS   Where is this enemy?
LYSISTRATA   Over there, by Demeter's shrine.
FEMALE CHORAGOS   Damned if he isn't. But who *is* he?

---

[42] A famous Athenian general.
[43] A famous Athenian misanthrope.

MYRRHINE   My husband.
   Kinesias.
LYSISTRATA   Oh then, get busy! Tease him!
      Undermine him!
   Wreck him! Give him everything—kissing, tickling,
      nudging,
   whatever you generally torture him with—: give him
      everything
   except what we swore on the wine we would not
      give.
MYRRHINE   Trust me!
LYSISTRATA   I do. But I'll help you get him started.
   The rest of you women, stay back.

   (*Enter* KINESIAS)

KINESIAS   Oh God! Oh my God!
   I'm stiff for lack of exercise. All I can do to stand up!
LYSISTRATA   Halt! Who are you, approaching our
      lines?
KINESIAS   Me? I.
LYSISTRATA   A man?
KINESIAS   You have eyes, haven't you?
LYSISTRATA   Go away.
KINESIAS   Who says so?
LYSISTRATA   Officer of the Day.
KINESIAS   Officer, I beg you,
   by all the gods at once, bring Myrrhine out!
LYSISTRATA   Myrrhine? And who, my good sir, are
      you?
KINESIAS   Kinesias. Last name's Pennison. Her
      husband.
LYSISTRATA   Oh, of course. I beg your pardon. We're
      glad to see you.
   We've heard so much about you. Dearest Myrrhine
   is always talking about "Kinesias"—never nibbles an
      egg
   or an apple without saying
   "Here's to Kinesias!"
KINESIAS   Do you really mean it?
LYSISTRATA   I do.
   When we're discussing men, she always says,
   "Well, after all, there's nobody like Kinesias!"
KINESIAS   Good God.—Well, then, please send her
      down here.
LYSISTRATA   And what do *I* get out of it?
KINESIAS   A standing promise.

LYSISTRATA   I'll take it up with her.

(*Exit* LYSISTRATA)

KINESIAS   But be quick about it!
Lord, what's life without a wife? Can't eat. Can't
     sleep.
Every time I go home, the place is so empty, so
insufferably sad! Love's killing me! Oh,
     hurry!

(*Enter* MANES, *a slave, with Kinesias' baby; the voice of*
MYRRHINE *is heard off-stage*)

MYRRHINE   But of course I love him! Adore him!—but
     no,
he hates love. No. I won't go down.

(*Enter* MYRRHINE, *above*)

KINESIAS   Myrrhine!
Darlingest little Myrrhine! Come down quick!
MYRRHINE   Certainly not.
KINESIAS   Not? But why, Myrrhine?
MYRRHINE   Why? You don't need me.
KINESIAS   Need you? My God, *look* at me!
MYRRHINE   So long! (*Turns to go*)
KINESIAS   Myrrhine, Myrrhine, Myrrhine!
If not for my sake, for our child! (*Pinches* BABY)
                          —All right, you: pipe up!
BABY   Mummie! Mummie! Mummie!
KINESIAS   You hear that?
Pitiful, I call it. Six days now
with never a bath; no food; enough to break your
     heart!
MYRRHINE   My darlingest child! What a father *you*
     acquired!
KINESIAS   At least come down for his sake!
MYRRHINE   I suppose I must.
Oh, this mother business! [44]

(*Exit*)

KINESIAS   How pretty she is! And younger!
She's so much nicer when she's bothered!

(MYRRHINE *enters, below*)

MYRRHINE   Dearest child,

you're as sweet as your father's horrid. Give me a
     kiss.
KINESIAS   Now you see how wrong it was to get
     involved
in this scheming League of women. All this agony
for nothing!
MYRRHINE   Keep your hands to yourself!
KINESIAS   But our house
going to rack and ruin?
MYRRHINE   I don't care.
KINESIAS   And your knitting
all torn to pieces by the chickens? Don't you care?
MYRRHINE   Not at all.
KINESIAS   And our vows to Aphrodite?
Oh, *won't* you come back?
MYRRHINE   No.—At least, not until you men
make a treaty to end the war.
KINESIAS   Why, if that's all you want,
by God, we'll make your treaty!
MYRRHINE   Oh? Very well.
When you've done that, I'll come home. But
     meanwhile,
I've sworn an oath.
KINESIAS   Don't worry.—Now, let's have fun.
MYRRHINE   No! Stop it! I said no!
                      —Although, of course,
I *do* love you.
KINESIAS   I know you do. Darling Myrrhine:
come, shall we?
MYRRHINE   Are you out of your mind? In front of the
     child?
KINESIAS   Take him home, Manes.

(*Exit* MANES *with baby*)

                            There. He's gone.
                                Come on!
There's nothing to stop us now.
MYRRHINE   You devil! But where?
KINESIAS   In Pan's cave. What could be snugger than
     that?
MYRRHINE   But my purification before I go back to the
     Citadel?
KINESIAS   There's always the Klepsydra.[45]
MYRRHINE   And my oath?

---

[44] A line that parodies Euripides' *Iphigenia at Aulis*, 917.

[45] A sacred spring near Pan's cave.

KINESIAS   Leave the oath to me.
After all, I'm the man.
MYRRHINE   Well . . . if you say so!
                              I'll go find a bed.
KINESIAS   Oh, bother a bed! The ground's good enough
   for me!
MYRRHINE   No. You're a bad man, but you deserve
   something better than dirt.

(*Exit* MYRRHINE)

KINESIAS   What a love she is! And how thoughtful!

(*Re-enter* MYRRHINE)

MYRRHINE   Here's your bed.
   Now let me get my clothes off.
                         But, good horrors!
   We haven't a mattress!
KINESIAS   Oh, forget the mattress!
MYRRHINE   No.
   Just lying on blankets? Too sordid!
KINESIAS   Give me a kiss.
MYRRHINE   Just a second.

(*Exit* MYRRHINE)

KINESIAS   I swear, I'll explode!

(*Re-enter* MYRRHINE)

MYRRHINE   Here's your mattress.
   Go to bed now. I'll just take my dress off.
                              But look—
   where's our pillow?
KINESIAS   I don't need a pillow!
MYRRHINE   Well, *I* do.

(*Exit* MYRRHINE)

KINESIAS   I don't suppose even Heracles
   would stand for this!

(*Re-enter* MYRRHINE)

MYRRHINE   There we are. Ups-a-daisy!
KINESIAS   So we are. Well, come to bed.
MYRRHINE   But I wonder:
   is everything ready now?
KINESIAS   I can swear to that. Come, darling!
MYRRHINE   Just getting out of my girdle.
                         But remember, now,

what you promised about the treaty!
KINESIAS   I'll remember.
MYRRHINE   But no coverlet!
KINESIAS   Damn it, I'll be
   your coverlet!
MYRRHINE   Be right back.

(*Exit* MYRRHINE)

KINESIAS   This girl and her coverlets
   will be the death of me.

(*Re-enter* MYRRHINE)

MYRRHINE   Here we are. Up you go!
KINESIAS   Up? I've been up for ages!
MYRRHINE   Some perfume?
KINESIAS   No, by Apollo!
MYRRHINE   Yes, by Aphrodite!
   I don't care whether you want it or not.

(*Exit* MYRRHINE)

KINESIAS   For love's sake, hurry!

(*Re-enter* MYRRHINE)

MYRRHINE   Here, in your hand. Rub it right in.
KINESIAS   Never cared for perfume.
   And this is particularly strong. Still, here goes!
MYRRHINE   What a nitwit I am! I brought you the
   Rhodian bottle! [46]
KINESIAS   Forget it.
MYRRHINE   No trouble at all. You just wait here.

(*Exit* MYRRHINE)

KINESIAS   God damn the man who invented perfume!

(*Re-enter* MYRRHINE)

MYRRHINE   At last! The right bottle!
KINESIAS   I've got the rightest
   bottle of all, and it's right here waiting for you.
   Darling, forget everything else. Do come to bed!
MYRRHINE   Just let me get my shoes off.
                         —And, by the way,
   you'll vote for the treaty?
KINESIAS   I'll think about it.

————
[46] From Rhodes.

(MYRRHINE *runs away*)

There! That's done it! Off she runs,
with never a thought for the way I'm feeling. I must
have *someone*, or I'll go mad! Myrrhine
has just about ruined me.
              And you, strutting little soldier:
what about you? There's nothing for it, I guess,
But an expedition to old Dog-fox's[47] bordello.
OLD MEN   She's left you in a sorry state:
            You have my sympathy.
        What upright citizen could bear
        Your pain? I swear, not I!
Just the look of you, with never a woman
To come to your aid! It isn't human!
KINESIAS   The agony!
MALE CHORAGOS   Well, why not?
        She has you on the spot!
FEMALE CHORAGOS   A lovelier girl never breathed, you
old sot!
KINESIAS   A lovelier girl? Zeus! Zeus!
        Produce a hurricane
        To hoist these lovely girls aloft
        And drop them down again
Bump on our lances! Then they'd know
What they do that makes men suffer so.

(*Exit* KINESIAS)

(*Enter a* SPARTAN HERALD)

HERALD   Gentlemen, Ah beg you will be so kind
as to direct me to the Central Committee.
Ah have a communication.

(*Re-enter* MAGISTRATE)

MAGISTRATE   Are you a man,
or a fertility symbol?
HERALD   Ah refuse to answer that question!
Ah'm a certified herald from Spahta, and Ah've
come
to talk about an ahmistice.
MAGISTRATE   Then why
that spear under your cloak?
HERALD   Ah have no speah!

MAGISTRATE   You don't walk naturally, with your
tunic
poked out so. You have a tumor, maybe,
or a hernia?
HERALD   No, by Castor![48]
MAGISTRATE   Well,
something's wrong, I can see that. And I don't like it.
HERALD   Colonel, Ah resent this.
MAGISTRATE   So I see. But what *is* it?
HERALD   A scroll
with a message from Spahta.
MAGISTRATE   Oh. I've heard about these scrolls.
Well, then, man, speak out: How are things in
Sparta?
HERALD   Hard, Colonel, hard! We're at a standstill.
Can't seem to think of anything but women.
MAGISTRATE   How curious! Tell me, do you Spartans
think
that maybe Pan's to blame?
HERALD   Pan? No. Lampito and her little naked
friends.
They won't let a man come near them.
MAGISTRATE   How are you handling it?
HERALD   Losing our minds,
if you want to know, and walking around hunched
over
like men carrying candles in a gale.
The women have sworn they'll have nothing to do
with us
until we get a treaty.
MAGISTRATE   Yes, I know.
It's a general uprising, sir, in all parts of Greece.
But as for the answer—
        Sir: go back to Sparta
and have them send us your Armistice Commission.
I'll arrange things in Athens.
        And I may say
that my standing is good enough to make them
listen.
HERALD   A man after mah own heart! Sir, Ah thank
you!

(*Exit* HERALD)

---

[47] Nickname for a famous procurer.

[48] One of Sparta's protective spirits.

Strophe

OLD MEN   Oh these women! Where will you find
                A slavering beast that's more unkind?
                    Where a hotter fire?
                Give me a panther, any day!
                He's not so merciless as they,
                    And panthers don't conspire!

Antistrophe

OLD WOMEN   We may be hard, you silly old ass,
                    But who brought you to this stupid pass?
                        You're the ones to blame.
                    Fighting with us, your oldest friends,
                    Simply to serve your selfish ends—
                        Really, you have no shame!

MALE CHORAGOS   No, I'm through with women for
    ever![49]

FEMALE CHORAGOS   If you say so.
    Still, you might put some clothes on. You look too
        absurd
    standing around naked. Come, get into this cloak.

MALE CHORAGOS   Thank you; you're right. I merely
        took it off
    because I was in such a temper.

FEMALE CHORAGOS   That's much better
    Now you resemble a man again.
                            Why have you been so horrid?
    And look: there's some sort of insect in your eye!
    Shall I take it out?

MALE CHORAGOS   An insect, is it? So that's
    what's been bothering me! Lord, yes: take it out!

FEMALE CHORAGOS   You might be more polite.
                                —But, heavens!
    What an enormous gnat!

MALE CHORAGOS   You've saved my life.
    That gnat was drilling an artesian well
    in my left eye.

FEMALE CHORAGOS   Let me wipe
    those tears away!—And now: one little kiss?

MALE CHORAGOS   Over my dead body!

FEMALE CHORAGOS   You're so difficult!

MALE CHORAGOS   These impossible women! How
        they do get around us!

---

[49] Parodies lines in Euripides' *Hippolytus*.

The poet was right: Can't live with them, or without
    them!
But let's be friends.
And to celebrate, you might lead off with an Ode.

Strophe

OLD WOMEN   Let it never be said
                    That my tongue is malicious:
                    Both by word and by deed
                I would set an example that's noble and gracious.
                        We've had sorrow and care
                        Till we're sick of the tune.
                    Is there anyone here
                    Who would like a small loan?
                        My purse is crammed,
                        As you'll soon find;
                And you needn't pay me back if the Peace gets
                    signed!
                        I've invited to lunch
                        Some Karystian rips—[50]
                        An esurient bunch,
                But I've ordered a menu to water their lips!
                    I can still make soup
                    And slaughter a pig.
                    You're all coming, I hope?
                    But a bath first, I beg!
                        Walk right up
                        As though you owned the place,
                And you'll get the front door slammed to in your
                    face!

(Enter SPARTAN AMBASSADOR, *with entourage*)

MALE CHORAGOS   The Commission has arrived from
    Sparta.
            How oddly
    they're walking!
                        Gentlemen, welcome to Athens!
    How is life in Laconia?

AMBASSADOR   Need we discuss that?
    Simply use your eyes.

OLD MEN   The poor man's right:
                        What a sight!

AMBASSADOR   Words fail me.

---

[50] The Karystians were allies of Athens at this time, but were dis-
dained for their primitive manners and loose morals.

But come, gentlemen, call in your Commissioners,
and let's get down to a peace.
MALE CHORAGOS   The state we're in! Can't bear
a stitch below the waist. It's a kind of pelvic
paralysis.
AN ATHENIAN   Won't somebody call Lysistrata?
She has the answer.
A SPARTAN   Yes, there, look at him.
Same thing.
          Seh, do y'all feel a certain strain
early in the morning?
ATHENIAN   I do, sir. It's worse than a strain.
A few more days, and there's nothing for us but
Cleisthenes,
that broken blossom!
MALE CHORAGOS   But you'd better get dressed again.
You know these prudes who go around Athens with
chisels,
looking for prominent statues.[51]
ATHENIAN   Sir, you are right.
SPARTAN   He certainly is! Ah'll put mah own clothes
back on.

(Enter ATHENIAN COMMISSIONERS)

AN ATHENIAN   They're no better off than we are!
          —Greetings, Laconians!
SPARTAN (To one of his own group)   Colonel, we got
dressed just in time.
          Ah sweah,
if they'd seen us the way we were, there'd have been
a new war
between the states.
ATHENIAN   Call the meeting to order.
          Now, Laconians,
what's your proposal?
AMBASSADOR   We'd lahk to consider peace.
ATHENIAN   Good. That's on our minds, too.
          —Summon Lysistrata.
We'll never get anywhere without her.
AMBASSADOR   Lysistrata?
Summon Lysis-anybody![52] Only, summon!
MALE CHORAGOS   No need to summon:
here she is, herself.

(Enter LYSISTRATA)

          Lysistrata! Lion of women!
This is your hour to be
hard and yielding, outspoken and sly, austere and
gentle. You see here
the best brains of Hellas (confused, I admit,
by your devious charming) met as one man
to turn the future over to you.
LYSISTRATA   That's fair enough,
unless you men take it into your heads
to turn to each other instead of to me. But I'd know
soon enough if you did!
          —Where is that goddess of Peace?
Go, some of you: bring her here.

(Exeunt two SERVANTS)

          And now,
summon the Spartan Commission. Treat them
courteously:
our husbands have been lax in that respect.
Take them by the hand, women,
or by anything else, if they seem unwilling.
          —Spartans:
you stand here. Athenians: on this side. Now listen
to me.

(Re-enter SERVANTS, staggering under the weight of a
more than life-size statue of a naked woman: this is
PEACE)

I'm only a woman, I know; but I've a mind,
and I can distinguish between sense and foolishness.
I owe the first to my father; the rest
to the local politicians.[53] So much for that.
Now, then.
What I have to say concerns both sides in this war.
We are all Greeks.
Must I remind you of Thermopylae? of Olympia?
of Delphi? names deep in all our hearts?
And yet you men go raiding through the country,
Greek killing Greek, storming down Greek cities—
and all the time the Barbarian across the sea
is waiting for his chance.—That's my first point.
AN ATHENIAN   Lord! I can hardly contain myself!

---

[51] Statues with prominent male sexual organs, or *phalloi.*
[52] Lysistrata's name means "dissolver of armies."

[53] The preceding four lines are probably quoted from Euripides'
Melanippe the Wise.

LYSISTRATA   And you Spartans:
    Was it so long ago that Pericleides
    came here to beg our help?[54] I can see him still,
    his white face, his sombre gown. And what did he
        want?
    An army from Athens! Messenia
    was at your heels, and the sea-god splitting your
        shores.
    Well, Kimon and his men,
    four thousand infantry, marched out of here to save
        you.
    What thanks do we get? You come back to murder
        us.
ATHENIAN   Can't trust a Spartan, Lysistrata!
A SPARTAN   Ah admit it.
    When Ah look at those legs, Ah sweah Ah can't trust
        mahself!
LYSISTRATA   And you, men of Athens:
    you might remember that bad time when we were
        down,
    and an army came from Sparta
    and sent Hippias and the Thessalians
    whimpering back to the hills. That was Sparta,
    and only Sparta; without Sparta, we'd now be
    cringing helots, not walking about like free men!

(*From this point, the male responses are less to* LYSIS-
TRATA *than to the statue of* PEACE)

A SPARTAN   An eloquent speech!
AN ATHENIAN   An elegant construction!
LYSISTRATA   Why are we fighting each other? Why not
    make peace?
AMBASSADOR   Spahta is ready, ma'am,
    so long as we get that place back.
LYSISTRATA   Place? What place?
AMBASSADOR   Ah refer to Pylos.[55]
MAGISTRATE   Not while I'm alive, by God!
LYSISTRATA   You'd better give in.
MAGISTRATE   But—what were we fighting about?
LYSISTRATA   Lots of places left.
MAGISTRATE   All right. Well, then:

----

[54] In 464 B.C. during a revolt in Sparta, when an earthquake had just severely damaged the city.

[55] A lost Spartan possession; for the moment political and sexual desires become confused.

Hog Island first, and that gulf behind there, and the
    land between
    the Legs of Megara.
AMBASSADOR   Mah government objects.
LYSISTRATA   Over-ruled. Why fuss about a pair of legs?

(*General assent; the statue of* PEACE *is removed*)

AN ATHENIAN   Let's take off our clothes and plow our
    fields.
A SPARTAN   Ah'll fertilize mahn first, by the Heavenly
    Twins!
LYSISTRATA   And so you shall,
    once we have peace. If you are serious,
    go, both of you, and talk with your allies.
ATHENIAN   Too much talk already. We'll stand
    together!
    We've only one end in view. All that we want
    is our women: and I speak for our allies.
AMBASSADOR   Mah government concurs.
ATHENIAN   So does Karystos.
LYSISTRATA   Good.—But before you come inside
    to join your wives at supper, you must perform
    the usual lustration. Then we'll open
    our baskets for you, and all that we have is yours.
    But you must promise upright good behavior
    from this day on. Then each man home with his
    woman!
ATHENIAN   Let's get it over with!
SPARTAN   Lead on: Ah follow!
ATHENIAN   Quick as a cat can wink!

(*Exeunt all but the* CHORUSES)

Antistrophe
OLD WOMEN   Embroideries and
        Twinkling ornaments and
        Pretty dresses—I hand
    Them all over to you, and with never a qualm.
        They'll be nice for your daughters
        On festival days
        When the girls bring the Goddess
        The ritual prize.
           Come in, one and all:
           Take what you will.
    I've nothing here so tightly corked that you can't
    make it spill!

You may search my house,
But you'll not find
The least thing of use,
Unless your two eyes are keener than mine.
Your numberless brats
Are half starved? and your slaves?
Courage, grandpa! I've lots
Of grain left, and big loaves.
I'll fill your guts,
I'll go the whole hog;
But if you come too close to me, remember: 'ware
the dog!

(*Exeunt* CHORUSES)

(*An* ATHENIAN DRUNKARD *approaches the gate and is
halted by a* SENTRY)

DRUNKARD   Open. The. Door.
SENTRY   Now, friend, just shove along!
So you want to sit down! If it weren't such an old
joke,
I'd tickle your tail with this torch. Just the sort of
thing
that this kind of audience appreciates.
DRUNKARD   I. Stay. Right. Here.
SENTRY   Oh, all right. But you'll see some funny
sights!
DRUNKARD   Bring. Them. On.
SENTRY   No, what am I thinking of?
The gentlemen from Sparta are just coming back
from supper.
Get out of here, or I'll scalp you!

(*Exit* DRUNKARD)

(*The general company re-enters; the two* CHORUSES *now
represent* SPARTANS *and* ATHENIANS)

MAGISTRATE   I must say,
I've never tasted a better meal. And those Laconians!
They're gentlemen, by the Lord! Just goes to show:
a drink to the wise is sufficient. And why not?
A sober man's an ass.
Men of Athens, mark my words: the only efficient
Ambassador's a drunk Ambassador. Is that clear?
Look: we go to Sparta,
and when we get there we're dead sober. The result?
Everyone cackling at everyone else. They make
speeches;

and even if we understand, we get it all wrong
when we file our reports in Athens. But today—!
Everybody's happy. Couldn't tell the difference
between *Drink to Me Only* and
the *Star Spangled Athens.*
                              What's a few lies,
washed down in good strong drink?

(*Re-enter* DRUNKARD)

SENTRY   God almighty,
he's back again!
DRUNKARD   I. Resume. My. Place.
A SPARTAN (*To an* ATHENIAN)   I beg you, seh,
take your instrument in your hand and play for us.
Ah'm told
you understand the intricacies of the floot?
Ah'd lahk to execute a song and dance
in honor of Athens,
                    and, of course, of Spahta.

(*The following song is a solo—an aria—accompanied by
the flute. The* CHORUS OF SPARTANS *begins a slow dance*)

DRUNKARD   Toot. On. Your. Flute.
SPARTAN CHORAGOS   Mnemosyne,[56]
Inspire once more the Grecian Muse
To sing of glory glory glory without end.
Sing Artemesion's shore,[57]
Where Athens fluttered the Persian fleet—
Alalai,[58] that great
Victory! Sing Leonidis and his men,
Those wild boars, sweat and blood
Down in a red drench. Then, then
The barbarians broke, though they had stood
A myriad strong before!
                    O Artemis,
Virgin Goddess, whose darts
Flash in our forests: approve
This pact of peace, and join our hearts,
From this day on, in love.
Huntress, descend!
LYSISTRATA   All that will come in time.

---

[56] Goddess of memory and mother of the Muses.
[57] Where in 480 B.C. the Athenian fleet successfully engaged the Persians, while Leonidas and his Spartans were making their famous stand at Thermopylae.
[58] A war cry.

But now, Laconians,
take home your wives. Athenians, take yours.
Each man be kind to his woman; and you, women,
be equally kind. Never again, pray God,
shall we lose our way in such madness.

        —And now

let's dance our joy! *(From this point the dance
becomes general)*
CHORUS OF ATHENIANS   Dance!

          Dance!

             Dance, you Graces!

Artemis, Dance!

        Dance, Phoebus, Lord of dancing!
Dance, Dionysus, in a scurry of Maenads!

        Dance, Zeus Thunderer!

Dance, Lady Hera,
Queen of the sky!

         Dance, dance, all you gods!
Dance for the dearest, the bringer of peace,
Deathless Aphrodite!
LYSISTRATA   Now let us have another song from
   Sparta.
CHORUS OF SPARTANS   From Taygetos' skyey summit,

     Laconian Muse, come down!
   Sing the glories of Apollo,

     Regent of Amyclae Town.

       Sing of Leda's Twins,
       Those gallant sons,
       On the banks of Eurotas—
        Alalai Evohe! [59]

Here's to our girls
   With their tangling curls,
    Legs a-wriggle,
    Bellies a-jiggle,
      A riot of hair,
     A fury of feet,
Evohe! Evohai! Evohe!

          as they pass
  Dancing,
     dancing,
        dancing,
          to greet
Athena of the House of Brass! [60]

---

[59] Now an orgiastic war cry.
[60] A famous temple on the acropolis of Sparta.

COMMENTS AND QUESTIONS

1. Like the tragedy *Oedipus Rex*, the comedy *Lysistrata* treats a selection of events taking place in a relatively short time. What, exactly, happens in *Lysistrata*? How has Aristophanes arranged the events? Where does the climax of the play fall, and how is it revealed?
2. Is the *tone* of *Lysistrata* entirely comic, or are there tragic or serious moments?
3. Do the characters in the play seem realistic to you? What makes them comic characters?
4. Which lines in the comedy seem especially funny to you? Why? Is the sexual explicitness in *Lysistrata* comic? Compare the treatment of sex here with the deadly seriousness of pornography. What is the difference?
5. *Lysistrata* is read more and more today as a play about women's liberation. Look for arguments both for and against this view in the play. What can you surmise about the actual social conditions of Greek women from this text? If the idea of the sex strike is not very realistic, the idea of women organizing themselves in order to achieve common goals is. What difficulties does Lysistrata encounter in the characters of the women themselves when she attempts to organize them? Can these be compared with the differences between "liberated" women and other women today? How are men viewed in this comedy?

4

CLASSICAL GREECE: PHILOSOPHY AND ETHICAL THOUGHT

The ancient Greeks were, as far as we know, the first to attempt to understand their universe as an order governed by a rational principle. From the late sixth century B.C. a group of thinkers, usually called the Pre-Socratics, looked beyond the arbitrary, willful gods worshiped by the masses, in order to define a universal principle of rationality. Whereas the popular gods were like human beings—only more powerful—the divine intellect postulated by the philosophers guaranteed the order and intelligibility of the world. Ancient Greek philosophy can be considered in one sense an effort to answer the question "what can be known?" If a statement reflects true knowledge, it cannot be true at one time and false at another. But the world about man appears always in a state of change; nothing remains the same for long. Consequently, any statements we make about the objects in this world are subject to contradiction when the objects change. True knowledge can only be of that which is itself immutable and eternal. Does this mean that, given the nature of knowledge, nothing in our experience can be known? Yet men are constantly making judgments about the world as if they had knowledge of absolute truths: they say that this man is better than that man, or more virtuous, or more honest.

Socrates

Socrates (470?–399 B.C.) set it as his task to make men aware of their assumptions about what they knew, not in order to make them skeptics but so that they might properly begin the pursuit of true knowledge. Knowledge begins with knowing what we do not know. So it was that the short, powerfully built, snub-nosed man, looking very much like a wrestler, spent most of his days in the streets of Athens, his native city, asking questions of his fellow citizens. Seemingly never satisfied with the first answer, he pushed his questions to the point where his companion in the dialogue had finally to admit that he did not know what he believed he knew at the outset. He became known as the gadfly of Athens—after the little gnat that pesters its object to desperation. Finally, he appeared so threatening to the traditions of his city that he was arrested and condemned to death for his detrimental influence on the youth of Athens.

Plato

Socrates never wrote a word, but his greatest disciple Plato (427?–347 B.C.) wrote volumes; in many of his writings, called *Dialogues*, he immortalized Socrates by making him the voice of the philosopher in the discussion. It is impossible to be certain how much of Plato's thought was borrowed from his master. At least the technique of seeking an immutable, eternal basis for our knowledge by interrogation certainly derived from Socrates, but it was probably Plato who formulated the technique into a method. The typical dialogue begins by Socrates asking for the definition of justice, or of courage, or of virtue itself. The person questioned responds usually with confidence, giving a traditional commonsense definition. Further questioning shows the answer to be inadequate, and a second definition is proposed—only to be rejected in turn—then a third and even a fourth without any results. At length the

discussant admits reluctantly that he is ignorant of what he believed himself to know. Perhaps the dialogue ends there, but frequently the interrogation continues until some positive conclusions are achieved.

Through this method of interrogation or *dialectic*, Plato eventually established the existence of two levels of reality. From eternity there were three elements in the universe: a demiurge or creator God; a world of eternal unchanging Ideas or patterns, perfect exemplars of truth, beauty, justice, all numbers, and geometrical shapes; and all natural things. The work of the demiurge was to model the receptacle into shapes resembling the eternal patterns of the Ideas or forms. Because the matter he worked with was mobile, his creations could never remain fixed for long; but at least the world he fashioned represented or imitated imperfectly the immutable exemplars of the transcendent world. Before this life man had lived as a soul in the world of the Ideas and had beheld them in their splendor. For the Greek, only like can know like: man could know the Ideas in this other world because he, like they, was divine.

Imprisoned at birth in a body, subject to the sensations of matter, the individual has forgotten that earlier life; nevertheless, enough remains to serve as the basis for judging experience. When we say that that thing is more beautiful than this thing, we are comparing both objects with a standard of beauty not found in our earthly experience but rather brought with us into this life from our contact in the upper world with the idea of pure beauty. The same is true with our judgment about other objects in our experience.

For Plato the soul is a divine entity, buried in a body from which at death it will escape. Because of our contact with the absolute beauty and good in a preexistence, we continue in this life to seek the experience we once had. Motivated by love of beauty and good, we strive to satisfy our needs through possession of material objects and other human beings. Only education can teach us the true end of our longing, directing our gaze away from the imperfect, transitory objects of this world to contemplation of the Ideas themselves of which these objects are but a dim reflection. Once in possession of the knowledge of mathematics, geometry, and other truths, we will come to look on our body and this world as a prison from which we will be freed at death.

The psychology of the philosopher constituted the first attempt to define various aspects of the human personality. Plato believed that the human soul consists of three fundamental parts: the reason that governs, moral courage that pursues the honorable even against great obstacles, and the appetite. The third part of the soul must be kept in close confinement; otherwise it would topple reason from its seat and create chaos in the life of the soul. Moral courage, on the other hand, is the ally of reason. A loyal member of a Greek city-state, Plato was convinced that the individual could not attain moral perfection or reach the stage where his reason contemplated the eternal realities while living in a corrupt community. Plato's ideal state reflects in its organization the three divisions of the soul. Like the soul it has its rational principle in the guardians, those who were to govern the whole. The auxiliaries, the soldiers, correspond to moral courage; and the artisans, who do most of the hard work in the society, reflect the appetitive principle. Just as in the individual soul, the whole is in harmony when reason rules, so in the state ruled by philosophers everyone keeps his place, performs his function, and is content.

An important characteristic of Plato's method was to illustrate profound philosophical ideas through use of stories, in the manner of myths. The selection below is taken from Benjamin Jowett's translation of *The Republic*, Plato's great dialogue on justice, illustrated by the perfect state. Commonly known as "The *Allegory* of the Cave," this passage endeavors to dramatize the predicament of mankind, which takes the shifting, temporary things of this world for ultimate reality. It also describes the problem of the philosopher, who has looked on the realm of the Ideas through contemplation and who yet has to return to live in this world among the shadows with which his fellow men are content.

PLATO

The Allegory of the Cave

"And now," I said,[1] "let me show in a figure how far our nature is enlightened or unenlightened. Behold! Human beings living in an underground den, which

_____
[1] The speaker is Socrates.

has a mouth open towards the light and reaching all along the den; here they have been from their childhood, and have their legs and necks chained so that they cannot move, and can only see before them, being prevented by the chains from turning round their heads. Above and behind them a fire is blazing at a distance, and between the fire and the prisoners there is a raised way; and you will see, if you look, a low wall built along the way, like the screen which marionette players have in front of them, over which they show the puppets."

"I see."

"And do you see," I said, "men passing along the wall carrying all sorts of vessels, and statues and figures of animals made of wood and stone and various materials, which appear over the wall? Some of them are talking, others silent."

"You have shown me a strange image, and they are strange prisoners."

"Like ourselves," I replied; "and they see only their own shadows, or the shadows of one another, which the fire throws on the opposite wall of the cave?"

"True," he said; "how could they see anything but the shadows if they were never allowed to move their heads?"

"And of the objects which are being carried in like manner they would only see the shadows?"

"Yes," he said.

"And if they were able to converse with one another, would they not suppose that they were naming what was actually before them?"

"Very true."

"And suppose further that the prison had an echo which came from the other side, would they not be sure to fancy when one of the passers-by spoke that the voice which they heard came from the passing shadow?"

"No question," he replied.

"To them," I said, "the truth would be literally nothing but the shadows of the images."

"That is certain."

"And now look again, and see what will naturally follow if the prisoners are released and disabused of their error. At first, when any of them is liberated and compelled suddenly to stand up and turn his neck round and walk and look towards the light, he will suffer sharp pains; the glare will distress him, and he will be unable to see the realities of which in his former state he had seen the shadows; and then conceive someone saying to him that what he saw before was an illusion, but that now, when he is approaching nearer to being and his eye is turned towards more real existence, he has a clearer vision—what will be his reply? And you may further imagine that his instructor is pointing to the objects as they pass and requiring him to name them,—will he not be perplexed? Will he not fancy that the shadows which he formerly saw are truer than the objects which are now shown to him?"

"Far truer."

"And if he is compelled to look straight at the light, will he not have a pain in his eyes which will make him turn away to take refuge in the objects of vision which he can see, and which he will conceive to be in reality clearer than the things which are now being shown to him?" [2]

"True," he said.

"And suppose once more, that he is reluctantly dragged up a steep and rugged ascent, and held fast until he is forced into the presence of the sun himself, is he not likely to be pained and irritated? When he approaches the light his eyes will be dazzled, and he will not be able to see anything at all of what are now called realities."

"Not all in a moment," he said.

"He will require to grow accustomed to the sight of the upper world. And first he will see the shadows best, next the reflections of men and other objects in the water, and then the objects themselves; then he will gaze upon the light of the moon and the stars and the spangled heaven; and he will see the sky and the stars by night better than the sun or the light of the sun by day?"

"Certainly."

"Last of all he will be able to see the sun, and not mere reflections of him in the water, but he will see him in his own proper place, and not in another; and he will contemplate him as he is."

"Certainly."

"He will then proceed to argue that this is he who gives the season and the years, and is the guardian of all that is in the visible world, and in a certain way the cause of all things which he and his fellows have been accustomed to behold?"

"Clearly," he said, "he would first see the sun and then reason about him."

"And when he remembered his old habitation, and the wisdom of the den and his fellow prisoners, do you not suppose that he would felicitate himself on the change, and pity them?"

"Certainly, he would."

"And if they were in the habit of conferring honors among themselves on those who were quickest to observe the passing shadows and to remark which of them went before, and which followed after, and which were together; and who were therefore best able to draw conclusions as to the future, do you think that he would care for such honors and glories, or envy the possessors of them? Would he not say with Homer, 'Better to be the poor servant of a poor master.' and to endure anything, rather than think as they do and live after their manner?"

"Yes," he said, "I think that he would rather suffer anything than entertain these false notions and live in this miserable manner."

"Imagine once more," I said, "such a one coming suddenly out of the sun to be replaced in his old situation;[3] would he not be certain to have his eyes full of darkness?"

"To be sure," he said.

"And if there were a contest, and he had to compete in measuring the shadows with the prisoners who had never moved out of the den, while his sight was still weak, and before his eyes had become steady (and the time which would be needed to acquire this new habit of sight might be very considerable), would he not be ridiculous? Men would say of him that up he went and down he came without his eyes; and that it was better not even to think of ascending; and if any one tried to loose another and lead him up to the light, let them only catch the offender, and they would put him to death."

"No question," he said.

"This entire allegory," I said, "you may now append,

---

[2] He will think the shadows to which he is accustomed more real than the puppets behind him that caused them. The puppets in turn he will find easier to look at than the living creatures in the world of sunlight outside, of which the puppets were but copies.

---

[3] Or "such a one going down again and taking his old position."

dear Glaucon, to the previous argument; the prison house is the world of sight, the light of the fire is the sun, and you will not misapprehend me if you interpret the journey upwards to be the ascent of the soul into the intellectual world according to my poor belief, which, at your desire, I have expressed—whether rightly or wrongly, God knows. But, whether true or false, my opinion is that in the world of knowledge the idea of good appears last of all, and is seen only with an effort; and, when seen, is also inferred to be the universal author of all things beautiful and right, parent of light and of the lord of light in this visible world, and the immediate source of reason and truth in the intellectual; and that this is the power upon which he who would act rationally either in public or private life must have his eye fixed."

"I agree," he said, "as far as I am able to understand you."

"Moreover," I said, "you must not wonder that those who attain to this beatific vision are unwilling to descend to human affairs; for their souls are ever hastening into the upper world where they desire to dwell; which desire of theirs is very natural, if our allegory may be trusted."

"Yes, very natural."

"And is there anything surprising in one who passes from divine contemplations to the evil state of man, misbehaving himself in a ridiculous manner; if, while his eyes are blinking and before he has become accustomed to the surrounding darkness, he is compelled to fight in courts of law, or in other places, about the images or the shadows of images of justice, and is endeavoring to meet the conceptions of those who have never yet seen absolute justice?"

"Anything but surprising," he replied.

"Anyone who has common sense will remember that the bewilderments of the eyes are of two kinds, and arise from two causes, either from coming out of the light or from going into the light, which is true of the mind's eye, quite as much as of the bodily eye; and he who remembers this when he sees anyone whose vision is perplexed and weak, will not be too ready to laugh; he will first ask whether that soul of man has come out of the brighter life, and is unable to see because unaccustomed to the dark, or having turned from darkness to the day is dazzled by excess of light. And he will count the one happy in his condition and

state of being, and he will pity the other; or, if he have a mind to laugh at the soul which comes from below into the light, there will be more reason in this than in the laugh which greets him who returns from above out of the light into the den."

"That," he said, "is a very just distinction."

"But then, if I am right, certain professors of education must be wrong when they say that they can put a knowledge into the soul which was not there before, like sight into blind eyes."

"They undoubtedly say this," he replied.

"Whereas our argument shows that the power and capacity of learning exists in the soul already; and that just as the eye was unable to turn from darkness to light without the whole body, so too the instrument of knowledge can only by the movement of the whole soul be turned from the world of becoming into that of being, and learn by degrees to endure the sight of being, and of the brightest and best of being, or in other words, of the good."

COMMENTS AND QUESTIONS

1. What in fact are the shadows in the cave for Plato?
2. Why does Plato stress the difficulty that the prisoners have in looking at the light of the sun?
3. Why do prisoners receive their returning colleague as they do? What does this tell us of the position of the philosopher in society?
4. In what ways does this allegory attack contemporary Greek education?

The state in *The Republic* is designed to utilize all the elements of culture for the perfection of the souls of both men and women. As opposed to the common Greek attitude toward females, Plato envisaged a basic equality of men and women, at least among the most talented of both sexes. Key aspects in the training of the youth are music and gymnastics. Proper physical exercise and diet not only make the body healthy and beautiful but also encourage the spiritual vigor of the individual. Education in the right kind of music makes the soul of the young person graceful and endows him or her with a true taste for beauty and proportion. With this power of discrimination the individual is able to judge the good and beautiful, the evil and ugly, and, while loving the first, to hate the latter. But neither music nor gymnastics are ends in themselves; in line with the classical ideal of "nothing too much," both must be integrated into the whole life of man and made to enhance the virtues of the soul. (Again the translator is Benjamin Jowett.)

PLATO

On Education

"Neither are the two arts of music and gymnastic really designed, as is often supposed, the one for the training of the soul, the other for the training of the body."

"What then is the real object of them?"

"I believe," I said, "that the teachers of both have in view chiefly the improvement of the soul."

"How can that be?" he asked.

"Did you never observe," I said, "the effect on the mind itself of exclusive devotion to gymnastic, or the opposite effect of an exclusive devotion to music?"

"In what way shown?" he said.

"The one producing a temper of hardness and ferocity, the other of softness and effeminacy," I replied.

"Yes," he said, "I am quite aware that the mere athlete becomes too much of a savage, and that the mere musician is melted and softened beyond what is good for him."

"Yet surely," I said, "this ferocity only comes from spirit, which, if rightly educated, would give courage, but, if too much intensified, is liable to become hard and brutal."

"That I quite think."

"On the other hand, the philosopher will have the quality of gentleness. And this also, when too much indulged, will turn to softness, but, if educated rightly, will be gentle and moderate."

"True."

"And in our opinion the guardians ought to have both these qualities?"

"Assuredly."

"And both should be in harmony?"

"Beyond question."

"And the harmonious soul is both temperate and courageous?"

"Yes."

"And the inharmonious is cowardly and boorish?"

"Very true."

"And, when a man allows music to play upon him and to pour into his soul through the funnel of his ears those sweet and soft and melancholy airs of which we were just now speaking, and his whole life is passed in warbling and the delights of song; in the first stage of the process the passion or spirit which is in him is tempered like iron, and made useful, instead of brittle and useless. But, if he carries on the softening and soothing process, in the next stage he begins to melt and waste, until he has wasted away his spirit and cut out the sinews of his soul; and he becomes a feeble warrior."

"Very true."

"If the element of spirit is naturally weak in him the change is speedily accomplished, but if he have a good deal, then the power of music weakening the spirit renders him excitable;—on the least provocation he flames up at once, and is speedily extinguished; instead of having spirit he grows irritable and passionate and is quite impracticable."

"Exactly."

"And so in gymnastics, if a man takes violent exercise and is a great feeder, and the reverse of a great student of music and philosophy, at first the high condition of his body fills him with pride and spirit, and he becomes twice the man that he was."

"Certainly."

"And what happens? if he do nothing else, and holds no converse with the Muses, does not even that intelligence which there may be in him, having no taste of any sort of learning or inquiry or thought or culture, grow feeble and dull and blind, his mind never waking up or receiving nourishment, and his senses not being purged of their mists?"

"True," he said.

"And he ends by becoming a hater of philosophy, uncivilized, never using the weapon of persuasion—he is like a wild beast, all violence and fierceness, and knows no other way of dealing; and he lives in all ignorance and evil conditions, and has no sense of propriety and grace."

"That is quite true," he said.

"And as there are two principles of human nature, one the spirited and the other the philosophical, some God, as I should say, has given mankind two arts answering to them (and only indirectly to the soul and body), in order that these two principles (like the strings of an instrument) may be relaxed or drawn tighter until they are duly harmonized."

"That appears to be the intention."

"And he who mingles music with gymnastic in the fairest proportions, and best attempers them to the soul, may be rightly called the true musician and harmonist in a far higher sense than the tuner of the strings."

"You are quite right, Socrates."

"And such a presiding genius will be always required in our State if the government is to last."

"Yes, he will be absolutely necessary."

COMMENTS AND QUESTIONS

1. How would Plato judge the physical education department of a large modern American college or university?
2. What opinion would he have of modern American education?
3. Why is music so important for Plato?

The *Phaedo* depicts Socrates' last hours. Having been tried and found guilty for corrupting the youth of Athens, he spends his time in prison philosophizing with his friends, proving to the satisfaction of all that the soul is immortal. He has been sentenced to die by drinking a cup of poison. At sunset, as the appointed hour for the execution approaches, Socrates' friends grow more and more concerned. One of them, Crito, asks, "And in what way shall we bury you?" With characteristic wit, Socrates responds, "In any way that you like; but you must get hold of me, and take care that I do not run away from you." Socrates then chides Crito for not having properly understood his reasoning: man is a soul and not a body. (Again Benjamin Jowett is the translator.)

PLATO

The Death of Socrates

Now the hour of sunset was near, for a good deal of time had passed while he was within. When he came out, he sat down with us again after his bath, but not much was said. Soon the jailer, who was the servant of the Eleven, entered and stood by him, saying:—To you, Socrates, whom I know to be the noblest and gentlest and best of all who ever came to this place, I will not impute the angry feelings of other men, who rage and swear at me, when, in obedience to the authorities, I bid them drink the poison—indeed, I am sure that you will not be angry with me; for others, as you are aware, and not I, are to blame. And so fare you well, and try to bear lightly what must needs be—you know my errand. Then bursting into tears he turned away and went out.

Socrates looked at him and said: I return your good wishes, and will do as you bid. Then turning to us, he said, How charming the man is: since I have been in prison he has always been coming to see me, and at times he would talk to me, and was as good to me as could be, and now see how generously he sorrows on my account. We must do as he says, Crito; and therefore let the cup be brought, if the poison is prepared: if not, let the attendant prepare some.

Yet, said Crito, the sun is still upon the hill-tops, and I know that many a one has taken the draught late, and after the announcement has been made to him, he has eaten and drunk, and enjoyed the society of his beloved; do not hurry—there is time enough.

Socrates said: Yes, Crito, and they of whom you speak are right in so acting, for they think that they will be gainers by the delay; but I am right in not following their example, for I do not think that I should gain anything by drinking the poison a little later; I should only be ridiculous in my own eyes for sparing and saving a life which is already forfeit. Please then to do as I say, and not to refuse me.

Crito made a sign to the servant, who was standing by; and he went out, and having been absent for some time, returned with the jailer carrying the cup of poison. Socrates said: You, my good friend, who are experienced in these matters, shall give me directions how I am to proceed. The man answered: You have only to walk about until your legs are heavy, and then to lie down, and the poison will act. At the same time he handed the cup to Socrates, who in the easiest and gentlest manner, without the least fear or change of colour or feature, looking at the man with all his eyes, Echecrates, as his manner was, took the cup and said: What do you say about making a libation out of this cup to any god? May I, or not? The man answered: We only prepare, Socrates, just so much as we deem enough. I understand, he said: but I may and must ask the gods to prosper my journey from this to the other world—even so—and so be it according to my prayer. Then raising the cup to his lips, quite readily and cheerfully he drank off the poison. And hitherto most of us had been able to control our sorrow; but now when we saw him drinking, and saw too that he had finished the draught, we could no longer forbear, and in spite of myself my own tears were flowing fast; so that I covered my face and wept, not for him, but at the thought of my own calamity in having to part from such a friend. Nor was I the first; for Crito, when he found himself unable to restrain his tears, had got up, and I followed; and at that moment, Apollodorus, who had been weeping all the time, broke out in a loud and passionate cry which made cowards of us all. Socrates alone retained his calmness: What is this strange outcry? he said. I sent away the women mainly in order that they might not misbehave in this way, for I have been told that a man should die in peace. Be quiet then, and have patience. When we heard his words we were ashamed, and refrained our tears; and he walked about until, as he said, his legs began to fail, and then he lay on his back, according to the directions, and the man who gave him the poison now and then looked at his feet and legs; and after a while he pressed his foot hard, and asked him if he could feel; and he said, No; and then his leg, and so upwards and upwards, and showed us that he was cold and stiff. And he felt them himself, and said: When the poison reaches the heart, that will be the end. He was beginning to grow cold about the groin, when he uncovered his face, for he had covered himself up, and said—they were his last words—he said: Crito, I owe a cock to Asclepius; will you remember to pay the debt? The debt shall be paid, said Crito; is there anything else? There was no answer to this question; but in a minute or two a movement was heard, and the attendants uncovered him; his eyes were set, and Crito closed his eyes and mouth.

Such was the end, Echecrates, of our friend; concerning whom I may truly say, that of all the men of his time whom I have known, he was the wisest and justest and best.

QUESTIONS

1. The death of Socrates has served for 2,500 years as the humanistic example of how a man should die. Is it a relevant example for our age?
2. What moral values does Socrates uphold?

Aristotle

For Plato knowledge was essentially *deductive*, that is, it came from within the human mind and was applicable to the world. Man brought his categories of organization to experience. In his later years Plato came increasingly to conceive of the world of the ideas in terms of mathematical relationships. From Plato derives, therefore, the conception that mathematics is the key to understanding nature. By contrast, his student Aristotle (384–322 B.C.) approached the universe not as a mathematician but as a biologist. Knowledge of man and nature in Aristotle's judgment was *inductive*. It was derived by the human intellect from nature itself.

Like Plato, Aristotle requires that knowledge, to be knowledge, must be eternally and immutably true. Accordingly, there can only be knowledge of that which is eternal and unchanging. At the same time, however, Aristotle in his mature work considered Plato's belief in a world of the ideas as nonsense. There are not two levels of reality—the world we know and the world of perfect forms or ideas—there is only one reality. But how is knowledge possible in such a world where all seems in a state of constant change? What in our experience is immutable and eternal when all about us is moving from place to place, being born, dying, becoming bigger or less, changing colors and the like? Aristotle's reply is that there is no need to postulate a world of ideal forms because this needlessly duplicates the forms already in nature. There are in the universe of Aristotle a finite if immense number of different kinds of things, which he calls forms or species. The species are eternal and never change, but they never exist apart from individual members of that species. Each individual member of the species, say of man, carries within himself the form of man-ness that makes him "be" what he is. Individuals of a species differ one from the other (that is, they are individuals) because they differ in their matter. Each is composed of a different mass of bone and flesh. Individual men are born, grow old, and die, but the form or species lives on, passing from generation to generation of men to all eternity. Thus, Aristotle has found the eternal forms *in* the things of this world themselves. We experience them in our encounter with each of the individual representatives of the species. In sense experience my intellect has the power to grasp the eternal form in the individual. When, for example, I see a tree, I know it is a tree because my mind perceives the form of tree-ness in it. Gradually, through experience with different trees, I can develop a knowledge of the various operations of the species; this knowledge will be immutable and eternal because the species in itself never changes. What I learn generally about these trees will be true for all trees.

How does Aristotle explain the cause of change in the universe? Why do streams flow, flowers grow, and the heavenly spheres circle? Each individual thing in the universe for Aristotle moves and changes because it is attempting in this way to realize perfection in its form. Indirectly, however, God is the ultimate cause of all movement. Aristotle sets the earth at the center of the universe, ringing it round with ten revolving spheres. The innermost sphere takes the moon around the earth, the next the sun, and so on, moving outward for each of the planets until we reach the tenth sphere, which holds the fixed stars. Beyond that sphere lies God. Aristotle's God is perfect mind who exists eternally thinking only of Himself and absolutely motionless. He knows nothing of the universe below Him. Like Him, the universe with its species is eternal. He did not create them. His only relationship to the universe is that all objects on earth and in heaven are attracted to Him and attempt to imitate His perfection by being themselves perfect. In order to do so, they must undergo change. He is perfect and therefore unmoving. The individual members of the countless species of things must constantly strive to perfect their particular species in themselves; thus, they move. Aristotle's God, consequently, is not a creator god but the underlying cause of all universal motion through the attraction He exerts for them.

What is the nature of man and his destiny in such a universe? Whereas everything in the universe consists of matter and form, in living things the form is called a soul. Plants and animals have souls, but not as complex as those of human beings. Man, as opposed to all other living things, has the power to know truth. He is endowed with a mind that can grasp the forms of things and can develop a body of knowledge about nature through reasoning and observation. On the basis of the axiom "like alone can know like," does the fact that the human mind can know the eternal form found in individual members of a species mean that man's soul as opposed to the other living souls is immortal? Although we cannot be certain, Aristotle seems to reject personal immortality. The part of the human mind that grasps the forms in the things is specifically designated as immortal, but Aristotle describes it in such a way that it does not really belong to us individually and that, while the personal elements of our soul perish at death, it departs from us. Thus, men—like every other thing on earth—bear the species for their time; and, as this generation passes away, another rises to replace it.

If there is no afterlife for the human being, what is the nature of happiness? Aristotle replies: Man's happiness lies in the perfection of his form as man. Man's distinctive characteristic is that he is a rational animal; therefore, his highest good lies in perfecting his reason. Such perfection occurs in two areas. First of all, man must control his life through reason. Such a life is a virtuous life. Honesty, courage, temperance, and the like are virtues; they are different aspects of the behavior of a rational man. The second area in which reason must be perfected in order to obtain happiness is in the intellectual sphere. Since the human reason has a capacity to learn the truth, the rational man must study the sciences, mathematics, and divine things if he is to fulfill his nature. Aristotle himself, following his inductive method of investigation, produced an immense number of works devoted to the widest range of subjects, including botany, zoology, astronomy, physics, rhetoric, psychology, physiology, and political science.

But the attainment of moral and intellectual virtues is not sufficient to create happiness. Aristotle willingly acknowledged that even the virtuous man could not be happy if he was poor and sick. Accordingly, Aristotle maintained that while virtue was the highest good for happiness, man needed both health and a degree of wealth in order to reach his end. The demands placed on the individual by this kind of ethic were obviously not overly rigorous and could easily be met by the upper class of the Greek polis.

While differing from Plato on the place of the forms and on the immortality of the human soul among other things, Aristotle was in complete agreement with the older man who had once been his teacher on the close relationship between ethics and politics. For Aristotle, as for Plato, the state was man written large. Man was only an animal outside the state; only through the state could he attain moral and intellectual perfection. But whereas for Plato the best form of government was a monarchy ruled by a philosopher king, Aristotle, rejecting what he considered Plato's purely theoretical approach, opted for republican government as the best form of government in the world as it was. Through participation in the political life of his state, the citizen could maximize his power and talents, thereby finding happiness.

Aristotle's discussion of the true gentleman presents the philosopher's ideal of the happy man in some detail. Virtue for Aristotle was fundamentally a mean between two extremes. Self-esteem was a mean between arrogance and humility. Generosity held the middle place between spendthriftiness and stinginess. The other virtues are similarly defined. Obviously again the classical ideal of balance, "nothing too much," is at work in Aristotle's ethics. The true gentleman must most of all cultivate the virtue of prudence: the ability to measure each situation and to determine the correct course of action. He must be able to establish the correct middle course for appropriate action. The resultant picture of the gentleman is very different from that of the later Christian ideal. We are clearly dealing with a member of the upper classes, affluent, confident, calculating, and disdainful of members of the lower classes, who have no hope of matching his standards of conduct. This selection from *Nicomachean Ethics* is translated by F. H. Peters.

ARISTOTLE

The High-Minded Man

High-mindedness would seem from its very name to have to do with great things; let us first ascertain what these are.

It will make no difference whether we consider the quality itself, or the man who exhibits the quality.

By a high-minded man we seem to mean one who claims much and deserves much: for he who claims much without deserving it is a fool; but the possessor of a virtue is never foolish or silly. The man we have described, then, is high-minded.

He who deserves little and claims little is temperate [or modest], but not high-minded: for high-mindedness [or greatness of soul] implies greatness, just as beauty implies stature; small men may be neat and well proportioned, but cannot be called beautiful.

He who claims much without deserving it is vain (though not every one who claims more than he deserves is vain).

He who claims less than he deserves is little-minded, whether his deserts be great or moderate, or whether they be small and he claims still less: but this little-mindedness is most conspicuous in him whose deserts are great; for what would he do if his deserts were less than they are?

The high-minded man, then, in respect of the greatness of his deserts occupies an extreme position, but in that he behaves as he ought, observes the mean; for he claims that which he deserves, while all the others claim too much or too little.

But now if he deserves much and claims much, and most of all deserves and claims the greatest things, there will be one thing with which he will be especially concerned. For desert has reference to external good things. Now, the greatest of external good things we may assume to be that which we render to the Gods as their due, and that which people in high stations most desire, and which is the prize appointed for the noblest deeds. But the thing that answers to this description is honour, which, we may safely say, is the greatest of all external goods. Honours and dishonours, therefore, are the field in which the high-minded man behaves as he ought.

And indeed we may see, without going about to prove it, that honour is what high-minded men are concerned with; for it is honour that great men claim and deserve.

The little-minded man falls short, whether we compare his claims with his own deserts or with what the high-minded man claims for himself.

The vain or conceited man exceeds what is due to himself, though he does not exceed the high-minded man in his claims.

But the high-minded man, as he deserves the greatest

things, must be a perfectly good or excellent man; for the better man always deserves the greatest things, and the best possible man the greatest possible things. The really high-minded man, therefore, must be a good or excellent man. And indeed greatness in every virtue or excellence would seem to be necessarily implied in being a high-minded or great-souled man.

It would be equally inconsistent with the high-minded man's character to run along swinging his arms, and to commit an act of injustice; for what thing is there for love of which he would do anything unseemly, seeing that all things are of little account to him? . . .

. . . the gifts of fortune also are commonly thought to contribute to high-mindedness. For those who are well born are thought worthy of honour, and those who are powerful or wealthy; for they are in a position of superiority, and that which is superior in any good thing is always held in greater honour. And so these things do make people more high-minded in a sense; for such people find honour from some. But in strictness it is only the good man that is worthy of honour, though he that has both goodness and good fortune is commonly thought to be more worthy of honour. Those, however, who have these good things without virtue, neither have any just claim to great things, nor are properly to be called high-minded, for neither is possible without complete virtue.

The high-minded man is not quick to run into petty dangers, and indeed does not love danger, since there are few things that he much values; but he is ready to incur a great danger, and whenever he does so is unsparing of his life, as a thing that is not worth keeping at all costs.

It is his nature to confer benefits, but he is ashamed to receive them; for the former is the part of a superior, the latter of an inferior. And when he has received a benefit, he is apt to confer a greater in return; for thus his creditor will become his debtor and be in the position of a recipient of his favour.

It is thought, moreover, that such men remember those on whom they have conferred favours better than those from whom they have received them; for the recipient of a benefit is inferior to the benefactor, but such a man wishes to be in the position of a superior. So he likes to be reminded of the one, but dislikes to be reminded of the other. . . .

It is characteristic of the high-minded man, again never or reluctantly to ask favours, but to be ready to confer them, and to be lofty in his behaviour to those who are high in station and favoured by fortune, but affable to those of the middle ranks; for it is a difficult thing and a dignified thing to assert superiority over the former, but easy to assert it over the latter. A haughty demeanour in dealing with the great is quite consistent with good breeding, but in dealing with those of low estate is brutal, like showing off one's strength upon a cripple.

Another of his characteristics is not to rush in wherever honour is to be won, nor to go where others take the lead, but to hold aloof and to shun an enterprise, except when great honour is to be gained, or a great work is to be done—not to do many things, but great things and notable.

Again, he must be open in his hate and in his love; for concealment shows fear.

He must care for truth more than for what men will think of him, and speak and act openly; he will not hesitate to say all that he thinks, as he looks down upon mankind. So he will speak the truth, except when he speaks ironically; and irony he will employ in speaking to the generality of men.

Another of his characteristics is that he cannot fashion his life to suit another, except he be a friend, for that is servile: and so all flatterers or hangers on of great men are of a slavish nature, and men of low natures become flatterers.

Nor is he easily moved to admiration; for nothing is great to him.

He readily forgets injuries; for it is not consistent with his character to brood on the past, especially on past injuries, but rather to overlook them.

He is no gossip; he will neither talk about himself nor about others; for he cares not that men should praise him, nor that others should be blamed (though, on the other hand, he is not very ready to bestow praise); and so he is not apt to speak evil of others, not even of his enemies, except with the express purpose of giving offence.

When an event happens that cannot be helped or is of slight importance, he is the last man in the world to cry out or to beg for help; for that is the conduct of a man who thinks these events very important.

He loves to possess beautiful things that bring no

profit, rather than useful things that pay; for this is characteristic of the man whose resources are in himself.

Further, the character of the high-minded man seems to require that his gait should be slow, his voice deep, his speech measured; for a man is not likely to be in a hurry when there are few things in which he is deeply interested, nor excited when he holds nothing to be of very great importance: and these are the causes of a high voice and rapid movements.

This, then, is the character of the high-minded man.

But he that is deficient in this quality is called little-minded; he that exceeds, vain or conceited.

QUESTIONS

1. Would you like to have this man for a friend?
2. How would a Christian criticize this ideal?
3. What information about Greek social structure does this passage give us?

While Aristotle wrote extensively concerning the ideal man, he ignored the matter of the ideal woman. Reflecting the prejudices of his society, Aristotle thought woman to be naturally inferior to man and not worthy of special analysis. In a treatise entitled "On the Generation of Animals," Aristotle writes that a female was simply a failed male. Nature in producing human beings aims at making a male offspring, but when the process is defective, a female is the result. Because the woman by nature is colder than the man, girls are usually born when the father is either young or old, that is, when he has not yet reached the heat of maturity or when past that point. This view of man as the most perfect creature in nature and of woman as a defective or second-rate man was to have long-range repercussions in Western culture. We will discuss some of them in the section on the Middle Ages. Yet one should not conclude that the ancient Greeks ignored women altogether in their view of "man." The goddesses in Greek mythology, the ideal female form in sculpture, and characters such as Lysistrata in comedy and Antigone in tragedy attest to the contrary. Plato, as we mentioned, envisaged equality between superior men and women in *The Republic*. And yet Aristotle's view was widely accepted. We might conclude that the Greeks initiated in Western culture complicated and contradictory values with which we are still grappling.

5
THE CULTURE OF ROME

Hellenistic and Roman History and Thought

Hellenistic Empires Already before the deaths of Plato and Aristotle, their political philosophies, assuming as they did the existence of the independent city-state, were becoming out of date. Athens was conquered by Sparta in 404 B.C., and for about thirty years Sparta controlled the leadership of the Greek city-state system. Sparta, however, was neither intellectually suited nor powerful enough to carry such a burden, and in 371 B.C. the Spartans were defeated by the Thebans, who in turn became the leading military force in Greece. But the Greek city-states were so isolated and divided by rivalries that they fell easy prey to the armies of Philip II of Macedon, a kingdom in the northern part of the Aegean peninsula. By 338 B.C. almost all Greece was under Philip's control, and, when he died in 336 B.C., his place was taken by his son Alexander (356–323 B.C.). With

Alexander, the West took the offensive against the East. The armies of Macedon and Greece invaded and conquered the Persian empire, and Greek rule was established in the Near East and Egypt. Educated in the ideas of Greek culture partially instilled in him by Aristotle, who acted as his tutor for a time, Alexander diffused the civilization and language of Greece wherever his armies went (see map).

In the process Greek culture became more cosmopolitan and sophisticated while remaining essentially Greek. Because of these modifications, however, the age beginning with Alexander is referred to as Greeklike, or Hellenistic. The dramatic power of the frieze for the Pergamon altar and the graceful nudity of the Cnidian *Aphrodite* are examples of the expansion and transformation of Greek art. In philosophy, in contrast to the wide-ranging interest of earlier thinkers, there was a tendency toward specialization. Euclid produced his masterful geometrical treatise, *The Elements*; Archimedes did basic work in statistics and hydrostatics; great advances were also made in biology, astronomy, geography, and city planning.

The expansion of the frontiers of Greek culture, moreover, had a dissolving effect on the political and cultural shell around the individual created by the polis. Individuals came increasingly to live on their own. They found themselves in a larger, more international community than the one they had known. However, freedom from the encompassing pressures of the integrated life of the polis made people uneasy. Eastern religions extending hope of personal immortality became popular. These cults often centered on a suffering god, who through his earthly death extended to his worshipers the hope of everlasting life. People in the Hellenistic empire also turned to philosophies focusing on the ethical conduct of the individual and providing a vision of political association more adapted to a period of world empire. These philosophies themselves gradually became more religious in nature.

Stoicism   Among the variety of new philosophical movements rising at the end of the fourth century, the one with the greatest future was Stoicism. First taught by Zeno (322–264 B.C.) at Athens, the Stoic doctrine taught that the principle of the world was reason. Reason was a divine essence that lay behind everything oc-

curring in the universe and was the ultimate cause of all that happened. Man was a rational creature whose soul, moreover, was a particle of that Divine Reason. Thus, all men were equal, one to the other, because each, whether slave or free, was a particle of the same divine substance. The Divine Reason operated according to certain laws. If man carefully examined his conscience, he would see in himself, as a particle of Divine Reason, the same laws. Every man, moreover, if he submitted himself to an honest examination, would produce the same conclusions: that it was wrong to kill, to steal, to hurt another human being. Thus, for the Stoic at the basis of every human mind lay the same principle of ethical action, a natural law, which was common to World Reason and the individual reason of man. What better kind of philosophy was there for a world state?

What of human happiness? Since the cause of the world was pure reason, everything had to happen for the best. Divine Reason was not a cold indifferent force but rather a providential goodness that aimed for the good of the whole. Man must learn to accept this external world as it is. The individual should not regret failures and lose control in times of success. Rather the individual must welcome everything calmly. To do so was to put oneself in accord with the World Reason and to follow one's own nature, which was essentially reason. Furthermore, because the principle of Divine Reason was beneficent, so the individual, truly following his own nature, would also be a force for good in the world and especially for other men. This doctrine gave a strong social direction to the followers of the school.

The early doctrine of the Stoics pictured the ethical ideal as apathy, indifference to all that was not concerned with virtue. The wise man was to do his duty regardless of the personal costs. Other "goods" of the soul, health and wealth (which for Aristotle were necessary for happiness), were irrelevant for the Stoic. Nor did the Stoic expect an eternal reward. At death the individual human soul of good and evil men alike would fall back into the reservoir of Divine Reason whence it came. With the centuries, however, Stoicism became less harsh, more reconciled to human weaknesses. By the first century B.C. adherents of the school rejected the ideal of apathy as inhuman and admitted that, if

Extent of the Empire
(and Dependent States)
→ Alexander's Route, 334-325 B.C.

not "goods," health and wealth were nonetheless useful for happiness. Increasingly Stoics also came to believe in some kind of personal immortality of the human soul even though it was difficult to reconcile that belief with the general structure of their thought.

The Rise of Rome   The great Macedonian empire of Alexander was unstable. When, after his death in 323, it was divided among his generals, disintegration set in. Throughout most of the third century B.C. a power vacuum existed in the Mediterranean area. By the beginning of the second century B.C. Rome gradually came to fill it. Founded sometime in the eighth century B.C. (the mythical date is 753 B.C.), Rome developed slowly. Only after five hundred years—after numerous wars and a series of annexation and treaty agreements—did Rome finally become mistress of Italy, around 260 B.C. But from there Roman frontiers expanded quickly. The Romans first expanded toward the south and west to Sicily and Spain, bringing themselves into conflict with Carthage, the great maritime power on the northern coast of Africa. They then moved toward the east, where by the mid-second century they had destroyed the kingdom of Macedon and annexed Greece as the province of Achaia. By 100 B.C. Rome was for all practical purposes mistress of the Mediterranean.

In the following century and a half the major interest of the state was to push back the frontiers from the coasts of the inland sea. On the east Rome expanded into Arabia, the Levant, and Persian territory; on the south into the deserts of North Africa and Egypt; on the north into southern Germany and southern Russia; while Roman legions from Gaul invaded and conquered England. At the height of its empire in the century after Christ, Rome controlled most of Western Europe, the Middle East, and North Africa. To the north stretched the German forests, to the east the decaying Persian empire, to the south the deserts of Africa, and to the west Ireland and the ocean (see map, p. 109).

Italy, like Greece, had an area where political power was divided among numerous little city-states. Rome had been only one of a number in central Italy; and, as the city expanded its authority, Rome merely absorbed one city-state after another. In its subsequent expansion outside of Italy, Rome followed very much the same policy of preserving the city-states as the local center of government; where no such organization existed, Rome created the city-state afresh. By the first century B.C. the Roman empire consisted of a grouping of dependent city-states into provinces, the governors of which were officials sent out from the city council (called the Senate) of the supreme city-state, Rome.

The ancient Romans, unlike the Greeks, were not given to speculation and abstract thinking. They were a practical people, religiously tolerant, ferocious fighters, and devoutly patriotic. But they proved themselves very adaptable. If initially Romans conquered Greece, they in their turn were conquered by Greek culture. Especially attractive to the Romans, now moving to a position of ruling a good portion of the world, was the philosophy of Stoicism, with its stern insistence on duty. The Stoic conception of man as a particle of Divine Reason, moreover, provided the Romans with just the sort of theoretical background for a legal system designed to integrate the disparate territories of the world state.

Roman Law   The Roman world, consisting of myriads of city-states, big and little kingdoms, was a legal nightmare. Each of these areas had its own law code, and the task of the conqueror was to develop some kind of legal system that would provide justice for the whole. From at least the first century B.C. on, Roman jurists began transforming the Stoic conception of a natural law present in the consciousness of all men into practical forms. This task took centuries, and the final codification of Roman law was not finished until centuries after the Roman empire in the west had fallen to the barbarians. While allowing each of the city-states to keep its own peculiar set of laws, the Roman state in matters of basic law and procedure forced all parts of its territory from England to Asia to follow the principles of the law of nations, the *jus gentium*, those principles of justice derived by Roman jurists and statesmen from the abstract natural law found in man's consciousness.

With time, following Rome's example, the individual city-states in other than basic principles of law tended as well to follow the law of Rome.

Cicero   Perhaps the most eloquent testimony to the faith in the essential equality of all men is found in the writings of the great Roman writer and statesman Marcus Tullius Cicero (106–43 B.C.). Besides being the most gifted orator of his day, Cicero also translated the terminology and ideas of Greek philosophers into Latin and composed numerous philosophical works of his own. Although skeptical of creating the vast systems of thought found in much of Greek philosophy, Cicero was vitally concerned with moral or ethical philosophy. He fervently believed that the eloquence of the orator, joined with moral philosophy, could have a tremendously positive effect on the hearts and minds of men. In a series of books devoted primarily to ethics and politics, *On Duties, On the Republic,* and *On the Laws,* he captured the Stoics' cosmopolitan vision of mankind, utilizing their conception of natural law as the background against which to judge the legal institutions and customs of his world. The selection from *On the Laws,* translated by Clinton Walker Keyes, concerns the nature of justice. Cicero (M) is the major speaker of the dialogue. His friend Atticus (A) is the other. Against the argument that the law is a matter of convenience and custom, Cicero maintains that it is rooted in the consciences of all mankind.

CICERO

On the Laws

M. . . . that animal which we call man, endowed with foresight and quick intelligence, complex, keen, possessing memory, full of reason and prudence, has been given a certain distinguished status by the supreme God who created him; for he is the only one among so many different kinds and varieties of living beings who has a share in reason and thought, while all the rest are deprived of it. But what is more divine, I will not say in man only, but in all heaven and earth, than reason? And reason, when it is full grown and perfected, is rightly called wisdom. Therefore, since there is nothing better than reason, and since it exists both in

THE ROMAN EMPIRE

man and God, the first common possession of man and God is reason. But those who have reason in common must also have right reason in common. And since right reason is Law, we must believe that men have Law also in common with the gods. Further, those who share Law must also share Justice; and those who share these are to be regarded as members of the same commonwealth. If indeed they obey the same authorities and powers, this is true in a far greater degree; but as a matter of fact they do obey this celestial system, the divine mind, and the God of transcendent power. Hence we must now conceive of this whole universe as one commonwealth of which both gods and men are members.

And just as in States distinctions in legal status are made on account of the blood relationships of families, according to a system which I shall take up in its proper place, so in the universe the same thing holds true, but on a scale much vaster and more splendid, so that men are grouped with Gods on the basis of blood relationship and descent. For when the nature of man is examined, the theory is usually advanced (and in all probability it is correct) that through constant changes and revolutions in the heavens, a time came which was suitable for sowing the seed of the human race. And when this seed was scattered and sown over the earth, it was granted the divine gift of the soul. For while the other elements of which man consists were derived from what is mortal, and are therefore fragile and perishable, the soul was generated in us by God. Hence we are justified in saying that there is a blood relationship between ourselves and the celestial beings; or we may call it a common ancestry or origin. Therefore among all the varieties of living beings, there is no creature except man which has any knowledge of God, and among men themselves there is no race either so highly civilized or so savage as not to know that it must believe in a god, even if it does not know in what sort of god it ought to believe. Thus it is clear that man recognizes God because, in a way, he remembers and recognizes the source from which he sprang.

Moreover, virtue exists in man and God alike, but in no other creature besides; virtue, however, is nothing else than Nature perfected and developed to its highest point; therefore there is a likeness between man and God. As this is true, what relationship could be closer or clearer than this one? For this reason, Nature has lavishly yielded such a wealth of things adapted to man's convenience and use that what she produces seems intended as a gift to us, and not brought forth by chance; and this is true, not only of what the fertile earth bountifully bestows in the form of grain and fruit, but also of the animals; for it is clear that some of them have been created to be man's slaves, some to supply him with their products, and others to serve as his food. Moreover innumerable arts have been discovered through the teachings of Nature; for it is by a skilful imitation of her that reason has acquired the necessities of life. Nature has likewise not only equipped man himself with nimbleness of thought, but has also given him the senses, to be, as it were, his attendants and messengers; she has laid bare the obscure and none too [obvious] meanings of a great many things, to serve as the foundations of knowledge, as we may call them; and she has granted us a bodily form which is convenient and well suited to the human mind. For while she has bent the other creatures down toward their food, she has made man alone erect, and has challenged him to look up toward heaven, as being, so to speak, akin to him, and his first home. In addition, she has so formed his features as to portray therein the character that lies hidden deep within him; for not only do the eyes declare with exceeding clearness the innermost feelings of our hearts, but also the countenance, as we Romans call it, which can be found in no living thing save man, reveals the character. (The Greeks are familiar with the meaning which this word "countenance" conveys,

though they have no name for it.) I will pass over the special faculties and aptitudes of the other parts of the body, such as the varying tones of the voice and the power of speech, which is the most effective promoter of human intercourse; for all these things are not in keeping with our present discussion or the time at our disposal; and besides, this topic has been adequately treated, as it seems to me, by Scipio in the books which you have read. But, whereas God has begotten and equipped man, desiring him to be the chief of all created things, it should now be evident, without going into all the details, that Nature, alone and unaided, goes a step farther; for, with no guide to point the way, she starts with those things whose character she has learned through the rudimentary beginnings of intelligence, and, alone and unaided, strengthens and perfects the faculty of reason.

A. Ye immortal gods, how far back you go to find the origins of Justice! And you discourse so eloquently that I not only have no desire to hasten on to the consideration of the civil law, concerning which I was expecting you to speak, but I should have no objection to your spending even the entire day on your present topic; for the matters which you have taken up, no doubt, merely as preparatory to another subject, are of greater import than the subject itself to which they form an introduction.

M. The points which are now being briefly touched upon are certainly important; but out of all the material of the philosophers' discussions, surely there comes nothing more valuable than the full realization that we are born for Justice, and that right is based, not upon men's opinions, but upon Nature. This fact will immediately be plain if you once get a clear conception of man's fellowship and union with his fellow-men. For no single thing is so like another, so exactly its counterpart, as all of us are to one another. Nay, if bad habits and false beliefs did not twist the weaker minds and turn them in whatever direction they are inclined, no one would be so like his own self as all men would be like all others. And so, however we may define man, a single definition will apply to all. This is a sufficient proof that there is no difference in kind between man and man; for if there were, one definition could not be applicable to all men; and indeed reason, which alone raises us above the level of the beasts and enables us to draw inferences, to prove and disprove, to discuss and solve problems, and to come to conclusions, is certainly common to us all, and, though varying in what it learns, at least in the capacity to learn it is invariable. For the same things are invariably perceived by the senses, and those things which stimulate the senses, stimulate them in the same way in all men; and those rudimentary beginnings of intelligence to which I have referred, which are imprinted on our minds, are imprinted on all minds alike; and speech, the mind's interpreter, though differing in the choice of words, agrees in the sentiments expressed. In fact, there is no human being of any race who, if he finds a guide, cannot attain to virtue.

The similarity of the human race is clearly marked in its evil tendencies as well as in its goodness. For pleasure also attracts all men; and even though it is an enticement to vice, yet it has some likeness to what is naturally good. For it delights us by its lightness and agreeableness; and for this reason, by an error of thought, it is embraced as something wholesome. It is through a similar misconception that we shun death as though it were a dissolution of nature, and cling to life because it keeps us in the sphere in which we were born; and that we look upon pain as one of the greatest of evils, not only because of its cruelty, but also because it seems to lead to the destruction of nature. In the same way, on account of the similarity between moral worth and renown, those who are publicly honoured are considered happy, while those who do not attain fame are thought miserable. Troubles, joys, desires, and fears haunt the minds of all men without distinction, and even if different men have different beliefs, that does not prove, for example, that it is not the same quality of superstition that besets those races which worship dogs and cats as gods, as that which torments other races. But what nation does not love courtesy, kindliness, gratitude, and remembrance of favours bestowed? What people does not hate and despise the haughty, the wicked, the cruel, and the ungrateful? Inasmuch as these considerations prove to us that the whole human race is bound together in unity, it follows, finally, that knowledge of the principles of right living is what makes men better.

QUESTIONS

1. What does Cicero mean by Law?
2. What effect would this belief have on one's approach to law and custom?
3. What is the basis of the natural equality of man?

Intimately connected with the theme of justice in this passage is that of the dignity of man, who, in his possession of consciousness of the law, is akin to the gods. Cicero, like the ancient philosophers before him, looked on the human predicament as essentially one of ignorance. In Cicero's case, man was divine but had lowered himself by his commitment to the passions. The salvation of the individual lay in becoming aware of one's true nature and of training oneself to conform with the commandments of reason. Thus, as for Plato, Aristotle, and the Stoics, human happiness was within man's grasp. The task of the philosopher was to educate individuals in the truth; the rest was up to them.

The Question of Slavery   Despite what might appear as the revolutionary tendencies of these doctrines of the basic equality of men and their common human dignity, neither Cicero nor his Stoic predecessors intended them to be attacks on the institution of slavery in their society. As opposed to Plato and Aristotle—who generally considered the state to be natural to man and political life to be the means by which the individual realizes his humanity—these later thinkers maintained that the state was a creation brought into being to meet the needs of men who were already human beings. By the time of Cicero it was widely believed that mankind had originally existed in a state of nature without formal government. Without property and forced subjection men had led lives of peace and harmony. At some point when this tranquility was disrupted by passion, the state was instituted as a means for restoring peace. Both slavery and property were essential ingredients of the new order. Thus, while slavery was not natural, it was a necessary institution designed to fit a corrupted human nature and was consequently legitimate. The only practical corollary of the doctrines of equality and human dignity in regard to the institution of slavery itself was the admonition to masters to be humane with their chattels and to treat them more as hired workers than as possessions.

From Republic to Empire   While Stoic beliefs continued to dominate the mentality of the Roman upper class in the centuries immediately after Cicero, the nature of Roman government was significantly altered at the center. By the first century B.C. Rome's republican institutions were breaking down under the pressure of groups of men competing for power in the state. Cicero struggled valiantly to preserve the old republican traditions, but in his lifetime he saw a number of individuals emerge briefly as de facto rulers of Rome. Had Julius Caesar (100–44 B.C.) not been assassinated, it seems likely that he eventually would have imposed himself on the state as its official master. As it was, after Caesar was murdered in 44 B.C., Rome had to suffer almost two decades of civil war before his nephew Octavius (whose title was Augustus Caesar) succeeded in establishing his authority.

Augustus Caesar   Although Augustus was designated as *imperator* among other titles, *imperator* merely meant that he was leader of the army. The title *princeps* ("foremost") best describes his place in the state. He was the first citizen of Rome. He had no wish to become a despot and honestly endeavored to restore the old republican institutions, especially the Senate, to a position of power and honor. In his own hands were concentrated the direction of the army and control over most state finance. He also directly appointed governors to a number of provinces. On the other hand, all public business was debated by the Senate, the *princeps* frequently consulted the Senate on policy, and the senators ruled over a number of provinces and held high positions in both the army and imperial civil service. Although gradually over the next two hundred years, the *princeps* assumed more power at the expense of the Senate, he usually tried to maintain at least the trappings of the republican institutions.

With the establishment of the Principate, the empire remained, as before, organized around hundreds of cities with the territory attached to them; it stayed so to the end of the imperial period, but now for the first time there was a truly unified authority at the center. In the last century of the Republic the Roman Senators sent out as governors of the provinces had often treated their charges as a means for self-enrichment. With Augustus and his successors the provincials felt that there was an overseer in the capital to whom they could appeal for justice. While a number of the emperors like Caligula and Nero were probably madmen, on the whole the provinces saw their general condition improve with the Principate. The Roman world, moreover, was tired of years of civil war and longed for peace. With Augustus' assumption of power as *princeps* began a two-hundred-year period of peace, the *Pax Romana*, which Gibbon, the eighteenth-century author of *The Decline and Fall of the Roman Empire*, characterized as "perhaps the happiest period in the history of the human race."

Roman Art and Architecture

The practical, orderly aspects of Roman life are reflected in Roman art and architecture. Although they adopted Greek forms and techniques, the Romans used their statues and buildings not primarily in pursuit of ideal beauty but to proclaim the Roman system to the world.

Roman Sculpture   A bronze from the first century B.C., called the *Arringatore (The Orator)*, presents a man who may have been a Roman official (Fig. 5-1). He stands before us as he might have stood in the forum any day of the week. His stance is simple and straightforward, as is the rendering of his features; here is a particular person, a physiognomy that could belong to no one but himself. He is not an ideal politician of any sort.

The realism that we see in *The Orator* is also evident in the many surviving portrait busts and heads. The Greeks did not accept the idea of portrait busts or heads, feeling that these detached objects were too reminiscent of a decapitated body. The Romans instituted the practice of taking portrait masks of the deceased, which were preserved at home and brought out for ceremonies. The patrician families sought to preserve their family's identity from generation to generation in this way.

By the time of Augustus the Romans had absorbed much from the Greek artists. Nevertheless, it is the combination of realism and the imperial ideal that makes distinctive portraits.

We know Augustus Caesar from statues, coins, and gems. As emperor he was priest-king, military leader, and ruler. It was important that he be represented in all the facets of his power not only to secure it for himself but also to make it legitimate. The statue of Augustus found at the imperial villa of Prima Porta is an excellent example of the military type of portrait (Fig. 5-2). Dressed in very decorative armor but without boots (therefore probably made after his death when he had been made a god and did not need boots), he stands alert but at ease, addressing his troops. The features are distinctively those of the emperor, virile and youthful. He has been ennobled and idealized by the absence of age, flaws, or any of the other makings of a fallible human. Compare the statue with *The Spearbearer* and *The Orator*. What has been taken from each, and what has been left behind in this effort to present Augustus, Imperator?

The *Ara Pacis Augustae*, (the Altar of the Peace of Augustus) probably begun in 13 B.C., was made to commemorate the peace brought about by the imperial might of Rome (Fig. 5-3). It is useful to compare it with the frieze of the Panathenaic festival (Fig. 2-9). At first sight it recalls the frieze, but there are subtle differences. First, the Greek procession is presented as an institutionalized event without regard to the particular individuals who participate. The *Ara Pacis* commemorates one specific historic moment—the moment when the altar was begun. Second, the figures of the *Ara Pacis* are more closely crowded together, as if they had indeed just gathered, giving them an air of immediacy and realism absent in the formal rhythms of the Parthenon frieze. Concentration is not directed toward the focal event but on the interaction between those who make up the event. This frieze has a false calm that seems comparable to the nobility and wisdom that overlay the ruthless Augustus. It was power and decisiveness that made the empire.

5–1   Right: Arringatore (The Orator). (Archaeological Museum, Florence—Alinari/ Editorial Photocolor Archives)

5–2   Far right: Augustus of Prima Porta. (Vatican Museum, Rome—Alinari/ Editorial Photocolor Archives)

5–3   Ara Pacis Augustae, Rome. Imperial Procession. (Alinari/Editorial Photocolor Archives)

In the reliefs of *The Spoils from the Temple at Jerusalem* (Fig. 5-4) on the Arch of Titus, we confront an almost reportorial scene of victory. The conquering Romans return to the city with captives and treasure, including the great, sacred menorah (seven-branched candelabra) from the temple. The sculpture is carved in low relief, and the space is filled with people and objects. This somewhat crowded quality gives the relief an air of urgency and energy that seems to symbolize the power of Rome. This is not myth or allegory but the direct reality of success. To the Roman mind this record of victory will ensure an immortality of which no divinity is capable. No Athenian of the fifth century would have dared to so memorialize himself.

Roman Architecture   As the Romans learned from the Greeks, so they also learned from other tribes and nations. Their system of building probably came from the Etruscans, a powerful tribe that lived in the peninsula until they were conquered by the Romans. To wall and post and lintel the Etruscans and then the Romans added the arch as a major building technique. It was not that arches were unknown before; it is simply that the Romans put them to multiple and innovating uses.

As a building system the true arch is a combination of *pier* (post) and a semicircle of material that replaces the *lintel* (Fig. 5-5). The arch itself is made of stones or bricks cut to fit so that they help hold each other in place. Erecting an arch requires a wooden scaffold with an arch-shaped top called a *centering*. This supports the arch while all the sections are being put into place. When the last top, center stone, the *keystone*, is inserted, the centering can be moved to the next arch. The diagram shows how an arch exerts pressure out-

5–4   Arch of Titus, Rome. The Spoils from the Temple at Jerusalem. (Alinari/Editorial Photocolor Archives)

ward and downward, necessitating pressure at those points to keep it from falling apart.

A series of arches produces a *barrel vault*. The weight of the vault rests equally along the wall. When two barrel vaults intersect at right angles, a *groin vault* results (Fig. 5-5); the weight of the vault then rests on the corner piers instead of along the wall, which can then be opened up for doors and windows. An arch rotated in space 360 degrees produces a *dome*. Like a barrel vault, a dome's weight rests equally on the wall, which is its circumference.

To this potentially very rich collection of forms, the Romans added a much cheaper, faster means of building—brick and rubble masonry fill. To make this, a sticky liquid mass is poured into a form in which small rocks, gravel, and stones are introduced to give greater density and strength. When dried, the surface is covered with plaster or a thin layer of marble or granite called a *veneer*.

The types of building that assumed great importance in Rome are not the same as those which were important for fifth-century Athens. When we think of Athens, we see the great Acropolian complex of sacred buildings towering over the city. The Roman city seems more of a piece, less divided between sacred and secular. The Romans were among the first to develop city planning on an extensive basis, and their methods of planning are in themselves a significant guide to their values.

If we had a Roman town or city perfectly planned and preserved, we would see first that the city itself was a rectangle, bounded by walls and traversed by major streets at right angles to each other (Fig. 5-6). These major streets were oriented to the cardinal points of the compass and traversed by other streets, also at exact right angles: this formed a grid pattern of city blocks, which were assigned different functions for living, markets, and areas of entertainment. The town would be

5-5a Roman Arch

5-5b Action of Forces in Arch

5-5c Barrel Vault

5-5d Groin Vault

5–6 Ideal Roman City. Groundplan.

1 Forum
2 Theater
3 Public Baths
4 Market
5 Temple
6 Typical Residential Block

reached by well-laid Roman roads and, if need be, fed water by aqueducts, like the Pont du Gard, still standing outside Nîmes in southern France (Fig. 5-7). At the center would be a *forum.*

The forum began as an open space with a rostrum for public speeches; but under Julius, then Augustus Caesar, it became a place for a temple with surrounding walkways. In time it included a law court *(basilica).* The forum was for the reading of proclamations, the promulgation of laws, and the celebration of triumphs and religious rites. It was a visible sign of Roman conquest, law, and administration.

The temple in the forum might have been dedicated to Jupiter or to the emperor. One of the best preserved Roman temples is the late republican *Maison Carrée* in southern France (Fig. 5-8). It is interesting to compare it with the Parthenon. The Roman temple has columns, a

portico, and a gable roof; but what are the major visible differences? The raised basement or podium with its long flight of steps, the absence of a colonnade, the much deeper portico, and the attached half-round columns on its sides and back all contrast with the Parthenon. What does this suggest to you? Look at the plan of the forum illustrated above (Fig. 5-6). Where is the temple in the complex? What role does it play in the space? The temple was not the focus of the complex, but a part, among several important buildings, in a system.

In a different section of the perfectly planned imaginary Roman city, we would find the buildings for entertainment—baths, theaters, and an arena. Though not the most perfect surviving example, the Colosseum in Rome is certainly the most famous of the great amphitheaters (Fig. 5-9). Here spectacles and gladiatorial

5–8   Maison Carrée, Nîmes. (Lauros-Giraudon, Paris)

5–7   Roman Aqueduct, Pont du Gard at Nîmes, France. (T. Lipscomb—Scala/Editorial Photocolor Archives)

5–9   Colosseum, Rome. (Alinari/Editorial Photocolor Archives)

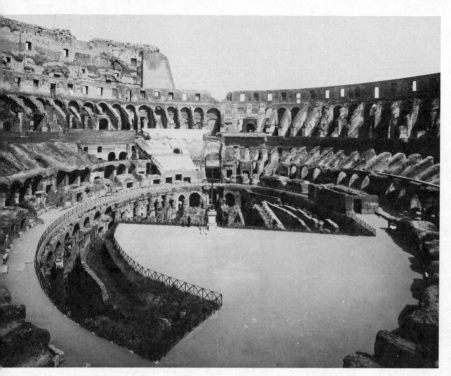

5–10   Interior of Colosseum, Rome. (Alinari/Editorial Photocolor Archives)

5–11   Exterior Arches, Colosseum, Rome. (Alinari/Editorial Photocolor Archives)

combat took place. A view of the interior of the building shows that the Colosseum is essentially made up of a series of groin vaults and barrel vaults on massive walls that support tiers of seats and provide passageways (Fig. 5-10). But the arches that open to the outside are framed with half-round columns of Greek orders—the Doric, the Ionic, and another, the Corinthian (Fig. 5-11). These have been applied to the piers between the arches for articulation and decoration. No longer supporting a lintel, the columns are used to emphasize the scale and height of the exterior. It is appropriate that the most massive, the Doric, is on the bottom, while at the topmost tier we find a thin, flattened column, a *pilaster*, with a rich flat capital. This use of the column is radically different from that employed by the Greeks. The Colosseum is not sacred at all, but a setting for man and his sports.

The Romans, in short, transformed whatever seemed adequate to fulfill their needs. Another example is the Pantheon, a temple to all the planetary deities, dedicated in Rome about 118–125 A.D. (Fig. 5-12). The plan (Fig. 5-13) shows us a great round, domed space contained within massive walls. Attached to the front is a deep portico that looks like one end of a Greek temple. The combination of circular and rectangular forms is among the first such combinations—a solution to give a sense of direction and ennobled entry to a round and therefore nondirectional space.

The interior presents us with the first important architectural space that is an interior (Fig. 5-14). The dome rises above the floor, and the only light spills in through the oculus, a round eye in the ceiling. This great hollow space creates a very different experience from the outdoor sanctuary of the Greeks or the Roman forum. It recalls the dome of heaven, the overarching sky; it seems to float or be suspended rather than to depend on the usual weight and support of the post and lintel system of building. The vital soaring quality of this majestic space and its accompanying technology will be influential for many centuries.

5–12   Pantheon, Rome.

5–13   Pantheon, Rome. Groundplan and Section.

5–14   "The Interior of the Pantheon," Giovanni Paolo Panini. (National Gallery of Art, Washington, D.C. Samuel H. Kress Collection)

5–15　Basilica of Maxentius, Rome, with Groundplan. (Photo: Alinari/Editorial Photocolor Archives)

The creation of great interiors joins with the Greek forms to make a rich supply of ideas. The basilica, another element of the forum, was also a majestic interior space, with long interior colonnades. Half-domes rose above the curved ends where judges sat to dispense the law (Fig. 5-15). This vision of earthly power and administration of justice could be allied with the sacred architecture of Greece to form a complex series of symbols and ideas.

Roman Literature

As in other aspects of their culture, the Romans looked to Greek models for their literature. Greek literature began before the Greeks as a people had any political importance; with Rome it was the opposite. The Romans had been too busy organizing, building, and conquering to write; they began to do so only when, in the third century B.C., they dominated Greece and discovered Greek literature. The first real example of a literary work in Latin is a translation of Homer's *Odyssey*. Toward the end of the third century Plautus put some Greek "new comedies" into Latin, but his bawdy plays like *The Braggart Soldier* have something distinctively Roman about them. The plays of Terence

(195–159 B.C.), who was a slave of African origins, are more subdued and more subtle in their humor, closer to the Greek ideal of new comedy. At the time of Terence, more and more Roman men of letters were seriously studying Greek literature.

Roman oratory and rhetoric, of which we have already seen an example from Cicero, arose during the first century B.C. This was also the time of the great philosophical poet Lucretius, who explained the philosophy of Epicureanism (a philosophy opposed to Stoicism) in a long poem entitled *De rerum natura (On the Nature of Things)*. Catullus, a poet who admired and imitated Sappho, gave the Latin language a new lyric power.

Virgil and the AENEID   Rome's greatest poet was undoubtedly Virgil (70–19 B.C.), whose Latin name is Publius Vergilius Maro. During Virgil's lifetime Julius Caesar was murdered and Augustus Caesar became the first of Rome's emperors. By uniting all of the lands conquered by Rome under one authority, Augustus, as we have seen, initiated that two-hundred-year era of peace and prosperity throughout the empire known as the *Pax Romana*. The years of Augustus' own reign, known as "the Augustan age," were viewed both by contemporaries and by later generations as Rome's golden years, comparable to Periclean Athens. These years indeed saw not only tremendous political and administrative achievements but also the finest Roman accomplishments in literature, as in other aspects of art and life. In the early years of this new era, Virgil wrote the great epic of Rome, named for its hero Aeneas, the *Aeneid*.

Highly conscious of living at a period of time when his native city was mistress of most of the known world and her glory was at its height, Virgil set out to write an epic poem in praise of Rome. Some even believe that Augustus might have commissioned him to write it. For an epic, there was only one model to which he could turn—Homer. Although Virgil's poem resembles both the *Iliad* and the *Odyssey* in that it is about a hero in battle and the wanderings of a hero and uses many similar literary devices, it differs in two basic ways. First, it is a literary, *written* work instead of an oral, *composed* one. Meant to be read instead of heard, it inaugurates the tradition of the written epic in Western literature. Second, Virgil's hero, Aeneas, is much less of an individual than is either Achilles or Odysseus. Homer's heroes represented the values of their culture in their own particular manner, but Virgil's hero seems to embody the values of his culture. Unlike Achilles or Odysseus, Aeneas is always sacrificing personal honor, glory, and happiness to some-

thing greater—and the "something greater" that seems to rule over the entire epic is the great destiny of Rome.

As in the case of the *Iliad*, the first lines of the *Aeneid* tell us a great deal about the poem as a whole. Here is the opening sentence in the original Latin:

> Arma, virumque cano, Troiae qui primus ab oris
> Italiam, fato profugus, Lavinaque venit
> litora—

Here are the first seven lines put into twelve lines of English (Latin is a more concise language) by a modern translator, Allen Mandelbaum:

> I sing of arms and of a man: his fate
> had made him fugitive; he was the first
> to journey from the coasts of Troy as far
> as Italy and the Lavinian shores.
> Across the lands and waters he was battered
> beneath the violence of High Ones, for
> the savage Juno's unforgetting anger;
> and many sufferings were his in war—
> until he brought a city into being
> and carried in his gods to Latium;
> from this have come the Latin race, the lords
> of Alba, and the ramparts of high Rome.

The outline of the story of Aeneas and Aeneas' place as an instrument of Roman destiny is presented in these opening lines. First Virgil gives his subject, *"arms"* and *"a man,"* as Homer's subject was "the anger of Achilles." The *Aeneid* is about both war and the struggles of Aeneas. Aeneas was predestined by Fate, a concept that looms larger than the gods, to come from Troy to Italy. According to legend he was a Trojan who, after the Trojan War, escaped from his defeated city, piously carrying his old father on his shoulders. After long years of various hardships and delays, he at last arrived in Italy. There he married Lavinia, the daughter of King Latinus, thus uniting the Trojan people with the native Latin people to found the Roman race. Aeneas' enemy in his wanderings and struggles is Juno, queen of the gods and rival of Aeneas' mother, Venus. His protector is the king of the gods, Jupiter, who, allied with Fate, is assured victory in the end. Every act of Aeneas will be determined by the destiny marked out for him. He is not a mere puppet of Jupiter's; but, since he is conscious that he has a greater will to accomplish, he struggles against the traps laid for him by Juno and sacrifices personal happiness and comfort to the greater good. Virgil's prologue goes beyond the scope of the *Aeneid* itself, which ends with a duel between Aeneas and one of his Italian opponents. Aeneas founds the city of Lavinium with his bride *after* the close of the epic. Thirty years later his son establishes a new city, Alba Longa. Some three hundred years after that, Romulus and Remus, princes of Alba, found Rome, which will ultimately rule over not only all of Italy but most of the known world. This perspective puts Aeneas in his proper place. He is not a mere individual; he is an instrument of the great destiny of Rome.

For many readers the most interesting part of the *Aeneid* is Book 4, in which Aeneas falls in love with Dido, the queen of Carthage (Rome's great rival city in North Africa). Aeneas' decision to leave Dido after he has been with her for some time, and her consequent suicide, make him a heartless character for some readers; but Virgil intended to show in this episode the great personal tragedies that a public destiny like Aeneas' entails. The poignancy of this sacrifice is stressed in Book 6, where Aeneas, allowed to descend into the underworld, visits the shades of illustrious dead people. He glimpses the shade of Dido, tries to embrace it, and calls out, "It was not of my own will, Dido, I left your land." But Dido, still proud and angry even as a ghost, turns away and disappears.

In the underworld Aeneas meets and converses with the shade of his father, Anchises. Anchises reveals to him the future of Rome, thus stressing the continuity between past and future of which Aeneas is a pivotal part. The passage printed below is Anchises' description of a parade of souls, witnessed by Aeneas, who will be born on earth at future dates and who will all contribute to the glory of Rome. Augustus, he tells us, will inaugurate Rome's "age of gold."

"More: Romulus, a son of Mars. He will
join Numitor, his grandfather, on earth
when Ilia, his mother, gives him birth
out of the bloodline of Assaracus.
You see the double plumes upon his crest:
his parent Mars already marks him out
with his own emblem for the upper world.
My son, it is beneath his auspices
that famous Rome will make her boundaries
as broad as earth itself, will make her spirit

the equal of Olympus, and enclose
her seven hills within a single wall,
rejoicing in her race of men: just as
the Berecynthian mother, tower-crowned,
when, through the Phrygian cities, she rides on
her chariot, glad her sons are gods, embraces
a hundred sons of sons, and every one
a heaven-dweller with his home on high.

"Now turn your two eyes here, to look upon
your Romans, your own people. Here is Caesar
and all the line of Iülus that will come
beneath the mighty curve of heaven. This,
this is the man you heard so often promised—
Augustus Caesar, son of a god, who will
renew a golden age in Latium,
in fields where Saturn once was king, and stretch
his rule beyond the Garamantes and
the Indians—a land beyond the paths
of year and sun, beyond the constellations,
where on his shoulders heaven-holding Atlas
revolves the axis set with blazing stars.
And even now, at his approach, the kingdom
of Caspia and land of Lake Maeotis
shudder before the oracles of gods;
the seven mouths of Nile, in terror, tremble.
For even Hercules himself had never
crossed so much of the earth, not even when
he shot the brazen-footed stag and brought
peace to the groves of Erymanthus and
made Lerna's monster quake before his arrows;
nor he who guides his chariot with reins
of vine leaves, victor Bacchus, as he drives
his tigers down from Nysa's steepest summits.
And do we, then, still hesitate to extend
our foree in acts of courage? Can it be
that fear forbids our settling in Ausonia?

From this parade of heroes, Anchises draws a lesson of Rome's mission:

For other peoples will, I do not doubt,
still cast their bronze to breathe with softer features,
or draw out of the marble living lines,
plead causes better, trace the ways of heaven
with wands and tell the rising constellations;
but yours will be the rulership of nations,
remember, Roman, these will be your arts:
to teach the ways of peace to those you conquer,
to spare defeated peoples, tame the proud."

Aeneas returns from the underworld inspired with love for the future greatness of his people. He is now more Roman than Trojan, and the rest of the epic will be devoted to his feats in "arms" necessary to the founding of Rome.

The cultural values asserted in this epic are clearly Roman. The Romans were on the whole a practical people, conscious that their real genius was not in the cult of individualism or in art for its own sake, but in the art of administrating and ruling. They did not see their imperialism in moralistic terms, as did European imperialists in Africa and Asia in the nineteenth century, who believed that destiny had sent them to "civilize" heathens. The Romans knew that the cultures they ruled in Greece, the Near East, and North Africa were in most cases more highly developed than their own. But they knew, too, that they gave the world an unparalleled peace and a system of law that could not have been obtained without their particular kind of imperialism. Americans are often compared to Romans because of their practical, administrative genius. (Has the United States ever seemed to have a concept of "imperial mission?" How would this be manifested in the twentieth century, and what are its dangers? Is there any American equivalent of the *Aeneid*?)

Horace and Satire   The other great poet of the Augustan Age was Horace (Quintus Horatius Flaccus, 65–8 B.C.). Horace was the son of an uneducated freedman (a former slave) who saw to it that his son received the best schooling that Rome could provide. Horace was in his early years an ardent republican but became just as ardent a supporter of the emperor. He is, in fact, often called Augustus' "poet laureate" because his later poems celebrate the emperor's policies and ideals. Interested, among other things, in literary criticism and theory, Horace formulated the basic tenet for Roman poets: poetry must be both *dulce* (pleasing) and *utile* (useful). The poet should combine patriotic, moral, or philosophical messages with sensuous beauty of rhythm and language. This idea that poetry should be useful is certainly more Roman than Greek.

Horace wrote lyrics (the *Epodes* and *Odes*) and later on *Epistles*, including *The Art of Poetry*. Here we have printed two examples from one of the early works, the *Satires*. We have chosen to concentrate on satire here because it is really the only literary form that is uniquely Roman and thus an important Roman cultural root.

Satire as a general human mode of expression was no more a Roman invention than comedy was a Greek one. The Romans, however, were responsible for giving satire artistic form. We saw how comedy developed from the *komos*; let us examine briefly the origins of satire.

What we now call satire seems to have its roots in ritual and magic. The desire to ridicule, or to expose human vices and follies, is universal. In certain cultures the process of ridiculing one's enemy with particularly vicious words was believed to have magical effects. It could actually injure the enemy or even cause him to kill himself and thus be used as a weapon of war. For example, the pre-Islamic Arabs, especially women, used invectives hurled against their enemies as magical, deadly curses. We still use words like caustic, biting, and venomous to describe words used in satire and ridicule. The magical and ritual origins of satire are evident here if we bear in mind that such descriptions were for many peoples not merely *metaphorical*.

The ancient Greeks also seem to have used satire for magical purposes. At the phallic ceremonies, which we mentioned in connection with old comedy, two ritual purposes were involved. One ceremony was intended to ensure fertility of land and people through the power of the phallus; the other was to expel evil spirits and influence through abuse. Out of the latter practice grew a tradition of composing *iambs*, short invective verses directed against a particular person. The practice of this kind of satire certainly influenced old comedy. Aristophanes held many important public figures, including Socrates and Euripides, up to devastating ridicule. In *Lysistrata* the invectives that the choruses of old men and old women hurl against each other are in the same satirical tradition.

No word for satire as such existed until the Romans gave it one: *satura*, which means both "full" and "a mixture of different things." In comparison to more refined and subtle forms of literature, satire is down-to-earth, hearty, and full of all kinds of things, like a good stew. For example, the satires of Horace contain lyrical poetry, philosophical arguments, folk tales, descriptions of everyday life, slapstick comedy, and obscene jokes. It is not surprising that this literary type should have developed among a people whose tastes were more practical and realistic than contemplative and abstract. Although the Roman writers of satire no longer believed in its magical effects, they believed that the function of satire to expose the vices and follies of individuals and society could be greatly therapeutic.

Roman satire, and basically all satire, is of two types. One, represented by Horace, is mild, humorous, and fundamentally optimistic. Horace claimed that the actions of some of his contemporaries impelled him to satirize—"Fools rush into my head, and so I write"—but that his purpose was to enable the "fools" to reform by exposing their foolishness rather than to punish them. The verses of a later Roman writer, Juvenal, who lived in a period when Roman society was more corrupt, represent the second type of satire. Juvenal's satire is truly biting: it exposes and castigates. Satirists like Juvenal seem to believe that evil is inherent in human nature and in the structure of society. It can be exposed, but not cured. These two types of satires—we might call them simply optimistic and pessimistic—can be found throughout the history of literature, in stage and media entertainment, and in ordinary conversation.

Roman verse satire, as we have already implied, is a particular literary form. The examples by Horace given here are fairly typical. Satires were written in hexameters, the six-foot Latin line (which the translator in this case has attempted to imitate). Horace's satires are usually in two parts: the first part exposes and attacks some kind of foolishness or viciousness; the second part upholds a norm or a virtue that contrasts with it. Often the poem is framed by a conflict between a satirist and an enemy. This is particularly clear in the second example, a dialogue between Horace and his slave, Davus. "The Town Mouse and the Country Mouse" frames a portrait of a typical day in Rome with evocations of peaceful and harmonious life in the country. It then presents the same contrast in the folk tale, used as a kind of allegory, with which it concludes. Both translations are by Smith Palmer Bovie.

HORACE

The Town Mouse and the Country Mouse

Hoc erat in votis: modus agri non ita magnus

This was what I had prayed for: a small piece of land
With a garden, a fresh-flowing spring of water at hand
Near the house, and, above and behind, a small forest
    stand.
But the gods have done much better for me, and
    more—
It's perfect. I ask nothing else, except to implore,
O Son of Maia, that you make these blessings my own
For the rest of my life. If my property has not grown
By my making a series of deals, neither will it shrink
By my mismanagement. If I'm not one of those who
    think:
"If only that corner were mine, that lies adjacent
To my strip, cutting in in a manner that's really
    indecent!"
Or, "If only some luck came my way, like the find
    which,
Leading the plowman to buried treasure, made him
    rich
Enough to buy the land he formerly plowed for hire,
Thanks to Hercules!" If what I have is all I desire
And makes me content, then to this one last wish I
    aspire:
Make my herd grow fat, and everything else I lay claim
    to,
Except my brains. And, Mercury, still be the same to
Horace as you have been, his great good guardian. To
    complete
My removal from city streets to mountain retreat,
What else should I do but celebrate it now satirically,
Dwelling, far from town (and far from lyrically),
In my pedestrian style, on how far from that bit of hell
Known as big city life is life in my citadel.
Social-climbing can't get me down here, or the lead-
    weight blows
Of siroccos, or for once and for all plague-laden falls
Lay me out, and enrich the layout in funeral halls.
    Instead, I begin this morning by addressing you,
    Monarch
Of Morning, or more openly, Janus, if you prefer it:

In allegiance to whom men begin all the work of their
     days—
For so heaven wills it. Be the principal source of my
     praise.
     At Rome the mornings are different: you rush me
     right off
To court to vouch for a friend. "Hey there! Get going!
Or someone else will answer this call before you!"
And I *have* to, whether the north wind is raking the
     land
Or winter drags snow-laden days through diminishing
     curves.
     After saying in court, good and loud, things that may
     some day
Incriminate me, I fight my way back through the
     crowd
In the streets, tripping over some slowpoke's toes.
     "What's up,
You blockhead? What gives?" some stupid assails me.
     "Oh, Horace,
It's you, is it, racing back home to Maecenas,[1] so full of
The fact that you knock over everything blocking your
     path!"
Well . . . the name of Maecenas *is* honey to me, I admit
     it.
     But as soon as I reach the depressing Esquiline
     Quarter,
A hundred conflicting concerns pour down on my
     head
And stream around me. "Roscius wants you to meet
     him tomorrow
Before seven in the morning, at Libo's Wall." "Oh,
     Quintus,
The clerks request you to remember to return to the
     Forum
Today for a big new matter of mutual interest."
"Do have Maecenas affix his seal to these papers."
If I say, "Well, I'll try," he insists, "You can *do* it if you
     want to."
     It is now seven years—actually, nearer the eighth—
Since Maecenas began to admit me into his company
Of friends, insofar as a friend is just good company

------

[1] Horace's patron.

On a trip, someone to talk to about such subjects as:
"What time is it?" . . . "Oh, about the fight: is the
     Thracian Bantam
A match for the Sheik?" . . . "These frosty mornings can
     nip you
If you don't wrap up." And small-change talk like this,
Which it's perfectly safe to deposit in leaky ears.
And the whole time, daily and hourly, our intimate
     Horace
Was *envied*. He watched the games from the stands
     with M.
He played some ball on the Campus, *and* with M.
"Fortune's Favorite Son," they thought in unison.
     A hair-raising rumor rolls through the streets from
     the Rostra,
And whoever bumps into me seeks my advice. "Dear
     fellow,
You ought to know, you live so much nearer the gods,
What's up in the Balkans?" "Nothing, as far as I know."
"Oh, you're still making fun of us!" But may the gods
     undo me
If I've heard a word. "What about the veterans'
     allotments
Of land Caesar promised? Will they be on the three-
     cornered isle,
Or Italian soil?" When I swear I know nothing about it,
They marvel at me for being the sole human being
Who knows how to keep an important unfathomable
     secret.
     Amid such lightweight concerns the light of my day
Sputters out, leaving me limp, only able to pray:

     Oh, countryside mine, when will I see you again,
     Read my favorite classical authors, and then
     Get some sleep and get back to my lazy routine of
     life,
     Of pleasure mercifully free from worry and strife?

When shall we dine on beans, Pythagoras' cousins,
And eat, cooked in bacon, country greens in their
     dozens?
Those nights and feasts of the gods! When friends and I
     sup
In *my lar*'s presence, while the saucy slaves lick up
What's left untouched on the plates. Each guest drains
     his cup,

Big or small, as it suits him: no Prohibition
To govern his choice except his free disposition
To toss off heroic amounts and keep a clear head,
Or gradually mellow with moderate potions instead.
And then we start talking, not about other men's lives
And property and assets but of things on which
　　wisdom thrives.
Not whether Lepos is really a good dancer or not
But whether happiness comes from the money you've
　　got
Or, rather, derives from virtue. What makes men
　　friends?
Self-interest, or rectitude? This subject lends
Interest to us: the good life, and its ends.
　　From time to time, my good old neighbor, Cervius,
Rattles off an old wives' tale, to make a point:
If someone praises Arellius' wealth, without knowing
What worries it brings, Cervius starts off like this:
　"Once upon a time, a country mouse
Welcomed a town mouse in his poor little hole of a
　　house
In the sticks, both host and guest being quite old
　　friends.
The country mouse roughed it, of course; he kept a
　　close eye
On his larder, but not so myopic he couldn't enlarge
His view, with a view to a friend's entertainment.
　　What else?
He was not the mouse to begrudge a friend the choice
　　chick-peas
Set aside in a special place, or the long grains of oats;
But, eager to conquer the fastidious disdain of a guest
Who tended to turn up his tooth after sampling each
　　dainty,
He brought in by mouth and served, to vary the meal,
A dried grape seed and some half-nibbled pieces of
　　bacon.
The master of the house, stretched out on his couch of
　　chaff
(New chaff), ate spelt and darnel, leaving the best
For his guest to digest. Finally, the town mouse spoke
　　up:

　　'What pleasure can it be for you, my friend,
　　Roughing it out here on the edge of a precipitous
　　　　forest?

Surely you put *people* and *the city* ahead of this
　　wildwood?
Take my advice, and my road, with me as your
　　guide.
All earthly creatures, after all, have drawn as their
　　lot
A mortal life: there is no escape from death
For large or small. Therefore, while you still can,
Enjoy a happy career, my good man, live well;
Live mindful of how short life really is.'

　　　　　　　　　　　　　　　When these words
Dawned on the yokel, he bounced off gaily from home,
And both set out together, according to plan,
Hoping to sneak through the walls of the city by night.
And night was poised, midway across the heavens,
When both set foot in a rich man's house, where
　　crimson
Coverings blazed against ivory couches, and leftovers
From last night's feast were stacked up high in the
　　baskets.
Well, the host then made his rural guest stretch out
On the crimson covers and began dashing madly about,
With his clothes tucked up like a waiter's, serving up
　　dish
After dish and taking a taste, as a proper slave does,
Of each course before serving it. The other mouse
　　meanwhile
Leaned back at ease, delighted with the change in
　　affairs
And with all this good living, and was playing to
　　perfection the part
Of the satisfied guest, when a sudden loud rattling of
　　doors
Shook them both right off of their couches. Frightened,
　　they scampered
Across the whole length of the room, and, even more
　　frightening,
The big house began to ring, at the very same time,
With the barking of colossal hounds. Says the country
　　mouse:

　　'I have no use for this kind of life. And good-by!
　　My woodland and hole, where I'm safe from traps
　　　　like these,
　　Will be quite good enough, my slim pickings quite
　　　　food enough.' "

COMMENTS AND QUESTIONS

1. Divide this satire into the two parts mentioned earlier: the exposure of the folly and the "sermon" on the contrasting virtue.
2. It is obvious that Horace is praising the virtues of country life over the more hectic and superficial city life. What values are associated with each? How would a Greek such as Pericles or Aristotle react to such a contrast?
3. How does Horace set up the contrast between town and country? Notice particularly the *tone* and the *rhythm* of the poetry in which each is conveyed. What poetic devices does Horace use to evoke the hustle and bustle of city life?
4. What kind of foolishness is Horace satirizing, and how does he convey his attitude?
5. What seems to be Horace's ideal "good life"? How does the fable of the mice serve to illustrate this?

The scene for the next satire is the Roman holiday at the end of December, the *Saturnalia*, which was characterized by a general freedom from work, normal duties, and normal social restraints. Slaves, during the Saturnalia, were supposed to be treated with great indulgence. Horace uses this setting to treat a theme prevalent in Stoicism: the true nature of freedom. Is the man of material wealth, apparently free, but enslaved to his greed and his passions, any freer than a slave? For the Stoics, only the philosopher, or the man whose mind was unencumbered by material wants, is truly free. A slave, in this sense, could be freer than his master. The Stoics were particularly fond of such paradoxes or apparent contradictions. As the slave lectures the master on freedom, the philosophical paradox becomes good material for satire. And here, of course, the object of the satire is the writer himself! During the course of the satire, Horace's portrayal of himself changes from that of a liberal to that of a tyrant. Like everyone else, he finds that the blows of satire, especially when they contain truth, can be wounding.

HORACE

My Slave Is Free to Speak Up for Himself

> Iamdudum ausculto et cupiens tibi dicere servus

Davus. I've been listening for quite some time now, wanting to have
A word with you. Being a slave, though, I haven't the nerve.
    Horace. That you, Davus?
    Dav.   Yes, it's Davus, slave as I am.
Loyal to my man, a pretty good fellow: *pretty* good,
I say. I don't want you thinking I'm too good to live.
    Hor. Well, come on, then. Make use of the freedom traditionally yours
At the December holiday season. Speak up, sound off!
    Dav. Some people *like* misbehaving: they're persistent and consistent.
But the majority waver, trying at times to be good,
At other times yielding to evil. The notorious Priscus
Used to wear three rings at a time, and then again, none.
He lived unevenly, changing his robes every hour.
He issued forth from a mansion, only to dive
Into the sort of low joint your better-class freedman
Wouldn't want to be caught dead in. A libertine at Rome,
At Athens a sage, he was born, and he lived, out of season.
    When Volanerius, the playboy, was racked by the gout
In the joints of his peccant fingers (so richly deserved),
He hired a man, by the day, to pick up the dice
For him and put them in the box. By being consistent
In his gambling vice, he lived a happier life
Than the chap who tightens the reins and then lets them flap.
    Hor. Will it take you all day to get to the bottom of this junk,
You skunk?
    Dav.   But I'm saying, *you're* at the bottom.
    Hor.   How so, you stinker?
    Dav. You praise the good old days, ancient fortunes, and manners,
And yet, if some god were all for taking you back,
You'd hang back, either because you don't really think

That what you are praising to the skies is all that
    superior
Or because you defend what is right with weak
    defenses
And, vainly wanting to pull your foot from the mud,
Stick in it all the same. At Rome, you yearn
For the country, but, once in the sticks, you praise to
    high heaven
The far-off city, you nitwit. If it happens that no one
Asks you to dinner, you eulogize your comfortable
    meal
Of vegetables, acting as if you'd only go out
If you were dragged out in chains. You hug yourself,
Saying how glad you are not to be forced to go out
On a spree. But Maecenas *suggests*, at the very last
    minute,
That you be his guest: "Bring some oil for my lamp,
    somebody!
Get a move on! Is everyone deaf around here?" In a
    dither
And a lather, you charge out. Meanwhile, your
    scrounging guests,
Mulvius & Co., make their departure from your place
With a few descriptive remarks that won't bear
    repeating—
For example, Mulvius admits, "Of course, I'm fickle,
Led around by my stomach, and prone to follow my
    nose
To the source of a juicy aroma, weak-minded, lazy,
And, you may want to add, a gluttonous souse.
But you, every bit as bad and perhaps a bit worse,
Have the gall to wade into me, as if you were better,
And cloak your infamy in euphemism?"
                     What if you're found out
To be a bigger fool than me, the hundred-dollar slave?
Stop trying to browbeat me! Hold back your hand,
And your temper, while I tell you what Crispinus'
    porter
Taught me.
            Another man's wife makes you her slave.
A loose woman makes Davus hers. Of us two sinners,
Who deserves the cross more? When my passionate
    nature
Drives me straight into her arms, she's lovely by
    lamplight,

Beautifully bare, all mine to plunge into at will,
Or, turning about, she mounts and drives me to death.
And after it's over, she sends me away neither
    shamefaced
Nor worried that someone richer or better to look at
Will water the very same plant. But when you go out
    for it,
You really come in for it, don't you? Turning yourself
    into
The same dirty Dama you pretend to be when you take
    off
Your equestrian ring and your Roman robes, and
    change
Your respectable self, hiding your perfumed head
Under your cape?
               Scared to death, you're let in the house,
And your fear takes turns with your hope in rattling
    your bones.
What's the difference between being carted off to be
    scourged
And slain, in the toils of the law (as a gladiator is),
And being locked up in a miserable trunk, where the
    maid,
Well aware of her mistress' misconduct, has stored you
    away,
With your knees scrunched up against your head?
    Hasn't the husband
Full power over them both, and even more over the
    seducer?
For the wife hasn't changed her attire or her location,
And is not the uppermost sinner. You walk open-eyed
Right under the fork, handing over to a furious master
Your money, your life, your person, your good
    reputation.
  Let's assume that you got away: you learned your
    lesson,
I trust, and will be afraid from now on, and be careful?
Oh, no! You start planning how to get in trouble again,
To perish again, enslave yourself over and over.
But what wild beast is so dumb as to come back again
To the chains he has once broken loose from?
                     "But I'm no adulterer,"
You say. And I'm not a thief when I wisely pass up
Your good silver plate. But our wandering nature will
    leap

When the reins are removed, when the danger is taken
    away.
  Are you my master, you, slave to so many
Other people, so powerful a host of other things, whom
    no
Manumission could ever set free from craven anxiety,
Though the ritual were conducted again and again?
    And besides,
Here's something to think about: whether a slave who's
    the slave
Of a slave is a plain fellow slave or a "subslave," as you
    masters
Call him, what am I your?[2] You, who command me,
Cravenly serve someone else and are led here and there
Like a puppet, the strings held by others.
                      Who, then, is free?
The wise man alone, who has full command of
    himself,
Whom poverty, death, or chains cannot terrify,
Who is strong enough to defy his passions and scorn
Prestige, who is wholly contained in himself, well
    rounded,
Smooth as a sphere on which nothing external can
    fasten,
On which fortune can do no harm except to herself.
  Now which of those traits can you recognize as one
    of yours?
Your woman asks you for five thousand dollars,
    needles you,
Shuts the door in your face and pours out cold water,
Then calls you back. Pull your neck from that yoke!
Say, "I'm free, I'm free!" Come on, say it. You can't! A
    master
Dominates your mind, and it's no mild master who
    lashes
You on in spite of yourself, who goads you and guides
    you.
  Or when you stand popeyed in front of a painting by
    Pausias,
You madman, are you less at fault than I am who
    marvel

At the posters of athletes straining their muscles in
    combat,
Striking out, thrusting, and parrying, in red chalk and
    charcoal,
As if they were really alive and handling these
    weapons?
But Davus is a no-good, a dawdler, and you? Oh,
    MONSIEUR
Is an EXPERT, a fine CONNOISSEUR of antiques, I ASSURE
    you.
  I'm just a fool to be tempted by piping-hot pancakes.
Does your strength of character and mind make much
    resistance
To sumptuous meals? Why is it worse for me
To supply the demands of my stomach? My back will
    pay for it,
To be sure. But do you get off any lighter, hankering
After delicate, costly food? Your endless indulgence
Turns sour in your stomach, your baffled feet won't
    support
Your pampered body. Is the slave at fault, who
    exchanges
A stolen scraper for a bunch of grapes, in the dark?
Is there nothing slavish in a man who sells his estate
To satisfy his need for rich food?
                    Now, add on these items:
(1) You can't stand your own company as long as an
    hour;
(2) You can't dispose of your leisure in a decent
    fashion;
(3) You're a fugitive from your own ego, a vagabond
    soul,
Trying to outflank your cares by attacking the bottle
Or making sorties into sleep. And none of it works:
The Dark Companion rides close along by your side,
Keeps up with and keeps on pursuing the runaway
    slave.
  Hor. "Where's a stone?"
  Dav.   "What use do you have for it?"
  Hor.   "Hand me my arrows!"
  Dav. The man is either raving or satisfying his
    craving
For creative writing.
  Hor.   If you don't clear out, instanter,
I'll pack you off to the farm to be my ninth planter.

---

[2] If Horace is himself a slave, Davus wonders what status he, as a
slave of a slave, has.

COMMENTS AND QUESTIONS

1. Which voice is really Horace's here, that of "Horace" calling "Where's a stone?" or that of "Davus" lecturing on the true nature of the wise man (the Stoic "philosopher")?
2. Does the writer's satire of the faults of the character "Horace" imply self-criticism or a sense of superiority? Or does it imply something about the nature of Horatian satire; that is, if you clearly see your own faults, you will understand the virtue with which you can remedy them?
3. What contrasts are set up between Horace and Davus? Does Davus claim that he is "really" free?
4. What aspects of Horace's self-portrait do you find particularly comic?
5. Think about the difficulties involved in writing a self-satire. The best way to appreciate these would be to try your hand at it.
6. Collect examples of satire from the media as well as from modern literature, and compare the techniques used with those of Horace.

Virgil and Horace represent two aspects of literature, and of art generally, that are typically Roman: grandeur and realism. A sense of pride and patriotism, a feeling for the magnificence of Rome's mission in the world, and a practical eye for the real and everyday were both characteristic of the Roman temperament. We have seen these qualities manifested in public architecture and in Roman portraiture.

THE GRECO-ROMAN ROOT: CONTINUITIES

The Classical Ideal The classical cultures, Greece and Rome, in spite of many differences, form together a unified system of cultural values and creations that has profoundly influenced the course of Western culture and is still with us today. In our focus on the "classical" phase of "classical" culture—Athens in the fifth century B.C.—we witnessed the aesthetic and moral values associated with the term. The Greek mentality of that century looks to human reason as the force giving order to the world. It is humanistic in that it stresses the dignity and worth of human individuals as such more than as part of a social or divine order. Yet it cautions against the dangers of human pride, *hubris.* "Nothing in excess" were the words of the oracle at Delphi, and we see this applied to Oedipus when he tries to outwit fate; in Pericles' description of the equilibrium between private and public good in Athens; in the monuments of sculpture and architecture that strive to balance or harmonize the real and the ideal; in Plato's emphasis on music *and* gymnastics in the ideal education; in Aristotle's "golden mean." Classical art is dynamic and pleasing because its proportions and symmetry represent an attempt to harmonize forces like body and soul, man and the gods, reason and emotion. When a classical work is copied and calculated from reason alone, it becomes lifeless. The Greeks very much admired the power of reason, but they were deeply interested in the *whole* human being.

Greek Logic and Mathematics The Greeks were the first to elaborate the logical structures of our thought, structures that have become so natural to the modern mind that we take them for granted. Greek logicians laid down the basic rules for determining when arguments are valid or invalid; that is, when conclusions follow from a given set of premises and when they do not. Greek terminology still predominates in textbooks of logic. Perhaps more significantly, the Greeks were the first to utilize logic and its companion mathematics for the systematic understanding of nature. These instruments of human reason were believed to work because the world was viewed as by nature intelligible and its functioning capable of being reduced to laws. Something of this same trust in the capability of man's intellect to solve the mysteries of nature motivates numbers of scientists and their supporters today. Even those of us less optimistic about the potentialities of man's mental faculties recognize the ability of intellect to organize large segments of human experience through the use of rational powers.

Greek Science and Politics Modern man, moreover, owes to the ancient Greeks most of the basic categories for ordering knowledge into disciplines, like physics, ethics, politics (all Greek words). The Greeks also defined and distinguished the methodologies or ways of investigating truth appropriate to various disciplines. Utilizing these methodologies, the Greeks made such advances that, in the sciences at least, Western Europe was not to surpass them until after roughly 1600. Greek political theorists provided an analysis of the basic constitutional forms of monarchy, tyranny, aristocracy, oligarchy, republican government, and democracy that still informs modern political science. The idea that true liberty is found in a democracy, or a state where men rule themselves, is a Greek one.

Greek Literature, Architecture, and Sculpture The Greeks created basic literary forms that influenced not only the course of Western literature but also the ways in which we think about life. The English language acknowledges its debt to Greek concepts with terms like *epic, lyric, tragedy,* and *comedy.* One has only to walk around Washington, D.C., to see how the architectural and sculptural forms first developed by the Greeks have become a permanent part of our environment.

Roman Expansion of Greek Culture Although the Greeks were undoubtedly the originators of most of the cultural forms we have been studying in this root, the term Greco-Roman makes sense because of what the Romans did with Greek culture. As the last and the greatest of the Hellenistic (Greeklike) empires, Rome spread Greek culture to the considerable area of the world that it occupied. Without Rome, Greek culture would have remained limited to a parochial group of city-states. The Romans, adding their own cultural forms to the Greek ones, adapted Greek culture to the needs of a larger world. The Greeks saw the world as divided between "Greek" and "barbarian"; the Romans were more cosmopolitan in outlook. The Greeks philosophized about the laws of nature, but the Romans realized them as a code of laws that became the basis for legal systems in the Western world. The Romans adapted Greek sculptural and artistic forms to more practical uses: the portrait, the forum, the triumphal arch, the colosseum. Our engineering and city planning derive from Roman innovation.

Greek/Roman Cultural Values   The differences between Homer's *Iliad* and Virgil's *Aeneid* are indicative of the shift in emphasis between Greek and Roman cultural values. Achilles is a hero because of his pride, strength, and daring: he may embody Greek cultural values but is still primarily an individual. Aeneas is praised for his *pietas*, or loyalty to family and nation. It is his task to serve the destiny of Rome, not primarily to excel himself. Our concept of patriotism (from the Latin *patria*) is primarily Roman.

Latin Language and Literature   The Romans reworked the Greek literary forms to their own taste and added a new one, verse satire. Latin became the literary language of the West for many centuries, and the Romans were consequently responsible for transmitting Greek concepts and forms to Western culture. The Latin language was also a major influence in the development of modern languages, including English.

It has been argued that the Greco-Roman emphasis on man, human reason, and secular glory has had detrimental as well as beneficial effects on Western culture. Pushed to its extreme, it can result in a spiritual vacuum. Hebraic cultural values, at the base of the Judeo-Christian root, are, as we shall see, of a different order.

PART TWO

THE JUDEO-CHRISTIAN ROOT

6

JUDAISM AND EARLY CHRISTIANITY

In moving to the second root culture of the Western world, we shift from a culture primarily centered on man to one primarily centered on an all-powerful, unique God. The creators of this world-view and its system of values were the ancient Hebrews, who have left their legacy in the Bible and in the other cultural manifestations of Judaism. As Christianity developed from Judaism, it brought elements of Greco-Roman culture to bear on the Hebraic core. We will examine a few important monuments of the culture of Christianity in our focal point for Part Two, the European High Middle Ages. First we will look briefly at the seminal Hebraic culture.

The Ancient Hebrews and the Bible

Modern Christian versions of the Bible include the scriptures of Judaism, called the Old Testament, and the scriptures of Christianity called the New Testament. Originally, however, the Bible referred only to the Old Testament. It can be defined as a collection of religious literature written in Hebrew (with some parts in other Middle Eastern languages) from about 1000 B.C. to 100 A.D. Like the Homeric epics, biblical literature first existed as *oral* narratives and poetry. The written Bible contains a wealth of different kinds of literature: history, short stories, drama, lyric poetry, and philosophical meditation.

What of the people who composed these greatly influential works? The Hebrews were originally a Middle Eastern tribe belonging to the racial group known as Semites, a group that includes the Arabs. Their early history can be divided into three parts: (1) the period of the patriarchs or founding fathers: Abraham, his son Isaac, and his son Jacob; (2) the captivity of the Hebrews (now called Israelites) in Egypt; and (3) the Exodus or deliverance from Egypt to the promised land of Canaan.

Abraham Abraham, who probably lived about four thousand years ago, is traditionally looked on as the original founder of the Jewish people. His most important contribution was to establish the worship of one God—not a god of nature, of the sun, wind, or rain, as was common in other Middle Eastern religions, but a truly personal God who took a direct interest in His chosen people, the Israelites. The relationship between Abraham and his God came to be known as the covenant.

According to this agreement, God promised that Abraham's clan would be led to a new land and would become a great nation. In return, the Israelites were to place their trust and faith in God. Abraham's grandson Jacob, driven by famine out of the Israelites' land of Canaan, settled with his clan in Egypt. Although the Egyptians were originally tolerant of them, the Israelites eventually became slaves until they were delivered by Moses, around 1200 B.C.

Moses Moses led the Israelites to Mount Sinai, where a new covenant between the God of Israel and His people was made. God revealed Himself to Moses under the name of "Jahweh," which means in Hebrew "he brings into existence." Jahweh was not only the creator of everything but could also enter into history to influence the course of human events. This idea of God gave the Israelites their strong sense of destiny. They were the chosen people—God would take care of them. In the covenant at Mount Sinai, Jahweh promised His protection and gave the Israelites the Ten Commandments to follow. The first of these is, of course, "Thou shalt have no other gods before me." The principle of one supreme personal God was firmly established, as it has been in Judaism ever since.

The Kings Moses' successor, Joshua, brought his people to the promised land of Canaan, and at that point the Israelites became a settled, rather than a nomadic people. The next phase of their history is called the period of kings, for they had not had one king over them earlier. The first king was Saul; the second and most famous, David. David founded the capital at Jerusalem, establishing a splendid court there with a luxury never known to the Israelites previously. It is during the reign of David that the Hebrew literature we know as the Bible was first written down. Up until that time, the legends of the patriarchs, the account of the creation, and so on, had been passed along orally.

Solomon Writing of biblical literature continued under the reign of the next king, Solomon. Solomon's court and kingdom were the most lavish and splendid that Israel ever knew. He taxed the people heavily for his extravagant building and also maintained a harem —although the hundred wives attributed to him is probably an exaggeration. He was reputed to be the wisest man in the world and a poet as well. Most scholars now think that this is probably a legend and especially that the Song of Songs, the great Hebrew poem also called the Song of Solomon, was not written by Solomon but by a later author; still, it seems to fit the splendor of Solomon's court. Solomon's power and splendor did not continue after him. When he died in 922 B.C., Israel was split into two kingdoms and foreign conquests of the Israelites began again. The Jews were exiled in Babylonia, then conquered by the Egyptians, by the Syrians, and finally, shortly before the birth of Jesus, by the Romans.

Genesis   The first biblical text we have included here is one that may appear all too familiar, but a student of the humanities should be able to approach it with new questions. All cultures of the world have myths of creation. Compare this Hebrew account of the beginnings of things in Genesis with the Greek one that we reviewed briefly in the section on Greek mythology and with the African accounts in Part Three. Which culture gives the most importance to the active role of the creator God, and how is this manifested? All of the biblical passages are from the King James translation of 1611, itself a cultural monument of great importance to the formation of the English language.

GENESIS

The Creation

CHAPTER 1

1 In the beginning God created the heaven and the earth.

2 And the earth was without form, and void; and darkness was upon the face of the deep. And the Spirit of God moved upon the face of the waters.

3 And God said, Let there be light: and there was light.

4 And God saw the light, that it was good: and God divided the light from the darkness.

5 And God called the light Day, and the darkness he called Night. And the evening and the morning were the first day.

6 And God said, Let there be a firmament in the midst of the waters, and let it divide the waters from the waters.

7 And God made the firmament, and divided the waters which were under the firmament from the waters which were above the firmament: and it was so.

8 And God called the firmament Heaven. And the evening and the morning were the second day.

9 And God said, Let the waters under the heaven be gathered together unto one place, and let the dry land appear: and it was so.

10 And God called the dry land Earth; and the gathering together of the waters called he Seas: and God saw that it was good.

11 And God said, Let the earth bring forth grass, the herb yielding seed, and the fruit tree yielding fruit after his kind, whose seed is in itself, upon the earth: and it was so.

12 And the earth brought forth grass, and herb yielding seed after his kind, and the tree yielding fruit, whose seed was in itself, after his kind: and God saw that it was good.

13 And the evening and the morning were the third day.

14 And God said, Let there be lights in the firmament of the heaven to divide the day from the night; and let them be for signs, and for seasons, and for days, and years:

15 And let them be for lights in the firmament of the heaven to give light upon the earth: and it was so.

16 And God made two great lights; the greater light to rule the day, and the lesser light to rule the night: he made the stars also.

17 And God set them in the firmament of the heaven to give light upon the earth,

18 And to rule over the day and over the night, and to divide the light from the darkness: and God saw that it was good.

19 And the evening and the morning were the fourth day.

20 And God said, Let the waters bring forth abundantly the moving creature that hath life, and fowl that may fly above the earth in the open firmament of heaven:

21 And God created great whales, and every living creature that moveth, which the waters brought forth abundantly, after their kind, and every winged fowl after his kind: and God saw that it was good.

22 And God blessed them, saying, Be fruitful, and multiply, and fill the waters in the seas, and let fowl multiply in the earth.

23 And the evening and the morning were the fifth day.

24 And God said, Let the earth bring forth the living creature after his kind, cattle, and creeping thing, and beast of the earth after his kind: and it was so.

25 And God made the beast of the earth after his kind, and cattle after their kind, and every thing that creepeth upon the earth after his kind: and God saw that it was good.

26 And God said, Let us make man in our image, after our likeness: and let them have dominion over the fish of the sea, and over the fowl of the air, and over

the cattle, and over all the earth, and over every creeping thing that creepeth upon the earth.

27 So God created man in his own image, in the image of God created he him; male and female created he them.

28 And God blessed them, and God said unto them, Be fruitful, and multiply, and replenish the earth, and subdue it: and have dominion over the fish of the sea, and over the fowl of the air, and over every living thing that moveth upon the earth.

29 And God said, Behold, I have given you every herb bearing seed, which is upon the face of all the earth, and every tree, in the which is the fruit of a tree yielding seed; to you it shall be for meat.

30 And to every beast of the earth, and to every fowl of the air, and to every thing that creepeth upon the earth, wherein there is life, I have given every green herb for meat: and it was so.

31 And God saw every thing that he had made, and, behold, it was very good. And the evening and the morning were the sixth day.

CHAPTER 2

1 Thus the heavens and the earth were finished, and all the host of them.

2 And on the seventh day God ended his work which he had made; and he rested on the seventh day from all his work which he had made.

3 And God blessed the seventh day, and sanctified it: because that in it he had rested from all his work which God created and made.

4 These are the generations of the heavens and of the earth when they were created, in the day that the Lord God made the earth and the heavens,

5 And every plant of the field before it was in the earth, and every herb of the field before it grew: for the Lord God had not caused it to rain upon the earth, and there was not a man to till the ground.

6 But there went up a mist from the earth, and watered the whole face of the ground.

7 And the Lord God formed man of the dust of the ground, and breathed into his nostrils the breath of life; and man became a living soul.

8 And the Lord God planted a garden eastward in Eden; and there he put the man whom he had formed.

9 And out of the ground made the Lord God to grow every tree that is pleasant to the sight, and good for food; the tree of life also in the midst of the garden, and the tree of knowledge of good and evil.

10 And a river went out of Eden to water the garden; and from thence it was parted, and became into four heads.

11 The name of the first is Pison: that is it which compasseth the whole land of Havilah, where there is gold;

12 And the gold of that land is good: there is bdellium and the onyx stone.

13 And the name of the second river is Gihon: the same is it that compasseth the whole land of Ethiopia.

14 And the name of the third river is Hiddekel: that is it which goeth toward the east of Assyria. And the fourth river is Euphrates.

15 And the Lord God took the man, and put him into the garden of Eden to dress it and to keep it.

16 And the Lord God commanded the man, saying, Of every tree of the garden thou mayest freely eat:

17 But of the tree of the knowledge of good and evil, thou shalt not eat of it: for in the day that thou eatest thereof thou shalt surely die.

18 And the Lord God said, It is not good that the man should be alone; I will make him a help meet for him.

19 And out of the ground the Lord God formed every beast of the field, and every fowl of the air; and brought them unto Adam to see what he would call them: and whatsoever Adam called every living creature, that was the name thereof.

20 And Adam gave names to all cattle, and to the fowl of the air, and to every beast of the field; but for Adam there was not found a help meet for him.

21 And the Lord God caused a deep sleep to fall upon Adam, and he slept; and he took one of his ribs, and closed up the flesh instead thereof.

22 And the rib, which the Lord God had taken from man, made he a woman, and brought her unto the man.

23 And Adam said, This is now bone of my bones, and flesh of my flesh: she shall be called Woman, because she was taken out of man.

24 Therefore shall a man leave his father and his mother, and shall cleave unto his wife: and they shall be one flesh.

25 And they were both naked, the man and his wife, and were not ashamed.

COMMENTS AND QUESTIONS

1. The two different accounts of creation in Genesis have caused biblical scholars to believe that each was written at a different time and by a different author. What are the two accounts? Where does one end and the other begin?
2. What principles of the Jewish religion are evident in this passage?
3. How do the two accounts of the creation of woman differ? How might these accounts have influenced ways in which we think about the nature of woman?

The following text is central to the Judaic and Christian concepts of man's relationship to God and to the problem of evil. Whereas the first two chapters of Genesis show man as a part of the totality of creation and in harmony with it, in this chapter the human beings, quite unlike the other living things in the created world, begin to act on their own: to make their own decisions apart from God. They have *free will:* they are given an orderly and harmonious world but are capable of creating disorder in it.

GENESIS

The Fall

CHAPTER 3

1 Now the serpent was more subtile than any beast of the field which the Lord God had made. And he said unto the woman, Yea, hath God said, Ye shall not eat of every tree of the garden?

2 And the woman said unto the serpent, We may eat of the fruit of the trees of the garden:

3 But of the fruit of the tree which is in the midst of the garden, God hath said, Ye shall not eat of it, neither shall ye touch it, lest ye die.

4 And the serpent said unto the woman, Ye shall not surely die:

5 For God doth know that in the day ye eat thereof, then your eyes shall be opened, and ye shall be as gods, knowing good and evil.

6 And when the woman saw that the tree was good for food, and that it was pleasant to the eyes, and a tree to be desired to make one wise, she took of the fruit thereof, and did eat, and gave also unto her husband with her; and he did eat.

7 And the eyes of them both were opened, and they knew that they were naked; and they sewed fig leaves together, and made themselves aprons.

8 And they heard the voice of the Lord God walking in the garden in the cool of the day: and Adam and his wife hid themselves from the presence of the Lord God amongst the trees of the garden.

9 And the Lord God called unto Adam, and said unto him, Where art thou?

10 And he said, I heard thy voice in the garden, and I was afraid, because I was naked; and I hid myself.

11 And he said, Who told thee that thou wast naked? Hast thou eaten of the tree, whereof I commanded thee that thou shouldest not eat?

12 And the man said, The woman whom thou gavest to be with me, she gave me of the tree, and I did eat.

13 And the Lord God said unto the woman, What is this that thou hast done? And the woman said, The serpent beguiled me, and I did eat.

14 And the Lord God said unto the serpent, Because thou hast done this, thou art cursed above all cattle, and above every beast of the field; upon thy belly shalt thou go, and dust shalt thou eat all the days of thy life:

15 And I will put enmity between thee and the woman, and between thy seed and her seed; it shall bruise thy head, and thou shalt bruise his heel.

16 Unto the woman he said, I will greatly multiply thy sorrow and thy conception; in sorrow thou shalt bring forth children; and thy desire shall be to thy husband, and he shall rule over thee.

17 And unto Adam he said, Because thou hast hearkened unto the voice of thy wife, and hast eaten of the tree, of which I commanded thee, saying, Thou shalt not eat of it: cursed is the ground for thy sake; in sorrow shalt thou eat of it all the days of thy life;

18 Thorns also and thistles shall it bring forth to thee; and thou shalt eat the herb of the field:

19 In the sweat of thy face shalt thou eat bread, till thou return unto the ground; for out of it wast thou taken: for dust thou art, and unto dust shalt thou return.

20 And Adam called his wife's name Eve; because she was the mother of all living.

21 Unto Adam also and to his wife did the Lord God make coats of skins, and clothed them.

22 And the Lord God said, Behold, the man is become as one of us, to know good and evil: and now, lest

he put forth his hand, and take also of the tree of life, and eat, and live for ever:

23 Therefore the Lord God sent him forth from the garden of Eden, to till the ground from whence he was taken.

24 So he drove out the man: and he placed at the east of the garden of Eden cherubim, and a flaming sword which turned every way, to keep the way of the tree of life.

COMMENTS AND QUESTIONS

1. How does this story reconcile the idea of God's infinite justice with the presence of evil in the world?
2. How does God appear in this story in relation to man?
3. What, specifically, tempts Eve and then Adam to eat the forbidden fruit? What does this tell you about the Hebrews' concept of the nature of human beings?
4. Compare the relationship between human curiosity and divine power here with the treatment of the same theme in *Oedipus Rex*.
5. Do you as a reader feel admiration or scorn for the human desire to eat the fruit?

Genesis goes on to recount the rise of the tribe of Israel. The following passage is illustrative of God's relationship with His "chosen people," here in the person of their founding father, Abraham.

GENESIS

The Sacrifice of Isaac

CHAPTER 22

1 And it came to pass after these things, that God did tempt Abraham, and said unto him, Abraham: and he said, Behold, here I am.

2 And he said, Take now thy son, thine only son Isaac, whom thou lovest, and get thee into the land of Moriah; and offer him there for a burnt offering upon one of the mountains which I will tell thee of.

3 And Abraham rose up early in the morning, and saddled his ass, and took two of his young men with him, and Isaac his son, and clave the wood for the burnt offering, and rose up, and went unto the place of which God had told him.

4 Then on the third day Abraham lifted up his eyes, and saw the place afar off.

5 And Abraham said unto his young men, Abide ye here with the ass; and I and the lad will go yonder and worship, and come again to you.

6 And Abraham took the wood of the burnt offering, and laid it upon Isaac his son; and he took the fire in his hand, and a knife; and they went both of them together.

7 And Isaac spake unto Abraham his father, and said, My father: and he said, Here am I, my son. And he said, Behold the fire and the wood: but where is the lamb for a burnt offering?

8 And Abraham said, My son, God will provide himself a lamb for a burnt offering: so they went both of them together.

9 And they came to the place which God had told him of; and Abraham built an altar there, and laid the wood in order, and bound Isaac his son, and laid him on the altar upon the wood.

10 And Abraham stretched forth his hand, and took the knife to slay his son.

11 And the Angel of the Lord called unto him out of heaven, and said, Abraham, Abraham: and he said, Here am I.

12 And he said, Lay not thine hand upon the lad, neither do thou any thing unto him: for now I know that thou fearest God, seeing thou hast not withheld thy son, thine only son, from me.

13 And Abraham lifted up his eyes, and looked, and behold behind him a ram caught in a thicket by his horns: and Abraham went and took the ram, and offered him up for a burnt offering in the stead of his son.

14 And Abraham called the name of that place Jehovah-jireh: as it is said to this day, In the mount of the Lord it shall be seen.

15 And the Angel of the Lord called unto Abraham out of heaven the second time,

16 And said, By myself have I sworn, saith the Lord, for because thou hast done this thing, and hast not withheld thy son, thine only son,

17 That in blessing I will bless thee, and in multiplying I will multiply thy seed as the stars of the

heaven, and as the sand which is upon the sea shore; and thy seed shall possess the gate of his enemies;

18 And in thy seed shall all the nations of the earth be blessed; because thou hast obeyed my voice.

COMMENTS AND QUESTIONS

1. This is a *narrative:* a tight, brief and simple one based on the old principle of suspense. In order to understand simply how it functions as a narrative, it may be useful to break it down into parts as follows:
   1. (verses 1–6) A straightforward account of events.
   2. (verses 7–8) *Almost* a breakdown. Suspense introduced.
   3. (verses 9–12) The climax.
   4. (verses 13–19) The resolution, a happy ending.
2. Analyze the contrast between the simple way in which the events are narrated and the underlying emotions. What are these emotions, and how does the writer convey them?
3. Why is God testing Abraham? What is Abraham's reaction?
4. Would the story be more or less effective if the writer described Abraham's inner feelings in more detail?
5. What attitude on the part of man in relation to God is advocated here? Compare this attitude with the Greek one.
6. Refer back to Matthew Arnold's distinction between Hebraic "right acting" and Hellenic "right thinking" in Chapter 1, page 13. Does this story, contrasted with Greek attitudes, support that distinction?

The Song of Songs Obviously Hebraic literature has influenced our culture primarily through the religious views that are developed in it and, along with them, a concept of morality. One book of the Bible, however, has been influential in quite different ways and represents a unique form of biblical literature. This is the Song of Songs, called in the King James Bible the Song of Solomon. Its authorship is unknown, but because of King Solomon's reputation for wisdom and poetic gifts, it was attributed to him. It is unique in the Bible in that God is never mentioned in it. What it appears to be is a passionate love poem, or more likely several love lyrics that were at some point (scholars speculate by the fifth century B.C.) collected together. Sometimes the speaker is the lover, or bridegroom, sometimes the beloved, or bride. In the course of the poems they are united, separated, sought by each other, found. The awakening of love is closely allied with the awakening of nature in springtime. The lovers celebrate each other's physical beauty and the marvel of being in love, all with a direct and sensuous imagery.

One may well ask how such a poem found its way into a collection of sacred scripture. No one has the definitive answer to this question, but it has puzzled scholars for centuries. Both Jewish and Christian commentators have attempted to explain away its sensuous, physical aspects by *allegorical* interpretations. In the Jewish tradition, the lover was said to represent Jahweh and the beloved his people, Israel. In the Christian version of the *allegory*, the lover becomes Christ; the beloved, his church. In the selections from the King James Bible that follow, the Christian allegorical interpretation is given at the heading of each chapter. We shall see how important this allegorical way of thinking is to the Christian mentality of the Middle Ages.

More recent scholars believe that the poems in the Song of Songs are what they appear to be—celebrations of human love. They were probably originally folk poems, and they may have been sung at weddings. In any case, they have become a part of our lyric tradition and have influenced the ways in which we express love between man and woman.

The Song of Songs

CHAPTER 1

1 The church's love unto Christ. 5 She confesseth her deformity, 7 and prayeth to be directed to his flock. 8 Christ directeth her to the shepherds' tents: 9 and shewing his love to her, 11 giveth her gracious promises, 12 The church and Christ congratulate one another.

1 The Song of songs, which is Solomon's.

2 Let him kiss me with the kisses of his mouth: for thy love is better than wine.

3 Because of the savour of thy good ointments thy name is as ointment poured forth, therefore do the virgins love thee.

4 Draw me, we will run after thee: the King hath brought me into his chambers: we will be glad and rejoice in thee, we will remember thy love more than wine: the upright love thee.

5 I am black, but comely, O ye daughters of Jerusalem, as the tents of Kedar, as the curtains of Solomon.

6 Look not upon me, because I am black, because the sun hath looked upon me: my mother's children were angry with me; they made me the keeper of the vineyards; but mine own vineyard have I not kept.

7 Tell me, O thou whom my soul loveth, where thou feedest, where thou makest thy flock to rest at noon: for why should I be as one that turneth aside by the flocks of thy companions?

8 If thou know not, O thou fairest among women, go thy way forth by the footsteps of the flock, and feed thy kids beside the shepherds' tents.

9 I have compared thee, O my love, to a company of horses in Pharaoh's chariots.

10 Thy cheeks are comely with rows of jewels, thy neck with chains of gold.

11 We will make thee borders of gold with studs of silver.

12 While the King sitteth at his table, my spikenard sendeth forth the smell thereof.

13 A bundle of myrrh is my well beloved unto me; he shall lie all night betwixt my breasts.

14 My beloved is unto me as a cluster of camphire in the vineyards of Engedi.

15 Behold, thou art fair, my love; behold, thou art fair; thou hast doves' eyes.

16 Behold, thou art fair, my beloved, yea, pleasant: also our bed is green.

17 The beams of our house are cedar, and our rafters of fir.

CHAPTER 2

1 The mutual love of Christ and his church. 3 The hope, 10 and calling of the church. 14 Christ's care of the church. 16 The profession of the church, her faith and hope.

1 I am the rose of Sharon, and the lily of the valleys.

2 As the lily among thorns, so is my love among the daughters.

3 As the apple tree among the trees of the wood, so is my beloved among the sons. I sat down under his shadow with great delight, and his fruit was sweet to my taste.

4 He brought me to the banqueting house, and his banner over me was love.

5 Stay me with flagons, comfort me with apples: for I am sick of love.

6 His left hand is under my head, and his right hand doth embrace me.

7 I charge you, O ye daughters of Jerusalem, by the roes, and by the hinds of the field, that ye stir not up, nor awake my love, till he please.

8 The voice of my beloved! behold, he cometh leaping upon the mountains, skipping upon the hills.

9 My beloved is like a roe or a young hart: behold, he standeth behind our wall, he looketh forth at the windows, shewing himself through the lattice.

10 My beloved spake, and said unto me, Rise up, my love, my fair one, and come away.

11 For, lo, the winter is past, the rain is over and gone;

12 The flowers appear on the earth; the time of the singing of birds is come, and the voice of the turtle is heard in our land;

13 The fig tree putteth forth her green figs, and the vines with the tender grape give a good smell. Arise, my love, my fair one, and come away.

14 O my dove, that art in the clefts of the rock, in the secret places of the stairs, let me see thy countenance, let me hear thy voice; for sweet is thy voice, and thy countenance is comely.

15 Take us the foxes, the little foxes, that spoil the vines: for our vines have tender grapes.

16 My beloved is mine, and I am his: he feedeth among the lilies.

17 Until the day break, and the shadows flee away, turn, my beloved, and be thou like a roe or a young hart upon the mountains of Bether.

CHAPTER 3

1 The church's fight and victory in temptation. 6 The church glorieth in Christ.

1 By night on my bed I sought him whom my soul loveth: I sought him, but I found him not.

2 I will rise now, and go about the city in the streets, and in the broad ways I will seek him whom my soul loveth: I sought him, but I found him not.

3 The watchmen that go about the city found me: to whom I said, Saw ye him whom my soul loveth?

4 It was but a little that I passed from them, but I found him whom my soul loveth: I held him, and would not let him go, until I had brought him into my mother's house, and into the chamber of her that conceived me.

5 I charge you, O ye daughters of Jerusalem, by the roes, and by the hinds of the field, that ye stir not up, nor awake my love, till he please.

6 Who is this that cometh out of the wilderness like pillars of smoke, perfumed with myrrh and frankincense, with all powders of the merchant?

7 Behold his bed, which is Solomon's; threescore valiant men are about it, of the valiant of Israel.

8 They all hold swords, being expert in war: every man hath his sword upon his thigh because of fear in the night.

9 King Solomon made himself a chariot of the wood of Lebanon.

10 He made the pillars thereof of silver, the bottom thereof of gold, the covering of it of purple, the midst thereof being paved with love, for the daughters of Jerusalem.

11 Go forth, O ye daughters of Zion, and behold king Solomon with the crown wherewith his mother crowned him in the day of his espousals, and in the day of the gladness of his heart.

CHAPTER 4

1 Christ setteth forth the graces of the church. 8 He sheweth his love to her. 16 The church prayeth to be made fit for his presence.

1 Behold, thou art fair, my love; behold, thou art fair; thou hast doves' eyes within thy locks: thy hair is as a flock of goats, that appear from mount Gilead.

2 Thy teeth are like a flock of sheep that are even shorn, which came up from the washing; whereof every one bear twins, and none is barren among them.

3 Thy lips are like a thread of scarlet, and thy speech is comely: thy temples are like a piece of a pomegranate within thy locks.

4 Thy neck is like the tower of David builded for an armoury, whereon there hang a thousand bucklers, all shields of mighty men.

5 Thy two breasts are like two young roes that are twins, which feed among the lilies.

6 Until the day break, and the shadows flee away, I will get me to the mountain of myrrh, and to the hill of frankincense.

7 Thou art all fair, my love; there is no spot in thee.

8 Come with me from Lebanon, my spouse, with me from Lebanon: look from the top of Amana, from the top of Shenir and Hermon, from the lions' dens, from the mountains of the leopards.

9 Thou hast ravished my heart, my sister, my spouse; thou hast ravished my heart with one of thine eyes, with one chain of thy neck.

10 How fair is thy love, my sister, my spouse! how much better is thy love than wine! and the smell of thine ointments than all spices!

11 Thy lips, O my spouse, drop as the honeycomb: honey and milk are under thy tongue; and the smell of thy garments is like the smell of Lebanon.

12 A garden inclosed is my sister, my spouse; a spring shut up, a fountain sealed.

13 Thy plants are an orchard of pomegranates, with pleasant fruits; camphire, with spikenard,

14 Spikenard and saffron; calamus and cinnamon, with all trees of frankincense; myrrh and aloes, with all the chief spices:

15 A fountain of gardens, a well of living waters, and streams from Lebanon.

16 Awake, O north wind; and come, thou south; blow upon my garden, that the spices thereof may flow out. Let my beloved come into his garden, and eat his pleasant fruits.

COMMENTS AND QUESTIONS

1. The best known, most often quoted part of this poem is in Chapter 2, verses 10–17. How would you explain its appeal?

2. The association between love and spring is, of course, by now an overworked cliché. Is the statement made here nevertheless still fresh and powerful?

3. Why is the beloved (both the man and the woman) so often compared to or invited to a garden? Can you think of other garden images in literature about love?

4. Compare these love lyrics with those of Sappho (Chapter 1). Which is richer in imagery? If you were to paint your impressions of them, which would have more color and more varied *textures*?

5. Compare Sappho's concept of love to that of the author of the Song of Songs. Note that, in the Greek view, love is sometimes seen almost as a sickness (indeed in some tragedies it is a "curse" of Aphrodite).

6. How would you describe the relationship between man and woman as it appears in the Song of Songs?

7. Do you see any justification for the Jewish or the Christian allegorical interpretations?

There are many other types of biblical literature that we do not have space to represent here. The book of Job, which deals with human suffering in a way similar to Greek tragedy but in an Hebraic context, makes an interesting comparison with *Oedipus*. The "wisdom" literature, such as the books of Proverbs and Ecclesiastes, has been influential throughout the Western tradition; so have the poems (attributed to King David) in Psalms. For Christianity the most important books of the Old Testament were those of the prophets (see for example Isaiah 11), who predicted that from the house of David would come the Messiah, or Savior, who would redeem Israel and bring about an era of peace and justice on earth. It is this promise that the followers of Jesus of Nazareth found that their leader fulfilled. The hope of a Messiah yet to come, however, still remains at the core of Judaism.

Early Christianity

Jesus of Nazareth was born during the age of the Emperor Augustus. Nazareth was a part of Judea, a Roman province ruled over by a Roman governor; but Judea was also the kingdom of the Jews and had a Jewish king, Herod. The followers of Jesus were all Jews and did not intend to establish a separate religion but to carry out a radical reform of Judaism. Not only did they view him as the Messiah prophesied to redeem Israel, they also wanted to extend the message of salvation beyond God's chosen people to all mankind.

After Jesus' crucifixion his disciples became an active sect in Jerusalem among their fellow Jews. It was Saint Paul, a convert to the sect of Jesus, who spread the word of the resurrected Christ (a Greek word meaning "anointed") throughout the Greek-speaking world. Coming to Rome in 60 A.D., Paul had much success there. The followers of Jesus, who now included more non-Jews than Jews, were by this time called Christians, after the name of their founder. In 64 A.D. much of Rome was destroyed by fire. The emperor, Nero, may have set it himself (to clear large areas in the center city where he intended to build a new palace complex); but he blamed the destruction on the Christians, whom he accused of "hatred of the human race." Christianity then became illegal and went underground. The Christians were accused of disloyalty to the emperor; of refusing to worship the state gods; of practicing incest, black magic, and cannibalism ("eating" their god in the communion rite); and of generally causing all sorts of misfortunes. The Roman persecution of Christian martyrs is well known, especially in its popular film versions. To be Christian in Rome was to be an antiestablishment, radical member of an underground organization—to risk imprisonment or death. If this was so, why did Christianity appeal to so many people and spread so rapidly? To answer this question is also to determine why the Christians were so easily marked out for harassment by the Roman authorities, who were usually tolerant of religious differences.

Official Roman religion at the time that the Christian message was being spread was fairly similar to the Greek religion. Generally, while adding a few state gods of their own, the Romans simply took over most of the Greek gods, giving them Latin names. Like the Greek gods and goddesses, the Roman ones were blown-up people who had their favorites among mortals and their sexual adventures. To have a happy love affair, an easy childbirth, a safe trip, or a good business deal, one might pray for help to one god or another but would not expect much more of them. The average lower-class person, for example, would not get any help from the gods at the hour of death. The pagan Greeks and Romans believed in something resembling a heaven called the Elysian Fields—a sort of happy hunting ground—but it was off-limits for the lower classes. The slave or former slave (freedman) could only hope to cross a dark river and then, as a shade, to wander eternally in the kingdom of the dead. This kind of religion had obviously satisfied the Romans for hundreds of years, but already in the last century of the Roman Republic before the advent of Caesar Augustus a change in religious interests was beginning to take place.

The change occurring in Greek religious and philosophical thought from the third century B.C. on has already been noted. The spread of Greek culture to the East was balanced by a gradual penetration of Eastern mystery religions into Europe. These religions extended to their adherents hope for a personal immortality beyond the grave and tended to deemphasize the importance of success in this earthly life. Philosophies too, like Stoicism, increasingly came to look on God not merely as some kind of principle of rationality needed to explain the nature of the world as it was but also as a personality who exercised a providential power over man's destiny.

By the reign of Augustus, while the official religion remained centered on the pagan gods, this same movement was well underway in the western half of the Roman empire as well. It affected men and women at all levels of society. Large numbers of Romans were rejecting the classical ethos that death in the service of the motherland was the highest moral end of the citizen. Even members of the upper class began to regard the state as a primarily negative force designed to keep order so that men could go about their central task of finding spiritual fulfillment in religious worship or philosophical contemplation of a divine being who promised individual salvation.

With so many mystery religions to choose from, like the worship of the "Great Mother" Isis or Persian Mithraism, why did Christianity prove so attractive to so many and ultimately triumph over its competitors? The Christians saw in their victory the vindication of their claims to be the true religion, but there are obvious historical explanations for the rapid growth of the sect and the intensive persecution of its members.

Of the Eastern mystery religions only Christianity was exclusive. Adherents to Isis, Mithras, or Cybele could belong to cults worshiping these gods and at the same time sacrifice to the gods of Rome. Christians forbade any worship of other gods. More than this, they condemned all other religions as sinful and inferior. Thus, while they offered their membership eternal life, Christians also claimed that theirs was the only way to heaven. This exclusiveness must have attracted many, while it made enemies of others who could not understand Christian intolerance.

In a sense the Christians were like the Jews in their unwillingness to participate in public religious ceremonies and to take an oath of loyalty to the emperor. But Judaism was an established religion with a limited potential for membership. Christians by contrast were bursting with missionary zeal. They claimed that the souls of all, whether slave or free, man or woman, were equal in God's sight. This message of equality, love, and charity had a tremendous attraction, especially among the poor and enslaved. Rome, however, was a society founded on the institution of slavery; its upper classes could never forget the horrors of the great slave revolt of Spartacus, in the last century of the Republic, that had threatened to incite slaves throughout Italy to murder their masters. If mere yokels—workers and slaves—became preoccupied with the personal salvation of their souls and believed that they possessed truth through their religion, would this not endanger their obedience to their masters and thus endanger the whole structure of Roman society? The new religion must be destroyed. But the more the state persecuted, the more the faith grew.

With the growth of that faith we find the first stirrings of an art that gives expression to the central ideas of the movement. Unlike the Greeks and Romans, or the Jews with their synagogues, the early Christians had no specific building or architectural setting for their celebrations. Without money or power, all they had was their sense of separateness and community within the great world. They met then in homes or rented rooms; but, as persecution grew, it became necessary to seek a safer place for the celebration of the Eucharist (Holy Communion)—the central rite that affirmed fellowship and God's presence among men.

Outside Rome were underground chambers for burial; in these catacombs the Christians met in secret. The walls were decorated with paintings that tell stories from the Old and New Testaments, especially about miracles, persecutions, and Christ's saving grace. The painting reproduced here (Fig. 6-1) shows Christ as the Good Shepherd. What is the motive behind this representation? Compare the figure with other male figures that we have seen. Is he like an emperor or more like a young athlete? This person, the Good Shepherd, who "lays down" his life for his sheep is the same Christ who speaks in the Sermon on the Mount, the New Testament text that best introduces the Christian message.

MATTHEW

The Sermon on the Mount

CHAPTER 5

1 And seeing the multitudes, he went up into a mountain: and when he was set, his disciples came unto him:

6–1 "The Good Shepherd." Catacomb of St. Callixtus, Rome. (Hirmer Fotoarchiv München)

2 And he opened his mouth, and taught them, saying,

3 Blessed are the poor in spirit: for theirs is the kingdom of heaven.

4 Blessed are they that mourn: for they shall be comforted.

5 Blessed are the meek: for they shall inherit the earth.

6 Blessed are they which do hunger and thirst after righteousness: for they shall be filled.

7 Blessed are the merciful: for they shall obtain mercy.

8 Blessed are the pure in heart: for they shall see God.

9 Blessed are the peacemakers: for they shall be called the children of God.

10 Blessed are they which are persecuted for righteousness' sake: for theirs is the kingdom of heaven.

11 Blessed are ye, when men shall revile you, and persecute you, and shall say all manner of evil against you falsely, for my sake.

12 Rejoice, and be exceeding glad: for great is your reward in heaven: for so persecuted they the prophets which were before you.

13 Ye are the salt of the earth: but if the salt have lost his savour, wherewith shall it be salted? it is thenceforth good for nothing, but to be cast out, and to be trodden under foot of men.

14 Ye are the light of the world. A city that is set on an hill cannot be hid.

15 Neither do men light a candle, and put it under a bushel, but on a candlestick; and it giveth light unto all that are in the house.

16 Let your light so shine before men, that they may see your good works, and glorify your Father which is in heaven.

17 Think not that I am come to destroy the law, or the prophets: I am not come to destroy, but to fulfill.

18 For verily I say unto you, Till heaven and earth pass, one jot or one tittle shall in no wise pass from the law, till all be fulfilled.

19 Whosoever therefore shall break one of these least commandments, and shall teach men so, he shall be called the least in the kingdom of heaven: but whosoever shall do and teach them, the same shall be called great in the kingdom of heaven.

20 For I say unto you, That except your righteousness shall exceed the righteousness of the scribes and Pharisees, ye shall in no case enter into the kingdom of heaven.

21 Ye have heard that it was said by them of old time, Thou shalt not kill; and whosoever shall kill shall be in danger of the judgment:

22 But I say unto you, That whosoever is angry with his brother without a cause shall be in danger of the judgment: and whosoever shall say to his brother, Raca, shall be in danger of the council: but whosoever shall say, Thou fool, shall be in danger of hell fire.

23 Therefore if thou bring thy gift to the altar, and there rememberest that thy brother hath ought against thee;

24 Leave there thy gift before the altar, and go thy way; first be reconciled to thy brother, and then come and offer thy gift.

25 Agree with thine adversary quickly, whiles thou art in the way with him; lest at any time the adversary

deliver thee to the judge, and the judge deliver thee to the officer, and thou be cast into prison.

26 Verily I say unto thee, Thou shalt by no means come out thence, till thou hast paid the uttermost farthing.

27 Ye have heard that it was said by them of old time, Thou shalt not commit adultery:

28 But I say unto you, That whosoever looketh on a woman to lust after her hath committed adultery with her already in his heart.

29 And if thy right eye offend thee, pluck it out, and cast it from thee: for it is profitable for thee that one of thy members should perish, and not that thy whole body should be cast into hell.

30 And if thy right hand offend thee, cut it off, and cast it from thee: for it is profitable for thee that one of thy members should perish, and not that thy whole body should be cast into hell.

31 It hath been said, Whosoever shall put away his wife, let him give her a writing of divorcement:

32 But I say unto you, That whosoever shall put away his wife, saving for the cause of fornication, causeth her to commit adultery: and whosoever shall marry her that is divorced committeth adultery.

33 Again, ye have heard that it hath been said by them of old time, Thou shalt not forswear thyself, but shalt perform unto the Lord thine oaths:

34 But I say unto you, Swear not at all; neither by heaven; for it is God's throne:

35 Nor by the earth; for it is his footstool: neither by Jerusalem; for it is the city of the great King.

36 Neither shalt thou swear by thy head, because thou canst not make one hair white or black.

37 But let your communication be, Yea, yea; Nay, nay: for whatsoever is more than these cometh of evil.

38 Ye have heard that it hath been said, An eye for an eye, and a tooth for a tooth:

39 But I say unto you, That ye resist not evil: but whosoever shall smite thee on thy right cheek, turn to him the other also.

40 And if any man will sue thee at the law, and take away thy coat, let him have thy cloke also.

41 And whosoever shall compel thee to go a mile, go with him twain.

42 Give to him that asketh thee, and from him that would borrow of thee turn not thou away.

43 Ye have heard that it hath been said, Thou shalt love thy neighbour, and hate thine enemy.

44 But I say unto you, Love your enemies, bless them that curse you, do good to them that hate you, and pray for them which despitefully use you, and persecute you;

45 That ye may be the children of your Father which is in heaven: for he maketh his sun to rise on the evil and on the good, and sendeth rain on the just and on the unjust.

46 For if ye love them which love you, what reward have ye? do not even the publicans the same?

47 And if ye salute your brethren only, what do ye more than others? do not even the publicans so?

48 Be ye therefore perfect, even as your Father which is in heaven is perfect.

CHAPTER 6

1 Take heed that ye do not your alms before men, to be seen of them: otherwise ye have no reward of your Father which is in heaven.

2 Therefore when thou doest thine alms, do not sound a trumpet before thee, as the hypocrites do in the synagogues and in the streets, that they may have glory of men. Verily I say unto you, They have their reward.

3 But when thou doest alms, let not thy left hand know what thy right hand doeth:

4 That thine alms may be in secret: and thy Father which seeth in secret himself shall reward thee openly.

5 And when thou prayest, thou shalt not be as the hypocrites are: for they love to pray standing in the synagogues and in the corners of the streets, that they may be seen of men. Verily I say unto you, They have their reward.

6 But thou, when thou prayest, enter into thy closet, and when thou hast shut thy door, pray to thy Father which is in secret; and thy Father which seeth in secret shall reward thee openly.

7 But when ye pray, use not vain repetitions, as the heathen do: for they think that they shall be heard for their much speaking.

8 Be not ye therefore like unto them: for your Father knoweth what things ye have need of, before ye ask him.

9 After this manner therefore pray ye: Our Father which art in heaven, Hallowed be thy name.

10 Thy kingdom come. Thy will be done in earth, as it is in heaven.

11 Give us this day our daily bread.

12 And forgive us our debts, as we forgive our debtors.

13 And lead us not into temptation, but deliver us from evil: For thine is the kingdom, and the power, and the glory, for ever. Amen.

14 For if ye forgive men their trespasses, your heavenly Father will also forgive you:

15 But if ye forgive not men their trespasses, neither will your Father forgive your trespasses.

16 Moreover when ye fast, be not, as the hypocrites, of a sad countenance: for they disfigure their faces, that they may appear unto men to fast. Verily I say unto you, They have their reward.

17 But thou, when thou fastest, anoint thine head, and wash thy face;

18 That thou appear not unto men to fast, but unto thy Father which is in secret: and thy Father, which seeth in secret, shall reward thee openly.

19 Lay not up for yourselves treasures upon earth, where moth and rust doth corrupt, and where thieves break through and steal:

20 But lay up for yourselves treasures in heaven, where neither moth nor rust doth corrupt, and where thieves do not break through nor steal:

21 For where your treasure is, there will your heart be also.

22 The light of the body is the eye: if therefore thine eye be single, thy whole body shall be full of light.

23 But if thine eye be evil, thy whole body shall be full of darkness. If therefore the light that is in thee be darkness, how great is that darkness!

24 No man can serve two masters: for either he will hate the one, and love the other; or else he will hold to the one, and despise the other. Ye cannot serve God and mammon.

25 Therefore I say unto you, Take no thought for your life, what ye shall eat, or what ye shall drink; nor yet for your body, what ye shall put on. Is not the life more than meat, and the body than raiment?

26 Behold the fowls of the air: for they sow not, neither do they reap, nor gather into barns; yet your heavenly Father feedeth them. Are ye not much better than they?

27 Which of you by taking thought can add one cubit unto his stature?

28 And why take ye thought for raiment? Consider the lilies of the field, how they grow; they toil not, neither do they spin:

29 And yet I say unto you, That even Solomon in all his glory was not arrayed like one of these.

30 Wherefore, if God so clothe the grass of the field, which to day is, and to morrow is cast into the oven, shall he not much more clothe you, O ye of little faith?

31 Therefore take no thought, saying, What shall we eat? or, What shall we drink? or, Wherewithal shall we be clothed?

32 For after all these things do the Gentiles seek: for your heavenly Father knoweth that ye have need of all these things.

33 But seek ye first the kingdom of God, and his righteousness; and all these things shall be added unto you.

34 Take therefore no thought for the morrow: for the morrow shall take thought for the things of itself. Sufficient unto the day is the evil thereof.

CHAPTER 7

1 Judge not, that ye be not judged.

2 For with what judgment ye judge, ye shall be judged: and with what measure ye mete, it shall be measured to you again.

3 And why beholdest thou the mote that is in thy brother's eye, but considerest not the beam that is in thine own eye?

4 Or how wilt thou say to thy brother, Let me pull out the mote out of thine eye; and, behold, a beam is in thine own eye?

5 Thou hypocrite, first cast out the beam out of thine own eye; and then shalt thou see clearly to cast out the mote out of thy brother's eye.

6 Give not that which is holy unto the dogs, neither cast ye your pearls before swine, lest they trample them under their feet, and turn again and rend you.

7 Ask, and it shall be given you; seek, and ye shall find; knock, and it shall be opened unto you:

8 For every one that asketh receiveth; and he that seeketh findeth; and to him that knocketh it shall be opened.

9 Or what man is there of you, whom if his son ask

bread, will he give him a stone?

10 Or if he ask a fish, will he give him a serpent?

11 If ye then, being evil, know how to give good gifts unto your children, how much more shall your Father which is in heaven give good things to them that ask him?

12 Therefore all things whatsoever ye would that men should do to you, do ye even so to them: for this is the law and the prophets.

13 Enter ye in at the strait gate: for wide is the gate, and broad is the way, that leadeth to destruction, and many there be which go in thereat:

14 Because strait is the gate, and narrow is the way, which leadeth unto life, and few there be that find it.

15 Beware of false prophets, which come to you in sheep's clothing, but inwardly they are ravening wolves.

16 Ye shall know them by their fruits. Do men gather grapes of thorns, or figs of thistles?

17 Even so every good tree bringeth forth good fruit; but a corrupt tree bringeth forth evil fruit.

18 A good tree cannot bring forth evil fruit, neither can a corrupt tree bring forth good fruit.

19 Every tree that bringeth not forth good fruit is hewn down, and cast into the fire.

20 Wherefore by their fruits ye shall know them.

21 Not every one that saith unto me, Lord, Lord, shall enter into the kingdom of heaven; but he that doeth the will of my Father which is in heaven.

22 Many will say to me in that day, Lord, Lord, have we not prophesied in thy name? and in thy name have cast out devils? and in thy name done many wonderful works?

23 And then will I profess unto them, I never knew you: depart from me, ye that work iniquity.

24 Therefore whosoever heareth these sayings of mine, and doeth them, I will liken him unto a wise man, which built his house upon a rock:

25 And the rain descended, and the floods came, and the winds blew, and beat upon that house; and it fell not: for it was founded upon a rock.

26 And every one that heareth these sayings of mine, and doeth them not, shall be likened unto a foolish man, which built his house upon the sand:

27 And the rain descended, and the floods came, and the winds blew, and beat upon that house; and it fell:

and great was the fall of it.

28 And it came to pass, when Jesus had ended these sayings, the people were astonished at his doctrine:

29 For he taught them as one having authority, and not as the scribes.

QUESTIONS

1. What does Jesus demand of his followers, and what does he promise?
2. What kind of a leader, what kind of personality, is Jesus?
3. Why do you think he speaks in parables and "similitudes"? What is the effect of the comparisons made?

The End of Antiquity

While Christianity grew ever stronger in the first three centuries after the death of its founder, the Roman empire itself in the third century began a rapid decline. The middle half of the century saw almost continuous civil war between at least fifty claimants to the imperial throne.

The decline of Rome was temporarily halted in the last quarter of the century by a number of strong emperors who, through a series of reforms and careful management of resources, kept the empire together for another hundred years. However, the move of the capital from Rome to Constantinople by Emperor Constantine (280?–337) indicates the displacement of political and economic power from the western to the eastern half of the empire by the fourth century.

Foundation of the Christian Church Given the divisive tendencies at work in the empire in the third century, the conversion of Emperor Constantine to Christianity in the early fourth century strikes the observer as politically opportune. In the three hundred years of its growth the Church under the pressure of persecution had created a kind of state within a state. Christians settled disputes among themselves within the Christian community; treasuries were created for the purposes of providing for the poor, orphans, and widows. By A.D. 200 almost every major city in the empire had its bishop and its body of priests, chosen by the community. From this time as well, the bishop of

Rome, the Roman pope, asserted his claim to be the spiritual leader of the whole church. His claim rested on the scriptural passage in which Christ tells Peter, his disciple:

> Thou art Peter . . . and upon this rock I will build my church; and the gates of hell shall not prevail against it. And I will give unto thee the keys of the Kingdom of heaven; and whatsoever thou shalt bind on earth shall be bound in heaven; and whatsoever thou shalt loose on earth shall be loosed in heaven. (Matthew 16:18–19)

Saint Peter was believed to have been the first bishop of Rome; as a result, his successors in that office were thought to have inherited this power of binding and loosing men's souls on earth and in heaven. Although these claims were hotly disputed, especially by bishops in the eastern half of the empire, by the fourth century the leadership of Rome was generally recognized in the western portion.

At the time of Constantine's conversion, only about 10 percent of the population in the Roman empire, most of them city dwellers, were Christian. Constantine and his successors were able to support the failing imperial machine with the vital, dynamic organization of the Christian Church. From the beginning the emperors looked on the Church as another branch of the imperial government. They influenced the election of bishops and even that of the pope himself. Clerics were treated as public officials, and the emperors drew on the various Church treasures when the need arose. Thus Christianity developed into something totally different from its beginnings: from an underground sect it became a state religion.

The First Church Buildings   The alliance of Christianity with the state is immediately evident in the appearance of churches–specific complexes for the preaching, teaching, and propagation of the faith. Old Saint Peter's in Rome (Fig. 6-2) was built in the early fourth century (333). Archaeological reconstructions show us a complex of buildings—a great gate, an open courtyard, a roofed porch (narthex), and then the church itself—a large simple building with a central space, the nave, for the congregation. Parallel to the nave on each side are two passageways, aisles. These

6–2   Reconstruction of Old St. Peter's, Rome.

reinforce the directional quality of the nave that focuses on the altar at the east end, supposedly placed above the bones of Saint Peter. Columns separating the nave and aisles support the roof and walls rising above. The roofs of the aisles do not rise the full height of the nave so that there is a story left free for windows before we reach the combinations of beams called trusses of the roof. These windows, in what is called the clerestory, provided light. Candles and lamps were used for night services.

Before the east end is reached, another space crosses the nave at right angles. The transept was for the pulpit and separated the nave from the altar. The semicircular east end, called the apse, had a half-dome above it. The clerics and the bishop would sit here during services.

In addition to the church and courtyard there was a round building called a baptistery. Walls were probably painted with stories like those of the catacombs. The exterior would have been fairly plain since the significant events took place in the interior space.

Compare this building plan (Fig. 6-3) with that of a Roman basilica (Fig. 5-15). How are they different? Why do you think the law court plan might have been a source for this kind of building? What is particularly Greek? Roman?

Early Christian Sculpture   Other important monuments that document the spread and power of Christianity are the numerous sarcophagi (caskets) that were found in Rome and in other Christian sites.

A Nave
B Transept
C Apse
D Aisle
E Atrium

6–3 Old St. Peter's, Rome. Groundplan.

Decorated with scenes from the Christian story, they emphasize the importance of its association with life, death, and afterlife. An excellent example is the *Sarcophagus of Junius Bassus*, a Roman noble (Fig. 6-4). Along the side represented here we see scenes that will appear again and again in Christian art.

The sarcophagus is divided into two registers or rows with five scenes each; each scene is separated by a column giving each a strong architectural framework. In the top register from left to right are the sacrifice of Isaac; Saint Peter taken prisoner; Christ enthroned between Saint Peter and Saint Paul; and Christ before Pontius Pilate (the last two scenes). In the bottom register we see Job and his comforters; Adam, Eve, and the serpent (the Fall of Man); Christ's entry into Jerusalem; Daniel in the lions' den; and Saint Paul led to his martyrdom. The artist has combined Old and New Testament scenes emphasizing sin, martyrdom, and death. These are mitigated by the two central scenes— Christ the heavenly king (he sits on a personification of the firmament) and Christ the earthly king, cheered as he enters Jerusalem. How does this sculpture differ from that we have considered? Is it classical? Do you

6–4 Sarcophagus of Junius Bassus, c. 359 A.D. Vatican Museums. (Alinari—Scala)

feel the presence of other needs and aims in the presentation of these scenes? How is Christ presented—youthful or dignified, imperial or divine? How do the nude bodies of Adam and Eve compare with the Greek *Spearbearer* or the Cnidian *Aphrodite?* What accounts for the differences?

If these questions are difficult to answer, it is because art and architecture were at this point in a state of transition. Artists and thinkers were searching for the best means to convey new and important ideas at a time when there were no clear patterns for the presentation of these ideas. Greek and Roman art were sources that acted as strong influences but were not the perfect match for making images of Christianity's beliefs. Moreover, what does faith, Christianity's basic tenet, look like? Visual art could only provide examples of the acts of people who had taken the path of faith.

The Barbarian Influence in the Roman World

The barbarians, who invaded the Roman empire in the fifth century, left many of these art objects and buildings intact. Primarily of Germanic origin, they had been in contact with Roman civilization for centuries. Their intention was not to destroy a civilization but to garner its fruits for themselves. In the eastern half of the empire the emperors were strong enough to resist the attackers; there the empire survived until its destruction by the Turks in 1453. But in the western provinces the emperors lost control; barbarian rulers assumed the position of authority in different areas.

Most of the barbarians were already Christian or were converted to Christianity soon after settling on Roman soil. Those converting in the homeland, however, had done so largely under the influence of heretical preachers and, once in the empire, had to be converted to the Catholic faith. Although the central role of kings in the tribe was a religious one and war chiefs supervised military expeditions, the pressures of invading the empire created a need for more central direction and led to a significant increase in the king's military powers. To an extent, the conversion of the various tribes to Christianity reduced the significance of the king as a religious leader, although throughout most of the Middle Ages the office retained something of its sacred, priestly qualities.

In the wreckage of the old imperial structure, what had been the Roman empire became a series of smaller kingdoms (see map). Because of their original Germanic religious associations, the kings were able not only to assert control over the churches but also over another important religious institution, the monastery.

Monasticism   From the first century of Christianity men and women who rejected life in the world had moved out into the wilderness individually to worship God in isolation. They called themselves hermits. Others who would have liked to withdraw from the world, however, felt unable to endure the loneliness of such a retreat or believed that isolation contradicted the Christian's duty to love one's neighbor. A communal retreat seemed to such Christians preferable to a solitary one. Thus, by the second century, communities of like-minded men and women came into existence, normally founded in remote places, and emphasizing common worship and mutual service. Often these *monasteries*, as they were eventually called, became the object of rich donations in land and money and grew to be powerful economic and political forces in the society.

In the confusion following the disintegration of the western Roman empire, monasticism flourished as never before. Centers of learning sometimes as well as of piety, offering physical as well as spiritual safety, monasteries were places of refuge in a dangerous world. An ideal plan for a monastery, drawn up about 800, the Saint Gaul plan (Fig. 6-5) shows a basilica, dormitories, dining room, library, hospital, hostel, cemetery, and gardens. It resembles a small, self-contained city. Given the wealth and importance of the great monasteries, it is easy to understand why the kings in the centuries after the invasions were concerned to assert some control over the resources of these foundations and to regulate the election of abbots.

Decline of Roman Centralization   Yet, even with the support of the local churches and monasteries, the barbarian rulers after A.D. 500 proved unable to keep the old Roman institutions running. The Roman conception of political power enshrined in the imperial institutions of government was a public one; that is, the Romans considered political authority to be a series of magistracies. Obedience was owed to a magistrate

THE BARBARIAN SUCCESSION STATES
About 500 A.D.

not as a person but as an official representing the majesty of the Roman people. The most effective political bonds in Germanic society were, on the other hand, the personal ones between a war chief and his followers, established by an oath. The warrior obeyed the chief not because the latter represented the tribe but because the warrior had sworn to follow this particular man. As has been seen, the tendency to local autonomy had already set in under the late emperors; the coming of the barbarians only accentuated the development. In a period of insecurity, when men must seek protection wherever they can, the private conception of political power almost inevitably comes to dominate

governmental relationships. By the seventh and eighth centuries a large portion of Europe's population found itself involved in a welter of political and economic relationships founded on oaths involving promises to obey or to protect.

The Germanic and surviving Roman aristocracies were the chief beneficiaries of this proliferation of power because they alone had the military might to maintain order at the local level. This group also seized control of churches and monasteries in their various regions, using them to advance their families. Whereas under the late empire and the early barbarian kings, the Church had been a tool in the hands of the central

A Church Nave	**E** Public Entrance	**J** Refectory
B Choirs	**F** Guest House	**K** Cloister
C Main Altar	**G** School	**L** Cemetery
D Towers	**H** Abbot's House	**M** Gardens, Barns

6–5 Schematic plan for an ideal monastery at St. Gall, Switzerland, c.819 A.D. (Drawing after a 9th. century manuscript, Chapter Library, St. Gall, Switzerland)

governments, now it had ten thousand masters. The papacy at Rome as well fell under the control of the Roman nobility. The effort of the Carolingian rulers of France in the eighth and early ninth centuries to reunite authority over a large expanse of territory had only a temporary effect on the process of political disintegration in most areas. Central government required a vigorous economic basis, but until the eleventh century Western Europe had, generally speaking, a localized subsistence economy.

7

MEDIEVAL EUROPE: CULTURE AND THE CATHEDRAL

The focus of our treatment of the Judeo-Christian root falls roughly on the period 1000 to 1350, sometimes called the High Middle Ages. Within this time period we can speak with some assurance of a civilization of the Middle Ages. Before 1000 medieval culture was still in formation, while after 1350 new currents (which historians generally label as characteristic of the Renaissance) were becoming dominant. Medieval society was doubtless affected by survivals of primitive Germanic, Italic, and Celtic folk culture, together with admixtures of sophisticated pagan philosophy and literature; but the informing ideas centered around belief in a transcendent, all-powerful God who, through the God-man Christ, offered redemption to the sinful race of men. Most cultural forms tended to be manifestations and expressions of this Christian (as developed from the Judaic) conception of God and the human predicament.

Prior to examining the productions in the arts and literature of this society, we will take up medieval developments in economics, in the Church, in political history, and in intellectual history generally. The early eleventh century in all these four areas initiated revivals that were interrelated. After five hundred years of progressive decline and relative stabilization at a low plateau, Western Europe by 1000 began to stir with new life.

Medieval Revivals

Economic Revival   Already by the end of the tenth century the tempo of economic life was changing. The development of the castle had finally provided the population with a source of security. Agricultural techniques and inventions like the horse collar gradually came into widespread use, leading to an increase in agricultural productivity and ultimately to an enormous population rise between 1000 and 1250. The distribution of the population was also altered; because food was easier to produce, a portion of the population could be spared from direct employment in agriculture for other things. Established towns grew in size, and new ones were founded. While by 1300 only about 10 percent of Europe's population lived in towns over 2000, nonetheless, the towns, serving as they did as focuses of economic and cultural life, played a role in medieval society much greater than this percentage would suggest. Silver deposits were exploited by mining; and when the bullion produced poured into the economy as currency, there was further expansion. International markets developed again, and large-scale production was encouraged.

Religious Revival   This renewed vitality in the economy was paralleled by a revival of religious interests. The great outpouring of European crusades toward the East from the end of the eleventh century is a reflection of a society bursting with creative energy and religious enthusiasm. In the decades after 1050 the popes at Rome initiated a program to dislodge the churches and monasteries from the hands of secular powers and to make them independent. The whole present relationship of the Church to the secular power, they argued, was sinful. Men of the world dominated the men of God. The soul is superior to the body, yet those who by divine command are to control bodily things now dominate heavenly ones. The priest is in fact superior to the king because his realm is higher. The priest controls the sacraments, that is, rites like baptism and communion, which are the channels through which divine, life-giving grace pours. The pope, at the very pinnacle of the channels of grace, can let it flow or cut it off from whom he deems unworthy. The other priests act by his authority. For all his earthly power, the greatest monarch of Christendom will perish eternally if he is separated from the divine source; it depends on the priest and, first of all, the pope to decide whether he is worthy to receive the sacraments.

On the basis of this theory the papacy from the mid-eleventh century embarked on a policy of removing secular lords—kings and princes included—from power over the churches in their areas. Bishops, priests, abbots and monks were to give ultimate obedience to the pope, the vicar of Christ in Rome. Every Christian was commanded to follow divine law as it was interpreted by the papacy, and kings who disobeyed God's rule were to cease being kings. The result of the development was that by the early thirteenth century the Roman pope was the most powerful figure in Christendom. Not only did he effectively supervise all the churches and monasteries, but he also acted as the conscience of the secular rulers and their governments.

Political Revival   These same centuries also witnessed a political revival. The economic revival intensified contact between the different regions of a kingdom and created a tendency for political integration. In the long run this served the cause of the secular rulers. Princes came increasingly to stress the public nature of political power and the obligations of subjects to obey them not on the basis of a personal oath but because the ruler was the prince in a given territory. In the course of the twelfth and thirteenth centuries the monarchies gradually asserted their authority at the local level and subordinated that of the nobility.

Increased central government, however, required money to pay for an army, a bureaucracy, and a royal court. This meant taxes. The king could not seize the money of his subjects. The Germanic conception of private political power founded on an oath was coupled with an implicit understanding that the leader would protect his follower's person and property. By the eleventh century there was a general recognition of the lord's right to demand aid from his followers in certain cases, but both the lord and his men had to agree in council when such circumstances existed and to work out the obligations of each man to his lord. Roman law, studied in Europe again from the eleventh century, also stipulated that "what touches all must be approved of by all." This was interpreted to mean, that when levying a tax for the good of the country, the king had to consult with important individuals and with representatives of various segments of the population. Thus, the desire of the monarchs to increase their power over the country led to the need for taxation, and this called into being consultative assemblies. Almost everywhere in Europe a tradition of consent of the people to taxation was developing.

By the fourteenth century the political revival would significantly hinder the effectiveness of papal intervention in international politics. Already in the twelfth, monarchies were diverting loyalties of their peoples to themselves not only away from local nobility but also away from the Christian republic led by the pope. But even by the first half of the thirteenth century this process was still only underway: if the glory was a fragile one, the papacy remained the most important political force in Europe.

Intellectual Revival Along with the political, economic, and religious revival beginning in the eleventh century came an intellectual revival. In its early stages in the eleventh and twelfth centuries, this revival can generally be described as a process of ordering knowledge in an effort to control experience. The initial step in this development around the year 1000 was the introduction of elementary texts of Aristotle's logic. From the ancient Greek system of logic, Europeans learned the idea of subordinating one idea to another, the part to the whole. Logic instructed them in the process of arriving at new truth and of organizing their knowledge into categories. Trained in logic, Europeans were able to present systematically pieces of knowledge that before were a confused jumble. A great European logician, Peter Abelard, wrote a book in the first half of the twelfth century called *Yes and No* in which he asked hundreds of central questions regarding human life and theology such as, "Is it right to murder another?" and "Does God exist?" After each question he placed the answers given by ancient great authorities, both pagan and Christian writers. Logic was also an aid in the reorganization of the highly confused laws of the Church. The scholars of the twelfth century gave an ordered form to church or canon law, besides systematically presenting in concise fashion the fruits of numerous commentaries on the Holy Bible. All these endeavors gave men a confidence in the power of reason to understand the universe and offered them a possibility of eventually controlling it.

In the centuries between the fall of Rome and the eleventh century, learning was centered in the monasteries of Europe. With the revival of the towns, however, the cathedrals came to dominate intellectual life. Every cathedral had a school for instructing the young clerics who sang there and served in various capacities around the altar. The first organized teaching of Aristotle's basic logical works occurred around the year 975 in a cathedral school, that of Rheims. From this point until the twelfth century the initiative in education belonged to these schools. By the twelfth century the number of students had increased to such a degree that in places like Paris and Oxford the cathedral was no longer able to contain the classes; then private teachers opened up their own schools in the vicinity. In the next century, as organization was given to this diversified instruction, the university was born.

The term *scholasticism* is usually applied to the scientific, theological, and philosophical learning taught in these schools and universities. First of all, this kind of learning was a monopoly of the schools, rather than of private scholars or secluded groups. The method, moreover, of presenting the thought in question-and-answer form was that followed in actual schoolroom teaching. But the term also applied to a common assumption of the thinkers of this three-hundred-year period. There was among them an implicit confidence that there was no conflict between the conclusions produced by reason and those accepted on faith, that the two sets of truth were compatible.

Initially with the introduction of Aristotelian logic the primary question became: to what extent could reason be employed to understand faith? As Christians, Europeans were committed to belief in the need of divine revelation to know certain truths. By the fifth century A.D. the basic doctrines of the Christian Church had been worked out on the basis of God's revealed word in the Bible, as follows: (1) the belief in a Trinity composed of Father, Son, and Holy Ghost, three persons in one divine substance. How this could be without making them three separate gods was acknowledged as divine mystery. (2) The belief in the creation of the universe out of nothing by an all-powerful God. (3) The doctrine of the fall of man into evil through his own free will. (4) The belief in heaven as a final resting place for the good and in a hell as the place for punishment of the evil. (5) The belief in Christ, human and divine, as the redeemer of man. Because he was God, he could live on earth without sin, and by virtue of his humanity he could redeem sinful, fallen mankind. (6) The doctrine of eternal life for the soul in paradise and the resurrection of the body through redemption. (7) Redemption was promised to those who believed in Christ as the Lord and who did good work on earth. (8) The necessity of God's grace for salvation. Whether some men are predestined by God to believe in Christ and do good work with God's grace doing everything, or whether grace is offered to all and men must cooperate with it in the process of salvation, was a debated point. The overwhelming tendency in the Church, however, was to stress the power and responsibility of men to cooperate.

The most congenial philosophic school of antiquity for early Christian thinkers had been that of Plato and his followers. Christians were attracted by the Platonic doctrine of two levels of reality, the world of the Ideas and that of the senses. Plato embraced the idea of the immortality of the soul; and the negative attitude of Platonists to the body, which they considered a prison, also proved attractive to Christians eager to dominate bodily lusts. The Christians were so influenced by these ascetic impulses that they often overlooked their own doctrine that the body, too, would be raised to heaven with the soul. Plato seemed so close to Christianity in some things he wrote that many Christian scholars believed that he had written either under the influence of the Holy Ghost or with knowledge of the work of the Hebrew prophets.

Stoicism also proved attractive to Christians, at least in its moral doctrines. Stoic stress on indifference to worldly success or failure seemed to be helpful to believers in their efforts to turn to God from the false joys of the world. The late Stoic view of government as having largely negative functions of keeping order reappeared in the works of the Church Fathers. As reformulated by the latter, the duty of the state was to prevent sinners from killing one another while the Church went about saving men's souls. The sword of kings was to be at the service of the Church: monarch and bishop were to work in harmony to bring men to seek righteousness.

The Church Fathers of the second to the fifth century, therefore, utilized the writings of Platonists and Stoics both as aids in elaborating Christian theological, philosophical, and moral ideas and as witnesses to the truth of Christian doctrine. While the writings of ancient Latin Stoics like Seneca survived in numbers between the fifth and the eleventh century, almost all of Plato was lost; and the Europeans' knowledge of his thought came mainly from what the Church Fathers had written about him. Aristotle's thought had not been popular in late antiquity and had had little effect on Christian doctrine in its formative stages. However, the craze for Aristotelian logic beginning in the eleventh century added a third ancient Greek influence to Christian thought. Working with Latin translations of Aristotle's elementary logic texts and ancient commentaries on these, European scholars were eager to sharpen their newfound intellectual instruments on the Christian faith. The danger to divine mystery was clearly perceived by critics of such efforts. Pious Christians in the twelfth century were especially alarmed at what appeared to be the assumption of some theologians that God's mind, working by the same processes, was subject to the same rules and conditions in its operations as was the human mind and that it was thus possible for the human mind to understand why God had operated as he did. Did this not detract from God's all-powerful nature and will? But what, then, were the limits of reason?

The recovery in the course of the thirteenth century of all of Aristotle's philosophical, moral, and scientific writings made the problem of faith and reason even more acute. Aristotle's logical works had been only an introduction to this masterpiece of thought. Medieval Europe was particularly weak in scientific work; but, with the introduction of Aristotle's body of writings, Europeans became aware of a system of thinking, ultimately reducible to a few basic principles, that had something to say about almost everything in the universe. Aristotle answered questions that they had not yet even learned to ask.

In the course of the thirteenth century, as they came to understand what Aristotle had written—and his work was and is very difficult to read—Christian thinkers came, however, to see that Aristotle believed in an eternal world and in a God who did not create the universe but who served only to explain why things in it moved. Moreover, he also seemed to believe that the human soul died with the human body. Aristotle appeared to be the culmination of the power of human reason; yet the results of his investigation, conducted according to the procedures of his logic (on which they too relied), seemed to point to some conclusions that contradicted the faith. Was the Christian faith therefore irrational? God was supposed to be truth, yet reason's conclusions apparently were not those of revelation.

Thomas Aquinas   The most influential attempt to reconcile reason and revelation in the thirteenth century was that of Thomas Aquinas (died 1274). Thomas showed, first of all, that Aristotle's proof for the eternity of the world was not a conclusive one. In fact, he maintained that there is no way by reason to prove either the eternity or the creation of the universe. We know that it was created, but that knowledge comes from faith. In the matter of Aristotle's position on the immortality of the human soul, Aquinas argued that Aristotle himself is ambiguous. Thus, he concluded, there is no proof that reason contradicts faith. Quite the contrary.

There are, according to Thomas Aquinas, many truths about the world that reason can discover: the causes of the rainbow, the source of locomotion in animals, and the like. More than this, there are certain truths revealed to us by God that could also be known by reason; for instance, that God exists and that he is one God. After all, some ancient pagans knew this through the use of their reason. Then there are truths

about God that no pagan could have known, such as the existence of the Trinity. Thus, for Aquinas the two spheres of truth, that established by reason and that by revelation, overlap.

If we follow reason according to the rules of logic, we can know many things about God and heaven; and, at the very pinnacle of this kind of truth, reason duplicates the lowest truths of revelation. Moreover, even the truths of revelation not open to human reason are not in themselves illogical, irrational. When reason examines them, in fact, they are quite reasonable. If man utilizes his reason according to the proper procedures of logic, he will gradually define a body of truth that at its greatest heights demands to be completed by the truths of faith.

Accordingly Aquinas and thinkers like him were able to construct enormous systems of thought beginning with our awareness of ourselves and the world and integrating all aspects of our internal and external experience. Every natural phenomenon from the falling of the raindrops to the movement of the stars can be set within a framework of explanation that literally requires the truths of revelation to cap it with ultimate meaning. Just as these edifices of human thought presented a world where all truth pointed heavenward, so did the great stone cathedrals that dotted the landscape of Western Europe in the thirteenth century.

Medieval Art and the Church: The Gothic Cathedral

Art in the ninth, tenth, and eleventh centuries, like learning, was centered in the court and monastery. These two institutions had the means, personnel, and time to produce creative work. Painting, sculpture, and architecture were viewed as ways to enhance and explain Christian doctrine. It is also true that both princes and churchmen realized the power of beauty and wealth to enhance their respective positions.

Along with the economic, religious, political, and intellectual revivals of Europe in the twelfth and thirteenth centuries, an artistic growth flourished. This gave rise to the Gothic style in art and architecture, a style whose forms and conventions would be practiced all over northern Europe and in the British Isles. Two particular occurrences were of great significance for

EUROPE AND THE CRUSADER STATES
about 1140

- → Routes of the Crusades: 1096-1204
- ∘∘∘∘ Pilgrimage Route: Paris to Santiago de Compostela
- Crusader states

this development: the pilgrimage and the crusades. Both activities united people and provided them with profound new experiences.

Pilgrimages Since every Christian could not be a monk, nun, priest, or in some other way directly affiliated with the church, it fell to the great numbers of lay

Catholics to seek other ways to ensure their salvation. The immediate means open was the performance of good works, which usually meant contributions of time and wealth to the local church, cathedral, or monastery. Another was the route of penance—the undertaking of a pilgrimage to Rome, the Holy Land, or another shrine to seek the aid of a saint or saints. Along the route, the pilgrim could visit the relics and shrines of important local saints, who would then act on behalf of the sinner.

For Frenchmen and Germans one of the most favored pilgrimages was to Santiago de Compostela in northern Spain. This was the site of the tomb of Saint James, the son of Zebedee, one of Christ's chosen disciples. We know of it as a pilgrimage site as early as the mid-ninth century. By the mid-tenth century, clerics and laity were making the journey in increasing numbers. The map shows the route followed. Chaucer's *Canterbury Tales*, set on an English pilgrimage to Thomas à Becket's shrine, reflects the spirit of comradeship that pilgrimages instilled.

Movement in a pilgrimage was slow, fifteen or twenty miles a day, mostly on foot. Monasteries and churches provided accommodations along the road and broke the monotony of the trip by their beauty. As pilgrims came from many directions to Santiago, churches and cathedrals began to develop specific regional types. In the great burst of building activity many architectural ideas were tried, discarded, and elaborated.

A brief look at one of the great pilgrimage churches in France will be of help in understanding the Gothic tradition that developed after the eleventh and twelfth centuries. Saint Sernin, located at Toulouse, in southern France, was one of many great churches built in the eleventh and twelfth centuries in response to the pilgrimages and to growing wealth, mobility, and ambition. All over France and Germany and in England, many builders employed the means of Roman architecture to create new feelings and form. We generally call this art *Romanesque* because of its relation to Roman architecture (Fig. 7-1).

The plan of Saint Gaul (Fig. 6-5) showed a church with rounded ends, nave, and two apses. Entrance was from the side, with no clearly defined transepts. Two round stair towers were located at one end outside the apse. Local parish churches were even simpler. They might have an apse; a crypt below ground for treasure, burial, and relics; and a simple nave with entry at the west end.

The plan of Saint Sernin at Toulouse (Fig. 7-2) represents a shape called the Latin cross. There is a clearly defined entrance porch that opens into a nave with

7–1 St. Sernin, Toulouse, east end. (© ARCH. PHOT. PARIS/ S.P.A.D.E.M., 1980)

7–2 Groundplan of St. Sernin, Toulouse, c. 1100.

double aisles on each side. The transept and apse are sharply defined. On the east side of the transept and around the apse are separate, clearly defined small apses, which are called chapels. These are all related to each other by an aisle which goes all the way around the transept arms and around the apse itself. This passageway is called an *ambulatory*. From the outside we see that Saint Sernin is a brick and stone building with clearly defined roof forms. There is the nave roof and, lower down, the roofs over the aisles and the separately roofed apse and chapels.

On entering, we would see a church meant to accommodate not only the monastery (of which it was a part) but also crowds of pilgrims. The arrangement of nave and aisles is comparable to that of Old Saint Peter's (Fig. 6-2), but the ceiling is composed of barrel and groin vaults like those used in the Colosseum (Fig. 5-10).

Crusades   The Crusades, those holy wars designed to free the great sites of Christianity from "heathen" hands, afforded another opportunity for churchmen and laity to gain wider knowledge of buildings and building techniques. Churches in Jerusalem, Constantinople, and southern Italy encouraged builders to seek greater splendor. The medieval crusades, like the pilgrimages fostering exchange of ideas and expertise from one region to another, similarly contributed to the rise of the Gothic style.

The Rise of Gothic Architecture   Many villages in France today still give the impression that an enormous church dominates the small houses, shops, and other buildings around it. Fantastic energy was put into the construction of these great stone works. Usually everyone in the village, from the lords and ladies down to the peasants, joined the professional stonemasons in doing their part to construct an edifice to the glory of God and to the representation of the Church on earth (Fig. 7-3).

Why did medieval people devote such time, energy, and money to the construction of these huge and complex buildings? It is hard to find anything comparable in the lives of modern people. We must try to remember that churches were not merely places to go on Sunday or decorations for a town; they represented a vital aspect of everyone's spiritual life. They were not only dwellings for God on earth but also a kind of bridge between the physical and spiritual realms. They began as heavy stone set on the ground, but they soared upward toward heaven. They contained something for everyone. For the common people, many of whom could neither read nor write, they offered a kind of visual religious education. The fifteenth-century poet François Villon wrote a ballade about his mother in which he described her simple faith, in particular her devotion to the Virgin Mary, and the way the art in her parish church influenced this faith. The translation is by William Frederic Giese.

FRANÇOIS VILLON

Ballade

For His Mother to Our Lady

Queen of the skies and regent of the earth
And sovran empress of the realms of hell,
Receive me, Mary, though of little worth,
Yet heavenward bent, a child of Christian birth;

7–3   Chartres. (© ARCH. PHOT. PARIS/S.P.A.D.E.M., 1980)

Through your grace only can I enter in—
For your great goodness, as I know full well,
Is greater than the burden of my sin.
O queen of heaven, your servitor am I,
And in this faith I mean to live and die.

Tell your blest Son I am His own, and thus,
Even as Egyptian Mary was forgiven
Or that most learnèd clerk, Theophilus,
Who once did seal a compact with the devil—
May God forbid I fall into like evil!—
So may I also be absolved and shriven;
For I hold true, howe'er unworthily,
Since I am weak, and sinful too alas,
The holy things that I have heard at Mass,
And in this faith I mean to live and die.

I am a woman poor and very old,
Who cannot read and nothing know at all,
But in the cloister, when my beads I've told,
I see God's paradise upon the wall,
All gay with harps and lutes, and, underneath,
A flaming hell where damned souls boil and seethe.
Hell frightens me, and heaven fills with joy:
O heavenly goddess, let the joy be mine,
For you to every sinner are benign
Whose faith is free of weakness and alloy—
And in this faith I mean to live and die.

Envoi

Virgin and blest princess without stain,
Thy Son was He who shall forever reign,
Jesus, who, wrought on by our feebleness,
Left His bright heaven to succor our distress
And offered on the cross His lovely youth.
Our Lord is He: this do I hold for sooth—
And in this faith I mean to live and die.

The illiterate old lady in this poem finds her religious faith and her religious fears confirmed in the paintings on the walls of her parish church. She then turns to the Virgin Mary, the kindly intercessor between lowly human beings and God Almighty. The Virgin, as we shall see, played a highly important role in medieval Christianity, and many cathedrals were dedicated to her. Like the church itself, she seemed an almost physical presence who could lead the soul toward the abstract and spiritual realm.

Many of the paintings that adorned the church walls, such as the ones referred to in the poem, are now lost; but the stained-glass windows, the sculptures, and the architectural design of the churches built in the twelfth and thirteenth centuries tell us a great deal about the values and beliefs of the people who built them and worshiped in them. The term *Gothic*, used to describe their style, was coined in the Renaissance. Until the eighteenth century it was a derogatory term, implying that a style created by the descendants of the Goths, one of the barbarian tribes that overran the Roman empire, was uncivilized and greatly inferior to the classical style. (In a similar way, Westerners once considered African art barbaric until European artists in the early part of our century began to appreciate its originality.) Certainly one can say that the aesthetic impression felt inside a Gothic cathedral is *different* from the impression one has inside a Roman building like the Pantheon, but most modern viewers would not at all agree with the Renaissance belief that this difference constitutes inferiority. Preference here is largely a matter of taste and temperament. Before we begin our analysis of some of the technical and artistic features of the Gothic cathedral, formulate some of your own impressions by comparing the interior and exterior of the Pantheon (Figs. 5-12, 5-13, 5-14) with Notre Dame of Chartres (Figs. 7-4, 7-5). Consider the actual size, the importance of interior or exterior for the user, the purpose of each, the arrangement of interior spaces, and the materials.

Gothic buildings, like all other architecture, evolved from the technology, needs, and ideals of a particular time and place. The patrons and master craftsmen who created these great churches drew on the current architectural solutions and skills while experimenting with and expanding both structural and formal capabilities. Masons, carpenters, and other craftsmen followed the routes of the crusades and pilgrimages.

The monastery church of Saint Denis (Fig. 7-6), in the Ile-de-France, near Paris, and the cathedral of Notre Dame (Our Lady) of Chartres, which we will consider in this chapter, document the origin and extraordinary capacities of the period for visual expression of metaphysical and deeply religious ideas.

7–4 Chartres, west front. (Lauros-Giraudon, Paris)

7–5 Chartres, nave. (Giraudon, Paris)

Suger and Saint Denis   In 1120 a monk named Suger was named abbot of the Abbey of Saint Denis, one of the oldest and most venerable monastic foundations in France. Named for the founding saint of French Catholicism, it was also associated with the Capets, successors to Charlemagne, many of whom were buried there. Suger had been at Saint Denis since childhood and had grown up with Louis VI, the Capetian king. A dynamic, ambitious, and highly intelligent individual, he had already distinguished himself as a diplomat for the papacy before becoming abbot. In 1147, when Louis VII left for the Second Crusade, Suger was made regent of the kingdom. But Suger did not seek power for its own sake. His association of the abbey with secular power came from his Christian desire to bring order and spiritual enlightenment to the poor and to the powerful. These beliefs, in combination with other factors (the church was in disrepair and crowded on feast days), caused Suger to begin to work on rebuilding the church at Saint Denis.

Descriptions of churches seen on Crusades provided Suger with some ideas; but most important were those derived from his own theology, which developed in the years before the work at Saint Denis began. It was heavily Neoplatonic, for it was based on the writing of Dionysius, a sixth-century Greek mystic who was mistakenly associated with Saint Denis (A.D. 200s), the patron saint of France. Suger's ideas were also related to those of Aristotle and the scholastics. The two central themes with which he worked were harmony and light. Suger believed that all matter in some degree partakes of God and in some way reflects ultimate reality. Visible light is, therefore, the analogy for the light of God, and thus symbolic of the unity of all creation. As natural light infuses and transforms, so we are transformed by this heavenly light, illumination, knowledge. Suger also believed that the contemplation of the truly beautiful "worthy materials" of gold, gemstones, chalices, and altars could transport one from the world here below to the heavenly one. In 1144 he wrote:

> Thus, when out of my delight in the beauty of the house of God—the loveliness of the many-colored gems has called me away from external cares, and worthy meditation has induced me to reflect, transferring that which is material to that which is immaterial, on the diversity of the sacred virtues—then it seems to me that I see myself dwelling, as it were, in some strange region of the universe which neither exists entirely in the slime of the earth nor entirely in the purity of Heaven; and that, by the grace of God, I can be transported from this inferior to that higher world.

It became his ambition to make his church such a means of transcendence, to fill it with light and to give it a spiritual significance as great as that of its saint and the French kingdom.

We do not know how Suger conveyed his ideas to the master builders who undertook the work. But we do know the combination of his visions and the hired technical skill produced a number of important changes in church design and construction that were absorbed at once by builders in the area around Saint Denis.

Perhaps the most significant innovation was a new system of *piers* and *vaults*, employing pointed arches that allowed the enlargement of the east end, creating a large *choir* (a rectangular space for the clergy between the transept and apse) surrounded by an aisle (ambulatory) with seven chapels spaced equidistantly on its outer edge (Fig. 7-7). These were roofed with vaults. Most important of all, however, the outside walls of the chapel and the clerestory above were now largely glass. This glass was richly colored—reds, blues, yellows, and some white. The small pieces of glass were arranged in patterns, figures, and stories. Joined together by lead strips, the panels were then set within a framework of stone. The east end of the church became a vessel for the transmission of divine, transforming light.

7–6 St. Denis, west front. (Giraudon, Paris)

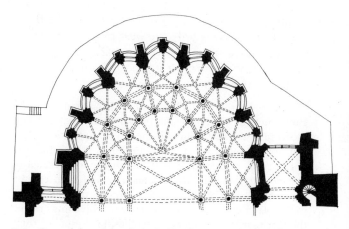

7–7 Groundplan of the choir, St. Denis, near Paris, c. 1140.

165

Once the new rear part [east end] is joined to the part in front, the church shines with its middle part brightened. For bright is that which is brightly coupled with the bright. And bright is the noble edifice that is prevaded by the new light.

The church, filled with light, was a bridge to the ultimate reality of divine revelation, the harmonious and orderly world. The windows transformed light, as God's light transformed the dull heaviness of matter. Uplifted by this created light within the church, the worshipers' souls would rise to seek God, its uncreated source.

This new way of building will be explored further in the rebuilding of the cathedral of Notre Dame of Chartres (Fig. 7-4), which is among the finest examples of Gothic design and construction.

The Cathedral at Chartres   The village of Chartres seems almost inundated by the fields of grain that spread out from the town, but the cathedral dominates the horizon. The church, dedicated to the Virgin, was founded before 743 (the first sure date associated with it). Its chief relic, the tunic of the Virgin, had been given by King Charles the Bald. This gift made Chartres the center of the cult of the Virgin in Western Europe, and the deep devotion it engendered is revealed by the successive buildings on the site. Documents tell of numerous fires, and we can follow successive rebuildings up to this great monument. A new basilica had been erected in the eleventh century. In the early twelfth century another fire occasioned the erection of the three entrances and tower bases at the west end. Then in June 1194 a fire devastated the basilica and town, leaving only the west front intact. From this anonymous account, written early in the thirteenth century, we can get a good idea of the role of this church in the life of the people.

> Therefore, in the year 1194 after the Incarnation of the Lord, since the church at Chartres had been devastated on the third of the Ides of June [June 10] by an extraordinary and lamentable fire making it necessary later, after the walls had been broken up and demolished and leveled to the ground, to repair the foundations and then erect a new church.... The inhabitants of Chartres, clerics as well as laymen, ... considered as their chief misfortune, the fact that they, unhappy wretches, in justice for their own sins, had lost the palace of the Blessed Virgin, the spe-

cial glory of the city, the showpiece of the entire region, the incomparable house of prayer...

> Indeed, when for several days they had not seen the most sacred reliquary of the Blessed Mary, the population of Chartres was seized with incredible anguish and grief, concluding that it was unworthy to restore the structures of the city or the church, if it had lost such a precious treasure, [which was] indeed the glory of the whole city. At last, on a particular holy day, when the entire populace had assembled by order of the clergy at the spot where the church had stood, the above mentioned reliquary was brought forth from the crypt.... The fact must not be passed over that when, at the time of the fire, the reliquary frequently referred to had been moved by certain persons into the lower crypt (whose entrance the laudable foresight of the ancients had cut near the altar of the Blessed Mary), and they had been shut up there, not daring to go back out because of the fire now raging, they were so preserved from mortal danger under the protection of the Blessed Mary that neither did the rain of burning timbers falling from above shatter the iron door covering the face of the crypt, nor did the drops of melted lead penetrate it, nor the heap of burning coals overhead injure it.... And after such a fierce conflagration, when men who were considered already dead from smoke or excessive heat had come back unharmed, all present were filled with such gladness that they rejoiced together, weeping affectionately with them.

> ... When, following the ruin of the walls mentioned above, necessity demanded that a new church be built and the wagons were at last ready to fetch the stone, all beckoned as well as exhorted each other to obey instantly and do without delay whatever they thought necessary for this construction or [whatever] the master workers prescribed. But the gifts or assistance of the laymen would never have been adequate to raise such a structure had not the bishop and the canons contributed so much money, as stated above, for three years from their own revenues. For this became evident to everyone at the end of the three-year period when all finances suddenly gave out, so that the supervisors had no wages for the workmen, nor did they have in view anything that could be given otherwise. But I recall that at that moment someone said—I know not by what spirit of prophecy—that the purses would fail before the coins needed for the work on the church of Chartres [were obtained]. What is there to add? Since, in view of the utter failure of human resources, it was necessary for the divine to appear, the blessed Mother of God, desiring that a new and incomparable church be erected in which she could perform her miracles, stirred up the power of this son of hers by her merits and prayers. When there was

a large gathering of people there, she openly and clearly exhibited a certain new miracle, one unheard of for a long time past, seen by all for the first time. As a result, news of the miracle spread far and wide through the whole of Gaul and made it easier to give credence to succeeding miracles.

Out of despair the people, clerics, and nobility of Chartres created an enduring act of devotion by making this palace for the queen of heaven. The new church was occupied by 1220 and dedicated in 1260—an astonishingly short time given the technology of the age. Its form embraced the changes that Suger had made at Saint Denis, creating a harmonious, substantial expression of belief rendered into visible form.

Standing before the west front (Fig. 7-8), you feel that the building looks somewhat familiar. The central doors suggest that the nave and aisles lie behind, and at the end of the nave may be seen an apse. Turning to the right, moving across the front, and looking down the south side, you see a wing that joins the nave at right angles. The church has a transept that can be entered through a graceful three-part porch and doors. Standing before the porch of the transept, looking west, toward the front towers, you see the wall of the aisle, its roof sloping up slightly to meet the walls of the nave and clerestory that rise above it (Figs. 7-9, 7-12).

7–9 Chartres, south aisle. (LEFEVRE-PONTALIS/© ARCH. PHOT. PARIS/S.P.A.D.E.M., 1980)

7–8 Chartres, west front, Royal Portal. (Lauros-Giraudon, Paris)

Extension of the Building   Topping the aisle wall is a row of columns carrying arches and a lintel. This *parapet* partially conceals the aisle roof. The aisle wall is divided into seven regular intervals expressed by six large, single, pointed windows and a passageway. The wall of the nave rising above the aisle repeats the intervals, but the single window is replaced by pairs of tall pointed windows topped with a round one. These are the windows of the clerestory of the nave with its sharply pointed lead-covered roof. The exterior walls, however, seem less like walls than elaborate piers, and in the spaces between each window are carefully cut and laid towers of stone called *buttresses* (Fig. 7-10). Each buttress continues to rise vertically but becomes thinner and lighter as it is stepped in toward the clerestory wall. Beginning at the gabled opening with its figure, a section of stone arch reaches out to join the stone pier between the clerestory windows. Finally, as each buttress towers almost to the parapet of the nave roof, another arch reaches out to the clerestory pier. These are the *flying buttresses*, arches of stone reaching across space to help transfer the weight of wall and roof to the foundations. This is the building framework: a great skeleton of stone. Light and air pass over it freely, moving among the details of moldings, angles, and arches and over the surfaces of the great windows themselves. As you move around the apse (Fig. 7-11), you note that the walls and windows deflect in and out, responding to the location of the chapels around the apse. There are also flying buttresses around the apse, supporting its great windows that rise, like the nave clerestory, above the ambulatory below. The exterior of Saint Denis may have looked like this; Chartres resembles it in plan and, in all probability, idea. Walking around the choir to the north, you reach the other entrance to the transept. Both transept entrances are towered and columned, quite different from the west front, which was built before the fire of 1194, and therefore long before the north and south transepts. Completing the circuit of the church shows its familiar basilican plan (Fig. 7-12) but also demonstrates that it is realized in a new way: in a structure that seems to stand outside the walls of windows, windows that fill the interior with light.

To understand the physical achievement that made the building possible, we must remind ourselves of Ro-

7–10   Chartres, nave. (Lauros-Giraudon, Paris)

7–11   Chartres, choir. (© ARCH. PHOT. PARIS/S.P.A.D.E.M., 1980)

man vaulting. The *barrel* and *groin vaults* of the Romans were semicircular in section, and the *bay* had to be regular (Fig. 7-13). Moreover, the tops of the arches had to be the same height. Piers, columns, and walls carried the vaults, and windows were small. Centering was used to erect the vaults; and, as a basilica grew, bay by bay, it became a series of separate units of space.

Study the plan of the apse of Chartres (Fig. 7-12). Pay particular attention to the dots and dark areas that indicate columns and piers. The diagonal lines on the plan indicate the joining of sections of the vaults. There are seven vaults of four sections each for the ambulatory; each of the side chapels contains vaults of five parts, but the bays of the ambulatory and chapels are irregular—they become larger as one moves from the apse out to the bounding wall. Regular Roman vaults would not permit this, nor would the system permit such irregularity in the size of pier and column. What permitted this new configuration in the plan? First, the arches of the vaults are not semicircular in

7–13a Groin vaults normally require square bays. When a rectangular bay is needed, the arches on the shorter sides (1) must be raised to keep the four sides of the vault equal in height. This is not a very satisfactory solution.

7–13b The pointed arch permits the arches of the short (1), long (2), and diagonal (3) spans to accommodate a rectangular bay with greater efficiency.

section, but pointed; second, the vaults are joined by pointed ribs that act as a permanent centering for the vaults (Figs. 7-5, 7-13).

It is not as if pointed arches were unknown. They had been used before and have the advantage of being more self-supporting: the two sides lean on each other. Ribs had been used before. What was important was the combination of pointed arch and rib to make a vaulting system that was lighter and much more flexible, permitting more and more wall to be opened for

7–12 Groundplan, Chartres.

glass. The outward, downward thrust of the vaults is carried away from the walls by the pier and flying buttresses that rise above the roofs. The new system makes Chartres' ambulatory a space with no sharp delineations, as between ambulatory and chapel, or apse and aisle. The separate cells of space made by the chapels at Saint Sernin (Fig. 7-2) have been replaced by a greater unity—a whole greater than its parts. This system of pointed arches, ribs, and flying buttresses made possible this accomplishment.

At the west front again, the towers seem to squeeze the portals between them, and the airy complexity of the south and north porches is replaced by a majestic weightiness, reinforced by the three round arched windows above the doors and the single huge, round window (Fig. 7-4). The south tower was finished about 1155, but the north tower spire was added only in the

7–14 Chartres, west front, right tympanum, Incarnation of Christ. (Giraudon, Paris)

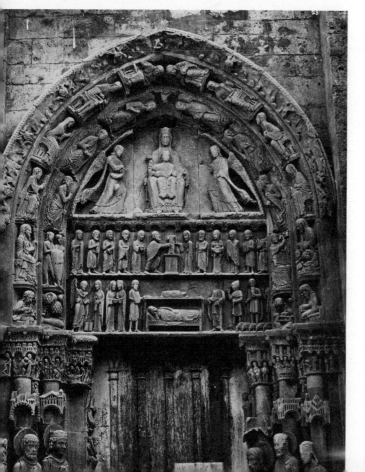

early sixteenth century. The three entrance doors are decorated with sculpted figures; and, as we examine the sculpture of the west front, we can begin to understand more about the church as a whole, this palace for the Virgin, this place of transportation from earthly to heavenly life.

For modern man it is difficult to think of art as a teaching tool; but for the man of the Middle Ages, art, like everything else, had a purpose in the divine scheme of things. The cathedral, like the philosophical system of Thomas Aquinas, was concerned with God, the world, and man—with the accumulation of human knowledge and speculation and their relation to divine knowledge and revelation.

Exterior Sculptures   The three doors of the west front, called the Royal Portal (Fig. 7-8), sit in round arches deep in the thick wall. The wall from the door to the outer wall face, the *jamb*, is slanted outward; these jambs are decorated with columns and figures. The columns have richly decorated bases, and their *capitals* are carved, providing a horizontal contrast to the jamb figures (Fig. 7-8). Above the doors are sculptured lintels, and above the lintel is the *tympanum*, the sculpture-filled panels that reach to the top of the opening. In the slanted area above the lintel from the arch to the wall's outer surface are stones called *archivolts*, also sculpted. All these sculptures, like Greek sculpture, would have been painted, gilded, and decorated to enhance and intensify the specific qualities of figure and setting.

The sculptures of the west front present the fundamentals of the Christian dogma with directness and clarity. Let us look more closely at each section to see how the sculptor presents his images and relates them to each other and to the architectural framework. You might also ask how this sculpture differs from that we saw in Athens on the Parthenon and in Rome.

Beginning with the tympanum of the right door, we see a crowned, haloed Virgin seated on a throne, the Christ Child in her lap (Fig. 7-14). On either side of the central figures is an angel swinging a censer, a container for burning incense. The Virgin and Child face us directly; the folds of their garments fall symmetrically and emphasize this frontality. The angels, seen in profile, are almost identical, their poses giving the composition great repose. These heavenly attendants, the throne, and the pose tell us that we are before the Virgin as the queen of heaven.

The lintel below is divided into two registers containing the following scenes: lower register, left to right, the Annunciation (Gabriel visits Mary to tell her that she will conceive and bear a son, Jesus); the Visitation (Mary visits Elizabeth, the mother of John the Baptist); the Nativity and the angels announcing Jesus' birth to the shepherds; in the upper register, the presentation of Jesus in the temple. All the figures in the scenes seem stocky and somewhat ill-proportioned; their clothes are simplified, and the faces all resemble each other. The figures in both rows share a simple rhythmical relation, spaced equidistantly apart and almost symmetrically. Was naturalism this artist's goal? What was his goal? Can we read the story with clarity and ease?

In addition to the apparent subjects, these representations were filled with much deeper meaning for medieval man—meanings that have been discovered in medieval treatises and sermons. For example, seeing Christ as child and in young manhood reminds us that he was human and present with us, as well as being God. Mary, his mother, is human and divine also, the queen of heaven and the motherly intercessor for us. In the nativity scene we see Mary resting on what looks like a bed. The medieval person would have recognized it as an altar, and placing the child in the manger on the bed's top edge alludes to Christ, the sacrifice, the Eucharist. The scene of the presentation in the temple repeats the idea; Christ stands in the center on an altar-like form. Thus, the sculptures not only represent scenes from the life of Jesus, they also serve as reminders of the complex nature of Christ, as God made man and as the sacrifice for mankind's salvation.

In the archivolts around the tympanum are personifications of the seven liberal arts: grammar, dialectic, rhetoric, arithmetic, music, geometry, and astronomy. The cathedral at Chartres was a seat of great learning, and the inclusion of the liberal arts in the sculptural program is a natural allusion to this and the major concern of the schools: to forge the links in knowledge from the human to the divine, from the systematics of Aristotle to the mystical transcendence of faith. These sculptures should also remind us that Christ is wisdom

7-15   Chartres, west front, left tympanum, Ascension of Christ. (Lauros-Giraudon, Paris)

incarnate, the *logos*, the word of God made man.

The other two tympana expand the story begun in the right portal. In the left portal is the Ascension of Christ. In its tympanum, Christ, supported by angels, is drawn up into heaven on a cloud (Fig. 7-15). In the upper register of the lintel four angels announce his second coming to the Apostles seated below. The archivolts are carved with signs of the zodiac and the labors of the months—Christ as man was in time; Christ as God *is* time, the beginning and the end—seasons, labors, and life will stop at his coming again. Compare these figures to those on the right, Incarnation portal. Do words like simplicity, order, clarity, symmetry apply? Look at the clouds and the angels' drapery. How do these figures compare with the Panathenaic festival? Those on the *Ara Pacis?*

The central tympanum shows Christ in majesty, one hand raised in blessing, surrounded by the four symbols of the Evangelists: Mark's lion, John's eagle, Matthew's man (or angel), and Luke's bull (Fig. 7-16). Angels and church elders in the archivolts and the apostles in the lintel witness the Second Coming—to

7–16 Chartres, west front, central tympanum, Second Coming of Christ. (Giraudon, Paris)

refer to heavenly rule—earthly kingship and priesthood. The female figures may be the ancestors of the Virgin.

Our knowledge of the subject matter of the sculpture and windows and the architecture at Chartres derives not only from it but also from the programs of decoration at numerous other cathedrals and churches. It is important to know that the work at Chartres is not an isolated phenomenon but reaches backward to earlier programs at other buildings and is subsequently influential in the creation of later programs, both in form and content. Chartres is a paradigm for many such buildings—the cathedrals at Rheims, Amiens, Paris, Rouen, Laon, Cologne, and Strasbourg and for churches in Paris and many other cities in France, Germany, and England.

These great doors on the west, illuminated by the setting sun, must have been perceived as palatial, heavenly gates, the entry to the court of Mary, the queen of heaven, for one enters acutely aware of the majesty and presence of this person and her Son.

judge the quick and the dead. Christ is seated and crowned with a halo, his ultimate kingship emphasized by the two angels who hold the crown at the top of the archivolts.

The capitals on the columns below show scenes from the life of Mary and Jesus. They connect the subjects of the three portals both narratively and visually. This is indeed a presentation of sacred history.

The remaining figures are the elongated columnar ones on the jambs. Only nineteen remain of the original twenty-four, male and female, crowned and uncrowned, neither ancient nor youthful. They share the stylized drapery and physical simplification of the other portal figures. But their scale and location give them a vibrating tension as they seem poised before the doors (Fig. 7-17).

The absolute identification of these figures has never been agreed upon, but we think them to be kings and prophets of the Old Testament. It is as if these are the ancestors of the sacred history of the New Testament revealed above. In these figures we may also perceive the close ties between church and state, kingship and priesthood. The crowned and uncrowned figures may

7–17 Chartres, west front, Old Testament figures. (Lauros-Giraudon, Paris)

Interior   Passing from the exterior into the nave is like leaving one world to enter another. The nave arcade rises to support a row of shallow arched openings, and above these the clerestory rises to the vaults 118 feet above the floor (Fig. 7-5). The great piers that make up the nave arcade and separate the nave from the aisles are not single columns, like those of the Parthenon, but seem to be created from a collection of individual shafts. Each pier has a central shaft, and centered on each face is a smaller shaft: one faces the aisle, one faces the nave, and one faces the pier behind or in front of it. These are gathered at the base, rise to the capital, and then disperse in the nave and aisle vaults. The nave is seven bays long, the transept spreads left and right, and the choir, apse, and ambulatory seem distant and light-filled. As you move down the nave, radiant with the colored light spilling in from the stained-glass windows of the clerestory above, you remember the complex and weighty stone skeleton that supports this light-filled and awesome space. The interior is the final expression of the diversity and unity of a system of building with arches and ribs, piers and columns.

Look at one pier and one bay of the nave (Fig. 7-5). Compare it with a column of the Parthenon and the bay of the pilgrimage church, Saint Sernin. What is immediately different? The base of the Gothic pier has not one, but a variety of simple moldings that unite the small shafts attached to the central column. Because of the attached columns and their capitals, the pier does not seem to face squarely into the nave or aisle. The different locations of the attached columns cause your eyes to move across, around, and behind the pier so that the nave and aisle interlock. Follow the attached shafts as they rise upward. Those two that face each other and decorate the arch of the nave arcade carry a series of curved moldings (Fig. 7-5). The shaft facing in the aisle carries smaller shafts that rise to become the aisle vault ribs. The shaft facing the nave bursts into five clearly articulated smaller shafts that rise to become the ribs of the nave vault. One shaft reaches the vault and crosses transversely; another crosses the vault diagonally to a pier on the other side of the bay. Where the two diagonal ribs meet, their flow is gathered into a circular *keystone*. Moreover, as each rib springs across the vault, it is multiplied into three or more curving

ribs—not a flat rib. Between the ribs are the smooth surfaces of the vaults. Looking up, you see the vault of a single bay, which looks like this ╳ ; yet it merges into the next bay in a shape that looks like this ◇ . The experience produced is one of a constant fluid merging of separate but totally dependent units of space. The bays of the aisles, like those of the nave, melt into a whole. Reaching the light-filled apse, you experience an absorbing, objective order and consistency of building form that does not intimidate or overwhelm but absorbs you as an integral part of the whole, just as every base, shaft, capital, and molding is essential.

The structural knowledge and expertise that produced the cathedral is not a matter of speculation. It was the product of the guilds and lodges of master masons who worked for the cathedral or monastery. These men were conversant with the knowledge of engineering, stone masonry, and mathematics necessary to make the building stand up. More specifically, we can say that the medieval mason proportioned his cathedral on a sure foundation of mathematics. The mason worked from a constant proportion, established in the beginning and capable of determining the measure of every member and element. This was not just a pragmatic tool; the mason, like the philosopher and theologian, believed that numbers and therefore harmony were reflections of the divine order of the world. From Aristotle and Pythagoras the mason drew knowledge of certain simple ratios as being the most sure reflections of that harmony, and these he applied to plan and elevation. If we do not immediately see, we sense overriding appropriateness of height to width and of equal correctness of division within. Thus, the Gothic cathedral is a concrete example of the use of reason in the service of faith, comparable to the philosophies of Abelard and Aquinas mentioned earlier in this chapter. The culture of the High Middle Ages was both practical and intellectual, but these two aspects were subordinated to man's primary purpose in life: the aspiration of the soul toward salvation by God, to be accomplished through the Church.

Stained-Glass Windows   Harmony and light, then, are the two binding physical motifs of Chartres: harmony of building—its spaces and forms—and light, the luminescence of the translucent window wall, stretching thin webs between the stones. These two values, harmony and light, are presented perhaps most completely in the stained glass of Chartres, where the art reached a level of unusual perfection. Unlike a painting, which reflects light, the windows transmit and transform light. The varicolored light conceals, reveals, and warms the spare stone of the building. The jewellike windows adorn the building as gold and gems adorn the vessels of the sacrament and cross of the altar. The Madonna herself is enthroned in the central window of the west front, and she is the subject of the windows of the north transept. But it is in a window in the south ambulatory, called *Notre Dame de la Belle Verrière* (Color Plate I), that we sense the profound adoration that her people felt for her. This window is the oldest and was probably saved from the debris of the fire. Like the Virgin on the west front, she sits enthroned, holding her child on her knees. Angels bearing censers and candles fill the panels on either side. We see a loving and supporting intercessor. The deep ruby glass seems to fall slightly behind the blue of the Virgin's robe and warms the air around her. The deep, intense-blue side panels have ruby niches that house the angels. Their smaller scale, the more intricate gowns and poses give them an animation and vitality contrasting with the stable order that they surround. Mother and child, heavenly and earthly love are permanent images.

The other windows in the basilica organize and present all facets of medieval knowledge—Old and New Testament, lives of the saints, fundamentals of Christian doctrine, labors of the months, signs of the zodiac, vices and virtues, and the activities of the guilds. Like the sculpture on the west front, and that on the north and south transepts (which we will consider finally), the same events are repeated and elaborated—man and God in time and at the end of time.

Moreover, in the windows at Chartres we see once again the deep relationship between churchman and lay person. The townspeople depended for their economic vitality on the cathedral, the fairs, and the pilgrims who came because of the relics of the Virgin. They held meetings on the church's steps, sold wine from the crypt, gathered to seek jobs in the nave, attended plays presented before the west front, social-

ized, loved, and were baptized and buried from Our Lady's chapels. To these people we owe many of the windows. The five great windows of the apse honoring the Virgin were paid for largely by the butchers and bakers. The Saint James Major window was given by the merchant tailors who appear in the bottom corners in two scenes from a tailor's shop (Color Plate II). In another window a banner with a red stocking tells us that the hosiers gave it, while the Charlemagne window, which relates the origins of the French monarchy, was given by the furriers.

Perhaps it seems unfair to say so little about the glass at Chartres, particularly because the architectural arrangements seem to evolve in order to permit the creation of more and more windows. But it is the most magical of the aspects of the building and the least susceptible to reproduction, either visual or verbal. The subjects of the windows are high up and not easily read; rather what is supremely important are the rich patterns of light that fall on the floors and play over the piers and ribs, transforming the entire space into a light-filled, unearthly one meant for contemplation and celebration. In the morning light the east end is filled with the new day, the church brightens with the noonday light, and the windows at the west end glow in the low setting sun. They reflect the passage of time, the church triumphant in this world, and beyond this world.

Transept Door Sculptures　While it is not really possible to bring the experience of Chartres to a conclusion, it is appropriate to end with the latest sculpture (ca. 1250–1270), that of the transept doors. The climactic scenes are found in the central tympana of each, and their meaning is enhanced by the subsidiary scenes in the doors on either side.

On the north portal concentration is on the *Virgin's* life, death, and assumption into heaven. The south portal presents the Christian Church on earth, in heaven, and ending in time on the day of the Last Judgment. The central portal shows the Last Judgment in the tympanum, the Twelve Apostles along the jambs, with Christ standing on the post between the doors (Fig. 7-18). The left portal is dedicated to the *martyrs* (persons killed for their beliefs) and the right one to the *confessors* (persons who gave special witness to the faith).

Formally, the figures of both the north and south portals show a steady increase in the degree of humanization, naturalism, and individuality. Compared to the much earlier figures of the west front, they grow in bulk, gain weight and volume, and fill the space. The drapery articulates the forms of the body. Faces, hands, and feet become more convincing, yet a balance is always maintained between these figures and their architectural setting. Like the great stone framework itself, these figures are individual yet integral, separate parts of a great whole.

The complex of building, sculpture, and stained glass at Chartres is, for many who have experienced it, an almost perfect harmony between reason and emotion, order and complexity, the spiritual and the worldly.

7–18   Chartres, south, central portal, Last Judgment. (© ARCH. PHOT. PARIS/S.P.A.D.E.M., 1980)

Music and Drama in the Cathedral:
THE PLAY OF DANIEL

The combined visual arts of the great Gothic cathedrals—architecture, painting, sculpture, and stained glass—exemplify the medieval Catholic belief (quite opposed to later, puritanical ones) that spiritual truths could be apprehended through physical, sensuous beauty. This same belief seems to underlie the service of the mass and the music developed for it. Earlier, in the monasteries, one-voiced *(monophonic)* chants, called Gregorian chants (after Pope Gregory the Great) were sung at masses and at the monks' spiritual exercises during the day. In the Gothic period, individual singers were used along with a choir, and a many-voiced *(polyphonic)* type of music for the mass developed. The resonance provided by the soaring vaults of the cathedral gave this music a special richness that it would not have in another setting. The performance of the mass, with its procession of priests and choirs, the play of light through the stained glass, the burning of incense, and the reverberations of music and oratory from the stones must have been an experience to delight both senses and spirit.

Each cathedral, as mentioned earlier, had a school for instructing the young clerics who sang in the choir and performed other services in the church. The school and the rest of the cathedral were administered and cared for by the chapter, a group of clergy associated with the cathedral and subject to a rule, or canon, that ordered their way of life. One of the duties of the chapter, and the boys in its school, was to provide music for the services of the church. Medieval musicians were always part of a community, either religious or secular; and the music they wrote and performed was composed for purposes other than a purely musical one, just as the purposes of medieval sculptors, painters, and architects were never purely artistic. In this regard they were unlike modern composers and performers who sell their wares as individuals to the public on an open market, for it was the community that imposed rules and requirements both on their daily lives and on their musical activities.

The demands of the community did not seem to restrict the musicians' creativity—on the contrary, medieval people seemed to be eager for more and more elaborate forms. It is perhaps because of this kind of demand that a type of drama developed out of the mass. This form, called *liturgical drama* because it was probably a part of the worship service, represented the same religious stories from the Old and New Testaments as were represented on the windows, walls, and niches of the cathedral; it acted on the imaginations of the faithful in much the same way. *The Play of Daniel*, which we will study here, is an example of liturgical drama; it must be understood both as music and as drama. This would, of course, ideally be true of Greek drama too, but at least we are fortunate enough to have manuscripts of medieval music (preserved in monasteries and cathedral schools) that give us some idea, if not a totally accurate one, of how it was performed. Medieval liturgical drama, in some ways stranger to the modern mind than Greek tragedy, is an important phenomenon in our cultural history because it developed at a time when the theater was all but dead in the Western world and thus made possible the growth of modern drama. Let us look briefly at the situation of drama during the "dark" ages and at how the new form developed.

The theater, as it was known in the classical world, was in effect killed by the combined influence of barbarians and Christianity. The invaders of the Roman empire had no idea what a theater was, and by the time of the "fall" of Rome, drama survived only in the form of bloody spectacles or rituals associated with pagan feasts. Seeing these survivals as corruptions of the body and spirit, Christians attempted to wipe them out; actors were, in fact, excommunicated from the Church. Nevertheless, it is a tribute to the human desire to participate in or to observe shows—to mime the outside world—that some form of dramatic activity continued throughout the dark ages in spite of repression. Wandering minstrels, jugglers, tumblers, and other showmen continued to entertain willing audiences in village squares.

Ironically, after centuries of hostility, it was within the Church itself that drama was reborn as an art form. It is as if the Church at last recognized the human need for imitation and spectacle and thus incorporated it for spiritual purposes. The mass itself is dramatic in character: it is a reenactment of the sacrifice of Christ. Processions, such as those held on Palm Sunday and Easter, added to its spectacular qualities. In line with the Gothic tendency to elaborate and enrich, evident in the art of the cathedral, the mass itself became more complex and decorative. Choirs began to sing in alternation with one another, a process called *antiphony* that is already somewhat dramatic. Then, in the early tenth century, lengthened musical passages and elaborations on the text of the mass were added, called *tropes;* to them is attributed the rebirth of drama. An Easter trope, called "Quem quaeritis?" (Whom do you seek?) is, as far as we know, the first "drama" within the church. Here (translated from Latin) is the entire text:

Angel: Whom do you seek in the tomb, O Christians?
The Three Marys: Jesus of Nazareth, the crucified,
O celestial ones.
Angel: He is not here, he is risen as he predicted.
Go and tell that he is risen from the tomb.

Probably this text was sung by antiphonal choirs and did not involve actors. It is admittedly not much of a drama, but from it an entire new tradition was born. By the twelfth century, musical drama as part of the mass reached the point at which it involved characters, choruses, and real dramatic action, as in *The Play of Daniel*. This musical drama was created in the twelfth century for the cathedral of Beauvais, a flourishing city of medieval France just northwest of Paris.

According to the prologue of *The Play of Daniel*, this music was written by the young scholars of Beauvais.

Ad honorem tui, Christe,
Danielis ludus iste,
In Belvaco est inventus,
Et invenit hunc juventus.

In your honor, Christ,
This play of Daniel
Was created in Beauvais;
The youth created it.

The language is Latin (with some phrases in Old French), and this is not surprising, for the affairs of the church were conducted in Latin as, most likely, were the classes that these young men attended. At the end of the play appears the rubric, or performance instruction:

Hic auditis, cantores
incipient Te Deum
Laudamus.

After hearing this, the singers
intone the "Te Deum
Laudamus."

This is the clue informing us that this play was probably performed at Matins, a religious service celebrated
daily by the chapter in the early hours of the morning
before dawn. Matins is normally a long service, for it
contains the chanting of nine complete Psalms and
their antiphons as well as the reading of nine scriptural
lessons and the singing of nine Responses and the Te
Deum. Obviously, the addition of a complete drama
would occur only for a special holiday; and, from references in the text, including the final prophecy of Daniel (which Christians interpret as foretelling the birth
of Christ), we conclude that it was written for the
Christmas season, probably performed at the end of
matins for Christmas morning.

The Play of Daniel has many features that made it
particularly attractive to twelfth-century Christians.
Coming at the time of the first Crusades, the story includes the great historical personages of the Persian empire, King Belshazzar and King Darius, a subject most
in keeping with current political interest. Then, the
story of the miracle of Daniel's salvation from the terror of the lions' den provides an opportunity for the
dramatization of a spectacular event for people who fervently believed in the miraculous. The pageantry of
the processions and the rituals of the Persian court
were also affairs that could be related to the regular activities of the chapter but that were elevated to a higher
level by being unusual or extraordinary. Lastly, the music itself had its own fascination. Each of these elements, when understood within the context of the
whole, can speak to us directly when we listen to, and
witness a performance of, *The Play of Daniel*.[1]

The music of the play is divided into nine sections,
and it is possible that it substituted for, or replaced
parts of, the nine sections of matins. The following divisions outline the Daniel story:

1. Prologue. Introduction of characters and synopsis of
the story.

2. Belshazzar commands a feast and orders his wise
men to interpret the riddle, "Mene, Tekel, Peres,"
which a mysterious hand has written on the wall.
3. The queen arrives, suggests asking Daniel, and he is
called before the king.
4. Daniel prophesies doom for Belshazzar but is rewarded for having spoken the truth.
5. The procession of Darius the Great arrives, Belshazzar is slain, and the musicians celebrate the ascendancy of the new ruler.
6. Darius calls for Daniel, raises him to high office, and
Daniel pledges allegiance.
7. The jealous counselors find a way to force the king
to condemn Daniel.
8. Daniel is saved from the lions by an angel, and he
delivers his prophecy of the coming of the Son of
Man.
9. Epilogue. An angel announces the birth of Christ,
and the Te Deum is sung.

What about the music of the play? After all, it is radically different from current musical sounds. If we take
the version recorded by the New York Pro Musica as a
fair representation of the way it might have been performed during the twelfth century,[2] we are immediately struck by the presence of instruments no longer
used in modern orchestras, a singing style that is certainly not common now, music that does not use *harmony*, and a language that is no longer spoken. Where
does one begin in order to understand and enjoy? Perhaps first with the *dynamics*, the volume level of the
performance.

Nothing in *The Play of Daniel* is loud. Europeans of
the twelfth century were accustomed to a quiet unknown to us, and their hearing was sensitive to minute
aural detail. The words of a solo voice at speaking level
are much easier to understand and carry the excitement of the story line more effectively and intimately
than an amplified voice artificially enhanced with electronic reverberation. Besides, the cathedral walls were
reverberant enough. The listeners had no ear pollution
from electronic rock music, jet landings, and freeway
traffic, or from background sounds of air conditioning,

---

[1] The reader is advised to listen to *A Twelfth Century Music Drama:
The Play of Daniel,* recorded by the New York Pro Musica directed
by Noah Greenberg (Decca DL 9402). Specific listening assignments
refer to this album.

[2] The scoring and editing is a modern reconstruction, for the original
source does not indicate instruments, dynamics, voices, and so on.

electric typewriters, and screaming radio disc jockeys. This awareness of subtle variations in melody, in the *timbre* (or tonal color) of instruments, and in performer *inflection* is reflected in the music that they composed to glorify their world and their God. Medieval man did not need volume to hear; he was more interested in finesse and detail.

Even the instruments play softly. The straight trumpet (fifteenth century!) used for this performance could in no way match the gross dynamics of a twentieth-century orchestral trumpet. What does play a significant role in medieval orchestration and replaces volume as an important factor of instrumental sonority is timbre, or tone color. Medieval musicians delighted in the variety, rather than the unity, of the instrumental sounds. The rebec is a little bowed fiddle with a thin nasal sound; the vielle a larger bowed string instrument with a more open tone; the minstrel's harp a stringed instrument that is plucked rather than bowed, and the psaltery another type of plucked string instrument. There were many different sounds from the percussion: jingles, triangles, finger cymbals, cymbals, tambourine, bells, and drums of varying size and pitch; likewise with the wind instruments: portative organ, recorders, and bagpipes. These instruments were not designed to blend but to stand apart and remain distinct. Medieval people heard and enjoyed the differences, and we can, too. Perhaps nineteenth-century America was striving for sameness, but twentieth-century America is beginning to cultivate, preserve, and appreciate individuality that is much in keeping with the way that medieval man—and medieval musicians—viewed their world.

In the same way that twelfth-century listeners would distinguish individual voices and separate timbres, they could also isolate different song types. Some kinds of music were appropriate for one action or emotion; other kinds were suitable for different situations. In *The Play of Daniel* two distinct musical types are easily discerned: songs and processionals. There are others, but let us study those two as the most important in this work. Daniel's lament, upon being condemned to the lions, reads:

Heu, heu, heu!
Quo casu sortis venit haec
    damnatio mortis?

Heu, heu, heu!
Scelus infandum!
Cur me dabit ad lacerandum
Haec fera turba feris?
Sic me, Rex, perdere quaeris?
Heu!
Qua morte mori me cogis?
Parce furori.

Woe, woe, woe!
By what chance of fate do I receive this
    condemnation to death?
Woe, woe, woe!
Unspeakable calamity!
Why will this savage multitude
Give me to be torn by wild beasts?
Thus, O King, do you seek to kill me?
Woe!
To what death do you compel me?
Spare your fury.

The music is *through-composed* to emphasize the emotional intensity of each portion of the text. No repeated passages appear that would use the same music for different words, and, in this case, the beginning is nonmelodic (that is, it opens on a monotone) to underline the cry of despair, *"Heu, heu, heu!"*

As you listen to the recording, note that the composers further clarify the text of this lament by basically setting the text one syllable to one pitch. In ecstatic passages of celebration and jubilation, it was customary to sing florid groups of notes, thus giving the music a sense of freedom and release. Here the opposite is true, for the sense of fear, uncertainty, and self-doubt calls for restraint and reflection.

A contrasting type of composition is a *conductus* or processional, and an excellent example is the procession of the queen coming to King Belshazzar: *"Cum doctorum."*

Cum doctorum et magorum
    omnis adsit contio
Secum volvit, neque solvit,
    quae sit manus visio.

Ecce prudens, styrpe cluens,
    dives cum potentia;
In vestitu deaurato
    conjux adest regia.

Haec latentem promet vatem
    per cujus inditium
Rex describi suum ibi
    noverit exitium.

Laetis ergo haec virago
    comitetur plausibus;
Cordis, orisque sonoris
    personetur vocibus.

All the throng of learned
    and wise men is present.
They ponder, but cannot explain,
    the appearance of the hand.

Behold the prudent, well-born,
    rich in power,
Gold-clad spouse
    of the King is here.

She will reveal the unknown prophet
    by whose information
The King will learn and know
    of his destruction.

Let this heroine be accompanied
    with joyful applause;
With strings and voices,
    let loud songs resound.

First notice that the Latin text is strophic; that is, it is written in verse form. The words are both metrical and rhymed, and so is the music. The meter for the first verse is:

```
/ ˘ / ˘ / ˘ / ˘
/ ˘ / ˘ / ˘ /
/ ˘ / ˘ / ˘ / ˘
/ ˘ / ˘ / ˘ /
```

This is the basic meter of all the verses, but a few poetic changes in verses 3 and 4 are regularized by the music, which was probably composed with verse 1 in mind.

In listening, notice that the melody for *"Cum doctorum"* is the same as that for *"Ecce prudens," "Haec latentem,"* and *"Laetis ergo."* In other words, the form is similar to some folk songs, modern hymns, a few "pop" songs, and many Country and Western tunes in which several verses are sung to the same melody. Music written this way is easily remembered; and, if it has a good beat (as this one does), it carries the listener along in a forward movement of insistent rhythm. It cannot express the precise meaning of the text as well as a through-composed piece, but that is not important in this case, for this *conductus* was not written to express deep feelings and heighten a monologue but to accompany a parade. In other words, the medieval composer used different compositional means to accomplish quite different artistic ends.

It should be apparent by now that the music of this play is not just one long, continuous, undifferentiated monophonic song but a logical series of discrete artistic songs, balanced and blended into a recipe that produces effective music drama. The wedding of drama with music was certainly not new—we saw it with the Greeks, although their music is lost to us. (It is, rather, drama without music that is a recent form.) Although Greek tragedy may also have had its origin in religious ritual, it differs profoundly from medieval liturgical drama; yet both forms went into the making of the drama as we know it today. The following translation is by George C. Yehling, III.

The Play of Daniel   ●

(Prologue)

BELSHAZZAR'S PRINCE:
    Ad honorem tui, Christe,
    Danielis ludus iste,
    In Belvaco est inventus,
    Et invenit hunc juventus.

In your honor, Christ,
This Play of Daniel
Was created in Beauvais;
The youth created it.

THE COURT:

Astra tenenti cunctipotenti	To the Almighty One who holds the stars,
Turba virilis et puerilis	The crowd of men and mob of boys
Contio plaudit,	Gives praise.
Nam Danielem multa fidelem	For they hear how faithful Daniel
Et subiisse atque tulisse	Undergoes and bears many things
Firmiter audit.	With constancy.
Convocat ad se Rex sapientes	The King calls the wise men to him
Gramata dextrae qui sibi dicant	That they may explain
Enucleantes.	The handwriting.
Qui, quia scribae non potuere	But they could not solve it,
Solvere, regi ilico muti	And they fell silent, on the spot,
Conticuere.	Before the King.
Sed Danieli Scripta legenti	But to Daniel, upon reading the writing,
Mox patuere quae prius illis	The words, which had been a mystery to them,
Clausa fuere.	Soon became clear.
Quem quia vidit prevaluisse	Because Belshazzar saw him surpass them,
Balthasar illis, fertur in aula	He was exalted in the assembly,
Praeposuisse.	It is told.
Causa reperta non satis apta	An insufficient case, brought to trial,
Destinat illum ore leonum	Delivered him to the lions' mouths
Dilacerandum.	To be torn apart.
Sed, Deus, illos ante malignos	But you, O God,
In Danielem tunc voluisti	Wanted Daniel's enemies
Esse benignos.	To be good to him.
Huic quoque panis, ne sit inanis,	Also, that he might not hunger,
Mittitur a te praepete vate	You sent a prophet on wings
Prandia dante.	To give him food.

(The Play Proper Begins)

THE COURT:

Rex, in eternum vive!	O King, live forever!

BELSHAZZAR:

Vos qui paretis meis vocibus,	You who obey my voice,
Afferte vasa meis usibus	Bring, for my use, the vessels
Quae templo pater meus abstulit,	Which my father carried off from the temple
Judaeam graviter cum percutit.	When he smote Judaea mightily.

THE COURT:

Jubilemus Regi nostro magno ac potenti!
Resonemus laude digna voce competenti!
Resonet jocunda turba solemnibus odis!
Cytharizent, plaudant manus, mille sonent modis!

Let us rejoice in our King, great and powerful!
Let us sing his worthy praise in a suitable voice!
Let the joyous crowd resound with solemn odes!
Let them play harps, clap hands, make a thousand
    noises.

Pater ejus destruens Judaeorum templa,
Magna fecit, et hic regnat ejus per exempla.
Pater ejus spoliavit regnum Judaeorum;
Hic exaltat sua festa decore vasorum.

His father, who destroyed the temple of the Jews,
Did great things, and this one rules by his example.
His father despoiled the kingdom of the Jews;
This one celebrates, appropriately, with their vessels.

Haec sunt vasa regia quibus spoliatur
Jerusalem, et regalis Babylon ditatur.
Praesentemus Balthasar ista Regi nostro
Qui sic suos perornavit purpura et ostro.
Iste potens, iste fortis, iste gloriosus,
Iste probus, curialis, decens et formosus.
Jubilemus Regi tanto vocibus canoris;
Resonemus omnes una laudibus sonoris;
Ridens plaudit Babylon, Jerusalem plorat;
Haec orbatur, haec triumphans Balthasar adorat.

These are royal vessels, which were plundered
From Jerusalem to enrich royal Babylon.
Let us present them to Belshazzar our King,
Who has adorned his servants with purple.
He is mighty, he is strong, he is glorious,
Virtuous, courtly, handsome, and fair.
Let us rejoice in such a King with melodious voice;
Let all resound his loud praises in unison;
Babylon applauds, laughing, Jerusalem weeps.
The latter is despoiled; the former, triumphant,
    worships Belshazzar.

Omnes ergo exultemus tantae potestati.
Offerentes Regis vasa suae majestati.

Let us all, therefore, exult in such a mighty one,
Offering the King's vessels to His Majesty.

Ecce sunt ante faciem tuam.

Behold, here they are before you.

(A hand writes "MENE, TEKEL, PERES" on the wall)

BELSHAZZAR:

Vocate mathematicos Chaldaeos, et ariolos.
Auruspices inquirite,
Et magos introducite.

Call the Chaldean mathematicians and astrologers.
Find the soothsayers,
And bring the wise men in!

TWO WISE MEN:

Rex, in eternum vive!
Adsumus ecce tibi.

O King, live forever!
Here we are.

BELSHAZZAR:

Qui scripturam hanc legerit
Et sensum aperuerit
Sub illius potentia
Subdetur Babylonia
Et insignitus purpura
Torque fruetur aurea.

Whoever shall read this writing
And disclose its meaning,
Under his power
Babylonia shall be placed,
And he shall wear purple
And a golden necklace.

THE TWO WISE MEN:
Nescimus persolvere nec dare consilium,
Quae sit superscriptio, nec manus indicium.

We do not know, nor can we explain,
What the writing is, nor what the hand means.

THE QUEEN AND HER ATTENDANTS:
Cum doctorum et magorum
    omnis adsit contio
Secum volvit, neque solvit,
    quae sit manus visio.

All the throng of learned
    and wise men is present.
They ponder, but cannot explain,
    the appearance of the hand.

Ecce prudens, styrpe cluens,
    dives cum potentia;
In vestitu deaurato
    conjux adest regia.

Behold the prudent, well-born,
    rich in power,
Gold-clad spouse
    of the King is here.

Haec latentem promet vatem
    per cujus inditium
Rex describi suum ibi
    noverit exitium.

She will reveal the unknown prophet
    by whose information
The King will learn and know
    of his destruction.

Laetis ergo haec virago
    comitetur plausibus;
Cordis, orisque sonoris
    personetur vocibus.

Let this heroine be accompanied
    with joyful applause;
With strings and voices,
    let loud songs resound.

THE QUEEN:
Rex, in eternum vive!

O King, live forever!

Ut scribentis noscas ingenium,
Rex Balthasar, audi consilium.
Cum Judaeae captivis populis
Prophetiae doctum oraculis.
Danielem a sua patria
Captivavit patris victoria.
Hic sub suo vivens imperio,
Ut mandatur, requirit ratio.
Ergo mana ne sit dilatio,
Nam docebit quod celat visio.

That you may know the writer's meaning,
King Belshazzar, hear my advice.
With the captive people of Judaea,
Daniel, learned in prophetic oracles,
Was brought from his country,
A prisoner of your father's victory.
He lives here under your rule,
And reason demands that he be called.
Therefore send for him without delay,
For he will show you what the vision conceals.

BELSHAZZAR:
Vos Danielem quaerite,
Et inventum adducite.

Seek Daniel and bring him here
When he has been found.

THE COURTIERS:
Vir propheta Dei Daniel,
V'yen ahl Roy,
Veni, desiderat

O Daniel, man and prophet of God
Come to the King.
Come, he wishes

Pahrlehr ah toy.
Pavet et turbatur, Daniel,
V'yen ahl Roy.
Vellet quod nos latet savoyr par toi.
Te ditabit donis, Daniel,
V'yen ahl Roy.
Si scripta poterit savoir par toi.

To speak to you.
He is fearful and disturbed, Daniel,
Come to the King.
He wants to learn from you what is a secret to us,
He will make you rich with gifts, Daniel,
Come to the King.
If he can learn from you the meaning of the writing.

DANIEL:
Multum miror cujus consilio
Me requirat regalis jussio.
Ibo tamen, et erit cognitum
Per me gratis quod est absconditum.

I wonder greatly by whose advice
The King's command seeks me out.
I will go, however, and he shall know from me,
At no cost, what is hidden.

THE COURTIERS:
Hic verus Dei famulus,
Quem laudat omnis populus;
Cujus fama prudentiae,
Est nota regis curiae.
Cestui manda lee Royce pahr nos.

This is God's true servant,
Whom all people praise,
The fame of whose prudence
Is known in the King's court.
The King sends for him by us.

DANIEL:
Pauper et exulans envoyce ahl Roy pahr vos.

Poor, and an exile, I go to the King by your request.

THE COURTIERS:
In juventutis gloria,
Plenus celesti gratia
Satis excellit omnibus
Virtute, vita, moribus.
Cestui manda lee Royce pahr nos.

In the glory of youth,
Full of heavenly grace,
He greatly excels all men
In virtue, in living, in his habits.
The King sends for him by us.

DANIEL:
Pauper et exulans envoyce ahl Roy pahr vos.

Poor, and an exile, I go to the King by your request.

THE COURTIERS:
Hic est cujus auxilio
Solvetur illa visio,
In qua scribente dextera,
Mota sunt Regis viscera.
Cestui manda lee Royce pahr nos.

This is he whose help
Will explain that vision,
In which the writing of a hand
Disturbed the King deeply.
The King sends for him by us.

DANIEL:
Pauper et exulans envoyce ahl Roy pahr vos.

Poor, and an exile, I go to the King by your request.

(Daniel appears before the King)

Rex, in eternum vive!

O King, live forever!

BELSHAZZAR:

Tune Daniel nomine diceris,
Huc adductus cum Judaeae miseris?
Dicunt te habere Dei spiritum
Et praescire quodlibet absconditum.
Si ergo potes scripturam solvere,
Immensis muneribus ditabere.

Are you he who is called Daniel,
Brought here with the wretched of Judaea?
They say that you have the spirit of God,
And that you know whatever is hidden.
If, therefore, you can explain the writing,
Huge rewards will be given to you.

DANIEL:

Rex, tua nolo munera;
Gratis solvetur litera.
Est autem haec solutio:
Instat tibi confusio.
Pater tuus prae omnibus
Potens olim potentibus,
Turgens nimis superbia
Dejectus est a gloria.
Nam cum Deo non ambulans,
Sed sese Deum simulans,
Basa templo diripuit
Quae suo usu habuit.
Sed post multas insanias
Tandem perdens divitias,
Forma nudatus hominis,
Pastum gustavit graminis.
Tu quoque ejus filius,
Non ipso minus impius,
Dum patris actus sequeris
Vasis eisdem uteris;
Quod quia Deo displicet,
Instat tempus quo vindicet,
Nam scripturae indicium
Minatur jam supplicium.
Et MANE, dicit Dominus,
Est tui regni terminus.
THECHEL libram significat
Quae te minorem indicat.
PHARES, hoc est divisio,
Regnum transportat alio.

King, I do not want your rewards.
The writings will be explained for no fee.
Now this is the solution:
Your destruction is at hand.
Your father was once mighty
Above all others.
Greatly puffed up with pride,
He was cast down from his glory.
For not walking with God,
But making himself like God,
He snatched the vessels from the temple
For his own use.
But after many excesses,
He finally lost his riches,
And divested of human form,
He ate grass for fodder.
You too, his son,
Are no less impious,
For you follow after his deeds
And use his vessels.
But whatever displeases God
Has a time for retribution,
And now the handwriting
Threatens a punishment.
And God says, MENE,
Your reign is at an end.
TEKEL means scales,
Which show you to be lacking.
PERES is distribution,
Your rule is given to another.

BELSHAZZAR:

Qui sic solvit latentia
Ornetur veste regia.
Tolle vasa, princeps militiae,
Ne sint mihi causa miseriae.

Let him who thus has solved the mystery
Be clothed in a royal garment.
Take away the vessels, prince of the army,
Lest they be a source of misery to me.

Plate I Chartres, stained glass window, "Notre Dame de la Belle Verrière." (Giraudon, Paris)

Plate II Chartres, stained glass window, "St. James Major." (Giraudon, Paris)

Plate III Florence, c. 1490. Carta della
catena, Museo di Firenze com'era.
(Scala/Editorial Photocolor Archives)

Plate IV Master of the Fogg Pieta, "Lamentation over the Dead Christ," c. 1330. (Courtesy of the Fogg Art Museum, Harvard University. Gift of Paul J. Sachs in memory of Miss Grace Norton)

Plate V Giotto, "The Lamentation." (Arena Chapel, Padua—Scala/Editorial Photocolor Archives)

Plate VI   Masaccio, "The Tribute
Money." (Brancacci Chapel, Florence—
Scala/Editorial Photocolor Archives)

THE QUEEN AND HER ATTENDANTS:

Solvitur in libro Salomonis
Digna laus et congrua matronis.
Pretium est ejus si quam fortis
Procul et de finibus remotis.
Fidens est in ea cor mariti
Spoliis divitibus potiti.
Mulier haec illi comparetur
Cujus rex subsidium meretur.
Ejus nam facundia verborum
Arguit prudentiam doctorum
Nos quibus occasio ludendi
Hac die conceditur solemni,
Demus huic praeconia devoti,
Veniant et concinent remoti.

There is recorded, in the book of Solomon,
Fitting and proper praise of woman.
Her value is that of a strong man
From far and distant lands.
Her husband's heart trusts in her;
He possesses abundant riches.
Let this woman be compared
To one whose king is worthy of support.
For the eloquence of her words
Overcomes the wisdom of the learned.
Let us who are performing this play
On this solemn day
Give to her devout praise;
Let the ends of the earth come and sing.

THE MEN OF THE COURT:

Regis vasa referentes
Quem Judaeae tremunt gentes,
Danieli applaudentes,
Gaudeamus! Laudes sibi debitas
Referamus!
Regis cladem praenotavit
Cum scripturam reseravit,
Testes reos comprobavit
Et Susannam liberavit,
Gaudeamus!
Laudes sibi debitas
Referamus!
Babylon hunc exulavit
Cum Judaeos captivavit,
Balthasar quem honoravit.
Gaudeamus!
Laudes sibi debitas
Referamus!
Est propheta sanctus Dei,
Hunc honorant et Chaldaei
Et gentiles et Judaei.
Ergo jubilantes ei
Gaudeamus!
Laudes sibi debitas
Referamus!

Carrying the vessels of the King
Before whom the peoples of Judae tremble,
And giving praise to Daniel,
Let us rejoice! Fitting praises
Let us bear him!
He foretold the King's downfall
When he explained the writing;
He proved the witnesses guilty
And freed Susannah.
Let us rejoice!
Fitting praises
Let us bear him!
Babylon exiled him,
When the Jews were taken captive
Whom Belshazzar honors.
Let us rejoice!
Fitting praises
Let us bear him!
He is a holy prophet of God.
Honored by Chaldeans
And Gentiles and Jews.
Therefore, making merry before him,
Let us rejoice!
Fitting praises
Let us bear him!

(King Darius and his soldiers and courtiers now enter, having overthrown Belshazzar)

DARIUS'S SOLDIERS AND COURT:

Ecce Rex Darius
Venit cum principibus,

Behold! King Darius
Comes with his princes,

Nobilis nobilibus.	The noble one with his nobles.
Ejus et curia	And his court
Resonat laetitia,	Resounds with joy,
Adsunt et tripudia.	And there is dancing.
Hic est mirandus,	He is awesome,
Cunctis venerandus.	Venerated by all.
Illi imperia	Empires are
Sunt tributaria.	His tributaries.
Regem honorant	All honor him as King
Omnes et adorant.	And worship him.
Illum Babylonia	The land of Babylonia
Metuit et patria.	Fears him, also.
Cum armato agmine	With his armed troops,
Ruens et cum turbine.	Descending like a whirlwind,
Sternit cohortes,	He crushes armies
Confregit et fortes.	And destroys the strong.
Illum honestas	Honesty and nobility
Colit et nobilitas.	Are his endowments.
Hic est Babylonius	He is the noble King,
Nobilis Rex Darius.	Darius of Babylonia.
Illi cum tripudio	Let this throng
Gaudeat et haec contio	Rejoice in him with dancing
Laudet et cum gaudio	And praise with joy
Ejus facta fortia	His mighty deeds,
Tam admirabilia.	So wondrous.
Simul omnes gratulemur;	Let us all be glad together;
Resonet et tympana;	Let the drums sound,
Citharistae tangant cordas;	Let harpists pluck their strings;
Musicorum organa	Let the musicians' instruments
Resonent ad ejus praeconia.	Resound his praises.

(Darius is seated on the throne. All acclaim him, saying)

Rex, in eternum vive!	O King, live forever!

TWO COUNSELORS:

Audite, principes, regalis curiae,	Hear us, you princes of the King's court,
Qui leges regitis totius patriae.	Who administer the laws throughout the land.
Est quidam sapiens in Babylonia,	There is a certain wise man in Babylonia,
Secreta reserans deorum gratia.	Who by the gods' grace reveals secret things.
Ejus consilium regi complacuit,	His advice pleased the King,
Nam prius Balthasar scriptum aperuit.	For he explained the writing to Belshazzar.
Ite velociter, ne sit dilatio;	So quickly, let there be no delay—
Nos uti volumus ejus consilio.	We want to make use of his counsel.
Fiat, si venerit, consiliarius	If he will come, let him be made counselor
Regis, et fuerit in regno tertius.	To the King, and he shall rank third in the kingdom.

(Three messengers are sent to Daniel)

MESSENGERS:

Ex regalis venit imperio,	Our embassy comes by command of the King,
Serve Dei, nostra legatio.	O servant of God.
Tua Regi laudatur probitas.	Your uprightness is praised to the King;
Te commendat mira calliditas,	Your amazing skill commends you.
Per te solum cum nobis patuit	Through you alone was explained
Signum dextrae quod omnes latuit.	The apparition of a hand which was a mystery to everyone.
Te Rex vocat ad suam curiam,	The King calls you to his court,
Ut agnoscat tuam prudentiam.	That he may acknowledge your discretion.
Eris, supra ut dicit Darius,	You shall be, according to what Darius says,
Principalis consiliarius.	His principal adviser.
Ergo veni, jam omnes curia	Therefore come, for the whole court
Praeparatur ad tua gaudia.	Is being readied for your pleasure.

DANIEL:

Genvois al Roi.	I will go to the King.

(Daniel is led before Darius)

COUNSELORS, MESSENGERS, COURTIERS:

Congaudentes celebremus natalis solemnia;	With great rejoicing let us celebrate the Christmas solemnities;
Jam de morte nos redemit Dei sapientia.	God's Wisdom has now redeemed us from death.
Homo natus est in carne, qui creavit omnia,	He who created all things is born man, in the flesh;
Nasciturum quem praedixit prophetae facundia.	His birth was foretold by the words of the prophet.
Danielis jam cessavit unctionis copia;	The old anointing of Daniel's time had ended;
Cessavit regni Judaeorum contumax potentia.	The dispensation of the Jews is over.
In hoc natalitio,	On this Christmas,
Daniel, cum gaudio	With joy, O Daniel,
Te laudat haec contio.	This crowd praises you.
Tu Susannam liberasti de mortali crimine,	You freed Susannah from a capital charge;
Cum te Deus inspiravit suo sancto flamine.	God inspired you by his holy spirit.
Testes falsos comprobasti reos accusamine;	You proved the witnesses guilty by their own accusations;
Bel draconem peremisti coram plebis agmine.	You destroyed the dragon Bel in the sight of the people.
Et te Deus observavit leonum voragine.	And God guarded you from the lion's pit.
Ergo sit laus Dei Verbo genito de Virgine.	Therefore, praised by the Word of God, born of a Virgin.

DANIEL:

Rex, in eternum vive!	O King, live forever!

DARIUS:

Quia novi te callidum,	Because I know your prudence,
Totius regni providum,	Daniel, I give you responsibility

Te, Daniel, constituo,
Et summum locum tribuo.

Over the entire kingdom
And award you the highest place.

DANIEL:

Rex, mihi si credideris,
Per me nil mali feceris.

King, if you trust in me,
You will do no evil by following my advice.

TWO ENVIOUS ADVISERS:

Rex in eternum vive!
Decreverunt in tua curia
Principandi quibus est gloria,
Ut ad tui rigorem nominis
Omni spreto vigore numinis,
Per triginta dierum spatium
Adoreris ut Deus omnium: O Rex

O King, live forever!
It was decreed in your court
By the rulers who are glorious
That, by the power of your name,
Every god should be rejected
For the space of thirty days,
And that you should be adored as God by all, O King!

Si quis ausu tam temerario
Renuerit tuo consilio,
Ut praeter te colatur deitas,
Judicii sit talis firmitas,
In leonum tradatur foveam;
Sic dicatur per totam regiam, O Rex!

If anyone should be so rash
As to disregard your command
And to prefer another god above you,
The punishment should be
That he be delivered to the lion's pit;
Let this be proclaimed throughout your realm, O King!

DARIUS:

Ego mando et remando
Ne sit spretum hoc decretum. Ohez!

I command and ordain
That this decree be obeyed. Hear it!

(Daniel worships his own God in spite of the decree)

TWO ENVIOUS ADVISERS:

Numquid, Dari, observari statuisti omnibus,

Qui orare vel rogare quicquam a numinibus,
Ni te Deum, illum reum daremus leonibus;
Hoc edictum sic indictum fuit a principibus.

Do you remember, Darius, the observance you commanded,
That whoever is guilty of praying to any god but you
For anything will be given to the lions?
This law was proclaimed by your princes.

DARIUS:

Vere jussi me omnibus
Adorari a gentibus.

It is true that I commanded
All people to worship me.

TWO ENVIOUS ADVISERS:

Hunc Judaeum suum Deum Danielem vidimus
Adorantem et precantem, tuis spretis legibus

We saw this Jew, Daniel, worshiping
And praying to his God in defiance of your laws.

DARIUS:

Nunquam vobis concedatur
Quod vir sanctus sic perdatur.

May it never be granted you
That that holy man should be so destroyed.

TWO ENVIOUS ADVISERS:

Lex Parthorum et Medorum jubet in annalibus

The law of the Medes and the Persians in the annals commands

Ut qui sprevit quae decrevit Rex, detur leonibus.

That whoever scorns the King's decree be given to the lions.

DARIUS:

Si sprevit legem quam statueram
Det poenas ipse quas decreveram.

If he has disobeyed the law that I made,
Let him receive the punishment that I decreed.

(Daniel is seized and brought to the lions' den)

DANIEL:

Heu, heu, heu!
Quo casu sortis venit haec damnatio mortis?

Woe, woe, woe!
By what chance of fate do I receive this condemnation to death?

Heu, heu, heu!
Scelus infandum!
Cur me dabit ad lacerandum
Haec fera turba feris?
Sic me, Rex, perdere quaeris?
Heu!
Qua morte mori me cogis?
Parce furori.

Woe, woe, woe!
Unspeakable calamity!
Why will this savage multitude
Give me to be torn by wild beasts?
Thus, O King, do you seek to kill me?
Woe!
To what death do you compel me?
Spare your fury.

DARIUS:

Deus quem colis tam fideliter
Te liberabit mirabiliter.

The God whom you worship so faithfully
Will deliver you miraculously.

(Daniel is thrown into the lions' den)

DANIEL:

Hujus rei non sum reus;
Miserere mei Deus; eleyson.
Mitte, Deus, huc patronum
Qui refrenet vim leonum; eleyson.

I am not guilty of this crime;
God have mercy on me, eleyson.
To this place, O God, send a defender
Who will restrain the power of the lions, eleyson.

(An angel is sent to protect Daniel from the lions. Another angel comes to Habakkuk, far away)

ANGEL:

Abacuc, tu senex pie,
Ad lacum Babyloniae,
Danieli fer prandium;
Mandat tibi Rex omnium.

Habakkuk, pious old man,
Bring food to Daniel,
To the pit in Babylonia;
The King of all commands it of you.

HABAKKUK:

Novit Dei cognitio
Quod Babylonem nescio,
Neque lacus est cognitus
Quo Daniel est positus.

God in his wisdom knows
That I know nothing of Babylon,
Nor of the pit
Into which Daniel has been put.

(The angel leads him there)

HABAKKUK:

Surge, frater, ut cibum capias;	Arise, brother, and take food;
Tuas Deus vidit angustias;	God has seen your sufferings;
Deus misit, da Deo gratias,	God has sent me, give thanks to him
Qui te fecit.	Who made you.

DANIEL:

Recordatus es mei, Domine;	You have remembered me, Lord;
Accipiam in tuo nomine, Alleluia!	I accept this in your name, Alleluiah!

(Darius approaches the pit)

DARIUS:

Tene, putas, Daniel,	Do you think, Daniel,
Salvabit, ut eripiaris	That he whom you revere and worship
A nece proposita,	Will save you and rescue you
Quem tu colis et veneraris?	From the death to which you are sent?

DANIEL:

Rex, in eternum vive!	O King, live forever!
Angelicum solita misit pietate patronum,	With his accustomed pity, God sent an angelic protection
Quo Deus ad tempus conpescuit ora leonum.	To close the lions' mouths for the time being.

DARIUS:

Danielem educite,	Bring Daniel out,
Et emulos immittite.	And throw the envious ones in.

(His princes proclaim the command)

Danielem educite,	Bring Daniel out,
Et emulos immittite.	And throw the envious ones in.

THE TWO ENVIOUS ADVISERS:

Merito haec patimur,	We suffer this deservedly, for we have
Quia peccavimus in sanctum Dei,	Sinned against a holy man of God;
Injuste egimus,	We have acted unjustly
Iniquitatem fecimus.	And have done evil.

DARIUS:

Deum Danielis qui regnat in saeculis	I command all people to worship
Adorari jubeo a cunctis populis.	Daniel's God, who rules the world.

DANIEL:

Ecce venit sanctus ille,	Behold, the holy one shall come,
Sanctorum sanctissimus,	The holiest of the holy,
Quem Rex iste jubet coli	Whom this king, powerful and mighty,
Potens et fortissimus.	Commands us to worship.

Cessant phana, cesset regnum,
Cessabit et unctio;
Instat regni Judaeorum
Finis et oppressio.

Temples, anointings,
This kingdom shall cease;
The end of the Kingdom of Judaea,
And of its oppression, is at hand.

(An angel appears to announce the fulfillment of Daniel's prophecy)

ANGEL:
Nuntium vobis fero de supernis:
Natus est Christus, Dominator orbis,
In Bethleem Judae,
Sic enim propheta dixerat ante.

I bring you a message from on high:
Christ, the ruler of the world, is born
In Bethlehem in Judah,
As the Prophet foretold.

(The entire company sings the "Te Deum laudamus")

Te Deum laudamus:
Te Dominum confitemur.
Te aeternum Patrem
Omnis terra veneratur:
Tibi omnes Angeli
Tibi caeli et universae potestates:
Tibi Cherubim et Seraphim incessabili voce
    proclamant:
Sanctus, sanctus, sanctus,
Dominus Deus Sabaoth:
Pleni sunt caeli et terra majestatis gloriae tuae.
Te gloriosus Apostolorum chorus,
Te Prophetarum laudabilis numerus,
Te Martyrum candidatus laudat exercitus.
Te per orbem terrarum sancta confitetur Ecclesia,

Patrem immensae majestatis;
Venerandum tuum verum et unicum Filium;
Sanctum quoque Paraclitum Spiritum.
Tu Rex gloriae, Christe,
Tu Patris sempiternus es Filius.
Tu, ad liberandum suscepturus hominem,
Non horruisti Virginis uterum.
Te, devicto mortis aculeo,
Aperuisti credentibus regna caelorum

Tu ad dexteram sedes, in gloria Patris.

Judex crederis esse venturus.
Te ergo quaesumus, tuis famulis subveni,
Quos pretioso sanguine redemisti.
Aeterna fac cum sanctis tuis in gloria numerari.

Salvum fac populum tuum, Domine,

We praise thee, O God;
We acknowledge thee to be the Lord.
All the earth doth worship thee,
The Father everlasting.
To thee all Angels cry aloud;
The Heavens and all the Powers therein;
To thee Cherubim and Seraphim continually do cry:

Holy, holy, holy,
Lord God of Sabaoth;
Heaven and earth are full of the Majesty of thy glory.
The glorious company of the Apostles praise thee.
The goodly fellowship of the Prophets praise thee.
The noble army of Martyrs praise thee.
The holy Church throughout all the world doth
    acknowledge thee;
The Father of an infinite Majesty;
Thine adorable true and only Son;
Also the Holy Ghost the Comforter.
Thou art the King of Glory, O Christ.
Thou art the everlasting Son of the Father.
When thou tookest upon thee to deliver man,
Thou didst humble thyself to be born of a Virgin.
When thou hadst overcome the sharpness of death,
Thou didst open the Kingdom of Heaven to all
    believers.
Thou sittest at the right hand of God, in the glory of
    the Father.
We believe that thou shalt come to be our Judge.
We therefore pray thee help thy servants,
Whom thou hast redeemed with thy precious blood.
Make them to be numbered with thy Saints in glory
    everlasting.
O Lord, save thy people

Et benedic haereditati tuae.

Et rege eos, et extolle illos usque in aeternum.

Per singulos dies benedicimus te.

Et laudamus nomen tuum in saeculum et in
saeculi.

Dignare Domine die isto sine peccato nos custodire.

Miserere nostri, Domine, miserere nostri.

Fiat misericordia tua Domine super nos,

Quemadmodum speravimus in te.

In te Domine speravi:

Non confundar in aeternum.

And bless thine heritage.

Govern them, and lift them up for ever.

Day by day we magnify thee;

And we worship thy Name ever world without end.

Vouchsafe, O Lord, to keep us this day without sin.

Have mercy upon us, O Lord, have mercy upon us.

O Lord, let thy mercy be upon us,

As our trust is in thee.

O Lord, in thee have I trusted;

Let me never be confounded.

COMMENTS AND QUESTIONS

1. Read the Book of Daniel in the Old Testament, asking yourself what the author has done with the biblical story. Has he Christianized any of its specifically Jewish aspects? Has he added anything to the
various characters or depicted them more clearly
than they are in the story?

2. What other biblical stories might have appealed to
medieval Christians for dramatization with music?
(There are liturgical dramas on Christ's resurrection, miracles, and birth.)

3. In noting the differences between the story of Daniel in the Bible and the way that it is handled in the
play, you may be able to see something of the same
process of transformation of myth into drama that
was at work in Sophocles' creation of *Oedipus Rex*.
Does the hero of *The Play of Daniel* show the same
internal development or character transformation as
Oedipus does? Are the other characters as well defined? Why or why not?

4. From a comparison of these two plays, what inferences can you make concerning the differences between the classical and the medieval aesthetic, particularly concerning the view of the place of human
beings held by each culture?

5. Could *Daniel* have been written as a tragedy? What
keeps it from being a tragedy? Would a tragic view of
life be alien to the Judeo-Christian view of the
world?

6. Is the music of *Daniel* dramatic in the same sense as
more familiar modern music? How does this affect
the action, the timing, the impact of the words?

7. In what ways do the lack of harmony and orchestration affect the function of the melody in the
Daniel play?

8. Even though you might not recognize distinctive
melodies as such in *The Play of Daniel*, do you hear
sounds that are more appropriate for one kind of action or emotion than for another?

8

DIVINE AND HUMAN LOVE

The cathedral of Notre Dame de Chartres, built as a palace for the queen of heaven, containing a relic of her tunic, full of images of her in stone and stained glass is, among other things, a testament to the enormous importance that the Virgin Mary had in the spiritual and daily lives of medieval men and women. And Chartres was not the only such palace. Romanesque churches were dedicated to a variety of saints, but in the Gothic period the greatest cathedrals of France—Amiens, Rheims, Laon, Rouen, and Paris— were called for Mary *Notre Dame* (Our Lady). We witnessed in François Villon's "Ballade: For His Mother to Our Lady" (though it was written later, in the fifteenth century) the sense of help and solace that a simple, unlettered woman found in her devotion to the Virgin. Why did the Virgin play such an important part in medieval lives, and what were the effects of this cult?

Popular Devotion to Mary   The devotion to Mary is part of a general humanizing trend in religion taking place in the eleventh and twelfth centuries. Monastic literature of this time begins to emphasize the theme of tenderness and compassion for Jesus' sufferings. Jesus was portrayed as more and more human—the representations of him in art reflect this. Whereas early medieval portrayals of the Christ Child had been somewhat allegorical, making the baby look already like the king of the world, twelfth-century artists began to portray a more childlike child and with him a mother who could express the tenderness of human, as well as divine, love. The artists who represented this divine mother took care to represent her as a lady of great beauty, combining physical attractiveness with a more ethereal quality. In the language of Mary's devotees, the praise of spiritual and physical beauty was often intermingled. Mary was seen as a queen but also as a mother—a kind and warm woman full of compassion for human sufferings and shortcomings, able and willing to intercede between individuals and God and thereby to save souls. A great many stories about miracles done by the Virgin circulated orally in the twelfth century; some were written down. The following examples illustrate the common man's view of the Virgin's compassion and power.

A clerk at Chartres led an unchaste life, but often prayed to the Virgin. When he died, he was buried outside the churchyard because of his bad reputation. The Virgin appeared to one of his colleagues, asked him why her "chancellor" had been so badly treated, and ordered that he be reburied in the churchyard.

A certain thief named Ebbo was devoted to the Virgin, and even hailed her when he went out to steal. He was finally arrested and hanged [a common punishment for thieves] but the Virgin supported him for two days and when the hangmen tried to tighten the rope, she put her hands around his throat and prevented them. Finally he was let go.

One of the spiritual leaders most responsible for promoting the cult of the Virgin in theology, along with popular devotion, was Saint Bernard (1090–1153). Bernard, abbot of Clairvaux and a close associate of the abbot Suger, was a Cistercian monk who emphasized in his teachings the value of the inner life and self-knowledge as part of a mystical ascension to God. Divine love, the essential attribute of the Virgin, could aid the soul in its progressive ascent from the love of bodily things, to the love of spiritual things, to the selfless love of God. The Virgin, human and yet the mother of God, could aid human beings in their progress from carnal to spiritual love.

Influence of Devotion to Mary on Love Poetry: Dante   Bernard and his followers created a whole language of mystical love and adoration for the Virgin in their prayers and songs. These expressions in turn influenced secular love poetry. Poets began to write of their lady loves in terms more religious than amorous—as if they were worshiping them more than merely loving or admiring them. The elevation of the lady in twelfth-century lyrics and romances gave rise to two trends in literature as well as in art and music. One, which we will examine later in this chapter, treats earthly love as a parody of heavenly love and demonstrates the destructive qualities of the former. The other, which continues into the Renaissance, etherealizes the lady into a symbol of divine love, or a kind of Platonic Idea. Dante Alighieri (1265–1321) wrote love poetry in this tradition. His adored lady was Beatrice, a real girl whom Dante knew and loved (from afar) in his native Florence, Italy, but whose name means "she who blesses." When she died, around the age of twenty-five, Dante dedicated to her a series of sonnets called *La Vita Nuova (The New Life)*, describing a spiritual reawakening through love. Later, when he was to write his great work, *La Divina Commedia (The Divine Comedy)*, he determined to do for Beatrice what had never been done for another woman. Beatrice, while never losing entirely her identification as a woman once loved on earth by Dante, there becomes a soul in heaven who will be the instrument of the poet's salvation. She is also an *allegory* for divine revelation. Dante's love for her will lead him to experience the love of the Virgin Mary, and then to God himself. We will see in the passages below how Dante's adoration of Beatrice is close to his adoration of the Virgin, but first we should say a word about the whole of *The Divine Comedy*.

The Divine Comedy

It is hard to describe exactly what this "comedy" is. It is certainly not a comedy in the usual sense—but it is in a way the opposite of a tragedy because it begins in despair and ends in bliss. It is often classified as an epic; but, though it is strongly influenced by Virgil's *Aeneid*, it is not at all concerned with the external adventures of heroes and wars. It might best be described as a spiritual epic, for it is essentially the story of the poet's quest for salvation. It is a long (three books) and complex work that contains everything: sordid descriptions of the dregs of humanity, gross comedy, political satire, poignant friendships, subtle philosophy, and the most spiritual poetry ever written. It is undoubtedly the greatest literary achievement of the Middle Ages. Like the philosophical system of Thomas Aquinas and the great cathedrals such as Chartres, it is an edifice that embraces and builds upon almost every conceivable aspect of life, in this world and the next, with the whole pointing toward God.

The first book, called *Inferno* (hell), begins with the poet's description of himself at age thirty-five in the year 1300, "lost in a dark wood." In his long search for the "true path" that will lead him to salvation, he undertakes a visionary journey into the other world. Virgil, the Latin poet, comes to serve as his guide on a journey through hell, where Dante witnesses every form of human sin and its punishment, suffering intensely himself. In the second book, *Purgatorio*, Virgil and Dante begin the ascent of the mountain of Purgatory, the place (in Catholic theology) where penitent sinners must work their way to heaven. Virgil represents not only himself in the poem but, allegorically, human reason as well. Since reason (as in Aquinas) can go only so far to help man obtain salvation, Virgil is replaced at the top of the mountain by Beatrice, allegorically divine revelation, who will serve as Dante's guide through paradise in the third book, *Paradiso*.

In the medieval world-view that Dante held, earth was believed to be at the center of the universe and the heavens a series of spheres around it from the closest sphere of the moon to the farthest Empyrean sphere, the dwelling place of God. When Dante and Beatrice reach the Empyrean, she prepares to leave the pilgrim to return to her place in heaven, entrusting him to Saint Bernard (Bernard of Clairvaux, the devotee of Mary mentioned above). Dante sings his final song of praise for Beatrice, conceding (though he praises his own poetic powers in the *Inferno*) that her heavenly beauty utterly undoes his art. Bernard promises Dante a vision of God, to be attained through the intercession of the Virgin Mary. Dante raises his eyes to the center of the mystic rose (a symbol of Mary, like the rose windows in the cathedrals) and, while experiencing unearthly bliss, sees the queen of heaven herself enthroned. Saint Bernard then offers a prayer to the Virgin, asking her to intercede for Dante, and Dante experiences a final rapture as he gazes directly on God. God is the source of all love—"the Love that moves the Sun and the other stars" are the final words of the poem— and the Eternal Light. Light, bearing much the same significance as it did for Suger when he created his cathedral, is the dominant image in paradise. It is a tribute to Dante's genius that he was able to render the ineffable in human language.

In Dante's time the standard language for the Church and for "serious" writing (history, philosophy) was still Latin; nevertheless, literature had begun to flourish all over Europe in the vernacular (the language actually spoken in daily life). Dante chose this vehicle for his great epic, writing in Tuscan, his native dialect, which thereafter became the standard Italian language.

The passages below are from the translation of *The Divine Comedy* by a modern American poet, John Ciardi. In the first, the beginning of Canto 30 of *Paradiso*, Dante praises Beatrice as she leads him into the Empyrean, the heaven of pure light.

When, as may be, the sun's noon heat is shed
 six thousand miles away, while, where we are,
 earth's shadow makes an almost level bed;

when, at our zenith, the sky begins to show
 such changes that a star or two begins
 to fade from the eyes of watchers here below;

and as the sun's most radiant serving maid
 comes nearer yet, and heaven puts out its lamps
 one by one, till the loveliest, too, must fade—

just so that Triumph that forever races
    around the blinding ray of the fixed Point
    that seems embraced by what Itself embraces,

faded from sight, degree by slow degree;
    at which I turned my eyes from the lost vision
    to Beatrice, as love commanded me.

If all that I have said of her below
    were gathered now into a single paean,
    that would be scant praise of her beauty now.

The beauty I saw there transcends all measure
    of mortal minds. I think only her Maker
    can wholly comprehend so great a treasure.

Here I concede defeat. No poet known,
    comic or tragic, challenged by his theme
    to show his power, was ever more outdone.

As feeblest eyes, struck by the sun, go blind,
    so the remembrance of my lady's smile
    strikes every recognition from my mind.

From the first day I looked upon her face
    in this life, to this present sight of her,
    my song has followed her to sing her praise.

But here I must no longer even try
    to walk behind her beauty. Every artist,
    his utmost done, must put his brushes by.

So do I leave her to a clarion
    of greater note than mine, which starts to draw
    its long and arduous theme to a conclusion.

She, like a guide who has his goal in sight
    began to speak again: "We have ascended
    from the greatest sphere to the heaven of pure light.

Light of the intellect, which is love unending;
    love of the true good, which is wholly bliss;
    bliss beyond bliss, all other joys transcending;

here shall you see both hosts of Paradise,
    one of them in the aspect you shall see
    when you return the day all bodies rise."

As a flash of lightning striking on our sight
    destroys our visual spirits, so that the eye
    cannot make out even a brighter light;

just so, an aureole burst all about me,
    swathing me so completely in its veil
    that I was closed in light and could not see.

QUESTION

How does this poem function both on a literal level (as the praise of a beautiful woman) and an allegorical level (as the description of the soul's encounter with divine revelation)?

    In the next passage (from Canto 31) Dante, seeing Beatrice for the last time, offers a kind of prayer of thanks to her. He is then left in the custody of Saint Bernard, who introduces him to a vision of the Virgin Mary. As Beatrice allegorically represents divine revelation, Bernard represents contemplation.

"O lady in whom my hope shall ever soar
    and who for my salvation suffered even
    to set your feet upon Hell's broken floor;[1]

through your power and your excellence alone
    have I recognized the goodness and the grace
    inherent in the things I have been shown.

You have led me from my bondage and set me free
    by all those roads, by all those loving means
    that lay within your power and charity.

Grant me your magnificence that my soul,
    which you have healed, may please you when it slips
    the bonds of flesh and rises to its goal."

Such was my prayer, and she—far up a mountain,
    as it appeared to me—looked down and smiled.
    Then she turned back to the Eternal Fountain.

And the holy Elder said: "I have been sent

---

[1] Beatrice descended to limbo, the uppermost part of hell reserved for virtuous pagans, to summon Virgil to guide Dante.

by prayer and sacred love to help you reach
the perfect consummation of your ascent.

Look round this garden, therefore, that you may
by gazing at its radiance, be prepared
to lift your eyes up to the Trinal Ray.

The Queen of Heaven, for whom in whole devotion
I burn with love, will grant us every grace
because I am Bernard, her faithful one."

As a stranger from afar—a Croat, if you will—
comes to see our Veronica, and awed
by its ancient fame, can never look his fill,[2]

but says to himself as long as it is displayed:
"My Lord, Jesus Christ, true God, and is this then
the likeness of thy living flesh portrayed?"—

just so did I gaze on the living love
of him who in this world, through contemplation
tasted the peace which ever dwells above.

"Dear son of Grace," he said, "you cannot know
this state of bliss while you yet keep your eyes
fixed only on those things that lie below;

rather, let your eyes mount to the last round
where you shall see the Queen to whom this realm
is subject and devoted, throned and crowned."

I looked up: by as much as the horizon
to eastward in the glory of full dawn
outshines the point at which the sun went down;

by so much did one region on the height
to which I raised my eyes out of the valley
outshine the rays of every other light.[3]

And as the sky is brightest in that region
where we on earth expect to see the shaft
of the chariot so badly steered by Phaeton,

while to one side and the other it grows dim—
just so that peaceful oriflamme lit the center
and faded equally along either rim.

And in the center, great wings spread apart,
more than a thousand festive angels shone,
each one distinct in radiance and in art.

I saw there, smiling at this song and sport,
she whose beauty entered like a bliss
into the eyes of all that sainted court.

And even could my speech match my conception,
yet I would not dare make the least attempt
to draw her delectation and perfection.

Bernard, seeing my eyes so fixed and burning
with passion on his passion, turned his own
up to that height with so much love and yearning

that the example of his ardor sent
new fire through me, making my gaze more ardent.

QUESTION

What similarities do you see between Dante's portrayal
of Beatrice and his portrayal of Mary? What differences
do you note?

The last passage is from Canto 33—the final canto of
The Divine Comedy. It opens with Saint Bernard's
prayer to the Virgin, surely the purest expression of this
kind of spiritual worship ever written. Dante then as-
cends to the direct vision of God and, returning to
himself as if awakening from a dream, ponders what he
has learned.

"Virgin Mother, daughter of thy son;
humble beyond all creatures and more exalted;
predestined turning point of God's intention;[1]

---

[2] Dante here describes the feeling a Christian from a far-off land
(such as Croatia) must have when he sees the famous relic, in Saint
Peter's Church, of the handkerchief with which Veronica wiped the
blood from Christ's face. He then compares this feeling to his own
in gazing on Saint Bernard. Dante, like Virgil, uses many of these
long comparisons, or epic *similes*.

[3] Another long comparison. Mary outshines heaven, bright as it is, as
the east outshines the west at daybreak.

---

[1] Through Mary, God became man; thus, he made her the pivot of
his plan of redemption for mankind.

thy merit so ennobled human nature
  that its divine Creator did not scorn
  to make Himself the creature of His creature.

The Love that was rekindled in Thy womb
  sends forth the warmth of the eternal peace
  within whose ray this flower has come to bloom.

Here, to us, thou art the noon and scope
  of Love revealed; and among mortal men,
  the living fountain of eternal hope.

Lady, thou art so near God's reckonings
  that who seeks grace and does not first seek thee
  would have his wish fly upward without wings.

Not only does thy sweet benignity
  flow out to all who beg, but oftentimes
  thy charity arrives before the plea.

In thee is pity, in thee munificence,
  in thee the tenderest heart, in thee unites
  all that creation knows of excellence!

Now comes this man who from the final pit
  of the universe up to this height has seen,
  one by one, the three lives of the spirit.[2]

He prays to thee in fervent supplication
  for grace and strength, that he may raise his eyes
  to the all-healing final revelation.

And I, who never more desired to see
  the vision myself than I do that he may see It,
  add my own prayer, and pray that it may be

enough to move you to dispel the trace
  of every mortal shadow by thy prayers
  and let him see revealed the Sum of Grace.

I pray thee further, all-persuading Queen,
  keep whole the natural bent of his affections[3]

and of his powers after his eyes have seen.

Protect him from the stirrings of man's clay;[4]
  see how Beatrice and the blessed host
  clasp reverent hands to join me as I pray."

The eyes[5] that God reveres and loves the best
  glowed on the speaker, making clear the joy
  with which true prayer is heard by the most blest.

Those eyes turned then to the Eternal Ray,[6]
  through which, we must indeed believe, the eyes
  of others do not find such ready way.

And I, who neared the goal of all my nature,
  felt my soul, at the climax of its yearning,
  suddenly, as it ought, grow calm with rapture.

Bernard then, smiling sweetly, gestured to me
  to look up, but I had already become
  within myself all he would have me be.

Little by little as my vision grew
  it penetrated further through the aura
  of the high lamp which in Itself is true.

What then I saw is more than tongue can say.
  Our human speech is dark before the vision.
  The ravished memory swoons and falls away.

As one who sees in dreams and wakes to find
  the emotional impression of his vision
  still powerful while its parts fade from his mind—

just such am I, having lost nearly all
  the vision itself, while in my heart I feel
  the sweetness of it yet distill and fall.

So, in the sun, the footprints fade from snow.
  On the wild wind that bore the tumbling leaves

---

[2] Dante has been through the pit of hell, climbed the mountain of purgatory, and gone through the heavens of paradise.
[3] Protect his reason and emotions from being completely overwhelmed by what he sees.

[4] Protect him from human weaknesses, especially pride.
[5] Mary's eyes.
[6] God, source of all light. Light, as a symbol for God and heavenly things, is as prevalent in Bernard's mysticism and Dante's poetry as it was in Suger's theories for rebuilding the church at Saint Denis.

the Sybil's oracles were scattered so.[7]

O Light Supreme who doth Thyself withdraw
   so far above man's mortal understanding,
   lend me again some glimpse of what I saw;

make Thou my tongue so eloquent it may
   of all Thy glory speak a single clue
   to those who follow me in the world's day;

for by returning to my memory
   somewhat, and somewhat sounding in these verses,
   Thou shalt show man more of Thy victory.

So dazzling was the splendor of that Ray,
   that I must certainly have lost my senses
   had I, but for an instant, turned away.

And so it was, as I recall, I could
   the better bear to look, until at last
   my vision made one with the Eternal Good.

Oh grace abounding that had made me fit
   to fix my eyes on the eternal light
   until my vision was consumed in it!

I saw within Its depth how It conceives
   all things in a single volume bound by Love,
   of which the universe is the scattered leaves;[8]

substance, accident, and their relation
   so fused that all I say could do no more
   than yield a glimpse of that bright revelation.

I think I saw the universal form
   that binds these things, for as I speak these words
   I feel my joy swell and my spirits warm.

QUESTIONS

1. Describe the *structure* and the *tone* of Bernard's prayer (lines 1–39).

2. What images are used to describe Mary in the prayer? How do these reinforce or add to the vision of her?
3. What spiritual and emotional states does Dante express in lines 40–69? What are the difficulties involved in describing these in poetry?
4. How does this translation of Dante use *images, symbols, similes, rhythm,* and *rhyme* for expressive purposes?

The Literature and Music of "Courtly Love"

The idealization, or spiritualization, of man's love for woman, as we have seen it portrayed in Dante's *Paradiso,* represents one trend resulting from the intermingling of language used in the worship of the Virgin Mary with the expression of love for an elevated lady. Another trend, which flourished in the twelfth and thirteenth centuries and has deeply influenced our modern culture's views on love, is represented by the love stories and poems with music that later came to be called "courtly."

The medieval view of love was formed primarily from classical expressions of ideal friendship (Cicero's *De Amicitia*) and of destructive passion (Ovid's *Heroides* and *Metamorphoses*) combined with biblical expressions of mystical love (Song of Songs) and of charity (1 Corinthians). By the twelfth century, love was the primary subject of the new vernacular (modern European languages, not Latin) literatures of Western Europe. Although stories about heroes, or epics, had been composed from as early as the seventh century—first in Anglo-Saxon—the main literary language of the early Middle Ages was still Latin. But by the twelfth century the vernacular was increasingly the vehicle for literature; and the new form, romance—a term originally signifying a composition in a romance (from Roman) language, French, Italian, or Spanish—was fast becoming the dominant form of *narrative.*

The Romance—Fiction, Not Fact   In romances the main characters were knights and ladies, and the concerns were chivalry and love rather than heroic combat (as in the epic). But though the characters may have suggested ideals of courtesy and nobility, neither they nor their actions should be thought of as reflecting daily life at the time. They, their deeds of chivalry,

---

[7] The Cumean Sybil, who figures in Virgil's *Aeneid*, gave out oracles written on leaves, one letter to a leaf, and scattered to the wind.
[8] This idea comes from Plato (see "The Allegory of the Cave" in Chapter 4). The true form of all created things exists in the mind of God. What we see are merely examples of the real forms.

and their loves were all fictions. And though the love that dominates these romances, as well as the new vernacular lyric poetry, is easily taken at face value, it was grounded more in fiction than in fact. The knight languishing in love for years and unable to bring himself to tell his lady of his feelings was a conventional literary figure. Around the fifteenth century, it is true that men started acting as they were described in the romances, but this was a case of life imitating art.

The medieval view of man, grounded in the classical and Christian insistence on the need to be guided by reason, would hardly permit an audience to find admirable a swooning lover, unable to act or even to think clearly. Such a figure would represent a ridiculous distortion of man created in the image of God and provide a vivid example of the folly of allowing passion to overcome reason. Whereas the language of what has been popularly known as courtly love (though the term is a modern invention) was at times similar to that used to express love of God or devotion to the Virgin, the application of such language to earthly love, necessarily transitory and changing, served neither to elevate the earthly nor to lower the divine. Rather, instead of making the earthly lady appear like the Virgin Mary, this effusive praise emphasized the inappropriateness of the comparison. The use of religious language to describe a lady love could only seem like a strange, distorted overstatement. The fiction of courtly love, with the lady functioning as an object of adoration and the man acting as her humble servant, parodied not only the veneration of the Virgin but also the sacrament of marriage, in which the woman promised to love, honor, and obey her husband, who was properly her lord. For man to be controlled by woman was, in the medieval view, for him to give up his responsibilities, as asserted by his religion, and to create a situation that would have been regarded as inverted and perverted, hardly one to be taken seriously.

There exist several medieval handbooks on love. One of the most popular, by Andreas Capellanus (late twelfth century), contains two parts on seduction (with instructions and models). In the third and final part, however, Andreas writes that if one is concerned with his salvation, he should forsake all such loves and turn to God. That man, even in the twelfth century, was not about to give up readily the pleasures of the flesh was clear to medieval writers: and one of the most

important books of the Middle Ages, the thirteenth-century French narrative called *The Romance of the Rose*, shows in its dream *allegory* the lover ignoring the advice of Reason and continuing to pursue his earthly love. The final consummation—on the literal level a happy ending—is especially ironic, for the lover has allowed his passion to overcome his reason and has even jeopardized his salvation.

Even when the lover and the beloved are in accord, and even when their love seems good, it will fail—as medieval writings insist over and over—if they view it as the most important thing in their lives. As medieval Christianity emphasized, human love is properly a way of loving God and is good when it uses love of created things as a way of loving the Creator. If, on the other hand, the love is so consuming that it makes the lovers oblivious of anything outside themselves, including God, then it is what in Church tradition was called cupidity, wrong loving, not at all an expression of right loving, or charity.

Though from the twelfth century well into the Renaissance love provided the dominant subject of narratives and lyrics, the literature should not be viewed as celebrating this passion or sentiment. Rather, love provided a focal point for examining human folly and self-destruction; and the lover who regarded his own good ahead of what his religion taught him to be the common good was to be laughed at for his folly rather than pitied for his frustration.

The "Ways of Love"   The following medieval English poems, in a modern version by Edmund Reiss, were found on the same page of a thirteenth-century manuscript. They illustrate well the interrelationship in medieval literature of the religious and the secular. Whatever the precise relationship between the two pieces—whether the first, urging love of God, provides a basis for understanding the earthly love of the second, or whether the complaint of earthly love is a parody of the overtly religious poem, simultaneously calling up ideal love and making clear the inadequacy of earthly passion—it is clear that the two together offer two sides of an issue, two perspectives that must be taken into account by the audience. Together, especially through their parallel language and verses, they create an ambiguous statement of love that demands solution or reconciliation.

The Way of Christ's Love

Little knows any man
The love by which he is bound,
Whose heart's blood for us ran
And who saved us with his wound.
His love for us has made us sound
And cast the devil to the ground.
  Ever and always, he has us in his thought;
  He will not lose what he so dearly bought.

He bought us with his holy blood,
What could he do more?
He is so meek and mild and good
That he never sinned therefore.
The sins we do we should rue sore,
And cry to Jesus, "Christ, thy ore!"
  Ever and always, etc.

He saw his father full of pain
At man's most grievous fall.
With sad heart he swore again
That we should pay for all.
His sweet son he did call
And prayed him die for us all.
  Ever and always, etc.

He brought us all out of death
And did a friend's good deed.
Sweet Jesus of Nazareth,
You give us heaven's meed.
Why do we not of him take heed?
His fresh wounds so grimly bleed.
  Ever and always, etc.

His deep wounds bleed so fast,
We ought to care for him.
Out of hell he has us cast
And brought us out of sin.
For love of us his cheeks grow thin
His heart's blood he gave for his kin.
  Ever and always, etc.

The Way of Woman's Love

Little knows any man
How secret love can be,
Until he desires a fair woman
Who has been loved previously.
The love of such does not last long;
She promises love but treats me with wrong.
  Ever and always sorrow weighs on me,
  I long for her whom I seldom see.

Today I would utter her name
If to say it I should dare.
She has by far the greatest fame
Of all those who are fair.
Unless she love me she will sin;
Woe is he who loves what he cannot win.
  Ever and always, etc.

Before her I fall on my knees
And cry, "Lady, thy grace!"
Lady, give my love some ease
And show me a fair face.
Unless you do, it will grieve me sore;
Love afflicts me so, I can live no more.
  Ever and always, etc.

Merry it is inside her tower
With knights and servants attending.
So it is in her bower
With mirth and pleasure unending.
Unless she love me, it will me rue;
Woe is he who loves a love untrue.
  Ever and always, etc.

Fairest creature of all such,
My good love, I salute you,
As many times and as much
As there are drops of dew,
Or stars in the sky, or grasses sweet and sour;
Whose love is untrue is seldom content an hour.
  Ever and always, etc.

The Troubadour Song One of the most stylized expressions of courtly love is found in the poetry and the music of the troubadours. The troubadours were poet-composers who worked and entertained in the region of southern France known as Provence, and they wrote in the regional dialect, Provençal, or *langue d'oc*. The themes of troubadour love poetry are nearly always the same: they concern a beautiful, idealized lady for whom the poet languishes with love but who does not return his love. Like the poets of ancient Greece and the modern folk singer, these artists entertained their (usually aristocratic) audience with solo voice, accompanied by a stringed instrument, the lute.

Perhaps the most famous troubadour was Bernart de Ventadorn, son of a mercenary soldier and a serving lady in the castle of the earl of Ventadorn. As an adult, he worked as a member of the court of Elinor of Aquitaine, so his presence was known in northern France as well. Bernart's travel surely contributed to the spread of the troubadour's art throughout France.

Although the poems of the troubadours concerned themselves with many subjects—morality, courtly love, politics—the preserved songs of Bernart seem to deal only with love. The stylized notions of chivalric love are matched by the stylized poetic and musical forms employed by the troubadours. Bernart's chanson, *Be m'an perdut*, has only three musical *phrases*—that is, only three very short melodic ideas—and the first two are identical. This construction results in an *AAB* musical form, a common secular music pattern known in the Middle Ages as *barform*. Notice in the music that the end of the third phrase is repeated and that these are the same notes as the endings of the first two phrases. All this repetition creates easily remembered tunes, and, after all, we are dealing with song that is somewhat analogous to today's popular music. If the tune is not catchy, it will fail in its function of light and pleasant entertainment music.

The poet uses the same approach and care with the poetic devices of rhyme and *meter* in his composition. These qualities disappear in the translation, but their presence in the original allows an easy match of words and music as well as creating an ingenious and clever "way with words."

> Be m'an perdut lai enves Ventadorn
>   Tuih mei amic, pois ma domna no m'ama;
> Et es be dreihz que jamais lai no torn,
>   C'ades estai vas me salvatj' e grama.

˘ ˜ / ˜ / ˜ / ˜ /
˘ / ˜ / ˜ / ˜ / ˜
˘ ˜ / ˜ / ˜ / ˜ /
˘ / ˜ / ˜ / ˜ / ˜

The syllables in each line are grouped by units of length (short–long, short–long . . .), and this is matched to the metrical style of the day, the *modal* rhythm of long–short groupings.

Like many popular songs and folk songs of today that tell a story, this piece has several verses sung to the same melody. Notice in the translation (by Carl Parrish) that the male singer, the troubadour, sings about a rather unapproachable lady and refers to familiar images (the regions of Ventadorn and Provence as well as the lord of Beaucaire) in addition to fanciful creations of his imagination.

BERNART DE VENTADORN

Be m'an perdut

I am indeed lost from the region of Ventadorn
To all my friends, for my lady loves me not;
With reason I turn not back again,
For she is bitter and ill-disposed toward me.
See why she turns a dark and angry countenance
    to me:
Because I take joy and pleasure in loving her!
Nor has she aught else with which to charge me.

So, like the fish who rushes to the lure
And suspects nothing until caught upon the hook,
Once I rushed to the overpowering love
And was not aware until I was in the flame
That burns hotter than ever furnace did.
And yet I cannot free my hands from it,
So greatly does my love hold and chain me.

I marvel not that love holds me fast,
For a more entrancing form, I believe, was never seen;
Beautiful and white she is, and fresh and smooth,
And wholly as I wish and desire her.
I can say no ill of her, for there is none in her;
Yet gladly would I say it if I knew any,
But I know none, and so forbear to speak it.

Ever shall I wish her honor and good,
And shall be her aid, her friend and servant,
And shall love her whether it please her or not,
For one cannot gainsay one's heart without
    destroying it.
I know no lady, whether she will or nor,
Whom I could not love if I wished.
They all can bring one to grief, though.

To others, then, I am in forfeit;
Whichever will can draw me to her
On condition that what honor and benefit
She thinks to do me will not be sold too dearly,
For the seeking is grievous if sought in vain.
From experience I speak, for I have suffered,
And beauty has betrayed me badly.

To Provence I send joy and greeting
And more of good than I could speak.
And it is a wonder that I do this;
For I send that which I have not;
I have no joy save what is brought me
By my beauteous vision, and Sire Enchantment, my
    confident,
And Sire Pleasure, the Lord of Beaucaire.

Tornada

My beauteous vision, God works such wonder
    through you
That no one seeing you would not be enraptured
Who knew what to tell you and what to do.

Obviously a song of this kind might use four verses or ten, depending on the patron's disposition, the poet's improvisational ability, and other circumstances of the moment; but whenever the last verse is sung, the musician uses a closing device, the *tornada*, a set of words sung to the music of the last phrase signaling the end by breaking the regular pattern.

The music (p. 204) is tuneful, easily sung, rhythmically simple, and generally memorable. It fits the conditions required for courtly entertainment, and the music exemplified in this song, *Be m'an perdut*, is typical of much of the art of the medieval courtly singers. The techniques of the troubadour, having originated in southern France, spread to many parts of Europe, and the musicians became known by different names—*trouvère* and *Minnesinger*. The origins of the troubadour song remain unknown, but this genre of extemporized vocal music surely had a history in Europe long before our earliest notated examples. By the time of Bernart, the courtly love song was a highly refined art, and it has had a deep and long-lasting influence on the secular songs of Europe and America. The music of *Be m'an perdut* is singable, easily playable on any instrument, and available on a professional recording.[1] With familiarity, it can be almost as enjoyable today as it was six hundred years ago.

The LAIS of Marie de France   While the musician-poets of southern France excelled in the short lyric, those of Brittany, in northern France, specialized in longer narrative songs called *lais*. These were probably composed orally, and none of them has survived, but a woman of exceptional education (for her time) and talent made the *lai* into a written literary form. Her name was Marie de France, and we know nothing more about her except that she wrote in French at the Norman court in England during the late twelfth century. She probably derived the plots of her twelve *lais* from those of the Breton singers. All were written in verse, and they represent different explorations of love and its effects on men and women. "Equitan," which appears below in a modern prose translation by Edmund Reiss, demonstrates especially vividly the destructiveness of illicit passion that was, as mentioned

---

[1] *A Treasury of Early Music*, Vol. 1 (Haydn Society Records HSE 7-9100), No. 6 [side 2, band 1].

BERNART DE VENTADORN

Be m'an perdut

earlier, a prime concern in this period. By being so concerned with pleasure, the king in this story is unable to rule justly. Not only does he seek to murder his loyal seneschal, or field marshal, he also ultimately brings about his own death as well as that of his lady.

The tale also shows a blend of the courtly and the ludicrous, especially at the end with the action centering on the bath. Here what had seemed noble and even beautiful is undercut so successfully that the deaths of the lovers do not result in our feeling any sense of tragedy. In fact, the fate of the two lovers may be seen as a *parody* of the conventional tragic ending of lovers who are ultimately ennobled by being joined together in death.

MARIE DE FRANCE

Equitan

Many noble lords have lived in Brittany. In times past, through their prowess, courtesy, and nobility they would compose lays of various adventures that they had heard so that these could be held in mind and not forgotten. They made one, which I have heard told and which should not be neglected, about Equitan, lord of Nantes, who was very courteous, just, and royal.

Equitan was held in great esteem and loved much in his country. He delighted in pleasure and love-making, which to him constituted chivalry. Those who love

without sense or measure place their lives at nought;
such is the rule of love that no one who feels passion
can maintain his reason.

Equitan had a seneschal, a good knight, worthy and
loyal, who administered all his land and ruled it justly,
for the king was concerned only with hunting, hawk-
ing, and love-making, and would not leave these pur-
suits except to wage war.

The seneschal had married a woman from whom
great evil came to the country. The lady was exception-
ally beautiful and of very good breeding. She had a fine
body and a lovely figure which Nature had taken pains
to fashion. Her eyes were clear and her face beautiful,
her mouth lovely, and her nose well shaped. There was
none her equal in the entire kingdom. The king often
heard her praised, and frequently he sent her his greetings as well as gifts. Even though he had never seen her,
he desired her and wished that he could speak with
her.

One day, to amuse himself, he secretly went hunting
in the country where the seneschal lived. At night,
when the king returned from his sport, he took his
lodging at the castle where the lady was. There he
could talk with her as much as he wished and reveal to
her his heart and his desire. He found her to be very
courteous and wise, beautiful of body and of face, well-
mannered and cheerful. Love had taken him into His
household. Love had shot an arrow at him, which
made a great wound where it lodged in his heart. Love
had no need for craft or subtlety. The king was so overcome by the lady that he became mournful and pen-
sive. Now when he needed most to understand, he
could not help himself. That night he neither slept nor
rested, but blamed and accused himself.

"Alas!" he said. "What destiny has brought me into
this country? Because of this lady whom I have seen I
have an ache in my heart and all my body is trembling.
I thought I would never fall in love, and if I love now I
shall do evil. This is the wife of my seneschal. I should
love and keep faith with him just as I wish him to do
with me. If through some mishap he should learn of
my passion, I know well that it would disturb him
greatly. Nevertheless, it would be worse for me if I
should go mad because of him. And it would be a
shame if such a beautiful lady was without a lover.
What would happen to her courtesy if she did not have
a lover? There is no man on earth who would not bene-

fit greatly from her love. Even if the seneschal should
hear about it, he should not be too heavy-hearted. He
should not have all of that treasure for himself alone;
indeed, I wish to share it with him."

When he had said these things, the king sighed, then
tossed and turned, and thought more. Finally he said,
"Why am I so upset and so afraid? I still do not know,
and have not tried to learn, whether she will have me
for her lover. I will soon find out, and if she feels what I
feel, I will be rid of this sorrow. God, it is so long until
daylight! I still cannot sleep, and it has been so long
since I went to bed last night."

The king stayed awake until dawn, which he
awaited with great discomfort. He went out as though
he planned to hunt, but soon he returned, saying that
he felt ill. He went to his room and went to bed. The
seneschal was concerned about him; he did not know
what the sickness was that was causing the king to
tremble so. But his wife was the real cause of it. The
seneschal had her go talk with the king in order to
amuse and comfort him. The king opened his heart to
her and let her know that he was dying because of her.
She could either bring him comfort or give him death.

"Sir," the lady replied, "I must have some time to
think. This is the first time I have been in this position.
You are a king of great nobility. I am not so rich that
you should approach me with love. If you do take your
desire, I know truly that it will lead to nothing. You
will soon leave me, and I will be ruined. If it should be
that I love you and grant your request, love would not
be equally divided between the two of us, for you are a
powerful king, and my husband is one of your vassals.
You would think to have mastery in this love, and love
is not worthy if it is not among equals. A poor man
who is honest, if he has sense and worth, is better than
a prince or king who is not honest; the poor man will
also have greater joy in love. She who loves above her
station will be insecure in every way. The rich man believes that nothing can take away from him the love
that he has acquired through his position."

Equitan replied, "Lady, please! Say no more to me!
These words are not refined or courteous but are rather
the business dealings of a merchant, who for gain or
property devotes his efforts to an unworthy cause.
There is no lady on earth, if she is wise, courteous, and
generous of heart, provided she set a high value on her
love and not be fickle, who, if she had nothing more

than a rich prince of a castle under her mantel, would not suffer for him and love him loyally and well. Those who are fickle in love and who turn to deceit are in turn scorned and deceived. We have seen several of these false lovers; it is no wonder that they lose what they have earned through their efforts. My dear lady, I surrender myself to you. Do not take me as your king, but as your servant and your friend. I swear to you that I will do your pleasure. Do not cause me to die for you. You will be the lady and I the servant, you the proud lord and I the suppliant."

The king spoke to her so long and begged mercy so much that he finally assured him of her love and gave up her body to him. With their rings they pledged themselves to each other and swore their loyalty to each other. They desired each other greatly and loved each other fervently. Through their passion they died and came to their end.

For a long time their love affair lasted, for it was not known by anyone. At the time of their meetings— when they would speak together—the king told his people that he was to be bled privately. The doors of his chamber were closed, and you could not have found a man so daring as to enter unless summoned by the king. The seneschal held the court to hear the various pleas and petitions.

The king loved the lady for a long time and desired no other woman. He did not wish to marry anyone; indeed he did not wish to hear the subject spoken of. The people disliked this greatly, so much so that the wife of the seneschal often heard about it. It weighed on her heavily, and she feared losing the king. When she was able to speak with him—at a time when she should have been happy kissing, hugging, embracing, and playing with him—she wept sorely and expressed great sadness. The king asked what was wrong.

The lady answered, "Sir, I weep for our love which for me has turned to great sorrow. You will take a wife, the daughter of a king, and so you will leave me. I have heard it said often, and I know it well. And alas, what will become of me? Because of you I will die, for I know no other comfort."

The king said to her with great love, "Fair friend, do not be afraid. Indeed, I will not take a wife or leave you for another. Know this truly and believe it. If your husband were dead, I would make you my wife and queen. I swear, for no other will I leave you."

The lady thanked him and said he had made her very happy. And since he had assured her that he would not leave her for another, she would bring about the death of her husband right away. It would be easy to accomplish if the king would help her. He answered that he would do so. In fact there was nothing he would not do for her if it lay in his power, no matter whether it were wise or foolish.

"Sir," she said, "if it please you, come to hunt in the forest in the country where I live. Stay at the castle of my lord; there you will be bled and, three days later, bathed. My husband will be bled and also bathed along with you. Be sure to command him, without fail, to accompany you. And I will have the baths heated and the two tubs brought. His bath will be so boiling hot that no man on earth could sit in it without being scalded and killed. As soon as he is dead, call your men and his, and show them how he died suddenly in his bath."

The king agreed that he would do her will in everything.

Not three months passed before the king went hunting in the country. He had himself bled, on account of his illness. Along with him went his seneschal. On the third day the king said that he wished to bathe; the seneschal wished likewise.

"Bathe with me," said the king.

The seneschal said, "Gladly."

The lady had the baths heated and the two tubs brought and placed by each bed as planned. She had the boiling water poured in the seneschal's tub. That gentleman had arisen and gone out for his ease. The lady came to speak to the king who sat her down beside him. They lay on the bed of the seneschal and amused themselves playing with each other. They played together by the tub of scalding water which was in front of them. They had posted a servant girl to guard the door. The seneschal returned shortly and found his way blocked. He became so angry that he flung it open and discovered the king and his wife lying on the bed embracing each other. The king saw the seneschal as soon as he came in, and to cover up his villainy, he jumped into the tub with his feet together. There he was scalded and died. All his evil came back on them, and the seneschal remained safe and well. He had seen what happened to the king and immediately seized his wife and pushed her head first into the same bath. There both died, the king first and the lady after him.

Whoever wishes to understand the meaning of this can discover a lesson here. Those who pursue evil toward another will find all this evil returned on them. This happened as I have told you. The Bretons made a lay of it, about Equitan, how he and the lady whom he loved so much came to their end.

QUESTIONS

1. What feelings, as a reader, do you have toward the two lovers? Is the author's portrayal of them ambivalent in any way?

2. Do you find any contradiction between the story and the moral?

3. What elements of comedy or parody do you see in this story, and what do you think medieval people would have seen?

4. Could you write a modern version of this tale? How do you think the portrayal of love here might have influenced our ideas of love?

5. How did our term *romance* derive from such stories?

6. What meanings are attached to terms like *refined* and *courteous*, and what have these values to do with the idea of courtly love?

Courtly Love in a Bawdy Version: Chaucer's "Miller's Tale"

The love of noble knights for noble ladies was not the only aspect of passion that interested medieval people. As we have indicated above, they were well aware of the comic aspects of romantic entanglements. Sex, as we saw with *Lysistrata*, has universal potential for comedy. Geoffrey Chaucer, writing in England at the end of the Middle Ages, was interested in a wide range of people and topics, among them the comedy of sex.

It has been said that if we possessed nothing of medieval literature other than Chaucer's narrative poem *The Canterbury Tales* (1390–1400), we would still have represented all the major types of medieval narrative. Representing three days of tale telling by pilgrims on their way to Canterbury Cathedral, *The Canterbury Tales* develop by presenting apparent truths that are then undercut to seem not entirely valid. Chaucer's method enables him both to give *mirthe* and to provide

doctryne or instruction. By insisting that his audience be aware of the complexities and ramifications of actions, especially those having moral significance, he forces them to participate in the creation of meaning and to look beyond the surface appearance of things.

Each of the tales is told by a different pilgrim, reflecting its narrator's personality in its tone and content. Our selection is a prose version, rendered into modern English by Edmund Reiss, of the tale told by the miller. Although the Miller's Tale might seem to be on the surface a bawdy tale, Chaucer has used this unlikely vehicle to undercut the noble appearance of courtly love, as brought out in "The Knight's Tale," which immediately precedes it. The situation of the piece is one typically ripe for sexual hanky-panky, with the old husband, John, married to the young woman, Alison. But even though John is jealous and worried about being cuckolded, he is apparently oblivious of their lodger, the young cleric Nicholas. In a sense John's unconcern is understandable, for clerics were supposed to be contemplatives, loving God and the Virgin, and being beyond the concerns of the flesh. But when Nicholas casts his eyes heavenward, it is only to deceive. Instead of using things of this world as means of getting to eternal verities, Nicholas ironically reverses the process, using the other world as a means of obtaining his love in this world. The incongruous blend of contemplative and worldly may be seen when Nicholas embraces Alison and at the same time speaks to her as a subservient courtly lover and also when he uses a fictitious vision of the Second Deluge to effect his deception of the old husband. Although Noah's Flood was a traditional symbol of cleansing and purification, it is here ironically used as a vehicle for lechery. But John, the old husband, is so foolish that he cannot be pitied, for he does not even know God's covenant with man after the original Deluge that He would never again flood the earth.

The illicit love of Nicholas and Alison is not only contrasted with the inadequate but licit marriage, it is also the basis for the love expressed by Absolon, another cleric. When Absolon sings outside the bedroom window urging Alison to love, he employs language clearly recognizable from the Song of Songs. Chaucer's point is far from burlesquing this mystical love; rather, by including it in an obviously inappropriate situation, he calls up the ideal love lacking in the bawdy sexuality at hand and makes the amorous passion of Absolon seem as inadequate as Absolon himself is ridiculous. It is at least as inappropriate for him to refer to Alison in terms of the imagery of mystical love as it is for Nicholas at the beginning of the tale to ask her for the "mercy" traditionally associated with prayers to the Virgin.

GEOFFREY CHAUCER

The Miller's Tale
(Modern English version by Edmund Reiss)

Once upon a time there dwelled at Oxford a rich churl who took in lodgers, and who was a carpenter by trade. With him there lived a poor scholar who had studied the arts but whose fancy had been turned completely to astrology. He knew the procedures for answering questions at different times about whether there should be drought or rain and about what should happen to men in various instances; I cannot list them all.

This clerk was called gentle Nicholas. He knew about secret love and pleasure, and in these matters he was sly and cunning, though he looked as meek as a maiden. He had a chamber in that house where he lived alone. His room was neatly decorated with sweet herbs, and he himself was as sweet as licorice root or ginger. His various books of astrology, great and small, were laid out along with his astrolabe and his calculating stones, on shelves above his bed. His cupboard was covered with a coarse red cloth, and on top lay a merry harp on which he made such sweet melody at night that all the chamber rang. He sang *The Angel to the Virgin* and afterwards *The King's Note*; his merry throat was often blessed. And thus this sweet clerk spent his time living on his income and the money given him by friends.

This carpenter had recently taken a wife, only eighteen years of age, whom he loved more than his life. He was jealous and kept her closely confined, because since she was young and he was old, he judged himself likely to be a cuckold. He was uneducated and did not even know Cato, who wrote that men should wed their counterparts. Men should wed in accord with their situations, because youth and age are often in conflict. But since he had fallen in the snare of love, he had to endure his misfortune just like other people.

This young wife was pretty, with a body as graceful and small as a weasel's. She wore a belt of striped silk, and also a full apron, white as morning milk, upon her loins. Her smock was white and embroidered in front and back, inside and out, as well as on the collar with coal-black silk. The ribbons of her white cap were of the same material as her collar; her hair band of silk was set high on her head; and indeed she had a lecherous eye: her two brows were plucked thin and bent and were black as a sloe berry. She was more pleasant to look on than is the blossoming pear tree and softer than the wool of a lamb. And by her belt hung a purse of leather decorated with silk tassels and brass beads. In all this world if you searched far and wide, you could not find anyone so ingenious as to imagine so pretty a doll or such a wench. Her complexion was brighter than the newly minted coin in the Tower, and her singing was as loud and lively as that of a swallow sitting on a barn. She could skip and play like a kid or calf following after his mother, and her mouth was as sweet as honeyed ale or mead or as a pile of apples laid in hay or heather. She was as frisky as a young colt, tall as a mast, and straight as a bolt. Low on her collar she wore a brooch as broad as the center boss of a shield. Her shoes were laced high up her legs. She was a primrose, a pig's eye, for any lord to lay in his bed or for any good yeoman to wed.

Now, sirs, it so happened that one day this gentle Nicholas began to behave wantonly with this young wife while her husband was away at Oseney, for clerks are very clever and crafty. And he slyly caught her by the crotch and said, "Unless I have my will, through my secret longing for you, love, I'll die!" And he held her hard by the buttocks, and said, "Sweetheart, make love to me right now, or, by God, I'll die!"

She sprang away as a colt does at the smithy and twisted her head aside, saying, "I will not kiss you, by my faith! Let go, I said! Let go, Nicholas, or I'll cry for help! Take away your hands for the sake of courtesy!"

Nicholas begged for mercy and spoke so well and stated his case so vigorously that at last she granted him her love and swore an oath by St. Thomas of Kent that she would be at his disposal whenever she found the chance. "My husband is so full of jealousy that unless you watch out and be secret, I know well that I'm as good as dead," she said. "You must be careful in this matter."

"Nay! Don't worry about that," answered Nicholas. "A clerk would have used his time poorly if he couldn't deceive a carpenter."

And so they were agreed and swore to watch for their chance, as I said. When Nicholas had finished talking and had stroked her well about the loins, he kissed her sweetly and took his harp and vigorously made melody.

Later it happened on one holy day that this good wife went to the parish church to perform Christ's own work. Here forehead shone as brightly as the sun, for she had washed it well after her work. In that church there was a parish clerk named Absolon. His hair was curly and shone like gold; it spread out like a broad fan from a straight part down the middle. His complexion was ruddy, and his eyes gray as a goose. His shoes were cut with open-work designs like those in the windows at St. Paul's, and his red stockings showed elegantly. He was dressed neatly and properly in a coat of light blue, decorated with many laces, and over this he wore a handsome surplice as white as a blossom on a sprig. He was a merry fellow, by God! He knew well how to let blood, cut hair, and shave, and also to draw up a charter or a quit-claim deed. He knew how to dance in twenty styles, after the school of Oxford though, and with his legs to leap to and fro. He could play songs on a small fiddle and sometimes accompanied himself in a loud falsetto; and he could play as well on a guitar. In all the town there was not an ale house with a pretty barmaid that he failed to visit for his amusement. But to tell the truth, he was a bit squeamish about farting and was fastidious in his speech.

This Absolon, who was so jolly and merry, would go on holy days with a censer and diligently cense the parish women. He cast many loving looks on them, especially on the carpenter's wife. It seemed to him a merry life just to gaze on her, for she was so good-looking, and sweet, and appetizing. I dare say that if she had been a mouse and he a cat, he would have pounced on her right away. This parish clerk, this jolly Absolon, had in his heart such love-longing that he would not take any offering from any other women. Because of courtesy, he said, he would have none.

That night when the moon shone brightly, Absolon took his guitar and went looking for adventures in town. Forth he went, jolly and amorous, till he came to the carpenter's house, a little after the cock had crowed, and took his stand by a casement window that was in the bedroom wall.

He sang with a gentle soft voice, "Now, dear lady, if it be your will, I pray you to have pity on me," and harmonized well with his guitar.

The carpenter awoke and, hearing him sing, said to his wife, "What's this, Alison? Don't you hear Absolon singing outside our bedroom window?"

And she answered her husband, "Yes, by God, John. I hear it all."

And so it went on; what more could you expect? Day after day jolly Absolon wooed her so much that he was woebegone. He stayed awake all night and all day, combing his hair elaborately and dressing himself elegantly. He wooed her through go-betweens and stand-ins, and swore to be her own servant. He sang, quavering like a nightingale. He sent her sweet wine, mead, and spiced ale, and wafers piping hot from the oven. And because she was from town, he offered her money, for some people are won by riches, some by blows, and some by courtesy. Sometimes to show his versatility and skill he played Herod on the stage. But what was the use of it all? She loved gentle Nicholas so much that Absolon might just as well go blow a horn. He got nothing but scorn for his labors. Thus she made a fool out of Absolon and turned all his seriousness into a joke. The proverb that men say is true: "The nearby sly one will cause the distant dear one to be hated." No matter how insane or angry Absolon became, he was still far from her sight, and nearby Nicholas cast his shadow on him. Now bear yourself well, gentle Nicholas, for Absolon must wail and sing "Alas."

And so it happened one Saturday that the carpenter went to Oseney. Gentle Nicholas and Alison were in agreement that Nicholas should contrive a plan to deceive the foolish jealous husband. If the game went as planned, she would sleep in his arms all night, for such was his desire and hers also. And without more words or further ado Nicholas secretly took food and drink for a day or two to his room and told her to tell her husband, if he asked for Nicholas, that she did not know where he was and that she had not seen him all day long, but she thought he must be sick since he did not answer any of her maid's calls.

All that Saturday Nicholas stayed quietly in his chamber, eating and sleeping and doing whatever he pleased until Sunday evening. The foolish carpenter was greatly concerned about Nicholas and wondered what could be wrong with him.

He said, "I'm afraid, by St. Thomas, that things aren't going right with Nicholas. God forbid that he all of a sudden died! this world is so uncertain. Just today I saw a corpse carried to church that only last Monday I saw at work. Go up," he said to his servant. "Call at his door, or knock on it with a stone. See how things are and tell me right away."

The servant went up resolutely and, standing at the chamber door, he cried out and knocked as though he were mad: "What's up? Ho! What's going on, Master Nicholas? How can you sleep all day long?"

But all was for nothing; he heard not a word. He found a hole, low on a broken board, where the cat crept in. And through this hole he peered in and at last caught sight of Nicholas. He sat gazing upward as though he had looked on the new moon. Down the servant went and at once told his master what state Nicholas was in.

The carpenter crossed himself and said, "Help us, St. Frideswide! A man little knows what may happen to him! Through his astronomy this man has fallen into some madness or some fit. I always thought this would happen! Men should not pry into God's secrets. Blessed be the uneducated man who knows nothing but his Creed! So fared another clerk with his astronomy. He walked in the fields peering at the stars to find out what was going to take place and fell into a dung pit. He couldn't even see that! But yet, by St. Thomas, I feel sorry for gentle Nicholas. If I can, by Jesus, king of heaven, I'm going to scold him for all this studying! Get me a staff, so that I can pry under the door, while you, Robin, lift it up. He'll come out of his trance, I guess!"

And he went immediately to the chamber door. His servant was a strong churl and by the hasp he heaved it up at one try. The door fell onto the floor, but throughout all this Nicholas sat as still as a stone and continually gaped upward into the air.

The carpenter thought he must be in a trance and seized him by the shoulders, shaking him mightily and crying out loudly, "Hey, Nicholas! Hey! Look down! Awake and think on Christ's passion! I'll protect you from elves and evil spirits!"

And he recited the night spell at all four corners of the house and at the threshold of the outside door:

"Jesus Christ and St. Benedict, Bless this house from every wicked creature. Against the spirits of the night, the White Pater Noster. And where have you gone, St. Peter's sister?"

At last gentle Nicholas began to sigh deeply and said, "Alas, shall all the world now be lost again?"

The carpenter answered, "What are you saying? What? Think on God as we men who work do!"

Nicholas answered, "Fetch me drink and afterwards I will speak in private of certain things that touch you and me. I will tell it to no other person."

The carpenter went downstairs and returned with a large quart of strong ale. And when each of them had drunk his share, Nicholas shut the door and sat down by the carpenter.

He said, "John, my landlord, beloved and dear to me. You must swear to me here upon your honor that you will not reveal this secret to anyone. It's Christ's own secret that I'm going to tell you, and if you reveal it to anyone you will be utterly lost; such vengence will fall on you if you betray me that you will go mad."

"Nay, God forbid! By his holy blood!" said this foolish man. "I'm no blabber. Though I say so myself, I don't hold with gossip. Say what you will; I will never tell it to man, woman, or child, by Him who harrowed hell!"

"Now, John," said Nicholas, "I will not lie. I have discovered through my astrology, as I looked at the bright moon, that next Monday, a quarter way through the night, the rain will fall so wildly and furiously that it will be twice as bad as Noah's flood. In less than an hour," he said, "this world will be drowned, so terrible will the rain be. Through it all mankind will drown and lose their lives."

The carpenter answered, "Alas, my wife! Is she to drown? Alas, my Alison!" In his sorrow he almost fell down and said, "Is there no remedy for this?"

"Why, yes, thank God!" said gentle Nicholas, "if you will follow my instructions and counsel, and not your own inclinations. For so says Solomon, who was so wise, 'Follow advice and you will never be sorry.' And if you will follow my good advice, I promise you that even without mast or sail I'll save Alison, you, and myself. Haven't you heard how Noah was saved when our Lord warned him beforehand that all the world would be destroyed by water?"

"Yes, indeed," said the carpenter, "a long time ago."

"Haven't you also heard" said Nicholas, "the trouble Noah and his companions had getting his wife on board the ark? I'll wager he would have given all his black rams if she could have had a ship to herself. So you know what is best to do. This requires haste, and in matters of haste there is no time for preaching or making delays.

"Go right away and bring to this house a kneading trough or else a shallow tub for each of us. But be sure that these are large enough so that we can float in them as in a boat and have enough provisions for a day— don't worry about the rest. The water will recede and go away about nine o'clock the next morning. But Robin, your servant, must not know anything about this and I can't save your maid, Jill. Don't ask me why, for even if you should, I wouldn't tell you God's secrets. You should be satisfied, unless your wits are addled, to have as much grace as Noah had. I'll save your wife, without a doubt. Get going now and be quick about it.

"But when you've gotten the three kneading tubs for the three of us, then you must hang them high up under the roof, so that no one may discover our plans. And when you have done what I've said and have put our provisions in them, and also an ax to cut the ropes in two when the water comes so that we can start, and when you have broken a hole high in the gable over the stable, toward the garden, so that we can pass forth on our way without hindrance, when the great rain is ended, then you will float as merrily, I expect, as the white duck does after the drake. Then I shall call out, 'Ho, Alison! Ho, John! Be merry, for the flood will soon pass away.' And you will say, 'Hail master Nicholas! Good morning, I see you clearly for it is day.' And then we shall be lords of the world all our life, just like Noah and his wife.

"But I must warn you of one thing. We must be careful on the night when we board our ships that we don't speak a word, or call, or cry out, except in prayer, for this is God's special command.

"Your wife and you must hang far apart so that there will be no sin between you, not in look or in deed. This order is clear. God speed you. Tomorrow night when everyone else is asleep, we will creep into our kneading tubs and sit awaiting God's grace. Get going now. I don't have time to talk more about this. Men say, 'Act wisely and say nothing.' You are so wise it's not neces-

sary to instruct you further. Go, save our lives, I beseech you!"

This foolish carpenter went his way. Often he said, "Alas" and "Woe is me!" He told his secret to his wife, though she was fully aware and knew better than he what all this curious business was about. But nevertheless, she acted as though she was going to die and said, "Alas! Hurry! Help us escape or we will both be dead. I am your true, sweet, wedded wife. Go, dear husband, and help save our lives!"

Oh, what a great thing emotion is! Men can die from mere imagination, so deeply their fancies can affect them. This foolish carpenter began to shake. It seemed to him that he could see Noah's flood come surging upon him like the sea to drown Alison, his honey dear. He wept, wailed, looked grief-stricken, sighed many a sorrowful sigh, and went and got a kneading trough, a vat, and a tub, which he secretly sent to his house and hung from the roof. With his own hand he made three ladders, complete with rungs and uprights, to climb on to the tubs hanging in the beams. In all of them he put provisions—bread, cheese and good ale in a jug—sufficient for a day. But before he made all these arrangements, he sent his servant and also his maid to London on business. And on Monday, when it grew dark, he shut his door and, without any light, prepared everything as it should be. And soon all three of them climbed up and sat quietly in the tubs. "Now, an Our Father, and then mum," said Nicholas. And "Mum" said John, and "Mum" said Alison.

The carpenter said his prayers, then sat silently, then said more prayers, waiting to hear the rain. Because he was weary from his work a deep sleep fell on him near curfew time, I guess. Because of his troubled spirit, he groaned sorrowfully and soon began to snore for his head was turned awry. Down the ladder crept Nicholas, and Alison softly followed. Without further words they went to bed where the carpenter usually slept. There they made revel and melody! And there lay Alison and Nicholas busy with mirth and pleasure until the early morning when the bell of lauds rang and the friars went to sing in their church.

The parish clerk, amorous Absolon, who was so woebegone for love, was at Oseney that Monday with friends, making sport and playing, and by chance he asked a cloisterer about John the carpenter.

He drew him aside out of the church and said, "I

don't know. I haven't seen him at work since Saturday. I expect he went to get some timber for our abbot; and when he goes for timber, he usually stays at the farm for a day or two. Or else he is at home. But I really can't say where he is."

Absolon was jolly and light-hearted, and thought, "Now it's time to stay up all night, for I'm sure I didn't see him stirring about his door since dawn. As I hope to prosper, at cock's crow I'll knock secretly at the casement window that stands low on his bedroom wall. Now I'll make known all my love-longing to Alison. I'm sure I won't miss getting some comfort from her, at least a kiss. My mouth has itched all day long, and that's a sign of kissing at least. Also all night I dreamed I was at a feast. Therefore, I'll go to sleep for an hour or two and then stay awake and play all night long."

When the first cock crowed, up rose this jolly lover Absolon and carefully put on all his finery. But first, before he combed his hair, he chewed cardamon and licorice to make his breath sweet, and under his tongue he placed a clover, which he hoped would make him lucky. He strolled to the carpenter's house and quietly stood in front of the casement window, which was so low that it reached to his chest.

Softly he coughed under his breath: "Where are you, honey comb, sweet Alison, my fair bird, my sweet cinnamon? Awake, my love, and speak to me! You think too little on my woe, and because of love for you I sweat when I walk. It's no wonder that I swelter and sweat. I pine as much as a lamb does for the teat. Truly, love, I feel such love-longing that my lament is like a turtledove's. I cannot eat more than a little girl."

"Get away from the window, you fool!" she said. "So help me, God, you're not going to kiss me. I love another better than you, and why shouldn't I, by Jesus, Absolon! Get out of here, or I'll throw a stone at you. I want to sleep and you can go to the devil!"

"Alas," said Absolon, "and woe is me! It's a shame that true love should be treated so badly. At least kiss me since it cannot be otherwise, for love of Jesus and for love of me."

"Will you get out of here then?" she said.

"Yes, indeed, love," replied Absolon.

"Then get ready," she said. "Here I come." And she added softly to Nicholas, "Now be quiet and you will laugh your fill."

Absolon got down on his knees and said, "I am a master at all the steps of love, and after this I hope to have more. Love, give me grace, and, sweet bird, your mercy!"

She undid the window quickly. "Come on!" she said. "Let's go! Hurry up before the neighbors see you."

Absolon wiped his mouth dry. The night was dark as pitch, black as coal; and out the window she thrust her hole. And Absolon, as Fortune had in store for him, with his mouth kissed her naked ass with relish before he knew what was happening. He started back and thought something was wrong, for he knew well that women do not have beards and he had felt something rough and long-haired.

He said, "Fy! Alas! What have I done?"

"Teehee!" said she, and slammed the window shut. And Absolon went forth in sorrow.

"A beard! A beard!" cried gentle Nicholas. "By God's body, this went well."

Foolish Absolon heard everything and bit his lip in anger. He said to himself, "I'll pay you back!"

Who now scrubbed his lips with dust, sand, straw, cloth, and chips? Who but Absolon who often cried, "Alas! I'll sell my soul to Satan. I had rather be avenged for this insult," said he, "than own all this town. Alas!" he said, "Alas I did not turn aside!"

His hot love was now cooled and quenched. From the time he had kissed her ass he did not care a bit about making love. He was healed of his malady and cursed lovers often, and wept as a child who has been beaten. He went quietly through the streets to a blacksmith named Gervase, who worked on plow fittings at his forge and busily sharpened plowshares and cultours.

Absolon knocked softly and said, "Open up quickly, Gervase."

"What! Who is it?"

"It's me, Absolon."

"What, Absolon? What's going on? By Christ's sweet tree, why are you up so early? Eh? Bless me, what ails you? Some gay girl, God knows, must have brought you out on the prowl. By St. Neot, you know what I mean!"

Absolon did not care a bean about all his playing and did not even bother to banter with him. He had more on his mind than Gervase knew, and said, "Dear friend, lend me that hot coulter in the forge here. I have some use for it, and I'll bring it back to you right away."

Gervase answered, "Why, if it were gold or a bag of money it would be yours, as I'm an honest smith. But, by Christ's foe, what do you want it for?"

"Let that be as it may," answered Absolon. "I'll tell you all about it tomorrow." And he took the coulter by the cool handle and quickly went out the door and to the wall of the carpenter's house. He coughed first and then knocked on the window, just as he had done before.

Alison answered, "Who's that knocking? I bet it's a thief."

"Why, no," he said. "God knows, my sweet beloved, it's your Absolon, my darling. I've brought you a ring of gold," he said. "My mother gave it to me, so help me God. It's very fine and nicely engraved. I'll give it to you if you give me a kiss."

Nicholas had gotten up to piss and thought he could improve on the joke. He would have Absolon kiss his ass before he left. He quickly raised the window up and slyly thrust his ass far out, buttocks and all, even to the haunches.

Then Absolon said, "Speak, sweet bird. I don't know where you are."

Nicholas at once let fly a fart as great as a thunder clap, that almost blinded Absolon. But he was ready with his hot iron and smote Nicholas in the middle of his ass.

Off went the skin a hand's breadth around. The hot coulter had so burnt his rump that he thought he would die of the pain. Like a madman he cried, "Help, water! Water, help! For God's sake!"

The carpenter started out of his sleep and heard someone cry "Water!" as though he were mad. He thought, "Alas! Now Noel's Flood is coming!" He sat up without more ado and with his ax cut the rope in two. Down went everything, without a stop, until it landed on the floor. And there he lay unconscious.

Up started Alison and Nicholas, and cried "Look out!" and "Help!" in the street. All the neighbors, rich and poor, ran in to stare at the carpenter who lay in a swoon, pale and wan, for in the fall he had broken his arm. But he must accept responsibility for his misfortune. When he tried to explain, he was shouted down by gentle Nicholas and Alison. They told everyone that he was crazy, that in his fantasy he feared "Noel's Flood," and that he had bought three tubs which he hung from the roof and had begged them for the love of God to sit up under the roof with him.

The folks laughed at this fantasy. Up at the roof they gawked and gaped, and turned all his misfortune into a joke. For no matter what the carpenter answered, it was no use. No one would listen to him. He was sworn at with great oaths and considered mad by all the town, for one clerk will naturally stand with another. They said, "The man is crazy, my dear brother," and everyone laughed at the commotion.

Thus was the carpenter's wife screwed in spite of all his care and jealousy; and Absolon kissed her lower eye; and Nicholas was burned in the rump. This tale is done and may God bless everyone!

QUESTIONS

1. How do you react to "The Miller's Tale"? Does it have appeal for modern readers?
2. How deeply do you become involved with each of the characters? Is it necessary to remain detached from them? Why or why not?
3. Are these characters more or less realistic than those in earlier medieval literature, such as *The Play of Daniel?*
4. Compare the comedy of sex in this tale with that in *Lysistrata.* What differences are attributable to the differences in culture?
5. What impact does Chaucer's Christianity have on his comedy?
6. Compare the expressions of love in this tale with those in "Equitan." What justification can you find for the interpretation that this tale represents a parody of "courtly" love?

THE JUDEO-CHRISTIAN ROOT: CONTINUITIES

Judeo-Christian and Greco-Roman In some ways it does not make sense to speak of "Judeo-Christian" as a continuum, or as a cultural root in opposition to the Greco-Roman one. If the Hellenic/Hebraic distinction is fairly clear, one must remember that Christianity (and, for that matter, Judaism from the second century B.C.) was strongly influenced by Greek ways of thinking. The New Testament is itself a document of Greek literature, containing Greek philosophical terms; and the influence of Plato and Aristotle on the development of Catholic theology was enormous. Nor can one neglect the Roman contribution to Christian culture. Without the political, economic, and legal structures provided by the Roman empire, Christianity might well have remained a small Middle Eastern sect instead of the dominant cultural influence in Europe. We have seen how the Christian church, God's house on earth, grew out of the Roman basilica.

Once this is said, however, it is nonetheless evident that certain aspects of Christianity, deriving from Judaism, differentiate it profoundly from the classical values of Greece and Rome. Foremost of these is the Hebraic concept of Jahweh, the one, supreme God who takes a personal interest in His chosen people, Israel: "Thou shalt have no other gods before me." The God of the Jews and the Christians is a creator who made the world as we know it from nothing and a law-giver who dictates to His creation, man, the fundamental principles of morality. Socrates determined what is right and good according to the dictates of reason; the Jew or Christian accepts the Ten Commandments or the Sermon on the Mount as moral law because it is the word of God. The contrast between Protagoras' dictum "Man is the measure of all things" and the words of the psalmist, "What is man, that Thou art mindful of him?" is indicative: one culture is man-centered, the other God-centered.

Opposing itself to the values of the Greco-Roman world as a small, radical group, Christianity demanded allegiance to Christ before allegiance to the Roman emperor and the gods of the state; yet, once Emperor Con-stantine converted, it was able to use the empire to its advantage. The Middle Ages witnessed the growth of two spheres of allegiance for every European, the spiritual and the temporal.

Culture and the Church In the twelfth and thirteenth centuries, our focus of attention here, the Church claimed the right to act as the conscience of Christian rulers and their subjects, to determine proper Christian belief, and to judge offenses against the faith. While allowing discussion within broad limits, the Church permitted no questioning of basic doctrines. As it was, few had any desire to do so. Temporal rulers were advised not to interfere in matters of belief and morals and to support the judgment of the spiritual in such cases. Recognition of this area as off-limits to temporal powers continued in later centuries, even after the Reformation when religious authorities were no longer able to exercise close control over it. In the eighteenth and nineteenth centuries, thinkers came to define this spiritual sphere as within the province of the individual conscience and independent of the constraints of government action. While the Reformation itself had, as we will see, a good deal to do with this evolution, the origins of this demand for freedom of individual conscience began with the Church's demarcation of its sphere of authority.

Monarchy and the Modern State By the twelfth and thirteenth centuries a new form of temporal power, the medieval monarchy, had developed; it was to serve as the basis for our modern state. There were essentially two kinds of states in the ancient period, the small, tightly knit city-state and the sprawling empire that controlled a variety of separate peoples by means of a relatively small elite. To expand as the city-states Athens and Rome did was to become an empire, because the city-state had no means of integrating the new populations into its intensive political life. Thus, it had to govern subject peoples with a corps of officials sent out from the mother city.

The medieval monarchy, on the other hand, was both larger than the city-state and more cohesive than the empire. Closely tied to the rise of the monarch's power was the development of representative institutions both at the local level and at the center, ultimately making subjects feel part of a greater whole. When a new area was incorporated into the country, *its* population, too, became involved in the political processes and a sense of common identity arose. Utilizing this sense of identity, the monarch could mobilize a far greater population than could the rulers of the city-state; he could demand a greater degree of loyalty from them than could the emperor. While in the centuries since the Middle Ages the supreme executive has become at least nominally an elected official, the European medieval monarchy with its representative element has served as the ancestor for the modern state adopted throughout the world.

Germanic Contributions   We have not emphasized the Germanic or "barbarian" contributions to our cultural roots, but we have at least mentioned their importance in the formation of medieval civilization. The personal sense of loyalty to the lord and the lord's responsibility to his men were essential ingredients in the rise of the medieval monarchy. The ruler could expect obedience, but the follower would normally be consulted in the decision process. Together with principles of Roman law, Germanic custom limited the ruler's freedom of action and encouraged him to act in cooperation with larger and larger groups of his subjects in extending the operations of the state.

The Cathedral as Center   We have centered our study of medieval culture on the cathedral because it was such an important part of medieval life. We have looked at four cultural forms connected with the cathedral: the schools and the philosophy taught there; the Gothic architecture, sculpture, stained-glass painting, and theory behind them; the music and drama performed at worship services; and the cult of the Virgin Mary, to whom the cathedrals were dedicated.

The art and thought in and around the cathedral show an extraordinary diversity and creativity and a love of elaboration quite different from the simplicity and restraint of classical art and thought. Three of the great systems of the Middle Ages—the philosophy of Thomas Aquinas, Chartres Cathedral, and Dante Alighieri's *Divine Comedy*—seem to encompass everything in this world and the next in their province, while organizing their edifice so that the whole is directed toward God. The belief that the sensual and intellectual realms of being can serve as steps into the spiritual realm is at the heart of all three of these systems. This belief also explains the medieval love of *symbolism, allegory,* and suggestion. Modern art forms owe much to their medieval predecessors, both in their use of symbols (that is, the suggestion of "another world" through physical reality) and in their use of form to express feeling. The neoclassicists of the eighteenth century thought the distorted sculptures on medieval cathedrals much inferior to the naturalistic, proportioned Greek and Roman ones. In the twentieth century we are well aware that apparent distortion is one means for expression.

"Gothic" was a disparaging term given by the neoclassicists to medieval architecture. But the nineteenth century rediscovered its beauty to such an extent that the United States, like other Western countries, became dotted with neo-Gothic churches, cathedrals, and universities. Today, when most people think of a religious edifice, they think of some form of Gothic style. Our universities, not only the neo-Gothic ones, stand as testimonies that the roots in the cathedral schools have flourished.

Medieval and Modern Music and Drama   The vocal and instrumental music composed in the monasteries and cathedral schools was the first truly Western music. Much of it is still used in religious services today; and the great musical elaboration of medieval Europe, *polyphony,* is not only the basis of all modern music but is also the distinctive feature identifying Western music from all other forms. While legend labels chant as the gift of God, history records polyphony as the creation of man. The drama written along with medieval chant was also the first European drama, emerging within the cathedral at a time when the dramatic form in the Western world was almost dead. Drama, like other forms of medieval art, pointed toward the promise of salvation, or redemption, thereby breaking with the classical forms. Unlike those, drama in the Middle Ages often combined comic and tragic elements. We will see that the medieval (along with the classical) dramatic tradition went into the making of Shakespeare's plays and from there influenced the whole development of modern drama and film.

Views of Women   The cult of the Virgin Mary, a major element in medieval art and life and in Catholicism, has profoundly influenced our society's conception of women. We have seen how the Virgin was represented in twelfth- and thirteenth-century literature and art as a divine mother, an object of the highest form of spiritual love, an intercessor between man and God. The portrayal of earthly ladies in the same period, strongly influenced by the cult of the Virgin, became either so etherealized that the lady became a symbol and the lover's feeling for her purely spiritual, or else she became a parody of the Virgin and the lover—an example of the destructiveness of earthly passion. Later centuries, however, took these parodies of swooning lovers worshiping their ladies quite seriously. As life began to imitate art, women became in a sense objects of veneration. In order to merit this attitude, they were supposed to be pure, chaste, and unattainable, not creatures of flesh and blood. Men developed the idea that women could be placed in two categories: pure (on a pedestal) and "fallen," so corrupted and irresponsible that they had to be controlled by men. We are only now changing the residues of this attitude.

Some of the gestures that stem from the courtly or chivalric tradition—men opening doors for women, holding out chairs for them, paying for their entertainment on dates—are still with us. So are some of our notions about love. Later centuries, as we shall see, took seriously the literary "courtly" type that presented love as an all-consuming, irresistible passion. From this came the "romantic" search for constant ecstasy and the resultant idea that adultery is necessarily more passionate than marriage. The idealization of the power and value of romantic love is very much a Western cultural value. More stable, traditional societies (as we will see in our study of Africa) view romantic love as exaggerated.

Transition to Renaissance   We have seen in our example from Marie de France that the courtly tradition, while portraying the irresistible aspects of love, also showed its ludicrous and destructive qualities. The medieval mind (such as we saw it in the philosophy of Aquinas) could hardly accept the notion that earthly passions were superior to the love of God or to human reason, which could reach up to revelation. Love, or sex, was frequently an object of comedy in the Middle Ages. Chaucer's tales are there to remind us that medieval men and women were full, real people who enjoyed a good laugh for some of the same reasons that we do. By Chaucer's time the period we call medieval was drawing to a close. In both art and literature, human beings and the natural world were being observed and portrayed more realistically and less symbolically in transition between the God-centered culture and the more human-centered one that we call the Renaissance.

PART THREE
RENAISSANCE AND REFORMATION: FUSION OF THE ROOTS

9

HUMANISM AND THE EARLY ITALIAN RENAISSANCE

Students of history used to learn that everything in the Middle Ages was "obscure" or "superstitious," or that the minds of people were dominated by the Church and that suddenly in the Renaissance "light" burst forth, and culture, as in antiquity, flourished once again. By now the Middle Ages have come into their own and are seen as a culture with its own values and creations, highly important ones, in fact, for our cultural roots. Many scholars now also see the change from the Middle Ages to the Renaissance as gradual rather than revolutionary. There are many continuities to be found in philosophy, politics, and the fine arts; and, despite the much-publicized shift from God to man, the culture of the European Renaissance remained fundamentally within the Judeo-Christian tradition. The subjects of painting, sculpture, music, and the other arts were predominantly religious. At least in the first century of its development, humanism, the leading intellectual movement of the Renaissance, viewed its major task as making the men and women of the time better Christians. Daily life in the Renaissance, as in the Middle Ages, was intimately tied to the rituals and calendar of the Church.

Nevertheless, despite these continuities, there is no doubt that something new happened in Western culture in the years 1350–1600. Our whole modern view of reality would not be the same without the Renaissance. What was this new view of the world, and how did it manifest itself in cultural achievements?

An Italian Phenomenon Whereas the center of medieval culture was located in northern France and southern Germany, the Renaissance from 1350 to 1500 was dominated by Italy. During the Middle Ages Italy had been the commercial center of Western Europe, and Italians were well known for their administrative abilities in the Church. Culturally, however, the area was a kind of backwater; Italian universities claimed preeminence only in medicine and in the study of Roman and Church law. The figure of Dante, coming at the end of the thirteenth century, is an exception. In contrast to its secondary role in medieval culture, Italy dominated in the Renaissance. If after 1500 the Renaissance has become a European movement, it was largely an Italian phenomenon in the first 150 years.

The Crisis of the Fourteenth Century The fourteenth century was a time of trouble for Europe. By 1300 Western Europe was overpopulated for the technological level of the society. The costs of food and food-bearing land were high, wages were low, and a good percentage of the population was undernourished. When a terrible famine, the worst of the Middle Ages, struck the subcontinent between 1314 and 1318, about 10 percent of the people died and the losses were not made up. Beginning in 1348 the Black Death struck repeatedly over a wide area for the next fifty years. By 1400 Europe had only about 60 percent of the population that it had in 1300. The population was to remain at this low level until the last decades of the century, when a spectacular rise in population began. This great human loss resulted in an economic contraction, a rise in labor costs, and a drop in rents and food prices. The overall effect on the upper classes of Europe who earned their income from trade or agriculture was adverse.

Although, like the rest of Europe, Italy was affected by the plague and the economic contraction, it remained the commercial center and did not suffer economic stagnation to the same degree as the north. Indeed, it appears that an imbalance in trade favorable to Italy existed in the fourteenth and fifteenth centuries. Quantities of gold and silver flowed into the peninsula from the north in exchange for luxury goods that Italians produced or imported from the East. The drain from the north could not go on forever; and, as purchases of Italian goods by northerners slowed down, investment opportunities in business narrowed in Italy. Part of the stocks of surplus precious metals, with no profitable outlet available, were subsequently funneled into culture; they paid for architecture, for art objects, and for patronage to scholars and writers.

The Rise of Mysticism Not coincidentally, the fourteenth century, a period of enormous loss of life and dislocation, was the time when intellectual forces critical of the scholastic synthesis of faith and reason made themselves heard. The scholastic systems made sense in a period of economic and political integration like the twelfth and thirteenth centuries, but the great famine and the holocaust of the Black Death made a mockery of such approaches. In the north, theological and philosophical movements assaulted scholasticism for its attempt to build bridges of reason reaching up to God himself. These movements rejected the possibility of defining God through an analysis of His creation. For these new thinkers there was no way to argue back from what God created to Him as creator because, had He willed, He could have made everything in the universe different from what it is. The realms of faith and reason were seen to be absolutely separate. Human beings could know of God only what He had decided to tell in the Bible and through the operations of the Holy Spirit. Reason's work was limited to the created world. Aquinas' neat conception of continuity and overlap between the two was, therefore, rejected.

Confronted with famine and repeated outbreak of plague, the thinkers of the fourteenth century understandably magnified God as absolute will and the world as completely dependent on Him at every moment.

Understandable, too, is the importance of *mysticism* in the fourteenth century. Mysticism was an effort to transcend outward experience in order to join oneself immediately with the divine while still within the body. While mysticism was throughout the Middle Ages an acceptable element in the spiritual life of the Church, the misery and high mortality of this century made the mystic ascent very desirable.

Humanism

Another response to the crisis of the fourteenth century was humanism. Humanism was clearly an outgrowth of the urban culture of central and northern Italy. As contrasted with the monarchies of the north, the Italian peninsula was a land of city-states. Whereas only about 10 percent of the northern population lived in towns of over two thousand people, in Italy the figure was close to 40 percent. The intense city life of these city-states encouraged public speaking, while the frequent contact between the little states not only made eloquent ambassadors a necessity but also produced a climate that favored well-written public correspondence.

The inhabitants of the Italian city-state were in many ways the most likely to appreciate the achievements and spirit of the ancient world. Roman and Greek monuments dotted the peninsula as nowhere else in Europe, and Roman law was the basic law of all the city-states; politically, Italy in the fourteenth century was organized like the ancient world around the city-state. Whereas northern European culture was primarily agricultural, the Italian, like the ancient, was urban. Consequently, it was easy for the Italian humanists of the fourteenth to the sixteenth centuries to see themselves as the descendants of the ancient Roman orators and writers who dominated the intellectual lives of their own cities.

Essentially the humanists were rhetoricians interested in Greek and Latin literature, grammar, history, and *ethics*. These subjects constituted the *studia humanitatis*, or those disciplines that made man truly human. Man, for the humanist, distinguished himself from all other animals in his capacity to use words to express himself. If this was the basic human characteristic, then the man who best expressed himself in words was the most human. The humanists also assumed that outer speech was a reflection of one's inner state. If the inner man was calm and in harmony with his nature, then his speech would be fluent and harmonious. True eloquence stemmed from a fine soul just as the highest degree of moral virtue was closely tied to eloquence. Of course, one could be virtuous and still stutter, but virtue could be realized only by helping others to become virtuous as well. The individual Christian had a responsibility to other men to aid them to be good Christians; this could best be done by eloquent speech that inspired the will and heart to do the right.

Since the humanists considered the ancient pagan writers to have achieved excellence in speaking and writing, they believed that the study of Greek and Roman literature could best teach effective oral and written expression. They also thought that the writings of the pagans contained moral teachings urged with such forcefulness that they could not but influence their readers to become virtuous. In reading these writings, therefore, the humanists sharpened their moral sensibilities as well as their literary technique. They, in turn, would use their eloquence and virtue to persuade and train others.

Admittedly, the truth found in the pagan authors—fragmentary and based on reason—had to be interpreted in the context of the overarching truths of the Judeo-Christian tradition. The humanists, however, saw no incompatibility between what the Bible told man about God and about the nature of the human soul and the moral lessons taught by the ancient writers. The eloquence and learning of the ancients, consequently, coupled with the greater vision provided by divine revelation, could be a tremendous force for Christian reform.

On the whole, the humanists were hostile to scholasticism. Unlike the northern critics of the movement, who attacked scholasticism because it seemed to limit God's free will (by assuming that human reason could define His basic nature through an examination of the created world), the humanists simply felt that elaborate philosophical and theological systems were unnecessary. God gives us in revelation what we need to know about Christian truth: the real task of man is not to make systems but to live better Christian lives. The humanists also attacked the language of the scholastics as too technical and awkward. Such a style could never inspire men to improve their lives. There was an enormous difference between knowing the truth and carrying out its lessons in practice. Eloquent speech was the means of making truth active in the world.

The Use of Classical Authors Because ancient eloquence was central to their scheme of education, the humanists from the fourteenth century on devoted enormous energy not only to recovering lost ancient writings but also to preparing good editions of those inherited from the Middle Ages. In the more than eleven or twelve hundred years since ancient Roman times, the works of the pagans, especially the most popular ones, had been copied thousands of times by thousands of scribes; thus, texts were terribly corrupted. It fell to the humanists to restore as fully as possible the words and phrases of the pagan writers by a systematic comparison of surviving manuscripts. If ancient eloquence was to serve as a basis of inspiration to the present generation, the texts must be restored to their original purity.

Medieval writers used the classics as a kind of quarry from which to borrow words and ideas in order to adorn and support their own schemes of thought. On the other hand, while concerned with using the ancient writers for their own purposes, the humanists were also interested in defining the personalities of the great men of antiquity. Rather than attribute attitudes and ideas to pagan writers on a piecemeal basis, they tried to form an integrated picture of their thought and personalities by a careful analysis of all of an individual writer's works. Because of the similarities between their own and the ancient culture, they were able to appreciate the thoughts and actions of the ancients as the Middle Ages never could. This awareness of an interest in the totality of a personality, moreover, motivated their approach not merely to historical personages but also to men of their own time.

Furthermore, all the comparison of words and phrases in the effort to obtain accurate texts taught the humanists a concept not well understood in the Middle Ages: languages change; they have a history. The same is true of institutions, customs, and ideas. Thus, the scholarly endeavors of the humanists led

them gradually to develop a sense of change and development, of historicity. This deepened their appreciation of the nature of human personality, permitting them to see the extent to which individuals were conditioned by circumstances of time and place. It also led them to a growing awareness that men are responsible for their history in large part and, subsequently, for their future as well. They came to see man as a doer, a maker, endowed with the godlike powers of reason and will to create his own culture.

Humanism and Science While by no means discarding the medieval ethos, which emphasized compassion, suffering, and humility, humanism in its essential tendencies moved toward a reevaluation of the human predicament by accenting the active, dynamic aspect of human nature. Originally biased against the natural sciences because of their focus on nature rather than man, the humanists nonetheless furnished the scientists with better texts of antiquity on which to base their investigations. By the sixteenth century, they were largely responsible for providing a vision of man and his creative capacities that encouraged scientific inquiry. Through the joint efforts of humanism and natural science, the task of improving human life materially as well as spiritually through a better understanding of man and his environment became increasingly viewed as a prime goal of learning.

Florence and Civic Humanism By the early fifteenth century Florence became the unrivaled center of humanistic studies as well as the artistic capital of Italy. Its population, varying between forty and sixty thousand throughout the century, was about half of what it had been before the Black Death of 1348. Florence, a city founded by the Romans, had been only one of the major towns of Italy until the twelfth century, when the economic revival gave the city, well situated on the trade routes, a new importance. Although formally under the sovereignty of the emperor, as were most of the other northern and central Italian towns, Florence like them had its own municipal government and was for all practical purposes self-governing. Gradually, as the city grew in commercial and industrial importance, it extended its authority out from the city walls; by 1400 Florence controlled a sizable portion of central Italy. The basis of Florentine prosperity in the thirteenth and fourteenth centuries was woolen cloth, but banking increasingly came to play a major role in the economy. Fourteenth-century Florence was the financial center of Europe.

The main form of government in the Italian towns of the northern and central portions of the peninsula in the thirteenth century had been republican; that is, ruled by a large body of citizens with the lower social elements excluded. In the fourteenth century, however, when the rule of one man or one family became common, Florence was one of a dwindling number of cities still governed by *republican* methods. The basis for citizenship and political participation in Florentine government from the late thirteenth century on was membership in one of the numerous guilds in the city; but the major guilds, those primarily concerned with international trade, like the woolmakers and the bankers, exercised an overriding influence.

By 1400 the sphere of active citizens had in effect narrowed to less than a hundred families. Although hundreds of other families shared in the more than two thousand public offices that had to be filled annually in the Florentine state, a narrower group of families controlled the key positions. Nonetheless, while Florence was realistically an *oligarchy*, the old republican institutions continued to function; and Florentine leaders considered themselves the defenders of a republican form of government against the assaults of the one-man tyrannical governments encircling their state. The Florentine humanists deserve the credit for being the first thinkers in Europe since the fall of Rome to develop a theory of republican government with which to justify the struggle of the Florentine Republic for its political existence in a period when one Italian state after another fell under monarchical rule. For that reason they are called *civic humanists*.

Petrarch   Francesco Petrarch (1304–1374) is generally considered the first of the Italian humanists. Although he was Florentine by descent and his first teacher was an exiled Florentine like his own father, Petrarch grew to manhood in France, not Italy. In the last half of his life, which he spent primarily in Italy, Petrarch saw the city of his ancestors only twice on brief visits. Petrarch's pioneering achievement was to formulate the basic humanistic conception of the intimate connection between ethics and eloquence just described and to develop an appreciation for ancient life and thought in its historical context.

In certain respects, however, Petrarch was still closely linked to medieval traditions. Medieval thinkers were fully committed to the belief that the contemplative life was the best form of existence for man and that monarchy was the best form of government. Like these thinkers, Petrarch, who spent most of his mature life in proximity to the new princely courts of northern Italy, considered the life of the citizen—the married man with business and civic responsibilities—unquestionably inferior to that of the solitary scholar or monk, who devoted his energies to the contemplation of divine truth. Moreover, like them he believed that monarchy was the ideal political constitution and that the Roman emperors had been established by God to replace the decaying Roman Republic.

Salutati and Bruni   After the death of Petrarch, the humanist and chancellor of Florence, Coluccio Salutati (1331–1406), helped to make Florence the center for humanistic studies. Both in his official work as Florentine secretary of state or chancellor and in his more scholarly writings, Salutati began to challenge the medieval theory of the superiority of monarchy. His disciple, Leonardo Bruni (1370–1444), was primarily responsible for formulating a theory of republican government that was to remain a living force down to the nineteenth century and beyond. He considered the rule of one man harmful to the common good. Since men realize themselves to the fullest in serving the state, republican government is natural to man and inherently stronger than monarchy. Rome reached its highest power under the Republic, not under the emperors; in fact, while some emperors might have been personally good men, as a group they destroyed Rome. Florence, founded in the days of the Roman Republic, inherited that tradition of liberty, and in contemporary Italy it served as the leader in the struggle of free men against *tyranny*.

The origins of Bruni's theory can be traced to the writings of Aristotle and Cicero. But Bruni's capacity to sense the republican spirit of these writers, which his predecessors had not perceived, stems from his personal experience as a part of a living republican society. His arguments rested both on his understanding of human nature and on the lessons he believed were found in history. The first European to formulate republican ideas with such clarity, he was followed over the next hundred years by a whole succession of writers, mainly Florentine, urging similar views.

Bruni was also one of the first of the humanists to learn Greek. Eminent Latin scholars like Petrarch and Salutati in the previous century did not know the other classic language. Aristotle's works had been translated hundreds of years before into Latin, but Bruni's knowledge of Greek gave him access to the rest of extant Greek literature. This learning was especially valuable to him in his work in political theory, as indicated in the following excerpt from one of Bruni's Latin orations (translated by Ronald Witt). This is a funeral oration written by Bruni in 1428 in honor of the Florentine general, Nanni Strozzi, who died fighting against Milan, Florence's bitter enemy. Pericles' funeral oration as reported by Thucydides was clearly an influence. The Florentine orator ascribes to the dead man and to Florence many of the virtues and qualities attributed by Pericles to the Athenian war dead and to the city for which they sacrificed their lives.

BRUNI

Funeral Oration

This is an exceptional funeral oration because it is appropriate neither to weep or lament. For we should be sorry for those who die having accomplished nothing which might bring comfort to those left behind. The life of this man was most enviable and his death was most glorious. We would be ungrateful to mourn a man who lived and died enjoying such a wealth of advantages. But in explaining the nature of his good fortune we must acknowledge that a good many things, the most important ones, were his by a kind of divinely ordained destiny. His first claim to fame is conferred on him because of his country's merit. For the homeland is the first and chief basis of human happiness and more worthy of our veneration than even our own parents. If we begin therefore by praising the motherland, we will be starting in the right order.

He was born in the most spacious and greatest of cities, wide-ruling and endowed with the mightiest power, without question the foremost of all the Etruscan cities.[1] Indeed, it is second to none of the cities of Italy either in origin, wealth, or size. The two most noble and outstanding races of people in Italy cooperated in its foundation, that is, the Tuscans, the former lords of Italy, and the Romans, who acquired domination of the whole world through their virtue and their military prowess. For our city was a Roman colony integrated with the native Tuscan population.[2] The Tuscans had been the chief people of Italy and supreme both in authority and wealth. Before the foundation of the Roman empire their power was so great that they had the seas on both sides of Italy under their control and governed the whole length of the country from the Alps to the Straits of Sicily for many centuries. Finally, this one people diffused the worship of the immortal gods as well as learning and letters throughout Italy. Other peoples of Italy borrowed their symbols of war and peace. As for the power of the Romans, their excellence, virtue, glory, magnanimity, wisdom and the size of their empire, it is better to say nothing than to have said only a few words.

What city, therefore, can be more excellent, more noble? What descended from more glorious antecedents? Which one of the most powerful cities is able to be compared with our own on these grounds? Our fathers, moreover, are worthy of commendation because inheriting this city in their turn, they so established and governed it that they were in no way inferior to their own fathers in virtue. Sustained by the most sacred laws, the state was ruled by them with such wisdom that they served as an example of good moral behavior for other peoples and had no need to take others as their model. With constant vigilance they either conserved their authority and power or even increased it with the result that in the memory of man this city

---

[1] Cities of the ancient Etruscans (as we saw in the section on Roman architecture in Chapter 5) dominated the central portion of the Italian peninsula before the rise of Rome. There is little indication that Florence was an Etruscan city, but Fiesole, a town on the heights above Florence, was founded by that people.

[2] The date of Florence's foundation is still controversial. It occurred sometime in the first century B.C.

has always been the foremost in Tuscany.

Worthy of praise as well are those who are its present-day citizens. They have augmented the power received from their predecessors even more by adding Pisa[3] and a number of other great cities to their empire through their virtue and valor in arms. But there is not time here to recall wars, battles, and feats of arms. This is extensive material indeed, and such things demand the labor and attention of not one day but many years. However, at this point with the discussion of external affairs either laid aside or already considered, let us stop to view and investigate in some detail the very body, so to speak, of the city.

Our form of governing the state aims at achieving liberty and equality for each and every citizen. Because it is equal in all respects, it is called a popular government. We tremble before no lord nor are we dominated by the power of a few. All enjoy the same liberty, governed only by law and free from fear of individuals. Everyone has the same hope of attaining honors and of improving his condition provided he is industrious, has talent and a good sober way of life. For our city requires virtue and honesty in its citizens. It considers anyone with these qualities to be noble enough to govern the state. The pride and haughtiness of the powerful are so hated that the city has passed more numerous and stringent laws against this kind of men than against anything else. As a result it has conquered the proud, as if binding them with unbreakable chains of the law, forcing them to bow their necks and to humble themselves to a moderate status. The result is that it is considered a benefit to transfer from the great families into the ranks of the common people.

This is true liberty and equality in a city: to fear the power of no one nor dread injury from them; to experience equality of law among the citizens and the same opportunity of ruling the state. These advantages cannot be had where one man rules or a few. For those who espouse kingly rule seem to imagine a degree of virtue in a king which they admit no man ever had. Has there ever been a king who did all of those things which are accomplished in a state on behalf of the people? Was there ever one who wanted nothing for himself except the empty glory of the name? Thus it is that praise of monarchy is like a thing false and shadowy, not clear and solid. Both good and evil people, says the historian,[4] are suspected by kings. The virtue of another is always frightening to them. Nor is it much different under the rule of a few.

Thus the popular remains the only legitimate form of governing the state. In a popular government are found true liberty and equity for all citizens; in it the desires for virtue can thrive without suspicion. This capacity for a free people to attain honors and this ability to pursue one's goals serve in a marvelous way to excite men's talents. For with the hope of honors extended, men raise themselves and surge upward; excluded they become lifeless. Since in our state men have this hope and the opportunity is offered, no wonder that talents and industry abound so exceedingly. Indeed our city has such a numerous multitude of citizens that, in addition to the countless population living in the homeland, an infinite number are diffused throughout the world.... There is no place in the world so remote or out of the way where some Florentine does not live ... Wherefore, if the whole multitude of our absent citizens variously diffused throughout the world be joined to those present in the city, an absolutely infinite and innumerable multitude would result, which no city in Italy could match. Our citizens excel so greatly in talents and intelligence that few equal them and none surpass them. They have vivacity and industry and alacrity and agility in acting with a greatness of spirit equal to all challenges.

We thrive not only in governing the republic, in domestic arts, and in engaging in business everywhere, but we are also distinguished for military glory. For our ancestors splendidly fought many wars on the dusty battlefield, overcoming all neighboring people with their military prowess. They shattered a thousand enemy battle wedges and set up almost innumerable trophies. Besides our city has furnished generals to the most powerful kings and produced skillful leaders of military science.

---

[3] Pisa was captured in 1406.

[4] Refers to the Roman historian Sallust (86–34 B.C.).

What now shall I say about literature and scholarship in which all concede that Florence is the chief and most splendid leader? Nor am I now speaking about those popular arts executed for money—although in these as well our people are foremost. But I am speaking about those more civilized and lofty studies which are considered more excellent and worthy of everlasting immortal glory. For who is able to name a poet in our generation or in the last one who is not Florentine? Who but our citizens recalled this skill at eloquence, already lost, to light, to practical use, and to life? Who but they understood Latin literature, already abject, prostrate and almost dead, and raised it up, restored and reclaimed it from destruction? Camillus[5] is rightly said to be the founder of the city of Rome, not because he established it at the beginning, but because he restored it when it was defeated and occupied by the enemy. For the same reason, should our city not merit being proclaimed the parent of the Latin language, which a short time ago it found lost and cast down, and which it restored to its brilliance and dignity? Furthermore, just as we attribute to Triptolemus,[6] who first produced wheat, whatever has grown since, so whatever literature and cultivated learning takes root anywhere ought to be credited to our city. Now the knowledge of Greek literature, which had decayed in Italy for more than seven hundred years, has been revived and restored by our city. Now we are able to confront the greatest philosophers, the admirable orators, and other men of outstanding learning, not through the obscurity of clumsy interpretations[7] but face to face. Finally, these humanities [studia humanitatis] most excellent and of highest value, especially relevant for human beings, necessary both for private and public life, adorned with a knowledge of letters worthy of free men, have originated in our city and are now thriving throughout Italy. The city enjoys such resources and wealth that I fear to arouse jealousy by referring to its inexhaustible supply of money. This is demonstrated by the long Milanese war[8] waged at an almost incredible cost, in

which we spent over 3,500,000 florins. Now at the end of the war men are more prompt in paying their taxes than they were at the beginning of the war. As if miraculously, the abundance of money seems to increase in the city daily.

Therefore, the man we praise belonged by birth to this most noble, laudably established, most populous, spirited, rich and glorious homeland. By the will of the immortal gods he (Strozzi) achieved in this way at the very beginning the greatest part of his happiness. . . . In this regard he could not have been more fortunate than he was in fact. . . .

QUESTIONS

1. Compare this praise of Florence with Pericles' praise of Athens (Chapter 2) and Virgil's praise of Rome in the *Aeneid* (Chapter 5). In what respects does Bruni seem to consider Florence comparable to the classical cities, and what new elements does he add?
2. Does Bruni's speech ever sound as though it could have been made by an American statesman? In what respects?
3. How does Bruni define the humanities? Why does he consider them vital to the life of the city?
4. Why does he think that popular government is superior to the rule of one or of a few?

The Medici; Neoplatonism   In the last decade of Bruni's life Florence came under the control of the Medici family and their supporters. An old Florentine banking family, the Medici by the early fifteenth century were the richest family in the city. In the early 1430s the head of the family, Cosimo, quarreled with the other leading members of the Florentine government and was sent into exile in 1433. The following year, when his enemies in the government proved themselves clearly incompetent, they were driven out and Cosimo was recalled. Though the republican institutions continued to function and Cosimo remained a private citizen, for all practical purposes he and his close friends were usually able to control both the internal and external policies of the republic.

When Cosimo died in 1466, his son, Piero the Gouty, inherited the authority; and, when three years later Piero died, he in turn was succeeded by his two

---

[5] Camillus freed Rome from the Gauls in the early fourth century B.C.

[6] According to legend Triptolemus was the founder of agriculture.

[7] Refers to the Latin scholastic translations of the twelfth and thirteenth centuries, for example, those of the works of Aristotle.

[8] This particular war with Milan began in 1425 and ended in 1429.

sons, Lorenzo and Giuliano, then twenty and eighteen respectively. After the assassination of Giuliano in 1478, Lorenzo alone directed the political life of the city until his own death in 1492. The years of Lorenzo's domination in Florence were also years of some of the highest cultural achievements in the city. Because of his exquisite taste and personal talents, Lorenzo became known in his own lifetime as Lorenzo the Magnificent.

The rise of the Medici and their political control over Florentine institutions rendered Bruni's emphasis on the active life of the citizen unrealistic. While a republican current persisted in the city, the mood was generally one of political quietism. Not by chance the last half of the fifteenth century marked the progress of a movement usually labeled Florentine Platonism.

As we have already seen, Greek studies were introduced in Florence at the beginning of the fifteenth century. One of the first goals of Greek scholars was to translate the complete works of Plato. Whereas Aristotle had been translated into Latin in the thirteenth century, until this time only a handful of Plato's writings were in that language. Now, along with Plato's works, writings of Plato's ancient followers were also put into Latin. The most famous of these followers was Plotinus, an Egyptian of the second century A.D., who had given Plato's philosophy a clearly mystical bent. Plotinus stressed that through proper training the soul, whose true home was beyond this world, could at times in this life return by a mystic ascent to the world of the Ideas. The ultimate step was to merge totally with the Platonic One or Idea of the Good. Besides those of Plotinus, other Platonic writings, many of them of a magical nature, became popular with late fifteenth-century intellectuals. This kind of literature fitted an age that was no longer interested in active participation in politics.

The following selection, translated by Ronald Witt, is taken from *Oration on the Dignity of Man*, by Pico della Mirandola (1463–1494). Pico was not a Florentine by birth but, heavily influenced by Florentine Platonism, spent the last years of his short life in the city. An ideal Renaissance type, Pico was handsome, brilliant, and heir to a little Italian principality. He knew Latin, Greek, Hebrew, and Arabic. This oration was written as the introduction to a list of nine hundred theological and philosophical propositions that (at the age of twenty) he volunteered to debate in Rome with anyone. The debate never occurred.

The oration begins with the presentation of an extraordinary conception of the creative free will of man. Formerly, in line with the doctrines of Plotinus, Florentine Platonists had conceived of man midway on a chain of being between the lowest material objects and God. They believed that man had the power either to rise to the highest reaches of being or to fall to the lowest depths. Pico's achievement was to view man as outside the chain of being linking earth with heaven. Man contains within himself the potentiality of being anything. His free will is complete. His being, in fact, is a microcosm of the whole universe.

PICO DELLA MIRANDOLA

Oration on the Dignity of Man

I have read, O venerable fathers, in the records of the Arabs that Abdala the Saracen,[1] when asked what he believed was the most admirable thing on the stage of this world, as it were, replied that there was nothing more admirable than man. Hermes Trismegistus supported this opinion when he said, "O Asclepius, man is a great miracle!" Yet when I consider the grounds for such sayings, the many justifications, given by many, for the outstanding qualities of human nature do not satisfy me: that man is intermediary between the creatures, a friend of the higher powers, king of the lower regions; capable of understanding nature with the sharpness of his senses, the penetration of his reason, and the light of his intelligence; the space between unchanging eternity and the flux of time, and (as the Persians say) the bond of the world, nay rather, its marriage bond, and, as David testifies, only less than the angels.[2] Indeed these are great qualities but not the principal ones, that is, those which rightly serve as the basis for such extraordinary admiration. But why should we not admire the very angels and the blessed chorus of the heavens more? At length I seemed to myself to have understood why man is the most fortunate animal and therefore worthy of universal admiration

---

[1] Abdala was presumably the cousin of Mohammed.
[2] Psalms 8:5.

and what his place in the order of the universe is that makes him an object of envy not only by brutes or by the stars, but even by minds beyond this world. It is an unbelievable and wonderful thing. Why should it not be? For on this account man is properly said to be a great miracle and a wondrous being. But now hear, Fathers, what it is and out of your kindness lend me your full attention.

The supreme father, God the architect, had already fabricated this house of the world which we see, the most illustrious temple of the divinity, according to the laws of His secret wisdom. He had adorned the place above the heavens with minds and animated the heavenly spheres with eternal souls; He had filled the excrementary and filthy places of the lower world with all manner of animals. But, with the work finished, the artisan wanted there to be someone who could contemplate the nature of so great a work, love its beauty and admire its magnitude. For this reason with all these things finished (as Moses and Timeaus[3] bear witness) only then did He think of creating man. But there was nothing among the archetypes from which He could model a new creature, nor in His treasuries was there an inheritance to bestow on His new son, nor was there any place left in the whole world where this contemplator of the universe could sit. Everything was already full; everything in the highest, middle, and lowest orders of being was already given out. But it was not in the Father's nature to fail as if worn out in this last creation; nor was His wisdom to waver without a plan in such a serious situation. Nor was it a part of His loving kindness that He, who would praise divine liberality in others, would condemn Himself for His lack of it. At length the consummate artificer decreed that the creature whom He could endow with no properties of its own should share in all those which the others possessed individually for themselves. Therefore, He took man, a creation of indeterminate form, and placing him at the midpoint of the world spoke to him in this way: "I have given you no fixed abode, no form of your own, no gifts peculiarly yours, O Adam, so that you might have and possess the abode, form and gifts you yourself desire according to your will and judgment.

The defined nature of other beings is confined by laws which I have prescribed. You, compelled by no limitations, according to your free choice in whose hands I have placed you, shall prescribe your own limits. I have set you in the center of the world, that you might more easily observe whatever there is in the world. We have made you neither heavenly nor terrestrial, neither mortal nor immortal, so that, free of constraint and more honorable as your own moulder and maker, you might give yourself whatever form you prefer. You can degenerate toward lower beings, which are brutes, or, if you will, you can be reborn among higher beings, which are divine."

Oh, the magnificent generosity of God the Father! Oh, the extraordinary and wondrous felicity of man, who was given the power to be that which he wanted! Brutes as soon as they are born bring with them from the mother's womb everything they are to have. The highest spiritual beings either from the beginning or soon thereafter are that which they will be for eternity. In the case of man, the Father bestowed on him at birth manifold seeds and germs of every kind of life. Whichever ones he cultivates will grow and bear their fruit in him. If he cultivates vegetative seeds, then he becomes a plant; if sensual ones, then a brute; if rational seeds, then he becomes a heavenly being. If intellectual ones, then he will be an angel and son of God. And if, unhappy with being a creature of any sort, he draws into the center of his own unity, his spirit will be made one with God, and in the solitary darkness of the Father, Who is above all things, he will distinguish himself beyond all things. Who does not admire this our chameleon? Could anything else be more an object of wonder?

QUESTIONS

1. What different sources does Pico appear to use in establishing the dignity of man?
2. Compare Pico's account of man's creation with that in Genesis (Chapter 6). To what extent does he remain within the Judeo-Christian tradition, and how does he differ?
3. What is the basis for man's dignity? In what respect is man more wonderful than the angels?
4. Compare Pico's glorification of man to that of Sophocles in the choral ode from *Antigone* (see the section "Humanism and Tragedy" in Chapter 3).

---

[3] Plato, *Timaeus.*

10

ART, ARCHITECTURE, AND MUSIC IN FLORENCE

Innovation Based on Antiquity   In 1436 when Leon Battista Alberti (1404–1472) published the Italian version of his Latin treatise *On Painting* (1435), he added a prologue, praising the great Florentine artists Donatello, Ghiberti, and Masaccio, and the architect Brunelleschi. These men, says Alberti, are responsible for returning to the study of nature as the source of art and have consequently brought great fame to Florence. In a passage that parallels Bruni's in the *Funeral Oration*, Alberti compares Florentine accomplishments in art to those of the ancients, reserving the greatest praise for the Florentines, since they had to create by first discovering the knowledge that the ancients had already attained.

This point of view stresses the sense of departure from the immediate past and that of courageous experiment and exploration which, to Alberti and his contemporaries, must have seemed characteristic of Florence in the mid-fifteenth century. Wealth, power, and the association of free men had produced the republic; these same conditions fostered the new forms and conventions in art and architecture.

Similarly, the successful artists of the fifteenth century had roots in Roman antiquity. Brunelleschi, Florence's architect, is reported to have visited Rome in the early 1400s, studying and measuring the remains of the Forum. He returned to create a conspicuously new architecture. Alberti, who knew Brunelleschi, was also an architect who studied ancient texts; he wrote about the ideals and intentions that made Roman and fifteenth-century architecture so different from that of the Middle Ages. His theory and Brunelleschi's practice were, as we will see, representative of the changes taking place in Florence and were largely responsible for the transmission of new ideas to the future.

The City of Florence   It is difficult to imagine the events of the fifteenth century without some feeling for the physical setting of Florence itself (Color Plate III). In the center of Italy, the city sits in a plain at the foothills of the Apennine Mountains, bisected by the Arno River. From almost any vantage point outside or within the city, one's view is dominated by the red-tiled octagonal dome of Saint Mary of the Flowers, or the *Duomo*, the cathedral of the city. The feeling created by this cathedral and its place within the city is vastly different from that of Notre Dame at Chartres. The *Duomo* sits in its own square (*piazza*) but within a city of other squares that belong to equally important old Christian churches or civic and mercantile enterprises. The *Palazzo Vecchio* (the old city hall) with its battlements and tower reminds one of the Gothic period (Fig. 10-1). It dominates the square where Michelangelo's *David* was originally placed.

The city has many centers of activity; there are distinguishable quarters for artisans, and the *Ponte Vecchio* (the old bridge) spanning the Arno still carries the many shops for luxury items that were there in the 1400s. Florence bustles with business activity—with the precious industries of gold, silver, silk, and leather still practiced today. The great food market near San Lorenzo and the small street stalls give the city an air of tantalizing fecundity.

Florence is dominated by narrow, cobbled streets and

10–1   Palazzo Vecchio, Florence. (Alinari/Editorial Photocolor Archives)

the thick walls of the palaces, banks, and apartments that rise three and four stories, keeping the blistering summer sun from the streets. In the winter the reds, yellows, browns, and tans of marble, stone, stucco, and brick glow wetly, contrasting with the black and white, gray, or green marble of the façades of many of the churches (Fig. 10-2). The city has a this-worldly intensity, a presence of now that is surely both a condition and creation of her fifteenth-century efflorescence.

Florentine Architecture

The cathedral dome that dominates Florence was designed by Filippo Brunelleschi (1377–1446), who won a competition for the commission. While not the most significant of Brunelleschi's accomplishments, it introduces the scientist, inventor, and designer that Brunelleschi had become. Technically he employed a system that suspended an interior shell from the exterior structure of ribs and concealed buttresses that originated in Roman and Gothic technology. Of almost equal importance to the city fathers were the machines and devices that Brunelleschi invented to erect the dome without an enormous quantity of wooden centering (see Roman and Gothic architecture). The *lantern* (cupola) based on his design was put in place after his death. Brunelleschi's influence on architecture was enormous. We can better appreciate some of the new ideas and vitality he gave to the art by considering two other works: the interior of San Lorenzo and the Pazzi Chapel.

The Church of San Lorenzo Brunelleschi designed a sacristy for the Medici family to be added to San Lorenzo, an essentially Gothic church. The Medici were so delighted with it that he was then commissioned to remodel the interior of the church (Fig. 10-3), a project that began in 1421 and went on for many years. San Lorenzo's great simplicity and directness emphasize the contrast between the Renaissance and the Middle Ages. The interior seems almost early Christian, but with a substantial difference. Imposed on the traditional plan of nave and aisles (Fig. 10-4) is a sense of mathematical harmony, the repetition of sizes and shapes that derive from, but achieve a form different from, that of Gothic or Roman buildings.

Perhaps the most significant obvious difference is the sense of definite measured units of space, individual and independent. The nave is separated from the aisles by arcades of smooth Corinthian columns that carry semicircular arches. Above the arches is an entablature marking off the clerestory walls that are broken by arched windows centered above the arches. The columns, arches, and entablature are all in a gray stone that contrasts sharply with the smooth white plaster walls. The aisles are roofed by shallow vaults, and shallow side chapels line the walls. These have semicircular arched openings with a decorative keystone and are

10–2   Baptistry, Florence. (Alinari/Editorial Photocolor Archives)

10–3   Interior, San Lorenzo, Florence. (Alinari/Editorial Photocolor Archives)

also flanked by pilasters with Corinthian capitals, thus repeating the column-arch combination of the nave arcade. The aisles are lit by small round windows, one centered above each side chapel (Fig. 10-5).

The division of the wall planes of the aisles and the nave arcade are reinforced by the pavement, which is arranged in squares (see plan, Fig. 10-4)—thus, two squares form a bay of the nave and equal the height of a column; one square equals a bay of the aisle and one-half square a chapel. The transept is made of four large squares that are approximately equal to four square bays of the aisles. The nave roof is flat and decorated with square coffers.

Space in San Lorenzo is clear and limited, strongly directional but ordered into a rigorous sequence of bays. Each column, perfectly articulated, marks the beginning and end of a bay, a space. The light is dim but not mysterious. The transept is a specific and different space, as is the square apse at the east end. The feeling is one of intellectual control, not mystic transcendence.

Alberti, the architectural theorist, wrote that a church should induce contemplation through order and harmony, reflecting the mathematical perfection of the universe. It should, he said, be plain and encourage one to focus inward on control of self for the attainment of right, Christian actions. Windows should be high, so that one could see only the sky and not be distracted by the external world. Brunelleschi seems to have anticipated these ideals.

The Pazzi Chapel   The Pazzi Chapel was commissioned by the wealthy Pazzi family for their own use and for the use of the monastery of which it is a part. Located in the cloister of Santa Croce, it forms a strong contrast to the church that is one of the few Gothic buildings in Florence. The façade, with its columns and portico, clearly recalls Roman architecture (Fig. 10-6).

Structurally the interior of the chapel is familiar also (Fig. 10-7). Brunelleschi has used a post and lintel and load-bearing wall system to carry barrel vaults and an arrangement of domes. The plan shows two major axes; that formed by the domical space of the portico (which is repeated in the dome over the apse) and that formed by the rectangular spaces of the barrel vaults that support the central dome (Fig. 10-8). The directional quality of each axis is resolved under the great dome of the

10–4   Groundplan, San Lorenzo, Florence.

10–5   Nave, San Lorenzo, Florence. (Alinari/Editorial Photocolor Archives)

hall. The resultant feeling is one of quiet serenity reinforced by the articulation of the wall planes, windows, door, and apse opening. Applied pilasters rising from a base carry an entablature on which rest the arches of the vaults. These members, like the other decorative elements (the blind arches opposite the windows, for

10–6   Pazzi Chapel, Florence. (Alinari/Editorial Photocolor Archives)

10–7   Groundplan and cross section, Pazzi Chapel, Florence.

example), are made of *pietra serena*, the gray stone that is also used on the interior surfaces of San Lorenzo. They form a strong contrast with the white plastered walls and the terra cotta plaques, which are predominantly blue and white. The impression of the interior is one of cool elegance, for each element is paired, or repeated, except for the central dome, which in its singularity acts to arrest all motion. Does the chapel remind you of Roman buildings that we have seen? How does it differ from a Greek temple, a Roman one? Can you compare this building with San Lorenzo, with Chartres?

It is easy to understand how Brunelleschi's work must have appeared to his colleagues. With its order, clarity, and use of elements from the antique, it must have seemed like Rome revived. Yet it is not based on simply copying from ruins that Brunelleschi had seen,

10–8   Interior, Pazzi Chapel, Florence. (Alinari/Editorial Photocolor Archives)

or from later uses of antique forms in early Christian and Romanesque buildings. Like Gothic art and architecture, the art and architecture of fifteenth-century Florence depend for their forms and ideals on a structure of knowledge and value, on a society that was not in ignorance of the meaning to be found in building. Alberti's Latin treatise *On Architecture* presents some of the ideas and principles that he certainly believed capable of communication in building. The model for his treatise was the text by Vitruvius, the first-century B.C. Roman architect and engineer, but the book itself was very much the product of Alberti and fifteenth-century Florentine thought. It is another important way to understand the art and architecture of that century.

Leon Battista Alberti and the Theory of Architecture   Alberti wrote that the architecture and the planning of cities should be based on a rational analysis of problems, needs, site, and climate. The city, he felt, would inspire its citizens through its propriety, order, harmony, and control. Buildings should be considered in a hierarchy based on significance. The ornaments of a city should be its churches. Of second importance are buildings of civic and mercantile nature, like guild halls, bridges, and squares; finally, one should consider housing. Private dwellings should constitute a self-effacing background for the public monuments to Christian and civic virtues.

Alberti not only advocated public housing for the lower classes but also admonished the city fathers to prevent conspicuous consumption. Rich men, he said, should not be permitted to call attention to themselves by the creation of lavish, individual buildings but should live in houses only somewhat better than the less fortunate city dwellers. Wealth should be used to create buildings that all could share, and buildings would contribute to the public good.

These ideas are consistent with Bruni's concept of man as a civic person whose ambitions and skills, intellect and passion should be turned to the benefit of the republic. Moreover, there is almost a parallel between the humanists' belief that eloquence should be cultivated to speak and persuade for the truth of Christian virtue and Alberti's idea that eloquent architecture, based on the great principles of nature, will enable a person to discover and lead a harmonious life.

In Alberti's text we find these proposals for eloquent architecture derived from a study of nature and of the antique. Man, Alberti says, is a creature of reason and appetite, of intellect and will. If he succumbs only to the forces of appetite and will, he may enjoy his life briefly but will not achieve goodness and virtue, the attributes of greatness. In fact, he says, it is only by use of reason and intellect that one can know how to act. These tools are sharpened and trained through the study of nature.

Perfection in architecture is achieved for Alberti by emulation of perfect forms—the square and circle—and by the application of the rules of harmony that govern that of music. Both geometrical and musical forms are divine in origin and occur throughout the universe. Beauty, says Alberti, is the result of the correct observation and application of rules of proportion derived from Pythagoras' system of musical harmony. Beauty is the creation of a whole to which nothing can be added and from which nothing can be subtracted without the destruction of that whole. Our minds, understanding that perfection intuitively, respond to harmony and order, producing actions that will grace life as monuments grace a city.

The belief that good buildings can make a good life is highly debatable. What cannot be denied is that the application of reason to art was one of the most powerful forces in the Renaissance. This will emerge more clearly as we study painting.

New Developments in Painting

Our study of the Middle Ages demonstrated that painting and sculpture depended upon formulas and conventions for the presentation of visual equivalents of important ideas and beliefs. The makers of stained glass increased the size of significant persons and ignored any illusions of weight or volume in the representation of figures. The illuminators who made manuscript pages emphasized intense color, flat surface, complex linear patterns, and stylized gestures to create their pictures. Also, the size and location of figures were determined by their importance. Rarely do we feel that the rules for making, the formal conventions, are inappropriate to or detract from the information to be conveyed. In fifth-century Athens emphasis was placed on an ideal representation of the human body as the best means to commemorate or perpetuate important events and beliefs. The sculptors of the Royal Portal at Chartres subordinated the visible world to symmetry, pattern, flatness, and distortion to teach and inform viewers of Christian dogma. At times the rules and their results may seem strange to us, but it is the successful marriage of means to ends that makes great art and architecture. With the art of fifteenth-century Florence we meet a new set of rules, of conventions for making, that were arrived at experimentally through trial and error, as were the other conventions we have studied. Alberti wrote about painting, describing the rules to make appropriate pictures. Giorgio Vasari (1511–1574), who was among the first biographers of the artists and architects of the Renaissance, was also an important critic of the intentions and development of their art. Like Alberti, he praised artists for their return to, and successful conquest of, the representation of nature.

Giotto   Vasari tells us that in the fourteenth century it was Giotto, an Italian fresco painter, who looked at nature for the source of his art. Compare the Gothic painting (Color Plate IV) with *The Lamentation* (Color Plate V) by Giotto, one of the many paintings of Christ's life in the Arena Chapel in Padua. Giotto has challenged the rules that governed earlier paintings. In *The Lamentation* his observation of the world is limited to a few visual clues for the location of the scene, but it is clearly outdoors. The figures themselves, now simply draped, have substantial weight and volume. There is nothing to interfere with our perception of gestures that indicate real human emotion. The figures act in a place and take up space much as our own bodies would. In a sense we seem to share the space of the action rather than being separated from it. The surface of the wall is no longer flat but somewhat transparent.

Masaccio   Compare Giotto's scene with *The Tribute Money*, a painting by another Florentine, Tommaso di Ser Giovanni, called Masaccio (1401–1428?). Made about a hundred years after *The Lamentation*, this painting is also a *fresco*, part of the wall decorations in the Brancacci Chapel in Santa Maria delle Carmine in Florence (Color Plate VI). The story is from Christ's life as told in Matthew 17:24–27. A tax collec-

tor has approached Jesus, who then instructs Peter to catch a fish from the Sea of Galilee; in its mouth will be a coin sufficient for the tax to be paid. The action of the story is stretched out in the painting. What are the major differences between Masaccio's fresco and that of Giotto? Is there a greater illusion of space around the figures and in which the figures move? What role does the landscape play? Is it day or night? Are weather conditions important? What is important to conveying the action? The figures casting shadows that fall around each other, on faces, and on hands focus our attention. Where is the light source? Does light seem to come into the space of the painting from the sky, or does it seem to originate outside of the painting? What kind of people are the disciples? Do they have personalities, or are they simply twelve images who stand for the Twelve? What has happened to enable Masaccio to delineate so easily a world similar to the one we see?

Masaccio, it would seem, has transformed the wall plane into a transparent surface that provides the space in which to stage a dramatic event. We see into the space where men move, light falls from the sky, figures cast shadows, people have personalities and are, therefore, like us, like the visible world of experienced reality.

Brunelleschi was responsible for the development of linear *perspective*, a tool for the accurate translation of three-dimensional space onto the two-dimensional plane of paper, panel, or wall (Fig. 10-9). Masaccio,

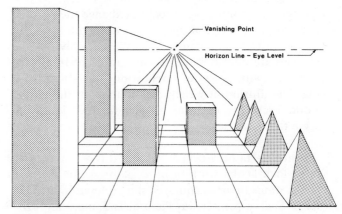

10–9   Simplified single-point perspective (after Brunelleschi).

learning from Giotto the importance of gesture and the feeling of weight, combined the two with his own ideas about shade and shadow, volume and location to create this dramatic scene. Obviously, Masaccio did not achieve this in one day (equally obviously he was not alone in his endeavors), but he gives us a scene that seems suddenly familiar to us. His work both transforms and presents a series of new conventions that we will see further explored and elaborated.

There is a close parallel between the development of perspective in painting and sculptural relief and the humanists' growing sense of the historical past. The fifteenth-century humanists were coming to understand the past as composed of a group of successive societies leading down to their own time. Increasingly they became aware of the differences between pagan Roman society and Christian Rome and of the changes that had occurred in thinking in the Middle Ages located between their own time and antiquity. In a sense they viewed history as a series of temporal planes corresponding to the spatial planes defined by the linear perspective. Just as the artist objectified space from the point of view of his eye, so the humanist defined the past in relationship to his own time. Similarly the humanists utilized this objectified time for their own purposes, in their case, the improvement of the present and the shaping of the future.

It is not enough, however, that we celebrate the conquest of illusion. To assume that this was the goal of Renaissance painting is to miss the point of this artistic development. Just as Brunelleschi and Alberti wanted to learn the principles of antique architecture in order to create new forms in response to new ideas, so perspective was a principle, a tool to enhance the purpose of Christian art. That purpose is to engage the viewer in the scene presented before him. We not only observe but also are moved by the event—an event in a place and time with powerful implications for our own being. The illusion of weight and volume, of the visible world itself, the creation of splendid individuals all serve this purpose.

Piero della Francesca   It is for this reason that we must look at the work of other painters, for the new conventions in art encouraged the exploration of these ideas. Such a painter was Piero della Francesca (1420–

1492). Born in southeastern Tuscany, he came to Florence as a painter's apprentice. When he left a few years later, he never returned but worked in the vicinity of his birth, Arezzo, Borgo San Sepolcro, and finally in Urbino, a small but wealthy mountain principality. We can see that the origins of his art lie in Masaccio's frescoes, but he gave to his painting a clarity and severe harmony that developed with his exploration of the principles of perspective and his use of bright, cool, clear colors.

Piero wrote a treatise in which he demonstrated the uses of perspective to delineate bodies and architectural forms. These he reduced to their most abstract geometrical components, seeing forms as variations on or combinations of spheres, cylinders, cones, cubes, and pyramids. We are reminded of Alberti's search for nature's perfect forms, and we can observe that Piero not only considered them but used this knowledge in the creation of his painting.

The frescoes *Discovery of the Wood from Which the True Cross Was Made* and *Meeting of Solomon and the Queen of Sheba*, from the *Legend of the True Cross* (c. 1453–1454) provide an example of Piero's work (Fig. 10-10). The two scenes are part of a series of frescoes that decorate the church of San Francesco in Arezzo, Italy. The story told is one in which events of the Old Testament and early Christianity are linked with Christ's story. In the first scene, on the left, the Queen of Sheba kneels before a wooden beam. She has foreknowledge that the beam will be used as the cross on which the Messiah will be crucified. On the right she is presented to Solomon, the great Jewish king, who is also Christ's ancestor. The scene on the right takes place in a *portico*, and the architecture with its Corinthian columns recalls Brunelleschi and Alberti. All the participants, presented in simplified "modern" dress, are arranged in orderly half-circles around Solomon and Sheba, who stand against a dark wall panel near the architectural and visual center of the space. The two figures nearest the viewer, a man (left) and woman (right) are turned away; their heads and faces are shown in profile. Then we see a man and woman in profile, and two figures almost full face. This arrangement of pairs of figures creates the half-circles and reinforces our sense of the depth of space of the portico. All the figures are substantial, weighty, three-dimensional

10-10 Piero della Francesca, "Discovery of the Wood from Which the True Cross was Made" and "Meeting of Solomon and the Queen of Sheba" from "Legend of the True Cross." (San Francesco, Arezzo—Alinari/Editorial Photocolor Archives)

forms. We can see shadows on faces, on the floor, and in the folds of drapery, but there is no strong sense of light coming from just one direction. Rather, light is fairly even and general.

The scene to the left takes place in a landscape. Here Piero uses the beam and a white horse seen from behind to carry our eyes back into space and create boundaries for the scene. But he also employs a half-circle of attendants to focus our attention on the queen. The procession, the trees, and the low hills are other devices that he uses to focus our attention. As in the portico scene, light appears to come from no specific direction; it is mostly an even, revealing light that is based on nature, but it is not natural light. What is the most pervasive quality or mood of these two scenes? Excitement, drama, serenity? Are the participants emotional; how do their faces and bodies reflect the mood? Of the work we have now seen, to what are these scenes comparable? Compare and contrast these figure groups with Masaccio's in *The Tribute Money.* How does the conquest of illusion serve as a means to

achieve the more effective presentation of different kinds of scenes?

Botticelli   Sandro Botticelli (1444–1510) was more interested in the expressive possibilities of a graceful and energetic line than in the structural problems of perspective. He had been apprenticed to an engraver, and from his experiences with those conventions came his reliance on draftsmanship. The favorite painter of the Medici family, Botticelli was very much interested in the ideas of humanism and Neoplatonism prevailing in the intellectual circles around Lorenzo. He was one of the first Florentine painters to represent subjects from classical mythology. Just as the humanists attempted to fuse Greco-Roman myths and ideas with Christian theology, Botticelli endowed his pagan subjects with a spirituality that derives from medieval painting and sculpture.

The large painting called *Primavera (Springtime)* or *The Realm of Venus* is an *allegory* of the rebirth of nature in spring under the power of love (Color Plate VII).

In the center stands Venus, who looks more like a madonna than a Greek love goddess. The fusion of the pagan goddess and the Christian saint would not have surprised the Neoplatonists, who believed that both could aid the soul in its ascent to God. Venus appears to give her blessing to the three Graces, who are dancing in a circle to her right. The rhythmical line for which Botticelli was so well known is nowhere more apparent than here. The folds of flowing drapery make one feel the movement of the dance. The seminude bodies are another classical inspiration—they could never have appeared in medieval art. Next to the Graces stands Mercury, raising his wand to the skies. To the viewer's right is Flora, in a dress abundantly covered with flowers, and another almost-nude nymph representing springtime, who is about to be seized by a young man personifying Zephyr, the wind. Above everyone flies the blindfolded Cupid with his bow and arrow. What about the setting of this painting? Although the flowers are exact copies of flowers that grow around Tuscany, Botticelli has certainly not portrayed a realistic natural setting. What kind of nature is he portraying, and what is he attempting to suggest by it? How would you characterize the colors? Make a schematic drawing to show how the *composition* works. Are the various elements of the painting held together in some way? Does the right side of the painting convey a different sort of feeling from that conveyed by the left side? How? Compare your reactions to this painting to your reactions to Piero della Francesca's paintings.

Primavera is the work that best states in visual terms the spirit of the Florentine Renaissance under Lorenzo de' Medici. Botticelli was inspired by a poem on the subject written by one of the Medici friends, Poliziano, and the painting decorated the Medici palace. It celebrates youth, beauty, and love with the same underlying melancholy that characterizes Lorenzo's own poems and carnival songs.

Lorenzo de' Medici's Carnivals and Carnival Songs

During the fifteenth century the city of Florence developed a tradition of outdoor public celebrations, feasts that probably had their intellectual origins in the pre-Christian pagan festivals celebrating the victory of spring over winter, the returning fertility of the earth. By the time of Lorenzo the Magnificent, two major carnivals occurred each year—a season of pre-Lenten revelry (which has its modern version in the Mardi Gras activities of New Orleans) and the *Calendimaggio*, which was an extended May Day celebration (from May 1 to June 24!).

The grandeur of Lorenzo's style of life earned him his nickname, "the Magnificent," and the carnivals received his strong encouragement because of his taste for opulence and probably also for political reasons. Carnivals kept the populace happy. Himself an accomplished poet and an ardent lover of music and display, he hired a musician from Flanders of international reputation, Heinrich Isaac, as his court composer and as tutor of his children.

Torchlight processions in which decorated wagons were pulled through the streets were the main feature of the carnivals. The wagons, or *carri*, were decorated by some of the best artists of the time in a manner similar to today's parade floats, and the themes of the decoration often represented stories from classical antiquity and popular legends. Lorenzo wrote carnival songs in Italian (many humanist poets wrote for an elite, in Latin), the most famous of which was "The Song of Bacchus," a poem written for a float depicting the triumph of Bacchus and Ariadne. According to a Greek myth Ariadne, a princess of Crete, ran off with her lover, Theseus of Athens. She was abandoned by him on an island but later rescued by Bacchus (Dionysus, the Greek god of love and wine), who fell in love with her and married her.

The usual themes associated with the "triumphs" depicted on the carnival floats were love, pleasure, and the enjoyment of life, but among them there was always a macabre "triumph of death," a terrifying float including men dressed as skeletons drawn by a team of black oxen. Thus during a part of the gaiety people were urged to repent—a Renaissance fascination with death amidst a proclamation of joy in life on earth is evident here. Even in Lorenzo's "Song of Bacchus," one can sense the urgent fear of time running out beneath the exhortation to love and pleasure. (The translation is by Mary Ann Witt.)

LORENZO DE' MEDICI

The Song of Bacchus

What a lovely time is youth,
    Yet how it slips away!
Be happy, if you will, today,
    Tomorrow is unsure.

Here are Bacchus and Ariadne,
    So fair, so deep in love,
Because time flies and cheats,
    They stay together happily.
These nymphs and other folk
    Are always merry and gay.
Be happy, if you will, today,
    Tomorrow is unsure.

These joyful little satyrs
    Enamoured of the nymphs,
Have for them in cave and wood
    Set a hundred traps.
Now, enflamed by Bacchus,
    They dance, they jump every way.
Be happy, if you will, today,
    Tomorrow is unsure.

The nymphs won't mind being caught,
    They're ripe for traps,
For only the rude and ungrateful
    Can guard against love.
Now mingling with one another,
    They pipe and sing alway.
Be happy, if you will, today,
    Tomorrow is unsure.

Here comes a big load, riding an ass.
    It's Silenus,
Old and drunk and glad,
    By now he's full of flesh and years.
He can't stand straight,
    But he'll laugh and play.
Be happy, if you will, today,
    Tomorrow is unsure.

Here comes Midas after them:
    Whatever he touches turns to gold.
What good does treasure do a man
    If it can't bring him joy?
And what contentment can Midas feel
    Who's thirsty forever, night and day?
Be happy, if you will, today,
    Tomorrow is unsure.

Everyone: open wide your ears!
    Let no one feed on tomorrow;
Men and women, young and old,
    Be happy today, each one!
Banish every sad thought
    But let the festival stay.
Be happy, if you will, today,
    Tomorrow is unsure.

Sweet ladies and young lovers, come,
    Long live Bacchus and long live love!
Let everyone play and dance and sing,
    And fill your hearts with joy.
Do not toil and do not grieve,
    What's to be will come anyway.
Be happy, if you will, today,
    Tomorrow is unsure.

Although we are uncertain about the identity of the composer of the music for "The Song of Bacchus," it is likely that Isaac himself composed this carnival song. Not only was he in the employ of Lorenzo during the last years of the patron's life (the most likely time for the creation of this work), but also the music reflects a mastery of technique that indicates the hand of a professional composer. The lilting melody and smooth-flowing harmonies reflect the best style of Italian secular music of the late fifteenth century.

The Song of Bacchus

QUESTIONS

1. How does the poet use characters from classical mythology to convey a message for the present?
2. Describe the *tone* of this poem and its music. How is a sense of the fear of death blended with that of joy in life?
3. Contrast the attitude expressed here with the medieval Christian doctrine that patient suffering in this life is necessary in order to achieve happiness in the afterlife.
4. Compare the feeling conveyed by this song with that conveyed by Botticelli's *Primavera.*

Music for the Death of Lorenzo

During the same year that Columbus made his first voyage to the New World, Lorenzo de' Medici died. He had been the ideal Renaissance prince: a consummate diplomat, intellectual leader, connoisseur and patron of the arts. His loss was felt deeply and personally by those poets and musicians who knew and worked for him and also loved and respected him.

One of the most beautiful and moving musical compositions written in the last years of the fifteenth century, the beginning of the High Renaissance in music, was Heinrich Isaac's *threnody*, a dirge or funeral song, in the Italian style on Angelo Poliziano's Latin verse lamenting the death of Lorenzo.

ANGELO POLIZIANO

Quis Dabit Capiti

Quis dabit capiti meo aquam?
Quis oculis meis fontem
    lachrimarum dabit?
Ut nocte fleam,
Ut luce fleam?

Sic turtur viduus solet,
Sic cygnus moriens solet,
Sic luscinia conqueri.
Heu miser, miser,
O dolor, dolor!

Laurus impetu fulminis
Illa illa jacet subito,
Laurus omnium celebris
Musarum choris,
Nympharum choris.

Sub cuius patula coma
Et Phebi lira blandius
Insonat et vox blandius,
Nunc muta omnia,
Nunc surda omnia.

Who will give my head water?
Who will give my eyes
    a fountain of tears?
That I may weep by night,
That I may weep by day?

Thus the lonely turtle-dove mourned,
Thus the dying swan,
Thus the nightingale.
Ah wretched, wretched me,
Oh grief, oh grief.

The laurel [Lorenzo] lies there,
Lies there, struck suddenly by a thunderbolt,
The laurel honored by the choir
Of all the Muses,
And all the nymphs.

Beneath whose spreading branches
The lyre of Phoebus more charmingly
Sounds and his voice more sweetly sings.
Now all is silent,
Now all is deaf.

Isaac's genius and sensitivity created a *motet* (a *polyphonic* composition for unaccompanied chorus based on a Latin sacred text) of moving solemnity, a four-voice composition scored in a low register to dramatize its function as a dirge. An intimate bond between word and tone was the goal of Renaissance composers working in the company of the Italian humanists, and Isaac masterfully sculpted his sounds in this musical elegy.

To make the opening statement incisive, to be certain the listener could understand every word, Isaac declaimed the text of the beginning syllabically in slow-moving chords, at first in hollow *open fifths*, all voices enunciating the syllables at the same time—"Who will give my head ..." Then, as the singers reach the word "water," the chords dissolve into flowing polyphonic lines, a musical gesture symbolizing the text being set.

The Medicis' love of pageantry is represented in this mural, whose subject is only ostensibly religious. The "king" riding the white horse is Lorenzo; behind him are Piero and the elderly Cosimo, who is riding a donkey. Note the "black moor" groom to the left of Cosimo.

He begins the second phrase in like manner but sets the "fountain of tears" with a base of three chordal notes (the solid base of an actual fountain comes to mind) over which, or out of which, flows a curving, almost liquid, soprano melodic line.

Harmonic modulation, as we know it today, was not a part of the composer's art in the late fifteenth century; but Renaissance *chromaticism*, the use of accidentals (flats and sharps) to displace the music slightly out of the regular *tonal* order of the style, was an expressive device reserved for moments of intense emotion. Isaac's harmonic progression from A to F to C and then B-flat strains and wrings the phrase *Sic cygnus moriens solet* ("Thus [mourns] the dying swan").

Although the motet begins with four vocal parts, the second section of the work beginning *Laurus impetu fulminis* ("The laurel, struck [suddenly] by a thunderbolt") uses only three vocal parts. However, in the original Renaissance choirbook in which this work is notated, a space with no notes is set aside in which is written *Laurus tacet* ("The Laurel is silent"). Lorenzo's absence, therefore, was painted graphically in music by a device detectable primarily by the composer and the singers but also by those who were trained and skilled in detecting the subtleties of Renaissance tone painting. Four-voice music and three-voice music have distinctive qualities that are identifiable aurally, and the

absence of a part could be felt by those in attendance who heard the change in *texture* and comprehended the meaning of the words.

At the same time that the texture of the piece drops from four to three parts, the lowest voice is given a part to sing whose words are neither the same as those being sung by the other singers nor from the text of Poliziano's poem. Instead, Isaac composed an insertion referring to the requiem service of the Church, *Et requiescamus in pace* ("And let us rest in peace"). The composer took this phrase, set it to a short bass melody, and slowly repeated it over and over as an *ostinato*, one step lower each time it enters—a certain symbolic representation of Lorenzo descending step by step into the grave. The emotion of the event, the words, and the music are focused and concentrated into a dramatic setting of intense grief.

When, in the third and final section of the motet, the fourth voice reenters, it is no longer a regular part but a single, unmoving note (which is held for eighteen measures in the modern edition), quite likely an aural *image* of death in a tomb. When finally this note is given a rest (literally a rest in the music), the other three parts sing of Phoebus Apollo's sweet-sounding voice, a godly song whose magic, according to Greek mythology, could give peace and healing to those in the underworld. Then, "Now all is silent, Now all is deaf," and the motet ends.[1]

----

[1] Two excellent, but different, recordings of Isaac's motet are available: *Ceremonial Music of the Renaissance* (Das alte Werk, SAWT 9524-B) and *Fifteenth-Century Netherlands Masters* (Decca DL 79413). The former employs chorus and antique instruments; the latter performs the work with voices only.

QUESTIONS

1. In what ways are the polyphonic carnival song and the funeral motet more or less expressive than the monophonic *Play of Daniel* or the troubadour song *Be m'an perdut?*
2. How might the change in society with an emerging middle class affect the role of the composer?
3. Scientific advances of the Renaissance had an effect on music. What would the invention of printing do for composers? How might this affect the music they wrote?

Renaissance man experienced his world passionately, and he proclaimed himself master of all he could touch, taste, see, and hear. Lorenzo (and Isaac?) expressed the joys of youth in *Quant'è bella giovinezza*, while Poliziano and Isaac voiced the bitterness of death in *Quis dabit capiti meo aquam*. But the latter did not portray the fear of judgment and punishment—concepts ever present in the thoughts of medieval man. It was the sadness of loss of life, of parting from the pleasures of this world that stirred the Renaissance man's soul to anguish. One can see, therefore, that both these compositions, as unlike as a carnival song and a dirge might seem at first glance, are similar in their philosophic basis. They both celebrate the joys of life and lament the end that comes all too quickly.

11

THE END OF THE FLORENTINE RENAISSANCE: MACHIAVELLI, LEONARDO, AND MICHELANGELO

The death of Lorenzo the Magnificent in 1492 came in a very troubled time not only for Florence but for the whole of Italy (see map). In 1495 the French invaded Italy, sweeping the length of the peninsula with their powerful armies. This was only the first of a whole series of foreign invasions over the next fifty years, during which time Italy became the battleground between the two rising national monarchies, France and Spain. The Medici were toppled from power with the arrival of the French in 1495, and a republic under French rule was established. But the waning of French influence over Italy in the following decade spelled the doom of the new regime, and the Medici returned to power in 1512. Except for a brief three-year interruption (1527–1530), they were to remain rulers of Tuscany down to the eighteenth century.

Already by Lorenzo's last years, Florence was sharing its position of cul-

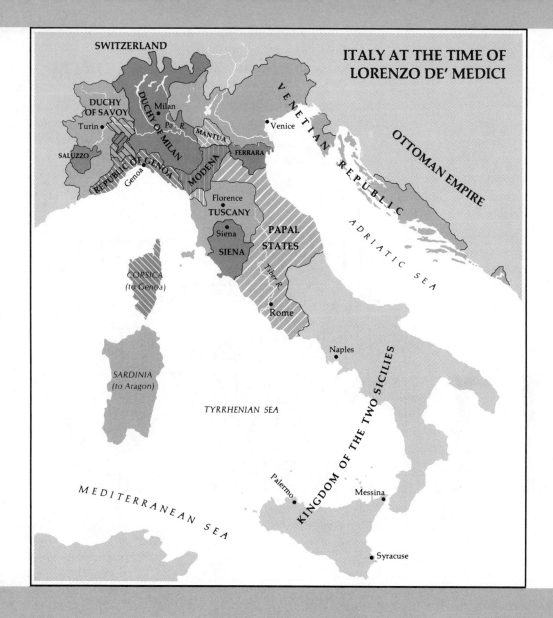

ITALY AT THE TIME OF LORENZO DE' MEDICI

tural dominance with Rome. From the early decades of the sixteenth century, moreover, northern European countries began to rival Italy's position of cultural leadership. Yet in this very period, Florence still managed to produce three great men, Niccolò Machiavelli (1469–1527), Leonardo da Vinci (1452–1519), and Michelangelo Buonarotti (1475–1564).

Machiavelli

The ease with which the Italians succumbed to Spanish and French arms shocked Italian thinkers and caused them to seek explanations. Many focused on the chaotic political structure of the peninsula as the major factor in Italian weakness. This atmosphere of questioning produced one of the greatest political theorists of all time, the Florentine Niccolò Machiavelli. Born in Florence in 1469, Machiavelli rose to a position of prominence in the republican government established in the city after 1495. Closely associated with that regime, Machiavelli fell into disfavor after the reestablishment of Medici power in 1512. He spent most of the last fifteen years of his life as a private citizen, composing his works on history and political theory.

At heart a republican, Machiavelli faced squarely the problem that confronts any political thinker, the conflict between liberty and order. To what extent can individuals be given freedom without disrupting authority? Although he would like to have seen Florence and other Italian states republican, he recognized that, given the corruption of Italian society, only a strong ruler was capable of establishing order; until order had been established, there was no hope of reforming the people to make them capable of self-government. He realized the risk: the kind of ruler ruthless enough to establish order was not likely to be the kind of prince willing to train the people in self-government. But in a peninsula divided into fifty to a hundred power centers, a prey to foreign invasions, strong authority had priority. Thus, although raised in the tradition of Florentine civic humanism derived from Bruni, Machiavelli gave first place to political realities.

Machiavelli's most famous work, *The Prince*, written in 1513, was designed to give lessons in statecraft to a prince with an eye to creating an authority capable of driving out the invaders and bringing peace to Italy. Although Machiavelli appeals to the selfish desire of the prince for power, the author's own motives are essentially altruistic. *The Prince* is intended to be a revolutionary "mirror of the prince," a medieval form of literature designed to instruct the prince on how to be a good ruler. However, whereas the traditional mirror of the prince endeavored to make the prince conform to common principles of Christian morality in his rule, the thesis of *The Prince* is that the morality of the successful ruler is unlike that of the private citizen. Indeed, the conduct required of a prince would frequently be reprehensible if that of a private individual. In Chapter 15 of *The Prince*, translated by Ninian Hill Thompson, Machiavelli explains how the prince

should *appear* to act, exploiting accepted forms of conduct for the advancement and protection of his own power:

MACHIAVELLI

The Prince

Of the qualities in respect of which men, and most of all Princes, are praised or blamed

It now remains for us to consider what ought to be the conduct and bearing of a Prince in relation to his subjects and friends. And since I know that many have written on this subject, I fear it may be thought presumptuous in me to write of it also; the more so, because in my treatment of it I depart widely from the views that others have taken.

But since it is my object to write what shall be useful to whosoever understands it, it seems to me better to follow the real truth of things than an imaginary view of them. For many Republics and Princedoms have been imagined that were never seen or known. It is essential, therefore, for a Prince who would maintain his position, to have learned how to be other than good, and to use or not to use his goodness as necessity requires.

Laying aside, therefore, all fanciful notions concerning a Prince, and considering those only that are true, I say that all men when they are spoken of, and Princes more than others from their being set so high, are noted for certain of those qualities which attach either praise or blame. Thus one is accounted liberal, another miserly (which word I use, rather than *avaricious*, to denote the man who is too sparing of what is his own, *avarice* being the disposition to take wrongfully what is another's); one is generous, another greedy; one cruel, another tender-hearted; one is faithless, another true to his word; one effeminate and cowardly, another high-spirited and courageous; one is courteous, another haughty; one lewd, another chaste; one upright, another crafty; one firm, another facile; one grave, another frivolous; one devout, another unbelieving; and the like. Every one, I know, will admit that it would be most laudable for a Prince to be endowed with all of the above qualities that are reckoned good; but since it is impossible for him to possess or constantly practise them all, the conditions of human nature not allowing it, he must be discreet enough to know how to avoid the reproach of those vices that would deprive him of his government, and, if possible, be on his guard also against those which might not deprive him of it; though if he cannot wholly restrain himself, he may with less scruple indulge in the latter. But he need never hesitate to incur the reproach of those vices without which his authority can hardly be preserved; for if he well consider the whole matter, he will find that there may be a line of conduct having the appearance of virtue, to follow which would be his ruin, and that there may be another course having the appearance of vice, by following which his safety and well-being are secured.

QUESTIONS

1. How would Machiavelli judge Bruni's *Oration*?
2. Do you consider Machiavelli's advice immoral or merely practical?

To critics who found this advice shocking and abhorrent, Machiavelli retorted that in the long run the ruthless government of his prince was less cruel and more humane than that of the rule of a kind and Christian prince that would invite rebellion and the well-known evils associated with anarchy. While publicly denounced throughout Europe, Machiavelli's book provided unacknowledged guidance to generations of princes and presidents for centuries to come.

In Machiavelli's view the state was not a product of undirected growth of authority; rather, it was a work of art, the creation of the prince who skillfully imposed a form of political order on the people, who served as the matter for his work. This kind of imagery indeed reflects the Renaissance preoccupation with defining the nature of the artist and his activity. It was in this period that people first began to take the word *artist* seriously and to look on the artist with respect.

The Renaissance Artist Who is an artist? Is he a maker, a thinker, a craftsman, a technician, a manipulator of emotions, a teacher? Is he a worldly, extroverted, confident, sophisticated personality or lonely, introverted, filled with self-doubt and scorn? These questions were asked by writers and artists in the Renaissance, and it is to them that we owe concepts of the artist and architect, as well as the inclusion of these arts in the "fine" or "liberal" as opposed to the mechanical arts. Not only theory but also the works of the artists themselves produced these ideas. In the contrasts between two of the greatest figures of Italian Renaissance art, we find two very different images of the artist.

Leonardo da Vinci

Both Leonardo and Michelangelo were Florentine, near contemporaries, and undeniable geniuses. Leonardo was splendidly handsome; Michelangelo was at times obsessed with his ugliness. When Leonardo offered his services to the duke of Milan, he gave primacy to his qualifications as a military and hydraulic engineer, architect, and sculptor, mentioning painting last. When Pope Julius II commanded Michelangelo to paint the frescoes on the ceiling of the Sistine Chapel (in the Vatican Palace), he replied that he was not a painter but a sculptor. Nevertheless, he fulfilled the commission and later became noted not only for his genius in painting and sculpture, but also in architecture. Both men seem to possess enormous ego and incredible versatility. In both we find characteristics that have contributed to our idea of the "Renaissance man"—a person of broad learning and skill. The complex nature of the accomplishments of both men makes their work difficult to confine to any generalizations; therefore, we will try only to show in a few examples how each contributed to the Renaissance.

Although Leonardo viewed painting as the least of his talents, until recently we knew him principally as painter and courtier. Now, since the discovery and publication of his notes and drawings, begun in the late nineteenth century, we can call him a scientist with equal correctness. Perhaps, above all, he was an investigator of nature through observation and practice. He was an architect, engineer, botanist, and musician; he studied hydraulics, geology, and human anatomy. The pages of his notebooks reveal a man obsessed with nature's beauty, power, and functional complexity. He sought answers to his questions neither in the Church nor in antiquity but in nature—that which was observable—and in the mind—that which asked and imagined. He studied the motion of water to capture its power to operate engines, but his drawings also reveal his respect for its awesome natural power in a flood or storm. He dissected bodies to understand human anatomy, which then became the source for the mighty bodies in a drawing or painting. But muscles were abstracted into the ropes of levers and pulleys (Fig. 11-1). He drew the fetus in the womb and anticipated Harvey's discovery of the circulation of the blood. His botanical drawings created a style for scientific illustration, and the plants reappear, lovingly delineated in his pictures. It is as if Leonardo could not satisfy a longing to know, to understand the principles of life—birth, transformation, change, and decay operating in the natural world. It is as if what he saw constantly assailed him with its incredible diversity, beauty, simplicity, and ugliness; and he sought rationally to control, order, and understand the vast potentialities open to human experience. He *attended* to *his* world; he wanted nothing to escape that questing, loving eye.

In his lifetime Leonardo finished few paintings. The *Mona Lisa* (or *La Gioconda*), a portrait of the enigmatic lady of the sublime smile, is perhaps the most familiar. Even more enigmatic to many is *The Madonna of the Rocks* (1483) in the Louvre—a soft, slightly mist-filled representation of the Virgin with the Christ Child, who, supported by an angel, blesses the kneeling John the Baptist presented by the Virgin (Color Plate VIII).

The Madonna of the Rocks Set in a curious cavelike opening on a ledge in a rocky landscape, the four figures interact with each other; yet the viewer is hard pressed to define the interaction. The light is soft and vague, the landscape shadowy and moist. The edges of the figures, their drapery, and their expressions lack clear definition. We do not doubt their presence in space, for the figures have a weight and volume that originated with Masaccio; yet there is a sense of fragility that is shared with Botticelli's *Primavera*. Nor do these figures possess Piero's intense abstraction—we are not sure what to look at in them. We seem forced by gesture and glance to look from face to face. The landscape itself is ambivalent, rocky, yet filled with beautiful plants and flowers. Light penetrates from behind

11–1 Leonardo da Vinci, drawing: "Anatomy of a shoulder, transformation into levers." (Royal Library, Windsor Castle, copyright reserved)

and falls in the foreground. Where are we? Precisely what do we see? Academically we know the picture may deal with the doctrine of the virgin birth of Christ, but that knowledge does not begin to explain the picture. Rather it is almost a sacred conversation—a moment suspended in time that alludes to events years hence. Or is time, in a chronological sense, of any consequence? This is a picture rich in ambivalences. Its brilliant *illusionism* is dependent on the experienced world, and on a technical mastery of the creation of subtle nuances of shade and shadow that was one of Leonardo's great accomplishments. Similarly, it is a knowledge of anatomy, the study of faces and gestures, of falling light, of air suffused with light that makes the vision possible. But technical expertise cannot account for the experience of the picture—a profound religious silence—where children who are touchingly childlike imitate the roles of their adulthood, and a mother's protective gesture reaches all of us. This splendid vision is so rich in nuance and idea that it is ever fresh to the eye and imagination. This is the end attained by the means that the fifteenth-century Florentines made possible—an end so filled with resonances that we are still compelled to discuss the picture and we struggle to know the painter's mind.

The Madonna of the Rocks is one of the few almost finished paintings by Leonardo. It is because of such a painting as this that we study the complex, unfinished *Adoration of the Magi* or the ruined *Last Supper* hoping to reconstruct not just the means but also the purpose of an artist who presents both a final statement and a vision of potentiality, of transformation. The vision is complete by Alberti's definition, but also ever ready, like nature itself, to provide a new experience, to stimulate the imagination with fresh questions. It is as if reason, finally, is not enough. One can control the will, guide intuition, define problems, comprehend mathematical harmonies, and draw the structure of the body; but one cannot determine the source of the life force or define the power of experience. Nor can one rule the imagination as it seeks knowledge of the work through the world. In this capacity, man is Godlike and transcendent, free of everything except death.

Leonardo's Comparison of the Arts   In a collection of writings called *The Comparison* (*Il Paragone*, translated here by Mary Ann Witt), Leonardo argues for the acceptance of art as a science and discusses the relations between painting and other arts—poetry, music, and sculpture. Probably intended as an introduction to his treatise on painting, this work is clearly a defense of painting as the greatest of all the arts. It is also one of the first recorded statements by a painter on his art.

LEONARDO DA VINCI

The Comparison

WHICH SCIENCE IS MOST USEFUL, AND IN WHAT DOES ITS USEFULNESS CONSIST?

The science whose fruit communicates most is the most useful and, by contrast, the one which communicates least is the least useful. The result of painting can be communicated to all generations of the universe because it is subject to the sense of vision. What comes through the ear to our understanding does not pass in the same way as what comes through the eye, and painting does not need interpreters for various languages as literature does: it gives immediate satisfaction to human beings, just as things produced by nature do. It satisfies not only humans, but other animals, as was manifested by a painting, representing a father, which infants still in their swaddling clothes caressed, together with dogs and cats of the same house—a wonderful sight.

Painting represents the works of nature to our understanding more truly and more accurately than do words or literature, but literature represents words to the understanding more truthfully than does painting. But we can say that the science which represents the works of nature is more admirable than one which represents the works of the worker, that is the words of men, as in poetry and the like, which pass through the human tongue.

OF THE EYE

The eye, in which the beauty of the world is reflected, is of such excellence that whoever consents to its loss deprives himself of the representation of all the works of nature. Because of the sight of these the soul is content to stay in the prison of the body, for through the eyes nature in all its variety manifests itself to the soul. . . .

Certainly there is no one who would not rather lose the senses of hearing and smell rather than that of sight. In losing hearing, one loses knowledge based on words, but not the beauty of the world. . . .

HOW PAINTING IS THE GREATEST OF ALL HUMAN WORKS

The eye, which is called the window of the soul, is the principal means by which the understanding can most abundantly and magnificently contemplate the infinite works of nature. The ear is second, for it acquires its worth by hearing what the eye has seen. If you historians, poets, or mathematicians had never seen things with your eyes, you would represent them badly in your writing. And if you, poet, tell a story by painting with your pen, the painter with his brush can tell it so that it will be more easily understood and give more complete satisfaction. And if you call painting mute poetry, the painter may call poetry blind painting. . . .

THE DIFFERENCE BETWEEN PAINTING AND SCULPTURE

I do not find any difference between painting and sculpture other than the fact that the sculptor does his work with more physical labor and the painter does his work with more mental labor. This can be proved, for the sculptor has to hammer with the strength of his arms in order to chip away the excess from the block of marble or other stone in which his sculpture is potentially contained. This involves very mechanical exertion often accompanied by a great amount of sweat mixed with dust which makes him very dirty. His face becomes so whitened with marble dust that he looks like a baker, he becomes covered with little chips which make it seem that snow has fallen on him, and his dwelling becomes soiled and messy. The painter, by contrast (and here we are speaking of the foremost painters and sculptors) sits with the greatest ease before his work, well dressed and moving his light pen with its lovely colors. His dwelling is clean and full of delightful pictures, sometimes musicians or readers of beautiful works accompany him, and he can hear them with great pleasure without being bothered by hammering and other noises.

WHY MUSIC SHOULD BE CALLED THE YOUNGER SISTER OF PAINTING

Music can only be called the sister of painting, for it depends on the sense of hearing, a sense inferior to sight. Its harmony is created by the union of proportioned parts, produced simultaneously, constrained to be born and to die in one or several harmonic chords. . . .

But painting is greater than music because it does not die immediately after it is created, as does unfortunate music. On the contrary, it remains, and appears to be alive, though in fact it is only a flat surface. O wonderful science, which can preserve the fleeting beauties of mortals and give them greater permanence than the works of nature, which are continuously changing with time, which leads them into inevitable old age.

The science of painting is comparable to Divine Nature, as individual paintings are to the creations of nature, and for this it is adored.

COMMENTS AND QUESTIONS

1. Leonardo was one of the first to argue that painting belonged with the humanities, or liberal arts, rather than with crafts, or manual arts, which was its status in the Middle Ages. Why does he call it a science and what arguments does he use to show that it is "scientific"?
2. How does he "prove" that painting is an art form superior to poetry, music, and sculpture? Which arguments are convincing to you, and which are not? What would you say in defense of each of the other arts to refute his ideas?
3. What seem to be his underlying beliefs about the nature of painting and the interrelationship of the arts?
4. How does Leonardo's concept of the artist's role resemble and/or differ from our idea about it today?

Leonardo's comments on his art raise some problems that are still with us. What is it in the combination of nature, imagination, skill, and communication that creates a successful or a great painting or, for that matter, any work of art? How does a work of art evoke resonance and sympathy in the viewer? We may agree that a particular painting moves us, yet not on why that happens. With Masaccio's paintings, it may be the still drama, enacted in a space that we share. Piero della Francesca certainly presents clarified images, harmonized in a world that he has made both more abstract and orderly. Botticelli speaks to our sensitivities with delicate color and linear harmonies. The powerful visual experience evoked by *The Madonna of the Rocks* is more difficult to define precisely. Leonardo's predecessors and peers reinstated the nude, the portrait, and the landscape; moreover, they created conventions of form and technique to achieve the presentation of Christian and pagan themes for personal edification. The possibilities for the artist must have seemed unlimited to them, maybe frightening in their limitlessness. Perhaps, in Leonardo's mind, it was the limits imposed by sculpture that made this art seem inferior, yet it was his greatest peer, Michelangelo, who defined limits so wide and so demanding that they changed the course of sculpture.

Michelangelo

In contrast to Leonardo, the handsome, graceful courtier with polished manners and mellifluous voice, Michelangelo seems like a difficult child. He was secretive, rude, dirty, and offensive. He wrote sonnets that detail the anguish generated by his love of the beautiful human body and his guilt over that love. Leonardo passionately embraced nature, while Michelangelo seems to have embraced his own genius, then God, as the path to immortality (both concerns far removed from Leonardo's elevation of the artist to the status of the gentleman). But both artists shared the power to imagine, make, and move. Both used nature—the visible world—but they transformed it, filling the objects made with immediate and universal meaning.

The squares of Florence were decorated by some of the city's great sculptors. The Loggia dei Lanzi, a great open porch to the right of the Palazzo Vecchio, is still filled with sculpture. To the left is the Neptune fountain, whose splashing water invigorates the humid summer air. Directly in front, on the raised terrace before the Palazzo is a copy of Michelangelo's *David* (the original was moved inside a museum in 1873). Light is intense in the square, and the high walls and tower of the Palazzo Vecchio intensify the experience. The figure silently commands the busy space and challenges your passage into the palace.

The *David* is marble, over thirteen feet tall (Fig. 11-2). The figure is completely nude; the limbs and torso, now aged by rain and sun, once had a smoothness that remains only on the surface of the face. Never painted or decorated, unlike the statuary of former times, its first impact is of intractable stone formed into a superhuman figure. But what is the boy like? The *Kritios Boy* (Fig. 2-8) and *The Spearbearer* (Fig. 2-12) are obvious idealizations of the human figure. How is David different from these two? Compare his face with that of Augustus and with a prophet from the doors at Chartres. Is this David an idealization of youth? His face is not symmetrical, the hands are enormous, and the arms and legs are too long. The body is awkward, like that of a tough youth, streetwise and confident. The brooding

11–2 Michelangelo, "David." (Academy, Florence—Alinari/ Editorial Photocolor Archives)

face is reticent but filled with a fierce courage. The body turns, a knee flexed; does the boy search the horizon for Goliath? The muscles of the neck and torso are tense, standing forth under the skin. The veins in arms, elbows, and hands rise to enliven the surface of the skin. The toes on one foot grasp the ground, while the toes of the other play over the rocky ledge. Has the stone been thrown, or does it lie in his curved fingers? Does he ready the sling, or does it lie on his shoulder, no longer useful, but used?

If you are unable to decide the precise moment or motivation, you have begun to experience the *David*—an experience deriving its power from ambiguity. He is splendidly beautiful without being idealized. The torso and limbs flow into his pose with ease and grace, yet show the tension of movement. He is youthful but confident, brooding but able to act. His face has an intellectual intensity, and his body is its physical complement. Over all lies a feeling of potential—to make, do, dream, and be—to live in the world, to challenge with mind and body the limits of our human nature. That is the enemy—not the giant Goliath but the struggle between intellect and will, self-interest and unselfishness, love and hate.

11–3 Michelangelo, "Captive Slave." Louvre, Paris. (© ARCH. PHOT. PARIS/S.P.A.D.E.M., 1980)

The *David* was placed before the entrance to the Florentine city hall in 1504, during the restoration of the Republic, as a visible sign of courage and purpose—qualities that had made the Republic possible. After the ascendancy of the Medici, it might have been a reminder of what had been and might be again. The shepherd boy became king, only to be destroyed by his pride.

Michelangelo populated Florence and Rome with giants like this one. He loved the stone that was his medium and hated the demands that it made. In his sonnets he writes of the conflict between his art with its glorification of the human body and his personal quest for the salvation of his soul, a quest that he felt his art contradicted. The great commissions produced in the sixty years after the *David* reflect stages not only in his art but also in the bent of his mind. There were the great papal commissions like the unfinished tomb for Julius II and the frescoes for the Sistine Chapel ceiling (1508–1512) and *The Last Judgment* (1536–1541) behind its high altar. Although he became the architect for the new Saint Peter's, redesigned the Capitoline Hill, and executed other architectural and painted commissions, his greatest vehicle for expression was the human body. In some figures he was able to attain a classicism almost Greek (Color Plate IX). In other figures, like the unfinished *Captive* (1527–28), whose body is still contained in the block, the imperfect stone seems expressive of those faults that must fall away if man is to become good and filled with grace (Fig. 11-3).

There was no sculptural or artistic convention of any kind that Michelangelo did not turn to his use. He was capable of making architecture as responsive as stone (Fig. 11-4), straining scale, distorting the body to carry the weight of meaning. The power of his art, like Leonardo's, seems to lie in the strength of the idea and the appropriation of form sufficient to give it visual realization.

In his unfinished works, like those of Leonardo, we sense the skill needed to manipulate the medium and the potential of the object for interpretations that reach beyond the accepted meaning. The bust of Brutus (the assassin of Julius Caesar), although made after 1537 (thus after the final demise of the Republic and return of the Medici to power), seems to carry on the spirit of republican Florence (Fig. 11-5). The head and face are

11–4 Michelangelo, Laurentian Library, Florence. (Alinari/ Editorial Photocolor Archives)

unfinished, the drape completed by one of Michelangelo's assistants. Compare it with similar works that we have seen. The ridges left by the chisel do not detract from the strong, heavy face. The folds of flesh that extend from the nostrils to the small but sensuous mouth, as well as the hollows of the cheeks, give the face a tension and purpose that come with age. The deep hollows of the simplified eyes hold shadow; they contrast with the broad ridge of the nose. This face could be that of any man with courage who has known fear, with purpose who has known discouragement. He is neither the purely detached imperial Augustus (Fig. 5-2) nor the political Arringatore (Fig. 5-1). He asks questions and seeks answers. He loves life but knows that death will come. He wants salvation but knows that it comes from sacrifice. Our responses to this face are varied, rich, and resonant. In it are recorded the marks of life and the need for meaning.

By the mid-sixteenth century, the search for meaning in human life had become problematic. Leonardo sought meaning in nature, Michelangelo in intense Christianity. Neither vision was to prove completely satisfactory; the struggle between them precipitated the changes in Italy and Europe that culminated in the crisis of belief—both in humanism and in Christianity.

11–5 Michelangelo, "Brutus." (Alinari/Editorial Photocolor Archives)

12 NORTHERN HUMANISM AND THE PROTESTANT REFORMATION

By 1500 humanism had northern European adherents. Generally speaking, northern humanism differed from the Italian variety in directing its attention to the ancient texts of the Christian religion rather than to the writings of Roman and Greek antiquity. Humanist philological techniques developed in preparing editions of Cicero, Plato, and others were now applied to editing the Bible and the writings of the Latin and Greek Church Fathers. Thus, the humanists in the north were responsible for directing the attention of learned men to the early history of Christianity and the sources of the Christian faith.

Erasmus

The leading northern humanist and doubtless the most important humanist of his generation was Desiderius Erasmus (1463–1536). Though born in the Low Countries, Erasmus lived most of his mature life in France, England, and Switzerland. Like his Italian humanist predecessors, he believed that ethics were more important than elaborate systems of philosophy and theology. Coupled with his extremely critical attitude toward current Church abuses, this insistence on the primacy of moral action became a powerful weapon for the reform of Christian life.

In Erasmus' opinion, the Church had overemphasized rituals and outward manifestations of piety. It had made too sharp a distinction between the status of a cleric and that of a layman. The central focus of Christianity should be on the spirit, on the cultivation of deep religious feeling rather than depending on its ceremonies. While not attacking the principle of monasticism as evil, he nevertheless maintained that the lay life, doing God's work in the world, was a more effective way of serving Christ than was that of the cloistered monk. Moreover, laymen, too, needed and had the right to read and discuss the sources of their faith. In short, as Erasmus himself said at one point: "The world has become my monastery."

Like the texts of pagan antiquity, those of Christian antiquity were highly defective. Erasmus chose as his first task the preparation of a new edition of the Greek New Testament with Latin translation, which he published in 1516. It was a courageous task to undertake. Over a thousand years of Christian scholarship had been based on the Vulgate, composed of early translations of the books of the Bible; now Erasmus showed that some of the key passages on which countless interpretations had been made were not actually in the Greek original or were mistranslated. In the same year he published his nine-volume edition of the works of Saint Jerome. This was the first humanist edition of the complete works of a Church Father, but many were to follow.

Erasmus was the first great European writer to make use of an important invention, the printing press. Although printing had been developed before his time—the Gutenberg Bible first appeared in 1455—the earlier books were primarily luxury items. Erasmus distributed his editions and his polemical pamphlets throughout Europe. Writing in Latin, he could be read by educated people in all countries; thus, he helped to create a culture of the printed word that has since dominated Western intellectual life.

Erasmus firmly believed that if all the sources of Christian truth could be published in an accurate form, the eloquence of the words, as they were originally written under the inspiration of the Holy Spirit, could not fail to move men to become better Christians. The goal of Erasmus' Christian scholarship was, therefore, to reform both individual Christians and the Church itself. He did not attack the dogma of the Church, but he did attack the effort of theologians to elaborate on the dogma and to claim certainty for their deductions. For him there were only a few absolutely certain principles in the Bible, and these were all men needed to believe in order to be saved. What was important for him was that Christian belief be reflected in one's life. True Christians acted like Christians. This was Erasmus' "philosophy of Christ" in essence. Accordingly, he was exceedingly tolerant of differing views of theology but severely critical of evil conduct.

The *Colloquies* were originally conceived by Erasmus as a device to teach children the art of Latin conversation, but he soon realized that the dialogue form could be an effective means for teaching his reform program. The colloquy printed below, "The Abbot and the Learned Woman," (translation by Mary Ann Witt) is illustrative of Erasmus' bias. The abbot has formally given himself to a religious life, yet in fact lives a worldly existence. The middle-class woman lives in the world but according to the inner guidance of reason and moral understanding. It is clear that Erasmus believed that using one's mind in humanistic study could lead to both a richer and more truly Christian life than would life in a monastery. And, against the common opinion of the day, he states here that women may benefit from learning as much as men do.

DESIDERIUS ERASMUS

The Abbot and the Learned Woman

CHARACTERS: ANTRONIUS and MAGDALIA

ANTRONIUS   I find this house strangely furnished.

MAGDALIA   Why? Is it not well furnished?

ANTRONIUS   I don't know what you call well, but it seems to me it isn't proper, either for a girl or a married woman.

MAGDALIA   And why not?

ANTRONIUS   Because there are *books* all over the place.

MAGDALIA   As if you, who have lived so long, and are an abbot and a courtier, had never seen books in a lady's room before. . . .

ANTRONIUS   Yes, I have seen French books, but here there are Greek and Latin ones!

MAGDALIA   Then is wisdom to be found only in French books?

ANTRONIUS   They are good pastimes for court ladies, who have nothing else to do.

MAGDALIA   So you would have only court ladies be women of understanding, and enjoy themselves.

ANTRONIUS   That's a mistake, to couple understanding with enjoyment. The first is not for a woman at all, and the second is only for a lady of quality.

MAGDALIA   But is it not everybody's business to live well?

ANTRONIUS   Beyond all question.

MAGDALIA   How can anyone enjoy life who does not live well?

ANTRONIUS   Rather, how can anyone enjoy life who does?

MAGDALIA   That is to say, you are for having a good time, no matter how badly one behaves.

ANTRONIUS   I am of the opinion, I must confess, that a pleasant life is a good life.

MAGDALIA   But what is it that makes life pleasant? Does it come from external things, or from the inner soul?

ANTRONIUS   From external things.

MAGDALIA   Spoken like a smart abbot, but a dull philosopher. Tell me now, what are those external enjoyments you speak of?

ANTRONIUS   Money, honor, eating, drinking, sleeping, and doing as you please.

MAGDALIA   But what if God should give you wisdom, along with all the rest? Would your life be any worse for it?

ANTRONIUS   Let me know first what you mean by wisdom.

MAGDALIA   Wisdom is the knowledge that human happiness lies in the goods of the mind and that the external advantages of family, honor, or wealth do not make us any happier or better.

ANTRONIUS   Then so much for wisdom.

MAGDALIA   But what if I take more delight in a good book than you do in hunting, playing dice, or drinking? Will you not allow me to have a pleasant life in my own way?

ANTRONIUS   That would not be a pleasant life to me.

MAGDALIA   The question is not what pleases *you* most, but what ought to be enjoyable.

ANTRONIUS   I assure you, I would not want my monks to be so bookish.

MAGDALIA   Yet my husband heartily approves of my studies. I do not see what you have against studiousness in your monks.

ANTRONIUS   It makes them undutiful! They end up by quoting from the canons and the decretals, appealing to Peter and Paul.[1]

MAGDALIA   But surely you don't have them do anything that goes against the decrees of Peter and Paul?

ANTRONIUS   I don't know anything about their doctrines. But I do hate monks who talk back to their superiors. Nor do I want any of my charges to know more than I do.

MAGDALIA   You have only to try to know as much as possible yourself.

ANTRONIUS   I have no time for that.

MAGDALIA   No time to be wise?

ANTRONIUS   No.

---

[1] The decrees and decretals were doctrines approved by the pope. Peter and Paul refer here to two medieval commentators, Petrus Baldus and Paul de Castro.

MAGDALIA   What prevents you?

ANTRONIUS   Lengthy prayers, my hunting, my horses, household duties, court functions.

MAGDALIA   So these things are more important to you than wisdom?

ANTRONIUS   It's a question of habit.

MAGDALIA   Now suppose some Jupiter gave you the power to turn yourself and all your monks into any animals whatever. Would you change yourself into a horse and them into a herd of swine?

ANTRONIUS   No, indeed.

MAGDALIA   And yet if you did, you would prevent any of your disciples from becoming wiser than you.

ANTRONIUS   I wouldn't really care what sort of animals the monks became, provided that I might still be a man myself.

MAGDALIA   But is he who is neither wise nor has any desire to be wise really a man?

ANTRONIUS   But, as long as I'm wise enough for my own business . . .

MAGDALIA   So are hogs.

ANTRONIUS   You sound like a philosopheress!

MAGDALIA   I won't say what you sound like. But what do you have against the furnishings of my house?

ANTRONIUS   A distaff and spindle would be more suitable.

MAGDALIA   Is it not a wife's duty to look after the household and raise the children?

ANTRONIUS   It is.

MAGDALIA   And can this job be managed without understanding?

ANTRONIUS   No, I suppose not.

MAGDALIA   I gain this understanding from my books.

ANTRONIUS   I have sixty-two monks under my care and not so much as one book in my cell.

MAGDALIA   Those monks are well cared for!

ANTRONIUS   I could stand some books, but not Latin ones.

MAGDALIA   And why not?

ANTRONIUS   That is not an appropriate language for women.

MAGDALIA   Why?

ANTRONIUS   It does little to protect their chastity.

MAGDALIA   French romances are no doubt more conducive to modesty.[2]

ANTRONIUS   Well, there's another reason too.

MAGDALIA   Out with it.

ANTRONIUS   Women are safer from priests if they don't know Latin.

MAGDALIA   But since you are so careful that the priests don't learn Latin, what's the danger?

ANTRONIUS   Public opinion is on my side. It's a rare and unusual thing for a woman to learn Latin.

MAGDALIA   Why talk to me of public opinion, that is never in the right? Or of custom, that gives authority to wickedness? We should apply ourselves to that which is good, and turn that which was unusual, unpleasant, and perhaps scandalous before, into the contrary.

ANTRONIUS   I hear you.

MAGDALIA   Is it suitable for a German lady to speak French?

ANTRONIUS   Yes it is.

MAGDALIA   For what reason?

ANTRONIUS   To converse with speakers of French.

MAGDALIA   And why may I not as well learn Latin in order to enjoy the company of so many wise and learned authors, so many faithful counselors and friends?

ANTRONIUS   But it is not good for women to wear out their brains on books—they have none to spare.

MAGDALIA   I don't know how many you have to spare, but I'd rather spend my small supply on studies than on mumbling prayers like a parrot or emptying dishes and beer glasses all night long.

ANTRONIUS   Too much learning can drive people mad.

MAGDALIA   Do drinkers, clowns, and buffoons keep you sane?

ANTRONIUS   They make the time pass merrily.

MAGDALIA   Why should such pleasant companions as the authors I converse with drive me mad?

ANTRONIUS   It's a common saying.

---

[2] For examples, the courtly love lais of Marie de France. Note that Magdalia uses irony frequently and that Antronius does not seem to know how to respond to it. Could this be a result of her "classical" education?

MAGDALIA   But facts tell us otherwise. It is more likely that intemperate eating, drinking, and carousing will drive you to distraction.

ANTRONIUS   I would not have a learned wife for anything.

MAGDALIA   But I congratulate myself on having a husband very unlike you. Learning makes us dearer to one another.

ANTRONIUS   But it takes so much time and trouble to get knowledge, and our lives are short, after all.

MAGDALIA   Tell me, if you were to die tomorrow, would you rather die a fool or a wise man?

ANTRONIUS   If I could have wisdom with no work. . . .

MAGDALIA   Nothing in this world is to be had without work. Yet whatever we have acquired, with no matter how much pain, we must in the end leave it behind. Why should we hesitate to spend our efforts on that most precious thing of all, whose fruits go with us into the other life?

ANTRONIUS   I have often heard it said, "One wise woman is two fools."

MAGDALIA   Some fools are of that opinion. A woman who is truly wise does not think herself so, but she who is not wise and yet thinks herself so is truly twice a fool.

ANTRONIUS   I don't know how it is, but in my opinion, a packsaddle fits an ox as well as learning fits a woman.

MAGDALIA   But you can't deny that a packsaddle fits an ox better than a miter[3] an ass or a pig. What's your opinion of the Virgin Mary?

ANTRONIUS   As high as possible.

MAGDALIA   Don't you think that she read books?

ANTRONIUS   Yes, but not books like yours.

MAGDALIA   What did she read, then?

ANTRONIUS   The canonical hours.[4]

MAGDALIA   Which canonical hours?

ANTRONIUS   Those for the service of the Benedictines.

MAGDALIA   Indeed! And what about Paula and Eustochium?[5] Were they not well versed in the holy scriptures?

ANTRONIUS   Yes, but that's a rare thing now.

MAGDALIA   Once an uneducated abbot was a rare bird; now nothing's more common. Even princes were once as eminent for their learning as they were for their authority. But it's not so rare as you think to find learned women. I can give you many examples from Spain, Italy, England, and Germany. If you don't watch out, we may take over your theological schools, your pulpits, and your miters.

ANTRONIUS   God forbid it should ever come to that!

MAGDALIA   How will *you* forbid it? If you continue as at present, people will put up with preaching geese rather than with dumb pastors. The stage of the world has been turned upside down. The actors must either play their parts or get off.

ANTRONIUS   How did I ever stumble on this woman? When you find time to pay *me* a visit, you will certainly be better entertained.

MAGDALIA   How?

ANTRONIUS   We'll dance, drink, hunt, play, and laugh.

MAGDALIA   I feel like laughing already.

COMMENTS AND QUESTIONS

1. What attitudes and lifestyle does Antronius (whose name suggests "ass" in Latin) represent? Is Erasmus satirizing the clergy in general or only certain aspects of it with this character?

2. Do you agree with Antronius or feel sympathy with him at any point, or is he merely ridiculous?

3. Which basic tenets of humanism does Magdalia defend?

4. What, specifically, enables Magdalia to win points over the abbot?

5. What seems to be the purpose of humanistic learning for Erasmus? How does it relate to human life?

---

[3] An ornamental headdress worn by abbots, as well as bishops and the pope.

[4] The canonical hours were prayers to be read in the monastery seven times a day. In stating that Mary read prayers designed for Benedictine monks, the abbot is, of course, making a foolish anachronism.

---

[5] Paula and Eustochium were two "spiritual daughters" of Saint Jerome (340–420), the Church Father who translated the Bible into Latin. They were taught by him.

6. What do Erasmus' views on women appear to be from this dialogue? Would you call him a feminist from a modern point of view?

Renaissance Women   In Erasmus' time some European women were, as Magdalia points out, beginning to receive a humanistic education. One should not, however, be misled into thinking that girls automatically received as good an education as boys did. The educated woman remained very much the exception, for most families believed that girls' education should be primarily in domestic arts. Erasmus was impressed with the way in which the English humanist Thomas More had educated his daughters in Greek and Latin, and he probably modeled Magdalia on More's eldest daughter, Margaret Roper. There were, of course, educated women before the Renaissance, but nearly all of them were from the upper classes or aristocracy (recall Marie de France). Magdalia, however, is obviously a middle-class woman; she is contrasted with the "court ladies." When the growth of printing and the book trade made possible new access to learning among those who were neither aristocrats nor clergy, many clergymen viewed books as truly dangerous. Would not people who read them form their own opinions instead of accepting doctrine from the authorities of the Church? Since women were commonly viewed as weak-minded, easily swayed, and virtuous only when obedient and submissive, it was believed to be particularly necessary to keep them away from books. Opposed to all intolerance and fanaticism, Erasmus adopted a reasonable and humane attitude, though not a very radical one, toward book learning and toward women's education in particular.

The Protestant Reformation

The reform tendencies present in Erasmus and other northern humanists were not unique to them. Rather, by 1500 in northern Europe a broad spirit of Christian reform prevailed, of which humanism was only one reflection. Intensive efforts were underway to reform monastic orders, and new orders were founded devoted to strict enforcement of the monastic vows. Pietistic movements like the Brethren of the Common Life, which included both laymen and clerics, aimed at in-

fusing in the daily life of all Christians a deep spirit of devotion. Against this background the Lutheran reform could be interpreted as only another manifestation of a universal concern. Martin Luther (Fig. 12-1) was different from the other reformers, however, in that he attacked not only abuses but doctrines as well.

Martin Luther   For Luther the Church in the past thousand and more years had been guilty of distorting the truth found in the Bible. In practice the Church had exalted the pronouncements of Church councils, popes, and learned men to a level equal to that of Scripture. For him these "truths" were human ones; men made mistakes and only the Bible was unquestionably true. Hence, he rejected the authoritative interpretations that the Church had placed on each passage of the Bible as concealing rather than revealing the Word of God found therein. Each man should have the power of coming to the text and reading it according to the dictates of his own conscience. When in 1521 Luther was called before the Catholic emperor, Charles V of Germany, at Augsburg to renounce his deviation from Catholic truth, he exalted the majesty of the individual human conscience in refusing:

> Since then Your Majesty and your lordships desire a simple reply, I will answer without horns and without teeth. Unless I am convicted by Scripture and plain reason—I do not accept the authority of popes and councils, for they have contradicted each other—my conscience is captive to the Word of God. I cannot and I will not recant anything, for to go against conscience is neither right nor safe. God help me. Amen.

By this, however, he did not mean that everyone's opinion about religion should be respected. The truth on important issues of the faith was so evident for Luther that no fair-minded person could differ with his interpretation. Accordingly, he was perfectly willing to persecute others who did not share his understanding of the basic principles found in the Bible.

A dominant tradition of the medieval Church had been, as we have seen, the belief that men could cooperate with God's grace in earning their own salvation. Through a succession of good works, product of the joint efforts of human will and grace, the individual could build up enough merits to earn a place in

12–1 Lucas Cranach, the Elder, "Portrait of Luther as an Augustinian Friar," engraving, 1520. (Courtesy of Fogg Art Museum, Harvard University. Francis Calley Gray Collection)

heaven. The sacraments controlled by the Church hierarchy were viewed as the channels through which life-giving grace poured to believers. The clerics (the priests who administered the sacraments and had care of souls) and the monks and friars (who had taken special vows to devote their life to God) were considered as a group to be on a higher spiritual level than were laymen. Their average chances for entering heaven were considered better than those of nonclerics; they were more likely to build up merits because of their profession.

Luther attacked the central thesis of this belief. No man can cooperate with God in his own salvation. Mortals are too sinful. God predestines some individ-

uals from all eternity to salvation. These men and women know who they are because they have faith that Christ's merits have been imputed to them for their salvation. They themselves did absolutely nothing to win this salvation; it was a free gift of God. Therefore, gone was the need for pilgrimages, penance, masses for the dead, and all the other rituals of the medieval Church designed to build up a sum of the good works requisite for salvation. Only after an individual is justified and knows that Christ is his savior can he really begin to do good works. Yet these count nothing for salvation: they are merely the fruits of knowing that God has already chosen one to be saved. The good works pour out as a product of love for God and one's fellow men because Christ is at work in the depths of the soul.

Consequently, no one is saved because of what he or she does. From this it follows that a shoemaker has just as good a chance of being saved as does the pope. In Luther's view, the whole spiritual hierarchy with the bishops, archbishops, cardinals, and pope was a man-made construction. He denied that Christ in committing the keys to Peter intended to make the bishop of Rome the head of the whole Church. The present hierarchical Church was a work of man, not God; and, since it was loaded with corruption and led by blind men, the edifice had to be destroyed. Luther's solution was that the territorial prince in each area should be the governor of the territorial Church.

The sources for Luther's thought, in addition to the Bible, included Saint Augustine and northern European critics of medieval scholasticism. Unlike Thomas Aquinas, Luther had little faith in the ability of human reason to establish truths about the divine nature. Luther's God was primarily Will, and men had no power to know anything more of him than the Bible conveyed. The reformer's insistence on the importance of the inner life as opposed to ceremonies was perhaps in part an inheritance from northern mysticism, but humanists like Erasmus also exercised an influence here. To humanism as well, Luther owed his training in the three major ancient languages, Latin, Greek and Hebrew, and his confidence in his critical powers when confronted with a text. Humanism placed at his disposal a set of philological tools and a tradition of independent judgment; Luther fearlessly applied these in an examination of the whole body of Christian doctrine.

Like Erasmus, Luther made extensive use of the medium of printing to distribute his ideas. The impact of his message was much greater, however, because whereas Erasmus wrote only in Latin, Luther championed his appeal to reform in eloquent German. To make the Bible more accessible to the layman, he translated the whole of the Old and New Testaments, a translation that served as the basis for the modern German language. A musician and poet, Luther composed literally hundreds of hymns, thus establishing the Protestant tradition of hymn singing in church. Through music and the popular word, Luther's thought had a widespread and profound influence.

While Luther embraced the doctrine of the freedom of conscience to interpret the Bible—confident that the Bible clearly supported his views—other reformers, using the same principle, held very different positions with similar certainty. For more than ten centuries the holy book of the Christian faith had been protected by authoritative commentaries on key words and phrases. And now Luther proclaimed a doctrine of interpretation that, contrary to his intention, encouraged religious anarchy.

John Calvin   Next to the Lutherans the single most important Protestant group were the Calvinists. John Calvin (1509–1564), a Frenchman, came to Geneva in Switzerland after the city had already converted from Catholicism; after 1540 under his able direction the city became the center of that variety of Protestantism bearing his name. A second-generation reformer, Calvin believed with Luther in God's predestination of the human soul either to heaven or to hell and in the uselessness of man's good works for salvation. But whereas Luther's preoccupation had been with the salvation of the sinner and its consequences for the individual, Calvin focused on the duty of the "elect" to glorify God in all their actions as instruments of God's work. The result of the difference was that, while Lutherans stressed the need of the saved to live as Christians in their daily life, the Calvinists viewed themselves as charged with responsibility to reform society so as to make it acceptable in the Lord's eyes. As exemplified in Geneva, Calvinism was against taverns, whorehouses, elaborate clothing, and any form of behavior that would detract from God's glory. For the same reason Calvinists proved much more active missionaries than did Lutherans. Moreover, although Calvin himself was politically conservative, his followers were born revolutionaries in countries where rulers were not Calvinists. After the founder's death, Calvinism was rapidly diffused in France and England as well as in Eastern Europe, especially Poland.

There is no place here to discuss the multitude of more radical Protestant sects that sprang up in the sixteenth century along with Lutheranism and Calvinism. Suffice it to say that throughout the century Catholics and Protestants, conservative Protestants and radical Protestants, tortured and killed one another in the name of their religious convictions. Religious toleration would come in the next century only because most of the European population was tired of civil wars and of anarchy created by religious struggles.

Cultural Relativism and Scepticism

Surely part of the reason for the massive participation of Europeans in the religious wars of the sixteenth century can be traced to the economic development of the subcontinent in that century and to the enormous population increases. The only previous European-wide religious phenomenon to match it was that of the Crusades in the twelfth and thirteenth centuries, the last great age of general economic boom and population increase. As in the earlier case, the vigor felt in the expanding society of the sixteenth century found an outlet to an extent in religious warfare, this time within Europe itself.

Economic Expansion   The causes of the economic expansion were various. Certainly the population increase itself was a major factor. But one element that cannot be discounted was the enormous increase in bullion stocks, which multiplied the currency of Europe, causing a price rise and stimulating production. From the early fourteenth century the Spanish and the Portuguese had been exploring the coast of Africa. By the end of the fifteenth century they managed to round the dangerous Cape of Good Hope and establish contact with the Far East. By the second half of that

EUROPE AT THE TIME OF THE PROTESTANT REFORMATION

Legend:
— The Holy Roman Empire
▪ Habsburg Family Dominions, 1519
○ Principal Protestant Centers

century significant supplies of gold were being imported into Europe from the gold mines south of the Sahara.

Through the voyages of Christopher Columbus from 1492 on, the crown of Castille laid claim to a whole new world beyond the Atlantic Ocean. In the sixteenth century the New World provided an almost unlimited stream of precious metals for Europe, raising prices and fueling the economy. Both agricultural and industrial production expanded. While most of the industrial goods were still produced in homes and small shops, an increasing number of people were involved in their manufacture. In a few areas like paper, glass, and cannon making, the mining of coal, ship building, and printing, there was significant investment made in the modes of production. The forerunners of modern factories were constructed.

The new discoveries in Africa, Asia, and the Americas had profound cultural as well as economic effects on Europeans. (See Hans Holbein's *Ambassadors,* Color Plate X.) Contact with different systems of religion, thought, government, and new customs challenged their view of what was "natural" to human nature. In a word, exploration encouraged cultural relativism.

Montaigne   The writings of one of the great minds of the late sixteenth century show the effects both of the geographical discoveries and of the religious wars. Michel de Montaigne (1533–1592) came to doubt not only the possibility of establishing any certitude in religion, but also the power of reason to establish laws of nature and society in the world. He was one of the few thinkers in history up to his time who seriously raised the question *What do I know?*

Son of a Catholic father and a Protestant-Jewish mother, Montaigne served for a time as the mayor of the modest French city of Bordeaux, but he preferred to remain away from the centers of power. His favorite place for his major activities—reading, writing, and thinking—was his book-lined study located in a tower. There, he not only read and commented on classical philosophers but also, in a more modern vein, looked inward in an attempt to understand himself. This he did, not because he considered himself an exceptional individual, but because he thought that an understanding of oneself could lead to an understanding of the human predicament. He certainly had no intention of establishing laws for human beings. Reason could not do that; men were each one different from the other. But, at least by the last years of his life, he came to believe that nature through pain and pleasure gives us some guidance in the conduct of our lives. While he relished his own peculiarities, he felt a kinship with other humans and a need to communicate his thoughts to them: "Every man bears the whole form of the human condition."

Montaigne called his writings essays, meaning "trials" or "experiences." He does not claim to impose a lesson but rather to invite the reader to participate in his "tryouts," his observations, his experiences. The essays might be called the journal of a man seeking wisdom. Although each one has a definite subject, Montaigne does not hesitate to go off on tangents when his reflections so lead him. The subjects he chooses may be philosophical, personal, or social. His essay on cannibals, most of which is reprinted below, represents one of his most daring social criticisms. He uses a society from a newly discovered land—in this case Indians in Brazil—to comment on the false sense of moral superiority in his own countrymen, or in Europeans in general. The theme of the "noble savage" (contrasted with decadent and corrupt "civilized" human beings) will become, as we will see, an even more popular theme in the eighteenth century. Montaigne was one of the first Europeans to understand and portray the cultural relativism that the new travels and discoveries made possible.

Montaigne's *Essays* were translated into English in 1603 by an Englishman of Italian extraction named John Florio. They were then widely read in England, most notably by Shakespeare, who quoted from them in at least one of his plays. Florio's English has the robust, somewhat rambling quality of Montaigne's French. It is essentially the English of Shakespeare and the King James Bible. The translation of the selection below is mostly Florio's, with spelling modernized and a few phrases simplified.

MICHEL DE MONTAIGNE

Of Cannibals

When King Pyrrhus came into Italy, after he had surveyed the marshalling of the army which the Romans sent against him, he said: "I know not what barbarous men these are" (for so the Greeks called all foreign nations) "but the disposition of this army, which I see, is nothing barbarous." . . . Thus should a man take heed, lest he follow vulgar opinions, which should be measured by the rule of reason, and not by the common report. I have had for a long time dwelling with me a man, who for the space of ten or twelve years had dwelt in that other world, which in our age was lately discovered in those parts where Villegaignon first landed, and surnamed Antarctic France.[1] The discovery of so in-

---

[1] Villegaignon landed in Brazil in 1557.

finite and vast a country seems worthy of great consideration. . . .[2]

This servant I had was a simple and rough-hewn fellow, a condition fit to yield a true testimony. For subtle people may indeed . . . observe things more exactly, but they amplify and gloss them, the better to persuade . . . they never represent things truly, but fashion and mask them according to the visage they saw them in. . . . I would have every man write what he knows, and no more. . . .

Now (to return to my purpose) I find (as far as I have been informed) there is nothing in that nation, that is either barbarous or savage, unless men call that barbarism which is not common to them. As indeed, we have no other measure of truth and reason, than the example and idea of the opinions and customs of the country we live in. There is ever the perfect religion, the perfect government, perfect and complete customs in all things. We call people savage, as we call fruits wild, which nature has produced by herself. Indeed, however, we should rather term savage those which we ourselves have altered by our artificial devices and diverted from their common order. In the former are the true and most profitable virtues, and natural properties most lively and vigorous, which in the latter we have bastardized, applying them to the pleasure of our corrupted taste. And if notwithstanding we find that the fruits of those lands that were never tilled are still more excellent, compared to ours, there is no reason why art should win the point of honor over our great and powerful mother nature. We have so much by our inventions surcharged the beauties and riches of her works that we have altogether overchoked her: yet wherever her purity shines, she makes our vain and frivolous enterprises wonderfully ashamed. . . . All our endeavor or wit cannot so much as represent the nest of the least little bird, its contexture, beauty, profit and use, nor even the web of a frail spider. "All things" (says Plato) "are produced, either by nature, by fortune, or by art. The greatest and fairest by one or other of the two first, the least and imperfect by the last."

Those nations therefore seem to me barbarous thus:

they have received very little fashioning from human ingenuity, and are yet near their original natural state. The laws of nature do yet command them, but little bastardized by ours, and that with such purity, that I am sometimes grieved that the knowledge of it no sooner came to light, when men better than we could have judged of it. I am sorry that Lycurgus and Plato had it not, for it seems to me that what in those nations we see by experience . . . exceeds all the pictures with which poetry has embellished the golden age. . . . They could not imagine a genuineness so pure and simple as we see by experience, nor ever believe our society might be maintained by so little art and human combination. It is a nation, I would answer Plato, that has no kind of traffic, no knowledge of letters, no intelligence of numbers, no name of magistrate, nor of political superiority, no use of service, of riches or of poverty; no contracts, no successions, no partitions, no occupation but idle, no kinship but common, no apparel but natural, no manuring of lands, no use of wine, corn or metal. The very words that import lying, falsehood, treason, dissimulations, covetousness, envy, belittling and pardon were never heard of amongst them. How different would he find his imaginary commonwealth from this perfection: *Men but recently born of the gods.*[3]

Furthermore, they live in a country of so exceeding pleasant and temperate situation, that as my testimonies have told me, it is very rare to see a sick body amongst them; and they have further assured me they never saw any man there, either shaking with the palsy, toothless, with eyes dropping, or crooked and stooped with age. They are situated along the sea coast. . . . They have great abundance of fish and flesh, that have no resemblance at all with ours, and eat them without any sauces, or skill of cookery, but plain boiled or broiled. The first man that brought a horse thither, although he had in many other voyages conversed with them, bred so great a horror in the land, that before they could take notice of him, they slew him with arrows. . . . They spend the whole day dancing. Their young men go hunting after wild beasts with bows and arrows. Their women busy themselves meanwhile with

---

[2] In the passage omitted here, Montaigne recounts Plato's account of the "lost continent," Atlantis, and wonders if the "new world" could once have been connected with the old.

[3] Seneca, *Epistles,* XC, 44. Montaigne uses many classical quotations in this essay (as in his others), some of which are omitted here.

warming their drink—that is their main occupation. Some of their old men, in the morning before they go to eat, preach in common to all the household, walking from one end of the house to the other, repeating the same sentence many times.... The preacher commends but two things to his listeners: first, courage against their enemies, and second, lovingness to their wives.... They are shaven all over, much closer and cleaner than we are, with no other razors than of wood and stone. They believe their souls to be eternal, and those that have deserved well of their gods to be placed in that part of heaven where the sun rises, and the cursed ones toward the west. They have certain prophets and priests which normally live in the mountains and very seldom show themselves to the people. When they do come down, a great feast is prepared .... The prophet speaks to the people in public, exhorting them to embrace virtue and follow their duty. All their moral discipline contains but these two articles: first an undaunting resolution in war, and second an inviolable affection to their wives....

They war against the nations that lie beyond their mountains, to which they go naked, having no other weapons than bows, or wooden swords, sharp at one end as our broaches are. It is an admirable thing to see the constant resolution of their combats, which never end but by effusion of blood and murder, for they know not what fear and routs are. Every victor brings home the head of the enemy he has slain as a trophy of his victory, and fastens it to the entrance of his dwelling. After they have treated their prisoners well for a long time, with all commodities, the master of them summons together a great assembly of his acquaintance, ties a cord to one of the prisoner's arms, by the end of which he holds him fast, though at some distance, for fear of being hurt. He then gives the other arm, bound in like manner, to his dearest friend, and both in the presence of all the assembly kill him with swords. This done, they roast and then eat him in common, and send some slices of him to their friends who are absent. It is not, as some imagine, to nourish themselves with it (as anciently the Scythians[4] used to do), but to represent an extreme revenge. We can prove it

thus: some of them saw the Portuguese, who had allied themselves with their adversaries, use another kind of death when they took them prisoners, which was to bury them up to the middle, and shoot arrows against the upper part of the body, and then when they were almost dead to hang them. They supposed that these people of the other world, they who had sowed the knowledge of many vices among their neighbors, and were much more cunning in all kinds of evil and mischief, did not undertake this manner of revenge without cause, and that consequently it was more painful and cruel than theirs. Thereupon they began to leave their old fashion to follow this one.

I am not sorry that we note the barbarous horror of such an action, but grieved that in prying so narrowly into their faults we are so blinded in ours. I think there is more barbarism in eating men alive than to feed upon them being dead; to mangle by tortures and torments a body full of lively sense, to roast him in pieces, to make dogs and swine gnaw and tear him (as we have not only read, but seen very recently, not among ancient enemies, but among our neighbors and fellow citizens, and what is worse, under the pretext of piety and religion[5]) than to roast and eat him after he is dead. Chrysippus and Zeno, arch-pillars of the Stoic sect, thought that there was no harm at all, in time of need, to make use of our carrion bodies, and to feed upon them, as did our forefathers, who being besieged by Caesar in the City of Alexia, resolved to sustain the famine of the siege with the bodies of old men, women, and other persons unserviceable and unfit to fight.

> Gascons (as fame reports)
> Liv'd with meats of such sorts.[6]

... We may then well call these people barbarous in respect to the rules of reason, but not in respect to ourselves, who exceed them in all kinds of barbarism.

Their wars are noble and generous, and have as much excuse and as much beauty as this human infirmity can: they aim at nothing but rivalry in valor. They do not contend for the gaining of new lands, for

---

[4] An ancient, nomadic, and warlike people who lived in southeastern Europe and Asia.

[5] Montaigne refers here to the tortures inflicted by both Protestants and Catholics on their enemies.

[6] Juvenal, *Satires*, XV, 93–94. The Gascons were a people of southwestern France (Montaigne's own region).

to this day they still enjoy that natural abundance and fruitfulness which without laboring toil furnishes them in plenteous abundance with all necessary things so that they need not enlarge their limits. They are still in that happy state of desiring no more than their natural necessities: anything beyond is superfluous to them.

Those that are about the same age call each other brethren, those that are younger are called children, and the aged are esteemed as fathers to the rest. They leave full possession of goods in common, without division, to their heirs, and no other claim or title but that which nature gives to all creatures as she brings them into the world.

If their neighbors chance to come over the mountains to invade them and are victorious over them, the victors' conquest is glory and the advantage to be and remain superior in valor and virtue. Otherwise, they have nothing to do with the goods and spoils of the vanquished, and so return to their country where they are not lacking in any necessary thing, and know how to enjoy their condition happily and be content with what nature supplies them. The others do the same when their turn comes. They require no other ransom of their prisoners but an acknowledgement and confession that they are vanquished. But it is impossible to find one in a whole century who would not rather embrace death than either by word or countenance yield one jot from the grandeur of an invincible courage. There is not one who would not rather be slain and devoured than to beg for his life or show any fear. . . .

The reputation and worth of a man consists in his heart and will: therein lies true honor. Valor is in the strength, not of arms and legs, but of mind and courage; not in the spirit and courage of our horse, nor of our arms, but in our own. He who falls persistent in his courage, "If he slip or fall, he fights upon his knee." [7] He who, in danger of imminent death, is in no way daunted in his assuredness, he that in yielding up his ghost beholds his enemy with a scornful and fierce look, he is vanquished, not by us but by fortune; he is slain, but not conquered. The most valiant are often the most unfortunate. So are there triumphant losses that rival victories. . . .

To return to our story, the prisoners, no matter how they are dealt with, are so far from yielding that during the two or three months they are kept they always keep cheerful and urge and defy their keepers to hasten their trial. They upbraid them with their cowardliness and with the number of battles they have lost. I have a song made by a prisoner which contains this clause: "Let them boldly come together and flock in multitudes to feed on him; for with him they shall feed upon their fathers and grandfathers that heretofore have served his body for food and nourishment. These muscles, this flesh, these veins, are your own, fools that you are, know you not that the substance of your forefathers' limbs is still tied to ours? Taste them well, for in them you shall find the relish of your own flesh." This is an invention that shows no barbarism. Those who describe them dying say that when they are put to execution, the prisoners spit in their executioners' faces and scowl at them. Truly, as long as breath is in their body, they never cease to brave and defy them, both in speech and countenance. Surely, in respect to us these are very savage men, for either they must be so or we must be so. There is a wondrous difference between their style and ours.

Their men have many wives; the more valiant they are reputed to be, the greater the number. The manner and beauty of their marriages is wondrously strange and remarkable. Just as our wives jealously try to keep us from the love and affection of other women, their try to obtain it. Being more concerned for their husbands' honor than for anything else, they endeavor to have as many rivals as they possibly can, since that is a testimony to their husbands' valor. Our women would count it a wonder, but it is not so. It is a properly matrimonial virtue, of the highest kind. In the Bible, Leah, Rachel, Sarah, and Jacob's wives brought their fairest maid servants to their husbands' beds. . . . And lest anyone should think that this is done out of simple and servile duty to custom, . . . or because they are so blockish and dull spirited . . . I must cite an example of their abilities. Besides what I have said of one of their war songs, I have a love song which begins like this: "Adder stay, stay good adder, that my sister may by the pattern of thy many-colored coat draw the fashion and work of a rich lace for me to give unto my love; so may thy beauty, thy nimbleness and disposition be ever pre-

---

[7] Seneca, *On Providence*, II.

ferred before all other serpents." The first couplet is the refrain of the song. I am familiar enough with poetry that I may judge that this invention has no barbarism at all in it, but is altogether Anacreontic.[8] Their language is a kind of pleasant speech, and has a pleasing sound, and some affinity with Greek in its endings.

Three of that nation, ignorant of how costly the knowledge of our corruptions will one day be to their repose, security and happiness, and how their ruin shall proceed from this commerce, which I imagine is already well advanced (miserable as they are to have let themselves be so deceived by a desire for new-fangled novelties and to have left the calmness of their climate to come and see ours) were at Rouen at the time of our late King Charles the ninth[9] who talked with them a great while. They were shown our fashions, our pomp, and the way a beautiful city looks. Afterwards, some demanded their opinion, and wished to know of them what noteworthy and admirable things they had observed among us. They answered three things, the last of which I have forgotten, and am very sorry for it, the other two I yet remember. They said that first they found it very strange that so many tall men with long beards, strong and well armed, around the person of the king (very likely they meant his Swiss guards) would submit themselves to obey a beardless child, and they wondered why we did not rather choose one among them to command the rest. Secondly, (they have a way of speaking whereby they call men "halves" of one another) they had perceived that there were men among us full gorged with all sorts of commodities, and others which hunger-starved, and bare with need and poverty, begged at their gates, and they found it strange that these needy "halves" could endure such an injustice, and that they did not take the others by the throat or set fire to their houses.

I talked a good while with one of them but had such a bad interpreter who understood my meaning so badly and was so foolish in his conceptions of my ideas, that I did not learn a great deal from him. When I asked

him what good he received from the superior position he had among his countrymen (for he was a captain and our sailors called him king) he told me that it was to march foremost in any war charge. When I asked him how many men followed him, he showed me a space of ground to signify as many as might be contained there which I guessed to be about four or five thousand men. Moreover, I asked, when all wars were ended, did his authority expire? He answered that only this much was left, that when he visited the villages dependent on him, the inhabitants prepared paths across the hedges of their woods for him to pass through at ease. All this is not very bad, but what of that? They wear no kind of breeches nor hose.

QUESTIONS AND COMMENTS

1. What does Montaigne seem to mean by "nature"? Would a modern anthropologist agree with his observations on people in a "natural" state?
2. Montaigne uses a great deal of *irony* in contrasting the cannibals' "natural" state with the European "civilized" one. Point out specific examples of irony.
3. What criticisms, implicit and explicit, does Montaigne make of his own culture? How does he convince the reader that cannibalism is a relative value rather than an absolute "barbarous" evil?
4. What seem to be Montaigne's positive values? His views on morality and religion? Would you call Montaigne a humanist?
5. Montaigne's references to Greek and Roman events or thinkers often have the effect of allying the ancients with the Brazilian Indians against modern Europeans, to the detriment of the latter. Show how this is done. Why would this be an effective technique for Montaigne's readers?
6. What is the impact of the last sentence of the essay?
7. Is the main subject of the essay really the cannibals? What would you say it is?
8. With Montaigne, we have obviously come a long way from Pico della Mirandola and Erasmus, with their faith in the achievements and potential of man in general and of European culture in particular. What specific differences can you point out?

---

[8] Anacreon was a Greek lyric poet who lived about a century later than Sappho.
[9] King Charles IX was only about twelve years old at the time.

13

SHAKESPEARE AND THE LATE RENAISSANCE

The world of Montaigne, fraught with religious dissension, stimulated and enlarged by travels and discoveries, was also fundamentally the world of Shakespeare, though England under the reign of Queen Elizabeth I had a dynamic culture very much its own. More has been written about Shakespeare than about any other writer, and with good reason. The universality of his genius is such that it is difficult not to fall into what Bernard Shaw called "bardolatry" when discussing him. There are writers whose works are more unified, more even, certainly more "classical" than Shakespeare's; but the dramatic power, the philosophical depth, and the superb characterization in Shakespeare's major plays have never been equaled. For English-speaking people, the way in which his poetry has enriched and amplified our language assures his place in our cultural roots. His language may seem difficult to us today; but, as we read Shakespeare, we become aware of his enormous impact on our everyday speech and writing.

While Shakespeare remains a writer for all times, he was also very much a man of his time. Many of the cultural and intellectual trends that we have seen developing throughout the Renaissance are synthesized in this playwright of Elizabethan England. He shares Montaigne's skeptical and relativistic view of the human condition, and he often displays a deep pessimism and doubt that would have been impossible under the more unified, God-centered culture of the Middle Ages. Yet he had also been influenced by the earlier humanists' glorification of human beings. This passage from one of Hamlet's soliloquies illustrates the two tendencies:

> What a piece of work is a man! how noble in reason! how infinite in faculty! in form and moving how express and admirable! in action how like an angel! in apprehension how like a god! the beauty of the world! the paragon of animals! And yet, to me, what is this quintessence of dust? Man delights not me.

Compare this portrayal of man to that in the passage from *Antigone* that we quoted in Chapter 3 and from Pico della Mirandola in Chapter 9. The whole span of Renaissance-Reformation culture is found in Shakespeare: the early humanistic confidence in human powers, bolstered by the revival of classical texts, and the doubt, deepened by the Reformation, that man's endeavors amounted to very much at all.

Shakespeare exemplifies another Renaissance characteristic: he was interested in everything. In spite of a contemporary's remark that he knew "little Latin and less Greek," he was, by our standards, well grounded in the classical humanities through his own reading as well as through formal education. Certainly he knew the Roman tragedies of Seneca and comedies of Plautus, which served as models for his own drama. Yet his interests ranged far beyond book-learning. Sound practical knowledge of military strategy, seafaring, business affairs, and all sorts of lore is evident in his plays. The discoveries beyond Europe interested him greatly. Something of a self-made man himself, he acquired a wide experience in acting and theater management in addition to his writing.

Elizabethan England was a time in which broad interests and creative development could flourish. Although Elizabeth, the Protestant daughter of Henry VIII, came to the throne when there was great rivalry between Protestant and Catholic factions, she was beloved by her subjects and proved to be a powerful and able ruler. Under the reign of Elizabeth, England changed from an island kingdom to an expanding empire that controlled the seas after the naval defeat of the greatest European power, Spain. England grew rich through trade. Sixteenth-century Englishmen traveled to the New World and to Africa. Music, dance, poetry, painting, and architecture flourished; but the art form in which Elizabethan England surpassed the rest of Europe (except perhaps Spain) was the theater.

In order to understand the development of this theater, we should go back for a moment to the discussion of medieval drama. There we saw that the theater, which had practically disappeared from Europe after the Roman empire, was revived as a part of the church service. As the plays representing stories from the Bible grew more elaborate, they moved to the exterior of the church. No longer a part of the service, the "mystery plays," as they were called, responded to popular taste by adding more and more comical elements, often gross ones. In England these were sponsored by various trade guilds and presented on stage-wagons that went from place to place. When the mystery plays began to lose their appeal, they were replaced by "morality" plays that had allegorical characters (such as Fellowship, Good Deeds, Beauty, Death) and always taught a moral. The best of these, *Everyman*, shows man preparing himself for death and God's judgment. Farces and clowning of various sorts continued alongside this more serious theater. In Italy these grew into the *commedia dell'arte*, an improvisational form with stock characters that would greatly influence the development of modern comedy.

The impact of the humanist resurrection of classical texts on the theater was great. Humanists in Italy translated Latin and Greek plays; then they wrote their own tragedies and comedies in the classical manner, first in Latin and, by the sixteenth century, in Italian. French, German, and Spanish writers turned to the classical models. In England schools and universities began to produce comedies and tragedies by Plautus, Terence, and Seneca. Soon writers associated with the universities were writing plays in English that combined classical and medieval, Roman and English elements. Companies of "strolling players" who had specialized in moralities began to stage the new plays. Professional actors, who had been viewed by English society as little better than vagrants or criminals, gradually came under the protection of the nobility. Licensed theater companies were formed; Shakespeare belonged to one of these.

The theater grew in popularity, despite disapproval by the Puritans and others. Public theaters were built, not inside the city limits but just outside, along with the brothels, taverns, and other places of entertainment. Theaters in Elizabethan England, like theaters in ancient Greece, were patronized by all social classes. The Globe Theatre, built in 1599, where many of Shakespeare's plays were performed, had a platform stage jutting out into a central courtyard. The audience sat around three sides of this platform—the lower-class people (who each paid a penny) in the "pit" and the wealthier spectators in the galleries above. The orchestra was on stage, as music was usually a significant part of the production. It is important to keep in mind as one reads the script that the *spectacle*—the costumes, scenery, singing, playing, and dancing, as well as the acting—was (and of course still is) essential to the total show. There was no lighting, however; plays were performed in the afternoon. Shakespeare knew his audience: his theater is addressed not just to the elite and educated but to all segments of society.

Shakespeare's plays have been classified in four categories: comedies, histories, tragedies, and romances. None of these are "pure" forms. The tragedies, for example, nearly all contain elements of history and comedy. We will concentrate here on Shakespeare's use of the tragic form in one of his major works, *Othello, the Moor of Venice*, first produced in 1604.

Tragedy in the Renaissance   One question often asked by literary historians is: what permitted tragedy, a dead form in the Middle Ages, to revive in the Renaissance? In the scheme of Judeo-Christian values, tragedy is hardly possible. The story of Adam and Eve's fall is basically tragic, but the believer sees it as part of a greater whole, a promise of redemption. Isaac's sacrifice is almost tragic, but Jahweh intervenes just in time. The passion of Jesus would be tragic without the knowledge of God's design. The literary work closest to tragedy in the Bible is the Book of Job, but it was amended by later authors to have a happy ending. *The Play of Daniel* is typical of medieval art: it portrays a near catastrophe that is averted by the power of God. It is not by accident that the greatest literary work of the Middle Ages was called *The Divine Comedy*. It is a "comedy" not because it is funny but because it ends in happiness, in fact in paradise.

Renaissance culture, as we have seen, remained basically Christian; but, with the revival of Greco-Roman elements, one often perceives in it a tension between the two sets of values. Shakespeare, for example, refers to Christian doctrines and symbols but at times almost seems to believe in something like the classical Fate. In any case, he was able to write of the fall of his heroes without reference to their possible redemption. *Othello*, while it contains references to religion, takes place in a secular scheme of things. Some commentators have argued that Shakespeare was without any religious belief, or at least was as skeptical toward religion as was Montaigne. His audience, in a theater freed from attachment to the Church, accepted non-Christian tragedy.

The sources of Shakespeare's plays range from classical history to contemporary romances. Like the Greek dramatists, he did not make up the basic plots himself but shaped those he found for his own purposes. The source that he used for *Othello* is a rather badly told tale by an Italian writer named Cinthio. Because Renaissance Italy interested Shakespeare greatly, as it did his countrymen, many of his plays are set there. *Othello* had an even more exotic element for the English audience: a black man as its hero. To understand the background of the tragedy, it will be helpful to know something about Venice and about Moors.

Venice   Venice was an independent Italian city-state that reached the height of its power in the fifteenth century. It was ruled by a duke (*doge*) with a senate. Its colonies included Crete, the Dalmatian coast (now part of Yugoslavia), and the island of Cyprus, in which most of *Othello* is set. The Venetians were frequently at war with the Turks, who finally captured their colonies. Venice as a trade center was full of people from faraway lands; it was a center of culture as well, especially noted for its painting. Italy, and Venice in particular, seemed to Englishmen a place of luxuriousness, corruption, and subtle political intrigue. It is no surprise that Iago, the most intelligent and the most evil of Shakespeare's villains, is a Venetian.

Europeans and Blacks   Renaissance Europeans called the people of North Africa "tawny Moors" and the people of sub-Saharan Africa "black Moors." Othello is clearly a black African. By the time Shakespeare wrote his tragedy, black people were not uncommon on the streets of London. Several Englishmen had been to Africa; various European travel accounts had found their way to England. Most of these are a mixture of fantasy and reality. There are tales of "headless men," descriptions of the legendary kingdom of Prester John, and what seem to be fairly accurate accounts of the splendor of the court of Benin (see Chapter 14). Some of the stereotypes that would inflame prejudices are present in these accounts: black Moors, or Negroes, were said to be "naked," "without religion," "uncivilized," "cruel." They were thought to be hot-blooded and highly sexed because they lived so near the sun. In addition, the term *black* in the English language already had strong connotations of unclean, evil, and ugly, contrasted with the pure and ideally beautiful white.[1]

These associations and stereotypes served the Elizabethan dramatists who created the Moor as something of a stage type. Usually the Moor was portrayed as a villain, lusty and cruel.[2] Cinthio, Shakespeare's source, emphasizing Othello's "hot-bloodedness" and weakness, moralizes that blacks should not marry whites.

Shakespeare's Use of Black and White   It was then something of a feat for Shakespeare, and a testimony to his genius, to present a black man as the hero of a tragedy. Playing upon his audience's preconceptions, Shakespeare makes an original, rich use of black and white symbolism throughout the play. It is the black man who is inwardly pure, and it is a seemingly honest white man (and a soldier, a type usually portrayed as genuinely honest) who is inwardly evil. The difficulty of distinguishing being from seeming is a ma-

jor theme in the play, brought out in part by the black-white symbolism. The alleged supersexuality of Africans also figures in the play: Iago calls Othello the "lusty Moor," describing him with images of animal sexuality. Other characters reflect similar prejudice. But, again, the popular stereotype is turned around. Othello loves his Venetian wife Desdemona (though by no means platonically) with romantic devotion; Iago is totally unable to understand that love is not simple lust. Othello's overriding concern with sex appears only when he has been infected by Iago's "poison" (another important type of image in the play). This gradual mental and emotional poisoning of Othello by Iago is the motivating force of the tragedy.

Othello as Tragic Hero   Othello, a typical tragic figure, moves from a position of power and good fortune to a degraded state in which he can no longer endure his life. Like Oedipus he experiences a powerful revelation of truth and self-knowledge; like Oedipus he turns his own hand on himself. But the combination of fate and character that caused Oedipus' tragedy is here replaced by the combination of Othello's character and the carefully plotted malignancy carried out by Iago. *Othello*, very tightly constructed, is in many ways the most classical of Shakespeare's tragedies, yet it differs substantially from Greek tragedy.

Poetic Form   The poetic form of most of this tragedy is *blank verse*, the verse line introduced in the sixteenth century and still considered the most natural to the English language. It consists of unrhymed lines in *iambic pentameter*, that is, five strong stresses and five weak stresses. For example:

It is the cause, it is the cause, my soul,—
Let me not name it to you, you chaste stars!

Not all of *Othello* is in blank verse, however; Shakespeare uses prose and rhyming verse for various purposes in the play.

As an aid to the reader, we have prefaced each act with a brief summary of its action and have footnoted some of the more obscure terms and references. The text is from the Collier Folio of 1632, edited by George Long Duyckinch.

---

[1] See Winthrop D. Jordan, *White Over Black*, (Chapel Hill; University of North Carolina Press, 1968), Chapter 1.

[2] See Eldred Jones, *Othello's Countrymen*, (London: Oxford University Press, 1965).

Rubens, "Heads of Negroes." (Musées Royaux des Beaux-Arts ©ACL Bruxelles)

WILLIAM SHAKESPEARE *Othello, The Moor of Venice*

CHARACTERS

Duke of Venice
BRABANTIO, *a Senator*
Two other Senators
GRATIANO, *Brother to Brabantio*
LODOVICO, *Kinsman to Brabantio*
OTHELLO, *the Moor*
CASSIO, *his Lieutenant*
IAGO, *his Ancient*
RODERIGO, *a Venetian Gentleman*
MONTANO, *Governor of Cyprus*
Clown, *Servant to Othello*
Herald
DESDEMONA, *Daughter to Brabantio, and Wife to Othello*
EMILIA, *Wife to Iago*
BIANCA, *a Courtesan of Venice*
Officers, Gentlemen, Messengers, Musicians, Sailors, Attendants, &c.

THE SCENE. *For the first Act, in Venice; during the rest of the Play, at a Sea-Port in Cyprus.*

ACT I

SYNOPSIS: 1. Roderigo, in love with Desdemona, discusses with Iago her elopement with Othello and claims that Iago now favors Othello over him. Iago protests that since he was passed over, and Cassio chosen as Othello's lieutenant, he has reason to hate the general. They wake Brabantio to tell him that his daughter has eloped with the Moor. 2. Iago joins Othello on another street; Cassio delivers a message from the duke summoning the general to a military council. Brabantio and Roderigo enter, violent. Brabantio accuses Othello of having bewitched his daughter. Othello, with calm and dignity, persuades Brabantio to take his case to the duke. 3. The duke and senators, in council, discuss reports of a Turkish fleet threatening Cyprus. Brabantio presents his accusation of witchcraft to the duke. The duke sends for Desdemona, who makes it clear that she chose

Othello as husband of her own free will. The duke attempts to persuade Brabantio of his son-in-law's merit, but Brabantio rejects his daughter. The duke appoints Othello to defend Cyprus and become its governor; Desdemona will embark with Iago and meet him there. Iago persuades the despondent Roderigo that he may yet win Desdemona if he gives him (Iago) money. Alone, he begins his plan of vengeance on the Moor.

SCENE I. *Venice. A Street.*

(*Enter* RODERIGO *in choler, and* IAGO)

RODERIGO   Tush! never tell me, I take it much
   unkindly,
   That thou, Iago, who hast had my purse,
   As if the strings were thine, shouldst know of this.

IAGO   'Sblood! but you will not hear me:
   If ever I did dream of such a matter, abhor me.

RODERIGO   Thou told'st me thou didst hold him in
   thy hate.

IAGO   Despise me, if I do not. Three great ones of the
   city,
   In personal suit to make me his lieutenant,
   Off-capp'd to him; and, by the faith of man,
   I know my price: I am worth no worse a place;
   But he, as loving his own pride and purposes,
   Evades them, with a bombast circumstance,[1]
   Horribly stuff'd with epithets of war;
   And, in conclusion,
   Nonsuits my mediators; "For certes," says he,
   "I have already chose my officer." And what was he?
   Forsooth, a great arithmetician,
   One Michael Cassio, a Florentine,
   A fellow almost damn'd in a fair wife;
   That never set a squadron in the field,
   Nor the division of a battle knows
   More than a spinster; unless the bookish theoric,
   Wherein the toged consuls can propose
   As masterly as he: mere prattle, without practice,
   Is all his soldiership. But he, sir, had th' election;
   And I,—of whom his eyes had seen the proof,
   At Rhodes, at Cyprus, and on other grounds,
   Christian and heathen,—must be be-lee'd and calm'd
   By debitor and creditor, this counter-caster:
   He, in good time, must his lieutenant be,
   And I, God bless the mark! his Moor-ship's ancient.[2]

[1] Evasively and pompously.
[2] Ancient = ensign.

RODERIGO   By heaven, I rather would have been his
   hangman.

IAGO   But there 's no remedy: 't is the curse of service,
   Preferment goes by favour and affection,
   Not by the old gradation, where each second
   Stood heir t' the first. Now, sir, be judge yourself,
   Whether I in any just terms am affin'd
   To love the Moor.

RODERIGO   I would not follow him, then.

IAGO   O, sir! content you;
   I follow him to serve my turn upon him:
   We cannot all be masters, nor all masters
   Cannot be truly follow'd. You shall mark
   Many a duteous and knee-crooking knave,
   That, doting on his own obsequious bondage,
   Wears out his time, much like his master's ass.
   For nought but provender; and when he 's old,
   cashier'd
   Whip me such honest knaves. Others there are,
   Who, learn'd in forms and usages of duty,
   Keep yet their hearts attending on themselves,
   And, throwing but shows of service on their lords,
   Do well thrive by them; and when they have lin'd
   their coats,
   Do themselves homage: these fellows have some soul
   And such a one do I profess myself. For, sir,
   It is as sure as you are Roderigo,
   Were I the Moor, I would not be Iago:
   In following him, I follow but myself;
   Heaven is my judge, not I for love and duty,
   But seeming so, for my peculiar end:
   For when my outward action doth demonstrate
   The native act and figure of my heart
   In compliment extern, 't is not long after
   But I will wear my heart upon my sleeve
   For daws to peck at: I am not what I am.

RODERIGO   What a full fortune does the thick-lips
   owe,
   If he can carry 't thus!

IAGO   Call up her father;
   Rouse him: make after him, poison his delight,
   Proclaim him in the streets: incense her kinsmen;
   And though he in a fertile climate dwell,
   Plague him with flies: though that his joy be joy,
   Yet throw such changes of vexation on 't,
   As it may lose some colour.

RODERIGO   Here is her father's house: I 'll call aloud.

IAGO   Do; with like clamorous accent, and dire yell,
  As when, by night and negligence, the fire
  Is spied in populous cities.
RODERIGO   What ho! Brabantio! signior Brabantio,
  ho!
IAGO   Awake! what, ho! Brabantio! thieves! thieves!
  thieves!
  Look to your house, your daughter, and your bags!
  Thieves! thieves!

(Enter BRABANTIO, above, at a Window)

BRABANTIO   What is the reason of this terrible
  summons?
  What is the matter there?
RODERIGO   Signior, is all your family within?
IAGO   Are your doors lock'd?
BRABANTIO   Why? wherefore ask you this?
IAGO   'Zounds! sir; you are robb'd; for shame, put on
  your gown:
  Your heart is burst, you have lost half your soul:
  Even now, now, very now, an old black ram
  Is tupping your white ewe. Arise, arise!
  Awake the snorting citizens with the bell,
  Or else the devil will make a grandsire of you.
  Arise, I say.
BRABANTIO   What, have you lost your wits?
RODERIGO   Most reverend signior, do you know my
  voice?
BRABANTIO   Not I: what are you?
RODERIGO   My name is Roderigo.
BRABANTIO   The worse welcome:
  I have charg'd thee not to haunt about my doors.
  In honest plainness thou hast heard me say,
  My daughter is not for thee; and now, in madness,
  Being full of supper and distempering draughts,
  Upon malicious bravery dost thou come
  To start my quiet.
RODERIGO   Sir, sir, sir,—
BRABANTIO   But thou must needs be sure,
  My spirit and my place have in them power
  To make this bitter to thee.
RODERIGO   Patience, good sir.
BRABANTIO   What tell'st thou me of robbing? this is
  Venice;
  My house is not a grange.
RODERIGO   Most grave Brabantio,
  In simple and pure soul I come to you.

IAGO   'Zounds! sir, you are one of those, that will not
  serve God, if the devil bid you. Because we come to
  do you service, and you think we are ruffians, you 'll
  have your daughter covered with a Barbary horse:
  you 'll have your nephews neigh to you; you 'll have
  coursers for cousins, and gennets for germans.
BRABANTIO   What profane wretch art thou?
IAGO   I am one, sir, that comes to tell you, your
  daughter and the Moor are now making the beast
  with two backs.
BRABANTIO   Thou art a villain.
IAGO   You are—a senator.
BRABANTIO   This thou shalt answer: I know thee,
  Roderigo.
RODERIGO   Sir, I will answer any thing. But I beseech
  you,
  If 't be your pleasure, and most wise consent,
  (As partly, I find, it is) that your fair daughter,
  At this odd-even and dull watch o' the night,
  Transported with no worse nor better guard,
  But with a knave of common hire, a gondolier,
  To the gross clasps of a lascivious Moor,
  If this be known to you, and your allowance,
  We then have done you bold and saucy wrongs;
  But if you know not this, my manners tell me,
  We have your wrong rebuke. Do not believe
  That from the sense of all civility,
  I thus would play and trifle with your reverence:
  Your daughter, if you have not given her leave,
  I say again, hath made a gross revolt,
  Laying her duty, beauty, wit, and fortunes,
  On an extravagant and wheedling stranger,
  Of here and every where. Straight satisfy yourself
  If she be in her chamber, or your house,
  Let loose on me the justice of the state
  For thus deluding you.
BRABANTIO   Strike on the tinder, ho!
  Give me a taper!—call up all my people!—
  This accident is not unlike my dream;
  Belief of it oppresses me already.—
  Light, I say! light!

(Exit from above)

IAGO   Farewell, for I must leave you.
  It seems not meet, nor wholesome to my place,
  To be produc'd (as if I stay I shall)
  Against the Moor: for, I do know, the state,—

However this may gall him with some check,—
Cannot with safety cast him; for he 's embark'd
With such loud reason to the Cyprus wars
(Which even now stand in act) that, for their souls,
Another of his fathom they have none,
To lead their business:[3] in which regard,
Though I do hate him as I do hell pains,
Yet for necessity of present life,
I must show out a flag and sign of love,
Which is indeed but sign. That you shall surely find
  him,
Lead to the Sagittary the raised search;
And there will I be with him. So, farewell.

(Exit)

(Enter BRABANTIO, *and Servants with Torches)*

BRABANTIO   It is too true an evil: gone she is;
  And what 's to come of my despised time
  Is nought but bitterness.—Now, Roderigo,
  Where didst thou see her?—O, unhappy girl!—
  With the Moor, say'st thou?—Who would be a
    father?—
  How didst thou know 't was she?—O! thou deceiv'st
    me
  Past thought.—What said she to you?—Get more
    tapers!
  Raise all my kindred!—Are they married, think you?
RODERIGO   Truly, I think, they are.
BRABANTIO   O heaven!—How got she out?—O,
    treason of my blood!—
  Fathers, from hence trust not your daughters' minds
  By what you see them act.—Are there not charms,
  By which the property of youth and maidhood
  May be abus'd? Have you not read, Roderigo,
  Of some such thing?
RODERIGO   Yes, sir; I have, indeed.
BRABANTIO   Call up my brother.—O, that you had
    had her!—
  Some one way, some another.—Do you know
  Where we may apprehend her and the Moor?
RODERIGO   I think, I can discover him, if you please
  To get good guard, and go along with me.
BRABANTIO   Pray you, lead on. At every house I 'll call,

I may command at most.—Get weapons, ho!
And raise some special officers of night.—
On, good Roderigo;—I 'll deserve your pains.

(Exeunt)

SCENE II.   *The Same. Another Street.*

(Enter OTHELLO, IAGO, *and Attendants, with Torches)*

IAGO   Though in the trade of war I have slain men,
  Yet do I hold it very stuff o' the conscience
  To do no contriv'd murder: I lack iniquity
  Sometimes, to do me service. Nine or ten times
  I had thought to have yerk'd him here, under the
    ribs.
OTHELLO   'T is better as it is.
IAGO   Nay, but he prated,
  And spoke such scurvy and provoking terms
  Against your honour,
  That, with the little godliness I have,
  I did full hard forbear him. But, I pray, sir,
  Are you fast married? for, be sure of this,
  That the magnifico[4] is much beloved;
  And hath, in his effect, a voice potential,
  As double as the duke's: he will divorce you;
  Or put upon you what restraint, or grievance,
  The law (with all his might t' enforce it on)
  Will give him cable.
OTHELLO   Let him do his spite:
  My services, which I have done the signiory,
  Shall out-tongue his complaints. 'T is yet to know,
  Which, when I know that boasting is an honour,
  I shall promulgate, I fetch my life and being
  From men of royal siege; and my demerits
  May speak, unbonneted, to as proud a fortune
  As this that I have reach'd: for know, Iago,
  But that I love the gentle Desdemona,
  I would not my unhoused free condition
  Put into circumscription and confine
  For the sea's worth. But, look! what lights come
    yonder?
IAGO   These are the raised father, and his friends:
  You were best go in.
OTHELLO   Not I; I must be found:

---

[3] Here it seems that Iago grudgingly admits Othello's merit.

[4] "The magnificent (or noble) one": Brabantio.

My parts, my title, and my perfect soul,
Shall manifest me rightly. Is it they?
IAGO   By Janus, I think no.

(Enter CASSIO, *and certain Officers with Torches)*

OTHELLO   The servants of the duke, and my
    lieutenant.
The goodness of the night upon you, friends.
What is the news?
CASSIO   The duke does greet you, general;
And he requires your haste, post-haste appearance,
Even on the instant.
OTHELLO   What is the matter, think you?
CASSIO   Something from Cyprus, as I may divine.
It is a business of some heat: the galleys
Have sent a dozen sequent messengers,
This very night, at one another's heels;
And many of the consuls, rais'd and met,
Are at the duke's already. You have been hotly call'd
    for;
When, being not at your lodging to be found,
The senate sent above three several quests,
To search you out.
OTHELLO   'T is well I am found by you
I will but spend a word here in the house,
And go with you.

(Exit)

CASSIO   Ancient, what makes he here?
IAGO   'Faith, he to-night hath boarded a land carack:
If it prove lawful prize, he 's made for ever.
CASSIO   I do not understand.
IAGO   He 's married.
CASSIO   To whom?

(Re-enter OTHELLO)

IAGO   Marry, to—Come, captain, will you go?
OTHELLO   Have with you.
CASSIO   Here comes another troop to seek for you.
IAGO   It is Brabantio.—General, be advis'd:
He comes to bad intent.

(Enter BRABANTIO, RODERIGO, *and Officers, with Torches
and Weapons)*

OTHELLO   Holla! stand there!
RODERIGO   Signior, it is the Moor.

BRABANTIO   Down with him, thief!

(They draw on both sides)

IAGO   You, Roderigo! come, sir, I am for you.
OTHELLO   Keep up your bright swords, for the dew
    will rust them.—
Good signior, you shall more command with years,
Than with your weapons.
BRABANTIO   O, thou foul thief! where hast thou
    stow'd my daughter?
Damn'd as thou art, thou hast enchanted her,
For I 'll refer me to all things of sense,
If she in chains of magic were not bound,
Whether a maid so tender, fair, and happy,
So opposite to marriage, that she shunn'd
The wealthy curled darlings of our nation,
Would ever have, to incur a general mock,
Run from her guardage to the sooty bosom
Of such a thing as thou; to fear, not to delight.
Judge me the world, if 't is not gross in sense,
That thou hast practis'd on her with foul charms;
Abus'd her delicate youth with drugs, or minerals,
That weaken motion.—I 'll have 't disputed on,
'T is probable, and palpable to thinking.
I, therefore, apprehend, and do attach thee
For an abuser of the world, a practiser
Of arts inhibited, and out of warrant.—
Lay hold upon him! if he do resist,
Subdue him at his peril.
OTHELLO   Hold your hands!
Both you of my inclining, and the rest.
Were it my cue to fight, I should have known it
Without a prompter.—Where will you that I go,
To answer this your charge?
BRABANTIO   To prison; till fit time
Of law, and course of direct session,
Call thee to answer.
OTHELLO   What if I do obey?
How may the duke be therewith satisfied,
Whose messengers are here about my side
Upon some present business of the state,
To bear me to him?
OFFICER   'T is true, most worthy signior;
The duke 's in council, and your noble self,
I am sure, is sent for.
BRABANTIO   How! the duke in council,

In this time of the night!—Bring him away.
Mine 's not an idle cause: the duke himself,
Or any of my brothers of the state,
Cannot but feel this wrong, as 't were their own;
For if such actions may have passage free,
Bond-slaves and pagans shall our statesmen be.

(Exeunt)

SCENE III.   *The Same. A Council-Chamber.*
The DUKE, *and Senators, sitting in state; Officers attending*

DUKE   There is no composition in these news,
  That gives them credit.
1 SENATOR   Indeed, they are disproportion'd;
  My letters say, a hundred and seven galleys.
DUKE   And mine, a hundred and forty.
2 SENATOR   And mine, two hundred:
  But though they jump not on a just account,
  (As in these cases, with the same reports,
  'T is oft with difference) yet do they all confirm
  A Turkish fleet, and bearing up to Cyprus.
DUKE   Nay, it is possible enough to judgment.
  I do not so secure me in the error,
  But the main article I do approve
  In fearful sense.
SAILOR *(Within)*   What ho! what ho! what ho!

(Enter an Officer, with a Sailor)

OFFICER   A messenger from the galleys.
DUKE   Now, what 's the business?
SAILOR   The Turkish preparation makes for Rhodes:
  So was I bid report here to the state,
  By Signior Angelo.
DUKE   How say you by this change?
1 SENATOR   This cannot be,
  By no assay of reason: 't is a pageant,
  To keep us in false gaze. When we consider
  The importancy of Cyprus to the Turk;
  And let ourselves again but understand,
  That, as it more concerns the Turk than Rhodes,
  So may he with more facile question bear it,
  For that it stands not in such warlike brace,
  But altogether lacks th' abilities
  That Rhodes is dress'd in:—if we make thought of
    this,
  We must not think the Turk is so unskilful,

To leave that latest which concerns him first,
Neglecting an attempt of ease and gain,
To wake, and wage, a danger profitless.
DUKE   Nay, in all confidence, he 's not for Rhodes.
OFFICER   Here is more news.

(Enter a Messenger)

MESSENGER   The Ottomites, reverend and gracious,
  Steering with due course toward the isle of Rhodes,
  Have there injointed them with an after fleet.
1 SENATOR   Ay, so I thought.—How many, as you guess?
MESSENGER   Of thirty sail; and now do they re-stem
  Their backward course, bearing with frank
    appearance
  Their purposes toward Cyprus.—Signior Montano,
  Your trusty and most valiant servitor,
  With his free duty recommends you thus,
  And prays you to believe him.
DUKE   'T is certain, then, for Cyprus.—
  Marcus Luccicos, is not he in town?
1 SENATOR   He 's now in Florence.
DUKE   Write from us to him; post, post-haste dispatch.
1 SENATOR   Here comes Brabantio, and the valiant
    Moor.

(Enter BRABANTIO, OTHELLO, IAGO, RODERIGO, *and
Officers)*

DUKE   Valiant Othello, we must straight employ you
  Against the general enemy Ottoman.—
  I did not see you; welcome, gentle signior;

(To BRABANTIO)

We lack'd your counsel and your help to-night.
BRABANTIO   So did I yours. Good your grace, pardon
    me;
  Neither my place, nor aught I heard of business,
  Hath rais'd me from my bed; nor doth the general
    care
  Take hold of me, for my particular grief
  Is of so flood-gate and o'er-bearing nature,
  That it engluts and swallows other sorrows,
  And it is still itself.
DUKE   Why, what 's the matter?
BRABANTIO   My daughter! O, my daughter!
DUKE and SENATORS   Dead?
BRABANTIO   Ay, to me

Plate VII Botticelli, "Primavera."
(Uffizi, Florence—Scala/Editorial
Photocolor Archives)

Plate X Hans Holbein, "Jean de Dinteville and Georges de Selve" (The Ambassadors). (Reproduced by courtesy of the Trustees, The National Gallery, London)

Plate VIII Leonardo da Vinci, "The Madonna of the Rocks," Louvre. (Clichés Musées Nationaux, Paris)

Plate IX Michelangelo, The Sistine Ceiling, detail, "God and Adam." (Sistine Chapel, Rome—Scala/Editorial Photocolor Archives)

Plate XI Gelede dancer, Meko.
(Copyright F. Willett, Glasgow)

Plate XII Gelede dance scene.
(Howard Wildman)

She is abus'd, stol'n from me, and corrupted
By spells and medicines bought of mountebanks;
For nature so preposterously to err,
(Being not deficient, blind, or lame of sense)
Sans witchcraft could not.

DUKE   Whoe'er he be that, in this foul proceeding,
Hath thus beguil'd your daughter of herself,
And you of her, the bloody book of law
You shall yourself read in the bitter letter,
After its own sense; yea, though our proper son
Stood in your action.

BRABANTIO   Humbly I thank your grace.
Here is the man, this Moor; whom now, it seems,
Your special mandate, for the state affairs,
Hath hither brought.

DUKE and SENATORS   We are very sorry for it.

DUKE   What, in your own part, can you say to this?

(*To* OTHELLO)

BRABANTIO   Nothing, but this is so.

OTHELLO   Most potent, grave, and reverend signiors.
My very noble and approv'd good masters,
That I have ta'en away this old man's daughter,
It is most true; true, I have married her:
The very head and front of my offending
Hath this extent, no more. Rude am I in my speech,[5]
And little bless'd with the soft phrase of peace;
For since these arms of mine had seven years' pith,
Till now, some nine moons wasted, they have us'd
Their dearest action in the tented field;
And little of this great world can I speak,
More than pertains to feats of broil and battle;
And, therefore, little shall I grace my cause,
In speaking for myself. Yet, by your gracious
    patience,
I will a round unvarnish'd tale deliver
Of my whole course of love; what drugs, what
    charms,
What conjuration, and what mighty magic,
(For such proceeding I am charg'd withal)
I won his daughter with.

BRABANTIO   A maiden never bold;

Of spirit so still and quiet, that her motion
Blush'd at herself; and she,—in spite of nature,
Of years, of country, credit, every thing,—
To fall in love with what she fear'd to look on!
It is a judgment maim'd, and most imperfect,
That will confess perfection so could err
Against all rules of nature; and must be driven
To find out practices of cunning hell,
Why this should be. I, therefore, vouch again,
That with some mixtures powerful o'er the blood,
Or with some dram conjur'd to this effect,
He wrought upon her.

DUKE   To vouch this is no proof
Without more evidence and overt test,
These are thin habits, and poor likelihoods
Of modern seeming, you prefer against him.

1 SENATOR   But, Othello, speak:
Did you by indirect and forced courses
Subdue and poison this young maid's affections,
Or came it by request, and such fair question
As soul to soul affordeth.

OTHELLO   I do beseech you,
Send for the lady to the Sagittary,
And let her speak of me before her father:
If you do find me foul in her report,
The trust, the office, I do hold of you,
Not only take away, but let your sentence
Even fall upon my life.

DUKE   Fetch Desdemona hither.

OTHELLO   Ancient, conduct them; you best know the
    place.—

(*Exeunt* IAGO *and Attendants*)

And, till she come, as truly as to heaven
I do confess the vices of my blood,
So justly to your grave ears I 'll present
How I did thrive in this fair lady's love,
And she in mine.

DUKE   Say it, Othello.

OTHELLO   Her father lov'd me; oft invited me;
Still question'd me the story of my life,
From year to year; the battles, sieges, fortunes,
That I had pass'd.
I ran it through, even from my boyish days,
To the very moment that he bade me tell it:
Wherein I spake of most disastrous chances,

---

[5] Is it true that Othello's speech is rude? How does Othello's self-concept as a military man unused to court life later serve Iago's purposes?

Of moving accidents, by flood, and field;
Of hair-breadth scapes i' th' imminent deadly
  breach;
Of being taken by the insolent foe,
And sold to slavery; of my redemption thence,
And portance in my travel's history:
Wherein of antres vast, and deserts idle,
Rough quarries, rocks, and hills whose heads touch
  heaven,
It was my hint to speak, such was the process;
And of the Cannibals that each other eat,
The Anthropophagi, and men whose heads
Do grow beneath their shoulders. This to hear,
Would Desdemona seriously incline:
But still the house affairs would draw her thence;
Which ever as she could with haste despatch,
She 'd come again, and with a greedy ear
Devour up my discourse. Which I observing,
Took once a pliant hour; and found good means
To draw from her a prayer of earnest heart,
That I would all my pilgrimage dilate,
Whereof by parcels she had something heard,
But not intentively: I did consent;
And often did beguile her of her tears,
When I did speak of some distressful stroke,
That my youth suffer'd. My story being done,
She gave me for my pains a world of sighs:
She swore,—in faith, 't was strange, 't was passing
  strange;
'T was pitiful, 't was wondrous pitiful:
She wish'd she had not heard it; yet she wish'd
That heaven had made her such a man: she thank'd
  me;
And bade me, if I had a friend that lov'd her,
I should but teach him how to tell my story,
And that would woo her.—On this hint I spake;
She lov'd me for the dangers I had pass'd,
And I lov'd her, that she did pity them.
This only is the witchcraft I have us'd:
Here comes the lady; let her witness it.

(Enter DESDEMONA, IAGO, *and Attendants)*

DUKE   I think, this tale would win my daughter too.
  Good Brabantio,
  Take up this mangled matter at the best:
  Men do their broken weapons rather use,

Than their bare hands.
BRABANTIO   I pray you, hear her speak:
  If she confess that she was half the wooer,
  Destruction on my head, if my bad blame
  Light on the man.—Come hither, gentle mistress:
  Do you perceive in all this noble company,
  Where most you owe obedience?
DESDEMONA   My noble father.
  I do perceive here a divided duty.
  To you, I am bound for life, and education:
  My life and education both do learn me
  How to respect you; you are the lord of duty;
  I am hitherto your daughter: but here 's my husband,
  And so much duty as my mother show'd
  To you, preferring you before her father,
  So much I challenge that I may profess
  Due to the Moor, my lord.
BRABANTIO   God be with you!—I have done.—
  Please it your grace, on to the state affairs:
  I had rather to adopt a child, than get it.—
  Come hither, Moor:
  I here to give thee that with all my heart,
  Which, but thou hast already, with all my heart
  I would keep from thee.—For your sake, jewel,
  I am glad at soul I have no other child,
  For thy escape would teach me tyranny,
  To hang clogs on them.—I have done, my lord.
DUKE   Let me speak like yourself; and say a sentence,
  Which, as a grise, or step, may help these lovers
  Into your favour.
  When remedies are past, the griefs are ended
  By seeing the worst, which late on hopes depended.
  To mourn a mischief that is past and gone
  Is the next way to draw new mischief on.
  What cannot be preserv'd when fortune takes,
  Patience her injury a mockery makes.
  The robb'd, that smiles, steals something from the
    thief;
  He robs himself, that spends a bootless grief.
BRABANTIO   So let the Turk of Cyprus us beguile;
  We lose it not, so long as we can smile.
  He bears the sentence well, that nothing bears
  But the free comfort which from thence he hears,
  But he bears both the sentence and the sorrow,
  That, to pay grief, must of poor patience borrow.
  These sentences, to sugar, or to gall,

Being strong on both sides, are equivocal:
But words are words; I never yet did hear,
That the bruis'd heart was pierced through the ear.
Beseech you, now to the affairs of state.

DUKE   The Turk with a most mighty preparation,
makes for Cyprus.—Othello, the fortitude of the
place is best known to you; and though we have
there a substitute of most allowed sufficiency, yet
opinion, a most sovereign mistress of effects, throws
a more safer voice on you: you must, therefore, be
content to slubber the gloss of your new fortunes
with this more stubborn and boisterous expedition.

OTHELLO   The tyrant custom, most grave senators,
Hath made the flinty and steel couch of war
My thrice-driven bed of down: I do agnize
A natural and prompt alacrity,
I find in hardness; and do undertake
These present wars against the Ottomites.
Most humbly, therefore, bending to your state,
I crave fit disposition for my wife;
Due reference of place, and exhibition,
With such accommodation, and besort,
As levels with her breeding.

DUKE   If you please,
Be 't at her father's.

BRABANTIO   I 'll not have it so.

OTHELLO   Nor I.

DESDEMONA   Nor I; I would not there reside,
To put my father in impatient thoughts,
By being in his eye. Most gracious duke,
To my unfolding lend a prosperous ear:
And let me find a charter in your voice,
T' assist my simpleness.

DUKE   What would you, Desdemona?

DESDEMONA   That I did love the Moor to live with
him,
My downright violence and storm of fortunes
May trumpet to the world: my heart 's subdued
Even to the very quality of my lord:
I saw Othello's visage in his mind;
And to his honours, and his valiant parts,
Did I my soul and fortunes consecrate.
So that, dear lords, if I be left behind,
A moth of peace, and he go to the war,
The rites for which I love him are bereft me,
And I a heavy interim shall support

By his dear absence. Let me go with him.

OTHELLO   Your voices, lords: 'beseech you, let her will
Have a free way.
Vouch with me, heaven, I therefore beg it not,
To please the palate of my appetite;
Nor to comply wi' the young affects of heat,
(In me defunct) and proper satisfaction;
But to be free and bounteous to her mind:
And heaven defend your counsels, that you think
I will your serious and great business scant,
When she is with me. No, when light-wing'd toys
Of feather'd Cupid foil with wanton dulness
My speculative and active instruments,
That my disports corrupt and taint my business,
Let housewives make a skillet of my helm,
And all indign and base adversities
Make head against my reputation!

DUKE   Be it as you shall privately determine,
Either for her stay, or going. Th' affair cries haste,
And speed must answer it: you must hence to-night.

DESDEMONA   To-night, my lord?

DUKE   This night.

OTHELLO   With all my heart.

DUKE   At nine i' the morning here we 'll meet again.
Othello, leave some officer behind,
And he shall our commission bring to you;
With such things else of quality and respect,
As do import you.

OTHELLO   Please your grace, my ancient;
A man he is of honesty, and trust:
To his conveyance I assign my wife,
With what else needful your good grace shall think
To be sent after me.

DUKE   Let it be so.—
Good night to every one.—And, noble signior,

(*To* BRABANTIO)

If virtue no delighted beauty lack,
Your son-in-law is far more fair than black.

1 SENATOR   Adieu, brave Moor! use Desdemona well.

BRABANTIO   Look to her, Moor, if thou hast eyes to
see:
She has deceiv'd her father, and may thee.[6]

---

[6] A foreshadowing warning, which Iago will use. Note the dramatic
irony in Othello's response.

(Exeunt DUKE, *Senators, Officers, &c.)*

OTHELLO   My life upon her faith.—Honest Iago,
My Desdemona must I leave to thee:
I pr'ythee, let thy wife attend on her,
And bring her after in the best advantage.—
Come, Desdemona; I have but an hour
Of love, of worldly matters and direction,
To spend with thee: we must obey the time.

(Exeunt OTHELLO *and* DESDEMONA*)*

RODERIGO   Iago.

IAGO   What say'st thou, noble heart?

RODERIGO   What will I do, thinkest thou?

IAGO   Why, go to bed, and sleep.

RODERIGO   I will incontinently drown myself.

IAGO   Well, if thou dost, I shall never love thee after
it. Why, thou silly gentleman!

RODERIGO   It is silliness to live, when to live is a torment; and then have we a prescription to die, when
death is our physician.

IAGO   O villainous! I have looked upon the world for
four times seven years, and since I could distinguish
betwixt a benefit and an injury, I never found a man
that knew how to love himself. Ere I would say, I
would drown myself for the love of a Guinea-hen, I
would change my humanity with a baboon.

RODERIGO   What should I do? I confess, it is my
shame to be so fond; but it is not in my virtue to
amend it.

IAGO   Virtue? a fig! 't is in ourselves that we are thus,
or thus. Our bodies are gardens, to the which our
wills are gardeners; so that if we will plant nettles, or
sow lettuce; set hyssop, and weed up thyme, supply
it with one gender of herbs, or distract it with many;
either to have it sterile with idleness, or manured
with industry; why, the power and corrigible authority of this lies in our wills. If the balance of our lives
had not one scale of reason to poise another of sen-
suality, the blood and baseness of our natures would
conduct us to most preposterous conclusions: but we
have reason to cool our raging motions, our carnal
stings, our unbitted lusts, whereof I take this, that
you call love, to be a sect, or scion.

RODERIGO   It cannot be.

IAGO   It is merely a lust of the blood, and a permission
of the will. Come, be a man: drown thyself? drown

cats, and blind puppies. I profess me thy friend, and I
confess me knit to thy deserving with cables of per-
durable toughness; I could never better stead thee
than now. Put money in thy purse; follow these
wars; defeat thy favour with an usurped beard; I say,
put money in thy purse. It cannot be, that Desdemona should long continue her love to the Moor,—
put money in thy purse;—nor he his to her: it was a
violent commencement, and thou shalt see an an-
swerable sequestration;—put but money in thy
purse.—These Moors are changeable in their wills;—
fill thy purse with money: the food that to him now
is as luscious as locusts, shall be to him shortly as bitter as coloquintida. She must change for youth:
when she is sated with his body, she will find the error of her choice.—She must have change, she must:
therefore, put money in thy purse.—If thou wilt
needs damn thyself, do it a more delicate way than
drowning. Make all the money thou canst. If sancti-
mony and a frail vow, betwixt an erring barbarian
and a supersubtle Venetian, be not too hard for my
wits, and all the tribe of hell, thou shalt enjoy her;
therefore make money. A pox of drowning thyself! it
is clean out of the way: seek thou rather to be
hanged in compassing thy joy, than to be drowned
and go without her.

RODERIGO   Wilt thou be fast to my hopes, if I depend
on the issue?

IAGO   Thou art sure of me.—Go, make money.—I
have told thee often, and I re-tell thee again and
again, I hate the Moor: my cause is hearted; thine
hath no less reason. Let us be conjunctive in our revenge against him: if thou canst cuckold him, thou
dost thyself a pleasure, me a sport. There are many
events in the womb of time, which will be delivered.
Traverse, go; provide thy money. We will have more
of this to-morrow. Adieu.

RODERIGO   Where shall we meet i' the morning?

IAGO   At my lodging.

RODERIGO   I 'll be with thee betimes.

IAGO   Go to; farewell. Do you hear, Roderigo?

RODERIGO   What say you?

IAGO   No more of drowning, do you hear?

RODERIGO   I am changed. I 'll sell all my land.

IAGO   Go to; farewell: put money enough in your
purse

(Exit RODERIGO)

Thus do I ever make my fool my purse;
For I mine own gain'd knowledge should profane,
If I would time expend with such a snipe,
But for my sport and profit. I hate the Moor;
And it is thought abroad that 'twixt my sheets
He has done my office: I know not if 't be true.
Yet I, for mere suspicion in that kind,
Will do as if for surety. He holds me well;
The better shall my purpose work on him.
Cassio 's a proper man: let me see now;
To get his place, and to plume up my will
In double knavery,—How, how?—Let 's see:—
After some time, to abuse Othello's ear
That he is too familiar with his wife:
He hath a person, and a smooth dispose,
To be suspected; fram'd to make women false.
The Moor is of a free and open nature,
That thinks men honest, that but seem to be so,
And will as tenderly be led by the nose,
As asses are.—
I have 't;—it is engender'd:—hell and night
Must bring this monstrous birth to the world's light.

(Exit)

ACT II

SYNOPSIS: 1. News comes to Cyprus that a storm has destroyed the Turkish fleet. Cassio, then Iago and Desdemona arrive in Cyprus. Othello's ship is delayed by the storm, and Desdemona is anxious. Iago plots to entrap Cassio. Othello arrives and is happily reunited with his bride. Iago convinces Roderigo that Desdemona loves Cassio and that he should pick a fight with the lieutenant. In a soliloquy Iago reveals that he suspects his own wife of being unfaithful with Othello and with Cassio. 2. Othello's herald announces a night of revel to celebrate the destruction of the Turkish fleet and the wedding. 3. The newlyweds retire for the night; Cassio is left in charge of the nightwatch. Iago, who knows Cassio's weakness for drink, succeeds in making him drunk. Roderigo then picks his fight and is wounded by Cassio. An alarm summons Othello to the scene of the brawl. He finds Cassio at fault and discharges him. Iago persuades Cassio that he can regain Othello's favor by asking Desdemona for help.

SCENE I.   *A Sea-port Town in Cyprus. A Platform.*

(Enter MONTANO *and Two Gentlemen)*

MONTANO   What from the cape can you discern at
  sea?

1 GENTLEMAN   Nothing at all: it is a high-wrought
  flood;
  I cannot, 'twixt the heaven and the main,
  Descry a sail.
MONTANO   Methinks, the wind hath spoke aloud at
  land;
  A fuller blast ne'er shook our battlements:
  If it hath ruffian'd so upon the sea,
  What ribs of oak, when mountains melt on them,
  Can hold the mortise? what shall we hear of this?
2 GENTLEMAN   A segregation of the Turkish fleet:
  For do but stand upon the foaming shore,
  The chidden billow seems to pelt the clouds,
  The wind-shak'd surge, with high and monstrous
    mane,
  Seems to cast water on the burning bear,
  And quench the guards of th' ever-fixed pole.
  I never did like molestation view
  On the enchafed flood.
MONTANO   If that the Turkish fleet
  Be not inshelter'd and enbay'd, they are drown'd;
  It is impossible to bear it out.

(Enter a Third Gentleman)

3 GENTLEMAN   News, lads! our wars are done.
  The desperate tempest hath so bang'd the Turks,
  That their designment halts: a noble ship of Venice
  Hath seen a grievous wreck and sufferance
  On most part of their fleet.
MONTANO   How! is this true?
3 GENTLEMAN   The ship is here put in:
  A Florentine, Michael Cassio,
  Lieutenant to the warlike Moor, Othello,
  Is come on shore: the Moor himself 's at sea,
  And is in full commission here for Cyprus.
MONTANO   I am glad on 't; 't is a worthy governor.
3 GENTLEMAN   But this same Cassio, though he speak
    of comfort,
  Touching the Turkish loss, yet he looks sadly,
  And prays the Moor be safe; for they were parted
  With foul and violent tempest.
MONTANO   Pray heaven he be;
  For I have serv'd him, and the man commands
  Like a full soldier. Let 's to the sea-side, ho!
  As well to see the vessel that 's come in,
  As to throw out our eyes for brave Othello,

Even till we make the main, and th' aerial blue,
An indistinct regard.
3 GENTLEMAN   Come, let 's do so;
For every minute is expectancy
Of more arrivance.

(Enter CASSIO, and several Islanders)

CASSIO   Thanks you, the valiant of the warlike isle
That so approve the Moor.—O! let the heavens
Give him defence against the elements,
For I have lost him on a dangerous sea.
MONTANO   Is he well shipp'd?
CASSIO   His bark is stoutly timber'd, and his pilot
Of very expert and approv'd allowance;
Therefore my hopes, not surfeited to death,
Stand in bold cure.

(Within)

A sail, a sail, a sail!

(Enter a Messenger)

CASSIO   What noise?
MESSENGER   The town is empty; on the brow o' the sea
Stand ranks of people, and they cry, "a sail."
CASSIO   My hopes do shape him for the governor.

(Guns heard)

2 GENTLEMAN   Thay do discharge their shot of
     courtesy:
Our friends, at least.
CASSIO   I pray you, sir, go forth,
And give us truth who 't is arriv'd.
2 GENTLEMAN   I shall.

(Exit)

MONTANO   But, good lieutenant, is your general
     wiv'd?
CASSIO   Most fortunately: he hath achiev'd a maid,
That paragons description, and wild fame;
One that excels the quirks of blazoning pens,
And in th' essential vesture of creation,
Does bear all excellency.[1]—How now! who has put
     in?

---

[1] As God made her, she is perfect. Cassio's speech is reminiscent of
the language of courtly love.

(Re-enter Second Gentleman)

2 GENTLEMAN   'T is one Iago, ancient to the general.
CASSIO   He has had most favourable and happy speed:
Tempests themselves, high seas, and howling winds,
The gutter'd rocks, and congregated sands,
Traitors ensteep'd to clog the guiltless keel,
As having sense of beauty, do omit
Their mortal natures, letting go safely by
The divine Desdemona.
MONTANO   What is she?
CASSIO   She that I spake of, our great captain's captain,
Left in the conduct of the bold Iago;
Whose footing here anticipates our thoughts,
A se'ennight's speed.—Great Jove! Othello guard,
And swell his sail with thine own powerful breath,
That he may bless this bay with his tall ship,
Make love's quick pants in Desdemona's arms,
Give renew'd fire to our extincted spirits,
And bring all Cyprus comfort.—O, behold!

*(Enter DESDEMONA, EMILIA, IAGO, RODERIGO, and
Attendants)*

The riches of the ship is come on shore.
Ye men of Cyprus, let her have your knees.—

. *(They kneel)*

Hail to thee, lady! and the grace of heaven,
Before, behind thee, and on every hand,
Enwheel thee round.
DESDEMONA   I thank you, valiant Cassio.
What tidings can you tell me of my lord?
CASSIO   He is not yet arriv'd; nor know I aught
But that he 's well, and will be shortly here.
DESDEMONA   O! but I fear.—How lost you company?
CASSIO   The great contention of the sea and skies
Parted our fellowship.
(Within)   A sail, a sail!
But, hark! a sail.

(Guns heard)

2 GENTLEMAN   They give their greeting to the citadel:
This likewise is a friend.
CASSIO   See for the news.—

(Exit Gentleman)

Good ancient, you are welcome.—Welcome,
  Mistress.—

(To EMILIA)

Let it not gall your patience, good Iago,
That I extend my manners: 't is my breeding
That gives me this bold show of courtesy.

(Kissing her)

IAGO   Sir, would she give you so much of her lips,
  As of her tongue she oft bestows on me,
  You 'd have enough.
DESDEMONA   Alas! she has no speech.
IAGO   In faith, too much;
  I find it still, when I have lust to sleep:
  Marry, before your ladyship, I grant,
  She puts her tongue a little in her heart,
  And chides with thinking.
EMILIA   You have little cause to say so.
IAGO   Come on, come on; you are pictures out of
    doors,
  Bells in your parlours, wild cats in your kitchens,
  Saints in your injuries, devils being offended,
  Players in your housewifery, and housewives in your
    beds.
DESDEMONA   O, fie upon thee, slanderer!
IAGO   Nay, it is true, or else I am a Turk:
  You rise to play, and go to bed to work.
EMILIA   You shall not write my praise.
IAGO   No, let me not.
DESDEMONA   What wouldst thou write of me, if thou
    shouldst praise me?
IAGO   O gentle lady, do not put me to 't,
  For I am nothing, if not critical.
DESDEMONA   Come on; assay.—There's one gone to
    the harbour?
CASSIO   Ay, madam.
DESDEMONA   I am not merry; but I do beguile
  The thing I am, by seeming otherwise.—
  Come; how wouldst thou praise me?
IAGO   I am about it, but, indeed, my invention
  Comes from my pate, as birdlime does from frize,[2]

It plucks out brains and all; but my muse labours,
  And thus she is deliver'd.
If she be fair and wise,—fairness, and wit,
  The one 's for use, the other useth it.
DESDEMONA   Well prais'd!—How, if she be black and
    witty?
IAGO   If she be black, and thereto have a wit,
  She 'll find a white that shall her blackness fit.
DESDEMONA   Worse and worse.
EMILIA   How, if fair and foolish?
IAGO   She never yet was foolish that was fair;
  For even her folly helps her to an heir.
DESDEMONA   These are old fond paradoxes, to make
  fools laugh i' the alehouse. What miserable praise
  hast thou for her that 's foul and foolish?
IAGO   There 's none so foul, and foolish thereunto,
  But does foul pranks which fair and wise ones do.
DESDEMONA   O heavy ignorance! thou praisest the
  worst best. But what praise couldst thou bestow on a
  deserving woman indeed? one that, in the authority
  of her merit, did justly put on the vouch of very mal-
  ice itself?
IAGO   She that was ever fair, and never proud;
  Had tongue at will, and yet was never loud;
  Never lack'd gold, and yet went never gay;
  Fled from her wish, and yet said,—"now I may":
  She that, being anger'd, her revenge being nigh,
  Bade her wrong stay, and her displeasure fly;
  She that in wisdom never was so frail,
  To change the cod's head for the salmon's tail;
  She that could think, and ne'er disclose her mind,
  See suitors following, and not look behind:
  She was a wight,—if ever such wight were,—
DESDEMONA   To do what?
IAGO   To suckle fools, and chronicle small beer.[3]
DESDEMONA   O, most lame and impotent conclusion!
  —Do not learn of him, Emilia, though he be thy hus-
  band.—How say you, Cassio? is he not a most pro-
  fane and liberal [4] censurer?
CASSIO   He speaks home, madam; you may relish him
  more in the soldier, than in the scholar.

(Talks apart with DESDEMONA)

---

[2] Frize—a coarse cloth. Its threads come out when birdlime, a sticky
  paste, is removed from it.

[3] Small beer—trivial events.
[4] Worldly and licentious.

IAGO *(Aside)*   He takes her by the palm: ay, well said, whisper: with as little a web as this, will I ensnare as great a fly as Cassio. Ay, smile upon her, do; I will gyve thee in thine own courtship. You say true; 't is so, indeed: if such tricks as these strip you out of your lieutenantry, it had been better you had not kissed your three fingers so oft, which now again you are most apt to play the sir in. Very good; well kissed! an excellent courtesy! 't is so indeed. Yet again your fingers to your lips? would, they were clys-ter-pipes[5] for your sake.—*(A Trumpet heard)* The Moor! I know his trumpet.

CASSIO   'T is truly so.

DESDEMONA   Let 's meet him, and receive him.

CASSIO   Lo, where he comes!

(Enter OTHELLO, and Attendants)

OTHELLO   O, my fair warrior!

DESDEMONA   My dear Othello!

OTHELLO   It gives me wonder great as my content,
   To see you here before me. O, my soul's joy!
   If after every tempest come such calms,
   May the winds blow, till they have waken'd death,
   And let the labouring bark climb hills of seas,
   Olympus-high, and duck again as low
   As hell 's from heaven. If it were now to die,
   'T were now to be most happy; for, I fear,
   My soul hath her content so absolute,
   That not another comfort like to this
   Succeeds in unknown fate.[6]

DESDEMONA   The heavens forbid,
   But that our loves and comforts should increase,
   Even as our days do grow!

OTHELLO   Amen to that, sweet powers!—
   I cannot speak enough of this content;
   It stops me here; it is too much of joy:
   And this, and this, the greatest discords be,

(Kissing her)

That e'er our hearts shall make!

IAGO *(Aside)*   O! you are well tun'd now;
   But I 'll set down the pegs that makes this music,
   As honest as I am.

---

[5] Tubes used for injection.
[6] This is an instance of dramatic irony.

OTHELLO   Come, let us to the castle.—
   News, friends; our wars are done, the Turks are
      drown'd.
   How does my old acquaintance of this isle?—
   Honey, you shall be well desir'd in Cyprus,
   I have found great love amongst them. O my sweet,
   I prattle out of fashion, and I dote
   In mine own comforts.—I pr'ythee, good Iago,
   Go to the bay, and disembark my coffers.
   Bring thou the master to the citadel:
   He is a good one, and his worthiness
   Does challenge much respect.—Come, Desdemona,
   Once more well met at Cyprus.

(Exeunt OTHELLO, DESDEMONA, and Attendants)

IAGO   Do thou meet me presently at the harbour.—Come hither.—If thou be'st valiant—as they say base men, being in love, have then a nobility in their na-tures more than is native to them,—list me. The lieutenant to-night watches on the court of guard.—First, I must tell thee this—Desdemona is directly in love with him.

RODERIGO   With him! why, 't is not possible.

IAGO   Lay thy finger—thus, and let thy soul be in-structed. Mark me with what violence she first loved the Moor, but for bragging, and telling her fantastical lies; and will she love him still for prating? let not thy discreet heart think it. Her eye must be fed; and what delight shall she have to look on the devil? When the blood is made dull with the act of sport, there should be,—again to inflame it, and to give sa-tiety a fresh appetite, loveliness in favour, sympathy in years, manners, and beauties; all which the Moor is defective in. Now, for want of these required con-veniences, her delicate tenderness will find itself abused, begin to heave the gorge, disrelish and abhor the Moor; very nature will instruct her in it, and compel her to some second choice. Now, sir, this granted, (as it is a most pregnant and unforced posi-tion) who stands so eminently in the degree of this fortune, as Cassio does? a knave very voluble; no far-ther conscionable, than in putting on the mere form of civil and humane seeming, for the better compass-ing of his salt and most hidden loose affection? why, none; why, none: a subtle slippery knave; a finder out of occasions; that has an eye can stamp and counterfeit advantages, though true advantage never present itself: a devilish knave! besides, the knave is handsome, young, and hath all those requisites in him, that folly and green minds look after; a pestilent complete knave, and the woman hath found him already.

RODERIGO   I cannot believe that in her: she is full of most blessed condition.

IAGO   Blessed fig's end! the wine she drinks is made of grapes: if she had been blessed, she would never have loved the Moor: bless'd pudding! Didst thou not see her paddle with the palm of his hand? didst not mark that?

RODERIGO   Yes, that I did; but that was but courtesy.

IAGO   Lechery, by this hand; an index, and obscure prologue to the history of lust and foul thoughts. They met so near with their lips, that their breaths embraced together. Villainous thoughts, Roderigo! when these mutualities so marshal the way; hard at hand comes the master and main exercise, the incorporate conclusion. Pish! But, sir, be you ruled by me: I have brought you from Venice. Watch you tonight; for the command, I'll lay 't upon you. Cassio knows you not:—I'll not be far from you: do you find some occasion to anger Cassio, either by speaking too loud, or tainting his discipline; or from what other cause you please, which the time shall more favourably minister.

RODERIGO   Well.

IAGO   Sir, he is rash, and very sudden in choler, and, haply, with his truncheon may strike at you: provoke him, that he may; for even out of that will I cause these of Cyprus to mutiny, whose qualification shall come into no true taste again, but by the displanting of Cassio. So shall you have a shorter journey to your desires, by the means I shall then have to prefer them and the impediment most profitably removed, without the which there were no expectation of our prosperity.

RODERIGO   I will do this, if I can bring it to any opportunity.

IAGO   I warrant thee. Meet me by and by at the citadel: I must fetch his necessaries ashore. Farewell.

RODERIGO   Adieu.

(Exit)

IAGO   That Cassio loves her, I do well believe it,
That she loves him, 't is apt, and of great credit:
The Moor—howbeit that I endure him not,—
Is of a constant, loving, noble nature,
And, I dare think, he'll prove to Desdemona
A most dear husband. Now, I do love her too,
Not out of absolute lust, (though, peradventure,
I stand accountant for as great a sin)
But partly led to diet my revenge,
For that I do suspect the lustful Moor
Hath leap'd into my seat; the thought whereof
Doth like a poisonous mineral gnaw my inwards,
And nothing can, or shall, content my soul,
Till I am even'd with him, wife for wife;
Or, failing so, yet that I put the Moor
At least into a jealousy so strong
That judgment cannot cure. Which thing to do,—
If this poor brach of Venice, whom I trash,
For his quick hunting, stand the putting on,—
I'll have our Michael Cassio on the hip;
Abuse him to the Moor in the rank garb,—
For I fear Cassio with my night-cap too;
Make the Moor thank me, love me, and reward me,
For making him egregiously an ass,
And practising upon his peace and quiet,
Even to madness. 'T is here, but yet confus'd:
Knavery's plain face is never seen, till us'd.

(Exit)

SCENE II.   *A Street.*

(Enter a Herald, with a Proclamation; People following)

HERALD   It is Othello's pleasure, our noble and valiant general, that upon certain tidings now arrived, importing the mere perdition of the Turkish fleet, every man put himself into triumph; some to dance, some to make bonfires, each man to what sport and revels his addiction leads him; for, besides these beneficial news, it is the celebration of his nuptials. So much was his pleasure should be proclaimed. All offices are open: and there is full liberty of feasting, from this present hour of five, till the bell hath told eleven. Heaven bless the isle of Cyprus, and our noble general, Othello!

(Exeunt)

SCENE III.   *A Hall in the Castle.*

(*Enter* OTHELLO, DESDEMONA, CASSIO, *and Attendants*)

OTHELLO   Good Michael, look you to the guard to-
night:
Let 's teach ourselves that honourable stop,
Not to out-sport discretion.
CASSIO   Iago hath direction what to do;
But, notwithstanding, with my personal eye
Will I look to 't.
OTHELLO   Iago is most honest.
Michael, good night: to-morrow, with your earliest,
Let me have speech with you. Come, my dear love:
The purchase made, the fruits are to ensue;

(*To* DESDEMONA)

That profit 's yet to come 'twixt me and you.—
Good night.

(*Exeunt* OTHELLO, DESDEMONA, *attended*)

(*Enter* IAGO)

CASSIO   Welcome, Iago: we must to the watch.
IAGO   Not this hour, lieutenant; 't is not yet ten
o'clock. Our general cast us thus early for the love of
his Desdemona, whom let us not therefore blame: he
hath not yet made wanton the night with her, and
she is sport for Jove.
CASSIO   She 's a most exquisite lady.
IAGO   And I 'll warrant her, full of game.
CASSIO   Indeed, she 's a most fresh and delicate
creature.
IAGO   What an eye she has! methinks it sounds a par-
ley of provocation.
CASSIO   An inviting eye; and yet methinks right
modest.
IAGO   And, when she speaks, is it not an alarum to
love?
CASSIO   She is, indeed, perfection.
IAGO   Well, happiness to their sheets! Come, lieutenant, I have a stoop of wine; and here without are a
brace of Cyprus gallants, that would fain have a
measure to the health of the black Othello.
CASSIO   Not to-night, good Iago. I have very poor and
unhappy brains for drinking: I could well wish
courtesy would invent some other custom of
entertainment.

IAGO   O! they are our friends; but one cup: I 'll drink
for you.
CASSIO   I have drunk but one cup to-night, and that
was craftily qualified too, and, behold, what innovation it makes here. I am unfortunate in the infirmity, and dare not task my weakness with any more.
IAGO   What, man! 't is a night of revels: the gallants
desire it.
CASSIO   Where are they?
IAGO   Here at the door; I pray you, call them in.
CASSIO   I 'll do 't, but it dislikes me.

(*Exit* CASSIO)

IAGO   If I can fasten but one cup upon him,
With that which he hath drunk to-night already,
He 'll be as full of quarrel and offense
As my young mistress' dog. Now, my sick fool,
    Roderigo,
Whom love has turn'd almost the wrong side
    outward,
To Desdemona hath to-night carous'd
Potations pottle deep; and he 's to watch.
Three elves of Cyprus,—noble, swelling spirits,
That hold their honours in a wary distance,
The very elements of this warlike isle,—
Have I to-night fluster'd with flowing cups,
And they watch too. Now, 'mongst this flock of
    drunkards,
Am I to put our Cassio in some action
That may offend the isle.—But here they come.
If consequence do but approve my dream,
My boat sails freely, both with wind and stream.

(*Re-enter* CASSIO, *with him* MONTANO, *and Gentlemen*)

CASSIO   'Fore heaven, they have given me a rouse
already.
MONTANO   Good faith, a little one; not past a pint, as
I am a soldier.
IAGO   Some wine, ho! (*Sings*)
    And let me the canakin clink, clink;
    And let me the canakin clink;
        A soldier 's a man;
        A life 's but a span;
    Why then let a soldier drink.[7]

————
[7] See the music to this song at the end of the play.

Some wine, boys!

(Wine brought)

CASSIO   'Fore heaven, an excellent song.

IAGO   I learned it in England, where (indeed) they are most potent in potting; your Dane, your German, and your swag-bellied Hollander,—Drink, ho!—are nothing to your Englishman.

CASSIO   Is your Englishman so exquisite in his drinking?

IAGO   Why, he drinks you, with facility, your Dane dead drunk; he sweats not to overthrow your Almain; he gives your Hollander a vomit, ere the next pottle can be filled.

CASSIO   To the health of our general.

MONTANO   I am for it, lieutenant; and I 'll do you justice.

IAGO   O sweet England! *(Sings)*
King Stephen was a worthy peer,
  His breeches cost him but a crown;
He held them sixpence all too dear,
  With that he call'd the tailor—lown.
He was a wight of high renown,
  And thou art but of low degree:
'T is pride that pulls the country down,
  Then take thine auld cloak about thee.
Some wine, ho!

CASSIO   Why, this is a more exquisite song than the other.

IAGO   Will you hear it again?

CASSIO   No; for I hold him to be unworthy of his place that does those things.—Well, heaven 's above all; and there be souls must be saved, and there be souls must not be saved.

IAGO   It is true, good lieutenant.

CASSIO   For mine own part,—no offence to the general nor any man of quality,—I hope to be saved.

IAGO   And so do I too, lieutenant.

CASSIO   Ay; but, by your leave, not before me; the lieutenant is to be saved before the ancient—Let 's have no more of this; let 's to our affairs.—Forgive us our sins!—Gentlemen, let 's look to our business. Do not think, gentlemen, I am drunk: this is my ancient;—this is my right hand, and this is my left hand.—I am not drunk now; I can stand well enough, and speak well enough.

ALL   Excellent well.

CASSIO   Why, very well, then; you must not think, then, that I am drunk.

(Exit)

MONTANO   To the platform, masters; come, let 's set the watch.

IAGO   You see this fellow, that is gone before:
He is a soldier, fit to stand by Caesar
And give direction; and do but see his vice.
'T is to his virtue a just equinox,
The one as long as th' other: 't is pity of him.
I fear, the trust Othello puts in him,
On some odd time of his infirmity,
Will shake this island.

MONTANO   But is he often thus?

IAGO   'T is evermore the prologue to his sleep:
He 'll watch the horologe a double set,
If drink rock not his cradle.

MONTANO   It were well,
The general were put in mind of it.
Perhaps, he sees it not; or his good nature
Prizes the virtue that appears in Cassio,
And looks not on his evils. Is not this true?

(Enter RODERIGO*)*

IAGO   How now, Roderigo?

(Aside to him)

I pray you, after the lieutenant; go.

(Exit RODERIGO*)*

MONTANO   And 't is great pity, that the noble Moor
Should hazard such a place as his own second,
With one of an ingraft infirmity:
It were an honest action to say
So to the Moor.

IAGO   Not I, for this fair island:
I do love Cassio well, and would do much
To cure him of this evil. But hark! what noise?

(Cry within,—Help! Help!)

(Re-enter CASSIO, *pursuing* RODERIGO*)*

CASSIO   You rogue! you rascal!

MONTANO   What 's the matter, lieutenant?

CASSIO   A knave!—teach me my duty?
I 'll beat the knave into a wicker bottle.

RODERIGO   Beat me!
CASSIO   Dost thou prate, rogue?

(*Striking* RODERIGO)

MONTANO   Nay, good lieutenant;

(*Staying him*)

I pray you, sir, hold your hand.
CASSIO   Let me go, sir,
  Or I 'll knock you o'er the mazzard.
MONTANO   Come, come; you 're drunk.
CASSIO   Drunk!

(*They fight*)

IAGO   Away, I say! (*Aside to* RODERIGO) go out, and
  cry a mutiny.

(*Exit* RODERIGO)

Nay, good lieutenant,—alas, gentlemen!—
Help, ho!—Lieutenant,—sir,—Montano,—sir;—
Help, masters!—Here 's a goodly watch, indeed!

(*Bell rings*)

Who 's that that rings the bell?—Diablo, ho!
The town will rise: God's will! lieutenant, hold!
You will be sham'd for ever.

(*Enter* OTHELLO, *and Attendants*)

OTHELLO   What is the matter here?
MONTANO   'Zounds! I bleed still: I am hurt to the
  death.

(*He faints*)

OTHELLO   Hold, for your lives!
IAGO   Hold, hold, lieutenant!—sir, Montano,—
  gentlemen!—
  Have you forgot all sense of place and duty?
  Hold, hold! the general speaks to you: hold, for
  shame!
OTHELLO   Why, how now, ho! from whence ariseth
  this?
  Are we turn'd Turks, and to ourselves do that,
  Which heaven hath forbid the Ottomites?
  For Christian shame, put by this barbarous brawl:
  He that stirs next to carve for his own rage,
  Holds his soul light; he dies upon his motion.—

Silence that dreadful bell! it frights the isle
From her propriety.—What is the matter, masters?—
Honest Iago, that look'st dead with grieving,
Speak, who began this? on thy love, I charge thee.
IAGO   I do not know:—friends all but now, even now
  In quarter, and in terms like bride and groom
  Divesting them for bed; and then, but now,
  (As if some planet had unwitted them)
  Swords out, and tilting one at other's breast,
  In opposition bloody. I cannot speak
  Any beginning to this peevish odds;
  And would in action glorious I had lost
  Those legs, that brought me to a part of it.
OTHELLO   How came it, Michael, you were thus
      forgot?
CASSIO   I pray you, pardon me; I cannot speak.
OTHELLO   Worthy Montano, you were wont be civil,
  The gravity and stillness of your youth
  The world hath noted, and your name is great
  In mouths of wisest censure: what 's the matter,
  That you unlace your reputation thus,
  And spend your rich opinion, for the name
  Of a night-brawler? give me answer to it.
MONTANO   Worthy Othello, I am hurt to danger:
  Your officer, Iago, can inform you,
  While I spare speech, which something now offends
      me,
  Of all that I do know; nor know I aught
  By me that 's said or done amiss this night,
  Unless self-charity be sometime a vice,
  And to defend ourselves it be a sin,
  When violence assails us.
OTHELLO   Now, by heaven,
  My blood begins my safer guides to rule;
  And passion, having my best judgment quelled,
  Assays to lead the way. If I once stir,
  Or do but lift this arm, the best of you
  Shall sink in my rebuke. Give me to know
  How this foul rout began, who set it on;
  And he that is approv'd in this offence,
  Though he had twinn'd with me, both at a birth,
  Shall lose me.—What! in a town of war,
  Yet wild, the people's hearts brimful of fear,
  To manage private and domestic quarrel,
  In night, and on the court and guard of safety?
  'T is monstrous.—Iago, who began it?

MONTANO   If partially affin'd, or leagued in office,
Thou dost deliver more or less than truth,
Thou art no soldier.
IAGO   Touch me not so near.
I had rather have this tongue cut from my mouth,
Than it should do offence to Michael Cassio;
Yet, I persuade myself, to speak the truth
Shall nothing wrong him.—Thus it is, general.
Montano and myself being in speech,
There comes a fellow crying out for help,
And Cassio following him with determin'd sword
To execute upon him. Sir, this gentleman
Steps in to Cassio, and entreats his pause:
Myself the crying fellow did pursue,
Lest by his clamour (as it so fell out)
The town might fall in fright: he, swift of foot,
Outran my purpose; and I return'd, the rather
For that I heard the clink and fall of swords,
And Cassio high in oath, which, till to-night,
I ne'er might say before. When I came back,
(For this was brief) I found them close together
At blow and thrust, even as again they were,
When you yourself did part them.
More of this matter can I not report:—
But men are men; the best sometimes forget:—
Though Cassio did some little wrong to him,
As men in rage strike those that wish them best,
Yet, surely, Cassio, I believe, received
From him that fled some strange indignity,
Which patience could not pass.
OTHELLO   I know, Iago,
Thy honesty and love doth mince this matter,
Making it light to Cassio.—Cassio, I love thee;
But never more be officer of mine.—

(Enter DESDEMONA, attended)

Look, if my gentle love be not rais'd up!—
I 'll make thee an example.
DESDEMONA   What 's the matter?
OTHELLO   All 's well now, sweeting; come away to
    bed.—
Sir, for your hurts, myself will be your surgeon.—
Lead him off.

(MONTANO is led off)

Iago, look with care about the town,

And silence those whom this vile brawl distracted.—
Come, Desdemona; 't is the soldier's life,
To have their balmy slumbers wak'd with strife.

(Exeunt all but IAGO and CASSIO)

IAGO   What, are you hurt, lieutenant?
CASSIO   Ay, past all surgery.
IAGO   Marry, heaven forbid!
CASSIO   Reputation, reputation, reputation! O! I have
lost my reputation. I have lost the immortal part of
myself, and what remains is bestial.—My reputation,
Iago, my reputation!
IAGO   As I am an honest man, I thought you had received some bodily wound; there is more offence in
that, than in reputation. Reputation is an idle and
most false imposition; oft got without merit, and lost
without deserving: you have lost no reputation at all,
unless you repute yourself such a loser. What, man!
there are ways to recover the general again: you are
but now cast in his mood, a punishment more in policy than in malice; even so as one would beat his of-
fenceless dog, to affright an imperious lion. Sue to
him again, and he 's yours.
CASSIO   I will rather sue to be despised, than to deceive so good a commander, with so light, so
drunken, and so indiscreet an officer. Drunk? and
speak parrot? and squabble? swagger? swear? and discourse fustian with one's own shadow?—O thou invisible spirit of wine! if thou hast no name to be
known by, let us call thee—devil.
IAGO   What was he that you follow'd with your
sword? What had he done to you?
CASSIO   I know not.
IAGO   Is 't possible?
CASSIO   I remember a mass of things, but nothing distinctly; a quarrel, but nothing wherefore.—O God!
that men should put an enemy in their mouths, to
steal away their brains! that we should, with joy,
revel, pleasure, and applause, transform ourselves
into beasts!
IAGO   Why, but you are now well enough: how came
you thus recovered.
CASSIO   It hath pleased the devil, drunkenness, to give
place to the devil, wrath: one unperfectness shows
me another, to make me frankly despise myself.
IAGO   Come, you are too severe a moraler. As the

time, the place, and the condition of this country stands, I could heartily wish this had not befallen; but, since it is as it is, mend it for your own good.

CASSIO   I will ask him for my place again: he shall tell me, I am a drunkard. Had I as many mouths as Hydra, such an answer would stop them all. To be now a sensible man, by and by a fool, and presently a beast! O strange!—Every inordinate cup is unblessed, and the ingredient is a devil.

IAGO   Come, come; good wine is a good familiar creature, if it be well used: exclaim no more against it. And, good lieutenant, I think you think I love you.

CASSIO   I have well approved it, sir.—I drunk!

IAGO   You, or any man living, may be drunk at some time, man. I'll tell you what you shall do. Our general's wife is now the general:—I may say so in this respect, for that he hath devoted and given up himself to the contemplation, mark, and devotement of her parts and graces:—confess yourself freely to her; importune her; she'll help to put you in your place again. She is of so free, so kind, so apt, so blessed a disposition, that she holds it a vice in her goodness, not to do more than she is requested. This broken joint between you and her husband entreat her to splinter, and my fortunes against any lay worth naming, this crack of your love shall grow stronger than it was before.

CASSIO   You advise me well.

IAGO   I protest, in the sincerity of love, and honest kindness.

CASSIO   I think it freely; and, betimes in the morning, I will beseech the virtuous Desdemona to undertake for me. I am desperate of my fortunes, if they check me here.

IAGO   You are in the right. Good night, lieutenant; I must to the watch.

CASSIO   Good night, honest Iago.

(*Exit* CASSIO)

IAGO   And what's he, then, that says I play the villain,
When this advice is free I give, and honest,
Probable to thinking, and, indeed, the course
To win the Moor again? For 't is most easy
The inclining Desdemona to subdue
In any honest suit: she 's fram'd as fruitful

As the free elements. And, then, for her
To win the Moor,—were 't to renounce his baptism,
All seals and symbols of redeemed sin,—
His soul is so enfetter'd to her love,
That she may make, unmake, do what she list,
Even as her appetite shall play the god
With his weak function. How am I, then, a villain
To counsel Cassio to this parallel course,
Directly to his good?—Divinity of hell!
When devils will their blackest sins put on,
They do suggest at first with heavenly shows,
As I do now; for whiles this honest fool
Plies Desdemona to repair his fortunes,
And she for him pleads strongly to the Moor.
I'll pour this pestilence into his ear,—
That she repeals him for her body's lust;
And, by how much she strives to do him good,
She shall undo her credit with the Moor:
So will I turn her virtue into pitch,
And out of her own goodness make the net,
That shall enmesh them all.—How now, Roderigo?

(*Enter* RODERIGO, *angrily*)

RODERIGO   I do follow here in the chase, not like a hound that hunts, but one that fills up the cry. My money is almost spent: I have been to-night exceedingly well cudgelled; and, I think, the issue will be—I shall have so much experience for my pains, and so, with no money at all, and a little more wit, return again to Venice.

IAGO   How poor are they, that have not patience!
What wound did ever heal, but by degrees?
Thou know'st, we work by wit, and not by witchcraft;
And wit depends on dilatory time.
Does 't not go well? Cassio hath beaten thee,
And thou by that small hurt hast cashier'd Cassio.
Though other things grow fair against the sun,
Yet fruits that blossom first will first be ripe:
Content thyself a while.—By the mass, 't is morning;
Pleasure and action make the hours seem short.
Retire thee; go where thou art billeted:
Away, I say; thou shalt know more hereafter:
Nay, get thee gone.

(*Exit* RODERIGO)

Two things are to be done.
My wife must move for Cassio to her mistress.
I 'll set her on:
Myself, the while, to draw the Moor apart,
And bring him jump where he may Cassio find
Soliciting his wife.—Ay, that 's the way:
Dull not device by coldness and delay.

(Exit)

ACT III

SYNOPSIS: 1. Cassio brings musicians to play for the newlyweds;
Othello's clown asks them to stop. Iago and Emilia arrange for Cassio
to meet with Desdemona. 2. Othello asks Iago to meet him to inspect
the fortification of the castle. 3. Desdemona promises Cassio to help
him all she can. Cassio leaves her as Iago and Othello enter. Iago begins his campaign to instill jealousy in Othello. Desdemona pleads
with her husband on Cassio's behalf. When he complains of a head-
ache, she attempts to soothe it with a handkerchief, which Othello
throws down. Emilia finds the handkerchief and gives it to Iago.
Othello demands of Iago proof of his insinuations that his wife is unfaithful. Iago tells him stories, and mentions that he has seen Cassio
with Desdemona's handkerchief. Enraged, Othello vows revenge with
Iago. He promotes Iago to lieutenant. 4. Desdemona speaks for Cassio
to Othello; he angrily accuses her of losing the handkerchief he gave
her. Cassio meets his mistress Bianca and gives her the handkerchief
(which Iago put in his room), asking her to copy the embroidery.

SCENE I. *Before the Castle.*

(Enter CASSIO, *and some Musicians*[1]*)*

CASSIO Masters, play here, I will content your pains:
    Something that 's brief; and bid good-morrow to the
    general.

(Music)

(Enter Clown)

CLOWN Why, masters, have your instruments been in
    Naples, that they squeak i' the nose thus?

1 MUSICIAN How, sir, how?

CLOWN Are these, I pray you, called wind instru-
    ments?

1 MUSICIAN Ay, marry, are they, sir.

CLOWN O! thereby hangs a tail.

1 MUSICIAN Whereby hangs a tale, sir?

CLOWN Marry, sir, by many a wind instrument that I

---

[1] It was an Elizabethan custom to entertain newlyweds with music.

know. But, masters, here 's money for you; and the
general so likes your music, that he desires you, for
love's sake, to make no more noise with it.

1 MUSICIAN Well, sir, we will not.

CLOWN If you have any music that may not be heard,
    to 't again; but, as they say, to hear music the general
    does not greatly care.

1 MUSICIAN We have none such, sir.

CLOWN Then put up your pipes in your bag, for I 'll
    away. Go; vanish into air; away!

(Exeunt Musicians)

CASSIO Dost thou hear, mine honest friend?

CLOWN No, I hear not your honest friend; I hear you.

CASSIO Pr'ythee, keep up thy quillets. There 's a poor
    piece of gold for thee. If the gentlewoman that at-
    tends the general's wife be stirring, tell her there 's
    one Cassio entreats her a little favour of speech: wilt
    thou do this?

CLOWN She is stirring, sir; if she will stir hither, I
    shall seem so to notify her.

CASSIO Do, good my friend.

(Exit Clown)

(Enter IAGO*)*

                                In happy time, Iago.

IAGO You have not been a-bed, then?

CASSIO Why, no; the day had broke
    Before we parted. I have made bold, Iago,
    To send in to your wife: my suit to her
    Is, that she will to virtuous Desdemona
    Procure me some access.

IAGO   I 'll send her to you presently;
    And I 'll devise a mean to draw the Moor
    Out of the way, that your converse and business
    May be more free.

(Exit)

CASSIO I humbly thank you for 't. I never knew
    A Florentine more kind and honest.

(Enter EMILIA*)*

EMILIA Good-morrow, good lieutenant. I am sorry
    For your displeasure; but all will soon be well.
    The general and his wife are talking of it,

And she speaks for you stoutly: the Moor replies,
That he you hurt is of great fame in Cyprus,
And great affinity, and that in wholesome wisdom
He might not but refuse you; but, he protests, he
    loves you,
And needs no other suitor but his likings,
To take the safest occasion by the front,
To bring you in again.
CASSIO   Yet, I beseech you,—
If you think fit, or that it may be done,—
Give me advantage of some brief discourse
With Desdemona alone.
EMILIA   Pray you, come in:
 I will bestow you where you shall have time
To speak your bosom freely.
CASSIO   I am much bound to you.

(Exeunt)

SCENE II.   *A Room in the Castle.*

(Enter OTHELLO, IAGO, *and Gentlemen)*

OTHELLO   These letters give, Iago, to the pilot,
And by him do my duties to the state:
That done, I will be walking on the works;
Repair there to me.
IAGO   Well, my good lord; I 'll do 't.
OTHELLO   This fortification, gentlemen,—shall we
    see 't!
GENTLEMEN   We wait upon your lordship.

(Exeunt)

SCENE III.   *Before the Castle.*

(Enter DESDEMONA, CASSIO, *and* EMILIA)

DESDEMONA   Be thou assur'd, good Cassio, I will do
All my abilities in thy behalf.
EMILIA   Good madam, do: I know it grieves my
    husband,
As if the case were his.
DESDEMONA   O! that 's an honest fellow.—Do not
    doubt Cassio,
But I will have my lord and you again
As friendly as you were.
CASSIO   Bounteous madam,
Whatever shall become of Michael Cassio,
He 's never any thing but your true servant.

DESDEMONA   O, sir! I thank you. You do love my lord;
You have known him long, and be you well assur'd,
He shall in strangeness stand no farther off
Than in a politic distance.
CASSIO   Ay, but, lady,
That policy may either last so long,
Or feed upon such nice and waterish diet,
Or breed itself so out of circumstance,
That, I being absent, and my place supplied,
My general will forget my love and service.
DESDEMONA   Do not doubt that: before Emilia here,
I give thee warrant of thy place. Assure thee.
If I do vow a friendship, I 'll perform it
To the last article: my lord shall never rest;
I 'll watch him tame, and talk him out of patience;
His bed shall seem a school, his board a shrift;
I 'll intermingle every thing he does
With Cassio's suit. Therefore, be merry, Cassio;
For thy solicitor shall rather die,
Than give thy cause away.

(Enter OTHELLO *and* IAGO, *at a distance)*

EMILIA   Madam, here comes my lord.
CASSIO   Madam, I 'll take my leave.
DESDEMONA   Why, stay, and hear me speak.
CASSIO   Madam, not now: I am very ill at ease;
Unfit for mine own purpose.
DESDEMONA   Well, do your discretion.

(Exit CASSIO)

IAGO   Ha! I like not that.
OTHELLO   What dost thou say?
IAGO   Nothing, my lord: or if—I know not what.
OTHELLO   Was not that Cassio parted from my wife?
IAGO   Cassio, my lord? No, sure, I cannot think it,
That he would steal away so guilty-like,
Seeing you coming.
OTHELLO   I do believe 't was he.
DESDEMONA   How, now, my lord!
I have been talking with a suitor here,
A man that languishes in your displeasure.
OTHELLO   Who is 't you mean?
DESDEMONA   Why, your lieutenant, Cassio. Good, my
    lord,
If I have any grace, or power to move you,
His present reconciliation take;

For if he be not one that truly loves you,
That errs in ignorance, and not in cunning,
I have no judgment in an honest face.
I pr'ythee, call him back.

OTHELLO   Went he hence now?

DESDEMONA   Ay, sooth; so humbled,
That he hath left part of his grief with me,
To suffer with him. Good love, call him back.

OTHELLO   Not now, sweet Desdemona; some other
time.

DESDEMONA   But shall 't be shortly?

OTHELLO   The sooner, sweet, for you.

DESDEMONA   Shall 't be to-night at supper?

OTHELLO   No, not to-night.

DESDEMONA   To-morrow dinner then?

OTHELLO   I shall not dine at home:
I meet the captains at the citadel.

DESDEMONA   Why then, to-morrow night; or Tuesday
morn;
On Tuesday noon, or night; on Wednesday morn:
I pr'ythee, name the time, but let it not
Exceed three days: in faith, he 's penitent;
And yet his trespass, in our common reason,
(Save that, they say, the wars must make examples
Out of our best) is not almost a fault
T' incur a private check. When shall he come?
Tell me, Othello: I wonder in my soul,
What you could ask me that I should deny,
Or stand so mammering on. What! Michael Cassio,
That came a wooing with you, and so many a time,
When I have spoke of you dispraisingly,
Hath ta'en your part, to have so much to do
To bring him in! Trust me, I could do much,—

OTHELLO   Pr'ythee, no more: let him come when he
will,
I will deny thee nothing.

DESDEMONA   Why, this is not a boon;
'T is as I should entreat you wear your gloves,
Or feed on nourishing dishes, or keep you warm,
Or sue to you to do a peculiar profit
To your own person: nay, when I have a suit
Wherein I mean to touch your love indeed,
It shall be full of poize and difficult weight,
And fearful to be granted.

OTHELLO   I will deny thee nothing.
Whereon, I do beseech thee, grant me this,
To leave me but a little to myself.

DESDEMONA   Shall I deny you? no, Farewell, my lord.

OTHELLO   Farewell, my Desdemona: I 'll come to thee
straight.

DESDEMONA   Emilia, come.—Be it as your fancies
teach you
Whate'er you be, I am obedient.

(*Exit, with* EMILIA)

OTHELLO   Excellent wretch! Perdition catch my soul,
But I do love thee, and when I love thee not,
Chaos is come again.

IAGO   My noble lord,—

OTHELLO   What dost thou say, Iago?

IAGO   Did Michael Cassio, when you woo'd my lady,
Know of your love?

OTHELLO   He did, from first to last: why dost thou ask?

IAGO   But for a satisfaction of my thought;
No farther harm.

OTHELLO   Why of thy thought, Iago?

IAGO   I did not think, he had been acquainted with it.

OTHELLO   O, yes; and went between us very oft.

IAGO   Indeed?

OTHELLO   Indeed! ay, indeed:—discern'st thou aught
in that?
Is he not honest?

IAGO   Honest, my lord?

OTHELLO   Honest? ay, honest.

IAGO   My lord, for aught I know.

OTHELLO   What dost thou think?

IAGO   Think, my lord?

OTHELLO   Think, my lord!
By heaven, he echoes me,
As if there were some monster in his thought
Too hideous to be shown.—Thou dost mean
something.
I heard thee say but now,—thou lik'dst not that,
When Cassio left my wife: what didst not like?
And, when I told thee, he was of my counsel
In my whole course of wooing, thou criedst,
"Indeed!"
And didst contract and purse thy brow together,
As if thou then hadst shut up in thy brain
Some horrible conceit.[2] If thou dost love me,

---

[2] Conceit—thought or fancy.

Show me thy thought.
IAGO   My lord, you know I love you.
OTHELLO   I think, thou dost;
   And,—for I know thou art full of love and honesty,
   And weigh'st thy words before thou giv'st them
      breath,—
   Therefore, these stops of thine fright me the more;
   For such things, in a false disloyal knave,
   Are tricks of custom; but in a man that 's just,
   They are close delations, working from the heart,
   That passion cannot rule.
IAGO   For Michael Cassio.
   I dare be sworn, I think that he is honest.
OTHELLO   I think so too.
IAGO   Men should be what they seem
   Or, those that be not, would they might seem none! [3]
OTHELLO   Certain, men should be what they seem.
IAGO   Why, then, I think Cassio 's an honest man.
OTHELLO   Nay, yet there 's more in this.
   I pray thee, speak to me as to thy thinkings,
   As thou dost ruminate; and give thy worst of
      thoughts
   The worst of words.
IAGO   Good my lord, pardon me:
   Though I am bound to every act of duty,
   I am not bound to that all slaves are free to. [4]
   Utter my thoughts? Why, say, they are vile and
      false,—
   As where 's that palace, whereinto foul things
   Sometimes intrude not? who has a breast so pure,
   But sometimes uncleanly apprehensions
   Keep leets, and law-days, and in session sit
   With meditations lawful?
OTHELLO   Thou dost conspire against thy friend, Iago,
   If thou but think'st him wrong'd, and mak'st his ear
   A stranger to thy thoughts.
IAGO   I do beseech you,—
   Though I, perchance, am vicious in my guess,
   (As, I confess, it is my nature's plague
   To spy into abuses, and oft my jealousy
   Shapes faults that are not)—that your wisdom yet,

---

[3] They should not pretend to be men when they are not worthy of the name.
[4] Even slaves are free to keep their thoughts to themselves.

From one that so imperfectly conceits,
   Would take no notice; nor build yourself a trouble
   Out of his scattering and unsure observance.
   It were not for your quiet, nor your good,
   Nor for my manhood, honesty, or wisdom,
   To let you know my thoughts.
OTHELLO   What dost thou mean?
IAGO   Good name, in man, and woman, dear my lord,
   Is the immediate jewel of their souls:
   Who steals my purse, steals trash; 't is something,
      nothing;
   'T was mine, 't is his, and has been slave to
      thousands;
   But he, that filches from me my good name,
   Robs me of that, which not enriches him,
   And makes me poor indeed.
OTHELLO   By heaven, I 'll know thy thoughts.
IAGO   You cannot, if my heart were in your hand;
   Nor shall not, whilst 't is in my custody.
OTHELLO   Ha!
IAGO   O! beware, my lord, of jealousy;
   It is the green-ey'd monster, which doth make
   The meat it feeds on: that cuckold lives in bliss,
   Who, certain of his fate, loves not his wronger;
   But, O! what damned minutes tells he o'er,
   Who dotes, yet doubts; suspects, yet fondly loves!
OTHELLO   O misery!
IAGO   Poor and content is rich, and rich enough;
   But riches fineless is as poor as winter,
   To him that ever fears he shall be poor.—
   Good heaven, the souls of all my tribe defend
   From jealousy!
OTHELLO   Why? why is this?
   Think'st thou, I 'd make a life of jealousy,
   To follow still the changes of the moon
   With fresh suspicions? No: to be once in doubt,
   Is once to be resolv'd. Exchange me for a goat,
   When I shall turn the business of my soul
   To such exsufflicate and blown surmises,
   Matching thy inference. 'T is not to make me
      jealous,
   To say—my wife is fair, feeds well, loves company,
   Is free of speech, sings, plays, and dances well;
   Where virtue is, these are more virtuous:
   Nor from mine own weak merits will I draw
   The smallest fear, or doubt of her revolt;

For she had eyes, and chose me: no, Iago;
I 'll see, before I doubt; when I doubt, prove;
And, on the proof, there is no more but this,
Away at once with love, or jealousy.

IAGO   I am glad of it; for now I shall have reason
To show the love and duty that I bear you
With franker spirit: therefore, as I am bound,
Receive it from me. I speak not yet of proof.
Look to your wife; observe her well with Cassio:
Wear your eye—thus, not jealous, nor secure:
I would not have your free and noble nature,
Out of self-bounty, be abus'd; look to 't.
I know our country disposition well:
In Venice they do let heaven see the pranks
They dare not show their husbands; their best
    conscience
Is, not to leave 't undone, but keep 't unknown.

OTHELLO   Dost thou say so?

IAGO   She did deceive her father, marrying you;
And, when she seem'd to shake, and fear your looks,
She lov'd them most.

OTHELLO   And so she did.

IAGO   Why, go to, then;
She that, so young, could give out such a seeming,
To seal her father's eyes up, close as oak,—
He thought, 't was witchcraft.—But I am much to
    blame;
I humbly do beseech you of your pardon,
For too much loving you.

OTHELLO   I am bound to thee for ever.

IAGO   I see, this hath a little dash'd your spirits.

OTHELLO   Not a jot, not a jot.

IAGO   Trust me, I fear it has.
I hope, you will consider what is spoke
Comes from my love.—But, I do see you are
    mov'd:—
I am to pray you, not to strain my speech
To grosser issues, nor to larger reach,
Than to suspicion.

OTHELLO   I will not.

IAGO   Should you do so, my lord,
My speech should fall into such vile success,
As my thoughts aim not at. Cassio 's my worthy
    friend.
My lord, I see you are mov'd.

OTHELLO   No, not much mov'd.—

I do not think but Desdemona 's honest.

IAGO   Long live she so; and long live you to think so!

OTHELLO   And yet, how nature erring from itself—

IAGO   Ay, there 's the point:—as,—to be bold with
    you,—
Not to affect many proposed matches,
Of her own clime, complexion, and degree,
Whereto, we see, in all things nature tends.
Foh! one may smell in such a will most rank,
Foul disproportion, thoughts unnatural.—
But pardon me; I do not in suspicion
Distinctly speak of her, though I may fear,
Her will, recoiling to her better judgment,
May fall to match you with her country forms,
And happily repent.

OTHELLO   Farewell, farewell.
If more thou dost perceive, let me know more;
Set on thy wife to observe. Leave me, Iago.

IAGO (Going)   My lord, I take my leave.

OTHELLO   Why did I marry?—This honest creature
    doubtless,
Sees and knows more, much more, than he unfolds.

IAGO (Returning)   My lord, I would I might entreat
    your honour
To scan this thing no farther; leave it to time.
Although 't is fit that Cassio have his place,
(For, sure, he fills it up with great ability)
Yet if you please to hold him off a while,
You shall by that perceive him and his means.
Note, if your lady strain his entertainment
With any strong or vehement importunity:
Much will be seen in that. In the mean time,
Let me be thought too busy in my fears,
(As worthy cause I have to fear I am)
And hold her free, I do beseech your honour.

OTHELLO   Fear not my government.

IAGO   I once more take my leave.

(Exit)

OTHELLO   This fellow 's of exceeding honesty,
And knows all qualities with a learned spirit
Of human dealings: if I do prove her haggard,
Though that her jesses[5] were my dear heart-strings,

---

[5] Jesses are thongs used for controlling a hawk.

I 'd whistle her off, and let her down the wind,
To prey at fortune.[6] Haply, for I am black,
And have not those soft parts of conversation
That chamberers have; or, for I am declin'd
Into the vale of years;—yet that 's not much
She 's gone; I am abus'd; and my relief
Must be to loath her. O, curse of marriage!
That we can call these delicate creatures ours,
And not their appetites. I had rather be a toad,
And live upon the vapour of a dungeon,
Than keep a corner in the thing I love
For others' uses. Yet, 't is the plague of great ones;
Prerogativ'd are they less than the base;
'T is destiny unshunnable, like death:
Even then this forked plague is fated to us,
When we do quicken. Desdemona comes.

(*Enter* DESDEMONA *and* EMILIA)

If she be false, O! then heaven mocks itself.—
I 'll not believe it.
DESDEMONA   How now, my dear Othello!
  Your dinner and the generous islanders,
  By you invited, do attend your presence.
OTHELLO   I am to blame.
DESDEMONA   Why is your speech so faint? are you not
    well?
OTHELLO   I have a pain upon my forehead here.
DESDEMONA   Faith, that 's with watching; 't will away
    again:
  Let me but bind it hard, within this hour
  It will be well.

(*Offers to bind his Head*)

OTHELLO   Your napkin is too little;

(*Lets fall her Handkerchief*)

Let it alone. Come, I 'll go in with you.
DESDEMONA   I am very sorry that you are not well.

(*Exeunt* OTHELLO, *and* DESDEMONA)

EMILIA   I am glad I have found this napkin.
  This was her first remembrance from the Moor:
  My wayward husband hath a hundred times

---

[6] Leave her to fend for herself.

Woo'd me to steal it; but she so loves the token,
(For he conjur'd her she should ever keep it)
That she reserves it evermore about her,
To kiss, and talk to. I 'll have the work ta'en out,
And give 't Iago: what he will do with it,
Heaven knows, not I;
I nothing, but to please his fantasy.

(*Enter* IAGO)

IAGO   How now! what do you here alone?
EMILIA   Do not you chide, I have a thing for you.
IAGO   A thing for me?—it is a common thing.
EMILIA   Ha?
IAGO   To have a foolish wife.
EMILIA   O! is that all? What will you give me now for
    that same handkerchief?
IAGO   What handkerchief?
EMILIA   What handkerchief!
  Why, that the Moor first gave to Desdemona;
  That which so often you did bid me steal.
IAGO   Hast stolen it from her?
EMILIA   No, 'faith: she let it drop by negligence;
  And, to th' advantage, I, being here, took 't up.
  Look, here it is.
IAGO   A good wench; give it me.
EMILIA   What will you do with 't, that you have been
    so earnest
  To have me filch it?
IAGO   Why, what 's that to you?

(*Snatching it*)

EMILIA   If it be not some purpose of import,
  Give 't me again: poor lady! she 'll run mad,
  When she shall lack it.
IAGO   Be not acknown on 't; I have use for it.
  Go; leave me.

(*Exit* EMILIA)

I will in Cassio's lodging lose this napkin,
And let him find it: trifles, light as air,
Are to the jealous confirmations strong
As proofs of holy writ. This may do something.
The Moor already changes with my poison:
Dangerous conceits are in their natures poisons,
Which at the first are scarce found to distaste;
But with a little act upon the blood,

Burn like the mines of sulphur.—I did say so:—

(*Enter* OTHELLO)

Look, where he comes! Not poppy, nor mandragora
Nor all the drowsy syrups of the world,
    Shall ever medicine thee to that sweet sleep,
    Which thou ow'dst yesterday.
OTHELLO   Ha! ha! false to me? to me?
IAGO   Why, how now, general! no more of that.
OTHELLO   Avaunt! be gone! thou hast set me on the
        rack.—
    I swear, 't is better to be much abus'd,
    Than but to know 't a little.
IAGO   How now, my lord!
OTHELLO   What sense had I of her stolen hours of lust?
    I saw it not, thought it not, it harm'd not me:
    I slept the next night well, was free and merry;
    I found not Cassio's kisses on her lips:
    He that is robb'd, not wanting what is stolen,
    Let him not know 't, and he 's not robb'd at all.
IAGO   I am sorry to hear this.
OTHELLO   I had been happy, if the general camp,
    Pioneers and all, had tasted her sweet body,
    So I had nothing known.—O! now, for ever,
    Farewell the tranquil mind; farewell content:
    Farewell the plumed troop, and the big wars,
    That make ambition virtue: O, farewell!
    Farewell the neighing steed, and the shrill trump,
    The spirit-stirring drum, the ear-piercing fife,
    The royal banner, and all quality,
    Pride, pomp, and circumstance of glorious war!
    And O! you mortal engines, whose rude throats
    Th' immortal Jove's dread clamours counterfeit,
    Farewell! Othello's occupation 's gone.
IAGO   Is it possible?—My lord,—
OTHELLO   Villain, be sure thou prove my love a
        whore,
    Be sure of it: give me the ocular proof,

(*Taking him by the Throat*)

    Or, by the worth of mine eternal soul,
    Thou hadst been better have been born a dog,
    Than answer my wak'd wrath.
IAGO   Is it come to this?
OTHELLO   Make me to see 't; or, at the least, so prove
        it,

That the probation bear no hinge, nor loop,
    To hang a doubt on, or woe upon thy life!
IAGO   My noble lord,—
OTHELLO   If thou dost slander her, and torture me,
    Never pray more: abandon all remorse;
    On horror's head horrors accumulate;
    Do deeds to make heaven weep, all earth amaz'd,
    For nothing canst thou to damnation add,
    Greater than that.

(*Releasing him*)

IAGO   O grace! O heaven defend me!
    Are you a man? have you a soul, or sense?—
    God be wi' you; take mine office.—O wretched fool,
    That liv'st to make thine honesty a vice!
    O monstrous world! Take note, take note, O world!
    To be direct and honest, is not safe.—
    I thank you for this profit: and, from hence,
    I 'll love no friend, since love breeds such offence.
OTHELLO   Nay, stay.—Thou shouldst be honest.
IAGO   I should be wise; for honesty 's a fool,
    And loses that it works for.
OTHELLO   By the world,
    I think my wife be honest, and think she is not;
    I think that thou art just, and think thou art not.
    I 'll have some proof: her name, that was as fresh
    As Dian's visage, is now begrim'd and black
    As mine own face. If there be cords, or knives,
    Poison, or fire, or suffocating streams,
    I 'll not endure it.—Would I were satisfied!
IAGO   I see, sir, you are eaten up with passion:
    I do repent me that I put it to you.
    You would be satisfied?
OTHELLO   Would! nay, I will.
IAGO   And may; but how? how satisfied, my lord?
    Would you the supervision! grossly gape on?
    Behold her topp'd?
OTHELLO   Death and damnation! O!
IAGO   It were a tedious difficulty, I think,
    To bring it to that prospect. Damn them then,
    If ever mortal eyes do see them bolster,
    More than their own! What then? how then?
    What shall I say? Where 's satisfaction?
    It is impossible you should see this,
    Were they as prime as goats, as hot as monkeys,
    As salt as wolves in pride, and fools as gross

As ignorance made drunk: but yet, I say,
If imputation, and strong circumstances,
Which lead directly to the door of truth,
Will give you satisfaction, you may have it.

OTHELLO   Give me a living reason she's disloyal.

IAGO   I do not like the office;
But, sith I am enter'd in this cause so far,
Prick'd to 't by foolish honesty and love,
I will go on. I lay with Cassio lately,
And being troubled with a raging tooth,
I could not sleep.
There are a kind of men, so loose of soul,
That in their sleeps will mutter their affairs:
One of this kind is Cassio.
In sleep I heard him say,—"Sweet Desdemona,
Let us be wary, let us hide our loves!"
And then, sir, would he gripe, and wring my hand,
Cry,—"O, sweet creature!" and then kiss me hard,
As if he pluck'd up kisses by the roots,
That grew upon my lips: then, laid his leg
Over my thigh, and sigh'd, and kiss'd; and then,
Cried,—"Cursed fate, that gave thee to the Moor!"

OTHELLO   O monstrous! monstrous!

IAGO   Nay, this was but his dream.

OTHELLO   But this denoted a foregone conclusion:
'T is a shrewd doubt, though it be but a dream.

IAGO   And this may help to thicken other proofs,
That do demonstrate thinly.

OTHELLO   I 'll tear her all to pieces.

IAGO   Nay, but be wise: yet we see nothing done;
She may be honest yet. Tell me but this:
Have you not sometimes seen a handkerchief,
Spotted with strawberries, in your wife's hand?

OTHELLO   I gave her such a one: 't was my first gift.

IAGO   I know not that: but such a handkerchief,
(I am sure it was your wife's) did I to-day
See Cassio wipe his beard with.

OTHELLO   If it be that,—

IAGO   If it be that, or any that was hers,
It speaks against her with the other proofs.

OTHELLO   O, that the slave had forty thousand lives!
One is too poor, too weak for my revenge.
Now do I see 't is true.—Look here, Iago;
All my fond love thus do I blow to heaven: 't is
    gone.—

Arise, black vengeance, from thy hollow cell!
Yield up, O Love! thy crown, and hearted throne,
To tyrannous hate! swell, bosom, with thy fraught,
For 't is of aspics' tongues!

IAGO   Pray, be content.

OTHELLO   O, blood, Iago, blood!

IAGO   Patience, I say: your mind, perhaps, may
    change.

OTHELLO   Never, Iago. Like to the Pontick sea,
Whose icy current and compulsive course
Ne'er knows retiring ebb, but keeps due on
To the Propontick, and the Hellespont;
Even so my bloody thoughts, with violent pace,
Shall ne'er look back, ne'er ebb to humble love,
Till that a capable and wide revenge
Swallow them up.—Now, by yond' marble heaven,
In the due reverence of a sacred vow

(Kneeling)

I here engage my words.

IAGO   Do not rise yet.—

(Kneeling)

Witness, you ever-burning lights above!
You elements that clip us round about!
Witness, that here Iago doth give up
The execution of his wit, hands, heart,
To wrong'd Othello's service. Let him command,
And to obey shall be in me remorse,
What bloody work soe'er.

OTHELLO   I greet thy love,
Not with vain thanks, but with acceptance
    bounteous,
And will upon the instant put thee to 't.
Within these three days let me hear thee say,
That Cassio 's not alive.

IAGO   My friend is dead: 't is done at your request;
But let her live.

OTHELLO   Damn her, lewd minx! O, damn her!
Come, go with me apart; I will withdraw,
To furnish me with some swift means of death
For the fair devil. Now art thou my lieutenant.

IAGO   I am your own for ever.

(Exeunt)

SCENE IV. *The Same.*

(Enter DESDEMONA, EMILIA, *and Clown)*

DESDEMONA Do you know, sirrah, where the lieutenant Cassio lies?

CLOWN I dare not say, he lies any where.

DESDEMONA Why, man?

CLOWN He is a soldier; and for one to say a soldier
lies, is stabbing.

DESDEMONA Go to. Where lodges he?

CLOWN To tell you where he lodges, is to tell you
where I lie.

DESDEMONA Can any thing be made of this?

CLOWN I know not where he lodges; and for me to devise a lodging, and say, he lies here, or he lies there,
were to lie in mine own throat.

DESDEMONA Can you inquire him out, and be edified
to report?

CLOWN I will catechize the world for him; that is,
make questions, and by them answer.

DESDEMONA Seek him; bid him come hither: tell
him, I have moved my lord in his behalf, and hope
all will be well.

CLOWN To do this is within the compass of man's
wit: and therefore I will attempt the doing it.

(Exit)

DESDEMONA Where should I lose that handkerchief,
Emilia?

EMILIA I know not, madam.

DESDEMONA Believe me, I had rather have lost my
purse
Full of cruzadoes; and but my noble Moor
Is true of mind, and made of no such baseness
As jealous creatures are, it were enough
To put him to ill thinking.

EMILIA   Is he not jealous?

DESDEMONA Who? he! I think the sun, where he was
born,
Drew all such humours from him.

EMILIA   Look, where he comes.

(Enter OTHELLO)

DESDEMONA I will not leave him now, till Cassio
Be call'd to him.—How is 't with you, my lord?

OTHELLO Well, my good lady.—*(Aside)* O, hardness
to dissemble!—
How do you, Desdemona?

DESDEMONA   Well, my good lord.

OTHELLO Give me your hand. This hand is moist, my
lady.

DESDEMONA It yet hath felt no age, nor known no
sorrow.

OTHELLO This argues fruitfulness, and liberal heart.
Hot, hot and moist: this hand of yours requires
A sequester from liberty, fasting and praying,
Much castigation, exercise devout;
For here 's a young and sweating devil here,
That commonly rebels. 'T is a good hand;
A frank one.

DESDEMONA You may, indeed, say so;
For 't was that hand that gave away my heart.

OTHELLO A liberal hand: the hearts of old gave hands,
But our new heraldry is—hands, not hearts.

DESDEMONA I cannot speak of this. Come now, your
promise.

OTHELLO What promise, chuck?

DESDEMONA I have sent to bid Cassio come speak
with you.

OTHELLO I have a salt and sudden rheum offends me.
Lend me thy handkerchief.

DESDEMONA   Here, my lord.

(Offering it)

OTHELLO That which I gave you.

DESDEMONA   I have it not about me.

OTHELLO Not?

DESDEMONA No, indeed, my lord.

OTHELLO   That is a fault.
That handkerchief
Did an Egyptian to my mother give;
She was a charmer, and could almost read
The thoughts of people: she told her, while she kept
it,
'T would make her amiable and subdue my father
Entirely to her love; but if she lost it,
Or made a gift of it, my father's eye
Should hold her loathed, and his spirits should hunt
After new fancies. She, dying, gave it me;
And bid me, when my fate would have me wive,

To give it her. I did so; and take heed on 't:
Make it a darling like your precious eye;
To lose or give 't away were such perdition,
As nothing else could match.

DESDEMONA   Is 't possible?

OTHELLO   'T is true: there 's magic in the web of it.
A sibyl, that had number'd in the world
The sun to course two hundred compasses,
In her prophetic fury sew'd the work;
The worms were hallow'd that did breed the silk,
And it was dyed in mummy, which the skilful
Conserv'd of maidens' hearts.

DESDEMONA   Indeed! is 't true?

OTHELLO   Most veritable; therefore look to 't well.

DESDEMONA   Then, would to heaven that I had never
seen it.

OTHELLO   Ha! wherefore?

DESDEMONA   Why do you speak so startingly and
rash?

OTHELLO   Is 't lost? is 't gone? speak, is it out o' the
way?

DESDEMONA   Heaven bless us!

OTHELLO   Say you?

DESDEMONA   It is not lost; but what an if it were?

OTHELLO   How?

DESDEMONA   I say, it is not lost.

OTHELLO   Fetch 't, let me see 't.

DESDEMONA   Why, so I can, sir; but I will not now.
This is a trick to put me from my suit:
I pray, let Cassio be receiv'd again.

OTHELLO   Fetch me that handkerchief: my mind
misgives.

DESDEMONA   Come, come;
You 'll never meet a more sufficient man.

OTHELLO   The handkerchief,—

DESDEMONA   I pray, talk me of Cassio.

OTHELLO   The handkerchief,—

DESDEMONA   A man that, all his time,
Hath founded his good fortunes on your love;
Shar'd dangers with you;—

OTHELLO   The handkerchief,—

DESDEMONA   In sooth, you are to blame.

OTHELLO   Away!

(*Exit* OTHELLO)

EMILIA   Is not this man jealous?

DESDEMONA   I ne'er saw this before.
Sure, there 's some wonder in this handkerchief:
I am most unhappy in the loss of it.

EMILIA   'T is not a year or two shows us a man:
They are all but stomachs, and we all but food;
They eat us hungerly, and when they are full,
They belch us.

(*Enter* IAGO *and* CASSIO)

                              Look you! Cassio, and my husband.

IAGO   There is no other way; 't is she must do 't:
And, lo, the happiness! go, and importune her.

DESDEMONA   How now, good Cassio! what 's the news
with you?

CASSIO   Madam, my former suit. I do beseech you
That by your virtuous means I may again
Exist, and be a member of his love,
Whom I, with all the office of my heart,
Entirely honour: I would not be delay'd.
If my offence be of such mortal kind,
That nor my service past, nor present sorrows,
Nor purpos'd merit in futurity,
Can ransom me into his love again,
But to know so must be my benefit;
So shall I clothe me in a forc'd content,
And shift myself upon some other course,
To fortune's alms.

DESDEMONA   Alas! thrice-gentle Cassio,
My advocation is not now in tune;
My lord is not my lord; nor should I know him,
Were he in favour, as in humour, alter'd.
So help me every spirit sanctified,
As I have spoken for you all my best,
And stood within the blank of his displeasure,
For my free speech. You must a while be patient:
What I can do, I will; and more I will,
Than for myself I dare: let that suffice you.

IAGO   Is my lord angry?

EMILIA   He went hence but now;
And, certainly, in strange unquietness.

IAGO   Can he be angry? I have seen the cannon,
When it hath blown his ranks into the air,
And, like the devil, from his very arm
Puff'd his own brother;—and can he be angry?
Something of moment, then: I will go meet him.
There 's matter in 't, indeed, if he be angry.

DESDEMONA   I pr'ythee, do so.

(*Exit* IAGO)

—Something, sure, of state,—
Either from Venice, or some unhatch'd practice,
Made demonstrable here in Cyprus to him,—
Hath puddled his clear spirit; and, in such cases,
Men's natures wrangle with inferior things,
Though great ones are their object. 'T is even so;
For let our finger ache, and it indues
Our other healthful members ev'n to that sense
Of pain: nay, we must think, men are not gods;
Nor of them look for such observances
As fit the bridal.—Beshrew me much, Emilia
I was (unhandsome warrior as I am)
Arraigning his unkindness with my soul;
But now I find, I had suborn'd the witness,
And he 's indicted falsely.

EMILIA   Pray heaven, it be state matters, as you think,
And no conception, nor no jealous toy,
Concerning you.

DESDEMONA   Alas, the day! I never gave him cause.

EMILIA   But jealous souls will not be answer'd so;
They are not ever jealous for a cause,
But jealous for they are jealous: 't is a monster,
Begot upon itself, born on itself.

DESDEMONA   Heaven keep that monster from
Othello's mind!

EMILIA   Lady, amen.

DESDEMONA   I will go seek him.—Cassio, walk
hereabout.
If I do find him fit, I 'll move your suit,
And seek to effect it to my uttermost.

CASSIO   I humbly thank your ladyship.

(*Exeunt* DESDEMONA *and* EMILIA)

(*Enter* BIANCA)

BIANCA   Save you, friend Cassio!

CASSIO   What make you from home?
How is it with you, my most fair Bianca?
I' faith, sweet love, I was coming to your house.

BIANCA   And I was going to your lodging, Cassio.
What, keep a week away? seven days and nights?
Eight score eight hours? and lovers' absent hours
More tedious than the dial eight score times?

O weary reckoning!

CASSIO   Pardon me, Bianca;
I have this while with leaden thoughts been press'd;
But I shall, in a more convenient time,
Strike off this score of absence. Sweet Bianca,

(*Giving her* DESDEMONA'S *Handkerchief*)

Take me this work out.

BIANCA   O, Cassio! whence came this?
This is some token from a newer friend:
To the felt absence, now, I feel a cause.
Is it come to this? Well, well.

CASSIO   Go to, woman!
Throw your vile guesses in the devil's teeth,
From whence you have them. You are jealous, now,
That this is from some mistress some remembrance:
No, in good troth, Bianca.

BIANCA   Why, whose is it?

CASSIO   I know not, sweet: I found it in my chamber.
I like the work well; ere it be demanded
(As like enough it will) I 'd have it copied:
Take it, and do 't; and leave me for this time.

BIANCA   Leave you! wherefore?

CASSIO   I do attend here on the general,
And think it no addition, nor my wish,
To have him see me woman'd.

BIANCA   Why, I pray you?

CASSIO   Not that I love you not.

BIANCA   But that you do not love me.
I pray you, bring me on the way a little;
And say, if I shall see you soon at night.

CASSIO   'T is but a little way, that I can bring you,
For I attend here; but I 'll see you soon.

BIANCA   'T is very good: I must be circumstanc'd.

(*Exeunt*)

ACT IV

SYNOPSIS: 1. Othello falls into an epileptic fit when Iago tells him that
Cassio has admitted making love with Desdemona. Iago has Othello
hide and watch him converse with Cassio. Cassio jokes about
Bianca's infatuation with him; Othello thinks he refers to Desdemona. Bianca enters and tells Cassio that she refuses to copy the embroidery in a present given by another woman. Othello is now convinced by this "proof." He agrees to strangle Desdemona in her bed,
and Iago agrees to kill Cassio. An ambassador from the duke, Lodovico, brings a letter appointing Cassio governor of Cyprus and ordering Othello home to Venice. Desdemona tells Lodovico of the breach

between Othello and Cassio. Othello loses control; strikes and taunts Desdemona. 2. Othello questions Emilia, who swears that Desdemona is faithful to him. Nevertheless, he accuses his wife, calling her a whore. Iago tells her that the general is disturbed by official matters. Iago convinces Roderigo to murder Cassio. 3. Othello orders Desdemona to bed. She sings her "swan song," "Willow." In contrast to Emilia, Desdemona swears she would never deceive her husband.

SCENE I.   *The Same.* (*Enter* OTHELLO *and* IAGO)

IAGO   Will you think so?

OTHELLO   Think so, Iago?

IAGO   What,
   To kiss in private?

OTHELLO   An unauthoriz'd kiss.

IAGO   Or to be naked with her friend abed,
   An hour, or more, not meaning any harm?

OTHELLO   Naked abed, Iago, and not mean harm?
   It is hypocrisy against the devil:
   They that mean virtuously, and yet do so,
   The devil their virtue tempts, and they tempt
      heaven.

IAGO   If they do nothing, 't is a venial slip;
   But if I give my wife a handkerchief,—

OTHELLO   What then?

IAGO   Why, then 't is hers, my lord; and, being hers,
   She may, I think, bestow 't on any man.

OTHELLO   She is protectress of her honour too:
   May she give that?

IAGO   Her honour is an essence that 's not seen;
   They have it very oft, that have it not:
   But, for the handkerchief,—

OTHELLO   By heaven, I would most gladly have forgot
   it.
   Thou saidst,—O! it comes o'er my memory,
   As doth the raven o'er the infected house,
   Boding to all,—he had my handkerchief.

IAGO   Ay, what of that?

OTHELLO   That 's not so good, now.

IAGO   What, if I had said, I had seen him do you
   wrong?
   Or heard him say,—as knaves be such abroad,
   Who having, by their own importunate suit,
   Or voluntary dotage of some mistress,
   Convinced or supplied them, cannot choose
   But they must blab—

OTHELLO   Hath he said any thing?

IAGO   He hath, my lord; but be you well assur'd,

No more than he 'll unswear.

OTHELLO   What hath he said?

IAGO   'Faith, that he did,—I know not what he did.

OTHELLO   What? what?

IAGO   Lie—

OTHELLO   With her?

IAGO   With her, on her; what you will.

OTHELLO   Lie with her! lie on her!—We say, lie on
   her, when they belie her. Lie with her! that 's ful-
   some. — Handkerchief, — confessions, — handkerchief!—To confess, and be hanged for his labour.—
   First, to be hanged, and then to confess:—I tremble
   at it. Nature would not invest herself in such shuddering passion without some instruction. It is not
   words, that shake me thus:—Pish!—Noses, ears, and
   lips.—Is it possible?—Confess!—Handkerchief!—O
   devil!—

(*Falls in a Trance*)

IAGO   Work on,
   My medicine, work! Thus credulous fools are
      caught;
   And many worthy and chaste dames, even thus,
   All guiltless, meet reproach.—What, ho! my lord!
   My lord, I say! Othello!

(*Enter* CASSIO)

               How now, Cassio!

CASSIO   What 's the matter?

IAGO   My lord is fallen into an epilepsy:
   This is his second fit; he had one yesterday.

CASSIO   Rub him about the temples.

IAGO   No, forbear.
   The lethargy must have his quiet course,
   If not, he foams at mouth; and, by and by,
   Breaks out to savage madness. Look, he stirs:
   Do you withdraw yourself a little while,
   He will recover straight: when he is gone,
   I would on great occasion speak with you.—

(*Exit* CASSIO)

   How is it, general? have you not hurt your head?

OTHELLO   Dost thou mock me?

IAGO   I mock you! no, by heaven.
   Would you would bear your fortunes like a man.

OTHELLO A horned [1] man 's a monster, and a beast.

IAGO There 's many a beast, then, in a populous city,
And many a civil monster.

OTHELLO Did he confess it?

IAGO   Good sir, be a man;
Think, every bearded fellow, that 's but yok'd,
May draw with you: there 's millions now alive,
That nightly lie in those unproper[2] beds,
Which they dare swear peculiar:[3] your case is better.
O! 't is the spite of hell, the fiend's arch-mock,
To lip a wanton in a secure couch,
And to suppose her chaste. No, let me know;
And, knowing what I am, I know what she shall be.

OTHELLO O! thou art wise; 't is certain.

IAGO Stand you awhile apart;
Confine yourself but in a patient list,
Whilst you were here, o'erwhelm'd with your grief,
(A passion most unfitting such a man)
Cassio came hither: I shifted him away,
And laid good 'scuse upon your ecstasy;
Bade him anon return, and here speak with me;
The which he promis'd. But encave yourself,
And mark the fleers, the gibes, and notable scorns,
That dwell in every region of his face;
For I will make him tell the tale anew,
Where, how, how oft, how long ago, and when
He hath, and is again to cope your wife:
I say, but mark his gesture.—Marry, patience,
Or I shall say, you are all-in-all in spleen,
And nothing of a man.

OTHELLO   Dost thou hear, Iago?
I will be found most cunning in my patience;
But (dost thou hear?) most bloody.

IAGO   That 's not amiss,
But yet keep time in all. Will you withdraw?

(OTHELLO *retires*)

Now will I question Cassio of Bianca,
A housewife, that by selling her desires,
Buys herself bread and clothes: it is a creature
That dotes on Cassio, as 't is the strumpet's plague,
To beguile many, and be beguil'd by one.

---

[1] In folklore, cuckolds grew horns.
[2] Not their own.
[3] Belonging to them.

He, when he hears of her, cannot refrain
From the excess of laughter:—here he comes.—

(*Re-enter* CASSIO)

As he shall smile, Othello shall go mad;
And his unbookish jealousy must construe
Poor Cassio's smiles, gestures, and light behaviour,
Quite in the wrong.—How do you now, lieutenant?

CASSIO The worser, that you give me the addition,
Whose want even kills me.

IAGO Ply Desdemona well, and you are sure on 't.
Now, if this suit lay in Bianca's power,

(*Speaking lower*)

How quickly should you speed!

CASSIO   Alas, poor caitiff!

OTHELLO Look, how he laughs already!

IAGO I never knew woman love man so.

CASSIO Alas, poor rogue! I think i' faith, she loves me.

OTHELLO Now he denies it faintly, and laughs it out.

IAGO Do you hear, Cassio?

OTHELLO   Now he importunes him
To tell it o'er. Go to; well said, well said.

IAGO She gives it out, that you shall marry her:
Do you intend it?

CASSIO   Ha, ha, ha!

OTHELLO Do you triumph o'er me? do you triumph?

CASSIO I marry her!—what, a customer? I pr'ythee,
bear some charity to my wit; do not think it is so un-
wholesome. Ha, ha, ha!

OTHELLO So, so, so, so. They laugh that win.

IAGO 'Faith, the cry goes, that you shall marry her.

CASSIO Pr'ythee, say true.

IAGO I am a very villain else.

OTHELLO Have you scored me? Well.

CASSIO This is the monkey's own giving out: she is
persuaded I will marry her, out of her own love and
flattery, not out of my promise.

OTHELLO Iago beckons me: now he begins the story.

CASSIO She was here even now; she haunts me in
every place. I was, the other day, talking on the sea-
bank with certain Venetians, and thither comes this
bauble; and, by this hand, she falls me thus about
my neck;—

OTHELLO Crying, O dear Cassio! as it were: his gesture imports it.

CASSIO So hangs, and lolls, and weeps upon me; so hales, and pulls me; ha, ha, ha!—

OTHELLO Now he tells, how she plucked him to my chamber. O! I see that nose of yours, but not that dog I shall throw it to.

CASSIO Well, I must leave her company.

IAGO Before me! look where she comes.

(*Enter* BIANCA)

CASSIO 'T is such another fitchew! marry, a perfumed one.—What do you mean by this haunting of me?

BIANCA Let the devil and his dam haunt you! What did you mean by that same handkerchief, you gave me even now? I was a fine fool to take it. I must take out the work!—A likely piece of work, that you should find it in your chamber, and know not who left it there. This is some minx's token, and I must take out the work? There, give it your hobby-horse: wheresoever you had it, I 'll take out no work on 't.

CASSIO How now, my sweet Bianca! how now, how now!

OTHELLO By heaven, that should be my handkerchief!

BIANCA An you 'll come to supper to-night, you may: an you will not, come when you are next prepared for.

(*Exit*)

IAGO After her, after her.

CASSIO 'Faith, I must; she 'll rail in the street else.

IAGO Will you sup there?

CASSIO 'Faith, I intend so.

IAGO Well, I may chance to see you, for I would very fain speak with you.

CASSIO Pr'ythee, come; will you?

IAGO Go to; say no more.

(*Exit* CASSIO)

OTHELLO (*Advancing*) How shall I murder him, Iago?

IAGO Did you perceive how he laughed at his vice?

OTHELLO O, Iago!

IAGO And did you see the handkerchief?

OTHELLO Was that mine?

IAGO Yours, by this hand: and to see how he prizes the foolish woman your wife! she gave it him, and he hath given it his whore.

OTHELLO I would have him nine years a killing.—A fine woman! a fair woman! a sweet woman!

IAGO Nay, you must forget that.

OTHELLO Ay, let her rot, and perish, and be damned to-night, for she shall not live. No, my heart is turned to stone; I strike it, and it hurts my hand. O! the world hath not a sweeter creature: she might lie by an emperor's side, and command him tasks.

IAGO Nay, that 's not your way.

OTHELLO Hang her! I do but say what she is.—So delicate with her needle!—An admirable musician! O! she will sing the savageness out of a bear.—Of so high and plenteous wit and invention!—

IAGO She 's the worse for all this.

OTHELLO O! a thousand thousand times. And then, of so gentle a condition.

IAGO Ay, too gentle.

OTHELLO Nay, that 's certain:—but yet the pity of it, Iago!—O, Iago! the pity of it, Iago!

IAGO If you are so fond over her iniquity, give her patent to offend; for if it touch not you, it comes near nobody.

OTHELLO I will chop her into messes.—Cuckold me!

IAGO O! 't is foul in her.

OTHELLO With mine officer!

IAGO That 's fouler.

OTHELLO Get me some poison, Iago; this night:—I 'll not expostulate with her, lest her body and beauty unprovide my mind again. This night, Iago.

IAGO Do it not with poison, strangle her in her bed, even the bed she hath contaminated.

OTHELLO Good, good; the justice of it pleases; very good.

IAGO And for Cassio, let me be his undertaker. You shall hear more by midnight.

(*A Trumpet within*)

OTHELLO Excellent good.—What trumpet is that same?

IAGO Something from Venice, sure. 'T is Lodovico, come from the duke; and, see, your wife is with him.

(*Enter* LODOVICO, DESDEMONA, *and Attendants*)

LODOVICO 'Save you, worthy general!

OTHELLO   With all my heart, sir.

LODOVICO   The duke and senators of Venice greet
   you.

(Giving him a Packet)

OTHELLO   I kiss the instrument of their pleasures.

(Opens the Packet, and reads)

DESDEMONA   And what 's the news, good cousin
   Lodovico?
IAGO   I am very glad to see you, signior:
   Welcome to Cyprus.
LODOVICO   I thank you. How does lieutenant Cassio?
IAGO   Lives, sir.
DESDEMONA   Cousin, there 's fallen between him and
   my lord
   An unkind breach, but you shall make all well.
OTHELLO   Are you sure of that?
DESDEMONA   My lord?
OTHELLO   "This fail you not to do, as you will"—

   (Reading)

LODOVICO   He did not call; he 's busy in the paper.
   Is there division 'twixt my lord and Cassio?
DESDEMONA   A most unhappy one: I would do much
   To atone them, for the love I bear to Cassio.
OTHELLO   Fire and brimstone!
DESDEMONA   My lord?
OTHELLO   Are you wise?
DESDEMONA   What! is he angry?
LODOVICO   May be, the letter mov'd him;
   For, as I think, they do command him home,
   Deputing Cassio in his government.
DESDEMONA   By my troth, I am glad on 't.
OTHELLO   Indeed.
DESDEMONA   My lord?
OTHELLO   I am glad to see you mad.
DESDEMONA   How, sweet Othello?
OTHELLO   Devil!

   (Striking her)

DESDEMONA   I have not deserv'd this.
LODOVICO   My lord, this would not be believ'd in
   Venice,
   Though I should swear I saw it. 'T is very much,
   Make her amends, she weeps.
OTHELLO   O devil, devil!

If that the earth could teem with woman's tears,
Each drop she falls would prove a crocodile.—
Out of my sight!
DESDEMONA   I will not stay to offend you.

(Going)

LODOVICO   Truly an obedient lady.—
   I do beseech your lordship, call her back.
OTHELLO   Mistress!
DESDEMONA   My lord?
OTHELLO   What would you with her, sir?
LODOVICO   Who, I, my lord?
OTHELLO   Ay; you did wish, that I would make her
   turn,
   Sir, she can turn, and turn, and yet go on,
   And turn again; and she can weep, sir, weep;
   And she 's obedient, as you say,—obedient,—
   Very obedient.—Proceed you in your tears.—
   Concerning this, sir,—O well-painted passion!
   I am commanded home.—Get you away;
   I 'll send for you anon.—Sir, I obey the mandate
   And will return to Venice.—Hence! avaunt!

(Exit DESDEMONA)

Cassio shall have my place. And,—sir, to-night,
I do intreat that we may sup together:
You are welcome, sir, to Cyprus.—Goats and
   monkies!

(Exit)

LODOVICO   Is this the noble Moor whom our full
   senate
   Call all-in-all sufficient?—This the noble nature
   Whom passion could not shake? whose solid virtue
   The shot of accident, nor dart of chance,
   Could neither graze, nor pierce?
IAGO   He is much chang'd.
LODOVICO   Are his wits safe? is he not light of brain?
IAGO   He 's that he is: I may not breathe my censure.
   What he might be,—if, what he might, he is not,
   I would to heaven, he were.
LODOVICO   What! strike his wife?
IAGO   'Faith, that was not so well; yet would I knew,
   That stroke would prove the worst.
LODOVICO   Is it his use?
   Or did the letters work upon his blood,

And new-create this fault?
IAGO   Alas, alas!
  It is not honesty in me, to speak
  What I have seen and known. You shall observe
    him;
  And his own courses will denote him so,
  That I may save my speech. Do but go after,
  And mark how he continues.
LODOVICO   I am sorry, that I am deceiv'd in him.

  (*Exeunt*)

SCENE II.   *A Room in the Castle*

  (*Enter* OTHELLO *and* EMILIA)

OTHELLO   You have seen nothing then?
EMILIA   Nor ever heard; nor ever did suspect.
OTHELLO   Yes, you have seen Cassio and her together.
EMILIA   But then I saw no harm; and then I heard
  Each syllable that breath made up between them.
OTHELLO   What! did they never whisper?
EMILIA   Never, my lord.
OTHELLO   Nor send you out of the way?
EMILIA   Never.
OTHELLO   To fetch her fan, her gloves, her mask, nor
    nothing?
EMILIA   Never, my lord.
OTHELLO   That 's strange.
EMILIA   I durst, my lord, to wager she is honest,
  Lay down my soul at stake: if you think other,
  Remove your thought; it doth abuse your bosom.
  If any wretch have put this in your head,
  Let heaven requite it with the serpent's curse,
  For if she be not honest, chaste, and true,
  There 's no man happy; the purest of their wives
  Is foul as slander.
OTHELLO   Bid her come hither:—go,—

  (*Exit* EMILIA)

  She says enough;—yet she 's a simple bawd,
  That cannot say as much.—This is a subtle whore.
  A closet-lock-and-key of villainous secrets:
  And yet she 'll kneel, and pray: I have seen her do 't.

  (*Re-enter* EMILIA, *with* DESDEMONA)

DESDEMONA   My lord, what is your will?
OTHELLO   Pray, chuck, come hither.

DESDEMONA   What is your pleasure?
OTHELLO   Let me see your eyes:
  Look in my face.
DESDEMONA   What horrible fancy is this?
OTHELLO   Some of your function, mistress;

  (*To* EMILIA)

  Leave procreants alone, and shut the door;
  Cough, or cry hem, if any body come:
  Your mystery, your mystery;—nay, despatch.

  (*Exit* EMILIA)

DESDEMONA   Upon my knee, what doth your speech
    import?
  I understand a fury in your words,

  (*Kneels*)

  But not the words.
OTHELLO   Why, what art thou?
DESDEMONA   Your wife, my lord; your true
  And loyal wife.

  (*Rises*)

OTHELLO   Come, swear it, damn thyself;
  Lest, being like one of heaven, the devils themselves
  Should fear to seize thee: therefore, be double-
    damn'd
  Swear thou art honest.
DESDEMONA   Heaven doth truly know it.
OTHELLO   Heaven truly knows, that thou art false as
    hell.
DESDEMONA   To whom, my lord? with whom? How
    am I false?
OTHELLO   O Desdemona!—away, away, away!
DESDEMONA   Alas, the heavy day!—Why do you
    weep?
  Am I the occasion of these tears, my lord?
  If, haply, you my father do suspect
  An instrument of this your calling back,
  Lay not your blame on me: if you have lost him,
  Why, I have lost him too.
OTHELLO   Had it pleas'd heaven
  To try me with affliction; had he rain'd
  All kinds of sores, and shames, on my bare head:
  Steep'd me in poverty to the very lips;
  Given to captivity me and my utmost hopes;

I should have found in some part of my soul
A drop of patience: but, alas! to make me
A fixed figure, for the hand of scorn
To point his slowly moving finger at;
Yet could I bear that too; well, very well:
But there, where I have garner'd up my heart,
Where either I must live, or bear no life,
The fountain from the which my current runs
Or else dries up; to be discarded thence,
Or keep it as a cistern, for foul toads
To knot and gender in!—turn thy complexion
   there,[4]
Patience, thou young and rose-lipp'd cherubin;
Ay, there, look grim as hell!

DESDEMONA   I hope, my noble lord esteems me
   honest.

OTHELLO   O! ay; as summer flies are in the shambles,
That quicken even with blowing. O thou weed!
Who art so lovely fair, and smell'st so sweet,
That the sense aches at thee, would thou hadst ne'er
   been born!

DESDEMONA   Alas! what ignorant sin have I
   committed?

OTHELLO   Was this fair paper, this most goodly book,
Made to write whore upon? What committed?
Committed?—O thou public commoner!
I should make very forges of my cheeks,
That would to cinders burn up modesty,
Did I but speak thy deeds.—What committed?
Heaven stops the nose at it, and the moon winks.
The bawdy wind, that kisses all it meets,
Is hush'd within the hollow mine of earth,
And will not hear it. What committed?—
Impudent strumpet!

DESDEMONA   By heaven you do me wrong.
OTHELLO   Are not you a strumpet?
DESDEMONA   No, as I am a Christian
If to preserve this vessel for my lord,
From any other, foul, unlawful touch,
Be not to be a strumpet, I am none.
OTHELLO   What, not a whore?
DESDEMONA   No, as I shall be saved.
OTHELLO   Is it possible?

----

[4] Change thy color.

DESDEMONA   O, heaven forgive us!

   (Kneeling)

OTHELLO   I cry you mercy, then.
I took you for that cunning whore of Venice,
That married with Othello.—You, mistress,

   (Re-enter EMILIA*)*

That have the office opposite to Saint Peter,
And keep the gate of hell; you, you, ay, you:
We have done our course; there 's money for your
   pains.
I pray you, turn the key, and keep our counsel.

   (Exit)

EMILIA   Alas! what does this gentleman conceive?
How do you, madam? how do you, my good lady?
DESDEMONA   'Faith, half asleep.

   (Rising)

EMILIA   Good madam, what 's the matter with my
   lord?
DESDEMONA   With whom?
EMILIA   Why, with my lord, madam.
DESDEMONA   Who is thy lord?
EMILIA   He that is yours, sweet lady.
DESDEMONA   I have none: do not talk to me, Emilia;
I cannot weep; nor answer have I none,
But what should go by water. Pr'ythee, to-night
Lay on my bed my wedding sheets,—remember;—
And call thy husband hither.
EMILIA   Here is a change, indeed!

   (Exit)

DESDEMONA   'T is meet I should be us'd so, very meet.
How have I been behav'd, that he might stick
The small'st opinion on my least misdeed?

   (Re-enter EMILIA, *with* IAGO*)*

IAGO   What is your pleasure, madam? How is it with
   you?
DESDEMONA   I cannot tell. Those, that do teach young
   babes,
Do it with gentle means, and easy tasks:
He might have chid me so; for, in good faith,
I am a child to chiding.

IAGO   What 's the matter, lady?

EMILIA   Alas! Iago, my lord hath so bewhor'd her,
Thrown such despite and heavy terms upon her,
As true hearts cannot bear.

DESDEMONA   Am I that name, Iago?

IAGO   What name, fair lady?

DESDEMONA   Such as, she says, my lord did say I was.

EMILIA   He call'd her whore: a beggar in his drink,
Could not have laid such terms upon his callat.

IAGO   Why did he so?

DESDEMONA   I do not know; I am sure, I am none
such.

IAGO   Do not weep, do not weep. Alas the day!

EMILIA   Has she forsook so many noble matches,
Her father, and her country, and her friends,
To be call'd whore? would it not make one weep?

DESDEMONA   It is my wretched fortune.

IAGO   Beshrew him for it!
How comes this trick upon him?

DESDEMONA   Nay, heaven doth know.

EMILIA   I will be hang'd, if some eternal villain,
Some busy and insinuating rogue,
Some cogging, cozening slave, to get some office,
Have not devis'd this slander; I 'll be hang'd else.

IAGO   Fie! there is no such man: it is impossible.

DESDEMONA   If any such there be, heaven pardon
him!

EMILIA   A halter pardon him, and hell gnaw his bones!
Why should he call her, whore? who keeps her
company?
What place? what time? what form? what likelihood?
The Moor 's abus'd by some most villainous knave,
Some base notorious knave, some scurvy fellow.—
O, heaven! that such companions thou 'dst unfold,
And put in every honest hand a whip,
To lash the rascals naked through the world,
Even from the east to the west!

IAGO   Speak within door.

EMILIA   O, fie upon them! some such squire he was.
That turn'd your wit the seamy side without,
And made you to suspect me with the Moor.

IAGO   You are a fool; go to.

DESDEMONA   O good Iago!
What shall I do to win my lord again?
Good friend, go to him, for, by this light of heaven.
I know not how I lost him. Here I kneel:

If e'er my will did trespass 'gainst his love,
Either in discourse of thought, or actual deed;
Or that mine eyes, mine ears, or any sense,
Delighted them in any other form;
Or that I do not yet, and ever did,
And ever will,—though he do shake me off
To beggarly divorcement,—love him dearly,
Comfort forswear me! Unkindness may do much;
And his unkindness may defeat my life,
But never taint my love. I cannot say whore:
It does abhor me now I speak the word;
To do the act that might the addition earn,
Not the world's mass of vanity could make me.

IAGO   I pray you, be content; 't is but his humour:
The business of the state does him offence,
And he does chide with you.

DESDEMONA   If 't were no other,—

IAGO   'T is but so, I warrant.

(Music)

Hark, how these instruments summon to supper!
The messengers of Venice stay the meat.
Go in, and weep not; all things shall be well.

(Exeunt DESDEMONA *and* EMILIA*)*

(Enter RODERIGO*)*

How now, Roderigo!

RODERIGO   I do not find that thou deal'st justly with
me.

IAGO   What in the contrary?

RODERIGO   Every day thou doff'st me with some device, Iago; and rather, as it seems to me now, keep'st
from me all conveniency, that suppliest me with the
least advantage of hope. I will, indeed, no longer endure it; nor am I yet persuaded, to put up in peace
what already I have foolishly suffered.

IAGO   Will you hear me, Roderigo?

RODERIGO   'Faith, I have heard too much; for your
words, and performances, are no kin together.

IAGO   You charge me most unjustly.

RODERIGO   With nought but truth. I have wasted myself out of my means: the jewels you have had from
me, to deliver to Desdemona, would half have corrupted a votarist: you have told me, she has received
them, and returned me expectations and comforts of
sudden respect and acquaintance; but I find none.

IAGO   Well; go to; very well.

RODERIGO   Very well! go to! I cannot go to, man; nor 't is not very well: by this hand, I say, it is very scurvy; and begin to find myself fobbed in it.

IAGO   Very well.

RODERIGO   I tell you, 't is not very well. I will make myself known to Desdemona: if she will return me my jewels, I will give over my suit, and repent my unlawful solicitation; if not, assure yourself, I will seek satisfaction of you.

IAGO   You have said now.

RODERIGO   Ay, and I have said nothing, but what I protest intendment of doing.

IAGO   Why, now I see there 's mettle in thee; and even, from this instant, do build on thee a better opinion than ever before. Give me thy hand, Roderigo: thou hast taken against me a most just exception; but, yet, I protest, I have dealt most directly in thy affair.

RODERIGO   It hath not appeared.

IAGO   I grant, indeed, it hath not appeared, and your suspicion is not without wit and judgment. But, Roderigo, if thou hast that within thee indeed, which I have greater reason to believe now than ever,—I mean, purpose, courage, and valour,—this night show it: if thou the next night following enjoyest not Desdemona, take me from this world with treachery, and devise engines for my life.

RODERIGO   Well, what is it? is it within reason, and compass?

IAGO   Sir, there is especial commission come from Venice, to depute Cassio in Othello's place.

RODERIGO   Is that true? why, then Othello and Desdemona return again to Venice.

IAGO   O, no! he goes into Mauritania, and takes away with him the fair Desdemona, unless his abode be lingered here by some accident; wherein none can be so determinate as the removing of Cassio.

RODERIGO   How do you mean removing of him?

IAGO   Why, by making him uncapable of Othello's place; knocking out his brains.

RODERIGO   And that you would have me do?

IAGO   Ay; if you dare do yourself a profit, and a right. He sups to-night with a harlotry, and thither will I go to him: he knows not yet of his honourable fortune. If you will watch his going thence, (which I will fashion to fall out between twelve and one) you may take him at your pleasure: I will be near to second your attempt, and he shall fall between us. Come, stand not amazed at it, but go along with me; I will show you such a necessity in his death, that you shall think yourself bound to put it on him. It is now high supper-time, and the night grows to waste: about it.

RODERIGO   I will hear farther reason for this.

IAGO   And you shall be satisfied.

(Exeunt)

SCENE III.   Another Room in the Castle

(Enter OTHELLO, LODOVICO, DESDEMONA, EMILIA, and Attendants)

LODOVICO   I do beseech you, sir, trouble yourself no farther.

OTHELLO   O! pardon me; 't will do me good to walk.

LODOVICO   Madam, good-night; I humbly thank your ladyship.

DESDEMONA   Your honour is most welcome.

OTHELLO   Will you walk, sir?—
O!—Desdemona,—

DESDEMONA   My lord?

OTHELLO   Get you to bed on the instant; I will be returned forthwith. Dismiss your attendant there: look, it be done.

DESDEMONA   I will, my lord.

(Exeunt OTHELLO, LODOVICO, and Attendants)

EMILIA   How goes it now? he looks gentler than he did.

DESDEMONA   He says, he will return incontinent.[5]
He hath commanded me to go to bed,
And bade me to dismiss you.

EMILIA   Dismiss me!

DESDEMONA   It was his bidding; therefore, good Emilia,
Give me my nightly wearing, and adieu:
We must not now displease him.

EMILIA   I would you had never seen him.

DESDEMONA   So would not I: my love doth so approve him,

---

[5] At once.

That even his stubbornness, his checks, and
    frowns,—
Pr'ythee, unpin me,—have grace and favour in them.

EMILIA   I have laid those sheets you bade me on the
    bed.

DESDEMONA   All 's one.—Good faith, how foolish are
    our minds!—
If I do die before thee, pr'ythee, shroud me
In one of those same sheets.

EMILIA   Come, come, you talk.

DESDEMONA   My mother had a maid call'd Barbara:
    She was in love; and he she lov'd prov'd mad,
    And did forsake her: she had a song of—willow,
    An old thing 't was, but it express'd her fortune,
    And she died singing it: that song, to-night,
    Will not go from my mind; I have much to do,
    Not to go hang my head all at one side,
    And sing it like poor Barbara. Pr'ythee, despatch.

EMILIA   Shall I go fetch your night-gown?

DESDEMONA   No, unpin me here.—
    This Lodovico is a proper man.

EMILIA   A very handsome man.

DESDEMONA   He speaks well.

EMILIA   I know a lady in Venice would have walked
    barefoot to Palestine for a touch of his nether lip.

DESDEMONA (*Singing*)

A poor soul sat sighing by a sycamore tree,[6]
    Sing all a green willow;
Her hand on her bosom, her head on her knee,
    Sing willow, willow, willow:
The fresh streams ran by her and murmur'd her
    moans;
    Sing willow, willow, willow:
Her salt tears fell from her, and soften'd the stones;
Lay by these.—
    Sing willow, willow, willow.
Pr'ythee, hie thee; he 'll come anon.—
    Sing all a green willow must be my garland.
    Let nobody blame him, his scorn I approve,—
Nay, that 's not next.—Hark! who is it that knocks?

EMILIA   It is the wind.

DESDEMONA

I call'd my love false love; but what said he then?
    Sing willow, willow, willow:

---

[6] See the music for this song at the end of the play.

If I court no women, you 'll couch with no men.
So, get thee gone; good night. Mine eyes do itch;
Doth that bode weeping?

EMILIA   'T is neither here nor there.

DESDEMONA   I have heard it said so.—O, these men,
    these men!—
Dost thou in conscience think,—tell me, Emilia,—
That there be women do abuse their husbands
In such gross kind?

EMILIA   There be some such, no question.

DESDEMONA   Wouldst thou do such a deed for all the
    world?

EMILIA   Why, would not you?

DESDEMONA   No, by this heavenly light.

EMILIA   Nor I neither by this heavenly light:
    I might do 't as well i' the dark.

DESDEMONA   Wouldst thou do such a deed for all the
    world?

EMILIA   The world is a huge thing: 't is a great price
    For a small vice.

DESDEMONA   In troth, I think thou wouldst not.

EMILIA   In troth, I think I should, and undo 't, when I
    had done. Marry, I would not do such a thing for a
    joint-ring, nor for measures of lawn, nor for gowns,
    petticoats, nor caps, nor any petty exhibition, but, for
    the whole world,—why, who would not make her
    husband a cuckold, to make him a monarch? I
    should venture purgatory for 't.

DESDEMONA   Beshrew me, if I would do such a wrong
    for the whole world.

EMILIA   Why, the wrong is but a wrong i' the world;
    and, having the world for your labour, 't is a wrong
    in your own world, and you might quickly make it
    right.

DESDEMONA   I do not think there is any such woman.

EMILIA   Yes, a dozen; and as many
    To the vantage, as would store the world they play'd
    for.
But, I do think, it is their husbands' faults,
If wives do fall. Say, that they slack their duties,
And pour our treasures into foreign laps;
Or else break out in peevish jealousies,
Throwing restraint upon us; or, say, they strike us,
Or scant our former having in despite,
Why, we have galls; and, though we have some
    grace,

Yet have we some revenge. Let husbands know,
Their wives have sense like them: they see, and
   smell,
And have their palates, both for sweet and sour,
As husbands have. What is it that they do,
When they change us for others? Is it sport?
I think, it is; and doth affection breed it?
I think, it doth. Is 't frailty, that thus errs?
It is so too: and have not we affections,
Desires for sport, and frailty, as men have?
Then, let them use us well; else, let them know,
The ills we do, their ills instruct us to.

DESDEMONA   Good-night, good-night: heaven me such
   uses send,
Not to pick bad from bad, but by bad mend.

(Exeunt)

ACT V

SYNOPSIS: 1. Roderigo attacks Cassio but is wounded by him. Iago, unseen, wounds Cassio in the leg. Othello hears Cassio cry out and believes that Iago has succeeded in murdering him. Iago comes with Lodovico to comfort Cassio; in the dark he fatally stabs Roderigo. Iago attempts to implicate Bianca. Emilia is sent off to tell Othello that Cassio and Roderigo are wounded. 2. Othello enters Desdemona's bedchamber, where she is nearly asleep. He "puts out the light" of his candle and, after a kiss, prepares to "put out the light" of Desdemona's life. Desdemona awakes and pleads, but he smothers her. Emilia comes to deliver Iago's message. With her last breath, Desdemona tells her that Othello is innocent. Othello tells her the truth and the reason: her husband proved his wife unfaithful. Emilia is horrified by Iago's deception and rushes out to proclaim the murder. Iago and others enter; the truth is gradually revealed. Iago kills his wife, Othello wounds Iago and stabs himself, dying with a last kiss to Desdemona.

SCENE I.   *A Street*

(Enter IAGO *and* RODERIGO*)*

IAGO   Here, stand behind this bulk; straight will he
   come:
Wear thy good rapier bare, and put it home.
Quick, quick; fear nothing; I 'll be at thy elbow.
It makes us, or it mars us; think on that,
And fix most firm thy resolution.

RODERIGO   Be near at hand; I may miscarry in 't.

IAGO   Here, at thy hand: be bold, and take thy stand.

RODERIGO   I have no great devotion to the deed;
And yet he has given me satisfying reasons.—

'T is but a man gone:—forth, my sword; he dies.

(Stands back)

IAGO   I have rubb'd this young quat almost to the
   sense,
And he grows angry. Now, whether he kill Cassio,
Or Cassio him, or each do kill the other,
Every way makes my game: live Roderigo,
He calls me to a restitution large
Of gold, and jewels, that I bobb'd from him,
As gifts to Desdemona;
It must not be: if Cassio do remain,
He hath a daily beauty in his life,
That makes me ugly; and, besides, the Moor
May unfold me to him: there stand I in much peril.
No, he must die:—be 't so; I hear him coming.

(Retiring)

(Enter CASSIO*)*

RODERIGO   I know his gait; 't is he.—Villain, thou
   diest.

(Rushing forward, and making a pass at CASSIO*)*

CASSIO   That thrust had been mine enemy indeed,
But that my coat is better than thou know'st:
I will make proof of thine.

(Draws, and wounds RODERIGO*)*

RODERIGO   O! I am slain.

*(*IAGO *starts forward, cuts* CASSIO *behind in the Leg, and exit)*

CASSIO   I am maim'd for ever.—Light, ho! murder!
   murder!

(Falls)

(Enter OTHELLO*, at a distance)*

OTHELLO   The voice of Cassio.—Iago keeps his word.
RODERIGO   O, villain that I am!
OTHELLO   It is e'en so.
CASSIO   O, help! ho! light! a surgeon!
OTHELLO   'T is he.—O brave Iago! honest, and just,
That hast such noble sense of thy friend's wrong;
Thou teachest me.—Minion, your dear lies dead,
And your unblest fate hies:—strumpet, I come.

Forth of my heart those charms, thine eyes, are
      blotted;
Thy bed, lust-stain'd, shall with lust's blood be
      spotted.

(*Exit* OTHELLO)

(*Enter* LODOVICO *and* GRATIANO, *at a distance*)

CASSIO   What, ho! no watch? no passage? murder!
      murder!
GRATIANO   'T is some mischance; the cry is very
      direful.
CASSIO   O, help!
LODOVICO   Hark!
RODERIGO   O, wretched villain!
LODOVICO   Two or three groan.—It is a heavy night.
      These may be counterfeits: let 's think 't unsafe
      To come in to the cry without more help.
RODERIGO   No body come? then, shall I bleed to
      death.

(*Enter* IAGO, *unready, with a Light*)

LODOVICO   Hark!
GRATIANO   Here 's one comes in his shirt, with light
      and weapons.
IAGO   Who 's there? whose noise is this, that cries out
      murder thus?
LODOVICO   We do not know.
IAGO   Did not you hear a cry?
CASSIO   Here, here! for heaven's sake, help me.
IAGO   What 's the matter?
GRATIANO   This is Othello's ancient, as I take it.
LODOVICO   The same indeed; a very valiant fellow.
IAGO   What are you here, that cry so grievously?
CASSIO   Iago? O! I am spoil'd; undone by villains:
      Give me some help.
IAGO   O me, lieutenant! what villains have done this?
CASSIO   I think that one of them is hereabout,
      And cannot make away.
IAGO   O treacherous villains!—

(*To* LODOVICO *and* GRATIANO)

What are you there? come in, and give some help.
RODERIGO   O, help me! here.
CASSIO   That 's one of them.
IAGO   O murderous slave! O villain!

(IAGO *stabs* RODERIGO)

RODERIGO   O damn'd Iago! O inhuman dog!—
IAGO   Kill men i' the dark!—Where be these bloody
      thieves?
      How silent is this town!—Ho! murder! murder!
      What may you be? are you of good, or evil?
LODOVICO   As you shall prove us, praise us.
IAGO   Signior Lodovico?
LODOVICO   He, sir.
IAGO   I cry you mercy. Here 's Cassio hurt by villains.
GRATIANO   Cassio?
IAGO   How is it, brother?
CASSIO   My leg is cut in two.
IAGO   Marry, heaven forbid!—
      Light, gentlemen! I 'll bind it with my shirt.

(*Enter* BIANCA)

BIANCA   What is the matter, ho? who is 't that cry'd?
IAGO   Who is 't that cry'd!
BIANCA   O my dear Cassio! my sweet Cassio!
      O Cassio, Cassio, Cassio!
IAGO   O notable strumpet!—Cassio, may you suspect
      Who they should be, that have thus mangled you?
CASSIO   No.
GRATIANO   I am sorry, to find you thus: I have been
      to seek you.
IAGO   Lend me a garter.—So.—O, for a chair,
      To bear him easily hence!
BIANCA   Alas! he faints.—O Cassio! Cassio! Cassio!
IAGO   Gentlemen all, I do suspect this trash
      To be a party in this injury—
      Patience a while, good Cassio.—Come, come.
      Lend me a light.—Know we this face, or no?

(*Looking at* RODERIGO)

Alas! my friend, and my dear countryman,
      Roderigo? no:—yes, sure. O heaven! Roderigo.
GRATIANO   What, of Venice?
IAGO   Even he, sir; did you know him?
GRATIANO   Know him? ay.
IAGO   Signior Gratiano? I cry you gentle pardon:
      These bloody accidents must excuse my manners,
      That so neglected you.
GRATIANO   I am glad to see you.
IAGO   How do you, Cassio?—O, a chair, a chair!

GRATIANO   Roderigo!
IAGO   He, he, 't is he.—O! that 's well said;—the
   chair.—

(A chair brought)

Some good man bear him carefully from hence;
I 'll fetch the general's surgeon.—For you, mistress,
(To BIANCA)

Save you your labour.—He that lies slain here,
   Cassio,
Was my dear friend. What malice was between you?
CASSIO   None in the world; nor do I know the man.
IAGO   What, look you pale?—O, bear him out o' the
   air.—

(CASSIO and RODERIGO are borne off)

Stay you, good gentlemen.—Look you pale, mistress?
Do you perceive the gastness of her eye?—
Nay an you stir:—we shall hear more anon.—
Behold her well, I pray you, look upon her:
Do you see, gentlemen? nay, guiltiness will speak,
Though tongues were out of use.

(Enter EMILIA)

EMILIA   Alas! what 's the matter? what 's the matter,
   husband?
IAGO   Cassio hath here been set on in the dark
   By Roderigo, and fellows that are scap'd:
   He 's almost slain, and Roderigo dead.
EMILIA   Alas, good gentleman! alas, good Cassio!
IAGO   This is the fruit of whoring.—Pr'ythee, Emilia,
   Go know of Cassio where he supp'd to-night.—
   What! do you shake at that?
BIANCA   He supp'd at my house; but I therefore shake
   not.
IAGO   O! did he so? I charge you, go with me.
EMILIA   O, fie upon thee, strumpet!
BIANCA   I am no strumpet; but of life as honest,
   As you that thus abuse me.
EMILIA   As I? fie upon thee!
IAGO   Kind gentlemen, let 's go see poor Cassio
   dress'd.—
   Come, mistress, you must tell 's another tale.—
   Emilia, run you to the citadel,
   And tell my lord and lady what hath happ'd.—

Will you go on, I pray? *(Aside)* This is the night,
That either makes me, or fordoes me quite.

(Exeunt)

SCENE II.   *A Bedchamber*
DESDEMONA *in Bed asleep. A Light burning*

(Enter OTHELLO, locking the Door after him)

OTHELLO   It is the cause, it is the cause, my soul,—
   Let me not name it to you, you chaste stars!—
   It is the cause.—Yet I 'll not shed her blood;
   Nor scar that whiter skin of hers than snow,
   And smooth as monumental alabaster.
   Yet she must die, else she 'll betray more men.
   Put out the light, and then—put out the light?
   If I quench thee, thou flaming minister,
   I can again thy former light restore,
   Should I repent me; but once put out thy light,
   Thou cunning'st pattern of excelling nature,
   I know not where is that Promethean heat,
   That can thy light relume. When I have pluck'd the
     rose,
   I cannot give it vital growth again,
   It needs must wither:—I 'll smell it on the tree.—

(Kissing her)

O balmy breath, that dost almost persuade
Justice to break her sword!—One more, one more.—
Be thus when thou art dead, and I will kill thee,
And love thee after.—One more, and this the last:
So sweet was ne'er so fatal. I must weep,
But they are cruel tears: this sorrow 's heavenly;
It strikes, where it doth love.—She wakes—
DESDEMONA   Who 's there? Othello?
OTHELLO   Ay, Desdemona.
DESDEMONA   Will you come to bed, my lord?
OTHELLO   Have you pray'd to-night, Desdemona?
DESDEMONA   Ay, my lord.
OTHELLO   If you bethink yourself of any crime,
   Unreconcil'd as yet to heaven and grace,
   Solicit for it straight.
DESDEMONA   Alas, my lord! what may you mean by
   that?
OTHELLO   Well, do it, and be brief; I will walk by:
   I would not kill thy unprepared spirit;
   No, heaven forfend, I would not kill thy soul.

DESDEMONA   Talk you of killing?

OTHELLO   Ay, I do.

DESDEMONA   Then, heaven
Have mercy on me!

OTHELLO   Amen, with all my heart.

DESDEMONA   If you say so, I hope you will not kill me.

OTHELLO   Humph!

DESDEMONA   And yet I fear you: for you are fatal
then,
When your eyes roll so. Why I should fear, I know
not
Since guiltiness I know not; but yet, I feel I fear.

OTHELLO   Think on thy sins.

DESDEMONA   They are loves I bear to you.

OTHELLO   Ay, and for that thou diest.

DESDEMONA   That death 's unnatural, that kills for
loving.—
Alas! why gnaw you so your nether lip?
Some bloody passion shakes your very frame:
These are portents; but yet, I hope, I hope,
They do not point on me.

OTHELLO   Peace, and be still!

DESDEMONA   I will so. What 's the matter?

OTHELLO   That handkerchief, which I so lov'd, and
gave thee,
Thou gav'st to Cassio.

DESDEMONA   No, by my life and soul!
Send for the man, and ask him.

OTHELLO   Sweet soul, take heed,
Take heed of perjury; thou 'rt on thy death-bed.

DESDEMONA   Ay, but not yet to die.

OTHELLO   Yes, presently:
Therefore, confess thee freely of thy sin;
For to deny each article with oath,
Cannot remove, nor choke, the strong conception,
That I do groan withal. Thou art to die.

DESDEMONA   Then, Lord, have mercy on me!

OTHELLO   I say, amen.

DESDEMONA   And have you mercy too!—I never did
Offend you in my life; never lov'd Cassio,
But with such general warranty of heaven
As I might love: I never gave him token.

OTHELLO   By heaven, I saw my handkerchief in 's
hand.
O perjur'd woman! thou dost stone my heart,
And mak'st me call, what I intend to do,

A murder, which I thought a sacrifice.
I saw the handkerchief.

DESDEMONA   He found it then;
I never gave it him.—Send for him hither;
Let him confess a truth.

OTHELLO   He hath confess'd.

DESDEMONA   What, my lord?

OTHELLO   That he hath—us'd thee.

DESDEMONA   How? unlawfully?

OTHELLO   Ay.

DESDEMONA   He will not say so.

OTHELLO   No, his mouth is stopp'd;
Honest Iago hath ta'en order for 't.

DESDEMONA   My fear interprets then.—What! is he
dead?

OTHELLO   Had all his hairs been lives, my great
revenge
Had stomach for them all.

DESDEMONA   Alas! he is betray'd, and I undone.

OTHELLO   Out, strumpet! Weep'st thou for him to my
face?

DESDEMONA   O! banish me, my lord, but kill me not.

OTHELLO   Down, strumpet!

DESDEMONA   Kill me to-morrow; let me live to-night.

OTHELLO   Nay, if you strive,—

DESDEMONA   But half an hour.

OTHELLO   Being done,
There is no pause.

DESDEMONA   But while I say one prayer.

OTHELLO   It is too late.

DESDEMONA   O Lord, Lord, Lord!

(He smothers her)

EMILIA *(Within)*   My lord, my lord! what ho! my
lord, my lord!

OTHELLO   What noise is this?—Not dead? not yet quite
dead?
I, that am cruel, am yet merciful;
I would not have thee linger in thy pain—
So, so.

(Stabs her)

EMILIA *(Within)*   What ho! my lord, my lord!

OTHELLO   Who 's there?

EMILIA *(Within)*   O, good my lord! I would speak a
word with you.

OTHELLO   Yes;—'t is Emilia.—By and by.—She 's
  dead.
  'T is like she comes to speak of Cassio's death;
  The noise was high.—Ha! no more moving?
  Still as the grave.—Shall she come in? Were 't good?
  I think she stirs again:—no.—What 's the best?
  If she come in, she 'll sure speak to my wife:
  My wife! my wife! what wife?—I have no wife:
  O insupportable, O heavy hour!
  Methinks it should be now a huge eclipse
  Of sun and moon, and that th' affrighted globe
  Should yawn at alteration.

EMILIA (Within)   I do beseech you, I may speak with
  you.
  O, good my lord!

OTHELLO   I had forgot thee. O! come in, Emilia.—
  Soft,—by and by:—let me the curtains draw,—
  Where art thou? What 's the matter with thee now?

(Unlocks the Door)

(Enter EMILIA)

EMILIA   O, good my lord! yonder 's foul murder done,
OTHELLO   What! now?
EMILIA   But now, my lord!
OTHELLO   It is the very error of the moon;
  She comes more near the earth than she was wont
  And makes men mad.
EMILIA   Cassio, my lord, has kill'd a young Venetian,
  Call'd Roderigo.
OTHELLO   Roderigo kill'd?
  And Cassio kill'd?
EMILIA   No; Cassio is not kill'd.
OTHELLO   Not Cassio kill'd? Then murder 's out of
  tune,
  And sweet revenge grows harsh.
DESDEMONA   O, falsely, falsely murder'd!
EMILIA   Alas! what cry is that?
OTHELLO   That! what?
EMILIA   Out, and alas! that was my lady's voice.—
  Help! Help, ho! help!—O lady, speak again!

(Going to the bed)

Sweet Desdemona! O, sweet mistress, speak!
DESDEMONA   A guiltless death I die.

EMILIA   O! who hath done
  This deed?
DESDEMONA   Nobody; I myself; farewell:
  Commend me to my kind lord. O farewell!

(Dies)

OTHELLO   Why, how should she be murder'd?
EMILIA   Alas, who knows.
OTHELLO   You heard her say herself, it was not I.
EMILIA   She said so; I must needs report a truth.
OTHELLO   She 's like a liar gone to burning hell:
  'T was I that kill'd her.
EMILIA   O! the more angel she,
  And you the blacker devil.
OTHELLO   She turn'd to folly, and she was a whore.
EMILIA   Thou dost belie her, and thou art a devil.
OTHELLO   She was false as water.
EMILIA   Thou art rash as fire to say
  That she was false: O! she was heavenly true.
OTHELLO   Cassio did top her; ask thy husband else.—
  O! I were damn'd beneath all depth in hell,
  But that I did proceed upon just grounds
  To this extremity.—Thy husband knew it all.
EMILIA   My husband?
OTHELLO   Thy husband.
EMILIA   That she was false to wedlock?
OTHELLO   Ay, with Cassio. Nay, had she been true,
  If heaven would make me such another world
  Of one entire and perfect chrysolyte,
  I 'd not have sold her for it.
EMILIA   My husband?
OTHELLO   Ay, 't was he that told me first:
  An honest man he is, and hates the slime
  That sticks on filthy deeds.
EMILIA   My husband?
OTHELLO   What needs this iteration, woman? I say,
  thy husband.
EMILIA   O mistress! villainy hath made mocks with
  love.—
  My husband say, that she was false?
OTHELLO   He, woman;
  I say, thy husband: dost understand the word?
  My friend, thy husband, honest, honest Iago.
EMILIA   If he say so, may his pernicious soul
  Rot half a grain a day! he lies to the heart:
  She was too fond of her most filthy bargain.

OTHELLO   Ha!

(Threatening her)

EMILIA   Do thy worst:
This deed of thine is no more worthy heaven,
Than thou wast worthy her.

OTHELLO   Peace! you were best.

EMILIA   Thou hast not half the power to do me harm,
As I have to be hurt. O gull! O dolt!
As ignorant as dirt! thou hast done a deed,—
I care not for thy sword; I 'll make thee known,
Though I lost twenty lives.—Help! help, ho! help!
The Moor has kill'd my mistress! Murder! murder!

(Enter MONTANO, GRATIANO, *and* IAGO*)*

MONTANO   What is the matter?—How now, general!

EMILIA   O! are you come, Iago? you have done well,
That men must lay their murders on your neck.

GRATIANO   What is the matter?

EMILIA   Disprove this villain, if thou be'st a man:
He says, thou told'st him that his wife was false.
I know, thou didst not, thou 'rt not such a villain.
Speak, for my heart is full.

IAGO   I told him what I thought; and told no more
Than what he found himself was apt and true.

EMILIA   But did you ever tell him, she was false?

IAGO   I did.

EMILIA   You told a lie; an odious, damned lie;
Upon my soul, a lie; a wicked lie.—
She false with Cassio!—Did you say with Cassio?

IAGO   With Cassio, mistress. Go to, charm your
tongue.

EMILIA   I will not charm my tongue; I am bound to
speak.
My mistress here lies murder'd in her bed.

ALL   O, heaven forfend!

EMILIA   And your reports have set the murderer on.

OTHELLO   Nay, stare not, masters: it is true, indeed.

GRATIANO   'T is a strange truth.

MONTANO   O monstrous act!

EMILIA   Villainy! villainy! villainy!
I think upon 't,—I think,—I smell 't:—O villainy!
I thought so then:—I 'll kill myself for grief.—
O villainy, villainy!

IAGO   What! are you mad? I charge you, get you
home.

EMILIA   Good gentlemen, let me have leave to speak:
'T is proper I obey him, but not now.—
Perchance, Iago, I will ne'er go home.

OTHELLO   O! O! O!

(Falling on the Bed)

EMILIA   Nay, lay thee down and roar,
For thou hast kill'd the sweetest innocent,
That e'er did lift up eye.

OTHELLO   O! she was foul—

(Starting up)

I scarce did know you, uncle: there lies your niece,
Whose breath, indeed, these hands have newly
stopp'd
I know, this act shows terrible and grim.

GRATIANO   Poor Desdemona! I am glad thy father 's
dead
Thy match was mortal to him, and pure grief
Shore his old thread in twain: did he live now,
This sight would make him do a desperate turn,
Yea, curse his better angel from his side,
And fall to reprobation.

OTHELLO   'T is pitiful; but yet Iago knows,
That she with Cassio hath the act of shame
A thousand times committed: Cassio confess'd it;
And she did gratify his amorous works
With that recognizance and pledge of love
Which I first gave her. I saw it in his hand;
It was a handkerchief, an antique token
My father gave my mother.

EMILIA   O heaven! O heavenly powers!

IAGO   Come, hold your peace.

EMILIA   'T will out, 't will out:—I hold my peace, sir?
no;
No, I will speak as liberal as the wind.[1]
Let heaven, and men, and devils, let them all,
All, all, cry shame against me, yet I 'll speak.

IAGO   Be wise, and get you home.

(Drawing)

EMILIA   I will not.

*(*IAGO *offers to stab* EMILIA*)*

_____
[1] As freely as the wind blows.

GRATIANO   Fie!
   Your sword upon a woman?
EMILIA   O thou dull Moor! that handkerchief thou
      speak'st of,
   I found by fortune, and did give my husband:
   For often, with a solemn earnestness,
   (More than, indeed, belong'd to such a trifle)
   He begg'd of me to steal it.
IAGO   Villainous whore!

(They hold him)

EMILIA   She give it Cassio! no, alas! I found it,
   And I did give 't my husband.
IAGO   Filth, thou liest.

(Stabs her, and exit instantly)

EMILIA   By heaven, I do not; I do not, gentlemen.
   O murderous coxcomb! what should such a fool
   Do with so good a wife?
OTHELLO   Are there no stones in heaven,
   But what serve for the thunder?—Precious villain!
GRATIANO   The woman falls: sure, he has kill'd his
      wife.
EMILIA   Ay, ay.—O, lay me by my mistress' side!
GRATIANO   He 's gone, but his wife 's kill'd.
MONTANO   'T is a notorious villain. Take you this
      weapon,
   Which I have here recover'd from the Moor.
   Come, guard the door without: let him not pass,
   But kill him rather. I 'll after that same villain,
   For 't is a damned slave.

(Exeunt MONTANO *and* GRATIANO)

OTHELLO   I am not valiant neither,
   But every puny whipster gets my sword.
   But why should honour outlive honesty?
   Let it go all.
EMILIA   What did thy song bode, lady?
   Hark, canst thou hear me? I will play the swan,
   And die in music:—*Willow, willow, willow.*—
   Moor, she was chaste; she lov'd thee, cruel Moor:[2]
   So come my soul to bliss, as I speak true;
   So speaking as I think, I die,—I die.

(Dies)

OTHELLO   I have another weapon in this chamber,
   It is a sword of Spain, the ice-brook's temper.[3]—
   O! here it is.—Uncle, I must come forth.
GRATIANO *(Within)*   If thou attempt it, it will cost
      thee dear:
   Thou hast no weapon, and perforce must suffer.
OTHELLO   Look in upon me, then, and speak to me,
   Or, naked as I am, I will assault thee.

(Re-enter GRATIANO)

GRATIANO   What is the matter?
OTHELLO   Behold! I have a weapon;
   A better never did itself sustain
   Upon a soldier's thigh: I have seen the day,
   That, with this little arm, and this good sword,
   I have made my way through more impediments
   Than twenty times your stop.—But, O vain boast!
   Who can control his fate? 't is not so now.—
   Be not afraid, though you do see me weapon'd;
   Here is my journey's end, here is my butt,
   And very sea-mark of my utmost sail.
   Do you go back dismay'd? 't is a lost fear;
   Man but a rush[4] against Othello's breast,
   And he retires.—Where should Othello go?—
   Now, how dost thou look now? O ill-starr'd wench
   Pale as thy smock! when we shall meet at compt,[5]
   This look of thine will hurl my soul from heaven,
   And fiends will snatch at it. Cold, cold, my girl;
   Even like thy chastity,—O, cursed slave!—
   Whip me, ye devils,
   From the possession of this heavenly sight!
   Blow me about in winds! roast me in sulphur!
   Wash me in steep-down gulfs of liquid fire!
   O Desdemona! Desdemona! dead? O! O!

(Enter LODOVICO *and* CASSIO)

LODOVICO   Where is this rash and most unfortunate
      man?
OTHELLO   That 's he, that was Othello: here I am.
LODOVICO   Where is that viper? bring the villain forth.

(Enter MONTANO *with* IAGO, *bound, and Officers)*

---

[2] In her anger, Emilia reverts to the stereotyped language on Moors.

[3] A sword from Spain, tempered in cold water.
[4] Hold but a reed.
[5] The Last Judgment.

OTHELLO   I look down towards his feet;—but that 's a
    fable:[6]
  If that thou be'st a devil, I cannot kill thee.

(OTHELLO *wounds* IAGO)

LODOVICO   Wrench his sword from him.
IAGO   I bleed, sir; but not kill'd.
OTHELLO   I am not sorry neither: I 'd have thee live;
  For, in my sense, 't is happiness to die.
LODOVICO   O thou Othello! that wert once so good,
  Fall'n in the practice of a damned slave,
  What shall be said to thee?
OTHELLO   Why, any thing:
  An honourable murderer, if you will;
  For nought I did in hate, but all in honour.
LODOVICO   This wretch hath part confess'd his
    villainy.
  Did you and he consent in Cassio's death?
OTHELLO   Ay.
CASSIO   Dear general, I never gave you cause.
OTHELLO   I do believe it, and I ask your pardon.
  Will you, I pray, demand that demi-devil,
  Why he hath thus ensnar'd my soul and body?
IAGO   Demand me nothing: what you know, you
    know.
  From this time forth I never will speak word.
LODOVICO   What! not to pray?
GRATIANO   Torments will ope your lips.
OTHELLO   Well, thou dost best.
LODOVICO   Sir, you shall understand what hath
    befall'n,
  Which, as I think, you know not. Here is a letter,
  Found in the pocket of the slain Roderigo;

(Showing it)

  And here another: the one of them imports
  The death of Cassio to be undertook
  By Roderigo.
OTHELLO   O villain!
CASSIO   Most heathenish, and most gross!
LODOVICO   Now, here 's another discontented paper,

(Producing it)

  Found in his pocket too; and this, it seems,
  Roderigo meant to have sent this damned villain,
  But that, belike, Iago in the interim
  Came in and satisfied him.
OTHELLO   O, the pernicious caitiff!—
  How came you, Cassio, by that handkerchief,
  That was my wife's?
CASSIO   I found it in my chamber;
  And he himself confess'd, but even now,
  That there he dropp'd it, for a special purpose,
  Which wrought to his desire.
OTHELLO   O fool! fool! fool!
CASSIO   There is, besides, in Roderigo's letter,
  How he upbraids Iago, that he made him
  Brave me upon the watch; whereon it came
  That I was cast: and even but now he spake,
  After long seeming dead,—Iago hurt him,
  Iago set him on.
LODOVICO   You must forsake this room, and go with
    us
  Your power and your command is taken off,
  And Cassio rules in Cyprus. For this slave,
  If there be any cunning cruelty
  That can torment him much, and hold him long,
  It shall be his. You shall close prisoner rest
  Till that the nature of your fault be known
  To the Venetian state.—Come; bring them away.
OTHELLO   Soft you; a word or two, before you go.
  I have done the state some service, and they know it;
  No more of that.—I pray you, in your letters,
  When you shall these unlucky deeds relate,
  Speak of me as I am; nothing extenuate,
  Nor set down aught in malice: then, must you speak
  Of one that lov'd, not wisely, but too well:
  Of one not easily jealous, but, being wrought,
  Perplex'd in the extreme; of one, whose hand,
  Like the base Judean[7] threw a pearl away
  Richer than all his tribe; of one, whose subdued
    eyes,
  Albeit unused to the melting mood,
  Drop tears as fast as the Arabian trees
  Their medicinal gum. Set you down this;

---

[6] The devil was said to have a cloven foot.

[7] Judas, who betrayed Jesus.

And say, besides, that in Aleppo once,
When a malignant and a turban'd Turk
Beat a Venetian, and traduc'd the state,
I took by the throat the circumcised dog,
And smote him—thus.

(Stabs himself)

LODOVICO   O bloody period!
GRATIANO   All that 's spoke is marr'd.
OTHELLO   I kiss'd thee, ere I kill'd thee:—no way but
    this
Killing myself, to die upon a kiss.

(Dies on the Bed)

CASSIO   This did I fear, but thought he had no
    weapon;
For he was great of heart.
LODOVICO *(To Iago)*   O Spartan dog!
    More fell than anguish, hunger, or the sea,
    Look on the tragic loading of this bed;
    This is thy work: the object poisons sight;
    Let it be hid—Gratiano, keep the house,
    And seize upon the fortunes of the Moor,
    For they succeed on you.—To you, lord governor,
    Remains the censure of this hellish villain;
    The time, the place, the torture:—O, enforce it
    Myself will straight aboard, and to the state
    This heavy act with heavy heart relate.

(Exeunt)

Music in *Othello*

Music in Shakespeare's drama had many uses: military fanfare and pageantry, accompaniment to dance, an enhancement to a social setting, a part of an intimate lyrical mood. In *Othello*, the instrumental music is associated with the world of action; the vocal music (folk ballads rather than art songs) with the inner world of character. Two examples of the latter appear on pages 324 and 325: Iago's drinking song, "And let me the cannakin clinke" (Act II, scene iii); and Desdemona's ballad, "The Willow Song" (Act IV, scene iii). Iago's song, like most of what he says, seems to be something that it is not and serves his purpose. Creating an atmosphere of drunken gaiety, the song is really intended to inebriate Cassio. Desdemona's ballad, once sung by a maid called Barbary (the name recalls Africa) who loved a man who went mad, allows her to express her subconscious forebodings of imminent death. The song's sad rhythms tell more vividly than Desdemona would in her speech of a deep love that somehow went wrong. It creates in the spectator a moment of agonized suspense over what will come next.

COMMENTS AND QUESTIONS ON *OTHELLO*

1. For what different purposes does Shakespeare use blank verse, prose, rhymed verse, and music?
2. In what ways do the dramatic purposes of the music for *Othello* differ from those of *The Play of Daniel*?
3. What effect do the songs have on you? Would you include them in a modern production of the play?
4. How do you interpret the character of Iago? The English Romantic writer and critic Coleridge described the evil in Iago as a "motiveless malignancy." Others have called him a kind of devil, a totally evil figure. Some argue that he has (in his own mind) real motives for hating Othello. What are these motives, and which are believable?
5. How does Iago manipulate Roderigo? Cassio? Othello?
6. What is the role and the significance of the handkerchief?
7. To what extent does racial prejudice influence Iago and the other characters?
8. Describe the character of Othello. What qualifies him as a tragic hero? What is Othello's social position as a black man in a white society? Does this contribute to his insecurity and to his jealousy?
9. Does Othello at any point apply racial stereotypes to himself? Is this Iago's doing?
10. Do you think that Othello's final assessment of himself, in the speech just before his suicide, is accurate? How do you think this scene should be acted?
11. What is Desdemona's role and character? Do you have the impression that she and Othello know each other well? To what extent is the love between

her and Othello endangered by their society, and to what extent is its destruction a result of Iago's manipulation?

12. Language, particularly images, plays an important part in *Othello*. We have mentioned images of black and white, animal images, and images related to poison. What effects do these have in the play? What other types can you find?

13. Compare Oedipus and Othello as tragic figures.

14. Do you find that *Othello* is a "depressing" tragedy,

as some readers do, or that it ends on a note of redemption, as does *Oedipus Rex*?

15. To what extent does Shakespeare's tragedy exemplify the humanist belief in the dignity of man, and to what extent does it show late Renaissance skepticism?

16. What does the play tell you about European perceptions of Africa and Africans?

17. In what ways does *Othello* seem relevant to our own time?

Iago's Drinking Song

The Willow Song

RENAISSANCE AND REFORMATION: ROOTS AND CONTINUITIES

In the section on the Italian Renaissance, we focused on its beginnings in Florence rather than on its "high" (early sixteenth-century) phase in Rome. It is in fifteenth-century Florence that we can best witness the radical departures from medieval mentality; the innovations in art, life, and thought; and the new fusion of Christian and classical traditions that laid the basis for much of our modern art, thought, and institutions. The roots of the humanities as we know them are certainly there. We have seen how Florentine humanism spread to northern Europe, influencing the development of a literature at least equal to its own, and how its original self-confidence underwent a crisis that is still with us.

Individualism   "The discovery of the individual was made in early fifteenth-century Florence," proclaims Kenneth Clark in his *Civilization* series, "Nothing can alter that fact." Certainly, when one looks at the portraits of Renaissance Florentines (the art of the portrait had been lost in Europe since Roman times!), or when one reads about their lives or views the different styles of each artist, one senses an individuality that was not present in the more collective and symbolic arts of the Middle Ages. The development of a more naturalistic way of portraying individual characters and their natural surroundings is part of this trend—we see its beginnings in the fourteenth century with Giotto.

Civic Sense   If fifteenth-century Florentines were highly conscious of themselves as individuals, they were also very much aware of being part of a community. Florence in many ways resembled a Greek city-state; and, like the ancient Athenians, the Florentines believed that participation in the affairs of state was essential for the realization of one's full humanity. But the men of the Renaissance needed to justify this clas-sical value in Christian terms. Whereas medieval people believed that the contemplative life, or the life devoted to God, was of highest value, the fifteenth-century Florentines believed that Christian ideals could be served just as well in a secular, active life. Their political ideal of republicanism, rule by a body of citizens, has served as a basis for modern political theory. Although the modern state developed out of the medieval monarchies, since the nineteenth century these states have been on the whole republican.

By the last half of the fifteenth century, Florence came under the more autocratic rule of the Medici family. An ardent republican, Machiavelli nevertheless saw that by this time the ideal form of government was no longer practical for Florence. Yet through the early sixteenth century the spirit of republicanism, as seen in Michelangelo's *David*, with his proud, youthful defiance of tyranny, and his *Brutus*, the defender of Roman liberty, remained identified with the city. Republicanism was a part of the civic humanism of which Florentines were proud. The Florentines with their urban-centered lifestyle created a city whose physical aspect expressed their values. The architecture and sculpture, which even today give Florence its distinctive character, reflect a sense of beauty and proportion keyed to the measure of man. City planning as we know it today was born in Florence with the treatises of Leon Battista Alberti.

Visual and Verbal Eloquence   Beautiful architecture was for the practitioner Brunelleschi and the theoretician Alberti what beautiful speech was for the Florentine humanists. Visual and verbal eloquence were means of using newly rediscovered classical values in the service of Christian truth. Brunelleschi and (after him) Michelangelo observed closely the remains of Roman buildings and statues; Petrarch, Salutati, and Bruni edited and studied Latin, and eventually Greek, texts. The use of language was for the humanists the art that made man most truly human; consequently, the studies that they called the humanities focused on literature.

Historical and Visual Perspective   In their study of ancient rhetoric, the humanists observed a truth that had seemed unimportant to the medieval mind: language and other human customs, institutions, and ideas change—they have a history. The notion of seeing oneself and one's culture in historical perspective, as part of a continuum of time, has become a habit with us; it has its origins in the humanists' new ways of thought. The ability to see with the perspective of time has its artistic parallel in the ability to see, and to draw, with the perspective of space.

There is no doubt that the technical development permitting artists to give the illusion of three dimensions on the flat surface of a canvas was a major step in the history of art. Renaissance painters established a formal visual language for their art that remained until recently the official standard of all Western art academies. Yet *perspective*, it must be remembered, was a means, not an end in itself. It permitted artists to represent what they observed, rather than to create symbols of the unseen. The sources of their observation were primarily two: nature (inanimate, animate, and human) and antiquity. From these they derived an art centered on the human being and the here-and-now; yet, like the humanists, they wished to put these new modes of expression to the service of Christian values. Leonardo, who stressed the scientific nature of painting and its worthiness to be placed among the liberal arts, created one of the most mystical Virgins ever painted.

Practicality   Leonardo was also a creator of tools and devices by which man could control his natural surroundings. In this he reflects the tendency in the Renaissance for the theoretical to become increasingly united with the practical. The great scientific advances of the seventeenth century would have been impossible without the creation of better instrumentation with which to measure, view, and manipulate the material world. Incidentally, as we will explain in the discussion of the Scientific Revolution, the development of Neoplatonism in the fifteenth century led to a new concern with mathematics, which also made a fundamental contribution to new approaches in natural science.

Developments in Music   In music, too, nature and antiquity were sources that helped new forms to flourish. Renaissance composers were not acquainted with the actual musical works of the Greeks and Romans, but they read their musical theory and were interested in the ways in which music could be wedded to words. We have seen how this was done in the Isaac composition; we have also seen how nature (such as the flowing fountain) and human emotion are "tone painted" in this piece. Today's composer would write different sounds to depict a fountain or to express grief and anguish, but the concept of musical sound affecting human emotions stretches continuously back through history to classical Greece. Much of Renaissance music was religious, but secular music gained prominence at this time. Isaac's death lament for Lorenzo and Poliziano's poem lament the passing of this life but do not refer to the next one, and the only god mentioned in the piece is Phoebus Apollo!

Non-Christian Subject Matter   The use of pagan, classical subjects in painting, sculpture, music, and literature represents a radical break with medieval culture. Much of this "pagan" art developed under the influence of Lorenzo de' Medici and the circle of Neoplatonic scholars around him. The lyrical Venuses and nymphs of Botticelli represent joy in this world but also an underlying melancholy. One senses in them a spiritual world beyond the visible forms. Similarly, Lorenzo's carnival song and the music accompanying it use a subject from classical mythology to urge people to enjoy life in the present—before it slips away. The medieval focus on the salvation of the immortal soul has shifted.

The Dignity of Man   One of Lorenzo's Neoplatonic acquaintances, Pico della Mirandola, made what is considered by many to be the classical Renaissance statement on the dignity and grandeur of man. Pico's attempt to fuse Judeo-Christian ways of thinking with

Greco-Roman ones is evident: he assigns man a place above the animals and below the angels not inconsistent with Christian doctrine; but he then describes how man's creative powers are more admirable than those of the celestial beings, thus sounding a note not heard since antiquity. Yet, when this brilliant, handsome prince of Mirandola died in Florence of fever at the age of thirty-one, he met death wrapped in the robes of a Dominican friar.

Northern Humanism   When Italian humanism spread to northern Europe, its Christian aspect was emphasized more than its pagan one. Humanists such as Erasmus read and delighted in the classical authors but turned their attention more toward the study and editing of Greek and Latin Christian texts. Erasmus believed strongly in the value of reading and study: through knowledge and the development of inner piety, individual Christians could help to reform the ignorance and emphasis on externals that pervaded the Church, especially its monasteries.

Northern Europe made its greatest contribution to our culture through the printed word. Ever since the development of printing we have relied on communications media for the circulation of news and ideas. Radio and television have, of course, speeded up the process enormously, and film has come to fuse visual with literary statements; but we still rely heavily on books for the dissemination of intellectual developments and for knowledge of the past. Books, such as those published by Erasmus, enabled more people to form intelligent opinions and thus to question authority. Humanistic educators still share Erasmus' faith in the printed word's capacity to aid in the process of creating well-informed, soundly reasoning, independently thinking human individuals.

Reformation   Martin Luther pushed Erasmus' emphasis on the study of texts and rejection of authority to what Erasmus considered a radical extreme. Trained in humanistic methods, Luther used his extensive knowledge of Hebrew, Greek, and Latin to study the Bible directly, without the official interpretations of the Church, and to translate it into German, thus making it available to his countrymen. Luther's studies led him to reject "on conscience" certain doctrines and practices of the Church and, with many other contributing factors, launched the Reformation. Although Luther became as doctrinaire as the authorities he had rejected, the impetus he gave to thinking independently of authority has had far-reaching influences on the culture of the modern world. There is a direct line from Luther to the twentieth-century individual's sense of isolation, lack of direction, and need, in a tangle of conflicting values, to find himself.

Cultural Relativism   Religious wars between Catholics and Protestants raged throughout Europe in the sixteenth century. Paradoxically, this period of religious troubles coincided with a tremendous economic boom, fueled in part by the importation of gold and silver from the New World. Swift economic change, population increase, and rapidly rising prices, however, probably added to the unsettling atmosphere created by religious controversy. At the intellectual level individuals like Montaigne reflect a new and very modern feeling that truth and belief are, after all, relative matters.

Cultural relativism became during the sixteenth century a corollary to relativism in matters of opinion. In this era of travel and exploration, Europeans discovered in America, Africa, and Asia people who lived with customs and institutions very different from theirs. Just as Mediterranean peoples had once viewed Europeans as barbaric, many Europeans now thought the newly discovered cultures uncivilized, vastly inferior to their own. Intelligent observers such as Montaigne used the different cultural values to reflect what was corrupt and unjust in European society. Cultural relativism has served self-criticism and social satire ever since.

European Contact with Africa   The travels of Europeans in Africa led whites to reflect on the strange phenomenon of the existence of black people and blacks, as we will see in Part IV, to reflect on the strange phenomenon of the existence of white people. Prejudice was reinforced by a black/white symbolism already built into European languages, with black generally representing evil and white good. We have seen how Shakespeare used this symbolism in English for his original purposes and how he created the first black hero of the European stage.

William Shakespeare embodies nearly all of the currents that we have witnessed in the Renaissance-Reformation period. Like Leonardo, Michelangelo, and Luther, he was a giant in an age of geniuses—one who discovered and mastered new worlds of thought and expression. His characters demonstrate a range of feel-ing from the early humanists' confidence in man's abilities and powers to late Renaissance skepticism and relativism and the Reformation's doubt that man can accomplish much of anything on his own. Shakespeare combined the medieval and the classical traditions to lay the basis for the modern theater. His Othello, conqueror and noble warrior, yet prey to unconscious passions, black in a white society, is both a hero of the late Renaissance and a representative modern man.

PART FOUR
THE AFRICAN CULTURAL ROOT

AFRICA TODAY

14

AFRICAN BACKGROUNDS

The cultures of Western Europe and those of Africa begin to mingle and to affect each other during the European age of exploration and expansion in the Renaissance. Since that time, and particularly with the beginning of the trans-Atlantic slave trade in the fifteenth century, European, American, and African civilizations have been inextricably intertwined. Our introduction of Africa into the humanities at this point indicates the time period during which the cultures of West Africa, in particular, became one of the cultural roots of Americans.

Africa has influenced the West economically, as well as in the social and cultural realms. Profits from trade with Africa contributed to the development of northern Europe leading to the Industrial Revolution. Subsequently, the pursuit of markets for the goods produced by this revolution was an important economic motivation for the partition of Africa and the onset of colonial rule in the late nineteenth century. Patterns of economic relationships stimulated by colonialism, wherein Africa continued to provide raw materials or primary agricultural products to the industrialized West, remained little changed by the fact of independence for most of the African states in the 1960s and 1970s.

Images of Africa in the West   As Europe and America passed through the Enlightenment and into the age of democracy and nationalism, Africa remained a persistent symbol of "the other," of a civilization founded on principles of thought and religious behavior that were perceived to be fundamentally different from those of the West. The "noble savage" of the eighteenth century became the "primitive savage" at the bottom of the evolutionary ladder in the annals of Darwinian thought. Social and religious movements springing from the latter spurred intense efforts to Christianize and to "civilize" Africans in the twentieth century. In America it underlay missionary appeals and the Tarzan image of Africa, shaken but still powerful in our day. Europeans and Americans involved in the effort to "tame" Africans, to make them more like themselves, often succumbed to the "heart of darkness" as it appears in the novel by Joseph Conrad and in the works of others like Graham Greene. This image, a creation of the European mind, was rarely informed by substantive knowledge or the capacity to accept the legitimacy of different civilizations. Nevertheless, the idea of Africa and the African exercised a significant cultural influence on Western art and thought and will appear as a theme in Volume II of this book.

Africa and America   Perhaps more relevant to our purposes here is the direct role that Africa has played in the formation of American culture. Between the sixteenth and nineteenth centuries, more Africans came to the Americas than did people of other lands. Although the African slaves were put under great pressure to forget all aspects of their own, very diverse cultures, an amazing number of their customs were able to survive. We will look closely at the African "survivals" in Afro-American culture (and their impact on the whole of American culture) at the end of Part Four and again in the chapter on Afro-American culture in Vol-

ume II. Let us turn now to the study of Africa itself, both before and after the crucial contact with the West.

The continent of Africa is so large—and so diverse in its geographical, racial, linguistic, and cultural aspects—that it is almost impossible to speak of it generally, as a whole. Although we will need to make some remarks about the entire continent, we will concentrate primarily on the area that was the homeland of most Africans sent to the New World: the western coast ranging from 20° north to 20° south of the equator and extending up to one thousand miles inland—roughly the areas comprising the coastline and the drainage basins of the two great rivers, the Niger and Congo (see map). We will look briefly at some important points in the history of this area, particularly the great empires that flourished around the time of the Renaissance in Europe. Our focus will then be on traditional arts, values, and systems of thought in the cultures of a few West African peoples. "Traditional" refers to non-Westernized, nonindustrialized Africa, as opposed to modern Africa, whose societies have been significantly transformed by the colonial experience. It is important to bear in mind that the concept of time in traditional African cultures is different from that in the West. Western art and thought, beginning with the Greeks, has been characterized by rapid change and a sense of evolution through time. African religions tend to emphasize the circularity, rather than the linearity, of time, and African artists put more value on community and tradition than on individuality and change. Thus, when we talk about a Yoruba style, we will not be particularly concerned with whether the work dates from the eighteenth or the twentieth century. In the case of oral poetry and tales, the dates of origin are usually not known. In the case of early African history, however, we will be interested in attempting to establish the times when the great civilizations flourished.

Stages in African History: The Great Empires

The systematic exploration of Africa by Europeans began in the fifteenth century. Europe had been in contact for hundreds of years with the north coast of Africa and in the fourteenth century had undertaken colonization of the Canary Islands off the mainland. But

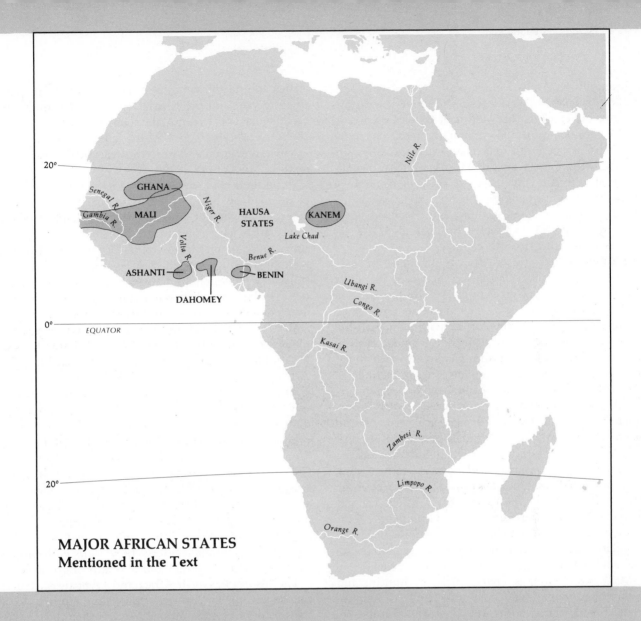

MAJOR AFRICAN STATES
Mentioned in the Text

in the middle decades of the fifteenth century, under the sponsorship of Prince Henry the Navigator (1394–1460), son of John I of Portugal, a succession of ambitious expeditions were undertaken. By the time of the prince's death, Europe's knowledge of Africa extended far down the Guinea coast. By 1497 Vasco da Gama had successfully rounded the Cape of Good Hope, traveled up the east African coast, and made his way to Calicut on the west coast of India. His safe return to Lisbon in September 1499 marked the establishment of a sea route to the East, ushering in a major era in the history of Europe's relationship with Africa and Asia. Because of the significance of the European contact, the history of Africa for our purposes is divided into two periods with the fifteenth century as the point of demarcation.

Early Africa The sources of knowledge of African history before the late fifteenth century are various. Most written evidence comes from travelers' accounts

—primarily by Arabs who regularly traded with sub-Saharan peoples in West Africa and along the eastern coast of the continent. Few African peoples used writing, but a good deal is known from oral traditions transferred from generation to generation by specialists entrusted with preserving the history of their people. Coupled with the conclusions of modern research in archaeology, anthropology, botany, and linguistics, these written and oral accounts have enabled historians in recent years to establish the outlines of Africa's history before the fifteenth century.

For most archaeologists Africa is the cradle of mankind, although the relationship between the early forms of man discovered in the Olduvai Gorge in Kenya and the peopling of the continents remains an unsolved question. On the African continent itself human society in the course of its development evolved an incredible array of cultures characterized by divergent languages and beliefs; a wide range of technological levels; and many political and social organizations.

The varying development of Africa's people is closely related to the vast diversity of ecological setting found on the continent. The major areas include North Africa, dominated by the Sahara Desert in the west; the Nile valley; the Savannah grasslands of eastern, central, and southern Africa; and the tropical rain forest of the West African coast and Congo River valley regions. The challenges of these different environments—their climates, soils, flora and fauna—have influenced the population growth, and the choices of economic, social, and political organization of Africa's peoples.

Stone Age groupings, characterized by hunting and gathering economies and small-scale bands as the principle of social organization, were the earliest form of society in evolutionary terms. The next major stage in human development led to the systematic cultivation of grains and root crops and the domestication of animals, known as the Neolithic Revolution. The significance of the Neolithic was that it created stable and sometimes surplus food supplies, enabling the expansion of population.

The lower Nile valley, where seasonal flooding inundated the nearby plains, was the first Neolithic site in Africa. Developing between the third and fourth millennia B.C., it nurtured the flowering of ancient Egypt. Spontaneous domestication of grains occurred in West Africa around the same time. The cultivation of crops like the yam and the banana, introduced through ancient contacts between Malaysian peoples and those of the southeastern coast of Africa, spread to the rain forest areas of central and western Africa by the beginning of the Christian era.

In northern and western Africa pastoralism, often accompanied by nomadic forms of social organization, emerged in ancient times in the grasslands and the steppe areas where agriculture was marginally successful because of precarious rainfall. Agriculturalist and pastoralist groups tended to be distinct, and relationships between sedentary farming and fishing communities and the pastoralists was a major factor in historical developments over the centuries for this area of Africa. Down the eastern half of the continent, however, techniques of agriculture and herding spread side by side within the same groups, and patterns of mixed farming evolved.

These stages in the development of African society can be dated only in the most general terms for most of the continent. With the introduction of metals, however, a more precise chronology of events is possible. The manufacture of metals meant more effective instruments for cultivating the field and better weapons. Greater production of food entailed population growth, and the military superiority of an army equipped with metal arms led to conquest and the creation of larger political organizations. Cities arose as political, religious, and economic centers; they were embellished with important buildings and a wealth of art objects.

The history of North Africa and Egypt in particular can be chronicled from the fourth millennium with the advent of first the Bronze Age and then the Copper Age.

Sub-Saharan Africa never produced either bronze or copper, but moved directly from the Stone Age into the Age of Iron. By the seventh or sixth century B.C., iron was being manufactured at Meroe, far up the Nile valley in modern-day Sudan. By the second century B.C., the trade routes served as the medium for diffusing the techniques of metal making as far as western Nigeria. Recent discoveries in the area north of the juncture of the Niger and the Benue rivers indicate that between 200 B.C. and A.D. 200 a rich civilization, referred to as the Nok, dominated an area three hundred miles long

14–1 Far left. Nok terra-cotta head. (Jos Museum, Nigeria; photograph by Eliot Elisofon, Museum of African Art, Eliot Elisofon Archives) Center. Ife bronze head. (Ife Museum, Nigeria; photograph by Eliot Elisofon, Museum of African Art, Eliot Elisofon Archives) Below. Benin bronze head. (The Metropolitan Museum of Art. The Michael C. Rockefeller Memorial Collection of Primitive Art.)

in this river valley. Clay heads of animals and human beings, some of them going back as far as the ninth century B.C., testify to the artistic originality of the Nok peoples (Fig. 14-1).

Together with the neolithic advances in the forest area the production of iron triggered what is now referred to as the Bantu expansion. In the area of the Cameroons and western Nigeria agricultural, fishing, and iron-working peoples expanding in population and equipped with superior weapons worked out from their homeland toward the south and eastward, conquering or expelling the bushmen and pygmies resident there. Although the process endured for more than a thousand years, modern linguistic studies of peoples speaking Bantu languages show that gradually the Bantu speakers gained domination in the whole of central and southern Africa. While each of the African peoples that we are going to study has its own language, they are all descended from Africans whose languages (like those of the Bantu speakers) ultimately derived from a common ancestral stock.

The secret of iron manufacture was only one of the items involved in African trade before the first century B.C. Trade between non-African peoples—Indians, Persians, and Arabs—and Africans along the eastern coast of the continent flourished in this period. At the same time Phoenician trading colonies in North Africa, centuries before the Roman conquest of this region, were active in exploring the Saharan oases and initiating commercial links with them. After the rapid spread of Islam across North Africa in the seventh century A.D., Arabs and Berber-speaking North Africans were the principal merchants engaging in trade with sub-Saharan Africa. Along the West African coast, Niger Delta peoples also traded in seagoing vessels with others as far west as modern-day Ghana. In the interior, cycles of regional markets extended the frontiers of contact, permitting the exchange of agricultural, craft, and some exotic products. Barter techniques—the exchange of one item for another—were widespread, but so were currencies. Some of the latter included cowrie shells, iron bars, salt, cloth, and gold. Such patterns of long-distance trade suggest the existence of other kinds of highly developed crafts in leather goods, iron implements, and cloth products.

Increasing complexity of social and political organization accompanied economic specialization. Complementarity of roles evolved between men and women as well as between whole subgroups within a given society. In contrast to the patterns of most Western societies, African women dominated agricultural production of subsistence economies. Men sometimes assisted in the preparation of fields for cultivation, but their main responsibilities lay in hunting and in the defense of their communities. Both men and women engaged in trade, although men tended to specialize in long-distance trade, including that with the Europeans when it began. These separate and complementary economic activities were buttressed by patterns of social organization sharply delineating men's and women's roles. For some societies descent was matrilineal; that is, inheritance of goods, access to land, and group leadership passed to the children through the family of the mother. In these societies women themselves, while still under the daily dominance of men, had greater control over their own lives than did those in patrilineal societies.

Other kinds of social distinctions existed in addition to that between men and women. A few societies already had slavery, but the onset of the trans-Atlantic slave trade would expand its institutionalization in African societies of the west coast. Some groups, often those with specialist knowledge of iron-working or traditional medicines, operated as distinct castes: they married only within their own group and were set apart by special rules of dress, residence, and religious taboos that regulated their relationships with others. Such groups were not pariahs, however, and often occupied critical political and religious roles within the larger society.

Diversity in forms of political organization also characterized African societies. Two poles of political organization have traditionally been identified: "stateless societies" and state systems. Any one society, however, might lie at a point somewhere along the continuum

between these two poles. "Stateless societies" were characterized by the predominance of kinship—family, lineage, and clan—as the basis of political organization. The units within which peoples interacted tended to be relatively small. There was little concentration of authority in the hands of any one person or group, spontaneous leadership emerging as the need arose. Residence patterns in "stateless societies" ranged from dispersed family homesteads to compact villages, but an important feature of such units was the equivalence of power between them; no one group could enforce its rules on another. There were some social institutions in "stateless societies" that extended across village boundaries. Age-group, religious, and initiation societies frequently were shared by others speaking the same language and sometimes by outsiders as well. The art and ideologies of ritual surrounding such organizations provided the potential for cultural unity of widely divergent groups despite the restricted range of political authority.

At the other extreme from the stateless societies lay the states characterized by a high degree of centralization of large territories; elaborate palace and government offices functioning in a wide range of economic and political tasks; court systems with constitutional and religious authorization to enforce their decisions; complex military organization; and close association between ritual and political authority most often focused on the king.

The Great Medieval Kingdoms

Ghana   The ancient empire of Ghana (700–1230) owed its rise to its control of the gold supply so vital to Muslim merchants engaged in the trans-Saharan trade between Morocco and the far western Sudan. Though its kings and citizenry in the early days of the empire were not Muslim themselves, the kings worked closely with the Arab merchant community. They came to adopt techniques of trade and administration, facilitated by literacy in Arabic learned through contacts with the Muslim strangers. Trans-Saharan trade and Islam spurred the emergence of other West African states like Kanem, the Hausa states, and the greatest of the successor states to Ghana, Mali. We will discuss the Mali empire in connection with the epic *Sundiata* in the next chapter.

Benin One of the first African states to engage in trade with the Europeans was Benin, centered in the forest area just north of the Niger Delta, beyond the influence of the trans-Saharan trade and Islam. Historians believe that sometime between 900 and 1000 people from the kingdom of Ife to the northwest merged with those of the forest area. Ife itself reached the height of its power in the following centuries. Benin traditions claim that the founder of the major dynasty of Benin kings was Oranmiyan, the son of Oduduwa, ruler of the Ife.

After a time of troubles, the peoples of Benin had sent messages to Oduduwa requesting that he send a wise prince to rule them. After some time Oranmiyan, accompanied by courtiers and a medical specialist, settled in a palace at a place called Usama. He married a beautiful woman named Erinwinde, who gave birth to a son. Oranmiyan, as the traditions state, did not remain in Benin long; having established proper government, he resigned, saying that only a son of the land could rule such a troublesome people, and returned to Ife. His son by Erinwinde, named Eweka, was chosen by Oranmiyan to succeed him; and, at the time of Eweka's coronation, royal regalia and other symbols of office were sent by his father from Ife. Ruling many years, Eweka I strengthened the kingdom and probably began to extend Benin's influence over other peoples by settling colonies of his relatives and officers among them. Although Benin was probably never subject to Ife's political authority, the ancient city's spiritual authority is clear: the kings of Benin adopted the title of *Oba* from Ife. They also adopted Ife's technique of brass and bronze casting.

Art in Benin The Benin bronzes, illustrated in Figures 14-1 through 14-6 are among the masterpieces of African art. The masks, heads, and plaques, reflecting prominent royal figures and scenes of the court, were closely associated with kingship and its rituals. For example, in Figure 14-6 can be seen the elaborate details of royal costume and paraphernalia, as well as the supreme power of the king in comparison to his subjects and servants (reflected in their relative degrees of prominence and position in the composition). Scenes of court life, including foreign visitors, were also portrayed, as illustrated by the figures of the merchant and the European soldier. The naturalism of Benin art

derived from its Ife heritage, and its representation of historical scenes sets it apart from other examples of traditional art to be studied later.

Creation of the bronzes was the sole preserve of craftsmen appointed by the king. They were made by a technique called the *cire perdu* or "lost wax" method. Over a solid clay core a fine layer of wax was pressed and then carved in intricate detail. The wax layer was then encased in another clay mold provided with core holes for the wax to drain out when the entire piece was heated. Molten metal was poured into the open

14-2 Mask from Wunmonijie, "Obalufon," bronze. (Reproduced by Courtesy of the Trustees of the British Museum)

14-3 Queen Mother of Benin, bronze. (Reproduced by Courtesy of the Trustees of the British Museum)

14-4   European soldier with crossbow and ammunition, Benin bronze plaque. (Reproduced by Courtesy of the Trustees of the British Museum)

14-6   The Oba and his Assistants, bronze plaque. (Reproduced by Courtesy of the Trustees of the British Museum)

14-5   Master Merchant, Benin bronze plaque. (Reproduced by Courtesy of the Trustees of the British Museum) space between the inner core and outer layer of the mold. Finally, after cooling, the clay molds would be broken away, revealing the bronze object ready for fine sanding and polishing. The delicate details and regal simplicity of earlier Benin bronzes gave way in the late seventeenth and eighteenth centuries to heavier, more elaborate, but still naturalistic objects. Some scholars believe that this apparent coarsening of the Benin style can be attributed to the surplus of casting metals acquired in greater abundance through the European trade.

At the apogee of its power and influence in the sixteenth and seventeenth centuries, Benin held authority over land and peoples in a triangle whose borders went deep into the delta in the east and as far as modern-day Benin (Dahomey) in the west (see map).

Culture of Benin   The traditions of the people of Benin and accounts by early European visitors, to which we now turn, illuminate the culture of a major African state as the worlds of Africa and Europe came together. The first three selections come from *A Short History of Benin*, containing the most famous collection of Benin oral traditions. The book was compiled in 1934 by Chief Jacob V. Egharevba, a member of a distinguished family in Benin and founder of the Benin Museum. Chief Egharevba's work itself is a synthesis of traditions from many groups within Benin: among others the *obas* themselves; *ihogbe*, historians of deceased kings; *ogbelaka*, Royal Bards; and *iguneronmwo*, the Royal Brass Smith. While most dates for the ancient period of Benin must remain relative, Chief Egharevba's work has been shown to be remarkably accurate when it can be compared to eyewitness accounts by travelers; it remains an indispensable source for the history of this African state. The fourth selection is a traditional poem extolling the oba and his office. It is taken from *African Poetry*, compiled and edited by Ulli Beier.

THE INTRODUCTION OF BRASS-CASTING FROM IFE

Oba Oguola wished to introduce brass-casting into Benin similar to various works of art sent him from Uhe Ife. He therefore sent to the Oghene of Uhe for a brass-smith and Igue-igha was sent to him. Igue-igha was very clever and left many designs to his successors and was in consequence deified and is worshiped to this day by brass-smiths. The practice of making brass-castings for the preservation of the records of events was originated during the reign of Oguola. He lived to a very old age.

EWUARE THE GREAT

After the murder of Uwaifiokun, Ogus was crowned the Oba of Benin with the title Ewuare (Oworuare) meaning "It is cool" or "The trouble has ceased." (His reign traditionally began in about A.D. 1440.) Prior to his accession he caused a great conflagration in the city which lasted two days and nights as a revenge for his banishment.

Ewuare was a great magician, physician, traveler and warrior. He was also powerful, courageous and sagacious. He fought against and captured 201 towns and villages in Ekiti, Ikare, Kukuruku, Eka and the Ibo country on this side of the river Niger. He took their petty rulers captive and caused the people to pay tribute to him.

He made good roads in Benin City and especially the streets known as Akpakpaya and Utantan. In fact the town rose to importance and gained the name "City" during his reign. It was he who had the innermost and greatest of the walls and ditches made around the City and he made powerful charms and had them buried at each of the nine gateways to the city, to nullify any evil charms which might be brought by people of other countries to injure his subjects.

Ewuare was the first Oba of Benin to come into contact with Europeans, for Ruy de Sigueira visited the Benin area in 1472 although it is not known whether he actually reached the city.

THE COMING OF THE PORTUGUESE TO BENIN

Guns and Coconuts

A Portuguese explorer named John Affonso d'Aveiro visited Benin City for the first time in 1485–1486. He introduced guns and coconuts into this country.

Missionaries

It is said that John Affonso d'Aveiro came to Benin City for the second time during this reign (of Oba

Esigie, which began in 1504). He advised the Oba to be-come a Christian, and said that Christianity would make his country better. Esigie therefore sent Ohen-okun, the Olokun priest at Ughoton, with him, as an Ambassador to the King of Portugal, asking him to send priests who would teach him and his people the faith. In reply the King of Portugal sent Roman Catholic mis-sionaries and many rich presents, such as a copper stool *(erhe)*, coral beads and a big umbrella, with an entreaty that Esigie should embrace the faith. At the same time he also gave presents to the Ambassador and his wife. The King of Portugal also sent some Portuguese traders who established trading factories at Ughoton, the old port of Benin. They traded in ivory, Benin cloths, pep-per and other commodities in the King of Portugal's in-terest. Owing to the unhealthy state of the country their commerce soon ceased.

But John Affonso d'Aveiro with the other mission-aries remained in Benin to carry on the mission work, and churches were built at Ogbelaka, Idumwerie and Akpakpava (Ikpoba Road), the last named being the "Holy Cross Cathedral." ... The work of the Mission made progress and thousands of people were baptized before the death of the great explorer John Affonso d'Aveiro, who was buried with great lamentations by the Oba and the Christians of Benin City.

The missionaries went with Esigie to the Idah war which took place in 1515–1516.

QUESTIONS

1. Discuss the significance of metal working and the origins of political power.
2. Note the characteristics of King Ewuare described in these selections: what values do they reflect?
3. What was the impression made by the early Portu-guese visitors on their hosts?
4. How did Benin react to Christianity?

THE OBA OF BENIN

He who knows not the Oba
let me show him.
He has piled a throne upon a throne.
Plentiful as grains of sand on the earth
are those in front of him.
Plentiful as grains of sand on the earth

are those behind him.
There are two thousand people
to fan him.
He who owns you
is among you here.
He who owns you
has piled a throne upon a throne.
He has lived to do it this year;
even so he will live to do it again.

QUESTIONS

1. What is the effect of *hyperbole* (figures of exagger-ation) in this poem?
2. Compare the portrait of the Oba in this poem with that of Ewuare the Great in the preceding texts.
3. Compare the portrayal of the Oba's power in this poem with the suggestions of his power in Figure 14-6.

European Accounts of Benin   The final selec-tions in this chapter are European accounts of Benin. Although the first European visitor was probably Ruy de Sigueira (who came, as noted in "Ewuare the Great," in 1472), John Affonso d'Aveiro was the first to engage Benin in sustained relationships with the Portu-guese ruler and his subjects. Trading contact was ini-tiated at Benin's port city of Gwato. The Portuguese de-scription of the early period of contact is told in an excerpt from Ruy de Pina's *Chronicle of John II* (1792), translated by J. W. Blake. Compare this version with Eg-harevba's: what are the differences and similarities be-tween them?

RUY DE PINA

Chronicle of John II

THE DISCOVERY OF THE KINGDOM OF BENIN

In this year [1486], the land of Beny beyond Myna to the Rios dos Escravos was first discovered by Joham Affom da Aveiro, who died there; whence there came to these kingdoms the first pepper from Guinee, whereof a great quantity was produced in that land; and presently samples of it were sent to Framdes [Flan-ders] and to other parts, and soon it fetched a great price and was held in high esteem. The king of Beny sent as ambassador to the king a negro, one of his captains, from a harbouring place by the sea, which is called Ugato [Gwato], because he desired to learn more about these lands, the arrival of people from them in his country being regarded as an unusual novelty. This ambassador was a man of good speech and natural wisdom. Great feasts were held in his honour, and he was shown many of the good things of these kingdoms. He returned to his land in a ship of the king's, who at his departure made him a gift of rich clothes for himself and his wife: and through him he also sent a rich present to the king of such things as he understood he would greatly prize. Moreover, he sent holy and most catholic advisers with praiseworthy admonitions for the faith to administer a stern rebuke about the heresies and great idolatries and fetishes, which the negroes practise in that land. Then also there went with him new factors of the king, who were to remain in that country and to traffic for the said pepper and for other things, which pertained to the trades of the king. But owing to the fact that the land was afterwards found to be very dangerous from sickness and not so profitable as had been hoped, the trade was abandoned.

The next selection describes some facets of Benin culture in the seventeenth century near the apogee of the kingdom's power, but at a time when rivals elsewhere, notably Oyo, were posing a challenge. The account is a letter written to Willem Bosman by David Van Nyendael and published in Bosman's *New and Accurate Description of the Coast of Guinea* (1705). Bosman was an employee of the Dutch West India Company; during his fourteen years in West Africa he served for a time as the chief factor at Axim in the Gold Coast.

WILLEM BOSMAN

New and Accurate Description of the Coast of Guinea

BENIN IN 1700

The Inhabitants of this Country, if possessed of any Riches, eat and drink very well; that is to say, of the best. The common Diet of the Rich is Beef, Mutton or Chickens, and Jammes (yams) for their Bread; which, after they have boiled, they beat very fine, in order to make Cakes of it: they frequently treat one another, and impart a Portion of their Superfluity to the Necessitous.

The meaner Sort content themselves with smoak'd or dry'd Fish, which, if salted, is very like what we in *Europe* call Raf or Reekel; their Bread is also Jammes, Bananas, and Beans; their Drink Water and *Pardon-Wine*, which is none of the best. The richer Sort Drink Water and Brandy when they can get it. The King, the Great Lords, and every Governor, who is but indifferently rich, subsist several Poor at their Place of Residence on their Charity, employing those who are fit for any Work, in order to help them to a Maintenance, and the rest they keep for God's sake, and to obtain the Character of being charitable; so that here are no Beggars: And this necessary Care succeeds so well, that we do not see many remarkably poor amongst them....

The King hath a very rich Income; for his Territories are very large, and full of Governors, and each knows how many Bags of Boesies (the Money of this Country) (cowries) he must annually raise to the King, which amounts to a vast Sum, which 'tis impossible to make any Calculation of. Others, of a meaner Rank than the former, instead of Money, deliver to the King Bulls, Cows, Sheep, Chickens, Jammes, and Cloaths; in short, whatever he wants for his Housekeeping; so that he is not oblig'd to one Farthing Expense on that account, and consequently he lays up his whole pecuniary Revenue untouch'd.

Duties or Tolls on imported and exported Wares are not paid here; but everyone pays a certain Sum annually to the Governor of the Place where he lives, for the Liberty of Trading; the Viceroy sends part of it to the King; so that his Revenue being determin'd and settled, he can easily compute what he hath to expect annually.

QUESTIONS AND COMMENTS

1. Compare Ruy de Pina's *Chronicle of John II* with Egharevba's account. What are the differences and similarities between them?

2. Look at Figure 14-4 for an African image of the European soldier. Compare this to the figure of the mas-

ter merchant or to that of the Oba (Figures 14-5, 14-6). What strikes you about the images portrayed?

3. What is the evidence of social and political stratification in the letter to Bosman? Was the Benin monarchy an oppressive one in the seventeenth century? What qualities in Benin society appealed to its Dutch observers?

The Decline of Benin   Other Europeans besides the Portuguese and the Dutch visited Benin, notably the English. William Hawkins first came to Benin in 1530. Thomas Windham in 1553 found that the king, "a Blacke moore," could easily converse in Portuguese. However, since the trading nations found more profitable sources of slaves elsewhere in Africa, Benin's direct contact with the Europeans diminished. The principal causes for the kingdom's decline remain unclear. It seems certain, however, that the trans-Atlantic slave trade engendered economic, political, and military rivals in Dahomey and Oyo in the seventeenth and eighteenth centuries. The monarchy at Benin nevertheless remained intact until the beginning of the colonial era.

Africa Since Contact with Europe   African history since the initial era of European contact in the fifteenth century has been one of uneven change and growth. The slave trade, followed by the shift to trade in natural products in the nineteenth century, affected those African peoples involved in it in many different ways. Kingdoms rose and fell, imported consumer goods replaced those of traditional manufacture, and the moral and social fabric was transformed by the loss of millions of individuals during their most productive years.

When powerful economic and political forces moved European countries to partition Africa in the late nineteenth century and to impose colonial rule, even those African peoples previously unaffected by Europe were now brought face to face with the West. Subjugated to the goals and needs of the colonial powers, African societies experienced much more intensive alteration of their political, economic, and social systems than in previous centuries. The science and technology of an industrialized Europe and a Christianity laden with Western interpretation and institutions were symbols of the Europeans' power over Africa. Some individuals and whole cultures adopted many Western forms in the hope of participating in that power; others resisted the new way. Both responses led to change in the ways that Africans perceived their world and acted in it. For the most part now independent, African countries that emerged in the twentieth century are attempting to overcome the colonial legacy of dependence and to combine material and technological progress with a nurturing of Africa's rich cultural heritage. It is to aspects of this traditional culture that we now turn.

15

WEST AFRICAN LITERATURE: THE ORAL TRADITION

African Languages The literary traditions of Africa are even more diverse than the literatures of Europe are. For one thing, the languages in which they are composed are more varied. Whereas nearly all European languages can be traced back to a common "proto" language (Indo-European) and thus belong to the same language family, Africa's languages are not only more than one thousand in number but also represent four major language families. These are: (1) Afro-Asiatic, including among others Arabic, Berber, Hausa, and Cushitic; (2) Nilo-Saharan; (3) Khoisan, the languages of the hunting and gathering peoples of southern Africa; and (4) Congo-Kordofanian. Most of the languages in our area of concentration spring from the latter family.

Written Literature in Africa Apart from Arabic, which has a rich tradition of written literature including some works by black Africans, only a few African languages were written before the nineteenth or twentieth centuries. These include Ge'ez, the liturgical tongue of the Ethiopian Christian church, and Amharic, for which the oldest documents date from the fourteenth century. Works in Swahili and Hausa dating from the eighteenth and nineteenth centuries respectively can be found written in Arabic script. Modern African writers write either in their own language in Arabic or Roman script or, in order to reach a wider audience, in French, English, or Portuguese.

Oral Literature The rich body of oral literature, however, permits us to understand the primary tradition of West Africa. A century ago the expression "oral literature" seemed a contradiction in terms. "Literature," to those educated in the Western humanistic tradition, meant something written down, a book in a library. Recent studies, however, have shown that European literature included many works composed orally, most notably, as we have seen, the epics of Homer. This fact has perhaps enabled Westerners to appreciate the fact that poetry and prose of great beauty and complexity can be composed and passed down through the generations without being in written form.

The existence of an oral tradition implies a mentality very different from that of a society relying on documents. For one thing, the faculties of memory must be much more highly developed in an oral society. If the kingdom of Benin was able to rule a wide area without written documents, this was partly because it was able to rely on the extensive memories of its administrators. Most African societies have been able to preserve their histories through the *griot*, an official poet-historian whose job it is to tell and transmit the history of his people. These histories may take the form of an epic poem, as we shall see in the excerpts from *Sundiata*.

In addition to history and the epic, oral literature in Africa includes *myths*, *tales*, *riddles*, *proverbs*, and *lyric* poetry. The most widespread type of poetry is the praise poem. Found nearly everywhere in Africa, praise poems extol kings, courtiers, and prominent personalities in the society as well as the gods. Popular poetry is composed and recited, often spontaneously, for the entertainment of the public. All of these *genres* are represented in the examples that follow.

It must be kept in mind that the texts in this book are not only translations from languages very different from English, they are also written transcriptions of an oral event. In the recitation of tale or poem in Africa, the performer and the act of performance are as integral to the work as the arrangement of the words. Poetry, as with the ancient Greeks, is sung; and some types of poems are distinguished entirely by the style, pitch, and quality of voice associated with particular groups of singers. The merit of a poem is often judged not only by the skill of the artist-performer but also by the successful integration of words, music, and dance. Poetry and the epic histories are often the domain of specialists, but folk tales, riddles, and proverbs were and are available to all. Even with these forms, though, the skill of the teller is an important factor.

Appreciation of the written materials here will thus require some creative imagination on the part of the reader; yet, even divorced from performance and in translation, these works can be appreciated both for their literary qualities and for what they convey about African perceptions of the cosmos, creation, human dilemmas, and cultural priorities. We have included a few poems by modern African writers, written in English but drawing on the oral tradition. While several western and central African cultures are represented, three major and distinct civilizations, from which we have taken several examples, deserve further introduction. These are the Mande complex (with specific reference to the Mandinka peoples), the Hausa, and the Yoruba (see map opposite page).

Mande Mande is the name of a cultural complex and group of languages in western Sudan. Mande peoples were among the earliest to develop agriculture in sub-Saharan Africa. Mandinka (also called Mandingo or Malinke) is one of about twelve subgroups that make up the Mande group and that formed the core population of the Mali empire. Around the year 1200 several of them were joined together in revolt against the declining empire of Ghana. The remarkable leader of this revolt was a Mandinka man named Sundiata, the hero of the epic that follows. As a result of his mili-

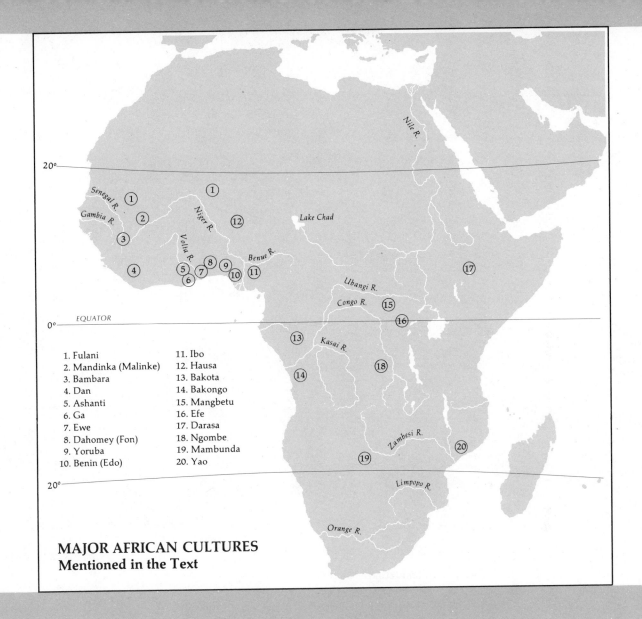

MAJOR AFRICAN CULTURES
Mentioned in the Text

1. Fulani
2. Mandinka (Malinke)
3. Bambara
4. Dan
5. Ashanti
6. Ga
7. Ewe
8. Dahomey (Fon)
9. Yoruba
10. Benin (Edo)
11. Ibo
12. Hausa
13. Bakota
14. Bakongo
15. Mangbetu
16. Efe
17. Darasa
18. Ngombe
19. Mambunda
20. Yao

tary victories, Mali flourished. With its economy based on the rich agricultural lands of the upper Niger and on secure control of the gold mines of Bambuk and Bure, Mali expanded to become the largest of the medieval African empires. Included within its boundaries were peoples and lands in parts of modern Guinea, Mali, Sierra Leone, Liberia, Ivory Coast, Senegal, northern Ghana, and Upper Volta.

The fabulous wealth and high culture of Mali became known to the outside world through the pilgrimage of Mansa Musa in 1324 (Fig. 15-1). He and succeeding mansas, or kings, attracted scholars from North Africa and the Middle East to Timbuktu, Mali's principal port city of the trans-Saharan trade. These scholars, together with the local people, created a great center of Islamic learning around the famous mosque of Sankore. Muslim traders of various Mande groups spread Islam far beyond the core areas around Niani, the capital, and Timbuktu, some reaching as far east as Hausaland. Succession disputes and aggressive neighbors

15-1 Catalan Map, 1375. (By permission of the British Library. *BL Maps Ref. A.6.(3)*)

nurtured internal tensions in the empire, which, nevertheless, survived until the seventeenth century.

Hausa Hausa is a linguistic term describing the several million peoples in West Africa who speak Hausa as their first language. Though their homeland is northern Nigeria and southern Niger, the Hausa have been engaged in long-distance trade for centuries; there are substantial Hausa-speaking communities in northern Ghana and in every major city in West Africa. Politically, the Hausa were long ago grouped into separate walled city-states to which the surrounding rural folk owed allegiance. From about the fourteenth century (perhaps stimulated by contact with Mande traders), Islam was the religion of the courts. In the early nineteenth century a holy war, or *jihad*, sparked a revolution that replaced the Hausa rulers with those from another group, the Fulani, and united them into a centralized state known as the Fulani empire. The Fulani empire included many non-Muslim groups from the lands north of the Benue and Niger rivers within its borders. By creating an area of unprecedented size within which trade, agriculture, travel, and communication could develop in relative peace, the empire imposed use of Hausa language and Islamic values on many more peoples than before.

Yoruba The Yoruba are an agricultural and trading people numbering several million who reside in southwestern Nigeria and the republic of Benin. Throughout most of the period of contact between Africa and Europe, the Yoruba were subjects of the Benin and Oyo empires. The latter was a kingdom of far-flung boundaries that disintegrated in the early nineteenth century. Oyo and the successor kingdoms were constitutional monarchies in which the power of the king was balanced by a council of state and an institutionalized priesthood. The richness of the Yoruba aesthetic is better known to outsiders than, perhaps, that of any other African people. The traditions of poetry, sculpture, and dance are founded on an elaborate system of religious beliefs and practices. The hierarchy and ritual among the Yoruba gods mirrors that of traditional Yoruba political structure. Yoruba religious beliefs have been remarkably successful in retaining their dynamism through accommodation with both Christian and Islamic practice. Perhaps one of the key reasons for this dynamism is the vitality of the poetry, myths, and proverbs (seen in the examples that follow) and their continued integration into social, political, and religious festivals of contemporary society.

The Epic

The original purpose of epic poetry, as we saw in the section on Homer in Chapter 1, was to "sing the famous deeds of men": to teach people in a pleasurable way about great heroes and historical events important to their culture. The epic hero, who exists or has existed in nearly all of the world's cultures, is a human being with certain superhuman qualities, someone who overcomes great obstacles and accomplishes both physical and spiritual triumphs for his people. Such a hero is Sundiata, whose legendary dimensions have informed the cultural identity of the Mande peoples down to the present time. The oral epic Sundiata was told by the griot Mamadou Kouyaté to Djibril Tamsir Niane, who transcribed it and translated it into French in 1960. What follows are excerpts from Niane's version, translated into English by G. D. Pickett.

from *Sundiata*

THE WORDS OF THE GRIOT MAMADOU KOUYATÉ

I am a griot. It is I, Djeli Mamadou Kouyaté, son of Bintou Kouyaté and Djeli Kedian Kouyaté, master in the art of eloquence. Since time immemorial the Kouyatés have been in the service of the Keita princes of Mali; we are vessels of speech, we are the repositories which harbour secrets many centuries old. The art of eloquence has no secrets for us; without us the names of kings would vanish into oblivion, we are the memory of mankind; by the spoken word we bring to life the deeds and exploits of kings for younger generations.

I derive my knowledge from my father Djeli Kedian, who also got it from his father; history holds no mystery for us; we teach to the vulgar just as much as we want to teach them, for it is we who keep the keys to the twelve doors of Mali.

I know the list of all the sovereigns who succeeded to the throne of Mali. I know how the black people divided into tribes, for my father bequeathed to me all his learning; I know why such and such is called Kamara, another Keita, and yet another Sibibé or Traoré; every name has a meaning, a secret import.

I teach kings the history of their ancestors so that the lives of the ancients might serve them as an example, for the world is old, but the future springs from the past.

My word is pure and free of all untruth; it is the word of my father; it is the word of my father's father. I will give you my father's words just as I received them; royal griots do not know what lying is. When a quarrel breaks out between tribes it is we who settle the difference, for we are the depositaries of oaths which the ancestors swore.

Listen to my word, you who want to know; by my mouth you will learn the history of Mali.

By my mouth you will get to know the story of the ancestor of great Mali, the story of him who, by his exploits, surpassed even Alexander the Great; he who, from the East, shed his rays upon all the countries of the West.

Listen to the story of the son of the Buffalo, the son of the Lion. I am going to tell you of Maghan Sundiata, of Mari-Djata, of Sogolon Djata, of Naré Maghan Djata; the man of many names against whom sorcery could avail nothing.

THE FIRST KINGS OF MALI

Listen then, sons of Mali, children of the black people, listen to my word, for I am going to tell you of Sundiata, the father of the Bright Country, of the savanna land, the ancestor of those who draw the bow, the master of a hundred vanquished kings.

I am going to talk of Sundiata, Manding Diara, Lion of Mali, Sogolon Djata, son of Sogolon, Naré Maghan Djata, son of Naré Maghan, Sogo Sogo Simbon Salaba, hero of many names.

I am going to tell you of Sundiata, he whose exploits will astonish men for a long time yet. He was great among kings, he was peerless among men; he was beloved of God because he was the last of the great conquerors.

Right at the beginning then, Mali was a province of the Bambara kings; those who are today called Mandingo, inhabitants of Mali, are not indigenous; they come from the East. Bilali Bounama, ancestor of the Keitas, was the faithful servant of the Prophet Muhammad (may the peace of God be upon him). Bilali Bounama had seven sons of whom the eldest, Lawalo, left the Holy City and came to settle in Mali; Lawalo had Latal Kalabi for a son, Latal Kalabi had Damul Kalabi who then had Lahilatoul Kalabi.

Lahilatoul Kalabi was the first black prince to make the Pilgrimage to Mecca. On his return he was robbed by brigands in the desert; his men were scattered and some died of thirst, but God saved Lahilatoul Kalabi, for he was a righteous man. He called upon the Almighty and jinn appeared and recognized him as king. After seven years' absence Lahilatoul was able to return, by the grace of Allah the Almighty, to Mali where none expected to see him any more.

Lahilatoul Kalabi had two sons, the elder being called Kalabi Bomba and the younger Kalabi Dauman; the elder chose royal power and reigned, while the younger preferred fortune and wealth and became the ancestor of those who go from country to country seeking their fortune.

Kalabi Bomba had Mamadi Kani for a son. Mamadi Kani was a hunter king like the first kings of Mali. It was he who invented the hunter's whistle; he communicated with the jinn of the forest and bush. These spirits had no secrets from him and he was loved by Kondolon Ni Sané. His followers were so numerous that he formed them into an army which became formidable; he often gathered them together in the bush and taught them the art of hunting. It was he who revealed to hunters the medicinal leaves which heal wounds and cure diseases. Thanks to the strength of his followers, he became king of a vast country; with them Mamadi Kani conquered all the lands which stretch from the Sankarani to the Bouré. Mamadi Kani had four sons—Kani Simbon, Kamignogo Simbon, Kabala Simbon and Simbon Tagnogokelin. They were all initiated into the art of hunting and deserved the title of Simbon. It was the lineage of Bamari Tagnogokelin which held on to the power; his son was M'Bali Nènè whose son was Bello. Bello's son was called Bello Bakon and he had a son called Maghan Kon Fatta, also called Frako Maghan Keigu, Maghan the handsome.

Maghan Kon Fatta was the father of the great Sundiata and had three wives and six children—three boys and three girls. His first wife was called Sassouma Bérété, daughter of a great divine; she was the mother of King Dankaran Touman and Princess Nana Triban. The second wife, Sogolon Kedjou, was the mother of Sundiata and the two princesses Sogolon Kolonkan and Sogolon Djamarou. The third wife was one of the Kamaras and was called Namandjé; she was the mother of Manding Bory (or Manding Bakary), who was the best friend of his half-brother Sundiata.

THE BUFFALO WOMAN

Maghan Kon Fatta, the father of Sundiata, was renowned for his beauty in every land; but he was also a good king loved by all the people. In his capital of Nianiba he loved to sit often at the foot of the great silk-cotton tree which dominated his palace of Canco. Maghan Kon Fatta had been reigning a long time and his eldest son Dankaran Touman was already eight years old and often came to sit on the ox-hide beside his father.

Well now, one day when the king had taken up his usual position under the silk-cotton tree surrounded by his kinsmen he saw a man dressed like a hunter coming towards him; he wore the tight-fitting trousers of the favourites of Kondolon Ni Sané, and his blouse oversewn with cowries showed that he was a master of the hunting art. All present turned towards the unknown man whose bow, polished with frequent usage, shone in the sun. The man walked up in front of the king, whom he recognized in the midst of his courtiers. He bowed and said, "I salute you, king of Mali, greetings all you of Mali. I am a hunter chasing game and come from Sangaran; a fearless doe has guided me to the walls of Nianiba. By the grace of my master the great Simbon[1] my arrows have hit her and now she lies not far from your walls. As is fitting, oh king, I have come to bring you your portion." He took a leg from his leather sack whereupon the king's griot, Gnankouman Doua, seized upon the leg and said, "Stranger, whoever you may be you will be the king's guest because you respect custom; come and take your place on the mat beside us. The king is pleased because he loves righteous men." The king nodded his approval and all the courtiers agreed. The griot continued in a more familiar tone, "Oh you who come from the Sangaran, land of the favourites of Kondolon Ni Sané, you who have doubtless had an expert master, will you open your pouch of knowledge for us and instruct us with your conversation, for you have no doubt visited several lands."

The king, still silent, gave a nod of approval and a courtier added, "The hunters of Sangaran are the best soothsayers; if the stranger wishes we could learn a lot from him."

The hunter came and sat down near Gnankouman Doua who vacated one end of the mat for him. Then he said, "Griot of the king, I am not one of these hunters whose tongues are more dexterous than their arms; I am no spinner of adventure yarns, nor do I like playing upon the credulity of worthy folk; but, thanks to the lore which my master has imparted to me, I can boast of being a seer among seers."

He took out of his hunter's bag twelve cowries which he threw on the mat. The king and all his entourage now turned towards the stranger who was jumbling up the twelve shiny shells with his bare hand. Gnankouman Doua discreetly brought to the king's notice that the soothsayer was left-handed. The left hand is the hand of evil, but in the divining art it is said that left-handed people are the best. The hunter muttered some incomprehensible words in a low voice while he shuffled and jumbled the twelve cowries into different positions which he mused on at length. All of a sudden he looked up at the king and said, "Oh king, the world is full of mystery, all is hidden and we know nothing but what we can see. The silk-cotton tree springs from a tiny seed—that which defies the tempest weighs in its germ no more than a grain of rice. Kingdoms are like trees; some will be silk-cotton trees, others will remain dwarf palms and the powerful silk-cotton tree will cover them with its shade. Oh, who can recognize in the little child the great king to come? The great comes from the small; truth and falsehood have both suckled at the same breast. Nothing is certain, but, sire, I can see two strangers over there coming towards your city."

He fell silent and looked in the direction of the city gates for a short while. All present silently turned towards the gates. The soothsayer returned to his cowries. He shook them in his palm with a skilled hand and then threw them out.

"King of Mali, destiny marches with great strides, Mali is about to emerge from the night. Nianiba is lighting up, but what is this light that comes from the east?"

"Hunter," said Gnankouman Doua, "your words are obscure. Make your speech comprehensible to us, speak in the clear language of your savanna.[2]"

"I am coming to that now, griot. Listen to my message. Listen, sire. You have ruled over the kingdom which your ancestors bequeathed to you and you have no other ambition but to pass on this realm, intact if not increased, to your descendants; but, fine king, your successor is not yet born. I see two hunters coming to your city; they have come from afar and a woman accompanies them. Oh, that woman! She is ugly, she is hideous, she bears on her back a disfiguring hump. Her monstrous eyes seem to have been merely laid on her face, but, mystery of mysteries, this is the woman you must marry, sire, for she will be the mother of him who will make the name of Mali immortal for ever. The child will be the seventh star, the seventh con-

---

[1] Honorific term for a great hunter; later applied to Sundiata.

[2] The language of those who live in the savannah grasslands is, like their environment, clear and bright.

queror of the earth. He will be more mighty than Alexander. But, oh king, for destiny to lead this woman to you a sacrifice is necessary; you must offer up a red bull, for the bull is powerful. When its blood soaks into the ground nothing more will hinder the arrival of your wife. There, I have said what I had to say, but everything is in the hands of the Almighty."

The hunter picked up his cowries and put them away in his bag.

"I am only passing through, king of Mali, and now I return to Sangaran. Farewell."

The hunter disappeared but neither the king, Naré Maghan, nor his griot, Gnankouman Doua, forgot his prophetic words; soothsayers see far ahead, their words are not always for the immediate present; man is in a hurry but time is tardy and everything has its season. . . .

Summary   After some time the old man's prophecy came to pass. One day two hunters came from the land of Do to present to the king a young girl who, though she was shrouded in traveling clothes, was apparently a hunchback. They related to the king and his court how the king of Do Mansa-Gnemo Dearra had promised to reward anyone who killed an astounding buffalo that had been destroying the fields in the area. Having set out themselves to find the buffalo, the two hunters had befriended an old woman who confessed that she was the Buffalo of Do. She told them how to capture and kill it on the promise that when offered the reward of a beautiful young maiden, they choose an ugly girl who would be seated in the crowd.

Events transpired as the old woman had predicted, and the hunters were laughed out of town when they chose the ugly girl, Sogolon Kedjou. Unable to possess her, the hunters only later thought to present her to the king of Mali. Recognizing the fulfillment of what the old man had foretold, Naré Maghan married Sogolon.

THE LION CHILD

A wife quickly grows accustomed to her state. Sogolon now walked freely in the king's great enclosure and people also got used to her ugliness. But the first wife of the king, Sassouma Bérété, turned out to be unbearable. She was restless, and smarted to see the ugly Sogolon proudly flaunting her pregnancy about the palace.

What would become of her, Sassouma Bérété, if her son, already eight years old, was disinherited in favour of the child that Sogolon was going to bring into the world? All the king's attentions went to the mother-to-be. On returning from the wars he would bring her the best portion of the booty—fine loin-cloths and rare jewels. Soon, dark schemes took form in the mind of Sassouma Bérété; she determined to kill Sogolon. In great secrecy she had the foremost sorcerers of Mali come to her, but they all declared themselves incapable of tackling Sogolon. In fact, from twilight onwards, three owls came and perched on the roof of her house and watched over her. For the sake of peace and quiet Sassouma said to herself, "Very well then, let him be born, this child, and then we'll see."

Sogolon's time came. The king commanded the nine greatest midwives of Mali to come to Niani, and they were now constantly in attendance on the damsel of Do. The king was in the midst of his courtiers one day when someone came to announce to him that Sogolon's labours were beginning. He sent all his courtiers away and only Gnankouman Doua stayed by his side. One would have thought that this was the first time that he had become a father, he was so worried and agitated. The whole palace kept complete silence. Doua tried to distract the sovereign with his one-stringed guitar but in vain. He even had to stop this music as it jarred on the king. Suddenly the sky darkened and great clouds coming from the east hid the sun, although it was still the dry season. Thunder began to rumble and swift lightning rent the clouds; a few large drops of rain began to fall while a strong wind blew up. A flash of lightning accompanied by a dull rattle of thunder burst out of the east and lit up the whole sky as far as the west. Then the rain stopped and the sun appeared and it was at this very moment that a midwife came out of Sogolon's house, ran to the antechamber and announced to Naré Maghan that he was the father of a boy.

The king showed no reaction at all. He was as though in a daze. Then Doua, realizing the king's emotion, got up and signalled to two slaves who were already standing near the royal "tabala."[3] The hasty beats of the

---

[3] Ceremonial drum.

royal drum announced to Mali the birth of a son; the village tam-tams took it up and thus all Mali got the good news the same day. Shouts of joy, tam-tams and "balafons"[4] took the place of the recent silence and all the musicians of Niani made their way to the palace. His initial emotion being over, the king had got up and on leaving the antechamber he was greeted by the warm voice of Gnankouman Doua singing:

"I salute you, father; I salute you, king Naré Maghan; I salute you, Maghan Kon Fatta, Frako Maghan Keigu. The child is born whom the world awaited. Maghan, oh happy father, I salute you. The lion child, the buffalo child is born, and to announce him the Almighty has made the thunder peal, the whole sky has lit up and the earth has trembled. All hail, father, hail king Naré Maghan!"

All the griots were there and had already composed a song in praise of the royal infant. The generosity of kings makes griots eloquent, and Maghan Kon Fatta distributed on this day alone six granaries of rice among the populace. Sassouma Bérété distinguished herself by her largesses, but that deceived nobody. She was suffering in her heart but did not want to betray anything.

The name was given the eighth day after his birth. It was a great feast day and people came from all the villages of Mali while each neighbouring people brought gifts to the king. First thing in the morning a great circle had formed in front of the palace. In the middle, serving women were pounding rice which was to serve as bread, and sacrificed oxen lay at the foot of the great silk-cotton tree.

In Sogolon's house the king's aunt cut off the baby's first crop of hair while the poetesses, equipped with large fans, cooled the mother who was nonchalantly stretched out on soft cushions.

The king was in his antechamber but he came out followed by Doua. The crowd fell silent and Doua cried, "The child of Sogolon will be called Maghan after his father, and Mari Djata, a name which no Mandingo prince has ever borne. Sogolon's son will be the first of this name."

Straight away the griots shouted the name of the infant and the tam-tams sounded anew. The king's aunt, who had come out to hear the name of the child, went back into the house, and whispered the double name of Maghan and Mari Djata in the ear of the newly-born so that he would remember it.

The festivity ended with the distribution of meat to the heads of families and everyone dispersed joyfully. The near relatives one by one went to admire the newly-born.

CHILDHOOD

God has his mysteries which none can fathom. You, perhaps, will be a king. You can do nothing about it. You, on the other hand, will be unlucky, but you can do nothing about that either. Each man finds his way already marked out for him and he can change nothing of it.

Sogolon's son had a slow and difficult childhood. At the age of three he still crawled along on all fours while children of the same age were already walking. He had nothing of the great beauty of his father Naré Maghan. He had a head so big that he seemed unable to support it; he also had large eyes which would open wide whenever anyone entered his mother's house. He was taciturn and used to spend the whole day just sitting in the middle of the house. Whenever his mother went out he would crawl on all fours to rummage about in the calabashes in search of food, for he was very greedy.

Malicious tongues began to blab. What three-year-old has not yet taken his first steps? What three-year-old is not the despair of his parents through his whims and shifts of mood? What three-year-old is not the joy of his circle through his backwardness in talking? Sogolon Djata (for it was thus that they called him, prefixing his mother's name to his), Sogolon Djata, then, was very different from others of his own age. He spoke little and his severe face never relaxed into a smile. You would have thought that he was already thinking, and what amused children of his age bored him. Often Sogolon would make some of them come to him to keep him company. These children were already walking and she hoped that Djata, seeing his companions walking, would be tempted to do likewise. But nothing came of it. Besides, Sogolon Djata would brain the poor little things with his already strong arms and none of them would come near him any more.

The king's first wife was the first to rejoice at Sogolon

---

[4] A type of xylophone in which the wooden keys are often mounted upon gourds.

Djata's infirmity. Her own son, Dankaran Touman, was already eleven. He was a fine and lively boy, who spent the day running about the village with those of his own age. He had even begun his initiation in the bush. The king had had a bow made for him and he used to go behind the town to practise archery with his companions. Sassouma was quite happy and snapped her fingers at Sogolon, whose child was still crawling on the ground. Whenever the latter happened to pass by her house, she would say, "Come, my son, walk, jump, leap about. The jinn[5] didn't promise you anything out of the ordinary, but I prefer a son who walks on his two legs to a lion that crawls on the ground." She spoke thus whenever Sogolon went by her door. The innuendo would go straight home and then she would burst into laughter, that diabolical laughter which a jealous woman knows how to use so well.

Her son's infirmity weighed heavily upon Sogolon Kedjou; she had resorted to all her talent as a sorceress to give strength to her son's legs, but the rarest herbs had been useless. The king himself lost hope.

How impatient man is! Naré Maghan became imperceptibly estranged but Gnankouman Doua never ceased reminding him of the hunter's words. Sogolon became pregnant again. The king hoped for a son, but it was a daughter called Kolonkan. She resembled her mother and had nothing of her father's beauty. The disheartened king debarred Sogolon from his house and she lived in semi-disgrace for a while. Naré Maghan married the daughter of one of his allies, the king of the Kamaras. She was called Namandjé and her beauty was legendary. A year later she brought a boy into the world. When the king consulted soothsayers on the destiny of this son he received the reply that Namandjé's child would be the right hand of some mighty king. The king gave the newly-born the name of Boukari. He was to be called Manding Boukari or Manding Bory later on.

Naré Maghan was very perplexed. Could it be that the stiff-jointed son of Sogolon was the one the hunter soothsayer had foretold?

"The Almighty has his mysteries," Gnankouman Doua would say and, taking up the hunter's words, added, "The silk-cotton tree emerges from a tiny seed."

One day Naré Maghan came along to the house of Nounfaïri, the blacksmith seer of Niani. He was an old, blind man. He received the king in the anteroom which served as his workshop. To the king's question he replied, "When the seed germinates growth is not always easy; great trees grow slowly but they plunge their roots deep into the ground."

"But has the seed really germinated?" said the king.

"Of course," replied the blind seer. "Only the growth is not as quick as you would like it; how impatient man is."

This interview and Doua's confidence gave the king some assurance. To the great displeasure of Sassouma Bérété the king restored Sogolon to favour and soon another daughter was born to her. She was given the name of Djamarou.

However, all Niani talked of nothing else but the stiff-legged son of Sogolon. He was now seven and he still crawled to get about. In spite of all the king's affection, Sogolon was in despair. Naré Maghan aged and he felt his time coming to an end. Dankaran Touman, the son of Sassouma Bérété, was now a fine youth.

One day Naré Maghan made Mari Djata come to him and he spoke to the child as one speaks to an adult. "Mari Djata, I am growing old and soon I shall be no more among you, but before death takes me off I am going to give you the present each king gives his successor. In Mali every prince has his own griot. Doua's father was my father's griot, Doua is mine and the son of Doua, Balla Fasséké here, will be your griot. Be inseparable friends from this day forward. From his mouth you will hear the history of your ancestors, you will learn the art of governing Mali according to the principles which our ancestors have bequeathed to us. I have served my term and done my duty too. I have done everything which a king of Mali ought to do. I am handing an enlarged kingdom over to you and I leave you sure allies. May your destiny be accomplished, but never forget that Niani is your capital and Mali the cradle of your ancestors."

The child, as if he had understood the whole meaning of the king's words, beckoned Balla Fasséké to approach. He made room for him on the hide he was sitting on and then said, "Balla, you will be my griot."

"Yes, son of Sogolon, if it pleases God," replied Balla Fasséké.

---

[5] A Muslim term for invisible spirits, supernatural agencies.

The king and Doua exchanged glances that radiated confidence.

THE LION'S AWAKENING

A short while after this interview between Naré Maghan and his son the king died. Sogolon's son was no more than seven years old. The council of elders met in the king's palace. It was no use Doua's defending the king's will which reserved the throne for Mari Djata, for the council took no account of Naré Maghan's wish. With the help of Sassouma Bérété's intrigues, Dankaran Touman was proclaimed king and a regency council was formed in which the queen mother was all-powerful. A short time after, Doua died.

As men have short memories, Sogolon's son was spoken of with nothing but irony and scorn. People had seen one-eyed kings, one-armed kings, and lame kings, but a stiff-legged king had never been heard tell of. No matter how great the destiny promised for Mari Djata might be, the throne could not be given to someone who had no power in his legs; if the jinn loved him, let them begin by giving him the use of his legs. Such were the remarks that Sogolon heard every day. The queen mother, Sassouma Bérété, was the source of all this gossip.

Having become all-powerful, Sassouma Bérété persecuted Sogolon because the late Naré Maghan had preferred her. She banished Sogolon and her son to a back yard of the palace. Mari Djata's mother now occupied an old hut which had served as a lumber-room of Sassouma's.

The wicked queen mother allowed free passage to all those inquisitive people who wanted to see the child that still crawled at the age of seven. Nearly all the inhabitants of Niani filed into the palace and the poor Sogolon wept to see herself thus given over to public ridicule. Mari Djata took on a ferocious look in front of the crowd of sightseers. Sogolon found a little consolation only in the love of her eldest daughter, Kolonkan. She was four and she could walk. She seemed to understand all her mother's miseries and already she helped her with the housework. Sometimes, when Sogolon was attending to the chores, it was she who stayed beside her sister Djamarou, quite small as yet.

Sogolon Kedjou and her children lived on the queen mother's left-overs, but she kept a little garden in the open ground behind the village. It was there that she passed her brightest moments looking after her onions and gnougous. One day she happened to be short of condiments and went to the queen mother to beg a little baobab leaf.

"Look you," said the malicious Sassouma, "I have a calabash full. Help yourself, you poor woman. As for me, my son knew how to walk at seven and it was he who went and picked these baobab leaves. Take them then, since your son is unequal to mine." Then she laughed derisively with that fierce laughter which cuts through your flesh and penetrates right to the bone.

Sogolon Kedjou was dumbfounded. She had never imagined that hate could be so strong in a human being. With a lump in her throat she left Sassouma's. Outside her hut Mari Djata, sitting on his useless legs, was blandly eating out of a calabash. Unable to contain herself any longer, Sogolon burst into sobs and seizing a piece of wood, hit her son.

"Oh son of misfortune, will you never walk? Through your fault I have just suffered the greatest affront of my life! What have I done, God, for you to punish me in this way?"

Mari Djata seized the piece of wood and, looking at his mother, said, "Mother, what's the matter?"

"Shut up, nothing can ever wash me clean of this insult."

"But what then?"

"Sassouma has just humiliated me over a matter of a baobab leaf. At your age her own son could walk and used to bring his mother baobab leaves."

"Cheer up, Mother, cheer up."

"No. It's too much. I can't."

"Very well then, I am going to walk today," said Mari Djata. "Go and tell my father's smiths to make me the heaviest possible iron rod. Mother, do you want just the leaves of the baobab or would you rather I brought you the whole tree?"

"Ah, my son, to wipe out this insult I want the tree and its roots at my feet outside my hut."

Balla Fasséké, who was present, ran to the master smith, Farakourou, to order an iron rod.

Sogolon had sat down in front of her hut. She was weeping softly and holding her head between her two hands. Mari Djata went calmly back to his calabash of rice and began eating again as if nothing had happened.

From time to time he looked up discreetly at his mother who was murmuring in a low voice, "I want the whole tree, in front of my hut, the whole tree."

All of a sudden a voice burst into laughter behind the hut. It was the wicked Sassouma telling one of her serving women about the scene of humiliation and she was laughing loudly so that Sogolon could hear. Sogolon fled into the hut and hid her face under the blankets so as not to have before her eyes this heedless boy, who was more preoccupied with eating than with anything else. With her head buried in the bed-clothes Sogolon wept and her body shook violently. Her daughter, Sogolon Djamarou, had come and sat down beside her and she said, "Mother, Mother, don't cry. Why are you crying?"

Mari Djata had finished eating and, dragging himself along on his legs, he came and sat under the wall of the hut for the sun was scorching. What was he thinking about? He alone knew.

The royal forges were situated outside the walls and over a hundred smiths worked there. The bows, spears, arrows and shields of Niani's warriors came from there. When Balla Fasséké came to order the iron rod, Farakourou said to him, "The great day has arrived then?"

"Yes. Today is a day like any other, but it will see what no other day has seen."

The master of the forges, Farakourou, was the son of the old Nounfaïri, and he was a soothsayer like his father. In his workshops there was an enormous iron bar wrought by his father Nounfaïri. Everybody wondered what this bar was destined to be used for. Farakourou called six of his apprentices and told them to carry the iron bar to Sogolon's house.

When the smiths put the gigantic iron bar down in front of the hut the noise was so frightening that Sogolon, who was lying down, jumped up with a start. Then Balla Fasséké, son of Gnankouman Doua, spoke.

"Here is the great day, Mari Djata. I am speaking to you, Maghan, son of Sogolon. The waters of the Niger can efface the stain from the body, but they cannot wipe out an insult. Arise, young lion, roar, and may the bush know that from henceforth it has a master."

The apprentice smiths were still there, Sogolon had come out and everyone was watching Mari Djata. He crept on all fours and came to the iron bar. Supporting himself on his knees and one hand, with the other hand he picked up the iron bar without any effort and stood it up vertically. Now he was resting on nothing but his knees and held the bar with both his hands. A deathly silence had gripped all those present. Sogolon Djata closed his eyes, held tight, the muscles in his arms tensed. With a violent jerk he threw his weight on to it and his knees left the ground. Sogolon Kedjou was all eyes and watched her son's legs which were trembling as though from an electric shock. Djata was sweating and the sweat ran from his brow. In a great effort he straightened up and was on his feet at one go—but the great bar of iron was twisted and had taken the form of a bow!

Then Balla Fasséké sang out the "Hymn to the Bow," striking up with his powerful voice:

"Take your bow, Simbon,
Take your bow and let us go.
Take your bow, Sogolon Djata."

When Sogolon saw her son standing she stood dumb for a moment, then suddenly she sang these words of thanks to God who had given her son the use of his legs:

"Oh day, what a beautiful day,
Oh day, day of joy;
Allah Almighty, you never created a finer day.
So my son is going to walk!"

Standing in the position of a soldier at ease, Sogolon Djata, supported by his enormous rod, was sweating great beads of sweat. Balla Fasséké's song had alerted the whole palace and people came running from all over to see what had happened, and each stood bewildered before Sogolon's son. The queen mother had rushed there and when she saw Mari Djata standing up she trembled from head to foot. After recovering his breath Sogolon's son dropped the bar and the crowd stood to one side. His first steps were those of a giant. Balla Fasséké fell into step and pointing his finger at Djata, he cried:

"Room, room, make room!
The lion has walked;
Hide antelopes,
Get out of his way."

Behind Niani there was a young baobab tree and it was there that the children of the town came to pick leaves for their mothers. With all his might the son of Sogolon tore up the tree and put it on his shoulders and went back to his mother. He threw the tree in front of the hut and said, "Mother, here are some baobab leaves for you. From henceforth it will be outside your hut that the women of Niani will come to stock up."

Sogolon Djata walked. From that day forward the queen mother had no more peace of mind. But what can one do against destiny? Nothing. Man, under the influence of certain illusions, thinks he can alter the course which God has mapped out, but everything he does falls into a higher order which he barely understands. That is why Sassouma's efforts were vain against Sogolon's son, everything she did lay in the child's destiny. Scorned the day before and the object of public ridicule, now Sogolon's son was as popular as he had been despised. The multitude loves and fears strength. All Niani talked of nothing but Djata; the mothers urged their sons to become hunting companions of Djata and to share his games, as if they wanted their offspring to profit from the nascent glory of the buffalo-woman's son. The words of Doua on the name-giving day came back to men's minds and Sogolon was now surrounded with much respect; in conversation people were fond of contrasting Sogolon's modesty with the pride and malice of Sassouma Bérété. It was because the former had been an exemplary wife and mother that God had granted strength to her son's legs for, it was said, the more a wife loves and respects her husband and the more she suffers for her child, the more valorous will the child be one day. Each is the child of his mother; the child is worth no more than the mother is worth. It was not astonishing that the king Dankaran Touman was so colourless, for his mother had never shown the slightest respect to her husband and never, in the presence of the late king, did she show that humility which every wife should show before her husband. People recalled her scenes of jealousy and the spiteful remarks she circulated about her co-wife and her child. And people would conclude gravely, "Nobody knows God's mystery. The snake has no legs yet it is as swift as any other animal that has four."

Sogolon Djata's popularity grew from day to day and he was surrounded by a gang of children of the same age as himself. These were Fran Kamara, son of the king of Tabon; Kamandjan, son of the king of Sibi; and other princes whose fathers had sent them to the court of Niani. The son of Namandjé, Manding Bory, was already joining in their games. Balla Fasséké followed Sogolon Djata all the time. He was past twenty and it was he who gave the child education and instruction according to Mandingo rules of conduct. Whether in town or at the hunt, he missed no opportunity of instructing his pupil. Many young boys of Niani came to join in the games of the royal child.

He liked hunting best of all. Farakourou, master of the forges, had made Djata a fine bow, and he proved himself to be a good shot with the bow. He made frequent hunting trips with his troops, and in the evening all Niani would be in the square to be present at the entry of the young hunters. The crowd would sing the "Hymn to the Bow" which Balla Fasséké had composed, and Sogolon Djata was quite young when he received the title of Simbon, or master hunter, which is only conferred on great hunters who have proved themselves.

Every evening Sogolon Kedjou would gather Djata and his companions outside her hut. She would tell them stories about the beasts of the bush, the dumb brothers of man. Sogolon Djata learnt to distinguish between the animals; he knew why the buffalo was his mother's wraith[6] and also why the lion was the protector of his father's family. He also listened to the history of the kings which Balla Fasséké told him; enraptured by the story of Alexander the Great, the mighty king of gold and silver, whose sun shone over quite half the world. Sogolon initiated her son into certain secrets and revealed to him the names of the medicinal plants which every hunter should know. Thus, between his mother and his griot, the child got to know all that needed to be known.

Sogolon's son was now ten. The name Sogolon Djata in the rapid Mandingo language became Sundiata or Sondjata. He was a lad full of strength; his arms had the strength of ten and his biceps inspired fear in his companions. He had already that authoritative way of

---

[6] In Mandingo religion, the double of a spirit. The spirit may leave the body and reincarnate itself in other persons or animals. In this case the mother's spirit became reincarnate in the buffalo.

speaking which belongs to those who are destined to command. His brother, Manding Bory, became his best friend, and whenever Djata was seen, Manding Bory appeared too. They were like a man and his shadow. Fran Kamara and Kamandjan were the closest friends of the young princes, while Balla Fasséké followed them all like a guardian angel.

But Sundiata's popularity was so great that the queen mother became apprehensive for her son's throne. Dankaran Touman was the most retiring of men. At the age of eighteen he was still under the influence of his mother and a handful of old schemers. It was Sassouma Bérété who really reigned in his name. The queen mother wanted to put an end to this popularity by killing Sundiata and it was thus that one night she received the nine great witches of Mali. They were all old women. The eldest, and the most dangerous too, was called Soumosso Konkomba. When the nine old hags had seated themselves in a semi-circle around her bed the queen mother said:

"You who rule supreme at night, nocturnal powers, oh you who hold the secret of life, you who can put an end to one life, can you help me?"

"The night is potent," said Soumosso Konkomba, "Oh queen, tell us what is to be done, on whom must we turn the fatal blade?"

"I want to kill Sundiata," said Sassouma. "His destiny runs counter to my son's and he must be killed while there is still time. If you succeed, I promise you the finest rewards. First of all I bestow on each of you a cow and her calf and from tomorrow go to the royal granaries and each of you will receive a hundred measures of rice and a hundred measures of hay on my authority."

"Mother of the king," rejoined Soumosso Konkomba, "life hangs by nothing but a very fine thread, but all is interwoven here below. Life has a cause, and death as well. The one comes from the other. Your hate has a cause and your action must have a cause. Mother of the king, everything holds together, our action will have no effect unless we are ourselves implicated, but Mari Djata has done us no wrong. It is, then, difficult for us to compass his death."

"But you are also concerned," replied the queen mother, "for the son of Sogolon will be a scourge to us all."

"The snake seldom bites the foot that does not walk," said one of the witches.

"Yes, but there are snakes that attack everybody. Allow Sundiata to grow up and we will all repent of it. Tomorrow go to Sogolon's vegetable patch and make a show of picking a few gnougou leaves. Mari Djata stands guard there and you will see how vicious the boy is. He won't have any respect for your age, he'll give you a good thrashing."

"That's a clever idea," said one of the old hags.

"But the cause of our discomfiture will be ourselves, for having touched something which did not belong to us."

"We could repeat the offence," said another, "and then if he beats us again we would be able to reproach him with being unkind, heartless. In that case we would be concerned, I think."

"The idea is ingenious," said Soumosso Konkomba. "Tomorrow we shall go to Sogolon's vegetable patch."

"Now there's a happy thought," concluded the queen mother, laughing for joy. "Go to the vegetable patch tomorrow and you will see that Sogolon's son is mean. Beforehand, present yourselves at the royal granaries where you will receive the grain I promised you; the cows and calves are already yours."

The old hags bowed and disappeared into the black night. The queen mother was now alone and gloated over her anticipated victory. But her daughter, Nana Triban, woke up.

"Mother, who were you talking to? I thought I heard voices."

"Sleep, my daughter, it is nothing. You didn't hear anything."

In the morning, as usual, Sundiata got his companions together in front of his mother's hut and said, "What animal are we going to hunt today?"

Kamandjan said, "I wouldn't mind if we attacked some elephants right now."

"Yes, I am of this opinion too," said Fran Kamara. "That will allow us to go far into the bush."

And the young band left after Sogolon had filled the hunting bags with eatables. Sundiata and his companions came back late to the village, but first Djata wanted to take a look at his mother's vegetable patch as was his custom. It was dusk. There he found the nine witches stealing gnougou leaves. They made a show of running away like thieves caught red-handed.

"Stop, stop, poor old women," said Sundiata, "what is the matter with you to run away like this. This garden belongs to all."

Straight away his companions and he filled the gourds of the old hags with leaves, aubergines and onions.

"Each time that you run short of condiments come to stock up here without fear."

"You disarm us," said one of the old crones, and another added, "And you confound us with your bounty."

"Listen, Djata," said Soumosso Konkomba, "we had come here to test you. We have no need of condiments but your generosity disarms us. We were sent here by the queen mother to provoke you and draw the anger of the nocturnal powers upon you. But nothing can be done against a heart full of kindness. And to think that we have already drawn a hundred measures of rice and a hundred measures of millet—and the queen promises us each a cow and her calf in addition. Forgive us, son of Sogolon."

"I bear you no ill-will," said Djata. "Here, I am returning from the hunt with my companions and we have killed ten elephants, so I will give you an elephant each and there you have some meat!"

"Thank you, son of Sogolon."

"Thank you, child of Justice."

"Henceforth," concluded Soumosso Konkomba, "we will watch over you." And the nine witches disappeared into the night. Sundiata and his companions continued on their way to Niani and got back after dark.

"You were really frightened; those nine witches really scared you, eh?" said Sogolon Kolonkan, Djata's young sister.

"How do you know," retorted Sundiata, astonished.

"I saw them at night hatching their scheme, but I knew there was no danger for you." Kolonkan was well versed in the art of witchcraft and watched over her brother without his suspecting it.

Summary Sogolon, knowing the danger that awaited her children in the court ruled by the jealous Sassouma, decided to leave until such time that Djata could return in safety to reign over Mali. In a parting act of malice Dankaran Touman sent Djata's griot, Balla Fasséké, on an embassy to the king of Sosso, Soumaoro Kanté, thereby depriving Djata of his friend and teacher. There Balla Fasséké remained along with Nana Triban until the eve of Soumaoro's major battle with Sundiata.

Vowing to return, Sogolon's son and his family began their seven years of exile during which Sundiata would grow to manhood. After brief stops in Djedeba and Tabon, they remained for a time at the court of the Cisse's at Wagadou. There Sundiata learned much from the merchants and officials engaged in the trans-Saharan trade. After a time the Cisse king sent them on to the king of Mema, his cousin. The king of Mema's hospitality was generous, and Sundiata quickly became a favorite at the court. His first military campaigns were fought on behalf of the king of Mema, and so valorous were his exploits that he soon was named viceroy.

SOUMAORO KANTÉ, THE SORCERER KING

While Sogolon's son was fighting his first campaign far from his native land, Mali had fallen under the domination of a new master, Soumaoro Kanté, king of Sosso.

When the embassy sent by Dankaran Touman arrived at Sosso, Soumaoro demanded that Mali should acknowledge itself tributary to Sosso. Balla Fasséké found delegates from several other kingdoms at Soumaoro's court. With his powerful army of smiths the king of Sosso had quickly imposed his power on everybody. After the defeat of Ghana and Diaghan no one dared oppose him any more. Soumaoro was descended from the line of smiths called Diarisso who first harnessed fire and taught men how to work iron, but for a long time Sosso had remained a little village of no significance. The powerful king of Ghana was the master of the country. Little by little the kingdom of Sosso had grown at the expense of Ghana and now the Kantés dominated their old masters. Like all masters of fire, Soumaoro Kanté was a great sorcerer. His fetishes had a terrible power and it was because of them that all kings trembled before him, for he could deal a swift death to whoever he pleased. He had fortified Sosso with a triple curtain wall and in the middle of the town loomed his palace, towering over the thatched huts of the villages.

He had had an immense seven-storey tower built for himself and he lived on the seventh floor in the midst of his fetishes. This is why he was called "The Untouchable King."

Soumaoro let the rest of the Mandingo embassy return but he kept Balla Fasséké back and threatened to destroy Niani if Dankaran Touman did not make his submission. Frightened, the son of Sassouma immediately made his submission, and he even sent his sister, Nana Triban, to the king of Sosso.

One day when the king was away, Balla Fasséké managed to get right into the most secret chamber of the palace where Soumaoro safeguarded his fetishes. When he had pushed the door open he was transfixed with amazement at what he saw. The walls of the chamber were tapestried with human skins and there was one in the middle of the room on which the king sat; around an earthenware jar nine heads formed a circle; when Balla had opened the door the water had become disturbed and a monstrous snake had raised its head. Balla Fasséké, who was also well versed in sorcery, recited some formulas and everything in the room fell quiet, so he continued his inspection. He saw on a perch above the bed three owls which seemed to be asleep; on the far wall hung strangely-shaped weapons, curved swords and knives with three cutting edges. He looked at the skulls attentively and recognized the nine kings killed by Soumaoro. To the right of the door he discovered a great balafon, bigger than he had ever seen in Mali. Instinctively he pounced upon it and sat down to play. The griot always has a weakness for music, for music is the griot's soul.

He began to play. He had never heard such a melodious balafon. Though scarcely touched by the hammer, the resonant wood gave out sounds of an infinite sweetness, notes clear and as pure as gold dust; under the skilful hand of Balla the instrument had found its master. He played with all his soul and the whole room was filled with wonderment. The drowsy owls, eyes half closed, began to move their heads as though with satisfaction. Everything seemed to come to life upon the strains of this magic music. The nine skulls resumed their earthly forms and blinked at hearing the solemn "Vulture Tune"; with its head resting on the rim, the snake seemed to listen from the jar. Balla Fasséké was pleased at the effect his music had had on the strange inhabitants of this ghoulish chamber, but he quite understood that this balafon was not at all like any other. It was that of a great sorcerer. Soumaoro was the only one to play this instrument. After each victory he would come and sing his own praises. No griot had ever touched it. Not all ears were made to hear that music. Soumaoro was constantly in touch with this xylophone and no matter how far away he was, one only had to touch it for him to know that someone had got into his secret chamber.

The king was not far from the town and he rushed back to his palace and climbed up to the seventh storey. Balla Fasséké heard hurried steps in the corridor and Soumaoro bounded into the room, sword in hand.

"Who is there?" he roared. "It is you, Balla Fasséké!"

The king was foaming with anger and his eyes burnt fiercely like hot embers. Yet without losing his composure the son of Doua changed key and improvised a song in honour of the king:

> There he is, Soumaoro Kanté.
> All hail, you who sit on the skins of kings.
> All hail, Simbon of the deadly arrow.
> I salute you, you who wear clothes of human skin.

This improvised tune greatly pleased Soumaoro and he had never heard such fine words. Kings are only men, and whatever iron cannot achieve against them, words can. Kings, too, are susceptible to flattery, so Soumaoro's anger abated, his heart filled with joy as he listened attentively to this sweet music:

> All hail, you who wear clothes of human skin.
> I salute you, you who sit on the skins of kings.

Balla sang and his voice, which was beautiful, delighted the king of Sosso.

"How sweet it is to hear one's praises sung by someone else; Balla Fasséké, you will nevermore return to Mali for from today you are my griot."

Thus Balla Fasséké, whom king Naré Maghan had given to his son Sundiata, was stolen from the latter by Dankaran Touman; now it was the king of Sosso, Soumaoro Kanté, who, in turn, stole the precious griot from the son of Sassouma Bérété. In this way war between Sundiata and Soumaoro became inevitable.

Summary The second half of the epic relates Sundiata's leave-taking of Mema in response to the pleas for rescue of a search party sent to find him, and tells of his triumphal series of battles against the terrible Soumaoro.

Allied with the armies of his childhood friends and with those who had offered him sanctuary during his exile, Sundiata led a massive force that included the cavalry of Mema and Wagadou; blacksmiths and the mountain Djallonkes; and groups under Fran Kamara of Tabon Wana. A victory at the valley of Tabon was followed by the first clash with Soumaoro's magic at Negueboria. The fame of Sundiata spread until all the sons of Mali were under his banner. But even a warrior like Sundiata was challenged to the limits by Soumaoro's sorcery. He was saved by the clever escape from Sosso of Balla Fasséké and Nana Triban; on the eve of the battle of Krina it was they who revealed Soumaoro's secret taboo. Reunited with his master, the griot Balla Fasséké sang the praises and history of Mali and challenged the assembled armies to prove themselves worthy of their heritage. At Krina, Soumaoro's power and magic were dissolved by Sundiata's mighty army and his destruction of Soumaoro's protective fetish. Despite hard-driven pursuit by Sundiata and Soumaoro's nephew Fakoli, Soumaoro avoided capture and ultimately disappeared into a mountain cave, never to be seen again. The city of Sosso was destroyed, and the rest of Soumaoro's allies now in disarray were vanquished.

The final sections relate the triumphal festival, the Kouroukan Fougan or the Division of the World, and the rebuilding of Sundiata's capital at Niani.

KOUROUKAN FOUGAN OR THE DIVISION OF THE WORLD

Leaving Do, the land of ten thousand guns, Sundiata wended his way to Ka-ba, keeping to the river valley. All his armies converged on Ka-ba and Fakoli and Tabon Wana entered it laden with booty. Sibi Kamandjan had gone ahead of Sundiata to prepare the great assembly which was to gather at Ka-ba, a town situated on the territory belonging to the country of Sibi. . . .

To the north of the town stretches a spacious clearing and it is there that the great assembly was to foregather. King Kamandjan had the whole clearing cleaned up and a great dais was got ready. Even before Djata's arrival the delegations from all the conquered peoples had made their way to Ka-ba. Huts were hastily built to house all these people. When all the armies had reunited, camps had to be set up in the big plain lying between the river and the town. On the appointed day the troops were drawn up on the vast square that had been prepared. As at Sibi, each people was gathered round its king's pennant. Sundiata had put on robes such as are worn by a great Muslim king. Balla Fasséké, the high master of ceremonies, set the allies around Djata's great throne. Everything was in position. The sofas,[7] forming a vast semicircle bristling with spears, stood motionless. The delegations of the various peoples had been planted at the foot of the dais. A complete silence reigned. On Sundiata's right, Balla Fasséké, holding his mighty spear, addressed the throng in this manner:

"Peace reigns today in the whole country; may it always be thus. . . ."

"Amen," replied the crowd, then the herald continued:

"I speak to you, assembled peoples. To those of Mali I convey Maghan Sundiata's greeting; greetings to those of Do, greetings to those of Ghana, to those from Mema greetings, and to those of Fakoli's tribe. Greetings to the Bobo warriors and, finally, greetings to those of Sibi and Ka-ba. To all the peoples assembled, Djata gives greetings.

"May I be humbly forgiven if I have made any omission. I am nervous before so many people gathered together.

"Peoples, here we are, after years of hard trials, gathered around our saviour, the restorer of peace and order. From the east to the west, from the north to the south, everywhere his victorious arms have established peace. I convey to you the greetings of Soumaoro's vanquisher, Maghan Sundiata, king of Mali.

"But in order to respect tradition, I must first of all address myself to the host of us all, Kamandjan, king of Sibi; Djata greets you and gives you the floor."

Kamandjan, who was sitting close by Sundiata, stood up and stepped down from the dais. He mounted his horse and brandished his sword, crying "I salute you all, warriors of Mali, of Do, of Tabon, of Mema, of Wagadou, of Bobo, of Fakoli . . . ; warriors, peace has returned to our homes, may God long preserve it."

"Amen," replied the warriors and the crowd. The king of Sibi continued.

---

[7] Army troops, often of slave origin.

"In the world man suffers for a season, but never eternally. Here we are at the end of our trials. We are at peace. May God be praised. But we owe this peace to one man who, by his courage and his valiance, was able to lead our troops to victory.

"Which one of us, alone, would have dared face Soumaoro? Ay, we were all cowards. How many times did we pay him tribute? The insolent rogue thought that everything was permitted him. What family was not dishonoured by Soumaoro? He took our daughters and wives from us and we were more craven than women. He carried his insolence to the point of stealing the wife of his nephew Fakoli! We were prostrated and humiliated in front of our children. But it was in the midst of so many calamities that our destiny suddenly changed. A new sun arose in the east. After the battle of Tabon we felt ourselves to be men, we realized that Soumaoro was a human being and not an incarnation of the devil, for he was no longer invincible. A man came to us. He had heard our groans and came to our aid, like a father when he sees his son in tears. Here is that man. Maghan Sundiata, the man with two names foretold by the soothsayers.

"It is to you that I now address myself, son of Sogolon, you, the nephew of the valorous warriors of Do. Henceforth it is from you that I derive my kingdom for I acknowledge you my sovereign. My tribe and I place ourselves in your hands. I salute you, supreme chief, I salute you, Fama of Famas.[8] I salute you, Mansa!"[9]

The huzza that greeted these words was so loud that you could hear the echo repeat the tremendous clamour twelve times over. With a strong hand Kamandjan struck his spear in the ground in front of the dais and said, "Sundiata, here is my spear, it is yours."

Then he climbed up to sit in his place. Thereafter, one by one, the twelve kings of the bright savanna country got up and proclaimed Sundiata "Mansa" in their turn. Twelve royal spears were stuck in the ground in front of the dais. Sundiata had become emperor. The old tabala of Niani announced to the world that the lands of the savanna had provided themselves with one single king. When the imperial tabala had stopped reverberating, Balla Fasséké, the grand master

of ceremonies, took the floor again following the crowd's ovation.

"Sundiata, Maghan Sundiata, king of Mali, in the name of the twelve kings of the "Bright Country," I salute you as 'Mansa.' "

The crowd shouted "Wassa, Wassa. . . . Ayé."

It was amid such joy that Balla Fasséké composed the great hymn "Niama" which the griots still sing:

Niama, Niama, Niama,
You, you serve as a shelter for all,
All come to seek refuge under you.
And as for you, Niama,
Nothing serves you for shelter,
God alone protects you.

The festival began. The musicians of all the countries were there. Each people in turn came forward to the dais under Sundiata's impassive gaze. Then the war dances began. The sofas of all the countries had lined themselves up in six ranks amid a great clatter of bows and spears knocking together. The war chiefs were on horseback. The warriors faced the enormous dais and at a signal from Balla Fasséké, the musicians, massed on the right of the dais, struck up. The heavy war drums thundered, the bolons gave off muted notes while the griot's voice gave the throng the pitch for the "Hymn to the Bow." The spearmen, advancing like hyenas in the night, held their spears above their heads; the archers of Wagadou and Tabon, walking with a noiseless tread, seemed to be lying in ambush behind bushes. They rose suddenly to their feet and let fly their arrows at imaginary enemies. In front of the great dais the Kéké-Tigui, or war chiefs, made their horses perform dance steps under the eyes of the Mansa. The horses whinnied and reared, then, overmastered by the spurs, knelt, got up and cut little capers, or else scraped the ground with their hooves.

The rapturous people shouted the "Hymn to the Bow" and clapped their hands. The sweating bodies of the warriors glistened in the sun while the exhausting rhythm of the tam-tams wrenched from them shrill cries. But presently they made way for the cavalry, beloved by Djata. The horsemen of Mema threw their swords in the air and caught them in flight, uttering mighty shouts. A smile of contentment took shape on Sundiata's lips, for he was happy to see his cavalry manoeuvre with so much skill.

---

[8] King of Kings.
[9] Emperor.

In the afternoon the festivity took on a new aspect. It began with the procession of prisoners and booty. Their hands tied behind their backs and in triple file, the Sosso prisoners made their entry into the giant circle. All their heads had been shaved. Inside the circle they turned and passed by the foot of the dais. Their eyes lowered, the poor prisoners walked in silence, abuse heaped upon them by the frenzied crowd. Behind came the kings who had remained faithful to Soumaoro and who had not intended to make their submission. They also had their heads shorn, but they were on horseback so that everyone could see them. At last, right at the back, came Sosso Balla, who had been placed in the midst of his father's fetishes. The fetishes had been loaded onto donkeys. The crowd gave loud cries of horror on seeing the inmates of Soumaoro's grisly chamber. People pointed with terror at the snake's pitcher, the magic balafon, and the king of Sosso's owls. Soumaoro's son Balla, his hands bound, was on a horse but did not dare look up at this throne, which formerly used to tremble with fear at mere talk of his father. In the crowd could be heard:

"Each in his turn, Sosso Balla; lift up your head a bit, impudent little creature!" Or else: "Did you have any idea that one day you would be a slave, you vile fellow!"

"Look at your useless fetishes. Call on them then, son of a sorcerer!"

When Sosso Balla was in front of the dais, Djata made a gesture. He had just remembered the mysterious disappearance of Soumaoro inside the mountain. He became morose, but his griot Balla Fasséké noticed it and so he spoke thus:

"The son will pay for the father, Soumaoro can thank God that he is already dead."

When the procession had finished Balla Fasséké silenced everyone. The sofas got into line and the tam-tams stopped.

Sundiata got up and a graveyard silence settled on the whole place. The Mansa moved forward to the edge of the dais. Then Sundiata spoke as Mansa. Only Balla Fasséké could hear him, for a Mansa does not speak like a town-crier.

"I greet all the peoples gathered here." And Djata mentioned them all. Pulling the spear of Kamandjan, king of Sibi, out of the ground, he said:

"I give you back your kingdom, king of Sibi, for you have deserved it by your bravery; I have known you since childhood and your speech is as frank as your heart is straightforward.

"Today I ratify for ever the alliance between the Kamaras of Sibi and the Keitas of Mali. May these two people be brothers henceforth. In future, the land of the Keitas shall be the land of the Kamaras, and the property of the Kamaras shall be henceforth the property of the Keitas.

"May there nevermore be falsehood between a Kamara and a Keita, and may the Kamaras feel at home in the whole extent of my empire."

He returned the spear to Kamandjan and the king of Sibi prostrated himself before Djata, as is done when honoured by a Fama.

Sundiata took Tabon Wana's spear and said, "Fran Kamara, my friend, I return your kingdom to you. May the Djallonkés and Mandingoes be forever allies. You received me in your own domain, so may the Djallonkés be received as friends throughout Mali. I leave you the lands you have conquered, and henceforth your children and your children's children will grow up at the court of Niani where they will be treated like the princes of Mali."

One by one all the kings received their kingdoms from the very hands of Sundiata, and each one bowed before him as one bows before a Mansa.

Sundiata pronounced all the prohibitions which still obtain in relations between the tribes. To each he assigned its land, he established the rights of each people and ratified their friendships. The Kondés of the land of Do became henceforth the uncles of the imperial family of Keita, for the latter, in memory of the fruitful marriage between Naré Maghan and Sogolon, had to take a wife in Do. The Tounkaras and the Cissés became "banter-brothers" of the Keitas. While the Cissés, Bérétés and Tourés were proclaimed great divines of the empire. No kin group was forgotten at Kouroukan Fougan; each had its share in the division. To Fakoli Koroma, Sundiata gave the kingdom of Sosso, the majority of whose inhabitants were enslaved. Fakoli's tribe, the Koromas, which others call Doumbouya or Sissoko, had the monopoly of the forge, that is, of iron working. Fakoli also received from Sundiata part of the lands situated between the Bafing and Bagbé rivers. Wagadou and Mema kept their kings who continued to bear the title of Mansa, but these two kingdoms acknowledged the suzerainty of the supreme Mansa. The Konaté of Toron became the cadets of the Keitas so that on reaching maturity a Konaté could call himself Keita.

When Sogolon's son had finished distributing lands and power he turned to Balla Fasséké, his griot, and said: "As for you, Balla Fasséké, my griot, I make you grand master of ceremonies. Henceforth the Keitas will choose their griot from your tribe, from among the Kouyatés. I give the Kouyatés the right to make jokes about all the tribes, and in particular about the royal tribe of Keita."

Thus spoke the son of Sogolon at Kouroukan Fougan. Since that time his respected word has become law, the rule of conduct for all the peoples who were represented at Ka-ba.

So, Sundiata had divided the world at Kouroukan Fougan. He kept for his tribe the blessed country of Kita, but the Kamaras inhabiting the region remained masters of the soil.

If you go to Ka-ba, go and see the glade of Kouroukan Fougan and you will see a linké tree planted there, perpetuating the memory of the great gathering which witnessed the division of the world.

.   .   .

With Sundiata peace and happiness entered Niani. Lovingly Sogolon's son had his native city rebuilt. He restored in the ancient style his father's old enclosure where he had grown up. People came from all the villages of Mali to settle in Niani. The walls had to be destroyed to enlarge the town, and new quarters were built for each kin group in the enormous army.

Sundiata had left his brother Manding Bory at Bagadou-Djeliba on the river. He was Sundiata's Kankoro Sigui, that is to say, viceroy. Manding Bory had looked after all the conquered countries. When reconstruction of the capital was finished he went to wage war in the south in order to frighten the forest peoples. He received an embassy from the country of Sangaran where a few Kondé clans had settled, and although these latter had not been represented at Kouroukan Fougan, Sun-

diata granted his alliance and they were placed on the same footing as the Kondés of the land of Do.

After a year Sundiata held a new assembly at Niani, but this one was the assembly of dignitaries and kings of the empire. The kings and notables of all the tribes came to Niani. The kings spoke of their administration and the dignitaries talked of their kings. Fakoli, the nephew of Soumaoro, having proved himself too independent, had to flee to evade the Mansa's anger. His lands were confiscated and the taxes of Sosso were payed directly into the granaries of Niani. In this way, every year, Sundiata gathered about him all the kings and notables; so justice prevailed everywhere, for the kings were afraid of being denounced at Niani.

Djata's justice spared nobody. He followed the very word of God. He protected the weak against the strong and people would make journeys lasting several days to come and demand justice of him. Under his sun the upright man was rewarded and the wicked one punished.

In their new-found peace the villages knew prosperity again, for with Sundiata happiness had come into everyone's home. Vast fields of millet, rice, cotton, indigo and fonio surrounded the villages. Whoever worked always had something to live on. Each year long caravans carried the taxes in kind to Niani. You could go from village to village without fearing brigands. A thief would have his right hand chopped off and if he stole again he would be put to the sword.

New villages and new towns sprang up in Mali and elsewhere. "Dyulas," or traders, became numerous and during the reign of Sundiata the world knew happiness.

There are some kings who are powerful through their military strength. Everybody trembles before them, but when they die nothing but ill is spoken of them. Others do neither good nor ill and when they die they are forgotten. Others are feared because they have power, but they know how to use it and they are loved because they love justice. Sundiata belonged to this group. He was feared, but loved as well. He was the father of Mali and gave the world peace. After him the world has not seen a greater conqueror, for he was the seventh and last conqueror. He had made the capital of an empire out of his father's village, and Niani became the navel of the earth.

COMMENTS AND QUESTIONS

1. What is the griot Djeli Mamadou Kouyaté's conception of his role of historian? How would he define history? Does his definition differ from ours?
2. What is the Malinke view of fate or destiny as expressed here?
3. In the section "Soumaoro Kanté, the Sorcerer King," you read, "His fetishes had a terrible power. . . ." *Fetish* means here an object believed to contain a supernatural power that may be used to protect the owner of the fetish or may be directed to harm another person. In this case Soumaoro used his fetishes to protect himself and to confuse his enemies. How does it appear that Soumaoro's power vanished when their secret was discovered?
4. What are the attributes of the hero as expressed in this Malian epic? How does it correspond with views expressed in the Greek epics?
5. What are the ideals of government and of good leadership?
6. Seek out some *proverbs* from the text. How do they inform us in a capsulized way of Malinke values?

Myths

Myths, as we saw in the section on Greek mythology (Chapter 1), are intimately allied with the religious beliefs and the values of a particular culture. Unlike legends or epics, they are not based on historical events but attempt rather to explain or clarify the primal mysteries of nature, creation, and man's relationship with the gods. African myths are primarily oral; they are told and sung. They are often used in religious rituals; but, because there are a great many African religions, there is also a tremendous variety in African mythology. It is possible, nevertheless, to identify certain common features in the religions of the West African peoples under consideration here and to trace fundamental themes in their mythology. Since religion is such an important and unifying element of African culture, an understanding of some of the basic African beliefs will be useful in studying all aspects of that culture.

African Religions: Some Generalizations All West African religions postulate the existence of a su-

preme God (whose name varies with the culture), associated with the creation of the universe. One of the great questions that the African myths ask is, Why is this God now so distant from the human world? The answer (as in the Judeo-Christian doctrine of the Fall) seems to lie in the fact of man's imperfection. African myths show in a variety of ways how the supreme deity, exasperated with human perversity or troublesomeness, simply withdrew from his creation, leaving the administration of it to lesser gods, natural spirits, or ancestors of living humans. Unlike the Judeo-Christian God, the African supreme being did not return to intervene in human affairs. People in Africa rarely worship the high God by direct means; rather they seek understanding and redress through lesser deities and spirits, each of whom represents an aspect of God. Communication between men and these highly charged spiritual forces is achieved through rituals in honor of them and through sacrifice.

Another important feature of African religion is the belief in the spiritual vitality of the natural world or, as it is called in the West, animism. According to this belief, supernatural spirits or "souls" (Latin, *anima*) may inhabit the bodies of animals or even inanimate parts of nature such as trees, rocks, forests, mountains, and rivers. These spirits are often guardian spirits who must be acknowledged and appeased, for some of them are capable of causing or controlling events in the natural world. The blessings of resident spirits must be sought, for example, when a new settlement is built.

The spirits inhabiting the natural world are nonhuman in origin and therefore close to the realm of the gods. Nearer to the world of men are the spirits of ancestors, the dead, whose souls are very much present in the everyday world and who may, for example, come to inhabit the body of a new baby. While the ancestral souls do not have "power" like the spirits, they do have "awareness" and can be communicated with. They may act as mediators between the living and the spirits.

All of the spirits are believed to be inherently neither good nor evil—they can affect human lives in either positive or negative ways. The beautiful and beneficent natural world can also be malevolent and destructive. To live in it, one must acknowledge those powerful forces that are outside of, but intrinsically part of, the cycles of one's life. Because of this complex relationship of people to the phenomena of the world, there is a profound duality that pervades every aspect of African life. For example, one may believe in sky spirits and earth spirits, and they may contradict each other. Some spirits, such as the "tricksters," may embody contradictory traits. It is up to human wit and ingenuity to learn to appease the spirits and to determine what course to take.

The myths that follow address themselves, in the context of African religion, to three basic questions: (1) How did the world begin? (creation); (2) What caused God to withdraw from the world of men? and (3) Why do people have to die? The two creation myths are Yoruba; they require a word of explanation on Yoruba religion, which will be discussed more fully in the poetry section. The highest God, named Oludumare or Olorun, has many aspects, which are represented by lesser deities called *orisha*. One of these is Obatala, god of creation.

Two Yoruba Myths of Creation

THE CREATION OF LAND

At the beginning everything was water. Then Oludumare the supreme god sent Obatala (or Orishanla) down from heaven to create the dry land. Obatala descended on a chain and he carried with him: a snail shell filled with earth, some pieces of crow and a cock. When he arrived he placed the crow on the water, spread the earth over it and placed the cock on top. The cock immediately started to scratch and thus the land spread far and wide.

When the land had been created, the other Orisha descended from heaven in order to live on the land with Obatala.

THE CREATION OF MAN

Obatala made man out of earth. After shaping men and women he gave them to Oludumare to blow in the breath of life.

One day Obatala drank palm wine. Then he started to make hunchbacks and cripples, albinos and blind men.

From that day onwards hunchbacks and albinos and all deformed persons are sacred to Obatala. But his worshipers are forbidden to drink palm wine.

Obatala is still the one who gives shape to the new babe in the mother's womb.

QUESTIONS

1. How is the role of the supreme God, Oludumare, distinguished from that of the orisha Obatala?
2. What similarities and differences do you find in these creation myths and the story of creation in Genesis?

Myths on the Separation of Man from God

[This myth comes from the Yao, one of a cluster of peoples speaking Bantu languages who live in northern Mozambique and adjacent lands in Tanzania. The translator of this myth, and those following, is Susan Feldmann.]

MULUNGU AND THE BEASTS

In the beginning man was not, only Mulungu and his people, the beasts. They lived happily on earth.

One day a chameleon found a human pair in his fish trap. He had never seen such creatures before and he was surprised. The chameleon reported his discovery to Mulungu. Mulungu said, "Let us wait and see what the creatures will do."

The men started making fires. They set fire to the bush so that the beasts fled into the forest. Then the men set traps and killed Mulungu's people. At last Mulungu was compelled to leave the earth. Since he could not climb a tree he called for the spider.

The spider spun a thread up to the sky and down again. When he returned he said, "I have gone on high nicely, now you Mulungu go on high." And Mulungu ascended to the sky on the spider's thread to escape from the wickedness of men.

[The following myth comes from the Ngombe, one of the many Mongo groups who live in the heart of the equatorial rain forest of Zaire. Their language and culture form part of the larger Bantu-speaking peoples of central and southern Africa.]

WITHDRAWAL OF GOD

Akongo was not always as he is now. In the beginning the creator lived among men; but men were quarrelsome. One day they had a big quarrel and Akongo left them to themselves. He went and hid in the forest and nobody has seen him since. People today can't tell what he is like.

[The next two are from the Ashanti peoples of modern Ghana. They are one of the populous Akan cultural complex, one of whose characteristics is matrilineal descent. The Ashanti state, founded around 1680, became a principal political power on the Gold Coast during the eighteenth and nineteenth centuries. Its greatness lay in part because of the European trade and in part because it integrated under its king (the *asantehene*) and ruling council many more of the Akan peoples into one state than had been achieved before. The Ashanti were also splendid craftsmen whose court art, textiles, and gold weights are among the highest achievements of West African art.]

THE TOWER TO HEAVEN

Long, long ago Onyankopon lived on earth, or at least was very near to us. Now there was a certain old woman who used to pound her mashed yams and the pestle kept knocking up against Onyankopon, who was not then high in the sky. So Onyankopon said to the old woman: "Why do you keep doing this to me? Because of what you are doing I am going to take myself away up in the sky." And of a truth he did so.

Now the people could no longer approach Onyankopon. But the old woman thought of a way to reach him and bring him back. She instructed her children to go and search for all the mortars they could find and bring them to her. Then she told them to pile one mortar on top of another til they reached to where Onyankopon was. And her children did so, they piled up many mortars, one on top of another, til they needed only one more mortar to reach Onyankopon.

Now, since they could not find another mortar anywhere, their grandmother the old woman said to them: "Take one out from the bottom and put it on top to make them reach." So her children removed a mortar from the bottom and all the mortars rolled and fell to the ground, causing the death of many people.

QUESTIONS ON MYTHS ON THE SEPARATION OF MAN FROM GOD

1. What generalization can you make from these myths about the basic cause of man's fall from his idyllic relationship with God?
2. What is the difference between the relationship between God and man and that between God and the animals in "Mulungu and the Beasts"?
3. What does "The Tower to Heaven" say about human ingenuity in relation to God? Compare the biblical story of the tower of Babel.

Myths on the Origin of Death

THE PERVERTED MESSAGE

In primeval times, God had familiar intercourse with men and gave them all they needed. This state, however, came to an end when some women who were grinding their food became embarrassed by God's presence and told him to go away, and beat him with their pestles. God then withdrew from the world, and left its government to the spirits.

Afterward God sent a goat from heaven to the seven human beings on earth with the following message: "There is something called death. One day it will kill some of you. Even if you die, however, you will not be altogether lost. You will come to live with me in the sky."

On the way, the goat lingered at a bush in order to eat, and when God discovered this he sent a sheep with the same message. But the sheep changed the message to the effect that men should die, and that as far as they were concerned this would be the end of all things. When the goat then arrived with her true message, men would not believe it. They had already accepted the message delivered by the sheep. Shortly afterward the first case of death took place, and God taught men to bury their dead. He also told them that as a foil to death they should be given the capacity to multiply.

According to another version, God sent the sheep with eternal life as a gift to men. But the he-goat ran on ahead and gave them death as a gift from God. They eagerly accepted this gift, as they did not know what death was. The sheep arrived after a while, but it was too late.

[The Efe are a small branch of the Mbuti hunting and gathering peoples who live in the Ituri forest of Zaire. They are seminomadic and often live in symbiotic relationships with nearby black African groups. This myth is from the Efe.]

FORBIDDEN FRUIT

God created the first human being Ba-atsi with the help of the moon. He kneaded the body into shape, covered it with a skin, and poured in blood. When the man had thus been given life, God whispered in his ear that he, Ba-atsi, should beget children, and upon them he should impress the following prohibition: "Of all the trees of the forest you may eat, but of the Tahu tree you may not eat." Ba-atsi had many children, impressed upon them the prohibition, and then retired to heaven. At first men respected the commandment they had been given, and lived happily. But one day a pregnant woman was seized with an irresistible desire to eat of the forbidden fruit. She tried to persuade her husband to give her some of it. At first he refused, but after a time he gave way. He stole into the wood, picked a Tahu fruit, peeled it, and hid the peel among the leaves. But the moon had seen his action and reported it to God. God was so enraged over man's disobedience that as punishment he sent death among them.

[The following myth comes from the Darasa, one of a cluster of ancient Cushitic peoples who practice intensive agriculture by irrigation and terracing of mountain slopes in southern Ethiopia.]

MAN CHOOSES DEATH IN EXCHANGE FOR FIRE

Formerly men had no fire but ate all their food raw. At that time they did not need to die for when they became old, God made them young again. One day they decided to beg God for fire. They sent a messenger to God to convey their request. God replied to the messenger that he would give him fire if he was prepared to die. The man took the fire from God, but ever since then all men must die.

[Madagascar, the source of this next myth, lies in the Indian Ocean off the southeastern coast of Africa. Its peoples include descendants of both mainland Africans and Malayo-Polynesians who probably followed the seasonal trade winds from southeast Asia to settle on the island around the beginning of the Christian era.]

MAN CHOOSES DEATH IN EXCHANGE FOR CHILDREN

One day God asked the first human couple who then lived in heaven what kind of death they wanted, that of the moon or that of the banana. Because the couple wondered in dismay about the implications of the two modes of death, God explained to them: the banana puts forth shoots which take its place and the moon itself comes back to life. The couple considered for a long time before they made their choice. If they elected to be childless they would avoid death, but they would also be very lonely, would themselves be forced to carry out all the work, and would not have anybody to work and strive for. Therefore they prayed to God for children, well aware of the consequences of their choice. And their prayer was granted. Since that time man's sojourn is short on this earth.

QUESTIONS ON MYTHS ON THE ORIGIN OF DEATH

1. Notice the closeness of animals to God in comparison to men. How do you interpret the significance of the "perverted message"?
2. Compare "Forbidden Fruit" with the similar story in Genesis. Is the religious message of the two stories the same?
3. What is the cultural significance of fire? Why would man choose it over immortality? Look up the Greek myth of Prometheus to compare it with this.
4. How are the importance of children and continuity of the community over time expressed? Notice the expression of this value in other aspects of African culture.

Tales (Hausa)

Myths have to do with gods, spirits, and religious questions; but *tales*, the second type of oral prose literature, are more concerned with the social world of human beings. All African oral literatures contain a large body of tales, divided into distinct types according to their purpose, the context in which they are told, and the status of the teller.

Taken from the oral literature of the Hausa, the following tales exemplify the two main types told by these people. *Tatsuniyoyi* are entertaining stories about animals and people, generally told by the older women to young children around the fire at night. They cloak lessons in social etiquette, morality, and personal values in amusing, memorable stories. The other type, *labarai*, are told by old men to each other and to young male adults. Their subject matter is most often cultural, family, and group history. While not to be taken literally, the labarai contain factual occurrences and represent for any given period of time the Hausa's view of their own past.

The labarai example below, "The Origin of All Kings"—sometimes called the Daura legend—relates the origin of the Hausa city-state political system. The legend probably developed in the eighteenth century at a time when Bornu, a kingdom to the east, exercised subtle political influence over the Hausa states. The attribution of Eastern origin (in this case Baghdad) is common among Islamic states in West Africa. The translator of this selection, and of the following tatsuniyoyi tales (with the exception of "The Kano Man," originally compiled by Frank Edgar) is Roberta Ann Dunbar.

Labarai Tale

THE ORIGIN OF ALL KINGS

This is the story of the first Kings of Daura, Kano, Katsina Gobir, Zazzau (Zaria) and Nuru (Rano), who descended from a man named Bayajibda, son of Abdullahi, King of Baghdad. Now the reason Bayajibda left Baghdad was that a heathen named Zidawa made war against them—a devastating war—and their land was divided into 40 parts.

Bayajibda went with twenty towards Bornu. Together with his soldiers they were a greater and more powerful force than the men of the King of Bornu. The Bornu king came from Syria. When Bayajibda's men realized they were more powerful than those of the King of Bornu they said to him, "Let's kill the King of Bornu so that you may succeed him."

But the King of Bornu hearing this was wary and could not be killed. The King of Bornu asked, "What is our plan for these intruders, my countrymen? The only plan I can see is to marry him off." So Bayajibda was given a daughter of the King named Magira to marry.

Peace and trust developed between them. When he went out on campaigns, Bayajibda would say to the King of Bornu, "Give me some of your men. I will take them to some villages and together we will conquer them." Sometimes he was given two thousand men; at others three thousand. But when he returned from war, he would not return with them. Rather, he set them up in towns in Bornu's territory.

After a time there were only two of Bayajibda's fellow countrymen left. He said to them, "Brothers, I want to look for a place for each of you to live." He set out with one of them and went to Kanem. He is King of Kanem. He set out with the other and went to Bagirmi. He is King of Bagirmi. Then Bayajibda, now alone, left, accompanied by his wife, the daughter of the King of Bornu, and his horse.

When the Bornu people saw that Bayajibda was alone, they kept trying to seek him out to kill him. Because of this he fled at great pace with his wife Magira who was pregnant. In this way they arrived at a certain town called Gabas. Bayajibda left his wife there as she was unable to travel further, and continued on his way. After his departure, she bore a son who was named Biram. He became King of Gabas, or as it was called Gabas of Biram.

When Bayajibda reached Daura, a queen was ruling there. Among the women who had ruled in Daura before, the first was Kufunu. After her the next was Gufunu, then Yakunu, Yakunya, Waizam, Waiwaina, Gidirgidir, Anagari, and Daura. It was she whom Bayajibda found ruling when he came.

When he arrived he alighted at the house of an old woman named Awaina and asked her to give him water. But she said to him, "Alas, my son, one can get water in this town only on Friday when people are gathered together." He replied, "I will draw water. Give me a bucket." She brought a bucket and gave him. It was nighttime when they spoke together about this.

When he had taken the bucket, he went to the well and dropped the bucket down inside. Now in the well lived a female snake. When the snake heard someone drop the bucket, she raised her head from the well and tried to kill Bayajibda. The name of the snake was Sarki. But he took out his sword, cut off her head and took the head and hid it. He drew water, drank and gave some to his horse. He took the rest to the old woman Awaina. He went into the house and lay down to rest.

At daybreak, people saw what this Arab from Syria had done. They were surprised at the size of what remained of the snake at the well. In a while the news reached Daura and she came with her warriors to the well site.

When the queen saw that the snake's head had been cut off and what remained behind, she was filled with wonder because this thing had so harassed the people. She said, "If I discover whoever has killed this snake, I will divide the kingdom in two and give him half." One man said, "I killed it." She asked, "Where is its head? If he doesn't show the head he is lying." So that man left. Another man came and exclaimed, "It was I who killed it." This one too was lying. Many men came forward, but each one was proclaiming himself falsely.

Then the old woman appeared and said, "Last night a stranger stopped at my house. He came with an animal, though whether it was an ox or a horse, I don't know. He took the bucket, drew water from the well, drank and gave some to his animal, bringing me the rest of it. Perhaps he is the one who killed the snake. We should find him and ask." So Bayajibda was summoned and Daura asked him, "Are you the one who killed the snake?" "It was I," he replied. She said, "Where is its head?" "Here it is," he said. Then the queen said, "I promised that for whoever did this thing, I would divide my town in two and give him half." He said, "Do not divide your town. As for me, I request your hand in marriage." So she married him and he lived in her house. She gave him a slave girl whom he took as a concubine. When people came to Daura's house they didn't say her name. Rather they said, "We are going to the house of Makas-Sarki, 'the killer of Sarki'." Thus it happened that she assumed the name Sarki [the Hausa word for chief].

After some time, the concubine became pregnant although Daura did not. The concubine gave birth to a son. Bayajibda sought Daura's permission and she gave it to name him Makarabgari (Receiver of the town). After this Daura became pregnant and when she gave birth to a son, she sought her husband's permission to name him. They agreed and the child was called Bawugari. He was the first of the kings.

When Makas-Sarki, his father, died, Bawugari inherited his father's dwelling place and bore six children. The first named Gazaura, was King of Daura. Another of the same mother named Bagauda became King of Kano. Another son named Gunguma became King of Zazzau and another by the same mother named Dami became King of Gobir. The last two, also of the same mother, were Kumayau who became King of Katsina and Zamgugu who was King of Rano.

Thus ends the story of the kings.

COMMENTS AND QUESTIONS

1. The marriage between an indigenous queen and a newcomer is not an uncommon motif in legends of origin and may reflect the transition from an earlier matrilineal or matriarchal stage to a patrilineal and patriarchal stage in society. This kind of marriage is also a frequent way of explaining accommodation between foreign invaders and local people over whom they had established hegemony. Compare the story of Oedipus.

2. Political power was recognized not only because of military conquest, but also because of technological expertise. Bayajibda killed the snake that had restricted Daura's water supply; he also came with an animal, the horse, unfamiliar to the old woman who gave him shelter. Does this suggest anything to you about levels of technology or modes of warfare in pre-Bayajibda Hausa society?

3. Compare this tale with the epic *Sundiata*. Is Bayajibda a hero in the same sense that Sundiata is? What is the difference in the way in which an epic and a tale present a hero?

Tatsuniyoyi Tales

DOG, HYENA, AND LIZARD

Dog got up from his sickbed and was hungry. He saw Lizard stealing some beans, grabbed him, and headed for home. On the way he ran into Hyena. Dog dropped Lizard and took to his heels. Hyena said, "Let me take this thing in hand home first before I come back to take that thing in the bush." So she picked up Lizard and carried him to her hole. Then she came back looking for Dog, but couldn't find him. She went home and Lizard was gone. Poor Hyena said,

"Alas, whatever you manage to get hold of in this world, if it is not your fate to have it, having gotten it is useless—you'll lose it anyway."

TWO FROGS

One day two frogs fell into a calabash of milk and couldn't get out. They swam around for a while, then one of them tired out and said,

"Today my days are finished."

So he gave up and sank to the bottom and died.

But the other frog kept on swimming and swimming. He churned the milk so hard with all of his swimming, that it turned into butter. The frog climbed on top of the ball of butter and jumped out of the calabash.

God said, "Rise so that I may help you."

SQUIRREL AND HEDGEHOG

One day it was raining. Hedgehog was wandering around when she came to the door of Squirrel's hole. She greeted him and said,

"I'm really cold. Is there any room there for me to take shelter?"

Squirrel said,

"There's a little space here, come on in."

They sat down together. After a while Squirrel said,

"Hey Hedgehog, our being together like this isn't very pleasant. Your body is all prickly. Why don't you go find another spot?"

Hedgehog said,

"Gee, this place is fine for me. Whoever doesn't find this place suitable, *he* should be the one to move!"

THE BLIND MAN WITH THE LAMP

A young man was strolling along one night when he caught sight of a man with a lamp. When he drew near he realized that the man was blind. The boy said,

"Hey blind man, have you lost your senses? What brings you to wandering around with a lamp? Aren't day and night all the same to you?"

The blind man said,

"Of course they are, stupid. Even at night I see better than you do. I don't carry this lamp for myself, but so that you silly people without eyes don't bump into me."

LIFE IS BETTER THAN WEALTH

Once there was a man who was so poor he didn't know what to do. So he went to the king and said,

"I don't have anything to eat for today, or for tomorrow either. I don't have anything at all in the world save this loincloth. I'm tired of living. I want you to kill me."

The king said,

"All right."

He called some soldiers and told them to kill the man so that he could find rest. The soldiers were about to dispatch him when another came by and said,

"If you kill him, please give me his loincloth."

When the poor man heard that he said,

"Stop! Take me back to the king. I have something to say."

So they took him back and the king asked them what happened. The poor man fell on his knees and said,

"Your highness, let me go. Today I have seen someone poorer than I am. Truly, life is great."

The king said,

"Be off with you and thank God that he has given you life and health."

HASARA AND RIBA

Hasara and Riba were sisters—same mother same father. Hasara was an extremely beautiful girl but poor Riba was ugly. Tinau and Sule sought their hands in marriage. Tinau was richer and better looking than Sule and he courted Hasara. So Sule proceeded to court Riba. The couples were married at the same time and each girl went to the home of her husband.

Now Hasara was proud and haughty. She liked elegant food, jewelry, and very expensive clothes. Riba, however, worked together with her husband. She helped him take goods to market and when they earned a profit, they put aside half of it, using the rest for their trading. Before a year was out Sule was a rich man. Tinau by that time was flat broke. To make a long story short, Tinau left Hasara with all her beauty. She married another and the same thing happened. Before the second year was past, Hasara had been married four times. But Riba is still there with her husband Sule. They are very prosperous and even have many cattle with shepherds to look after them. Whoever follows his heart's desire surely he will be wed to loss.

THE RIVALS

There were two boys who were courting the same girl. She couldn't decide which to accept, so she told them she would marry whichever one was the braver.

One day, the boys went to her place for a chat. When they got ready to go home, she accompanied them to the edge of the "bush." Suddenly, a leopard came upon them. The first boy hurled his spear at the leopard but missed it. The other did the same. They continued until all their spears were gone. Meanwhile the girl hid behind a tree. Then, one boy said to the other,

"Hurry home to my mother's house. There are some spears there near the bed. Gather them up and bring them back."

When the other boy departed, the one left behind fell on the leopard and wrestled with it. He got the leopard down and killed it. Then, he propped the leopard up, called to the girl, and told her to lie down in front of it. He then hid himself.

The other boy returned without any spears since they had already been borrowed by someone else. He came upon the leopard where he had left it and saw the girl lying on the ground in front of it. The boy said,

"Oh no, is that the way he is? He gets rid of me so that he can run off and lets the leopard kill the poor girl?"

Then he attacked the leopard with full force and grabbed it around the neck. The leopard's body fell over in a heap. The boy who had been hiding came out laughing.

So now, which one of them will the girl marry?

THE KANO MAN

This is the sharp fellow, the city slicker.

His character: A Kano man puts on a dark-blue gown, and a white Nupe one, and a black-and-white one; then he wears Kano-style trousers, either white or black-and-white; puts on a length of muslin for a turban; hangs a book over his shoulder and off he goes to school to recite the Koran; he takes a staff, a little gourd water-bottle, and away he goes. When he has fin-ished at school, he returns home. When it is time for market he goes to market. Returning from there, when it is night, he puts on a leather loincloth, picks up a rope-ladder, and off he goes to steal. Sometimes he gets shot or wounded with a sword, and sometimes dies, and sometimes gets better.

The Kano character is also, if a rich visitor arrives, to receive him joyfully, and give him a gown, or a turban or a length of cloth. Then they get together with one of the household where he is staying and start bringing shoddy stuff to sell him. When the householder sees it, he praises its quality. They abuse his trust in them and trick him. But if the visitor is shrewd, he rejects all the stuff they bring him, saying, "I'm not buying it," and waits till he gets to the market and buys what he wants.

Trickery and fraud are Kano characteristics. Whoever you are, a Kano man will trick you—unless he thinks it can't be done. For there is no one so cowardly.

COMMENTS AND QUESTIONS

1. A major characteristic of African tales evident in the Hausa tatsuniyoyi is their realism and recognition of the flaws in human nature and in society. Some tales exhort people to good behavior; others express stereotypes about people from different places or walks of life as seen here in "The Kano Man." Kano was and is a major commercial center. Its markets attracted merchants from all over West and North Africa. How does this tale's image of the Kano man—the quintessential merchant—compare with our own image of the "city slicker"?

2. *Hasara* and *Riba* are not usual Hausa names as suggested in that story. Rather they are respectively the Hausa words for "loss" and "profit." What does this tale tell you about values of work and discipline?

3. What other Hausa values are expressed in these tales?

4. What shows you that these tales are well grounded in the socioeconomic realities of the Hausa people?

5. What model is suggested in the tales "Hasara and Riba" and "The Rivals" for a proper relationship between husband and wife?

6. Do the morals to these tales appear to be "tacked on," or are they woven into the fabric of the story? Give examples.

Riddles

Riddles, like folk tales, are most often told at night around the fire. They, too, form the early associations in the mind of the young person with the wisdom and style of his elders. Frequently uttered as a statement rather than as a question, the essence of the idea and metaphors drawn instruct the young in the indirect but pithy aphorisms of life. In addition to allusions to the natural world that approach the poetic, riddles, like some poetry, allow explicit sexual references. The cleverness and wit of the stock phrases create the entertainment and memorability of the occasion. These riddles are reprinted from *Black Orpheus*, and the *Journal of American Folklore*.

Yoruba Riddles

A round calabash in the spear grass.
Ans.: Moon and stars.

We cut its head, we cut its tail. It still insists on performing the ritual of its ancestors.
Ans.: A piece of cassava. However small a piece you cut—it will still grow.

We tie a horse in the house, but its mane flies above the roof.
Ans.: Fire and smoke.

We invited him to warm himself in the sun—he came. We asked him to take his bath. He said: death has come.
Ans.: Salt.

One cooked yam all over the world.
Ans.: The moon.

They cut off his head; they cut off his waist; his stump says he will inherit the title of his father's house.
Ans.: Yam.

Children walking; mother crawling.
Ans.: Gourd.

It bears fruit, we cannot pick it; the fruit falls, we cannot gather it.
Ans.: Dew.

Fat wife inside many thorns.
Ans.: Tongue and teeth.

Ancient will of my father, ancient will of my father; if a child gets into it, it reaches his neck; if an elder gets into it, it reaches his neck.
Ans.: A shirt or gown.

We seize hold of it; the child in its womb walks away.
Ans.: Gun.

Who is it that goes down the street past the king's house without greeting the king?
Ans.: Rainwater.

My father complained that I was late coming back from the farm. I said the road divided into three and I had to travel on three paths simultaneously.
Ans.: Putting on trousers.

People run away from her when she is pregnant. But they rejoice when she has delivered.
Ans.: A gun.

Proverbs

Proverbs have a special place in oral literature. Rather than being told for entertainment like riddles and tales, they are most often used within conversation and, more formally, in the litigation of disputes within a community. The fluency with which a speaker can use proverbs is widely accepted as a measure of one's literary skill. Social relationships, philosophical observations, and ultimate moral values are illuminated in proverbs.

The Yoruba proverbs included below are keys to the values of the Yoruba people. They sometimes express a surprising candor about political relationships, hospitality, and attitudes toward the elderly—areas where candor outside of proverbial speech would be impolitic and rude. The translators are Bakare Gbadamosi and Ulli Beier.

Yoruba Proverbs

The egg eater does not think of the pain it cost the hen.

The dignified crawl of the earthworm arouses the envy of the cock.

A man has been beaten six times and is advised to be patient. What else is there for him to do?

When death is not ready to receive a man, it sends an expert physician at the right time.

A bachelor who asks for food too often will soon hear the price of vegetables.

The small hand of the child cannot reach the high shelf. The large hand of the adult cannot enter the neck of the calabash.

Only the man whom his child buries has really got a child.

It is the honour of the father that allows the son to walk about proudly.

We are talking about pumpkins. A woman asks what are we talking about. We say: this is a man's talk. But when we gather the fruit, who will break them and cook them?

Anger does not help. Patience is the father of character.

The river carries away an elderly person who does not know his own weight.

The thinking of a wolf is enough to tail a sheep.

What only stops a hawk from laughing will make the hen faint on her eggs.

The eagle makes the owner of the fowl go crazy.

The wisdom of others prevents a chief from being called a fool.

The god who favors a lazy man does not exist. It is one's hands that bring prosperity.

Everybody who comes to this world must become something. Only we don't know what.

The effort of forcing another man to be like oneself makes one an unpleasant person.

What causes a dog to bark is not sufficient to make a sheep gaze.

Having become king you prepare charms. Do you want to become a god?

One who takes another to court does not think that the other man has his own statement to make.

After the man has been cured, he beats the doctor.

The proud pond stands alone from the river, forgetting that water is common to both.

Mean people are common like trees in the forest.

An elderly man who cannot keep his mouth shut when he sees something strange, must use his mouth in court.

Do not be seen counting the toes of the man who has only nine.

QUESTIONS

1. What Yoruba social values and philosophical beliefs can you discern in the riddles? In the proverbs?
2. Attempt to define "riddle" as a literary genre. Which riddles here show evidence of a sophisticated wit?
3. Can you compare any of the proverbs here with those in the Bible?

Poetry

Most of the poems that follow have been taken from the rich oral tradition of the Yoruba language. They represent not only a wide variety of forms and subjects but also the intimate relationship that exists between poetry and everyday life in Africa. Two non-Yoruba poems illustrating this relationship are a Fulani love poem and the naming poem from the Ga people in Ghana. In addition, we have included three modern poems written in European languages but making use of traditional themes.

The ritual character of the first four Yoruba poems calls for a further explanation of Yoruba religion and traditional forms of Yoruba poetry. We saw in the mythology section that in Yoruba belief the first, high God, Olorun, is represented on earth by lesser deities called orisha. Orisha may also symbolize ancestor figures, ancient kings, and founders of cities. Each orisha is associated with some form of nature, or with a particular color or metal. Each of the four poems is a praise poem dedicated to one of the orisha. The first is about Obatala, god of creation (recall the Yoruba myths of creation); the second on Eshu, the unpredictable god of fate and the agent for change, good and bad. The subject of the third is Oshun, the mother goddess, protector of the town of Oshogbo and source of healing and fertility; and that of the fourth, Ogun, whose association with iron and war is linked to survival, innovation, and technology. These poems are classified as *oriki* by the Yoruba—meaning poems based on names given to gods, places, rulers, and important persons. The oriki poetry is performed by professional singers or, in the case of poems about deities such as these, by the priests of the particular deity whose oriki is being sung.

Yoruba poetry is classified by the style of specific groups of performers more than by subject matter or poetic form. Whereas the oriki are sung by priests, *ijala* are sung by hunters, and the *iwi*, represented by "Children," are poems sung by the *egungun*, the masqueraders. These have a specific religious function: they mediate between the community of the living and that of the recently dead. Masqueraders embody the spirit and imitate the voice of the person involved; during the ceremonial, dances are sacred. Reflecting the high degree of integration of religious beliefs with other aspects of social life, masqueraders may also entertain, sometimes offering social satires and commentaries.

In addition to being concerned with man's relationship to god and the spirits, all African poetry marks important experiences or transitions in the lives of people —as seen in the funeral, love, and naming poems. In the Ga naming poem, as in the Yoruba iwi on children, the fragility of life, the desirability of children, and their symbolic importance as links between the living and dead appear as critical elements of belief.

The final three poems—written by Birago Diop, a Senegalese who writes in French, and Chinua Achebe and Wole Soyinka, two Nigerians who write in English—illustrate the fact that modern African writers continue to draw inspiration from traditional beliefs and from the themes and styles of oral literature. The Yoruba poetry is translated by Bakare Gbadamosi and Ulli Beier; the Ga poem by Neils Augustine Hesse.

Oriki—Yoruba Praise Poems

ORIKI OBATALA

He is patient, he is not angry.
He sits in silence to pass judgement.
He sees you even when he is not looking.
He stays in a far place—but his eyes are on the town.

The granary of heaven can never be full.
The old man full of life force.

He kills the novice.
And wakens him to let him hear his words.
We leave the world to the owner of the world.
Death acts playfully till he carries away the child.
He rides on the hunchback.
He stretches out his right hand.
He stretches out his left hand.

He stands by his children and lets them succeed.
He causes them to laugh—and they laugh.
Ohoho—the father of laughter.
His eye is full of joy,
He rests in the sky like a swarm of bees.

We dance to your sixteen drums that sound jingin,
    jingin,
To eight of the drums we dance bending down,

To eight of the drums we dance erect.
We shake our shoulders, we shake our hips,
Munusi, munusi, munusi,
We dance to your sixteen drums.

Those who are rich owe their property to him.
Those who are poor, owe their property to him.
He takes from the rich and gives to the poor.
Whenever you take from the rich—come and give it to
    me!

Obatala—who turns blood into children.
I have only one cloth to dye with blue indigo.
I have only one headtie to dye with red camwood.
But I know that you keep twenty or thirty children for
    me
Whom I shall bear.

ORIKI ESHU

When he is angry he hits a stone until it bleeds.
When he is angry he sits on the skin of an ant.
When he is angry he weeps tears of blood.

Eshu, confuser of men.
The owner of twenty slaves is sacrificing,
So that Eshu may not confuse him.
The owner of thirty "iwofa" is sacrificing,
So that Eshu may not confuse him.
Eshu confused the newly married wife.
When she stole the cowries from the sacred shrine of
    Oya
She said she had not realized
That taking two hundred cowries was stealing.
Eshu confused the head of the queen—
And she started to go naked.
Then Eshu beat her to make her cry.
Eshu, do not confuse me!
Eshu, do not confuse the load on my head.

Eshu, lover of dogs.
If a goat gets lost in Ogbe,—don't ask me.
Do you think I am a thief of goats?
If a huge sheep is missing from Ogbe—don't ask me.
Do you think I am a thief of sheep?
If any fowl get lost in Ogbe—don't ask me.
Do you think I am a thief of birds?

But if a black dog is missing from Ogbe—ask me!
You will find me eating Eshu's sacrifice in a wooden
    bowl.

Eshu slept in the house.—
But the house was too small for him.
Eshu slept on the verandah—
But the verandah was too small for him.
Eshu slept in a nut—
At last he could stretch himself.

Eshu walked through the groundnut farm.
The tuft of his hair was just visible.
If it had not been for his huge size,
He would not have been visible at all.

Having thrown a stone yesterday—he kills a bird today.
Lying down, his head hits the roof.
Standing up he cannot look into the cooking pot.
Eshu turns right into wrong, wrong into right.

ORIKI OSHUN

We call her and she replies with wisdom.
She can cure those whom the doctor has failed.
She cures the sick with cold water.
When she cures the child, she does not charge the
    father.
We can remain in the world without fear.
Iyalode who cures children—help me to have my own
    child.
Her medicines are free—she feeds honey to the
    children.
She is rich and her words are sweet.
Large forest with plenty of food.
Let a child embrace my body.
The touch of a child's hand is sweet.

Owner of brass. Owner of parrots' feathers.
Owner of money.

My mother, you are beautiful, very beautiful.
Your eyes sparkle like brass.
Your skin is soft and smooth.
You are black like velvet.

Everybody greets you when you descend on the world.
Everybody sings your praises.

ORIKI OGUN

Ogun kills on the right and destroys on the right.
Ogun kills on the left and destroys on the left.
Ogun kills suddenly in the house and suddenly in the
    field.
Ogun kills the child with the iron with which it plays.
Ogun kills in silence.
Ogun kills the thief and the owner of the stolen goods.
Ogun kills the owner of the slave—and the slave runs
    away.
Ogun kills the owner of thirty "iwofa"—and his
    money, wealth and children disappear.
Ogun kills the owner of the house and paints the
    hearth with his blood.
Ogun is the death who pursues a child until it runs
    into the bush.
Ogun is the needle that pricks at both ends.
Ogun has water but he washes in blood.

Ogun, do not fight me. I belong only to you.
The wife of Ogun is like a tim tim.
She does not like two people to rest on her.

Ogun has many gowns. He gives them all to the
    beggars.
He gives one to the woodcock—the woodcock dyes it
    indigo.
He gives one to the coucal—the coucal dyes it in
    camwood.
He gives one to the cattle egret—the cattle egret leaves
    it white.

Ogun is not like pounded yam:
Do you think you can knead him in your hand
And eat of him until you are satisfied?
Ogun is not like maize gruel:
Do you think you can knead him in your hand
And eat of him until you are satisfied?
Ogun is not like some thing you can throw into your
    cap:
Do you think you can put on your cap and walk away
    with him?

Ogun scatters his enemies.
When the butterflies arrive at the place where the
    cheetah excretes,
They scatter in all directions.

The light shining on Ogun's face is not easy to behold.
Ogun, let me not see the red of your eye.

Ogun sacrifices an elephant to his head.
Master of iron, head of warriors,
Ogun, great chief of robbers.
Ogun wears a bloody cap.
Ogun has four hundred wives and one thousand four
    hundred children.
Ogun, the fire that sweeps the forest.
Ogun's laughter is no joke.
Ogun eats two hundred earthworms and does not
    vomit.

Ogun is a crazy orisha who still asks questions after 780
    years!
Whether I can reply, or whether I cannot reply.
Ogun please don't ask me anything.

The lion never allows anybody to play with his cub.
Ogun will never allow his child to be punished.
Ogun do not reject me!
Does the woman who spins ever reject a spindle?
Does the woman who dyes ever reject a cloth?
Does the eye that sees ever reject a sight?
Ogun, do not reject me!

COMMENTS AND QUESTIONS

1. In "Oriki Obatala" note the dualistic nature of Obatala. He is the creator, a kindly deity, who can also
   kill (as in line 7). Refer to the myth of Obatala earlier in this chapter. What characteristics are portrayed in both the myth and this poem?
2. Eshu, as the poem "Oriki Eshu" states, is the "confuser of men." In Yoruba cosmology he symbolizes
   disorder, the unexpected. And yet this quality permits him to turn "wrong into right." How does the
   poem express the contradictions of his character?
3. Is the *tone* of the poem on the feminine deity,
   Oshun, different from those on the masculine deities? How so?
4. How does the poetic principle of *anaphora*, the successive repetition of words or phrases, operate in all
   of the oriki and especially in "Oriki Ogun"? What
   would be the effect and usefulness of this device in
   oral poetry?

Ijala—The Poetry of Yoruba Hunters

ADIYE (FOWL)

One who sees corn and is glad.
The chicken wears its shin at the back.
We eat it with pounded yam.
Every fool will be buried in the cheek.
The foolish chicken has many relations:
Oil is its relative on the father's side.
Pepper and onion are its relatives on the mother's side.
If it does not see its friend salt even for a day
It will not sleep peacefully.

ETU-DUIKER (ANTELOPE)

Beautiful antelope with the slender neck.
Your thighs are worth twenty slaves.
Your arms are more precious than thirty servants.
Your neck is exquisite like a sacred carving.
You step out like a nobleman
Shaking the grass like bells.
Your facial marks are beautiful and bold
Even like those of the king of Ogbomosho.
You wash your body with white.
God has honoured you with white.
The hunter is happy when the owner of white appears.
I cannot be happy when I kill you,
Until I have found your body in the bush.
The pregnant woman demands your skin.
Lying on your skin she will bear a beautiful child.

NEW YAM

New yam causes the wife of yesterday to lose her
     manners,
New yam causes the head of the household to reject
     food.
It makes a rich person speak out.
Yam will pay its own debt.
"Lay me on a fine bed
And I will lay you on a fine lady."

COMMENTS AND QUESTIONS

1. What is the difference in tone between the poem on the chicken and the poem on the antelope? How do the poems render what the poets see as the essence of these two animals?

2. How is the antelope in "Etu-Duiker" personified? What dimension do *similes* give to the poem?

3. Yam, a root vegetable, is the staple food of many African peoples along the Guinea coast. While yam is relatively easy to grow, it may be ravaged by drought or, to the contrary, rotted by untimely rains. The annual harvest of the new yams, often following a time of hardship and meager food supply, is the occasion for celebration. It is often signaled by religious rituals of thanks and communal solidarity.

4. Explain the relation of the last two lines of "New Yam" to the first part of the poem.

Iwi—The Poetry of Yoruba Masqueraders

CHILDREN

A child is like a rare bird.
A child is precious like coral.
A child is precious like brass.
You cannot buy a child on the market.
Not for all the money in the world.
The child you can buy for money is a slave.
We may have twenty slaves,
We may have thirty labourers,
Only a child brings us joy,
One's child is one's child.
The buttocks of our child are not so flat
That we should tie the beads on another child's hips.
One's child is one's child.
It may have a watery head or a square head,
One's child is one's child.
It is better to leave behind a child,
Than let the slaves inherit one's house.
A child is the beginning and end of happiness.
One must not rejoice too soon over a child.
Only the one who is buried by his child,
Is the one who has truly born a child.
On the day of our death, our hand cannot hold a single
     cowrie.
We need a child to inherit our belongings.

COMMENTS AND QUESTIONS

1. Describe the style of this poem. What is the effect of the very short sentences?

2. What does this poem tell you about the importance of children in African society?

FUNERAL POEM I

Come nearer home,
Mother of Aina.
You knew how to produce children,
but never learned to chide them.
Come and receive the sacrifice
from your children.
You people of the road,
where did you meet her?
The mother of Kujusola
the mother of Alawede.
They met her on the road to Ede.
I thank the trees that did not fall on her.
I thank the river
that did not carry her away.
No one can bar her way
for she travels an underground path.
Like a new bride
She covers her head with a cloth.

FUNERAL POEM II

The hunter dies
and leaves his poverty to his gun.
The blacksmith dies
and leaves his poverty to his anvil.
The farmer dies
and leaves his poverty to his hoe.
The bird dies
and leaves its poverty to its nest.
You have died
and left me abandoned in the dark.
Where are you now?
Are you the goat
eating grass around the house?
Are you the motionless lizard
on the hot mud wall?
If I tell you not to eat earthworms
it's like asking you to go hungry.
But whatever they may eat in heaven
Partake with them.
A dead body cannot receive double punishment:
If there is not cloth to cover it—
There will always be earth to cover it.

COMMENTS AND QUESTIONS

1. What different emotions on the mourners' part are conveyed in these two poems, and how does the imagery express them?
2. How do the Yoruba beliefs that the dead live on as spirits or else are reincarnated appear in these poems?

Fulani Poetry
AMADOU HAMPATÉ BA

THE BELOVED

Diko,
of light skin, of smooth hair and long;
her smells sweet and gentle
she never stinks of fish
she never breathes sweat
like gatherers of dry wood.
She has no bald patch on her head
like those who carry heavy loads.
Her teeth are white
her eyes are like
those of a new born fawn
that delights in the milk
that flows for the first time
from the antelope's udder.
Neither her heel nor her palm
are rough; but sweet to touch
like liver; or better still
the fluffy down of kopok.

COMMENTS AND QUESTIONS

1. The Fulani, cattle-herding nomads, stem from the grasslands of the upper Senegal river, but have migrated over the centuries as far east as the Cameroons. How does the poet reflect here an intimate familiarity with nature and especially with the "bush" land?
2. The romantic idea of love does not play an important social role in African society. Husbands and wives may, of course, love each other; but the existence of love is not a prerequisite for marriage. Love is not a major theme in African poetry although

beautiful love lyrics, like the above, do exist. Fulani women have a reputation for being especially beautiful and exciting. What image of Diko, the beloved, do you have from this poem?

3. Compare the way in which the poet here uses imagery to describe his beloved and his feelings about her to similar techniques in the poems of Sappho (Chapter 1) and in the Song of Songs (Chapter 6).

Ga Poetry

NAMING POEM

May good fortune come
May our stools be clean
May our brooms be clean
In a circle of unity
    have we met
When we dig a well
May we find water
When of this water we drink
May our shoulders find peace
The stranger who has come
On his mother's head be life
On his father's head be life
Behind his back may
    darkness be
Before his face may
    all be bright
May his head the world respect
And his brethren may he know
May we have forgiveness
    to forgive him
May he work and eat
When he sees he has
    not seen
When he hears he has
    not heard
In black he has come
In white may he return
May good fortune come

COMMENTS AND QUESTIONS

1. In many African societies the naming of a child is surrounded with ceremony; it is the public recognition of the personhood of the newborn and the acknowledgment of his or her full membership in the community. The "naming" or "outdooring" does not occur usually until one or two weeks following birth, when it seems certain that the child will survive his entry into the world. On the chosen day, significant members of the youngster's family may whisper the name into the child's ear before announcing it publicly. Special blessings and prayers follow, and the day is filled with gift-giving and celebration by the many relatives and guests invited to share in the occasion.

2. The Ga are a southern Ghanaian people of the Ewe linguistic subgroup of Twi speakers (just as the Ashanti, discussed earlier, are members of the Akan subgroup of Twi languages). For many Ghanaian peoples there is a close link between the individual and his stool (line 2); for some, a person's soul is said to reside in his stool. (See the discussion of art objects in Chapter 16.) Many rites of passage in the individual's life are carried out in connection with his or her stool, so it is appropriate that "stools" appear in connection with the naming.

3. How does the invocation of this poem illustrate by a shift in focus the link between the child and the community?

4. What are the values that the community wishes for the child?

5. What do "darkness," "bright," "black," and "white" seem to signify?

BIRAGO DIOP

Forefathers

Listen more often to things rather than beings.
Hear the fire's voice,
Hear the voice of water.
In the wind hear the sobbing of the trees,
It is our forefathers breathing.

The dead are not gone forever.
They are in the paling shadows
And in the darkening shadows.

The dead are not beneath the ground,
They are in the rustling tree,
In the murmuring wood,
In the still water,
In the flowing water,
In the lonely place, in the crowd;
The dead are not dead.

Listen more often to things rather than beings.
Hear the fire's voice.
Hear the voice of water.
In the wind hear the sobbing of the trees.
It is the breathing of our forefathers
Who are not gone, not beneath the ground,
Not dead.

The dead are not gone forever.
They are in a woman's breast,
A child's crying, a glowing ember.
The dead are not beneath the earth,
They are in the flickering fire,
In the weeping plant, the groaning rock,
The wooded place, the home.
The dead are not dead.

Listen more often to things rather than beings.
Hear the fire's voice,
Hear the voice of water.
In the wind hear the sobbing of the trees.
It is the breath of our forefathers.

CHINUA ACHEBE

Generation Gap

A son's arrival
is the crescent moon
too new too soon to lodge
the man's returning.
His feast of re-incarnation
must await the moon's
reopening at the naming
ceremony of his
grandson.

COMMENTS AND QUESTIONS

1. Many African religions view human existence as a cyclical phenomenon wherein spirits may proceed through various phases of what we know as birth, life, and death in human, but sometimes animal form. This view, articulated in both traditional and modern poetry, reinforces man's sensitivity to, and awareness of, the natural world. Compare the metaphor of nature in "Forefathers" with that in the Yoruba funeral poems.

2. How is the cyclical nature of man's existence conveyed in "Forefathers," Achebe's "Generation Gap," and the iwi on children?

WOLE SOYINKA

Death in the Dawn

Traveller, you must set out
At dawn. And wipe your feet upon
The dog-nose wetness of the earth.

Let sunrise quench your lamps. And watch
Faint brush pricklings in the sky light
Cottoned feet to break the early earthworm
On the hoe. Now shadows stretch with sap
Not twilight's death and sad prostration.
This soft kindling, soft receding breeds
Racing joys and apprehensions for
A naked day. Burdened hulks retract,
Stoop to the mist in faceless throng
To wake the silent markets—swift, mute
Processions on grey byways. . . . On this
Counterpane, it was—
Sudden winter at the death
Of dawn's lone trumpeter. Cascades
Of white feather-flakes . . . but it proved
A futile rite. Propitiation sped
Grimly on, before.
The right foot for joy, the left, dread
And the mother prayed, Child
May you never walk
When the roads waits, famished.

Traveller, you must set forth
At dawn.
I promise marvels of the holy hour
Presages as the white cock's flapped
Perverse impalement—as who would dare
The wrathful wings of man's Progression. . . .

But such another wraith! Brother,
Silenced in the startled hug of
Your invention—is this mocked grimace
This closed contortion—I?

COMMENTS AND QUESTIONS

1. Wole Soyinka has consistently addressed human issues through the voice of Yoruba belief and expression. Although his works are masterpieces in English, and can be understood within the English
reading of them, their power and subtlety are magnified for the reader who understands something of
Yoruba culture. Ogun, the god of war and destruction, of the rains, of harvest, of disintegration and
death, is a favorite though not always explicit subject of Soyinka. In modern Nigeria, Ogun is god of
the road, a claimant of countless lives on over-
crowded highways; taxi and truck drivers are among
those who worship him. He is the real subject of
"Death in the Dawn." When the poet writes "May
you never walk/When the road waits, famished," it
is Ogun that one fears may be famished. "Death in
the Dawn" is not an oriki, but go back and reread
"Oriki Ogun" after you have read Soyinka's poem.
What traditional images of Ogun do you find in
Soyinka's poem?

16

VISUAL AND MUSICAL ARTS OF WEST AFRICA

Just as each African language has its own literary tradition, each African society has its own artistic and musical styles. We cannot hope to give even a bird's-eye view of the range and variety of African art and music in the present space. Rather, we will concentrate on the close observation of a few works in order to understand something of the African aesthetic. Since both African art and music have had a profound impact on their modern Western counterparts (see Chapter 36 in Volume II), we are already used to certain conventions, such as *abstraction* in art and the *pentatonic* ("jazz") *scale* in music, which shocked and puzzled earlier Western observers. We are not likely to view these arts, as did the European colonists, as awkward, tribal, or primitive. Nevertheless, there are characteristics of African art and music that make them significantly different from Western forms and that require our attention if we are to appreciate them. In spite of the great diversity of traditions and styles, even within West Africa alone, African art shares some common premises that we will examine first in the visual realm.

Visual Arts

Art and Communal Life   One of the basic differences between Western art and African art lies in the simple fact of classification. The art of the West is usually divided into "fine" and "applied" arts. In the first category are painting, sculpture, and architecture—the arts usually studied in the humanities. The second category includes more utilitarian objects such as furniture, ceramics, textiles, and clothing. This dichotomy does not exist in African art. For the African artist, the objects of everyday life may express beauty, harmony, and philosophical concepts as much or more than something to hang on a wall. The museum or the gallery does not exist in traditional Africa. While some Western and African arts are "useful" in the same way—palaces for kings, temples, objects for religious ceremonies—it must be kept in mind that *all* African art is in some way integrated into life in the community. At the same time, even the most humble object may manifest a complex relationship between people and society and their experiences and understanding of the world.

Understanding the world and interpreting one's experiences in it are the basis for art everywhere. The world of the traditional West African is one of close adherence to nature in all its manifestations; in the unchanging cycles of birth and death, planting and harvest, night and day, and the seasons. Yet circumstances may alter the seemingly permanent aspects of these events, and one is forced to assure their timely appearance. The seasonal migration of the herds that provide food and other staples of life, the natural cycles of fertility in animals, the beginning of the rainy seasons, the success of the planting and subsequent harvest, the normal, healthy birth of a child, are all subject to the vicissitudes of nature. This extraordinary awareness of inevitability and change in the face of natural phenomena is closely related to the *animism,* or belief in natural spirits, that characterizes African religions (see the "Myths" section of Chapter 15). The necessity to appease various spirits has been a motivating force for one type of African art. Objects, usually small statues, are created to invite a particular spirit, either "natural" or ancestor, to inhabit it. Great care is taken to make the object beautiful enough to entice the spirit to rest in it.

One might define the constant in African art and life as a tension between order and disorder, permanence and change. African societies place a great value on tradition; and ritual objects such as masks, costumes, and figurines pass on the values, laws, and beliefs of a people from one generation to another, as do the myths and tales of the oral tradition. This assures the permanence and the continuity of the community. On the other hand, the inevitability of change and the need to cope with it are reflected by the importance of *initiation* societies and the arts and rites associated with them. The process of the initiation is the passage of a boy or girl from childhood to adulthood, and the ritual takes place at the time of puberty. Women, in the case of girls, and men, in the case of boys, initiate the child by teaching certain practices, laws, and pieces of wisdom. The process recognizes the fact that the young adults will be agents of change within the community but assures that change will come about within the framework of tradition.

If most African art is religious in its orientation, that is not because it is all designed for cults or temples but because religion is so woven into the fabric of everyday African life. Just as the objects of African art are intimately related to that life, so they are also related to one other. The many rituals and festivals in Africa, one of which we will study in the next chapter, use masks, costume, music, poetry, and dance in the creation of a complete ensemble. Moreover, the stylistic principles in a mask, for example, are closely related to those in the other arts. We will also examine some of these aesthetic relationships while looking at the complete art of the festival. For the moment, let us consider some individual objects, bearing in mind that in so doing we are temporarily divorcing them from the total meaning of their context.

Masks and Headpieces   Masks and headpieces are usually worn by men in the context of the social and religious rituals of associations, sometimes referred to as secret societies. These societies function as the community's agents for social control, education (through initiation), and communication with spirits or the ancestors. They are particularly important and powerful in ethnic groups that do not have centralized chieftaincies or kingships. Secret societies may be very specialized in their function, although some also operate in a variety of situations. Usually the associations consist of several grades or ranks through which individuals of skill and prestige may rise to positions of great influence. They are "secret" because their specialist knowledge is reserved to initiates of the societies and because the members are anonymous to the public when performing the masked rituals or acting on behalf of the association. When an individual dons the mask, he becomes the receptacle for the spiritual force of whatever essence is portrayed and is identified as that essence by those who behold him.

The Chi Wara headpieces are found among the Bambara, who live near the upper Niger in Senegal, Guinea, and Mali (Fig. 16-1). Chi Wara (sometimes also spelled Tyiwara) is a legendary figure who taught the Bambara to cultivate with digging sticks. It is also the name of one of a series of graded associations for Bambara men. In preparation for clearing the fields, two members of the association wear these headpieces in imitation of the male and female antelope—the antelope having become identified with the Chi Wara figure. They engage in ritual play to please the spirits of the earth and to ensure the earth's fertility.

These beautiful wooden forms display one of the major characteristics of much African sculpture. The artist has exaggerated those features of the animals that are most important for recognition by those who use or observe the ritual and that call attention to each animal's particular important aspect. The female antelope's body is reduced to a simple flattened oval form, while the enlarged neck, head, and ears, which fit into tight curves, convey an impression of energy and strength. On her back rides a tiny young antelope whose form echoes that of his mother. The male antelope has a similar body; but his neck is formed of two curves with spiky extensions, his ears tilt backward, and his horns, stylized into a powerful upward thrust, tilt forward. The combination of curves with the antelope's spiky mane and the sharply contrasting direction

16–1 Above. Chi Wara headpiece, male antelope. Right. Chi Wara headpiece, female antelope. (Erle & Clyta Loran collection)

16–2   Above. Senufo. Kponiugo, fire-spitting mask. (Lowie Museum of Anthropology, University of California, Berkeley)

16–3   Right. Mambunda initiation mask. (© Livingstone Museum, Zambia)

of the ears and horns create a powerful sense of forward motion while the female's representation seems to recoil slightly from his onslaught. The distinguishing features of heads, body color, and texture are reduced or ignored. It is the power of procreation that is emphasized.

Another characteristic frequently evident in African sculpture that is also present in the Chi Wara headpieces is the sense of reduction of a single piece of wood—the trunk of a tree perhaps—from which the objects were carved. This is part of the explanation for the polar, columnar aspects of these figures.

A mask that seems to represent qualities in opposition to the forceful flowing motion of the Chi Wara, however, is the *kponiugo*, fire-spitting helmet (Fig. 16-2) of the Senufo. It is used by the Lo association, a group responsible for initiation schools among the Senufo of the Ivory Coast, Upper Volta, and Mali regions.

This rather fearsome visage is made up of the most important features of equally important animals. The teeth are those of the crocodile; the tusks represent the wart hog; the horns are those of the water buffalo or the antelope; and the chameleon, which perches on the head between the horns, is a symbol for the continuation of life. Sometimes these masks are also painted with leopard spots. Each of these animals represents a powerful spirit; and, combined in a powerful symmetry, they are said to represent the chaos of primordial times. As the wearer stalks through the night, tinder is struck under the chin to create the fire-spitting image. This wooden mask, probably cut from green wood for lightness, was blackened. Its wearer could both invoke and provoke powerful spirits.

Another initiation mask is this one used by the Mambunda of Zambia, a people who share many common institutions, like the *Mukanda* schools (Fig. 16-3).

During the instructional period of two to nine months, young boys between the ages of seven and fifteen are secluded. Among the dances performed and/or taught is one danced by the older men wearing these kinds of masks, which are used to evoke ancestral spirits and to drive away women and younger boys. It is a powerful mask that emphasizes the potential of facial curves for exaggeration. The pure symmetry of the form and the protruding mouth form sharp contrasts. The great expanse of forehead and the attached feathers across the scalp are another juxtaposition of opposites—smoothness with the ruffled feathers.

The white-faced masks, which may symbolize ancestor spirits or a young maiden, are worn by men of the Mmwo society of the Northern Ibo peoples near Onitsha and Awka (Fig. 16-4). Those representing male ancestral spirits are used at funerals, festivals, and initiation rites to cause fear and awe among nonmembers of the society. These kinds of masks remind us again of the importance of the benign presence of the ancestors of the tribe. One of the important stylistic features of these, as of other, masks is the reduction of features and their orderly composition into a symmetrical

16–5   Dan mask. (Copyright F. Willett, Glasgow)

16–4   Ibo. Mmwo mask. (Reproduced by permission of The University Museum, University of Pennsylvania)

whole. Since a spirit, not a person, is being evoked, naturalism of form, texture, and color are not prerequisites. We have here the principle of *abstraction* used for the representation of a being not of the natural world.

This Dan mask (Fig. 16-5) seems almost realistic when compared to the white-faced mask that we have just considered. The scale of the features and their realization seem much more human. But a brief consideration of the reduction of eyebrows to a single plane, the nose to perfect symmetry, the cheeks and chin to smooth planes, and the whole to this elegant oval shape contradicts the apparent naturalism. Like the masks of the Mmwo society and those of the Mambunda, masks of this type represent ancestral powers. They were often carried in miniature form by men as guardians and were also used to hide young boys in seclusion from the view of women.

Figurines The possible artistic range of the transformation of the human visage is only hinted at by the masks that we have considered, but they do suggest how terribly exciting such forms must have been to Western artists when they first saw them. Pablo Picasso, one of the first European artists to be inspired by African art, used this Bakota reliquary figure (Fig. 16-6) for a series of studies. How little he understood of its real importance is emphasized by the use to which it was actually put, that is, to drive away evil from the remains of the dead. The "head" of the figure is exaggerated to enormous size in proportion to what Picasso, concentrating on the object as a figure in space, interprets as a body. Actually, the "body" is the base, intended to hold a basket containing a skull or bones and thus to protect the remains of an ancestor. Compare this rendition of the head with that of the Mambunda mask. Notice particularly the use of incising, the way

16–7   Bakongo fetish statue. (Lowie Museum of Anthropology, University of California, Berkeley)

16–6   Bakota reliquary figure. (Lowie Museum of Anthropology, University of California, Berkeley)

in which facial features are stylized, and the way in which one seems volumetric and the other two-dimensional.

Another way in which ancestral forces could be evoked or released is shown in this Bakongo charm figure (Fig. 16-7). Cavities in the head or stomach were the receptacles for magical substances. These *fetishes*—or objects embodying supernatural power—could be used for benevolent or malevolent effects. The pose sometimes reflected the purpose. A stiffened pose, upraised arm, and grimacing face were used to make the forms more menacing, while nails or sharp iron studs were driven into the body to release malevolent forces. The fetishes used in voodoo have their origins in this kind of object.

Divination Tray Objects not representing the human figure and designed for specific, utilitarian purposes may also reflect religious principles. This Yoruba tray (Fig. 16-8) is used in the process of *divination*, foretelling the future or discovering secret knowledge. One of the features of Yoruba religion is the oracle of *Ifa*, a secret body of wisdom that may be made available to a believer through the intervention of a *babalawo*, or priest. The priest then interprets the secret body of poems, called *odu*, in various combinations, using the Ifa divination tray.

Following initial discussion and ritual cleansing, the petitioner who has come to the priest is seated opposite him. Between them lies the divination tray, which has a light layer of sand on the surface. The priest takes a number of palm nut kernels, tosses them into the air, and marks on the tray the number of those that he catches. At the end of a series of tosses he uses the number and arrangement of marks on the tray to select those odu poems to be interpreted. The interpretations reflect the ordered intentions of the deities and the ancestors. But there is always the element of chance and disorder. The face of Eshu, the god of unpredictable fate and change, is inevitably present on the border of the tray. Placed opposite the priest during the divination process, the face reminds both priest and petitioner of the potential in man's destiny for good or evil.

Stools The manifestation of African spiritual and political principles in utilitarian objects is perhaps best exemplified by the Ashanti stools (Fig. 16-9). The Ashanti, like other Akan peoples of Ghana and the Ivory Coast, believe that a person's spirit resides in his stool. When not in use, a stool is turned on its side so that no spirit other than the owner's will "sit" on the stool. Special stools are carved for an individual at important stages in his or her life such as at puberty or marriage.

This personal metaphor was extended to that of the state at the time of the founding of the Ashanti Confederacy by the king (*asantehene*) Osei Tutu in 1701. On a particular day when the king, subchiefs, and the Ashanti people were gathered together, Osei Tutu's chief priest summoned from the heavens a Golden Stool to enshrine and protect the soul of the new nation. The Golden Stool remains the single most important item of Ashanti court regalia: it stands for leadership and union. In this way stools also became symbols of political office for those with political authority delegated by the asantehene. The high status of members of the court, like the queen mother, is reflected in this ceremonial stool adorned with fine sculpture and a silver sheath overlay. The intricate surface designs frequently recall proverbs that the office-holder uses to convey a message or motto of his rule.

16–8 Left. Yoruba. Ifa tray. (Copyright F. Willett, Glasgow)

16–9 Above. Ashanti. Wooden stool for a queen mother. (Reproduced by Courtesy of the Trustees of the British Museum)

16–10 Left. Ashanti. Kente cloth (detail). (Reprinted from *African Art in Motion* by Robert Farris Thompson. Katherine Coryton White collection, UCLA Art Council, University of California, Los Angeles)

16–11 Above. Mangbetu pots. (Reproduced by Courtesy of the Trustees of the British Museum)

16–12 Below. Mangbetu woman. (Barbara W. Merriam)

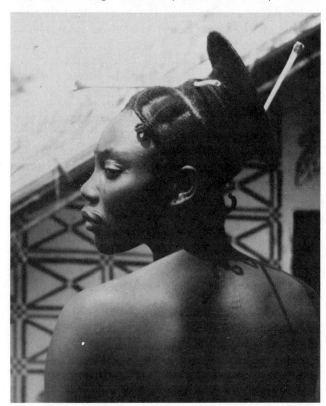

Ceremonial stools like this one are reserved for state occasions; others are specially carved for domestic and personal use. At the death of an Ashanti ruler his ceremonial stool is blackened with soot and becomes the object of propitiation in the state ancestor cult.

Kente Cloth   A further example of artistic accomplishment and political authority manifest in utilitarian objects is the *kente* cloth of the Ashanti and Ewe peoples of Ghana. Kente is a large cloth, draped for ceremonial dress, made out of narrow strips sewn together that have been woven from cotton, silk, or wool threads. While strip weaving is common in Africa, that which distinguishes kente is the elaboration of silk weft inlay designs that are geometric in character. There is a hierarchy of kente weavers and designs. At the pinnacle are the royal *asasia* cloths woven exclusively for the asantehene and his family, and for individuals granted a cloth as a symbol of loyalty or in return for services to the king. Pattern and color of the royal cloths carry special meanings appropriate to their owners. As do all kente, each asasia cloth has its name. The example shown here (Fig. 16-10) is called Everyone-Depends-on-Somebody. Its colors are gold, red, and blue. The gold and red are references to kingship and governmental power; blue refers to playfulness and humor. The equal intensity of the overall colors is coupled with the striking alternation of rectangles dominated by blue with those dominated by gold and red. The arrangement suggests the worth of both qualities in balance in the ideal society; power and authority must be matched by humor and simplicity.

Sculpture in Everyday Objects   While items of court regalia symbolize the authority of a ruler, other carved objects may commemorate a single person or group of persons, common and familiar. The Mangbetu of northeastern Zaire apply their excellent figurative sculpture to everyday objects rather than to statuary. Knife handles, harps, pipe bowls, and other containers are decorated with human heads and figures. Among them, the most famous of Mangbetu motifs are the pots carved to commemorate the bound heads and elaborate hairstyles of Mangbetu women (Figs. 16-11, 16-12). The coiffure itself is reminiscent of a woven basket. It consists of a fiber structure through which the hair is pulled, elongated with the addition of false hair, and then woven back through the fiber. The delicate woven lines of the coiffure are replicated in fine detail on the heads that sit atop the clay pots. The lower body of the pot reinforces the cylindrical shape of the head by curvilinear lines covering its surface.

QUESTIONS AND COMMENTS

1. How is exaggeration of natural features of human and animal form used to stress spiritual or social principles? Give examples.
2. As has been stated above, masks may have varied purposes: some are intended to invoke powers of natural or supernatural forces. They represent mystery and the potential for good or evil. These often rely upon images of the forest or bush to convey their meaning. Others symbolize civilization: man's imposition of pattern and order on the natural world or idealized human values. Review the objects presented in this section and identify ones that seem to you to bear out each of these two purposes.
3. The nature–civilization contrast may be seen in statues and other sculpted objects as well. Compare the reliance upon natural substance versus the reliance upon human reference in the images of the Bakongo

figure and the Ashanti stool. Identify the different images.
4. How does the form and placement during use of the Ifa divination tray suggest general principles of Yoruba cosmology?
5. There are many elements to consider in analyzing a work of sculpture: proportion; volume and dimension; compactness versus open space; surface texture (rough versus smooth, painted or unpainted). Of those objects that incorporate aspects of naturalism and stylized interpretation of the human form, which elements contribute to the effect of naturalism? Which to the effect of stylization?

African visual art may be utilitarian, decorative, symbolic, spiritual, or all of these at once. Masks and sculptures emphasize communication of spiritual forces and the interpretation of cosmic order to the human community; other objects symbolize or reinforce social relationships. There is, as we have seen, no dichotomy between "fine" and "applied" arts. Similarly, there is no division in African music between "concert" and "folk" music. Just as there are no museums in traditional Africa, there are no concert halls; music, like visual art objects, is intended to be used as part of the rituals and celebrations of everyday life.

African Music

The first observation that a careful observer of African music will surely make is some conclusion about the tremendous variety and complexity of the sounds emanating from this gigantic continent. The languages and cultures of the people of North Africa are closely related to those of the Arab world and the Middle East, traditions which differ—for geographic, economic, and political reasons—from those of South, Central, and West Africa. The music of this region, so oriental in its *modal, melodic,* and *improvisational* characteristics, although African for perhaps centuries, must be excluded from our consideration of indigenous African music, the music of black Africans. Likewise, one finds alongside the music of sub-Saharan Africa a tradition of Western music brought by the colonists from Europe, a practice that has its own traditions and has helped generate a new black African urban music called "high life," a chic modern music of the cities. Even when we dampen all the sounds that can be identified as "non-native" to the original peoples of Africa, we are still engulfed in an endless variety of musics and languages and peoples. The culture and the music of the Pygmies, Bushmen, and Saharan peoples are not the same as those of the Yoruba, Ashanti, and Susu ethnic groups. Here, as in the literature and art sections, we will concentrate on the music of West African societies. After discussing some general characteristics shared by the music of these societies, we will move on to a more detailed study of one specific example: music from the Festival of the Tohossuo, legendary princes of the royal family from the ancient kingdom of Dahomey.

Characteristics of West African Music: Similarities with Jazz   Most music performed by Africans is part of a social activity. Of course, individual music-making takes place in response to personal or ritual needs, but most musical performance accompanies the group activities of games, religious rites, feasts, festivals, and work. Music provides an opportunity for sharing in a communal creative experience. With the transferral of Africans to the New World, this West African music deeply influenced the development of jazz, with which, as we will see, it shares many characteristics. Because of a number of factors, black slaves in America were able to maintain much of their African musical heritage, all the while joining to it certain elements of the Euro-American musical tradition. The resulting hybrid had a markedly African base. The important points to keep in mind are these: the rich West African musical tradition; the comparative cultural isolation in which many black American slaves lived; the tolerance of musical activities among the slave communities accorded by white American masters; the compatibility of the important elements of West African music with the current tradition of Euro-American music. As West African music is communal in its basic approach, jazz, too, is a shared creative experience: those in the normal small group of musicians, the combo, respond improvisationally to one other's musical signals and the social signals of the audience or dance crowd in a way different from the performance practice of a Western string quartet or a chamber orchestra. African musicians, when composing collectively, are part of a social interaction that often communicates a group sentiment or message, an extramusical consideration that is found only rarely in music of the West.

Depending on the event and local customs, the performing groups may be made up of young or old, male or female, or mixed. However, there is usually a hierarchical differentiation among the players—leading roles are played by professional musicians or specialists; secondary roles are performed by the others in both choruses and instrumental ensembles. As the *Sundiata* epic indicated, in Africa the griot, or praise singer, is a highly respected musician-poet, usually a professional, in many of these societies. The leading blues singers and jazz musicians of black America are often seen to be held in the same esteem by the regular members of the black community.

Elements in African Music   Little, if any, traditional African music takes any interest in *harmony* as we know it in the West, but most African sounds are compatible with European harmonies. The leading elements of African music are *melody, rhythm, timbre* (the distinctive sound of the instruments and voices), and text. Although verbal art is intertwined with African musical art, some societies are able to convey specific messages by instrumental sounds alone. That is, *pitch* and rhythm can be explicitly equated to textual messages, for speech in some languages is musical in the sense that pitch variations affect word meanings. But "talking drums" and "talking winds" are not characteristic of the music of most of the peoples who were brought to America from Africa as slaves. Even though there may be a tendency to overemphasize this particular feature of African music because it is so unique and fascinating, we might be well advised to consider that most music is communicative in a general way once we have learned the conventions. For example, we are all familiar with the sounds of military music, love songs, sad songs, happy dance music, and so on. We know that words for one variety cannot be properly set to sounds of another, or, if they are, then a joke is intended, a mistake has been made, or something is out of kilter. In other words, the sound of the music without the words conveys a somewhat specific message anyway. In like manner, it is accurate to say that most African music communicates messages and feelings, ideas that are extramusical. But to the degree that particular sounds are wedded to specific social functions, it is probably true that African music is more communicative than most Western music.

Rhythm   The complex rhythms of most African drumming depend on the use of a recurring rhythmic pattern within the totality of the ensemble. This time-line in African music is what the jazz drummer refers to as "time," that unwavering sense of beat that must prevail regardless of what else is happening in solo or in ensemble. In its simplest form, the time-line can be projected by a "beat" or metronomic pulse that sounds audibly and continuously. But it can also function as an unsounded, but understood, quantity of the time-line part, which the musicians perceive as an *ostinato* or regularly recurring rhythm pattern. Another obvious conclusion at which the impartial observer of African music will arrive is the distinct bias toward percussion that is a part of the aesthetics of African music. As in jazz, there is a tendency to include a rhythm section in every instrumental ensemble, and surely the close association of African music and jazz with dance—both as part of the dance and as accompaniment for the dance—explains, or at least accounts for, the importance of rhythm as a chief feature of both musics. In fact, African drummers often perform on the move as part of the dance. Even when stationary, African drummers—and jazz drummers—have bodies in motion, with elbows flying, shoulders leaning, fingers tapping or pressing, and heads and mouths going.

Vocal Music: Call and Response   Although drumming and rhythm are probably preeminent in West African music, great stress is laid on vocal music. An exceptional variety may be found among the themes treated, such as war songs, hunting songs, play and work songs, religious and festival songs, and social commentary, a type not unlike the artifices of the American bluesman. Eileen Southern, renowned historian of the music of black Americans, cites the following as the earliest example of an African song text written down in a European language (1800):

The winds roared, and the rains fell;
The poor white man, faint and weary,
Came and sat under our tree.
He has no mother to bring him milk,
No wife to grind his corn.

Chorus:
Let us pity the white man.
No mother has he to bring him milk,
No wife to grind his corn.

The leader-and-chorus format of much African vocal music often displays a call-and-response mode of performance; this, too, is another characteristic eagerly seized by jazz historians seeking stylistic parallels between jazz and native African music. The typical jazz performance of the vocal and instrumental blues has a singer or lead instrument perform the first half of each phrase, only to be answered by another instrumentalist or the ensemble itself. The tie between the jazz blues and the African responsorial performance may be tenuous, but the leader-chorus performance among African vocal ensembles is, in fact, the norm and a characteristic to be savored. Much is lost if the words are not understood, of course; but the virtuosity of the leader, in contrast to the solidity and enthusiastic response of the remaining performers, is a distinctive sound of the black African tradition. As we read more about the cultural traditions of black Africa, we would also do well to keep in mind these observations:

> From the first African captives, through the years of slavery, and into the present century black Americans kept alive important strands of African consciousness and verbal art in their humor, songs, dance, speech, tales, games, folk beliefs, and aphorisms. . . . Cultural diffusion between whites and blacks was by no means a one-way street with blacks the invariable beneficiaries. . . . Black relationship to the larger culture was complex and multidimensional.[1]

Music from the Festival of the Tohossou   The princes of Dahomey are called the Tohossou, descendants of a legendary king; their worship is the object of a cult whose ceremonies are performed in the twenty temples of the city of Abomey, capital of the ancient

[1] Lawrence J. Levine, *Black Culture & Black Consciousness*, (London: Oxford University Press, 1977).

kingdom of Dahomey (Fig. 16-13). The music for portions of these ceremonies has been recorded. We should prepare ourselves to hear, in addition to the sounds of human voices, the music of three oblong drums, which are beaten by sticks on one side and the naked hand on the other; three iron bells struck with a short wooden stick; pairs of rattles contained in wicker baskets; and a small bell shaken by a priest. The festivities for one Tohossou last four days, and the recorded excerpts sample music from morning to nightfall of one festival day. Five groups of people, the entire community, participate: the priests, the princes (descendants of the royal line), men, women, and musicians. Even children have a part to play, and this day's ceremony will have dancing, singing, and sacrifice. As the day progresses, the bull will be bound, its throat will be slit, and a lamb will later be sacrificed to appease the spirit of the bull. The mysteries of all these ceremonies and ritual acts are not all known and entirely understood; but, since the Tohossou represent proud descendants of a warrior race, there are various songs, dances, and ritual acts dealing with the enemy, fallen brothers-in-arms, vengeance, and sacred deities. The first excerpt, "Song of Zomadonou," is sung by a young man portraying Zomadonou, a reincarnated prince, his words telling of the feats that made him famous. He is accompanied by one bell, struck in two places to obtain contrasting pitches, and the song of the bell creates the time-line ostinato: High (slow) High (slow) High (quick) Low (quick). Over and over again the pattern repeats as the prince sings his song to a *pentatonic* (five-note) *scale*. As Zomadonou sings, he is answered by the chorus, their response picking up the principal melodic figure of his solo song.

The second excerpt captures the voices of a male chorus grouped around the drums. It is basically a choral song meant to accompany a serpentine dance by the women as they snake their way three times around the sacred tree and sacrificial bull. The sound of the drums is not continuous, but the rattles keep a steady beat for the dance. Occasionally a solo voice will interject a brief exclamation, but the pattern of the music is choral song, not call and response. The music of this example is similar to the first in that the melody employs an abbreviated scale, ostinato patterns prevail, and tone production by the vocalists is full voiced, lusty, and somewhat strained.

16–13 First Day of the Yam Custom in Dahomey, 1818. From Edward Thomas Bowdich, *Mission from Cape Coast Castle to Ashantee,* 3rd ed. London: F. Cass & Co., Ltd. 1960. (Reproduced by permission of Frank Cass & Co., London; photo courtesy of the Trustees of the Boston Public Library)

Adomoussi, a priest devoted to the worship of the third Tohossou, performs the third excerpt himself. Striking a bell in two places, he follows with a short declamatory phrase—"O thou, when thou raise the saber it is to kill . . . Thou panther which avenges itself . . . Thou shark in the water . . . An enemy . . ." The pattern is simple—bell, statement, bell, statement—and one can see the parallel in the country bluesman who strums a chord to arrange his thoughts and follows with the simply sung phrase. The priest has something to tell his people; his bell and method of delivery catch their attention.

The choir for the next recorded example, "The Way Is Free," is entirely composed of women. Using a piercing chest tone, the leader sings short phrases to be answered by the remaining choir members. The percussion accompaniment, which is not heavy, seems to be but loosely attached to the singing of the women. Since no dance is employed at this point in the ceremony, the drums seem to act more as background than accompaniment. Not so for the Nifossousso dance that follows. The regular beat is stately and dignified; it accompanies a procession of women who have shed their brightly colored costumes for white loincloths in a slow procession to the temple. Following this, the men call Botro, a woman, to come and perform her dance. In the seventh example the woman advances to dance and to sing a warlike and frightening ritual with a stick that she finally plunges into the earth.

Throughout the performance of each of these snippets of music and ceremony it is obvious that certain musical sounds relate to general feelings in the same way that certain musical sounds of the Western tradition do. The priest who shouted his exclamations to

the accompaniment of a bell could not have been describing a quiet forest glade; the slow processional of the noble line of women moving to the temple would have been inappropriate to accompany the active dance of Botro. The sounds of African music, although different from those we are most accustomed to hear, open up to meaningful interpretation upon careful listening and a little reflection. Then, as the similarities to our own music begin to surface, we see the heritage that has blended with Euro-American music to form that American music called jazz. Only recently have American jazz musicians begun to take a new look at African roots in a search for further inspiration and replenishment, and we will see in Chapter 18 and in Volume II how another transformation in American music has taken place as our sense of history draws us to new ideas from our past.

17

AFRICAN ARTS IN FESTIVAL: THE EFE/GELEDE OF THE WESTERN YORUBA

The unity of the arts with one another and with the values and lifestyle of a particular culture is nowhere so evident as in the ways in which people celebrate together. We have seen how the festival of Dionysus in ancient Greece brought together wine drinking, love making, song, dance, mask, drama, and the architecture of the theater. The Romans honored Saturn, the god of agriculture, with a general feasting and unleashing of social restraints at the end of the year. Seeing that they could not do away with the Saturnalia, the Christians declared that Christmas would be celebrated at the end of December and retained certain pagan customs such as the yule log and the Christmas tree. Christian festivals also combined drama, music, visual effects, and dance, as we saw with *The Play of Daniel*, part of a Christmas celebration in the cathedral. The Christian holiday for "letting go" became carnival, the pre-Lent season, which in Renaissance Florence produced splendid festivals of poetry, song, dance, costumes, and painted floats.

Western peoples continued to put on festivals and celebrations in the early modern period, and in some instances (witness Mardi Gras in New Orleans) they continue today; but modern industrialism and individualism have tended to wipe out what once seemed a communal necessity. Many of us are forced to "celebrate" our holidays by turning on the TV. In traditional African societies, however, and in countries (like Brazil) where African influence is strong, festivals continue to be both a vital part of living and an important means of aesthetic expression. Even those Africans who are Christians or Muslim continue to participate in the festivals that have their roots in traditional religion.

The Yoruba culture, many aspects of which we have already studied, provides excellent examples of the synthesis of myth, poetry, dance, music, and visual arts in traditional festivals. One of these is the Efe/Gelede, celebrated by certain Yoruba subgroups in western Nigeria and the republic of Benin. The festival occurs annually before the beginning of the spring rains (between March and May) that will initiate the agricultural activities of the coming year. One of its purposes is thus to ensure the fertility of the earth. Women have always been symbols of fertility.

Significance of the Festival   In a patriarchal society where most ritual ceremonies reinforce the dominance of men over women, Efe/Gelede highlights the importance of women and serves as an occasion to recognize their spiritual powers. The specific context of Efe/Gelede derives from the importance of *Iyanla*, the Earth Mother or Great Mother, feminine counterpart of the supreme god Olorun or Oludumare.

Three Yoruba myths, all of which celebrate the mystical power and fertility of Iyanla, explain the background of the Efe/Gelede festival. The first tells that at the beginning of time when Oludumare sent Obatala, Ogun, and Iyanla, the first three orisha to earth, Iyanla complained that she, unlike the other two, had been given no special power. So Oludumare gave her the title "Mother of All," and presented her with a calabash containing a bird. The Great Mother promised to use her power by inflicting punishment on her enemies, but to those who appeased her she promised to grant wealth and children. In the second myth, the Great Mother, who had previously been blessed with many children, found that she could not bear any after her marriage to a man from Ketu (a Yoruba town in Benin). Upon consulting the oracle of Ifa, she was told to make sacrifices of corn and clay dishes and to dance with wooden figures on her head and metal anklets on her feet. She did so and promptly bore two children: a boy named Efe ("the Joker"), and a girl named Gelede. Her children found that when they grew up it was necessary for them, too, to dance with wooden images and iron anklets before they could have children. This dancing is reenacted in the festival.

The third myth recounts that another orisha, Orunmila, was told to sacrifice a wooden image, a waist-cloth, and metal anklets before he undertook a visit to the haven of the witches. He performed the sacrifice, made his journey, and returned safely, proclaiming that he had made friends with Sickness and Death and that he would die no more. The Yoruba believe that the destructive power of Iyanla is manifested through the witches, symbolized by the bird in the calabash. Elements of the Gelede costume recall this myth.

By honoring the great mother Iyanla and her children Efe and Gelede, the celebrants hope that the mystical powers granted to women by Iyanla may be channeled into constructive behavior of use to the community rather than into activity destructive of it. The festival thus in a sense honors and celebrates all women, especially mothers. It is generally performed over a two-day period. The first, the day of Efe, is devoted primarily to poetry, the songs of Efe. The second, the day of Gelede, places more emphasis on costumes and dancing.

First Day: Efe

The Efe ceremony takes place in the market area, a setting of social, religious, and economic activity primarily involving women. At one end of the arena a small enclosure with double arches of palms is constructed. It serves as the entrance for the principal performer, *Oro Efe*, literally the word of Efe. As the audience gathers, masqueraders and dancers perform in anticipation of the Oro Efe, whose songs will last throughout the night.

17–1 Far left. Oro Efe. Dressing of dancer. Layers of embroidered and appliqued cloth panels (gberi) are tied over a horizontally suspended bamboo hoop (agboja). (Henry John Drewal)

17–3 Left. Oro Efe in full dress. (Henry John Drewal)

Costume and Performance   The Oro Efe's elaborate costume, abounding in symbolism, includes leggings, iron gongs, and multicolored, appliqued cloth over a bamboo hoop (Figs. 17-1, 17-3). The headdress consists of a veil and a frontal view of the human face in mask. It is topped by an elaborate superstructure containing symbolic animal figures, colors, and suspended knives. The lions, leopards, and snakes connote strength and royalty, while the knives are associated with Soponnon, god of smallpox, and Ogun, god of iron. The goddess of the rainbow, Osumare, is connected with the python. The crowning symbol on the headdress is the bird of the mothers, alluding to the belief that mothers, like witches, can transform themselves into birds at night to fly about their business (Figs. 17-2, 17-3).

The Oro Efe is veiled to enhance his spiritual remove from the audience, but the cult head who summons him by striking the sacred bells calls him by name. A

17–2   Oro Efe mask. After a photograph of Oro Efe in performance at Ketu, April 24, 1971. (Henry John Drewal)

flute player also summons the Oro Efe, and the crowd awaits him in silence. The Oro Efe appears, swaying and sounding his leg rattles, swinging the whisks in his hand. His first words honor deities, ancestors, mothers, and elders. The angle of his body and slow pace express recognition and reverence to the spiritual powers. In the second stage of the ceremony, a chorus and, gradually, the audience join in the Oro Efe's songs. The public's participation symbolizes agreement with the Oro Efe's words; it strengthens the spiritual and social communality of the occasion. The performance continues throughout the night with occasional interludes offered by the drummers, who present praise poems, proverbs, jokes, and riddles. The Oro Efe departs near dawn while the audience is distracted by a stilted dancer in hyena masquerade, and the night's activities are over.

Efe Poetry   The poetry recited by the Oro Efe and in choral repetition is based on the belief that *ase*—power, authority, potential energy—can be embodied in words as well as in deities, living men and women, and the ancestors. Women are perceived to have a special ase that can be used for the good or the ill of the community. The voicing of poetry also contains ase and may be used to help direct that of the women toward potential good.

The types of poetry recited include invocation, social comment or satire, history, and funeral commemoration. Several of each type may be sung throughout the night; examples of some of these follow.

Invocation   One segment of the invocation requests blessing for the community as a whole. The songs invariably mention smallpox and cholera, scourges on the population. They plea for agricultural success, which means wealth, and for progeny. Since the mothers are associated with both procreativity and fertility of the earth, these are not surprising themes. In this example the singer prays for the end of unexpected deaths caused by farming accidents. He protests in the first line that he (the community) has offered *orijio*—medicinal leaves—to placate the mothers. Shango, god of thunder, would never strike one of his shrines; why should the progenitors *ose* and *aje* strike down their own offspring? Agbojo and Onidofoi, the ancestral spir-

its of the town, have been duly honored. Making his points, the singer displays his respect for the mothers and acknowledges their power by summoning the support of onlookers to join in his prayers.

Efe Poetry

INVOCATION

Orijio leaves charmed you to forgive my misdeeds.
Never have we suffered deaths from hoes, never from
    knives.
Have I lied?
Have I lied?
Never have we seen a thunderbolt strike a young *ose*
    tree.
Oso in the house were you not the one who gave birth
    to me?
Why do you not know us any longer?
Aje in the house, were you not the one who gave us
    birth?
Why do you not know us any longer?
Never have we seen a dog devour its child.
Never have we seen a dog devour its child.
Our mother, *opake*, forgive us our misdeed.
Our mother, do not allow me to falter
If a cult member has offended, expose him.
You joined our offering of thanksgiving to Agbojo,
Onidofoi was the one who saved us from death.
Young, old, households, and visitors, pray for my
    success.

Social Comment   In social comment songs the Oro Efe uses praises, cajolery, and condemnation to highlight events that have occurred in the community. The tone is ribald, the poetry often sarcastic, the images satirical, posing the opposite to their traditional meaning. Even though the Efe ceremony is to appease the mothers, male dominance is lauded; women who have shown too great an independence from their husbands are ridiculed. The second poem bewails two outrages: not only did the man decried commit adultery against Ogunsola, but Ogunsola was in addition his elder. In the third poem the Oro Efe also stresses the theme of respect for elders by admonishing youth to remember that age, not wealth or Western education, brings wisdom.

Efe Poetry

SOCIAL COMMENT I

For a husband to grind pepper and grate cassava.
For a husband to grind pepper and grate cassava.
For a husband to cook *eba* and wash pots.
For a husband to cook *eba* and wash pots.
The wife you married, Sango, is wonderful.
She threatened her husband with a cutlass at the
      market.
She threatened her husband with a cutlass at the
      market.
I heard him shout to all around "help me!"
She threatened her husband with a cutlass at the
      market.

SOCIAL COMMENT II

The conceited man with all his money is teasing his
      elder.
The conceited man with all his money is teasing his
      elder.
Did Ogunsola marry his wife for you?
Did Ogunsola marry his wife for you?
Wretched person who pulls on the snake's tail.
Wretched person who pulls on the snake's tail.
If the snake bites you should I be concerned?
Wretched person who pulls on the snake's tail.

SOCIAL COMMENT III

Ah, truly young children are very wise.
However I say they are not as wise as their elders.
We called you to get the soup, but you went to add
      water to it.
But you are not as wise as the one who cooked it.
A goat is different from a horse, a white man is
      different from a Hausa.
You are not as wise as the one who did the cooking.

Funerary Commemoration   This final type of
song delivered by the Oro Efe is a memorial for someone recently deceased, a person who in this case was
probably a singer and member of the cult. He challenges the chorus (*akijele*) to sing long and well. The
good character and positive influence of the deceased
is recalled by equating him with animals—the elephant
and hippopotamus who also, despite their greatness,

succumb to death. In the last line the permanence of
lineage is stressed with the allusion that the whisk—its
emblem—has been left behind for the deceased's
successors.

Efe Poetry

FUNERARY COMMEMORATION

I am looking at you to see how you do the ceremony.
You *akijele* have not sung enough.
Elephant died in the farm and the pot ate it up.
Hippopotamus died in the farm and the pot ate it up.
You sang well during Bello's performance.
All Oro Efe who are in the market,
We must all use mournful voice in singing.
We are calling upon you to come, come, father
      Adebayo, sleep no longer away from home.
We are calling upon you to come, come Akewe Bello,
      sleep no longer away from home.
He could no longer rise up, could no longer sing.
Father Labode, death caused the whisk to fall from the
      hand of the cult member.

The Efe poems again exemplify the close relationship
between word and performance in African literary art.
The dramatic convergence of the Oro Efe's costume,
voice, and gestures serves to heighten the spiritual and
emotional exhilaration of the ceremony, while the
poet's words command social discipline of the audience and remind them of the qualities that have enabled the community to survive. Together, they summon the ase of the community and lead the people in a
telling reaffirmation of faith.

The Gelede Celebration

The Gelede is performed on the afternoon following
the Efe festivities. Its purpose is to embody an approach
to the mothers that appeals to their positive attributes.
The priests and elders summon from the spectators attitudes necessary for the worship of the mothers: patience, indulgence, and composure. By upholding tradition and ridiculing those who offend it, the visual
symbols, along with the music and dance of Gelede, attempt to please and honor the mothers.

The main performers for Gelede are masqueraders.

While they are all men, they traditionally appear in pairs portraying males or females. The pairing probably alludes to the spiritual duality assigned to the mothers, and the males and females to the two children Efe and Gelede. The costumes, which consist essentially of mask, headwrap, and leg rattles (Fig. 17-4), exaggerate the sex characteristics of the male or female. Hoops and layers of cloth accentuate the chest of the male; a breastplate with elaborate carved breasts and wooden structures behind emphasize the female's physical attributes.

Masks consist of a head fitting over the upper portion of the masquerader's head and a superstructure above. The two components reflect different aesthetic values. The head is frontal, symmetrical, composed, and static, reflecting an ideal of patience, while the elaborate superstructure with its extended parts and asymmetrical design creates an effect of surprise. Colors in both parts are symbolic and frequently associated with the gods (Color Plate XI).

The elaborate art of the Gelede masks touches on all aspects of Yoruba life. Some of the motifs frequently occurring in them are animals, deities, social roles, historical personalities, fashion, and foreign elements. More than one motif may appear in a given mask. The principal animals of Gelede are the snake, bird, mongoose, tortoise, and lizard. Animal compositions may embody qualities of personality and behavior, as in Figure 17-5, where the snake symbolizes patience and "coolness" but is attacked by the "hot" or vengeful quadruped, a mongoose.

Goddesses, such as Oya, goddess of the Niger River (Fig. 17-6) are frequently represented in the Gelede part of the festival. Certain masks proclaim the hierarchical ordering in Yoruba social roles and religion. The mask represented in Figure 17-7 has a superstructure dominated by Yemoja, another name for Iyanla. Before the priestess is a figure prostrate in traditional greeting and at her side a small boy seeking her protection and support. This reiterates Yemoja's praises, which proclaim her the protector of children. The relative proportion suggests the religious hierarchical ordering, while the balance creates the notion of stability.

Foreigners—particularly Europeans with products of their culture such as cameras, sewing machines, cars, and trucks—often appear on the masks (Fig. 17-8). These elements of Western technology are used both for sheer entertainment and for satire, but they also imply a deeper spiritual message. Technological inventions are held by Yoruba commentators to be the result of the Europeans' spiritual power. Their appearance in Gelede masks may reflect a plea to the mothers to use their own spiritual powers in a positive way.

Dance   The visual imagery of the Gelede masks and costumes is enhanced by that of the dance, which is given great importance (Color Plate XII). Dance patterns in Africa, as elsewhere, evolve from habitual movements, posture, and gestures of work and play. Here the movements imitate qualities appropriate to

17-4   Female Gelede dancer with breastplate carved in the form of ibeji statues. Joga-Orile/Imasai, Northern Egbado, April, 1965. Regional Style Egbado. (Henry John Drewal)

17–5 Top left. Gelede mask: quadruped and snake. (Reproduced by Courtesy of the Trustees of the British Museum)

17–6 Above. Male Gelede mask. Oya. (Courtesy of Roger de la Burde)

17–7 Left. Female Gelede mask. Yemoja. (Reproduced by Courtesy of the Trustees of the British Museum)

17–8　Gelede mask. "The Lorry." (Federal Department of Antiquities, National Museum, Lagos, Nigeria)

the male or female sex, depending on the costume of the dancer. Like the words and performance of Efe and the dual composition of the masks, the dance heightens the tension inherent in this festival between male and female and between the perceived duality of the mothers. An example is the dance of the female masks performed by the young male dancer dressed as Tetede, wife of Efe. Tetede's costume with its pointed breasts emphasizes the male aggressive aspect of the feminine personality. The dance combines sequential deep knee bends, suggestive of a graceful curtsey, with a beating of shoulders and swaying of hips emphasizing female aggressivity. The dancer disguised as Efe also represents a male-female tension with both costume and mask. The heavy, layered costume suggests the ample figures of pregnant or mature women. Yet the Efe's dance, accompanied by the explosion of ceremonial guns, vigorously approaches abandon as the tempo increases and the dance reaches its culmination. This abandon, while masculine in tone, implies caricature and exaggeration

of movement and gesture associated with older women.

Through festival, as seen in both the Tohossou cult ceremony of the Dahomean kings and the Efe/Gelede of the western Yoruba, we have witnessed the interplay of many facets of African aesthetic expression. Poetry, music, song, sculptured mask, costume, and dance create together an experience of high drama for participants and observers, enhancing the social, spiritual, and moral concerns of the community. Entertaining and at times ribald, the performers nevertheless establish the priority of the spiritual powers that energize life on earth. They reinforce old values and symbols and acknowledge new realities. Audience and performers in communion celebrate the continuity of the community over time and affirm its vitality. While specific to certain groups of western Nigeria and Benin, these festivals evoke an essentially African mode of perception—the integration and wholeness of life.

COMMENTS AND QUESTIONS

1. African festivals—combining as they do music, costume, plastic art, and dance—confront all the senses with images and symbols of beliefs about human society and about spiritual forces. In reviewing this section, identify some of these in the case of Yoruba society by answering the following:
   (a) What elements of the masks are symbols of the Yoruba deities?
   (b) How is color used symbolically in mask and costume?
   (c) How does the organization of both Efe and Gelede segments of this festival illustrate the tension in Yoruba society between the roles of men and those of women? Who are the dancers? How do their costumes and dance styles convey the tension?
2. Think of other festivals that you have studied or know about from Western traditions. Can you identify similar components and purposes in them?
3. How does Gelede incorporate new experiences of cross-cultural contact of the Yoruba and integrate them into traditional Yoruba belief systems?

18

AFRICAN ROOTS AND CONTINUITIES

General Characteristics of the African Humanities

While a great diversity characterizes the many cultures on the continent of Africa and even within the area of West Africa studied here, there are certain modes of perception and cultural forms that may be characterized as African. These include, in the social realm, the veneration of elders, ancestors, and kinship ties generally, as well as the importance given to secret societies and initiation rites. We had seen that traditional religion, sometimes even among Muslim or Christian Africans, acts as a binding communal force. The close relationship with nature and the belief in a spirit world influencing it are primary motivating forces in the African arts and in the multifaceted art of the festival. African oral literature is devoted not only to religious ritual but also to moral instruction of the young and to the perpetuation of the history and traditions of a people. The griot, or oral historian-poet, plays a vital role in the latter aspect.

The traditional character of African art and culture makes the stylistic periodization that we have used in the study of Western culture somewhat irrelevant in terms of Africa. Aside from the sculptures of the Nok culture, and the arts of Ife and Benin, which can be dated, our examples of literature, art, and music have been drawn from several centuries of African experience including the present one. The festivals performed in the 1970s include modern elements while they derive from ancient forms and ideas. Similarly the poems of Diop, Achebe, and Soyinka express this continuity between ancient and modern.

Certain fundamental ideas and beliefs are shared across traditional African cultures. These include the commitment to a holistic view of life; the definition of community as the living, the dead, and the unborn; and a sensibility to the delicate balance between human society and natural forces in the universe—sometimes visible, sometimes invisible. If man must recognize the importance of natural and supernatural forces, his intelligence nevertheless is responsible for affecting his destiny. African ideas share with Western humanism a respect for the dignity of human beings and an acceptance of the foibles of human nature.

The African humanities exhibit perhaps even more than those of classical Greece a profound aesthetic and philosophical unity. Robert Farris Thompson, in his study *African Art in Motion*, has attempted to describe some of the basic principles that unite African arts and thought, particularly around the central art of dance. His conclusions, presented in brief form below, are well worth our consideration.

(1) Age and wisdom are venerated in African society. African art nonetheless shows a particular dynamic of age that would not in the West be associated with advanced years, for the elder is supposed to retain a certain youthful vitality. Even the terra cotta mask from the ancient Nok culture (see Fig. 14-1), while representing a high official who would necessarily be someone of advanced years, does not show the face of an aged man. The elder dancer who executes his performance with disciplined vitality is highly regarded.

(2) In dance, plastic art, and music, great attention is given to proportion and balance. Silence, or the "suspended beat" in music, and open space in art are not passive qualities but active components of the rhythmic flow. Balance is vitalized in perceiving the individual qualities and motions of body parts integrated into a whole. The ability to imagine and perform multiple rhythms in dance is an extension of this principle.

(3) Sharpness of line and a crisp beginning and ending characterize both dance and sculpture. The Ibo *Mmwo* mask (Fig. 16-4) demonstrates the clear boundaries of pattern that the carver's knife establishes.

(4) African arts portray an ideal of *resemblance* rather than *identity*. Sculptors, in particular, seek to represent a moral or spiritual force rather than to make an individual portrait. Although African art runs a gamut from the rather naturalistic Benin bronzes to abstract masks, it is never totally realistic or totally nonfigurative, but rather seeks a balance somewhere between the two poles.

(5) *Ancestorism*, which Thompson defines as "the belief that the closest harmony with the ancient way is the highest of experiences, the force that enables a man to rise to his destiny," is a powerful motivation in the African arts. The sculpture of the mask, mythology, music, and dance are used in rites to establish links between living sons and daughters and the community of ancestors.

(6) A final principle of "coolness," a word that has equivalents in many African languages, unites all the preceding ones. Aspects of "coolness" are visibility and openness, luminosity, and smoothness coupled with clarity. A dance, for example, may be characterized by extreme vitality but also by extreme control and by facial composure, the "mask of the cool." The belief in rebirth and reincarnation, which unites living vitality with orientation toward the ancestral, is an important component in "coolness." This unison of energy and balance, of "hot" movement and "cool" composure in African art, music, and dance is perhaps the most unique feature of African aesthetics.

African Survivals in Afro-American Culture

We have introduced Africa in this textbook between the European Renaissance and early modern period not only because this time saw the flourishing of the great West African empires, but especially because of the fact that it was at this point that the destinies of America and Europe became intertwined with that of Africa.

The fact that almost one million Africans, originating primarily in the western regions that we have studied, were imported to North America as a result of the slave trade has had profound effects on American culture. These effects have been transmitted to American culture as a whole by means of the continuities of African culture in Afro-American culture, and it is to these continuities or "survivals," as they are called, that we now turn.

African Survivals The term "African survival" is used by scholars to denote a specific form or function of an institution, ritual, belief, language, or art that is clearly identifiable with an African origin, although adapted to the New World situation. Such survivals have always been noticeable among black populations in South America and the Caribbean. North Americans of the white majority culture, however, along with many blacks, tended until recently to deny that there was anything African about Afro-American culture. For them, the American Negro had no past; his or her culture was purely a product of the slaves' adaptation to white America. In the early twentieth century, the black scholars W. E. B. DuBois and Carter Woodson were among the first to point out African survivals in the religious, social, and aesthetic life of Afro-Americans. An anthropologist, Melville H. Herskovits, continued the investigation of this question in his work *The Myth of the Negro Past,* published in 1941. Herskovits challenged the popularly held assumption that Afro-Americans had no cultural past. Outlining principal features of a "cultural complex" based on common patterns of behavior of the African cultures in the regions of slave origin, he identified certain features of Afro-American culture in the Americas and the Caribbean that evolved from African cultural institutions. Aspects of Afro-American culture that differed from comparable institutions of the white society would thus be explained by the different cultural heritage of black Americans rather than by their failure to imitate white behavior properly.

Other scholars, such as E. Franklin Frazier, argued that conditions of oppression were the real cause of the distinctive features of black culture, especially in regard to family structure. For example, the sale of family members to different masters during slavery and the need for black men to seek work away from home after emancipation resulted in an apparent predominance of single-parent and matriarchal households.

Numerous recent studies of both the African and the Afro-American past have defined more precisely both the types of African survivals to be found in Afro-American culture and the means by which they may have survived. The formation of Afro-American culture was a complex process indeed; but certain features of its social institutions, religious organizations, and beliefs, as well as its arts and letters, can now be identified as having distinctly African origins.

The Extended Family Identification with the extended (as opposed to the nuclear) family, the great importance of children to the sense of a community's continuity over time, and the special roles played by men and women in family life are African features that have persisted in Afro-American social life. Coupled with the latter is the acceptability of the economic independence of women. African women, unlike their European counterparts, could have rights in land and property. In certain circumstances, children born outside marriage were welcome additions to the woman's family. In many African societies children are often raised by people other than their own parents: sometimes grandparents, sometimes friends of their parents' generation. While preferences of these types may have been reinforced by the conditions of slavery and the plight of freed slaves, they provided adaptable models for a "normal" Afro-American family life, if different from those of the majority culture.

Groups and Associations Types of bonding and grouping characteristic of traditional African societies reappear in various ways in Afro-America. At the time of initiation, African boys and girls form close bonds with their agemates that continue, in the form of a society, throughout their lives. Age or initiation mates treat each other as brothers and sisters, granting reciprocal rights and obligations. Such groups are often the focus of festival, entertainment, and mutual support activities. Related to these groups are "titled" societies in which individuals can display their wealth and enhance their status by the purchase of a succession of "titles" bringing them recognition and respect. Titled societies also encourage cooperation in economic activities through the use of fees for insurance, burial, or investment purposes. Aspects of both the age-grade and titled societies may be seen in the structure and vitality of men's and women's groups, brotherhoods, and so on, among Afro-Americans. Even the organization of black American churches and their auxiliary societies reflects these African patterns of association.

Importance of Oral Eloquence   The Afro-American church, where permitted to develop independently, incorporated other social norms and roles of African society. Among these were leadership by elders and/or by individuals who were gifted speakers. In those African societies where leadership was informal or officially vested in a group of elders, individual influence and leadership were exercised through one's knowledge of custom and traditions as well as through sound judgment and rhetorical skill. Since the New World experience rarely permitted free and open public expression to black people, especially to men, these highly valued skills were developed in the single largest institution that the blacks had to themselves, the churches. Preachers in Afro-American churches have traditionally been political leaders in a society within a society. It is significant that many of the civil rights' leaders were first of all ministers in black churches. Martin Luther King, Jr., for example, was a gifted politician noted as well for his eloquence and his sense of history. As such, his leadership role in Afro-American society is reminiscent of that of the griot. In highly centralized states, the griots were important officials of the court. They exhorted troops to battle and counseled the ruler by recalling past heroes and events of their people's history. Their fate, as we have seen in the epic *Sundiata*, was closely bound to that of the king, who symbolized his people.

Oral Literature   The importance of the oral tradition in African life appears, as we have seen, not only in political and historical rhetoric but also in the tales used to transmit the wisdom of elders to the young. Some of the animal and human characters in African tales—notably Hare, Tortoise, and Spider—found their way to the New World in the tales told by African nursemaids to their children and to those of their mas-

ters. The transfer of animal characters was not the only African pattern to appear in this setting. The performance of the "uncle" and "auntie" figures who recited the tales was important. These stories utilized the theme of the trickster hare, common in African folklore, who outwitted those of superior physical strength (or social position) by his swiftness and cunning. The language of the tales was often replete with proverbs, riddles, and double meaning. They also sustained the pedagogical purpose of African tales: to impart a moral lesson or model of behavior.

Other kinds of Afro-American tales also reflect an African origin. For instance, there is a predominance of tales concerned with questions about the origin of the cosmos or, more generally, about how things came to be as they are. Religious tales containing plots about conjuring, voodoo, and natural phenomena reflect African religious practices that have been adapted to the New World setting. "Preacher" tales—ones by and about ministers—may combine elements of the trickster character with the primacy of the performance element. In the folk genre of the "black sermon" it is the preacher's skill in heightening the spiritual experience of his congregation through poetic use of the popular language that, more than the substance of the words, creates the popularity of the teller. Spirituals, Christian religious songs created in the context of slavery, often included actual hidden messages or codes. The importance of rhythm and verse is characteristic of Afro-American field hollers, riddles, and proverbs, as well as of some of the tales.

Written Literature   Many of the themes and stylistic devices of Afro-American folk literature mentioned above—trickster, animal, preacher subjects; moralistic purpose; the use of exaggeration, double meaning, hidden messages, rhythm, and verse—have been utilized by black American writers in their short stories, poetry, and novels. One of the earliest examples is Charles Waddell Chesnutt's *The Conjure Woman*, published in 1899, and widely read by white as well as black Americans. In this work a series of short stories develops around an elderly former slave named Uncle Julius. Uncle Julius, the epitome of deference and helpfulness toward his employer, frequently "explains things" to him through stories strongly reminiscent of the folk tale. The strange ways of nature, conjure, and animals are common subjects. Irony and satire provide the tales with various levels of meaning that belie Uncle Julius' innocence and simplicity. James Weldon Johnson's *God's Trombones: Seven Negro Sermons in Verse* is an excellent early example of the use of the black folk sermon in literature. The themes and literary techniques explored by Jean Toomer in *Cane*, Ralph Ellison in *Invisible Man*, and Richard Wright in *Native Son* are more recent examples of literature reflecting a great sensitivity to their African and Afro-American folk heritage by black American writers.

Language   African languages themselves have left their mark on the speech of Afro-American communities. Lorenzo Turner was the first to point out specific words from a variety of African languages in the speech of the Gullah communities off the South Carolina coast. More subtle—and, because of that, more persistent—linguistic influences were patterns of sentence construction. The speech of black Americans, long thought to be merely bad English, has been shown in recent years to be black English, the result of an English vocabulary superimposed on grammatical and syntactical patterns common to related African languages. It is strikingly similar to contemporary African dialects derived from contact with European languages. Other African linguistic influences are even more widespread.

Beliefs   African beliefs about the nature of the universe, about mankind's relationship to the world of nature, and about man's relationship to man have also survived in Afro-American cultures of the New World. Embodying what could be called aspects of religion, these survivals appear both within and without established black churches. Blacks in Latin America and the West Indies (and some influenced by them in the United States) worship and venerate numerous African deities, particularly those of the Yoruba. Often their names have been joined with those of the Christian saints whose personalities are perceived to be similar. In some instances the body of worshipers follow African patterns of cult organization, leadership, and ritual, although most have been altered by Christian forms.

We have seen how the spiritual vitality of the natural world and the belief in resident spirits influence all aspects of traditional African life. Acknowledgment of the spiritual power of water remains a recognizably African feature of Afro-American religion. It is not without reason that the Baptist church, which baptizes by immersion in water, is the most populous black American church. The spiritual potential of plants or of objects controlled by powerful spirits appears in the New World practices of "working roots" and of voodoo. Here a human agent, using herbs or objects as an intermediary, may direct powerful spirits to hinder or assist another person, often at the request of a third party. Inveighed against as superstitions or regarded more positively as folk medicine, such skills involve closely guarded secret knowledge and have rarely been studied in a systematic way. Credible witnesses testifying to the psychic power of such skills or forces at work have in recent years led modern scientists in the fields of pharmacology and psychiatry to study these phenomena in both Africa and the New World.

Music   African music and dance are the most well known African influences upon Afro-American and American culture in general. In Africa, the two arts are not easily distinguished from poetry and song, and none of these from the pervasive quality of ritual. Above all is the predominant role in African and Afro-American music of rhythm. It is varied and multiple in composition, often emphasizing the unexpected by the coincidence of otherwise differing rhythms upon a normally unaccented beat, called *syncopation*. Jazz music was founded upon this predominance of rhythm. In addition to rhythm, jazz musicians preferred harmonic scales, intervals of thirds, and the call-and-response pattern of solo instrument or voice with a chorus, all features widely used in Africa. Generally speaking, the African and Afro-American singing style uses the voice like an instrument, placing greater emphasis on its percussive role and on particular *timbres* of voice than European music does. The call-and-response pattern of leader and chorus was a distinctive feature of Afro-American spirituals, of course, before it was extended to the secular realm by jazz musicians.

Dance   While less studied than music, Afro-American dance can be seen to bear African characteristics of form, composition, and body stance. Preferences for group dancing in lines or in circles, with movement running counterclockwise in the latter, are typical in African dance continent-wide. A frontal pose of the face and the vigorous use of separate parts of the body to accent different rhythms of the dance were readily remarked by early European visitors to Africa. The survival of these features is generally, if not always precisely, noted by observers of Afro-American dance.

Interrelation of Arts   In traditional Africa poetry, song, music, and dance are always integrated into patterns of work and ritual as well as into those of sheer entertainment. Nothing is too sacred or too profane to be celebrated in art. Moreover, the participation in celebration, as we saw with the Efe/Gelede festival, serves to unite the community, to restore balance, and to reaffirm values. It seems likely that Afro-American artistic values and expression drew upon African content, form, occasion, and style; moreover, they also served to develop and sustain the slaves' self-conscious sense of community. Their extension and elaboration since slavery have created a distinctive Afro-American aesthetic and have greatly enriched American culture as well as Western culture as a whole.

Influence of Africa on Western Humanism Generally   The most direct impact of the African humanities on those of the West beyond Afro-America

has been in the fields of music and art. Artists like Picasso who "discovered" African sculpture in the early part of this century brought a vibrant, shocking, and refreshing set of aesthetic norms to Western art. Similarly, the African rhythms that Afro-Americans developed in jazz revitalized a tradition of Western music. Other aspects of Afro-American culture—dance, language and poetry, religion—that have their roots in Africa have been adopted or imitated by others in the West. More indirectly, Africa has influenced the humanities in Europe and America as a symbol, or an object of meditation. Black people appear in Western literature and art as evil, mysterious, savage, passionate, or as inherently noble, like Othello. Europe's contact with Africa was a source of the important theme of cultural relativity that began in the sixteenth century. The enormous burden of guilt which slavery left to the Western mind had its impact on the humanities. In Volume II we will see some examples of poets and philosophers in the eighteenth and nineteenth centuries who spoke out against the slave trade in various ways. The inhumaneness of such an institution called into question the very foundations of the humanities, and humanists were among the first to decry it. It is nonetheless true that the great flourishing of European culture, which dominated the world in the seventeenth century, was made possible in part by the exploitation of Africa.

GLOSSARY

Italics are used within the definitions to indicate terms that are themselves defined elsewhere in the glossary and, in a few cases, to distinguish titles of works or foreign words.

ABA Form MUSIC: A particular organization of parts used in a musical *composition* in which there are three units, the first and third of which are the same. See *Da capo aria.*

Abbey Religious body governed by an abbot or abbess, or the collection of buildings themselves, also called a monastery.

Abstract VISUAL ARTS: Not representational or *illusionistic.* Describes painting or sculpture which simplifies or distills figures from the material world into *forms,* lines, *colors.*

African Survival A specific form or function of an institution, ritual, belief, language, or art that is clearly identifiable with an African origin, although adapted to the situation of African descendants in the New World.

Allegory LITERATURE, VISUAL ARTS: The technique of making concrete things, animals, or persons represent abstract ideas or morals. A literary allegory usually takes the form of a *narrative* which may be read on at least two levels; for example, Dante's *Divine Comedy.* Medieval sculptures often have allegorical significance.

Altarpiece VISUAL ARTS: A painted or sculptured decoration on canvas or panels placed behind or above an altar.

Ambulatory ARCHITECTURE: A covered passageway for walking. In a church, the semicircular passage around the main altar.

Anaphora (ah-na'fo-rah) LITERATURE: A rhetorical figure which uses the repetition of the same word or phrase to introduce two or more clauses or lines of verse.

Animism The belief that parts of nature, such as water, trees, etc. have souls and can influence human events. The term is used by Westerners to describe African religions.

Antiphon MUSIC: In Gregorian chant, a short text from the Scriptures or elsewhere set to music in a simple *style,* and sung before and after a Psalm or a canticle.

Antiphonal MUSIC: See *Antiphony.*

Antiphony (an-ti'fo-ny) MUSIC: The sound produced by *choirs* or instruments "answering" one another. For instance, one choir will sing, and then it is "answered" by another choir.

Apse (aap'ss) ARCHITECTURE: A large semicircular or polygonal *niche,* *domed* or *vaulted.* In a Roman *basilica* the apse was placed at one or both ends or sides of the building. In a Christian church it is usually placed at the east end of the *nave* beyond the *choir.*

Arcade ARCHITECTURE: A covered walk made of *arches* on *piers* or *columns,* rather than *lintels.*

Arch ARCHITECTURE: 1. Commonly, any curved strutural member that is used to span an opening. 2. Specifically, restricted to the spanning members of a curved opening that are constructed of wedge-shaped stones called *voussoirs.* Arches may be of many shapes, basically round or pointed. See Roman Architecture (Ch. 5) and Gothic Architecture (Ch. 7).

Archaic 1. Obsolete. 2. In its formative or early stages.

Architrave (ahr'kuh-trave) ARCHITECTURE: A *beam* that rests directly on the *columns;* the lowest part of the *entablature.*

Aria (ah'ree-ah) MUSIC: An elaborate *composition* for solo voice with instrumental accompaniment.

Aristocracy Form of government from Greek word meaning "rule by the few for the common good."

Asantehene (a-sahn'tee-hee-nee) The Akan term for the King of the Ashanti state.

Ase (ah-say') Yoruba word meaning power, authority, potential energy.

Atmospheric Perspective See *Perspective.*

Aulos (ow'los) MUSIC: The most important wind instrument of the ancient Greeks. It is not a flute (as is often stated), but a shrill-sounding oboe. It originated in the Orient and was associated with the orgiastic rites of the god Dionysus.

Axis VISUAL ARTS: The imaginary line that can be passed through a building or a figure, around which the principal parts revolve. See *Balance.*

Balance VISUAL ARTS: The creation of an apparent equilibrium or *harmony* between all the parts of a *composition,* be it a building, painting, or sculpture.

Balustrade ARCHITECTURE: A rail or handrail along the top edge of a roof or balcony, made up of a top horizontal rail, a bottom rail, and short *columns* between.

Baptistry ARCHITECTURE: The building or room for performing the rite of baptism. Contains a basin or pool.

Barrel Vault See *Vault.*

Base ARCHITECTURE: 1. The lowest visible part of a building. 2. The slab on which some *column* shafts rest. See *Orders.*

Basilica (bah-sil'i-cah) ARCHITECTURE: A large, rectangular hall with a central space surrounded by aisles on the sides and an *apse* at one or each end or side. The basilica was used as a court of justice by the Romans and adopted by the early Christians as a church.

Bay ARCHITECTURE: One of a series of regularly repeated spaces of a building marked off by vertical elements.

Beam ARCHITECTURE: A large piece of squared timber, long in proportion to its breadth and thickness, used for spanning spaces. A *lintel* is a specific kind of beam.

Blank Verse LITERATURE: Unrhymed lines in *iambic pentameter.* A common form for dramatic verse in English. See Shakespeare (Ch. 13).

Boss ARCHITECTURE: The circular *keystone* at the crossing of diagonal *ribs.* May be richly carved and decorated.

Buttress ARCHITECTURE: The vertical exterior mass of masonry built at right angles into the *wall* to strengthen it and to counteract the lateral *thrust* of a *vault* or *arch.* Architecture of the Gothic period developed this *form* into the flying buttress, which is a combination of the regular or *pier*-like buttress and the arched buttress. See *Chartres* (Ch. 7).

Capital ARCHITECTURE: The uppermost or crowning member of a *column, pilaster,* or *pier* that forms the visual transition from the post to the *lintel* above. See *Orders.*

Caryatid (kahr'-ee-ah-tid) ARCHITECTURE: The name given a *column* when it is disguised as a female figure.

Casting SCULPTURE: A method of re-producing sculpture through the use of a mold that is the receptacle for a liquid which hardens when cooled. The method may be used to produce solid or hollow cast *forms.*

Cathedral Principal church of a diocese, literally the location of the bishop's throne, or cathedra.

Cella ARCHITECTURE: The principal chamber of a Greek or Roman temple, housing the cult image.

Centering ARCHITECTURE: The temporary wooden *structure* that supports an *arch* or dome while it is being erected.

Chapel ARCHITECTURE: 1. A small church. 2. A separate compartment in a large church that has its own altar.

Choir ARCHITECTURE: The part of the church reserved for clergy and singers, usually the space between the crossing and the *apse.* MUSIC: A group of singers in a church.

Chord MUSIC: The simultaneous sounding of three or more usually harmonious *tones.*

Chromatic MUSIC: Describes a scale progressing by half-tones instead of the normal degrees of the scale; e.g., in C major: c-c#-d-d#-e instead of c-d-e. VISUAL ARTS: Refers to the visual spectrum of hues. See *Color.*

Cire Perdu (seer pehr-doo') SCULPTURE: French expression meaning "lost wax." Technique for making bronze sculpture that involves molding wax over a clay mold, encasing it with another clay mold, heating the mold, then allowing the wax to drain out and replacing it with molten bronze.

Classic, Classical ALL ARTS: Recognized generally to be excellent, time-tested. LITERATURE AND VISUAL ARTS: 1. From ancient Greece or Rome. 2. From "classical" (fifth century B.C.) Greece or having properties such as *harmony, balance,* moderation and magnitude characteristic of art of that period. MUSIC: The musical *style* of the late 18th century. Leading composers in the classical style are Haydn, Mozart, and the early Beethoven.

Clerestory (clear'story) ARCHITECTURE: An upper story in a building that carries windows or openings for the transmission of light to the space beneath.

Coffer, Coffering ARCHITECTURE: Originally a casket or box, later, a recessed ceiling panel. Coffering is a technique for making a ceiling of recessed panels.

Colonnade ARCHITECTURE: A series of regularly spaced *columns* supporting a *lintel* or *entablature.*

Color VISUAL ARTS: A quality perceived in objects by the human eye that derives from the length of the light waves reflected by individual surfaces. The visible spectrum is divided into six basic hues: red, orange, yellow, green, blue, and violet. Red, yellow and blue are called the *primary colors;* the others, which result from mixing adjacent primary colors, are called *secondary colors.* White, black, and grays result from mixing these six hues and are not *chromatic:* they cannot be distinguished by hue, only by value. Value is the property of a color that distinguishes it as light or dark. Colors that are "high" in value are light colors; those that are "low" in value are dark colors. Adding white to a color will raise its value to make a *tint;* adding black to a color will lower its value to make a *shade.* Saturation is the property of a color by which its vividness or purity is distinguished. See also *Complementary Colors, Cool Colors, Warm Colors.*

Column ARCHITECTURE: A cylindrical, upright post or pillar. It may contain three parts: *base,* shaft, and *capital.*

Comedy LITERATURE: A drama that ends happily, intended to provoke laughter from its audience. Comedy often includes *satire* on types of characters or societies.

Complementary Colors Hues that form a neutral grey when mixed but, when juxtaposed, form a sharp contrast. The complementary of any *primary color* (red, yellow, or blue) is made by mixing the other two primaries. Example: The complementary of red is green, obtained by mixing yellow with blue.

Composition VISUAL ARTS: The arrangements of elements within the work in order to create a certain effect based on a variety of principles and conventions: e.g., *balance, color, contour, focal point, proportion, scale, symmetry, volume*. MUSIC: The putting together of elements such as *melody, harmony, rhythm,* and orchestration into a musical *form*. The term may be used similarly to denote a putting together of elements in a dance or film. LITERATURE: The act of composing an oral or written work.

Compound Pier ARCHITECTURE: A *pier* or post made up of attached *columns*. See *Chartres* (Ch. 7).

Content ALL ARTS: What the *form* contains and means. Content may include subject matter and theme. The quality of a work of art is often judged by the appropriateness, or apparent inseparability, of form and content.

Contour PAINTING, DRAWING: The visible edge or outline of an object, *form* or shape, used especially to suggest *volume* or mass by means of the distinctness, thickness, or color of the edge or line.

Contrapuntal (con-tra-pun'tal) MUSIC: In a *style* that employs *counterpoint*.

Cool Colors VISUAL ARTS: Blues, greens, and associated hues. Cool colors will appear to recede from the viewer in a picture, while *warm colors* will tend to project.

Cornice ARCHITECTURE: 1. The horizontal projection that finishes the top of a *wall*. 2. In classical architecture, the third or uppermost horizontal section of an *entablature*. See *Orders*.

Counterpoint MUSIC: Music consisting of two or more *melodies* played simultaneously. The term is practically synonymous with *polyphony*.

Crossing In a church, the intersection of the *nave* and *transept* in front of the *apse*.

Da Capo Aria (dah cah'poh ahr'ee-ah) MUSIC: A particular type of *aria* that developed in the baroque period (17th and 18th centuries). It consists of two sections, the first of which is repeated after the second. The result is the *ABA form*. See *Aria, ABA Form*.

Democracy From the Greek word meaning "rule by the people." A form of government in which the electorate is coincident with the adult population (sometimes only the adult males) of the community.

Despotism Government by a ruler with unlimited powers.

Dialectic PHILOSOPHY: 1. Platonic—A method of logical examination of beliefs, proceeding by question and answer. 2. Hegelian and Marxian—A logical method that proceeds by the contradiction of opposites (thesis, antithesis) to their resolution in a synthesis.

Dome ARCHITECTURE: A curved or hemispherical roof structure spanning a space and resting on a curved, circular, or polygonal *base*. Theoretically, a dome is an *arch* rotated 360 degrees around a central *axis*. See *Pantheon* (Ch. 5).

Drapery SCULPTURE: The clothing of a figure or *form* in a usually nonspecific but *tactile* and responsive material.

Drum ARCHITECTURE: The cylindrical or polygonal *structure* that rises above the body of a building to support a *dome*.

Duration MUSIC: The time-value assigned to a musical note; that is, how long it is to be played or sung.

Dynamics MUSIC: Words or signs that indicate the varying degrees of loudness in the music. For instance, *forte* (loud), *piano* (soft, quiet), *diminuendo* (decrease *volume* gradually).

Egungun (eh-goon-goon) Yoruba masqueraders concerned with mediating between the community of the living and that of the recently dead.

Elevation ARCHITECTURE: 1. Generally, a term that refers to one of the sides of a building. 2. Specifically, a drawing or graphic representation showing one face or side of a building. It can be of the interior or exterior.

Entablature ARCHITECTURE: The upper section of a classical *order* resting on the *capitals* of the *columns* and including *architrave, frieze, cornice,* and *pediment*.

Epic LITERATURE: A long *narrative* poem that recounts an event of importance in a culture's history and presents a hero of that culture. See section on Homer (Ch. 1).

Episode LITERATURE: In Greek tragedy, a section of action between two choruses. In drama and fiction generally, a group of events having unity in itself. A story is created from a series of related episodes. A fiction is said to be episodic if the episodes fall into no logical relationship.

Epithet LITERATURE: A short phrase used to modify a noun by pointing out a salient characteristic. Epithets (e.g., Homer's "swift-footed Achilles") are often used in epic poetry.

Eros In Greek mythology, son of Aphrodite and god of sexual love, called "Cupid" by the Romans.

Ethics PHILOSOPHY: The branch of philosophy dealing with problems of good and bad, right and wrong, in human conduct.

Façade (fa-sahd') ARCHITECTURE: A face of a building.

Fetish Statue or other object believed to embody supernatural power.

Fluting ARCHITECTURE: The grooves or channels, usually parallel, that decorate the shafts of *columns*. Fluting may run up and down a shaft or around the shaft in various directions.

Focal Point VISUAL ARTS: The place of major or dominant interest on which the eyes repeatedly focus in a painting, drawing, or architectural arrangement.

Foreshortening PAINTING: The method of representing objects or parts of objects as if seen from an angle so that the object seems to recede into space instead of being seen in a frontal or profile view. The technique is based on the principle of continuous diminution in size along the length of the object or figure. See *Perspective* and *Vanishing Point.*

Form ALL ARTS: The arrangement or organization of the elements of a work of art in space (visual arts) or time (literary, musical, performing arts). A form may be conventional or imposed by tradition (the Greek temple, the sonnet, the sonata, the five-act play) or original with the artist. In the latter case, form is said to follow from, or adapt itself to, *content.*

Fresco PAINTING: The technique of making a painting on new, wet plaster. Fresco painting was particularly favored in Italy from Roman times until the eighteenth century. See Ch. 10.

Frieze ARCHITECTURE: 1. Middle horizontal element of the classical *entablature.* See *Orders.* 2. A decorative band near the top of an interior wall that is below the *cornice* molding.

Gable ARCHITECTURE: The triangular space at the end of a building formed by the slopes of a pitched roof, extending from the *cornice* or eaves to the *ridge.* In classical architecture the gable is called a *pediment.*

Gallery ARCHITECTURE: A long, covered area, usually elevated, that acts as a passageway on the inside or exterior of a building.

Genre (john'ruh) LITERATURE: A literary type or form. Genres include *tragedy, comedy, epic, lyric,* novel, short story, essay.

Greco-Roman Belonging to the cultures of ancient Greece and Rome.

Griot (gree-oh') African oral poet, musician, and historian.

Groin Vault See *Vault.*

Groundplan ARCHITECTURE: A drawing of a horizontal *section* of a building that shows the arrangement of the *walls,* windows, supports and other elements. A groundplan is used to produce blueprints.

Ground Plane PAINTING: In a picture, the surface, apparently receding into the distance, on which the figures seem to stand. It is sometimes

thought of as comparable to a kind of stage space.

Harmony MUSIC: The chordal structure of music familiar to most Western listeners in popular music accompanied by guitars, in Romantic orchestral music, etc.

Hebraic Belonging to the Hebrews, Jews, or Israelites. Refers primarily to the culture of the ancient Hebrews of Biblical times.

Hebraism Hebrew culture, thought, institutions.

Hellenic Greek. Usually refers to the "classical" period of Greek culture; i.e., the fifth and fourth centuries B.C.

Hellenism The culture of ancient Greece.

Hellenistic Literally, "Greek-like." Refers to Greek history and artistic style from the third century B.C.

Homophonic (hawm-o-fon'ic) Characteristic of *homophony.*

Homophony (hoh-maw'foh-nee) MUSIC: A single *melody* line supported by its accompanying *chords* and/or voice parts. See *Monophony, Polyphony, Chord,* and Texture.

Hubris (hyoo'bris) A Greek word meaning arrogance or excessive pride.

Hue See *Color.*

Hyperbole (high-purr'boh-lee) LITERATURE: A figure of speech that uses obvious exaggeration.

Iamb (eye'amb) LITERATURE: A metrical "foot" consisting of one short (or unaccented) syllable and one long (or accented) syllable. Example: hĕllō.

Iambic Pentameter (eye-am'bic pentam'eh-ter) LITERATURE: The most common metrical line in English verse, consisting of five *iambs.* Example, from Shakespeare: "Shăll Ī cŏmpāre thĕe tō ă sŭmmĕr's dāy?"

Ifa (ee'fah) A Yoruba system of divination in which a priest advises his clients of proper courses of behavior based upon the casting of palm kernels and the interpretation of poems chosen for their numerical links to the patterns of thrown kernels.

Illusionism VISUAL ARTS: The attempt by artists to create the illusion of reality in their work. Illusionism

may also be called realism. It is important to remember that illusionism is not the motivating intention of all works of art.

Image ALL ARTS: The representation of sense impressions to the imagination. Images are a fundamental part of the language of art. They differ from the abstract terminology of science and philosophy in that they are a means whereby complex emotional experience is communicated. Images may be tactile, auditory, olfactory, etc., but the word is ordinarily used for visual impressions.

Imagery LITERATURE: Patterns of *images* in a specific work or in the entire works of an author. May refer to a specific type (animal imagery, garden imagery). VISUAL ARTS: The objects, *forms* or shapes depicted by the artist in a particular work.

Improvisation MUSIC: The art of performing music spontaneously rather than the practice of recreating written music.

Induction PHILOSOPHY: Reasoning from particular facts or cases to a general conclusion.

Initiation Ceremonies or rites by which a young person is brought into manhood or womanhood, or an older person is made a member of a secret society, brotherhood, etc.

Irony LITERATURE: A manner of speaking by which the author says the opposite of what he means, characteristically using words of praise to imply scorn. Dramatic or tragic irony means that the audience is aware of truths which the character speaking does not understand.

Iwi (ee'wee) Yoruba poems sung by Egungun masqueraders.

Jamb ARCHITECTURE: A vertical member at either side of a door frame or window frame. When sculpture is attached to this member it is called a jamb sculpture or jamb figure. See *Chartres* (Ch. 7).

Kente (ken'teh) Large ceremonial cloth from Ghana made of narrow strips sewn together and distinguished by elaborate, multicolored geometric designs of silk.

Keystone ARCHITECTURE: The central wedge-shaped stone of an *arch* that locks together the others.

Komos Greek word for a revel. Root of the word *comedy*.

Kouros (koo'rohs), **Kore** (koh'ray) SCULPTURE: Greek for a male nude votive figure, female votive figure.

Labarai (lah-bah-rye') Hausa tales told by old men, involving cultural, family, and group history.

Linear Perspective See *Perspective*.

Lintel ARCHITECTURE: The horizontal member or *beam* that spans an opening between two upright members, or posts, over a window, door, or similar opening.

Lyric LITERATURE: A short poem or song characterized by personal feeling and intense emotional expression. Originally, in Greece, lyrics were accompanied by the music of a lyre.

Matrilineal System of descent in which inheritance of goods, access to land, and group leadership pass to the children through the family of the mother.

Medium (pl. media) ALL ARTS: 1. The material or materials with which the artist works. Examples from VISUAL ARTS: paint, stone, wood, bronze, plaster, concrete. MUSIC: sound. LITERATURE: language. CINEMA: film. DANCE human body. DRAMA: language, costume, lighting, actors, sound, etc. 2. Modern means of communication (television, radio, newspapers). PAINTING: A substance such as oil, egg, or water with which *pigment* is mixed.

Melody MUSIC: A succession of musical *tones*. Often the melody is known as the "tune," and is not to be confused with the other accompanying parts of a song. See *Homophony*.

Metaphor LITERATURE: A figure of speech that states or implies an analogy between two objects or between an object and a mental or emotional state. Example: "My days are in the yellow leaf;/The flowers and fruits of love are gone" (Byron) makes an analogy between the poet's life and the seasonal changes of a tree.

Meter POETRY: A regularly recurring rhythmic pattern. Meter in English is most commonly measured by accents, or stresses, and syllables. MUSIC: A pattern of fixed temporal units. For example, $\frac{3}{4}$ meter means one beat to a quarter note and three beats to a measure. In a musical *composition* meter is the basic grouping of notes in time.

Metope (meh'toh-pay) ARCHITECTURE: The blank space of block between the *triglyphs* in the Doric *frieze*, sometimes sculpted in low *relief*. See *Orders*.

Modal MUSIC: Describes a type of music conforming to the scale patterns of the medieval Church *modes*. See *Modes*.

Modeling VISUAL ARTS: 1. The creation of a three-dimensional *form* in clay or other responsive material, such as wax, soap, soft bone, ivory, etc. 2. By analogy, in painting and drawing, the process of suggesting a three-dimensional *form* by the creation of *shade* and shadow.

Modes MUSIC: Melodic scales used for church music of the Middle Ages. The modes are organized according to *pitches* similar to our modern major and minor scales, yet different enough to set them apart from the modern scales.

Molding ARCHITECTURE: A member used in construction or decoration that produces a variety in edges or contours by virtue of its curved surface.

Monastery The dwelling place of a community of monks. See *Abbey*.

Monasticism A way of life assumed by those who voluntarily separate themselves from the world to contemplate divine nature. See *Monastery*.

Monophonic (mo-no-fohn'ic) Characteristic of *monophony*.

Monophony (mo-nof'o-nee) MUSIC: A simple *melody* without additional parts or accompaniment, such as the music of a flute playing alone or of a woman singing by herself. See *Homophony, Polyphony, Texture*.

Mosaic VISUAL ARTS: A *form* of surface decoration made by inlaying small pieces of glass, tile, enamel, or varicolored stones in a cement or plaster matrix or ground.

Motet (moh-tette') MUSIC: Usually an unaccompanied choral composition based on a Latin sacred text. The motet was one of the most important forms of *polyphonic* composition from the thirteenth through the seventeenth centuries.

Motif (moh-teef'), **Motive** (moh-teev') LITERATURE: A basic element that recurs, and may serve as a kind of foundation, in a long poem, fiction, or drama. A young woman awakened by love is the motif of many tales, such as *Sleeping Beauty*. VISUAL ARTS: An element of design repeated and developed in a painting, sculpture, or building. MUSIC: A recurring melodic phrase, sometimes used as a basis for variation.

Myth Stories developed anonymously within a culture that attempt to explain natural events from a supernatural or religious point of view.

Mythology The body of myths from a particular cultural group.

Naos (nah'ohs) ARCHITECTURE: Greek word for the *cella* or main body of a Greek temple.

Narrative LITERATURE: 1. (noun) Any *form* that tells a story or recounts a sequence of events (novel, *tale*, essay, article, film). 2. (adj.) In story form, recounting.

Narthex ARCHITECTURE: The entrance hall or porch that stands before the *nave* of a church.

Naturalism LITERATURE, VISUAL ARTS: Faithful adherence to the appearance of nature or outer reality.

Nave ARCHITECTURE: In Roman architecture, the central space of a *basilica;* in Christian architecture, the central longitudinal or circular space in the church, bounded by aisles.

Nave Arcade ARCHITECTURE: The open passageway or screen between the central space and the *side aisles* in a church.

Nemesis (neh'ma-sis) Greek goddess

of Fate. Word means retribution, punishment.

Neolithic The stage in the evolution of human societies when peoples began systematic cultivation and the domestication of animals.

Niche (nish) ARCHITECTURE: A semicircular or similarly shaped recess in a wall designed to contain sculpture, an urn, or other object. It is usually covered by a half-*dome*.

Oba Name for the chief ruler of Benin.

Oculus (ock'you-luhs) ARCHITECTURE: Circular opening at the crown of a *dome*. See *Pantheon* (Ch. 5).

Odu (oh'doo) A secret body of poetry used in the Yoruba *Ifa* divination process.

Oil Painting The practice of painting by using *pigments* suspended in oil (walnut, linseed, etc.).

Oligarchy (oh'lih-gar-key) Greek word meaning "rule by the few." Rule by the few where the state is primarily utilized to serve the interest of the governors. Traditionally contrasted with *aristocracy*, rule by the few for the common good.

Olorun (oh-low'roon), **Oludumare** (oh-loo-doo-mah'ray) The Yoruba term for the supreme high deity.

Open Fifths MUSIC: *Chords*, normally made of three sounds, with the middle *pitch* absent.

Orders ARCHITECTURE: Types of *columns* with *entablatures* developed in classical Greece. The orders are basically three: Doric, Ionic, and Corinthian. They determine not only the scale and therefore dimensions of a temple but also the experience generated by the building, or its *style*. See section on Greek Architecture and diagram of the orders (Ch. 2).

Oriki (ohr-ee'key) Yoruba term meaning praise poems based on names given to gods, places, rulers, and important persons.

Orisha (ohr-ee'sha) In Yoruba religion, lesser gods (below the chief god) and sometimes ancestor figures, ancient kings, and founders of cities who have been deified.

Ostinato (aw-stee-nah'toe) MUSIC: Italian for obstinate or stubborn; the persistent repetition of a clearly defined *melody*, usually in the same voice. This device is often used in a bass part to organize a *composition* for successive variations.

Oxymoron (ock-see-mohr'on) LITERATURE: A figure of speech that brings together two contradictory terms, such as "sweet sorrow."

Palazzo (pa-laht'so) ARCHITECTURE: Italian for palace, or large, impressive building.

Panel Painting A painting made on a ground or panel of wood, as distinguished from a *fresco* or a painting on canvas.

Parapet ARCHITECTURE: In an exterior *wall*, the part entirely above the roof. The term may also describe a low wall that acts as a guard at a sudden edge or drop, as on the edge of a roof, battlement, or wall.

Parody LITERATURE: A work that exaggerates or burlesques another, serious one. Often a parody pokes fun at an author and his style. The parody may be compared to a visual caricature or cartoon.

Pathos (pay'thaws) ALL ARTS: A quality that sets off deep feeling or compassion in the spectator or reader.

Patrilineal System of descent in which inheritance of goods, access to land, and group leadership passes to the children through the family of the father.

Pediment ARCHITECTURE: In classical architecture the triangular space at the end of a roof formed by the sloping ridges of the roof. The pediment was often filled with decoration which could be painted or sculpted or both.

Pentatonic Scale MUSIC: Five-note scale that occurs in the music of nearly all ancient cultures. It is common in West African music and is found in jazz.

Perspective VISUAL ARTS: Generally, the representation of three-dimensional objects in space on a two-dimensional surface. There are a variety of means to achieve this. The most familiar is that of "linear perspective" developed in the fifteenth century and codified by Brunelleschi, in which all parallel lines and edges of surfaces recede at the same angle and are drawn, on the picture plane, to converge at a single *vanishing point*. The process of diminution in size of objects with respect to location is very regular and precise. Other techniques, often used in combination with linear perspective, include: (a) vertical perspective—objects further from the observer are shown higher up on the picture, (b) diagonal perspective—objects are not only higher but aligned along an oblique *axis* producing the sensation of continuous recession, (c) overlapping, (d) *foreshortening*, (e) *modeling*, (f) *shadows*, and (g) atmospheric perspective, the use of conventions such as blurring of outlines, alternation of hue toward blue, and decrease of *color* saturation.

Phrase MUSIC: A natural division of the *melody*; in a manner of speaking, a musical "sentence."

Picture Plane PAINTING: The surface on which the picture is painted.

Picture Space PAINTING: The space that extends behind or beyond the picture plane; created by devices such as *linear perspective*. Picture space is usually described by foreground, middleground, and background.

Pier ARCHITECTURE: A *column*, post, or similar member designed to carry a great load; may also refer to a thickened vertical mass within the *wall* designed to provide additional support.

Pigment PAINTING: The grains or powder that give a *medium* its *color*. Can be derived from a variety of sources: clays, stones, metals, shells, animal and vegetable matter.

Pilaster (pih'lass-ter) ARCHITECTURE: A flattened engaged *column* or *pier* that may have a *capital* and *base*. It may be purely decorative or it may reinforce a *wall*.

Pitch MUSIC: A technical term identifying a single musical sound, taking into consideration the frequency of its fundamental vibrations. Some songs, or instruments, are pitched high and others are pitched low.

Plan See *Groundplan.*

Plane A flat surface.

Plasticity VISUAL ARTS: The quality of roundness, palpability, solidity, or three-dimensionality of a *form.*

Podium ARCHITECTURE: The high platform or *base* of a Roman temple, or any elevated platform.

Polis (poh'liss) The ancient Greek city-state.

Polyphonic (paul-ee-fon'ick) Characteristic of *polyphony.*

Polyphony (paul-if'o-nee) MUSIC: Describes *compositions* or *improvisations* in which more than one *melody* sounds simultaneously; that is, two or more tunes at the same time. Polyphony is characterized by the combining of a number of individual melodies into a harmonizing and agreeable whole. See *Homophony, Monophony,* and *Texture.*

Portico ARCHITECTURE: Porch or covered walk consisting of a roof supported by *columns.*

Post-and-Lintel ARCHITECTURE: An essential system of building characterized by the use of uprights—posts—which support horizontal *beams*—*lintels*—in order to span spaces. Used as supports for a window or door, the posts are the *jambs* and the *lintel* is the window head.

Primary Colors Red, Yellow, Blue—the three primary hues of the spectrum. See *Color.*

Pronaos (pro'nah-ohs) ARCHITECTURE: In classical architecture, the inner *portico* or room in front of the *naos* or *cella.*

Prose LITERATURE: Generally, may mean any kind of discourse, written or spoken, which cannot be classified as poetry. More specifically, prose refers to written expression characterized by logical, grammatical order, *style,* and even *rhythm* (but not *meter*).

Proverb A saying that succinctly and effectively expresses a truth recog-

nized by a community or a wise observation about life. Proverbs are most often transmitted orally.

Relief Sculpture Sculpture that is not freestanding but projects from a surface of which it is a part. A slight projection is called low relief (bas-relief); a more pronounced projection, high relief.

Republic A form of government in which ultimate power resides in the hands of a fairly large number of people but not necessarily the entire community. This power is exercised through representatives. The word derives from Latin meaning "public thing."

Response MUSIC: A solo-chorus relationship in which the soloist alternates performance with the chorus. The response is a particularly noteworthy device in traditional African music as well as in Gregorian chant.

Responsorial MUSIC: Describing the performance of a chant in alternation between a soloist and a chorus. (It is unlike *antiphonal* music, where alternating choruses sing.)

Rhythm ALL ARTS: An overall sense of systematic movement. In music, poetry, and dance this movement may be literally felt; in the visual arts it refers to the regular repetition of a *form,* conveying a sense of movement by the contrast between a form and its interval.

Rib ARCHITECTURE: Generally a curved structural member that supports any curved shape or panel.

Ribbed Vault ARCHITECTURE: A *vault* whose sections seem to be supported or are supported by slender, curved structural members that also define the sections of the vault. The ribs may run either transversely, that is from side to side, or diagonally, from corner to corner of the vault.

Riddle A form of popular, usually oral, literature that asks an answer to a veiled question. Riddles often make use of striking *images* and *metaphors.*

Ridge ARCHITECTURE: The line defined by the meeting of the two sides of a sloping roof.

Romanesque An artistic movement of the eleventh and twelfth centuries, primarily in architecture. The name comes from similarities with Roman architecture.

Rose Window ARCHITECTURE: The round, ornamental window frequently found over the entrances of Gothic cathedrals.

Sarcophagus (sahr-cough'a-gus) A large stone coffin. It may be elaborately carved and decorated.

Satire A mode of expression that criticizes social institutions or human foibles humorously. The Romans invented the verse satire, but satire may appear in any literary *genre,* in visual art, in film, mime, and dance.

Satyr (say'ter) **Play** LITERATURE: A light, burlesque play given along with *tragedies* and *comedies* at the festival of Dionysus in ancient Athens.

Scholasticism PHILOSOPHY: A way of thought that attempted to reconcile Christian truth with truth established by natural reason. Originating in the early Middle Ages, it reached its height in the thirteenth century in response to the recovery of Aristotle's scientific and philosophical writings.

Secondary Colors See *Color.*

Section ARCHITECTURE: The drawing that represents a vertical slice through the interior or exterior of a building, showing the relation of floor to floor.

Shade PAINTING: A *color* mixed with black. Mixing a color with white produces a *tint.*

Shading VISUAL ARTS: The process of indicating by means of graphics or paint the change in *color* of an object when light falls on its surface revealing its three-dimensional qualities. Shading can be produced not only by a change of color, but also by the addition of black, brown, or gray, or by drawing techniques.

Shadow VISUAL ARTS: The *form* cast by an object in response to the direction of light.

Shed Roof ARCHITECTURE: A roof

shape with only one sloping *plane*, such as the roof of a lean-to, or that over the *side aisle* in a Gothic or Romanesque church.

Side Aisle ARCHITECTURE: The aisles on either side of, and therefore parallel to, the *nave* in a Christian church or Roman *basilica*.

Simile (sim'eh-lee) LITERATURE: A type of *metaphor* which makes an explicit comparison. Example: "My love is like a red, red rose."

Span ARCHITECTURE: The interval between two posts, *arches, walls,* or other supports.

Stained Glass ARCHITECTURE: Glass to which a *color* is added during its molten state, or glass which is given a hue by firing or otherwise causing color to adhere to the glass.

Stele (stee'lee) ARCHITECTURE: In classical Greece a stone upright or slab used commemoratively; it may mark a grave or record an offering or important event.

Structure ALL ARTS: The relationship of the parts to the whole in a work of art. A structure may be mechanical (division of a play into acts, a symphony into movements) or may be more concealed and based on such things as the inter-relationships of *images, themes, motifs, colors,* shapes. In a *narrative* the structure usually refers to the arrangement of the sequence of events. In architecture structure may refer either to the actual system of building or to the relationships between the elements of the system of building.

Style ALL ARTS: Characteristics of *form* and technique that enable us to identify a particular work with a certain historical period, place, group, or individual. Painters in Florence in the 15th and 16th centuries used *perspective, color,* etc. in ways that allow us to identify a Renaissance style, but within that group we may distinguish the individual style of Leonardo from that of Raphael. Literary style is determined by choices of words, sentence *structure* and syntax *rhythm,* figurative language, rhetorical devices, etc. One

may speak of an ornate, simple, formal, or colloquial style; of a period style, or of an individual's style. Style is sometimes contrasted with *content.*

Subject ALL ARTS: What the work is about. The subject of a statue of Apollo is the god Apollo; the subject of *Sundiata* is that hero's life. MUSIC: The *melody* used as the basis of a *contrapuntal composition* (e.g., the subject of a fugue).

Symbol VISUAL ARTS, LITERATURE: An *image* that suggests an idea, a spiritual or religious concept, or an emotion beyond itself. It differs from *metaphor* in that the term of comparison is not explicitly stated. Symbols may be conventional; i.e., have a culturally defined meaning such as the Christian cross or the Jewish star of David. Since the nineteenth century, symbols have tended to denote a variety or an ambiguity of meanings.

Symbolism The use of symbol in any art.

Symmetry VISUAL ARTS: The balance of proportions achieved by the repetition of parts on either side of a central *axis.* The two sides may be identical, in which case we can speak of bilateral symmetry.

Syncopation MUSIC: A rhythmic device characterized as a deliberate disturbance of a regularly recurring pulse. Accented offbeats or irregular *meter* changes are two means of achieving syncopation.

Tactile VISUAL ARTS, LITERATURE: Refers to the sense of touch. In the visual arts, tactile *values* are created by techniques and conventions that specifically stimulate the sense of touch in order to enhance suggestions of weight, *volume* (roundness), visual approximation, and therefore three-dimensionality. Writers may also create tactile effects, as in the description of cloth or skin.

Tale LITERATURE: A simple *narrative,* whose subject matter may be real or imaginary, and whose purpose is primarily to entertain. Tales may also make use of "morals" to instruct.

Tatsuniyoyi (taht-soon-yoh'yee) Hausa tales about animals and people told by old women to entertain and instruct young children.

Tempera (tehm'per-ah) PAINTING: Technique in which the *pigment* is suspended in egg, glue, or a similar soluble *medium,* like water. Tempera paint dries very quickly and does not blend easily, producing a matte (flat, nonreflective) surface, because, unlike *oil paint,* it is essentially an opaque medium.

Texture VISUAL ARTS: Surface quality (rough, smooth, grainy, etc.) LITERATURE: elements such as *imagery,* sound patterns, etc. apart from the *subject* and *structure* of the work. MUSIC: The working relationship between the *melody* line and the other accompanying parts, or the characteristic "weaving" of a musical *composition.* There are three basic musical textures: *Monophonic* (a single line), *Homophonic* (a melody supported by *chords*), and *Polyphonic* (multiple melodic lines).

Theme VISUAL ARTS: A *color* or pattern taken as a subject for repetition and modification. Example: A piece of sculpture may have a cubical theme. MUSIC: A *melody* that constitutes the basis of variation and development. LITERATURE AND PERFORMING ARTS: An emotion or idea that receives major attention in the work. A novel or film may contain several themes, such as love, war, death. A dance may be composed on the theme of struggle, joy, etc. Theme is sometimes used in this sense for visual arts and music as well.

Threnody (threh'no-dee) MUSIC: A song of lamentation, a very mournful song.

Through-Composed MUSIC: Describes a type of song in which new music is provided for each stanza. A through-composed song is thus unlike most modern hymns, folk, and popular songs, which use the same tune for each stanza.

Thrust ARCHITECTURE: The downward and outward pressure exerted by a *vault* or *dome* on the *walls* supporting it.

Timbre (taam′bruh) MUSIC: The quality of "color" of a particular musical *tone* produced by the various instruments. For instance, the very "nasal" sound of the oboe is markedly different from the very "pure" sound of the flute.

Tint VISUAL ARTS: The *color* achieved by adding white to a hue to raise its *value*, in contrast to a *shade*, which is a hue mixed with black to lower its value.

Tone ALL ARTS: The creation of a mood or an emotional state. In painting, tone may refer specifically to the prevailing effect of a *color*. Thus, a painting may be said to have a silvery, bluish, light, or dark tone as well as a wistful, melancholy, or joyful tone. The term may also refer to *value* or *shade* (see *Color*). In literature, tone usually describes the prevailing attitude of an author toward his material, audience, or both. Thus a tone may be cynical, sentimental, satirical, etc. In music, "tone color" may be used as a synonym for *timbre*. Tone in music also means a sound of definite *pitch* and duration (as distinct from noise), the true building material of music. The notes on a written page of music are merely symbols that represent the tones that actually make the music.

Tornada (tore-nah′dah) MUSIC: In troubadour songs, a short stanza added at the end as a "send-off."

Tracery ARCHITECTURE: The curvilinear or rectilinear pattern of open stonework or wood that supports the glass or other transparent or translucent material in a window or similar opening. May also be used generally to refer to decorative patterns carved similarly on wood or stone.

Tragedy LITERATURE: A serious drama that recounts the events in the life of a great person which bring him or her from fortune to misfortune. Tragedies usually meditate on the relation between human beings and their destiny. Tragedies first devel-

oped in ancient Greece; other great periods of tragedy include Elizabethan England and France under Louis XIV. The word is sometimes used to describe a novel or story.

Transept ARCHITECTURE: The transverse portion of a church that crosses the central *axis* of the *nave* at right angles between the nave and *apse* to form a cross-shaped (cruciform) planned building.

Triglyph (try′glif) ARCHITECTURE: The block carved with three channels or grooves that alternates with the *metopes* in a classical Doric *frieze*. See *Orders*.

Triumphal Arch ARCHITECTURE: The monumental urban gateway, invented by the Romans, set up along a major street to commemorate important military successes. It may have one or three arched openings and is usually decorated with inscriptions, *reliefs*, and freestanding sculpture on the top.

Truss ARCHITECTURE: Originally a wooden structural member composed of smaller, lighter pieces of wood joined to form rigid triangles and capable of spanning spaces by acting as a *beam*.

Tympanum (tihm′pah-nuhm) ARCHITECTURE: The triangular or similarly shaped space enclosed by an *arch* or *pediment*.

Tyranny In ancient Greece, meant "rule of the strong man." Historically, came to mean arbitrary rule of one, but generally taken to mean arbitrary political rule of any kind.

Value See *Color*.

Vanishing Point PAINTING: The point or points of convergence for all lines forming an angle to the *picture plane* in pictures constructed according to the principles of linear *perspective*.

Vault ARCHITECTURE: The covering or spanning of a space employing the principle of the *arch* and using masonry, brick, plaster, or similar malleable materials. The extension of an arch infinitely in one plane creates a

barrel or tunnel vault. The intersection of two barrel vaults at right angles to each other produces a cross or groin vault. *Ribs* are sometimes placed along the intersections of a groin vault to produce a *ribbed vault*.

Veneer VISUAL ARTS: A thin layer of precious or valuable material glued or otherwise attached to the surface of another, less expensive, or less beautiful material. The Romans, for example, applied thin layers of marble to the concrete and rubble fill surfaces of their buildings to produce a more splendid effect. In this century, valuable woods like walnut or mahogany are applied as veneers to the surfaces of plywood.

Viewpoint The position or place from which the viewer looks at an object or the visual field.

Volume ARCHITECTURE: Refers to the void or solid three-dimensional quality of a space or *form* whether completely enclosed or created by the presence of forms which act as boundaries. Compare the "volume" of the *Parthenon* with the "volume" of the *Pantheon*.

Volute (vah-loot′) ARCHITECTURE: The spiral scroll that appears on Ionic and Corinthian *capitals*. By extension applied to any similar curvilinear form used in a similar way.

Voussoir (voo-swahr′) ARCHITECTURE: The wedge-shaped stone or masonry unit of an *arch*, wider at the top and tapering toward the bottom.

Wall ARCHITECTURE: A broad, substantial upright slab that acts as an enclosing *form* capable of supporting its own weight and the weight of *beams* or *arches* to span and enclose space.

Warm Colors VISUAL ARTS: The hues commonly associated with warmth—yellow, red, and orange. In *compositions* the warm colors tend to advance, in contrast to the *cool colors*, which tend to recede from the viewer.

INDEX